Hemmed In

Responses to Africa's Economic Decline

Hemmed In

Responses to Africa's Economic Decline

THOMAS M. CALLAGHY AND
JOHN RAVENHILL,
editors

COLUMBIA UNIVERSITY PRESS
NEW YORK

Columbia University Press
New York Chichester, West Sussex

Library of Congress Cataloging-in-publication Data
Hemmed in : responses to Africa's economic decline /
Thomas M. Callaghy and John Ravenhill, editors
p. cm.
Includes bibliographical references and index.
ISBN 0-231-08228-2 : — ISBN 0-231-08229-0 (pbk.) :
1. Economic assistance—Africa, Sub-Saharan. 2. Africa, Sub-Saharan—Economic policy. 3. Africa, Sub-Saharan—Economic conditions—1960-
I. Callaghy, Thomas M. II. Ravenhill, John.
HC800.H45 1994
338.967—dc20 93-19692
CIP

Casebound editions of Columbia University Press books are printed on permanent and durable acid-free paper.

Printed in the United States of America
c 10 9 8 7 6 5 4 3 2 1

To Carl G. Rosberg—Teacher, colleague, friend—With respect, appreciation and affection

Contents

List of tables x

Contributors xi

Preface and Acknowledgments xv

Introduction
Vision, Politics, and Structure: Afro-Optimism, Afro-Pessimism or Realism? 1
THOMAS M. CALLAGHY AND JOHN RAVENHILL

Chapter One
A Second Decade of Adjustment: Greater Complexity, Greater Uncertainty 18
JOHN RAVENHILL

Chapter Two
The IMF and the World Bank in Africa: How Much Learning? 54
REGINALD HERBOLD GREEN

Chapter Three
Debt, Conditionality, and Reform: The International Relations of Economic Policy Restructuring in Sub-Saharan Africa 90
DAVID F. GORDON

Chapter Four
Neither Phoenix nor Icarus: Negotiating Economic Reform in Ghana and Zambia, 1983–92 130
MATTHEW MARTIN

Chapter Five
The Political Repercussions of Economic Malaise 180
NAOMI CHAZAN AND DONALD ROTHCHILD

Chapter Six
The Future of the Manufacturing Sector in Sub-Saharan Africa 215
ROGER RIDDELL

Chapter Seven
Coping with Confusion: African Farmers' Responses to Economic Instability in the 1970s and 1980s 248
SARA BERRY

Chapter Eight
The Discovery of "Politics": Smallholder Reactions to the Cocoa Crisis of 1988–90 in Côte d'Ivoire 279
JENNIFER WIDNER

Chapter Nine
The Politics of Sustained Agricultural Reform in Africa 332
JEFFREY HERBST

Chapter Ten
The Politics of Nonreform in Cameroon 357
NICOLAS VAN DE WALLE

Chapter Eleven
Trading Places: Economic Policy in Kenya and Tanzania 398
MICHAEL F. LOFCHIE

Chapter Twelve
Political Passions and Economic Interests: Economic Reform and Political Structure in Africa 463
THOMAS M. CALLAGHY

Chapter Thirteen
How Hemmed In? Lessons and Prospects of Africa's Responses to Decline 520
THOMAS M. CALLAGHY AND JOHN RAVENHILL

Index 565

Tables

4.1. Comparative Economic Indicators, 1983–90 134
6.1. Production as a Percentage of Apparent Consumption, 1973–75 to 1981–83, Various Products 229
9.1. Percentage Change in Agricultural Production Per Capita Between 1979–81 and 1989 335
9.2. Percentage of Major Crops whose Yields Increased by more than 37%, 1979–1981 to 1988 343
10.1. Breakdown of Marketing Revenues: Robusta, Arabica and Cocoa, 1986/87 370
11.1. Kenya and Tanzania Economic Performance Compared 400
11.2. Kenya: Commodity Volume Increases 403
11.3. Official and Parallel Market Exchange Rates, Kenya and Tanzania 407
11.4. Kenya Nominal Protection Coefficients, Export Crops: 1967–85 410
11.5. Kenya Nominal Protection Coefficients, Grains, 1971–86 411
11.6. Tanzanian Export Crop Production, 1980–84, Production Average to Peak Period Production 419
11.7. Total Grain Imports, 1976–85 422
11.8. Tanzania Export Crop NPCs and Ratio of Prices to Kenya, 1967–80 425
13.1. Growth of Real GDP Per Capita, 1965–2000 542
13.2. Growth in Developing Countries, by Region and Analytic Group, 1965–89 and the 1990s. 543

Contributors

Sara S. Berry is Professor of History at the Johns Hopkins University. For over twenty-five years, she has specialized in the study of economic, social and agricultural change in Sub-Saharan Africa, with particular emphasis on southwestern Nigeria. She is author of *Cocoa, Custom and Socio-economic Change in Rural Nigeria* (1975) and *Fathers Work for Their Sons: Accumulation, Mobility, and Class Formation in an Extended Yoruba Community* (1985).

Thomas M. Callaghy is Associate Professor of Political Science, and the Max N. and Heidi L. Berry Term Professor in the Social Sciences at the University of Pennsylvania. He is author of *The State-Society Struggle: Zaire in Comparative Perspective* (1984) and editor of *South Africa in Southern Africa: The Intensifying Vortex of Violence* (1983). His current work centers on the politics of economic reform in the Third and former Second Worlds. As part of a six-person team he contributed to *Fragile Coalitions: The Politics of Economic Adjustment* (1989) and *Economic Crisis and Policy Choice: The Politics of Adjustment in the Third World* (1990), both edited by Joan Nelson.

Naomi Chazan is Professor of Political Science and African Studies at the Hebrew University of Jerusalem and a former director of its Harry S. Truman Institute. She is currently a member of the Israeli Knesset. She is author of *An Anatomy of Ghanaian Politics: Managing Political Recession* (1983), coauthor of *Politics and Society in Contemporary Africa* (2nd ed., 1992), and coeditor of *The Precarious Balance: State and Society in Africa* (1988) and *Civil Society and the State in Africa* (1993).

David F. Gordon is the senior Africa specialist on the staff of the Foreign Affairs Committee, U.S. House of Representatives. He was previously Associate Professor of International Relations and African Studies at Michigan State University. From 1989 to 1991 he served as the economic policy and governance advisor in USAID's regional office for east and southern Africa in Nairobi. He is author of *Decolonization and the State in Kenya* (1986) and coeditor of *Cooperation for International Development: The U.S. and the Third World in the 1990s* (1989).

Reginald Herbold Green is a Professional Fellow of the Institute of Development Studies (Sussex) and Senior Policy Advisor to the Mozambique Directorate of Planning. For over thirty years he has published extensively on the political economy of Sub-Saharan Africa. He is a regular consultant to UNICEF, the Southern African Development Community, and the African Development Bank. His current interests focus on livelihood rehabilitation and absolute poverty reduction.

Jeffrey Herbst is Assistant Professor at Princeton University's Woodrow Wilson School. He is the author of *The Politics of Reform in Ghana, 1982-1991* (1993), *State Politics in Zimbabwe* (1990), and articles on African politics. In 1992-93, he was a Fulbright Professor at the University of Cape Town and the University of the Western Cape in South Africa.

Michael F. Lofchie is a Professor of Political Science at the University of California, Los Angeles where he also served as Director of the James S. Coleman African Studies Center. Among his most recent books are *The Policy Factor: Agricultural Performance in Kenya and Tanzania* (1989) and (coeditor) *Africa's Agrarian Crisis: The Roots of Famine* 1986).

Matthew Martin is currently Senior Research Officer, External Finance for Africa, at the International Development Centre,

Oxford University, and advisor to two African governments on their external finance negotiations. He is author of *The Crumbling Facade of African Debt Negotiations: No Winners* (1991); he has also worked on the issues of aid, debt, and adjustment in Africa for the Overseas Development Institute, Swedish International Development Authority, UNCTAD, UNDP, and the World Bank.

Roger Riddell is a Senior Research Associate of the Overseas Development Institute (ODI) in London and has worked on African development issues for twenty years. He is author of *Manufacturing in Africa: Performance and Prospects of Seven Countries in Sub-Saharan Africa* (1990) and *Zimbabwe to 1996: At the Heart of a Growing Region* for the Economist Intelligence Unit. He is completing a book on the impact of NGOs on development for ODI and working with the African Development Bank on economic integration in a post-apartheid southern Africa.

John Ravenhill is Senior Fellow in the Department of International Relations, Research School of Pacific Studies, Australian National University. He is author of *Collective Clientelism: The Lomé Conventions and North-South Relations* (1985) and coauthor of *Politics and Society in Contemporary Africa* (2nd ed., 1992). He is editor of *Africa in Economic Crisis* (1986) and *No Longer an American Lake? Alliance Problems in the South Pacific* (1989) and coeditor of *Pacific Economic Relations in the 1990s: Conflict or Cooperation?* (1993).

Donald Rothchild is Professor of Political Science at the University of California, Davis, and a Visiting Fellow at the Brookings Institution for 1992-93. He is author of *Racial Bargaining in Independent Kenya* (1973) and coauthor of *Scarcity, Choice and Public Policy in Middle Africa* (1978) and *Politics and Society in Contemporary Africa* (2nd ed., 1992). He is also editor of *Ghana: the Political Economy of Recovery* (1991) and coeditor of *The Precarious Balance: State and Society in Africa* (1988).

Nicolas van de Walle is Assistant Professor of Political Science and a member of the African Studies Center at Michigan State University. He coauthored *Of Time and Power: Leadership in the Modern World* (1991). He is currently working on a book on the politics of economic reform in Cameroon.

Jennifer A. Widner is Associate Professor of Government at Harvard University. She is author of *The Rise of a Party-State in Kenya: From Harambee! to Nyayo!* (1993) and articles on the political economy of Kenya and Côte d'Ivoire. She is currently working on a book on the latter topic.

Preface and Acknowledgments

This volume is a collaborative outgrowth of John Ravenhill's 1986 edited volume *Africa in Economic Crisis*. It is meant to assess the record of responses in the 1980s and early 1990s to Africa's economic decline and to examine the prospects for the rest of the decade.

Thomas Callaghy is grateful to the Ford and Rockefeller Foundations for funding the research that constitutes the comparative background for his contributions to this volume. He is also appreciative of the support provided by the Research Foundation and the Public Policy Initiative Fund, both of the University of Pennsylvania. We would both like to extend special thanks to Kate Wittenberg and her fine staff at Columbia University Press, to the two anonymous reviewers of the manuscript, and to James Hentze, Wambui Mwangi, Srirupa Roy, and John Callaghy.

Carl Rosberg has been a teacher, colleague or friend of a number of the contributors to this volume. Some of us have been privileged to know him in all three capacities. We take great pleasure in dedicating this volume to him.

Carl Rosberg has been a pioneer in the study of African politics in the United States and has greatly influenced the careers of many who came later. After completing his D.Phil. at St. Antony's College, Oxford, Carl took up an assistant professorship in government at Boston University in 1955 and was a research associate in its new African Studies Program. In 1958 he moved to the University of California at Berkeley where he remained until his retirement in 1991. Among his many achievements at Berkeley was to build an African Studies Program. Not only was he chair of the Committee on African Studies in 1959–63 and 1966–67, but he also took a particular interest in the program during the long period (1973–89) that he was Director of the Institute of International Studies. Carl also served as Chairman of the Department of Political Science at Berkeley in 1969–74, guiding the department through a particularly difficult period.

Carl shouldered heavy administrative responsibilities for virtually all of his years at Berkeley. His ability to continue to publish throughout this period is testimony to his energy and to his enthusiasm for African politics. He traveled frequently to Africa; he had periods as Visiting Professor at Makerere University, the University of Nairobi, and the University of Dar es Salaam (where he was Head of the Department of Political Science for two years).

Carl's first book, *The Kenyatta Election: Kenya 1960–61* (1961), coauthored with George Bennett, examined the preindependence election in Kenya that moved it toward majority rule. But far better known is Carl's other major work on Kenya in the 1960s—*The Myth of "Mau Mau": Nationalism in Kenya* (1966), coauthored with John Nottingham. *The Myth of "Mau Mau"* was an exploration of the roots of Kenyan nationalism. By showing how Mau Mau was an integral part of an ongoing, rationally conceived nationalist movement, the book destroyed the credibility of the argument of white supremacists in Kenya that Mau Mau was an atavistic escape from modernity.

The decade of the 1960s was a particularly exciting time to be involved in the study of African politics. Countries were coming to independence; political parties were in transition; and there was considerable optimism about the prospects for regional integration. Some of the dynamism and energy of this period is captured in the book that Carl edited with his good friend, James S. Coleman, on *Political Parties and National Integration in Tropical Africa* (1964). This book became a standard authority for students in the field for many years. Many of the young scholars who contributed to the book subsequently went on to consolidate reputations as leading figures in the field of comparative politics.

In the same year that *Political Parties and National Integration in Tropical Africa* was published, Carl also edited the first of two volumes that he was to publish on socialism in Africa. *African Socialism*, coedited with William Friedland, became a standard work on the subject and, like *The Myth of "Mau Mau,"* it played an important role in demolishing myths—on this occasion about the "socialist" nature of Africa's parties. This statement applies a fortiori to the second volume on this topic, *Socialism in Sub-Saharan Africa: A New Assessment* (1979), coedited with Thomas M. Callaghy fifteen years after the publication of the first. With Africa experiencing the rise of a new wave of "socialist" parties in the former Portuguese colonies, this volume brought a timely reassessment of the meaning of socialism in Africa.

Carl has had a long-standing interest in the politics of South Africa and in encouraging a peaceful transition to black majority rule. A series of conferences was held under the auspices of the Institute of International Studies. Together with one of his former students and colleague in the Department of Political Science at Berkeley, Robert M. Price, Carl edited a volume on *The Apartheid Regime: Political Power and Racial Domination* in 1980.

As Africa's economic decline became clear in the late 1970s and early 1980s, political scientists sought an understanding of economic failure through an examination of the weaknesses of African political institutions. It would be no exaggeration to say that *Personal Rule in Black Africa: Prince, Autocrat, Prophet, Tyrant* (1982), coauthored with another of Carl's former students, Robert H. Jackson, was one of the most influential books in causing students of African politics to rethink the role and nature of government in African countries. A spinoff of this project was a 1982 article in *World Politics* on "Why Africa's Weak States Persist: The Empirical and the Juridical in Statehood"—a piece that was praised not only by students of Africa but by many international relations theorists as well.

Carl's willingness to collaborate in publishing with his students is indicative of his general concern for their careers and welfare. Many students of Africa, and many African students, owed their survival at Berkeley at least in part to research assistantships and other forms of support that Carl arranged. Carl's concern with the welfare of those he taught was regarded as eccentric by some of his colleagues. Carl devoted an enormous number of hours to seeking scholarships for African students, and helping them personally if they encountered problems with visas or with university or other authorities. Overseas students were invited to Thanksgiving and Christmas dinners with Carl and Elizabeth. Carl's door was always open to students and colleagues during the long hours that he spent in his office. His concern for people is a principal reason why so many people associated with him at Berkeley regard him as a friend as well as a colleague.

Thomas M. Callaghy, Swarthmore, Pennsylvania
John Ravenhill, Canberra, Australia

March 1993

Introduction

Vision, Politics, and Structure: Afro-Optimism, Afro-Pessimism or Realism?

THOMAS M. CALLAGHY AND
JOHN RAVENHILL

> Only with the emergence of African states that foster individual freedoms and market economies with complementary public sectors will the continent receive the attention it deserves. African societies might then graduate from being passive recipients of charity to full actors in global politics and economics.
>
> Michael Chege, "Remembering Africa"

> Africa's lag vis-à-vis the rest of the world is astronomical. We need good governance—that is meaningful participation by our people in the political process, transparent and accountable governmental systems with sensitivity to the sufferings of our people. When our people are motivated by good governance and fair rewards for their labors, African economies will then begin to grow at a pace which will ultimately see us catching up with the rest of the world or at least bridging the yawning gap. The continent of Africa is now so marginalized.
>
> Frederick Chiluba, President of Zambia[1]

These views, expressed here by a leading African scholar and a newly elected president, also double as a hope, and are now heard with increasing frequency from a wider range of Africans. As a vibrant form of Afro-optimism, they certainly represent a striking change from a decade ago, and, since the late 1980s, they have also become a prominent mantra of Western countries and international financial institutions (IFIs). Yet in the face of this hope, this vision, Africa remains distinctly "hemmed in" by its problems of decline. The 1980s were a lost decade for development in Africa. Per capita income in most African countries has now regressed to the levels prevailing at independence, more than thirty years ago.

One of the few positive factors to emerge from this decade of economic decline was the recognition by many African governments of the errors of previous policies, and the necessity to reorient their economic strategies. In varying degrees and ways, they have attempted to respond to decline. A significant impetus for this redirection of policy came from the need to reach agreement with Western donors on structural adjustment programs in order to secure badly needed external funding. At one time or another, the vast majority of African governments in the 1980s entered into structural adjustment agreements with the International Monetary Fund (IMF) and/or the World Bank, agreements that were implemented with varying degrees of enthusiasm and sincerity. Then, in the early 1990s, important democratization movements emerged in a wide range of African countries, posing new challenges for economic adjustment.

This volume surveys the major economic, political, and social aspects of Africa's first decade plus of adjustment to decline to derive lessons for African governments, the international financial institutions, bilateral donors, and all those who have an interest in the welfare of Africa's rapidly growing population, in short, for those concerned with Africa becoming less "hemmed in." By "hemmed in" we mean a situation in which the viable policy alternatives, and the capacities and resources needed to implement them, available to African governments are severely constrained as a consequence of volatile politics, weak states, weak markets, debt problems, and an unfavorable international environment. This volume will not, however, examine several other factors that also hem Africa in, and, in fact, intensify the ones investigated here—demographic, health, and ecological problems, drought and migration, and civil wars and interstate violence.

We believe that a realistic, hardheaded analysis of African conditions is in order, both for improved understanding and for better policy. Commentators representing a wide range of viewpoints often tend to pull back from important but difficult conclusions. Many Africans are still attempting to find "shortcuts" out of their problems, while many Western Africanists stretch to find optimistic conclusions in order to counteract negative views of the continent and what they see as unwarranted Afro-pessimism. At the same time, officials of the IMF, the World Bank, and the major Western donors often take an upbeat, almost "cheerleading" stance in order to encourage continued attempts at externally sponsored reforms they believe will bring major transformation. A realistic, even if not always agreeable, assessment—one that takes into account the synergy between the vision (and the policies that flow from it), politics and structure, one that avoids unproductive illusions but does so without underestimating or undervaluing the creativity of human agency—does better service to Africans as they confront their serious problems and to those outsiders who want to help them. An eventual backlash to varied false hopes and failed illusions might generate more Afro-pessimism than would a more realistic analysis of all positions now.

This volume consists of original essays, written by economists and political scientists but inevitably interdisciplinary in nature, which address a series of core questions. What are the economic and political factors that underlie Africa's economic decline? What are the political consequences of economic decline? How effective has the conditionality imposed by the international financial institutions and Western donors been in effecting a change in the policies of African governments? In what circumstances is policy reversal most likely to occur? What factors—and in particular, what political structures and coalitions—are necessary for adjustment to be sustained? To what extent has sufficient external support for African adjustment efforts been forthcoming? Will new domestic and external pressures for democratization facilitate or undermine adjustment efforts?

The chapters include both country case studies and sectoral studies. John Ravenhill and Reginald Green (chapters 1 and 2) provide overviews of the first decade of adjustment. David Gordon (chapter 3) focuses on how effective the conditionality used by the international financial institutions as part of structural adjustment programs has been. This issue is taken up in Matthew Martin's comparative study (chapter 4) of the effectiveness of IMF programs in Ghana and Zambia. Naomi Chazan and Donald Rothchild (chapter 5) review the political factors associated with economic decline, and the impact that structural adjustment programs have had on the political systems of Africa. Roger Riddell's contribution (chapter 6) is a study of manufacturing, in particular how this sector has been neglected in structural adjustment programs. The chapters by Sara Berry and Jennifer Widner (chapters 7 and 8) examine how farmers have responded to loss of income in poor economic times. Failures in the agricultural sector—in the production of export and food crops alike—are at the heart of Africa's recent economic decline. In the midst of widespread agricultural failure, there have, however, been some success stories. Jeffrey Herbst (chapter 9) looks at three cases where the agricultural sector has either performed reasonably well or where important pro-agriculture reforms have been undertaken—Kenya, Zimbabwe, and Ghana. He reviews the reasons underlying their success and the implications for other countries. The essays by Michael Lofchie (chapter 10) and Nicolas van de Walle (chapter 11) are detailed case studies that illustrate the reasons why adjustment has been more successful in some countries than others. Finally (in chapter 12), Callaghy places the African experience with adjustment in comparative perspective and examines the relationship between economic and political liberalization.

John Ravenhill's chapter introduces a number of the themes that recur throughout the volume. In particular, he notes that the keywords emerging from the first decade of adjustment have been complexity and uncertainty. Early optimism on the part of the international financial institutions that African economies could be revitalized through the application of a short, sharp shock treatment disappeared as the intractability of Africa's malaise become apparent. Increasingly, the complexity of the task of addressing Africa's problems was acknowledged. The World Bank's agenda for Africa has become much lengthier, has evolved to embrace issues of political as well as economic reform, and has moved from an emphasis on short-term measures to a medium- and long-term perspective. The cost of the new recognition of complexity, however, is a strong sense of uncertainty. The Bank and other external actors appear to be floundering in a sea of problems, uncertain as to how they might best be resolved and which should be given priority. Meanwhile, the debt overhang, unfavorable global economic conditions, and insufficient response from industrialized donors countries all limit the prospects for a sustained reversal of Africa's economic decline, to its becoming less "hemmed in."

Green's chapter is particularly concerned with the extent to which the major players in economic reform—the IMF, the World Bank, and African governments (and their continental representatives, the Organization of African Unity and the Economic Commission for Africa)—have learned from the first decade of attempted adjustment. Green notes that the Fund has failed to "structurally adjust" its approach to meet changing circumstances in Africa in the 1980s with the consequence that not only has it been in conflict with African governments but also that its stabilization programs have increasingly been in "antagonistic contradiction" to the World Bank's emphasis on adjustment with growth. The Bank, Green argues, is less monolithic and far more pragmatic than the Fund. It has learned from experience, and has changed course (which some critics have failed to acknowledge). Bank programs continue, however, to be characterized by dogmatism on issues such as user fees for social services, by inadequate analysis, and by overoptimism both on the funding reform programs require and on what will be provided by industrialized countries.

To date, the results of structural adjustment programs remain unclear; they have not been running long enough nor taken seriously enough in many countries for definitive conclusions to be reached. Nevertheless, Green asserts, there is no alternative to adjustment; the only debate can be over different emphases, timing, and the move to a longer-term focus on structural transformation. Although African organizations have helped to shape the agenda to focus increasingly on the longer-term and on basic needs, they have not produced a viable alternative strategy to the one advocated by the IMF and the World Bank.

Gordon's chapter begins by examining how African countries have come to depend so heavily on the international financial institutions (IFIs) for external finance. He argues that Africa's debt crisis had its origins in the failure of African countries after the first round of oil price increases in 1973–74 to use the foreign exchange they borrowed productively. In particular, and in contrast to Latin America, few of the funds were invested to increase export capacity. Consequently, when commodity prices slumped in the early 1980s, African countries were unable to service their debts, and entered into a vicious downward spiral of debt, decline, and rescheduling.

This cycle of decline provided the opening for the IFIs to become involved in shaping African governments's policy choices through attaching conditions to the debt relief that they provided. The role of the IFIs increased after it became obvious that the expectation of a quick revival of African economies was unrealistic. Reinforced by "policy dialogues," conditionality was widened in scope and changed from the IMF's emphasis on aggregate targets to a new focus on negotiating specific policy changes.

With the proliferation of required policy changes, Gordon argues, conditionality has become less effective, a view shared by Martin in his study of Ghana and Zambia. In part this is because the IFIs have failed to keep their part of the implicit conditionality compact to provide a substantial increase in external financing—both from their own resources and by acting as a catalyst for other official and private sources of foreign exchange. In addition, governments have discovered that most often few sanctions are imposed if they comply only partially with policy conditions. One reason for this is that the IFIs themselves came to have major institutional interests in proclaiming the apparent "success" of the reforms. Another reason is that the IFIs had insufficient capacity to monitor the proliferating conditions. Lastly, the IFIs are constrained by the fact that they are both instruments of reform and creditors with a vested interest in not declaring the countries to be in default.

Besides the prospect that African governments may well escape with only partial compliance, there are a number of other reasons why the prescribed reforms may not be fully implemented. First is the politics of reform coalitions: the likelihood that losers from structural adjustment are likely to mobilize more quickly and effectively than potential winners. Second, programs may not be implemented because of the limited technical skills available or because of bureaucratic obstruction. Third, in many instances African governments simply do not accept the technical analysis on which policy conditions were based. Like other authors in the volume, Gordon concludes that conditionality has worked most successfully where economic decline has been accompanied by regime change and, in particular, where the IFIs have been able to convince a group of influential technocrats and politicians or military officers of the value of the reform program.

Martin's comparative case study includes Ghana, the country most often held up as the success story of sustained, multisector adjustment, and Zambia, where economic reform was very limited and external financing for adjustment was dramatically canceled following disagreement over the implementation of an adjustment program. Martin's chapter seeks to explain why the effort in Ghana was broadly successful whereas the one in Zambia decidedly was not. He finds that the explanation lies in four groups of factors.

First are the differences in domestic politics between the two countries. Whereas the Jerry Rawlings military government enjoyed substantial autonomy as a consequence of the disorganized and disunited opposition, was pragmatic, and able to take rapid decisions, Kenneth Kaunda's long-lasting government was constrained by sectional groups and, in a country with (for Africa) an unusually urbanized population, feared that the implementation of some elements of the adjustment package, such as the reduction of food subsidies, would cause large-scale political protest. Zambian politics, Martin suggests, ultimately could not cope with the pace of adjustment.

A second factor was the design and implementation of the adjustment programs themselves. Although Martin finds fault in program design in both countries, the faults in the Zambian program were especially damaging. In particular, the Zambian program contained incorrect sequencing of adjustment measures, and proliferating (and often conflicting) conditions. A third difference lay in the capacity of the countries to adjust, in particular, the differential supply responses for their major export commodities. Here Zambia's dependence for the majority of its export earnings on copper mines that were coming toward the end of their profitable lives, coupled with the depressed state of the international copper market, constrained the possibilities for a swift increase in export earnings.

Finally, there was a crucial difference in the availability of foreign exchange in support of the two programs. Whereas Western donors eventually warmed to the Rawlings regime and were relatively generous in their support, the hostility and suspicion with which Kaunda's Zambia was viewed in international circles ensured that there was only grudging and inadequate external support for the Zambian adjustment program. As a result the Zambian program collapsed in part from import strangulation.

Martin concludes by drawing a number of lessons from the two cases for the design and implementation of adjustment programs. There is substantial room, he argues, for improvement in the negotiating process. All parties need to be better prepared for the talks, a larger role should be found for governments in program design, implementation should be more flexible, and there is a great need for additional and more timely external finance.

Chazan and Rothchild address the political factors underlying the economic crisis. The postcolonial African state, they argue, was characterized by hegemonic pretensions but an inability to penetrate society and extract resources from it. Overburdened state institutions were also unresponsive to popular demands. "Politics" was driven underground to be expressed primarily in the informal realm.

Excessive statism helped to bring on the economic decline of the 1980s. By the end of the second decade of independence, governments that were alternately too detached from society or too porous to societal demands were barely supported by weak, overextended, costly, and inefficient state structures. As the resources available to sustain a pattern of clientelist politics declined so popular unrest grew. The survival strategies pursued by social groups included disengagement from the state, a move which further curtailed the state's penetrative abilities.

Chazan and Rothchild note that state decline and, in some cases, attempted economic reform, facilitated straddling between the formal and informal sectors and permitted the emergence of entrepreneurs with sources of accumulation independent of the state. All of these processes helped to pluralize the institutional terrain, strengthened "civil society," and, in the late 1980s and early 1990s, generated major movements for democratization of Africa's long-standing authoritarian political structures.

Since agriculture has usually been made the centerpiece of structural adjustment programs (SAPs), manufacturing has often been neglected or relegated to a distinctly inferior position. Riddell tries to correct this imbalance; he suggests that policies toward manufacturing have moved from a radical pro-industry approach that was popular with many African governments immediately after independence to the polar opposite of the "harsh withdrawal" characteristic of SAPs. Neither approach, Riddell believes, is optimal for industrial promotion in Africa.

For Riddell, the "harsh withdrawal" advocated by the IFIs as part of the adjustment package is based on a faulty understanding of the manufacturing record in Africa. Although the level and share of manufacturing in GDP in Sub-Saharan Africa remained low, the rate of growth (albeit from a small base) in the 1960s and

1970s was higher than that of other developing countries. Africa's performance, if not startling, was at least respectable. A detailed examination of the data leads Riddell to conclude, first, that the manufacturing problem in Africa should not be treated in a fundamentally different way than in other developing countries; in other words, it should not be regarded as a lost cause. Second, the intercounty variations in performance suggest the need to tailor policies for specific countries. Success comes from the sustained provision of a supportive environment, but this environment has taken a number of forms, some of which have included substantial government intervention. Manufacturing in a few countries has remained internationally competitive despite an increase in protectionism.

Riddell suggests that the "harsh withdrawal" policies characteristic of many adjustment programs are fundamentally misguided. An increase in the level of manufactured exports will not be achieved merely by removing protection and exposing domestic manufacturers to the chill winds of international competition. If trade liberalization in itself is insufficient, so is privatization. The public sector is not necessarily less efficient than the private one; it all depends on the domestic environment. As structural adjustment programs have ignored supportive policies specific to the manufacturing sector, they, together with the recessions that they have induced, have led to "contraction without restructuring" in manufacturing. There is no evidence from the case studies that Riddell reviews of a link between adoption of structural adjustment programs and increased exports of manufactures.

Rather than "harsh withdrawal," Riddell suggests an alternative approach of "benign intervention." This is premised on the argument that in a era when low wages in themselves are of reduced significance in attracting manufacturing investment, the key to industrial development is to provide a stable environment and an expanding domestic production base. The implication is that SAPs should be concerned more with the medium- and long-term policies needed to promote industrial diversification and increasing competition among domestic companies. Riddell argues that while structural adjustment is necessary, programs must be adapted to include a variety of policies specifically designed to promote industry. Among these are short-term subsidies to production and consumption, and selected export incentives. Furthermore, the pace of trade liberalization should be far more gradual than that of existing adjustment programs; Riddell notes that a sheltered regional market has facilitated industrialization in some countries. Other factors important in providing an "enabling environment" include the encouragement of high levels of competency in management, engineering, and other skills. But the very clear message is that policies must be tailored to the circumstances of the individual country undergoing adjustment.

While much has been written about the need to revive agriculture as the foundation for renewed economic growth, we actually know relatively little about how farmers have responded to the problems generated by economic decline in the last two decades. This issue is addressed in the chapters by Berry and Widner.

Berry's starting point is to trace how social identities and access to land in Africa have been changed by colonialism, by commercialization, and by government action after independence. She argues that none of these influences has led to a revolution in African agriculture. Although all of them have increased the ambiguities of both social identity and the right of access to land, social identity and status within the community remain important as means of gaining wealth and power. Responses by farmers to the rural crisis, therefore, are constrained by their need to continue to make significant investments in acquiring or validating membership in key social networks.

Berry identifies four principal strategies farmers have used to cope with the uncertainties induced by economic decline. First, they have sought to increase off-farm income through such means as laboring for others, becoming traders, and engaging in other non-farm rural enterprise; or through migration. But in a period of general economic decline, non-farm income-generating opportunities may be scarce—a point emphasized by Widner, who argues that optimism about the opportunities offered by the informal sector can be misplaced. People require capital to enter many informal sector activities such as trading or establishing small workshops, and they need customers.

Second, farmers may attempt to reduce their vulnerability by planting crops that are more "liquid" (that is, those that are readily saleable and/or mature relatively quickly), or which make more flexible demands on their labor. A third strategy is also intended to increase flexibility in income generation and labor utilization:

making changes in the techniques of production such as staggering times of planting and harvesting. Finally, farmers may change the patterns of investment, again to reduce risk. This may include more investment in tradable commodities rather than capital goods, and more investment in social networks (although Berry notes that in times of crisis these cannot be expected to provide an adequate safety net).

Berry concludes by arguing that the instability that has characterized rural production in the last two decades weakens farmers' incentives and ability to think about the long term. Inevitably they focus on more liquid assets and tend to move toward production based on smaller farming units. The emphasis on immediate income tends to drive down crop prices (as farmers attempt to sell a larger proportion of their output), and wages (as more people seek off-farm employment) with the result being further impoverishment.

Widner extends Berry's analysis by examining how cocoa farmers in Côte d'Ivoire have responded politically to rural economic decline and, in particular, the factors that determine whether farmers will respond by engaging in organized political activities. Agrarian interests have typically been viewed as divided by various cleavages, of being incapable of exerting an effective influence on policy-making, and of more often pursuing, in Albert Hirschman's terminology, the "exit" rather than the "voice" option.[2]

Like Berry, Widner emphasizes that Africa's farmers face a narrowing range of options as a consequence of increasing land shortages and the breakdown of extended households. Farmers' frustrations at the obstacles they faced to diversification, and their lack of access to credit, led to a move from loyalty to the ruling *Parti Démocratique de Côte d'Ivoire* to an increasing resort to political voice. But the propensity to engage in political activities varied substantially among regions.

The increasing politicization of farmers was also precipitated by the decline in world cocoa prices in the second half of the 1980s which forced the Ivorian government to reduce farmgate prices in 1989. This was ironic, of course, because the World Bank was advocating across Africa that farmers should receive higher prices for their output. Unfortunately, the options available to farmers were strictly limited. The simultaneous fall in prices for other cash crops left little scope for diversification, and, while income was falling, farmers also faced higher prices for inputs for their crops. A retreat into subsistence production was impossible because of the households' need for cash to pay for items such as school fees. Borrowing money and off-farm employment were not options at a time of general economic decline.

Widner finds that farmers blamed government economic mismanagement for their plight, believing that the political elite's inept and often corrupt overinvestment in plantations had exacerbated the problem. Farmers increasingly sought new means of communicating their concerns to the administration, and a larger role in policy-making. Some farmers reorganized the largely defunct cooperatives for their own ends; others attempted to have a more direct input into policy-making by participating in grower delegations to Abidjan.

A combination of factors, Widner finds, explains differential rates of political activism. The most active areas were characterized by villages with ineffective chiefs, with "notables" who were on average younger and from more diverse cultural backgrounds, with more highly educated people, with a number of young men who had returned to the villages from urban areas, and with more interest in and access to local and national news. Widner argues, however, that there is little systematic evidence yet that the increased political activism of farmers is likely to be represented in party political form. The new political parties set up to contest the Ivorian elections had extremely limited resources and were not capable of systematically penetrating the countryside. Farmers remain a group that is difficult to mobilize for political purposes, although Widner expresses cautious optimism about a new national farmers union created in 1991.

How, then, can the necessary political support be generated to sustain a program of structural adjustment that puts agricultural revival at its core? This is the central question addressed by Herbst's chapter. He argues that the early World Bank emphasis on getting prices right has proved to be insufficient for reviving agriculture. To achieve this objective, a reform of economic institutions and the rebuilding of infrastructure are required. But for this to occur there must be a political system that favors agricultural interests.

Herbst suggests that there have been three principal examples in Africa of political systems that have provided sustained support for agricultural development—Kenya, Zimbabwe, and Ghana under Rawlings. In Kenya the principal factors leading to agriculture's favorable political treatment have been the ownership of farms by politicians, an electoral system that has held politicians accountable to their constituents, and the Harambee system. In Zimbabwe, agriculture has been well-treated in part because of the Robert Mugabe government's commitment to the rural sector forged during the guerrilla war, and because of the existence of a well-organized, well-informed white farmer group that has long enjoyed influence in a highly structured bargaining process with the government on agricultural prices. Finally, in Ghana, although agricultural interests have had no institutionalized representation in the policy-making process, the government's belief in the necessity of reinvigorating the agricultural sector and the conditionality imposed by the international financial institutions have ensured that favorable policies toward agriculture were implemented.

Can the experience of Kenya and Zimbabwe be replicated elsewhere in Africa? Herbst thinks not. Accordingly, favorable agricultural policies will likely depend on the influence of the international financial institutions in promoting agriculture and the empowerment of farmers. For this to be done more effectively, Herbst suggests, the World Bank needs to establish a larger local presence in African counties. Like Widner, Herbst is skeptical about the prospects for farmers being empowered by democratization given the transaction costs of organizing coalitions.

Two chapters follow which present detailed case studies of structural adjustment. The case of Cameroon, examined by van de Walle, is, like Zambia, an example of failed adjustment or nonreform. For van de Walle, the principal problem in Cameroon is what Miles Kahler has identified as the "orthodox paradox": the expectation that governments will implement reform programs that undermine the foundations of their political support and that a capable state is necessary to implement a neoclassical strategy of economic adjustment.[3] In Cameroon, the "hegemonic alliance" opposed reforms that threatened its control over state resources and rent-seeking activities, and it controlled a state apparatus with very weak capabilities. The country's oil wealth had obscured its fundamental economic problems, which included a costly and ineffective state sector. The decline in oil prices in the 1980s threatened the politics of elite accommodation at a time when recently installed President Paul Biya was attempting to consolidate his power. The regime's legitimacy and power ultimately were dependent on control over state resources, a control that would be undermined if the structural adjustment program were fully implemented.

Van de Walle argues that the regime survived by engaging in token implementation and the ritual games of political liberalization. In accordance with the comments made by Gordon in his review of conditionality, van de Walle found that the Cameroon government was able to play donors off against one another so that conditionality remained largely illusory. Although the token implementation of policies enabled the regime to buy time, it has had to rely increasingly on coercion and lacks any capacity for seriously implementing a structural adjustment program.

Lofchie's chapter compares two countries that have quite divergent economic records in the 1970s and 1980s—Kenya and Tanzania. Kenya, Lofchie argues, had a much more impressive economic record than its southern neighbor until the mid-1980s, largely because of its better agricultural performance. It consistently paid a larger share of world market prices to its agricultural producers than did Tanzania, and its currency was also much less overvalued. The reason for Kenya's relatively favorable treatment of export agriculture (although, Lofchie acknowledges, this was less so for food crops) was that identified by Herbst—concern for and investment in farming by political and bureaucratic elites. Favorable policies toward agriculture were facilitated by the proximity of Nairobi to the best farming land in the country, by the long tradition of private land ownership, and by the government's electoral and organizational accountability to smallholder interests. In contrast, Tanzania prevented public servants and politicians from purchasing land, and the best growing land was a long distance from the political center.

Lofchie argues that the difference in the economic records of the two countries is also explained by their differing attitudes toward economic policy and reform. Kenya, he suggests, had essentially been a structural adjuster on a voluntary basis since independence and often took the initiative in proposing policies to the international financial institutions. Tanzania, on the other hand, for a long time viewed the IFIs as "adversarial institutions," and sought their assistance only after prolonged economic decline. By the late 1980s, however, the two countries began to "trade places." New political logics in Kenya began to undermine economic performance, and a turnaround occurred in Tanzania as the balance of power in the government shifted from "socialists" to "pragmatists" because of the accumulated effects of decline and the influence of new ideas. Subsequently, devaluation, trade liberalization, and the reform of parastatals offered some prospect for economic recovery in Tanzania, although this remains constrained by the steepness of the country's decline, the breakdown of infrastructure, and the absence of private sector actors able to step in to replace government agencies.

Callaghy's chapter investigates the relationship between economic and political reform. Using experience from elsewhere in the Third World as a guide, he analyzes the political and institutional structures that have facilitated major economic transformation. These structures have been largely, but not exclusively, authoritarian. After sketching Africa's increasing marginalization and dependence, he examines three African cases—Ghana under Jerry Rawlings, Nigeria under Ibrahim Babangida, and Senegal under Abdou Diouf. These three cases range across a continuum from an authoritarian military regime that started economic reform well before initiating political liberalization (Ghana) to an authoritarian military regime that attempted economic reform while simultaneously carrying out a protracted, highly structured, and multistaged political liberalization process (Nigeria) to a civilian regime that attempted economic reform after important democratization had already been secured (Senegal). Ghana achieved considerable economic progress, at least by African standards; Nigeria made initial progress on economic reform and then faltered badly as the political transition approached; Senegal was unable to implement an economic reform program, but remained democratic.

Challenging the optimistic expectations of the current Western and African visions about the need for simultaneous economic and political change, Callaghy stresses the obstacles to both economic and political reform and argues that political liberalization might actually make economic reform even more difficult than it already is. He does, however, begin to explore the sequencing of reform and institutional arrangements that might facilitate the maintenance of sound economic policy under democratic conditions.

A number of themes emerge clearly from the chapters that point to fallacies in the conventional wisdom expressed by the IMF, the World Bank, and other external actors. Some of these have now been conceded by them—the fallacy that adjustment could quickly resolve Africa's economic woes, for instance. Beside the well-known fallacy of composition (the idea that what is good for one county acting alone is not necessarily beneficial if all countries pursue the same policy simultaneously), the chapters reveal the fallacy of a frictionless, flexible economy—the idea that resources and actors can move effortlessly into new and reformed sectors and that the private sector will step in to play the roles previously performed inefficiently by government agencies. Berry and Widner show that it is often not possible for farmers to move into nonrural activities because they lack the skill and capital to do so, especially in a time of general economic decline. Lofchie points out that in Tanzania, private actors are often not available to pick up the functions previously performed by parastatal organizations, and that there is a need to strike the right balance between public and private sectors if economic recovery is to succeed.

Another fallacy is that the pressure of competition—the "magic of the marketplace"— will succeed in forcing African manufacturing industries to become more efficient. Both Lofchie and Riddell argue that the current emphasis on trade liberalization has produced de-industrialization. Again, a less dogmatic approach is called for, a direction in which the World Bank appears to be heading in recent reports but which has yet to be implemented in the field.

A further fallacy is that democratization will inevitably lead to the empowerment of groups that benefit from economic reform and thus provide the political support necessary to sustain adjustment programs. It is far from certain that such support coalitions will emerge as the supply response may be much weaker than expected and the transaction costs of organizing such coalitions are formidable; some regimes have proved remarkably adaptable in the face of pressures for democratization. In addition, in the one clear case of attempted economic reform under democratic conditions, Senegal, the regime survived but economic reform failed, with the state seriously weakened in the process.

These and other fallacies are examined in the concluding chapter which attempts to assess just how "hemmed in" African countries really are, and does so from a larger comparative perspective. It integrates and evaluates the findings of the preceding chapters, in some cases providing a different interpretation of the material presented in order to provide as realistic an assessment as possible of Africa's prospects and the major lessons of the 1980s and the early 1990s.

The contributions to this volume make available a great deal of information about how African economies and polities have responded to serious conditions of decline. Our hope is that an improved knowledge base and a realistic assessment of these responses will help avoid some of the mistakes made in the first decade plus of Africa's adjustment to decline so that there is a better chance that the 1990s will not be a second "lost decade." If so, then Africa might become less "hemmed in" and move eventually to fulfill the visions of Michael Chege and Frederick Chiluba with which we started this introduction—something the region so greatly desires and deserves. In the short run, however, there may be more tension between fostering individual freedoms and good governance on the one hand and creating rapidly growing market economies on the other than many people might like to admit.

Notes

1. Michael Chege, "Remembering Africa," *Foreign Affairs*, 71, 1 (1992): 146; Frederick Chiluba, quoted in " `No One Else Will Solve Our Problems,' Chiluba Tells OAU," *Africa News*, 36, 7 (August 3–16, 1992): 6. Africa is used here and in the rest of the book to mean Sub-Saharan Africa minus South Africa.

2. Albert O. Hirschman, *Exit, Voice and Loyalty* (Cambridge: Harvard University Press, 1970).

3. Miles Kahler, "Orthodoxy and Its Alternatives: Explaining Approaches to Stabilization and Adjustment," in Joan M. Nelson, ed., *Economic Crisis and Policy Choice* (Princeton: Princeton University Press, 1990), pp. 33–61.

Chapter One

A Second Decade of Adjustment: Greater Complexity, Greater Uncertainty

John Ravenhill

Africa's economic decline has proved to be more prolonged and much more difficult to reverse than originally foreseen. More than a decade after the publication of the landmark Berg Report, which first focused the world's attention on Africa's economic problems,[1] few signs of sustained economic recovery are apparent. This chapter reviews Africa's experience with structural adjustment programs in the 1980s and suggests a number of lessons to be learned. Particular attention is given to the international financial institutions, as these have dominated the structural adjustment agenda.

In its first decade of structural adjustment Africa taken as a whole[2] has experienced further economic regression. Whereas the annual mean rate of growth of per capita income on the continent was 0.8% in the 1970s, it slumped to *negative* 2.2% per year from 1980 to 1989 and was projected to fall further in the first half of the 1990s.[3] Africa's total debt, which had reached \$55 billion in 1980, ballooned to \$160 billion by the end of the decade. Debt service accounted for 25% of the continent's exports of goods and services at the end of the decade; the ratio was projected to deteriorate further in the next few years. Economic decline was marked by import strangulation: import volumes in 1990 were only 84% of the level ten years earlier. And while imports declined and exports rose modestly, the deficit on the current account of the balance of payments amounted to more than 25% of the value of exports of goods and services.[4]

Africa's continuing economic decline cannot be blamed on the process of structural adjustment that the continent has been undergoing in the 1980s. Few countries have made a sustained effort at implementing adjustment programs while receiving external financial support in the volumes required for the programs to be successful. Other governments have adopted the new vocabulary of adjustment in the hope of qualifying for additional financial assistance, but they have not made a sustained commitment to policy reform. It would indeed be premature to suggest that structural adjustment has failed in Africa; in many places it has barely been implemented. Yet to argue that adjustment itself has been the cause of Africa's woes in the 1980s would be to posit a very optimistic counterfactual about the possible results of alternative policies. On the other hand, any expectations that adjustment would bring a swift turnaround in the continent's economic conditions have been dashed—despite the occasional claims by the World Bank to the contrary.

In 1989 the Bank in *Africa's Adjustment and Growth in the 1980s* proclaimed success for its programs of structural adjustment. Countries with strong adjustment programs were alleged to have experienced higher agricultural growth, faster export growth, stronger gross domestic product (GDP) growth, and more investment than other African countries. These were quite extraordinary assertions particularly as another Bank study, *Adjustment Lending: An Evaluation of Ten Years of Experience*, published in the previous year, had lamented the slow response of African countries to adjustment lending. That report had noted (p. 36) that "inadequate commitment has limited the seriousness of reforms, especially in Sub-Saharan Africa," and recorded that average GDP growth rates had fallen even in countries undertaking adjustment in this region.[5]

The belligerent tone of *Africa's Adjustment and Growth* signaled the ferocity of the debate that was going on within the Bank between hardliners, who blamed the inefficiencies of African governments for the continent's continuing decline, and moderates, who conceded African claims that the hostile external environment was a significant source of Africa's malaise. The report's denial of the importance of external factors, its argument that Africa had been unusually favored in receiving overseas aid, and its forthright claim of success for adjustment programs which, for the most part, had only recently been implemented, appeared to be an attempt to win continued support for the Bank's programs from Western donors and to head off criticism from the UN's Economic Commission for Africa (ECA) which was about to launch a proposed alternative framework for adjustment.

Africa's Adjustment and Growth proved to be an embarrassing exercise that not only damaged relations with African governments but also the credibility of the Bank's statistical analysis. The report's methodology was suspect. The ECA wasted no time in issuing a rejoinder claiming that the Bank had been able to reach its positive assessment of adjustment programs only by manipulating the data through such means as varying the choice of base year for time series analysis in order to pick the one most favorable to its conclusions, and by failing to weight the data so that the results for tiny Gambia were counted equally with those of Nigeria. As the ECA demonstrated, there were other ways to manipulate the data that could generate results quite different from those the Bank claimed.

Although indicative of one strand of thinking within the Bank, *Africa's Adjustment and Growth* was an aberration in the evolution of Bank commentary on Africa's problems.[6] As the various dimensions of Africa's malaise became evident in the 1980s, the Bank increasingly came to acknowledge the complexity of the situation that it was addressing. It also became more concerned with building bridges to African opinion, and with attempting to reach a consensus on policy measures to reverse economic decline (see chapter 2).

The design and implementation of structural adjustment programs in Africa has been very much a matter of learning by doing. Neither of the international financial institutions was well-equipped for the dominant role they were to play in Africa in the 1980s. The IMF, which had traditionally focused on short-term lending (usually no longer than three years) to correct payments imbalances, had very little experience with low-income countries. The short time period for which the Fund was authorized to lend money ensured that it could have very little concern with supply-side variables. The Fund assumed that supply in real terms would remain constant during the period of its program. Its primary focus was on easily quantifiable monetary aggregates. Although the Bank had far more experience with low-income countries, its focus until the late 1970s had been almost exclusively on project lending.[7] Structural adjustment lending was initiated in 1980; by the end of the decade the share of structural and sectoral adjustment loans in Bank lending had reached 25 percent.

The Bank's initial expectation was that a country's structural adjustment program would last for between three and five years by which time the economy would be restored to good health. A similar short time horizon was evident in the first of the Bank's major reports on Africa, *Accelerated Development*, which proposed a short, sharp shock treatment for African economies centered around "getting prices right." Of these the most important were the exchange rate, prices for commodity producers, domestic interest rates, and wages. The structural adjustment programs were intended to assist countries in overcoming balance of payments problems—in particular by providing finance for approved programs of policy reforms. The Bank's early approach dovetailed neatly with that of the International Monetary Fund, which became heavily involved in efforts to remedy Africa's balance of payments problems in the first half of the 1980s.

In a series of reports the Bank moved beyond the confrontational "get the prices right" and "get the government out of the economy" approach of *Accelerated Development*. *Toward Sustained Development*, issued in 1984, displayed a far greater awareness of the constraints—both internal and external—faced by African governments, and a greater sensitivity toward the aspirations of the Organization of African Unity for continental economic self-reliance. New emphasis was placed on the need for institution-building in Africa. *Financing Adjustment with Growth in Sub-Saharan Africa*, published in 1986, while continuing to emphasize the necessity of getting prices right, and for reducing the role of the state in the economy, made a powerful case that Africa's debt burden was "unmanageable" and that substantial rescheduling would be necessary to preclude widespread defaults, and asserted that domestic policy reforms would not succeed without a massive inflow of resources on concessional terms. It also admitted that aid policies toward the continent had been far from optimal and that donors had to accept some of the responsibility for the white elephants that had been constructed with their assistance. For the first time detailed attention was given to the necessity of reducing Africa's alarming rate of population growth.

Sub-Saharan Africa: From Crisis to Sustainable Growth, the Bank's November 1989 analysis of Africa's malaise, is its most comprehensive report yet.[8] In both substance and style it represents a victory for moderates within the Bank over hardliners. The 300-page report is a conscious attempt at bridge-building with African governments and their continental institutions; for the first time in the preparation of a major report, the Bank engaged in a lengthy process of consultation with African representatives. A Council of African Advisers was appointed, and 20 workshops were held in Washington and various parts of Africa to discuss the report.

The report does not retreat from the basic messages of the Bank's earlier work: price distortions have been a central factor in Africa's economic decline; poor public sector management lies at the heart of unproductive investment projects; higher levels of domestic savings are required which may be obtained, in part, through more user charges; structural adjustment programs are necessary and have produced positive albeit modest results. But in assessing Africa's decade of adjustment, the Bank goes beyond its earlier work:

- it admits that the adjustment process has been far slower than it anticipated at the beginning of the decade;
- it acknowledges that the external environment for African states has been significantly more adverse than it predicted and thus gives greater attention to the importance of declining terms of trade and unstable commodity prices than in previous reports;[9]
- albeit somewhat reluctantly, the Bank confesses that it participated in some poorly designed projects, and concedes that more than half of the completed rural development projects it financed have failed;
- while maintaining its faith in market mechanisms, it pays far more attention to non-price constraints on supply than in the past;
- (efficient) import substitution is back on the agenda ("an import substitution strategy can be combined with competitive pressures to ensure efficient production, as in the NICs" [p.111]);

- it places greater emphasis than previous reports on equitable growth, returning to the rhetoric of the McNamara Bank's basic human needs approach in asserting that "people must come first": less emphasis, therefore, is placed on reducing government expenditure and more on increasing investment to improve health, expand education, ensure food security, and create jobs;[10]
- special attention is given to women and to the urban poor;
- it emphasizes the importance of improving African capacities in particular through human resource development and building a stronger institutional framework;
- it endorses at length the OAU/ECA's call for regional economic integration, perceiving production for an expanded regional market as a stepping stone toward international competitiveness for African industries;
- it concedes that structural adjustment programs must be more flexible: "Structural adjustment is necessary, but it must be sustained—without dogmatism. It must be adjustment with a difference. Different in the sense that greater account is taken of its social impact" (p. 189); furthermore, "greater efforts should be made to internalize the process and to provide more *ex post* support for measures already adopted rather than *ex ante* conditionality based on promises of action to be taken in the future" (p. 181);
- it allows, after a decade of de-industrialization, that protection of industries may be necessary: "the challenge is to balance protection, which nurtures domestic industries, with competition, which forces firms to innovate, raise productivity, and reduce costs" (p. 116);
- it adopts a less ideological approach to privatization than in the past in asserting (p. 55) that "the division of responsibilities between the state and the private sector should be a matter of pragmatism—not dogma," and acknowledging (p. 121) that "operating by competitive rules is more important than outright ownership." On the other hand, it endorses what it terms a "Nordic" development paradigm in which the role of the state, it argues, should be confined to building human resources, and administrative and physical infrastructure;
- for the first time it explicitly acknowledges that Africa's economic crisis has its root in political malaise. Early drafts of the report used the terminology of one member of the Council of African Advisers in referring to Africa's "vampire" states—but this reference was removed before the publication of the final

draft. The Bank in more sober terminology calls for the establishment of the rule of law, and of independent institutions in order to ensure public accountability. It also endorses the ECA's call for a reduction in Africa's military expenditure (currently running at about 10 percent of government budgets, but constituting more than a quarter of those of strife-torn Ethiopia and Uganda).

The Bank's recognition of the complexity of the task that African countries face in rebuilding their economies is realistic. It comes, however, at the expense of the coherence of its message—a consequence both of its recognition of the multidimensionality of the problems and of its attempts to reach a consensus with African critics. Whereas the prescriptions of the Berg report were universal and clear-cut, those of *Sub-Saharan Africa: From Crisis to Sustainable Growth* are more nuanced and dependent on the circumstances of individual countries. The agenda has also been substantially lengthened. The new approach implicitly acknowledges that the Bank had earlier made faulty assumptions about the nature of the "crisis," especially about the potential malleability of African economic and social structures. There is now an explicit recognition that decline is rooted not only in faulty economic policies but also in sociopolitical structures. "Getting the prices right" can address only one dimension of the problem.

The Bank's program has become far more ambitious. But it has shown few signs of recognizing the linkages and tradeoffs between the different dimensions of the reforms it advocates. Indeed at times *From Crisis to Sustainable Growth* reads like a long wish list that is all too reminiscent of the OAU/ECA's *Lagos Plan of Action.*[11] The Bank increasingly gives the impression that it is floundering in a sea of overwhelming problems with no clear idea of which policies will work. And, to compound matters, the success of the strategies it advocates is dependent, as it acknowledges, on the provision of external funding at a level that appears to be unrealistically optimistic.

The Bank may have identified few policies that can assure success but Africa's continental organizations have not devised any viable alternatives. Much of their activity has been confined to sniping at the content of "orthodox" stabilization and structural adjustment programs. African governments, through their continental organizations, the Economic Commission for Africa, and the Organization of African Unity, have questioned the appropriateness of these programs for African economies which, they argue, are characterized by weak productive structures and imperfect markets. As a consequence, the ECA asserts in its *African Alternative: Framework to Structural Adjustment Programs for Socio-Economic Recovery and Transformation* (AAF-SAP), that the reforms adopted by African countries in the 1980s have failed to bring any significant economic improvement but rather have led to a further contraction in Africa's productive base, growing unemplcyment, greater malnutrition, and decreased expenditures on health and education. While acknowledging the necessity for adjustment, the ECA advocates a strategy of "adjustment with transformation" instead of what it regards as the rigidities of conventional Bank/Fund programs.

The objective of the ECA's strategy is to reduce African dependence on external trade and financing through re-orienting economies toward greater individual, regional, and continental self-reliance. On many issues the ECA is not far apart from the Bank's views as expressed in *From Crisis to Sustainable Growth*:

- emphasis is to be given to the agricultural sector;
- rehabilitation and rationalization of productive and infrastructural capacity must be promoted;
- enhancement of local entrepreneurial capability should take place;
- selective privatization must occur where the state has overextended itself;
- the scientific and technological base must be strengthened;
- greater regional self-reliance should be promoted;
- military expenditures must be reduced; and
- democratization promoted through local decentralization, grassroots initiatives, and community self-management.

The last two points represented a courageous step for the ECA in presenting a message that few of its clients on the continent wish to hear.

In addition to these proposals, the ECA report makes a number of useful criticisms of adjustment programs that the Bank appears to have taken on board in *From Crisis to Sustainable Growth*. In particular, the report condemns doctrinaire privatization, excessive dependence on market forces in situations where markets are structurally distorted, total import liberalization that threatens infant industries, and drastic reductions in expenditure on social services that threaten the welfare of the poorest groups. Furthermore, it is critical of the IFIs' preoccupation with short-term crisis management, and argues effectively for the necessity of a longer-term perspective.

Despite the overlap with the Bank's most recent report, there are significant differences between the two documents. In a number of respects the ECA report is flawed both in its analysis and prescriptions.

First, the ECA places excessive blame for deteriorating social and economic conditions on the continent on the effects of structural adjustment programs. Economic and social conditions were in serious decline in the 1970s, prior to the introduction of adjustment programs. In Ghana, for instance, in 1982—prior to the adoption of its structural adjustment program, real expenditures on health services were only 23 percent of the level in 1976. And, in many countries, governments have implemented programs in such a desultory manner that they can scarcely be said to have been given a chance to work. To be sure, by mandating budgetary reductions, structural adjustment programs have exacerbated cutbacks in social expenditures. But the Bank, and increasingly the Fund, have begun to acknowledge the need to address this problem even if the measures taken to date are far from adequate. The ECA makes no allowance for the evolution of the views of the international financial institutions over the decade, and mistakenly equates the programs of the Bank with those of the Fund.

Second, the ECA appears not to have shed the rhetoric of the New International Economic Order which controversially proclaimed the obligations of the industrialized world to assist the South. AAF-SAP (p.49) asserts, for instance, that "it is the *responsibility* of the international community" to support the alternative adjustment programs to be drawn up by African governments. Similarly, the ECA speaks of the marginalization of Africa as if this is a process in which African states have been entirely passive actors: in reality, African countries have largely marginalized themselves from the world economy.

Third, the ECA continues to maintain an excessive faith in the rationality of intra-African economic interactions and suspicion toward extra-continental actors. It asserts, for instance, that "the negative effects of the openness of the African economies should be seen only in the context of the region as a whole vis-à-vis the outside rather than in the context of individual African countries among themselves."[12] Why intra-African trade should be "less unequal" and therefore more beneficial than that with countries outside the continent is nowhere explained. The ECA thus continues to manifest a fear of the world economy, which causes it to conflate effective management of external economic relations with disengagement from the global economic system.

Fourth, the ECA continues to place great faith in statist prescriptions—which most analysts see as being at the heart of the problem in the first place. Its proposals for multiple exchange rates, selective trade policies, and administrative controls on prices open the way for the rent-seeking activities that underlie Africa's political malaise.

Coming to Terms with Complexity

Perhaps the single most important lesson learned from Africa's first decade of structural adjustment is how little we know not only about how African economies will respond to various policy measures but also about how key political actors will react to the hardships caused by stabilization programs. We are less certain than we once were about data on agricultural production[13], about the supply response to changes in producer prices, about the most appropriate timing and sequencing of elements of reform programs, and about the likely political response to economic decline.[14] Some generalizations can be made, however, from the 1980s experience.

Getting the Prices Right: Necessary but not Sufficient

The results from Africa's first decade of adjustment have generally provided support for the emphasis the Bank has placed on the necessity of getting prices right. They have also shown, however, a more complex interrelationship between prices in different sectors than was anticipated, and demonstrated that getting prices right alone will not provide the required boost to productive activities on the continent.

One of the most important prices is the exchange rate: overvalued rates were a significant factor holding back Africa's economic growth in the 1970s. In this period the high rates of domestic inflation generated by large budget deficits were not compensated for by devaluation. The major focus given by the Fund and the Bank to exchange-rate realignment has proved to be warranted. In Nigeria, for instance, the manufacturing sector made substantial gains in providing local substitutes for goods previously imported following the devaluation in 1986. Unfortunately, however, the magnitude of some currency realignments, and the way in which they have been achieved, has sometimes been disruptive and has directly undermined some of the other objectives—including the realignment of other prices—that were being pursued.

In some countries, massive devaluation has occurred. In Ghana the currency was depreciated by 6,000% in nominal terms (90% in real terms) over the period 1982/3–1987.[15] Since then the cedi has depreciated further; one dollar then equaled 90 cedis, while at present it buys more than 360 cedis. As the Bank itself has acknowledged, changes of this magnitude can be severely destabilizing: "sudden large changes in prices may themselves hinder adjustment, as in Ghana where industrial firms had great difficulty financing the working capital requirements of a ten-fold devaluation in 1983."[16] Not only were imported inputs much more expensive but the size of the devaluation also made it difficult for companies to obtain bank credit because many more cedis had to be borrowed against the unchanged value of local collateral.[17] Similarly, large currency realignments can dramatically increase the prices of essential inputs for agriculture, e.g., imported fertilizer. Instead of having the expected positive effect on investment by making available a larger quantity of foreign exchange, devaluation may actually have a negative impact by pushing up the prices of imported capital goods and other inputs.[18] Here the question of timing and sequencing is crucial: if producers are to invest for the future, higher prices for their produce must be achieved before they are faced with significant increases in the costs of their inputs.

As the Bank argues, while devaluation may be necessary, in itself it is by no means sufficient and must be accompanied by complementary policies such as tight fiscal and monetary policies and/or an incomes policy if it is to be sustained. The danger is that massive devaluation will trigger hyperinflation and generate expectations of a continuing vicious circle of devaluation, inflation, and further devaluation. Prices and wages must be stabilized if devaluation is to be a successful policy instrument—and few African governments have yet demonstrated that they have the capacity to do this.

The extent of the overvaluation of most African currencies in the 1980s strongly suggests that devaluation was necessary, particularly as a means of paying higher domestic currency prices to producers of agricultural exports. Critics of the Bank have argued that such measures will have little impact on economies like those of Africa where, given that consumer goods already constitute a very small percentage of imports (often less than 20%), there is limited scope for import substitution. These arguments have been boosted by a cross-national study by Bank economists suggesting that devaluation did not lead to an improvement in trade balances but, among other things, contributed to a fall in output as a consequence of economies' reduced ability to import critical inputs and spare parts.[19] Again the preliminary evidence from Ghana substantiates this argument—underlining the necessity of supporting adjustment programs through providing adequate foreign exchange.

Devaluations automatically provide protection to domestic producers against overseas competition. They thus work against another adjustment objective: to force domestic producers to become more efficient. Some reduction in tariffs and other restrictions on imports thus is necessary to force African enterprises to become more competitive in international markets. Again, however, it is a matter of striking a healthy balance between introducing competition and running the risk of destroying Africa's fragile industries. Although devaluation may provide protection, it increases the costs of imported inputs. Other components of stabilization programs such as tight monetary policies, high real interest rates, and more diligent collection of taxes may further significantly raise local manufacturing costs. The Bank has acknowledged the complexity of these interrelationships by backing away from its earlier dogmatic stand and accepting the case for some continued protection of local manufacturing.

A second major area where the Bank has insisted on getting prices right is agriculture. The Bank has long insisted that higher producer prices were necessary to increase agricultural output. Governments found that low producer prices were indeed counterproductive. Food crops were simply sold at higher prices in "parallel" (that is, nonofficial) markets so that one objective that underlay governments' offering low returns to producers—to make cheap food available to urban workers—was frustrated. Low prices for export crops simply led to producers withdrawing from production or to the smuggling of crops to neighboring countries that offered higher prices. In chapter 11, Lofchie documents how different producer pricing policies pursued by neighboring East African governments produced a generally healthy agricultural sector in Kenya and agricultural disaster in Tanzania.

Preliminary evidence suggests that higher producer prices introduced as part of adjustment programs may have stimulated increased production. In Ghana, the trebling between 1983 and 1987 of local currency producer prices for the main agricultural export, cocoa, generated an immediate and significant rise in exports. In Guinea, the Bank reported a "dramatic" rise in exports of coffee once producers received higher prices following the replacement of the government's coffee-marketing organization by the private sector. As usual, however, the data are open to a variety of interpretations. With perennial crops such as cocoa having a three to five year gestation period, higher producer prices would not be expected to generate an immediate increase in production.

Besides higher producer prices, other factors have contributed to the recent improvement in agricultural performance in some countries. The ECA has asserted that the primary reason for Africa's improved agricultural performance in the last years of the 1980s was good weather throughout the continent. Although this undoubtedly was a relevant factor, few would accept that it was the primary explanation for increases in export crop production. Some of the reported "production growth" in response to higher producer prices undoubtedly represents the return to official marketing channels of produce that was previously being smuggled across borders or sold on "parallel" markets. Green, for instance, estimates that as much as one-third of the reported increase in Ghana's cocoa output in 1983–1986/7 was actually production that had previously been smuggled and sold in neighboring countries where producer prices were higher.[20] Similarly, up to 40 percent of the reported increase in groundnut production in Senegal is estimated to be crops previously sold on parallel markets.[21]

A one-off increase in production can be achieved through raising producer prices. But whether significant additional gains can be made through price manipulation is open to doubt. Econometric studies have estimated that the long-term price elasticity of aggregate supply for agricultural crops in Africa is approximately 0.3, that is, for every 10% rise in prices, supply will increase by around 3%. In itself this suggests that higher prices will at best generate a modest increase in production. Higher prices thus are necessary but in themselves insufficient to achieve long-term agricultural growth. There is now almost universal agreement that non-price factors such as inadequate infrastructure, lack of availability of key inputs such as irrigation or fertilizers, and unproductive research and extension services are significant constraints on supply.[22] Furthermore, farmers are unlikely to respond to higher producer prices in the longer term unless there are consumer goods available on which to spend their higher incomes. Stabilization programs that depress government expenditures on infrastructure and support services for agriculture, and that curtail the availability of consumer goods, are counterproductive to longer-term goals of increasing agricultural supply. The various structural adjustment programs have yet to address supply side issues effectively.

To date, stabilization has come about predominantly through a reduction in demand rather than through a vigorous supply-side response.[23] The volume of African imports fell on average by eight percent *each year* in the period 1980–86; further declines were experienced in 1987 and 1988. The value of imports of machinery and transport equipment declined by 40 percent from 1981 to 1985–86.[24] Such falls do not bode well for economic growth in the future as economies are starved of the capital goods needed for future development. Export volumes grew by only 1.5% each year from 1980–86 but this increase was more than offset by declining terms of trade for Africa's commodities: as a consequence the purchasing power of exports fell each year in the 1980s so that at the end of the decade they stood at only 76.7% of the level of 1982.[25] In other words, movements in the terms of trade have cost African countries close to 25% of the purchasing power of their exports in the last decade.

Slow growth in demand from industrialized countries and intensified competition for market shares has caused commodity prices to tumble in real terms. These falls took place even though in the 1980s the industrialized world enjoyed its longest uninterrupted period of economic growth since the Second World War—a sign of the increasing delinking of the manufacturing sector from the primary producing sector. By 1986 average real commodity prices were the lowest recorded this century with the exception of 1932, the trough of the Great Depression.[26] And for two crops of vital importance for Africa, cocoa and coffee, prices fell even further between 1986 and 1989—by 48 and 55 percent respectively.

The ability of African governments to offer higher prices to producers of agricultural exports has been hampered by falls in world market prices. Côte d'Ivoire was forced in September 1989 to halve the price it paid to its cocoa farmers; Cameroon had earlier cut its producer price by 40 percent.[27] Recent trends in commodity prices support the argument of those who warned against the fallacy of composition in the Bank's prescriptions: the argument that what is good for one country acting individually is not necessary beneficial if a number of countries simultaneously pursue the same policy. The Bank has been encouraging higher levels of commodity output not only in Africa but also in other developing countries—for instance, it has supported the planting of cocoa not only in Africa but also in Brazil, Indonesia, and Malaysia. The result is that world output has risen far more rapidly than world consumption and is expected to continue to do so for most of the 1990s. As yields in Southeast Asia are often three times African levels,[28] these countries are able to produce profitably at price levels that would threaten the viability of African production.

The recent experience in many commodity markets casts doubt on the Bank's argument that "Africa has an immediate comparative advantage" in agriculture.[29] Africa, the Bank asserts, "cannot afford to adopt a passive role and lose even larger market shares to more aggressive Asian and Latin American exporters." But does Africa enjoy a comparative advantage over these other producers? In a world of unemployed or underutilized resources, the answer is probably negative. Given the macroeconomic instabilities generated by stabilization programs, investors are unlikely to be attracted to African countries in preference to, for instance, Malaysia (which, of course, already provides much better infrastructure).

And the debt problems of higher income developing countries will almost certainly guarantee that they will not voluntarily give up their gains in market shares from the last decade but will continue to market aggressively. The Bank's plea that "in negotiating commodity agreements, Africa's loss of market share should be seen as an argument for more favorable treatment"[30] reads like wishful thinking.

Cutting Budget Deficits and Reducing the Role of the State

The overextension of African states was reflected in the budget deficits that most African countries sustained throughout the 1970s—taxes seldom amounted to more than 70% of government expenditures. Budgetary deficits were inflationary as governments resorted to printing money, and tended to crowd out private investors from the market. The reduction of budgetary deficits thus was an important component of stabilization. The manner in which this has been achieved, however, has not been propitious for future growth.

Budget deficits have been reduced but this has occurred largely at the expense of investment expenditure—hardly a desirable outcome for the longer term prospects of the economy. In Senegal the agricultural budget was cut by 24 percent in real terms, and gross fixed capital formation as a share of GDP fell from around 30% in 1981 to less than 23% in 1984.[31] In Zambia, capital outlays were more than halved in real terms from 1982 to 1984; by the latter year they were more than 70% below the figure for 1974.[32] Governments have chosen soft targets for budget cuts, preferring to cut investment and maintenance outlays rather than personnel expenditures that sustain their patronage networks.[33] Van de Walle, in chapter 10, provides evidence of these trends from Cameroon. Consumption has been preserved at the cost of investment; expenditure on the military maintained at the expense of health and welfare. There is no evidence that reductions in public investment expenditure have been compensated by increased private investment. As the Bank has increasingly acknowledged, in many LDCs the problem is often not one of public investment "crowding out" private investment, but of insufficient public investment in infrastructure which is a necessary complement if not prerequisite for private investment.[34] The Bank noted in its second report on structural adjustment lending that the fall in investment in many African countries had been so severe that depreciating capital was not even being fully replaced.[35]

Another area of budgetary policy where there are potential tradeoffs between current stabilization and future growth is the Bank's and especially the Fund's insistence on the abolition of subsidies, and the Bank's concern with ensuring that governments recover part of the cost of programs through the user pays principle. A strong case can be made that many of the subsidies dispensed by African governments have been wasteful, part of the network of patronage whereby scarce resources were directed toward political supporters. Subsidies on agricultural inputs, for instance, usually were of primary benefit to the wealthier farmers. Universal food subsidies were wasteful, benefiting the poor and the wealthy alike. But complete abolition of food subsidies may cause considerable harm to the poor—especially in highly urbanized countries like Zambia—and directly threaten a government's legitimacy and prospects for political survival. Gradually the Bank has come to appreciate that a more nuanced approach—with continuation of subsidies but their targeting at the most needy—rather than a theological insistence on complete abolition may not only be consistent with improving human productivity in the long term but also the only politically feasible approach.

The Bank continues to insist, however, that countries attempt to recover costs of providing services through increased user charges. Again there is some justification for this: there is no good economic reason why scarce resources should be deployed on subsidizing services to those who can afford to pay for them. And user charges do provide an incentive to farmers to increase their output in order to have access to services. On the other hand, such charges may prevent the poor from gaining access to health, water, and education services—which again conflicts with the long-term goal of providing a healthy and educated workforce for development. And there must also be some doubt as to whether charging for some services is a cost-efficient means of raising revenue. Green cites internal Bank studies in suggesting that a realistic maximum of 10 to 20% of health and education services can be self-financing.[36]

Attempts by the Bank to insist on the privatization of state-owned enterprises—both for budgetary reasons and because of its preference for privatization—have generally met with resistance, one reason for which has been the threat that such action would pose to the state's patronage network, especially its ability to provide employment to urban school-leavers. Against this, however, governments have to balance the possibility that the sale of state corporations could itself become a source of patronage—in some countries where privatization has occurred, e.g., Senegal, the organizations have been sold cheaply to regime supporters.[37]

Divestiture has also been hampered by the lack of accurate information on the assets and liabilities of state corporations, the difficulty of valuing assets, and the inadequacies of local capital markets. Beside the threat to the government's patronage capacity, divestiture has also been unpopular politically, especially with organized labor, because it is seen as selling off the national patrimony. With governments implementing restrictive monetary policies and high real interest rates, foreign buyers may be much better placed than nationals to bid for the enterprises. As Gyimah-Boadi records from the Ghanaian experience, even local businesspeople who support privatization in principle have opposed divestiture where the program "favors the well-capitalized, better organized, and better-networked foreign investor."[38]

In many African countries where "crony capitalism" is the norm, the dividing line between the state and the private sector is far from distinct. Whether private monopolies—either under domestic or foreign control—will be any more efficient than the state monopolies they succeed remains to be demonstrated.

Adjustment, Poverty, and Redistribution

Structural adjustment programs inevitably have had significant redistributive effects. World Bank presidents' reports on structural adjustment lending have acknowledged that there are likely to be significant negative social effects in the short run from adjustment. Expenditure reduction policies often result in lower real wages and consumption levels. Public sector workers are often retrenched as part of expenditure reduction measures. Trade liberalization and tariff reforms may result in employment losses in inefficient enterprises that cannot withstand the new competition. And the poor may face higher prices, especially for food, and reduced access to social services because of cuts in social expenditures.[39]

These effects have been particularly pronounced in Africa. Here, structural adjustment programs had a conscious goal of engineering a major change in the urban-rural terms of trade in favor of rural producers—a trend that was already well under way by the end of the 1970s as a consequence of the rise in food prices and decline in manufacturing output. Urban wage earners have been the group most adversely affected by economic decline and subsequent stabilization. The index of real wages in Uganda fell from 100 in 1972 to 9 in late 1984; in Zaire the purchasing power of the minimum wage in 1982 was only 3% of the 1970 level. In many countries it appears that the flow of remittances from urban to rural areas has been reversed. Even though an increasing proportion of urban dwellers now grow part of their food requirements, there is evidence of growing malnutrition—in part because of Fund and Bank insistence on the dismantling of food subsidy programs.

Requirements for reductions in government expenditure have also led to major cuts in budgets for education and health care. UNESCO figures show a fall in education expenditure from $32 per capita in 1980 to $15 per capita in 1987 in a continent where more than one-quarter of the population is illiterate.[40] While not all of the decline in social expenditures can be blamed on adjustment programs, as the general economic crisis had already led to severe cuts in some states before adjustment programs were adopted, the dilemma is that the requirements for stabilization undermine the foundations—an educated, healthy population—for longer-term growth.

The Bank—under pressure from UNICEF—has increasingly acknowledged the problem and started to address the human dimension through such measures as the Programme to Mitigate the Social Costs of Adjustment in Ghana, and similar measures introduced in Côte d'Ivoire, Gambia, Guinea, Mauritania, and Senegal. The Bank's two reports on adjustment lending concluded that because domestic inefficiencies have proved to be more intractable than anticipated and external uncertainties have continued the focus of adjustment should be shifted from short-term crisis management and stabilization, which dominated the first decade of adjustment, to more fundamental issues of long-term growth, development, and poverty reduction. As noted above, this new emphasis is reflected in *From Crisis to Sustainable Growth*.

To date, however, the sums raised to finance human development fall far short of those required even to maintain previous real levels of expenditure. And a review of adjustment programs found that the conditions the Bank imposed for the release of successive tranches of adjustment loans seldom included the adoption of measures designed to improve social conditions.[41] In a continent where the Bank estimates that two-thirds of the population are living in absolute poverty, there is little scope for further downward pressures on living standards. Even under optimistic assumptions about growth in per capita incomes, the Bank projects that the number living in poverty in Sub-Saharan Africa will rise by 85 million to 265 million by the turn of the century: Africa will then account for more than 30% of the developing world's impoverished compared with 16% in 1985.[42]

Structural adjustment programs may well lead to increased levels of inequality in Africa. Much depends on the structure of production for the export crops that are being favored. Where they are grown primarily on plantations, as for instance in Malawi, or large farms, which usually enjoy the advantage of better transport links, then the benefits of higher producer prices may accrue disproportionately to a favored minority. Growing reliance on fertilizers and other expensive inputs may similarly favor the more prosperous farmer. In Ghana, for instance, Kraus estimates that 20–25% of cocoa farmers capture 50–55% of income; a 1987 survey of four villages in Ashanti found that 32% of farmers received 94% of gross cocoa income.[43] More specific targeting of poor rural producers will be necessary if the benefits of adjustment are to be widely disseminated.

Adjustment, Debt, and Financing

The generally slow supply response that has characterized the adjustment process in Africa, coupled with the financing requirements for new loans that donors have provided in support of countries that have adopted reform programs, has produced a worrying increase in indebtedness.[44] Ghana's total debt rose from $1.1 billion in 1980 to $3.4 billion in 1988; similarly Zambia, which canceled a structural adjustment agreement with the IMF in 1987, experienced an increase in total debt from $2,187m to $6,592m over the same period.[45] Debt service ratios rose accordingly—for both countries to in excess of 60% of total export earnings by 1987. Martin addresses these issues in chapter 4.

Another worrying dimension of the experience of countries that have implemented adjustment programs has been the low levels of investment experienced—both from domestic and foreign sources. As the Bank has acknowledged in its second report on adjustment lending, investment has suffered in the rush to restore external balances and maintain debt service. Where output has increased, this has often come from better use of existing capacity: if higher growth rates are to be maintained then greater investment will be required. Domestic investors, however, have been deterred by restrictive monetary policies, high interest rates, devaluations which increase the cost of imported inputs, and trade liberalization. Foreign investors, on the other hand, appear yet to be convinced that African economies have turned the corner and offer good investment prospects for the 1990s. In Ghana, where the PNDC government made vigorous efforts to attract foreign investment after 1985, there has been negligible interest other than in the financing of gold and timber exports.[46]

There is inevitably a time lag between the adoption of a structural adjustment program and a positive supply response. The Bank's second report on adjustment lending suggests that devaluation should lead to a positive output response in two to three years. Elsewhere, however, the report admits that the experiences of Korea, Chile, and Thailand suggest that it may be four to eight years before a country enters a "virtuous circle" in which adjustment induces a positive investment response.[47] Two perceptions will play an important role in investors' decisions: first, whether the potentially favorable conditions brought about by stabilization will be sustained (the continent's unhappy record of political instability which, as argued below, may well be exacerbated by current demands for democratization, gives potential investors few grounds for confidence); second, the extent to which the debt overhang will constitute a significant tax in the future on investment returns.[48]

Africa's growing debt problems and inadequate investment are in part a consequence of the poor response from industrialized countries in support of African governments that have embarked on painful adjustment processes. The argument about resource availability is not that countries would have been better off without adjustment nor that finance should be supplied regardless of whether appropriate adjustment measures are implemented, but rather that the necessary finance to sustain the import requirements of a growth-oriented adjustment process has yet to be provided—and made available on such concessional terms that it does not add to the continent's debt-servicing problems. Despite the widespread adoption of adjustment programs, African countries paid back more (a total of $1.8 billion) to the IMF in the years 1986–90 than they gained in new borrowing. More than 4% of Africa's exports were devoted to Fund charges and repurchases, the highest figure for any continent.[49] Nigeria, which adopted a rigorous adjustment program of its own design in 1986, recorded a net outflow to the World Bank of $34.9 million in 1989. The total net transfer by the World Bank and its soft-loan affiliate, the International Development Association, to the region in 1989 was $876.7 million after taking into account repayments and interest/charges amounting to $1.38 billion.[50]

Inflows from official creditors were used in part to finance a net outflow of private capital. Most recently, the Bank has allowed the International Development Association to provide funds to help countries no longer receiving World Bank loans to service their previous borrowing from the Bank. A complex paper chase has been under way in which credits and debits have been shuffled from one institution to another with little positive impact to date in terms of net inflows to African countries. Indeed, if debt relief and arrears are not taken into account, an IMF study has calculated that net inflows to the continent were less than $1 billion per year in 1986 and 1987.[51]

Given the unpromising investment climate, inflows of private capital to Africa have been negligible in the last decade. Only Kenya, Niger, Côte d'Ivoire, and Mauritius received net inflows of private external capital in 1987, while Nigeria and Ghana recorded net outflows. In 1981–87, foreign direct investment in all non-oil exporting African states (including North Africa) averaged less than $300m per year.[52] The last year in which Africa received a net positive inflow of officially supported export finance—which covers a larger share of capital flows to Africa from private financial sources than to higher-income developing countries—was 1983. In

1989, although Africa continued to experience a net outflow on export credit finance, there was an upturn in new commitments. But the share of transportation projects in these was 53% whereas industry received only 16%.[53]

With negligible net inflows of private capital and export credits, Africa has come to depend heavily on the international financial institutions for its financing needs. The danger of relying on borrowing from the IFIs is that such debt cannot officially be rescheduled. In practice, some rescheduling has taken place as the Bank has set aside 10% of IDA reflows and investment income to lend to countries pursuing adjustment programs that have outstanding debts to its main loan account, the International Bank for Reconstruction and Development. The IMF has also proposed a complex system whereby countries in arrears to the Fund that are pursuing approved adjustment programs would be able to accumulate borrowing rights from the Enhanced Structural Adjustment Facility (ESAF). These rights can be activated once other donors pay off the arrears. The ESAF funds would then be used immediately to pay back the donors. The net result of this scheme—designed to maintain the fiction that the IFIs do not reschedule loans—will be that the IMF's own ESAF funds are used to pay off a country's overdue obligations to the Fund. But this elaborate arrangement is clearly intended as an emergency measure designed to give access to the Fund to countries that otherwise would be ineligible—and is not designed to be a significant mechanism for rescheduling.[54]

Beside the rescheduling problem, IMF purchases, in accordance with the original intention of the Fund as a lender to help countries overcome "temporary disequilibriums," have traditionally been of strictly limited duration, and carry a market rate of interest (over 8%). The need to repay short-term IMF credits often produces a "bunching" of debt obligations that severely strains debt servicing capacity. The World Bank has advised some African countries against further borrowing from the IMF on conventional terms. In an attempt to overcome these problems, the Fund introduced in 1987 a Structural Adjustment Facility (SAF) and the Enhanced Structural Adjustment Facility. Loans from both have a five and a half year grace period, and must be repaid over the following five years including an interest rate of one half of one percent. For the SAF, loans cannot exceed 70% of a country's quota; for the ESAF the maximum loan is 250% of quota.[55] But these loans, even though they are on longer and softer terms than conventional IMF borrowing, are still relatively short-term. And there have been delays in disbursement: only 20% of the total resources of the SAF and ESAF had been disbursed during the first four years.

Substantially more finance on concessional terms is needed in order to relieve Africa's debt burden and to give adjustment programs a chance of achieving success. Africa is now the world's most heavily indebted continent in terms of the ratio of debt to GDP. With current debt-servicing requirements, much of the income from economic growth immediately flows back to the IFIs and Western donors—hardly a situation that is likely to engender popular support for the programs. By the end of 1989 a total of $6 billion of African debt had been canceled, but because this consisted mainly of loans that had been made on highly concessional terms, the debt cancellation reduced debt servicing payments by only about $100 million in 1990. Seventeen countries have benefited from consolidation of debt totalling $5 billion under the terms agreed at the G7 Toronto summit but again this provided savings of only $100 million on total debt servicing of over $9 billion per annum. A 1989 IMF study suggests that even if full rescheduling of forthcoming principal payments occurs over the next five years, and export earnings grow at about 3.5% each year, there will still be no growth in nominal import capacity.[56]

In *From Crisis to Sustainable Growth*, the Bank assumes that debt relief measures will keep debt service payments in the 1990s at or below the level of the 1980s. This is probably a reasonable assumption (even if official rescheduling is not forthcoming, countries will probably give themselves de facto "relief" by going further into arrears). But with debt payments still running at the high levels of the 1980s, and export prospects poor, the Bank is forced to place a great deal of faith in increased overseas development assistance (ODA) as a means of bridging the financing gap for the continent's development needs in the 1990s. The Bank asserts that ODA must grow at 4% each year in order to finance the program that it recommends. If funding fails to reach this level the Bank concludes that "Africa's decline is likely to continue in the 1990s." Yet the Development Assistance Committee of the Organization for Economic Cooperation and Development projected in its 1989 annual report that there would be only a *two* percent increase in ODA in real terms in the 1990s, and that this increase will be heavily dependent on continued growth in aid from Japan. Africa's share of global ODA disbursements has already grown from 23% in 1980 to 30% in 1987[57] and there are signs that "donor fatigue" has set in as industrialized countries become disillusioned with the slow progress in Africa. The ninth replenishment of the International Development Association—on which Africa draws disproportionately—only maintained its funding in real terms, whereas a significant increase had been hoped for; the EEC's funding for the fourth Lomé Convention also fell far short of expectations. Together IDA and Lomé provide 20% of all aid to Sub-Saharan Africa. Even if Western countries are willing to devote some of the "peace dividend" to fund additional ODA, the demands of the Eastern bloc for Western capital will inevitably compete with Africa's claims. The relatively modest flows of assistance to Africa can be compared to the $12 billion capital that Western countries have pledged to the newly formed European Bank for Reconstruction and Development, and the estimated $11 billion in new credits, grants, food aid, and loan and investment guarantees the Western countries have pledged to Eastern Europe—mainly Poland and Hungary—in the period since the overthrow of their communist regimes.[58]

Even if all of the Bank's optimistic assumptions are fulfilled, per capita income in Africa in the 1990s will rise by at most 1% per year. And, if the Bank's targets are to be met, this modest amount will not be available for consumption but rather must be used to raise the savings rate. Furthermore, for its scenario to be realized, the efficiency of investment must improve by about 50% over the levels of the 1970s, a similar increase of 50% must be achieved in domestic savings and net transfers as a percentage of GDP, and food production must increase at 4% a year (whereas agricultural production over the past 30 years has risen at only 2% a year). The Bank assumes that improving the income levels of the bottom 95% will occur through squeezing the consumption levels of the top 5% of the population—which is making a gigantic leap of faith in terms of political feasibility.

If the Bank's calculations of Africa's financing needs for the 1990s are correct then the continent's future looks very grim indeed. To increase per capita incomes even by only one per cent per year appears to require levels of financing substantially beyond those that can be expected from Western donors.

Building Political Coalitions in Support of Adjustment

The agenda for adjustment in Africa has been further complicated by the demands of Western donors and the World Bank, following on the collapse of communism in Eastern Europe, that African governments should not only liberalize their economic systems but also democratize their political systems. Pressure from external agencies has added to an unprecedented wave of popular protest throughout the continent against corrupt, authoritarian regimes. The restoration of democracy would be another leap into an area of great uncertainty. Africa's post-independence democratic experiment was short-lived and in most countries merely a prelude to prolonged political instability.

Structural adjustment inevitably imposes heavy burdens on politically significant sections of the population—urban dwellers, public servants, and employees of state-owned enterprises and, if the program is properly implemented, the military. Austerity is never popular—advocating it is unlikely to be an election-winning strategy. The problem is that the benefits from adjustment accrue slowly, while the losses are usually immediate and significant ones for politically influential groups.[59]

The evidence from Africa's first decade of structural adjustment suggests that people will tolerate austerity for a while—especially if economic and social conditions have become wretched under the previous regime. But tolerance for austerity has its limits; popular expectations are that adjustment will bring the desired improvements in welfare within a short period. As already noted, however, the process of adjustment in Africa has proved to be much lengthier than anticipated: while some degree of stabilization has been achieved in some countries, there is little sign of sustained economic improvement. As Herbst discusses in chapter 9, the problem then becomes one of building a coalition that is willing to support adjustment over the long haul.

Chazan makes a persuasive case that Africa's most sustained adjustment effort—Ghana under the Rawlings regime—has been facilitated by the insulation of the ruling PNDC from the demands of strong sociopolitical groups. This situation arose in part because such groups had been severely weakened by previous economic decline and in part because of the regime's deliberate decision to break with postcolonial elites.[60] Democratization would be likely to bring such groups back into the center of the political arena. The PNDC also has not hesitated to invoke authoritarian measures when faced with opposition to its policies.

The Bank's expectation appears to be that democratization would be likely to bring to power a pro-adjustment coalition in which rural elements, the anticipated beneficiaries of the ending of urban bias, would be dominant. The logic is reminiscent of the Maoist strategy of having the countryside encircle the towns. There may be fatal flaws to this logic, however. First, as already noted, the benefits from adjustment programs will not be evenly spread through the rural community. Those farmers who have to purchase food in some parts of the year may find that gains from higher export prices are offset by the increased cost of foodstuffs and may not be enthusiastic supporters of adjustment. Second, there is no assurance that in a political contest farmers will in fact be mobilized as farmers rather than along regional, ethnic, or religious lines.[61]

Farmers are notoriously hard to organize. The larger the number of small farmers, the more difficult it is to mobilize them. Whether in an open election they will give their support to an administration that has raised producer prices or whether they will support parties that attempt to capitalize on communal, linguistic, or religious cleavages is an empirical question that has yet to be answered. It is of course true that regimes may increase their legitimacy by holding elections—but full, open, national elections may place adjustment programs at risk. Democratic elections may increase legitimacy but so does good economic performance—the first may come at the expense of the second.

The Ghanaian model of holding local and district elections may prove to be a useful means of allowing popular participation and mobilizing rural support for the government while continuing to insulate the political center from group demands. "Getting politics right" will inevitably be a delicate balancing act. Cross-national studies have shown that adjustment under democratic regimes is not impossible; they do suggest, however, that newly democratized governments face special problems as a result of raised expectations—often compounded by the populist stance of the governments—and high levels of political participation.[62] Universal prescriptions for wholesale democratization may well be unhelpful at this stage of Africa's adjustment process.

There is no disputing the need for a stable investment environment if Africa's economic decline is to be reversed. This requires the establishment of a rule of law, which has been markedly absent from Africa's systems of personal rule. Good governance in the sense of political arrangements supportive of rapid economic growth, however, should not be equated with democratization; it can be provided through various types of political systems. And there have been plenty of examples of democratic political systems that have not provided a stable foundation for sustained economic growth. Indeed, the historical record suggests that successful industrialization since the middle of the 19th century has been associated far more often with authoritarian than with democratic regimes. These issues are taken up by Callaghy in chapter 12.

Africa requires not only a less personalized, more institutionalized form of rulership, but also greatly improved bureaucratic capacity. Again, the effects of stabilization policies in necessitating cutbacks in government expenditure including salary outlays for public servants may have a detrimental effect on the longer term prospects of the economy. Limits on expenditure in some countries have reportedly prevented governments from recruiting additional professionals. As Huntington suggested a quarter of a century ago, "the problem [is] not to hold elections but to create organizations."[63]

What Makes for Successful Adjustment?

Evidence from Africa's first decade of adjustment suggests that programs need a substantial amount of good luck in their early stages. In Ghana, the introduction of the program coincided with the ending of a drought—the subsequent good harvest provided much-needed foreign exchange and gave the program a morale-raising boost. In contrast, the introduction of Zambia's program occurred at a time when copper prices were undergoing yet a further fall; the resulting deterioration in the country's terms of trade immediately invalidated the calculations that had been made of the country's external financing needs (see Martin's discussion in chapter 4). Similarly, Gulhati argues that the positive impact of reforms in Malawi was swamped by negative developments: falling commodity prices, transport disruptions, and the inflow of refugees from the conflicts in Southern Africa.[64]

To be successful, programs require a genuine and sustained commitment on the part of governments to reform. This has clearly been lacking in a number of countries where governments made nominal commitments to programs to gain access to initial loan funding but had little intention of carrying through the conditions. Cancellation of the programs was fully expected with a subsequent impasse until governments and donors once again sat at the negotiating table. We may be witnessing a rerun of the "ritual dances" between African governments and the donor community that Callaghy observed in earlier negotiations on debt rescheduling.[65]

As the Bank has noted, reform programs will not be successful unless they are "owned" by the government concerned.[66] In what circumstances do governments make a genuine commitment to implement an adjustment program? Regimes that have just acceded to power have proved to be more committed to reform—Rawlings in Ghana, Babangida in Nigeria, the Mwinyi government in Tanzania, and the military junta in Guinea. Governments that have just assumed power have no vested interest in defending the policies previously pursued, probably have fewer key decisionmakers and clients who have materially benefited from the policies previously pursued, and enjoy a honeymoon period during which the population may be willing to accept tough measures. In contrast, those regimes which have been in office for a long period and which are least insulated from networks of clientelist relations have proved to be unwilling and/or unable to make a radical break with the past. Included in this category would be Kaunda's Zambia, Houphouët-Boigny's Côte d'Ivoire, Moi's Kenya, Mobutu's Zaire, and two francophone governments where new leaders inherited well-entrenched clientelist systems in the 1980s—Diouf's Senegal, and Biya's Cameroon.

Programs have been most successful where governments have maintained the same teams of economic advisers and given them consistent backing. This has been the case in Ghana and Nigeria, but not so in Zambia where President Kaunda sacked the two leading figures involved in the implementation of the IMF program, and eventually canceled it.[67] Moves by the Bank to insert its own officials in the administration of some African countries, most notably Liberia and Zaire, in an attempt to ensure compliance with program targets have been unsuccessful as these officials were simply bypassed by the local regimes. Indeed, the evidence suggests that programs have been most successful where local officials have played a major part in drawing them up—most notably Nigeria and Ghana. Elsewhere limited bureaucratic capacity and/or commitment has caused the programs to be drawn up in Washington and often presented on a take it or leave it basis by the IFIs. Representatives of some African governments have complained that the IFIs have made insufficient attempts to involve them in the design of adjustment programs.[68]

A combination of domestic political commitment and adequate external finance is necessary if programs are to have a reasonable chance of success. In the first decade of adjustment there were a number of instances where the necessary external financial support was not forthcoming. Real devaluation is unlikely to be sustained unless donors make available sufficient foreign exchange to enable import capacity to be maintained. The Bank now acknowledges that Zambia's termination of its programs with the Fund and Bank in 1987 was prompted in good part by the failure of donors to provide the foreign exchange promised in support of its introduction of exchange auctions. A former senior Bank official has complained that Western governments have frequently failed to come to the party, leading to serious underfunding of programs.[69] Improved performance by Western donors as well as African governments will be required if Africa's decline is to be reversed in the 1990s.

Conclusion

Looking back on Africa's first decade of structural adjustment and looking forward to the end of the century, there are few grounds for optimism. Few countries have been able to sustain a multi-sector program of adjustment, while, in those that have, several key economic indicators give cause for concern—especially the increasing levels of indebtedness, and the failure of investment to revive. Yet if adjustment has not brought the quick results that were hoped for, no viable alternative has been put forward. A counterfactual situation of sustained nonadjustment in Africa is simply untenable; it would produce an even more rapid decline. This is not to suggest that all elements of the adjustment packages pursued in the 1980s were either necessary or well-conceived; rather that the economic imbalances Africa faces have to be rectified.

The international financial institutions were ill-prepared for the dominant role they were to assume in Africa in the 1980s. In consequence, the decade has been very much an experience of learning by doing. In addition, the IFIs, while clearly unprepared for the complexity of the problems they would encounter, have increasingly acknowledged that the initial prescriptions of short-term stabilization and getting the prices right have provided a totally inadequate foundation on which to reconstruct Africa's economic trajectory.

The problem faced by African governments and by the IFIs is that the context is so unsupportive of economic growth. Among the main problem areas are:

- crumbling infrastructure;
- rapidly deteriorating ecology;
- a poorly educated and often malnourished population which is growing at an unsustainable rate;
- an agricultural sector which produces primarily for subsistence and for which there is little technology available that promises immediate productivity gains;
- an inefficient and uncompetitive manufacturing sector crippled by import strangulation;
- an inadequate domestic market for efficient manufacturing along with formidable barriers to regional integration;
- poor communications with external markets—often exacerbated by the apparent fear of elites of the global economy and their desire to withdraw from such markets;
- deteriorating terms of trade for many of Africa's principal exports brought about by global overproduction and by the decreased raw materials intensity of late 20th century manufacturing;[70]
- an unattractive investment climate in an era in which there is increasing competition for the world's savings;
- an unserviceable debt overhang;
- a public service with very limited competence; and
- unstable political systems now under intense internal and external pressure for (premature?) democratization.

As noted above, some elements of the context have been further weakened by the initial impact of adjustment measures: the fall in investment has affected not only manufacturing but also the social and physical infrastructure essential for future growth; the much-needed inflow of funds that has accompanied some adjustment programs nevertheless has had the negative effect of increasing countries' debt-servicing problems. It is scarcely surprising that the Bank commented that "Many people in and out of Sub-Saharan Africa feel a growing sense of hopelessness."[71]

Many of these contextual elements are interlinked. This produces the dilemma that corrections to many are necessary but—like getting prices right—in themselves insufficient to bring about economic growth. Much of the laundry list of contextual factors that is identified in the Bank's long-term perspective study is not amenable to short-term solution. The priority for Africa's second decade of adjustment must be to identify those elements that can be improved in the immediate future, and to provide the necessary finance to enable such improvement to be engineered.

Notes

1. World Bank, *Accelerated Development in Sub-Saharan Africa* (Washington, D.C.: World Bank, 1981).

2. In this chapter Africa is used as shorthand for Sub-Saharan Africa excluding South Africa.

3. Data for 1970s from *Accelerated Development*; for 1980–89 from *World Development Report 1990* (New York: Oxford University Press, 1990). According to the *World Development Report 1992* (New York: Oxford University Press, 1992), p. 32, per capita income fell by a further 2% in 1990 and a further 1% in 1991.

4. Data from International Monetary Fund, *World Economic Outlook May 1991*, (Washington, D.C.: International Monetary Fund, 1991).

5. Similarly, an earlier IMF report had found that only one-fifth of the African countries wth Fund programs had achieved the targeted levels of economic growth. Close to 20% of the programs had been canceled for noncompliance. Justin B. Zulu and Saleh M. Nsouli, *Adjustment Programs in Africa: The Recent Experience* (Washington, D.C.: IMF Occasional Paper No. 34, April 1985).

6. The Bank prepared a detailed rebuttal to the ECA document but decided, for political reasons, not to publish it.

7. The Bank itself acknowledges that "Some early SALs [Structural Adjustment Loans] caught the Bank quite unprepared to give specific advice in a number of instances." World Bank, *Adjustment Lending: An Evaluation of Ten Years of Experience* (Washington, D.C.: World Bank, 1988), p. 65.

8. World Bank, *Sub-Saharan Africa: From Crisis to Sustainable Growth* (Washington, D.C.: World Bank, 1989).

9. Some of the Bank's earlier projections proved to be far too optimistic. The Berg report had projected, for example, that the index of coffee prices (1980 = 100) would be 96.7 at the end of the decade; the actual figure was 36.1. Similarly cocoa prices, which were predicted to be at 66.2% of their 1980 level, had slumped to 39.2% by the end of the decade.

10. The Bank argues that investment rates should rise from their current level of about 16% of GDP to 25%. Expenditure on human resource development is targeted to increase from the current 4 to 5% of GDP to 8 to 10% annually. The Bank launched a Social Dimensions of Adjustment Program in December 1987. Its 1989 review, *Adjustment Lending*, concluded that programs designed to ameliorate the social costs of adjustment needed further intensification. According to the *Annual Report 1989* (pp. 87–88) the Bank's executive directors agreed that "economic growth, while necessary, was not sufficient to resolve the poverty problem. It was agreed that growth must be supplemented by additional efforts to ensure that development reaches the poor. Such efforts need not involve trade-offs with efficiency standards. . . ."

11. For criticism of the Lagos Plan see John Ravenhill, "Collective Self-Reliance or Collective Self-Delusion: Is the Lagos Plan a Viable Alternative?" in Ravenhill ed., *Africa in Economic Crisis* (New York: Columbia University Press, 1986), pp. 85–107.

12. United Nations Economic Commission for Africa, *African Alternative Framework to Structural Adjustment Programmes for Socio-Economic Recovery and Transformation (AAF-SAP)* [E/ECA/CM.15/6/Rev.3] (June 1989), p. 5.

13. Philip Raikes, *Modernising Hunger* (London: Catholic Institute for International Relations/James Currey, 1988).

14. Henry Bienen, "The Politics of Trade Liberalization in Africa," *Economic Development and Cultural Change* 38, 4 (July 1990): 713–732.

15. Simon Commander, John Howell and Wayo Seini, "Ghana 1983–7" in Commander ed., *Structural Adjustment and Agriculture* (London: Overseas Development Institute, 1989), p. 109.

16. World Bank, *Adjustment Lending* p. 51.

17. Jon Kraus, "The Political Economy of Stabilization and Structural Adjustment in Ghana" in Donald Rothchild ed., *Ghana: The Political Economy of Recovery* (Boulder: Lynne Rienner, 1991), p. 134.

18. Riccardo Faini and Jaime de Melo, "LDC adjustment packages," *Economic Policy* 11 (October 1990): 491–519.

19. *Ibid.*

20. Reginald Herbold Green, "Articulating Stabilisation Programmes and Structural Adjustment: Sub-Saharan Africa," in Commander ed., *Structural Adjustment and Agriculture*, p. 38.

21. Simon Commander, Ousseynou Ndoye and Ismael Ouedrago, "Senegal 1979–88" in Commander ed., *Structural Adjustment and Agriculture*, p. 156.

22. Jacobeit suggests that the massive investment in infrastructure and rehabilitation in Ghana after 1983 that connected farmers once again to the world market was a significant factor behind the growth of cocoa production in this period. Cord Jacobeit, "Reviving Cocoa: Policies and Perspectives on

Structural Adjustment in Ghana's Key Agricultural Sector" in Rothchild ed., *Ghana: The Political Economy of Recovery* p. 223.

23. Faini and de Melo, "LDC adjustment packages."

24. United Nations Secretary General's Expert Group on Africa's Commodity Problems, *Africa's Commodity Problems: Towards a Solution* (Geneva: UNCTAD, 1990), p. 23.

25. World Bank, *Annual Report 1989* (Washington, D.C.: World Bank, 1989), p. 33. IMF, *World Economic Outlook May 1991.* Sub-Saharan Africa's terms of trade fell by a further 3% in both 1990 and 1991. IMF, *World Economic Outlook May 1992* (Washington, D.C.: International Monetary Fund, 1992).

26. Overseas Development Institute, "Commodity Prices: Investing In Decline?" *Briefing Paper* (March 1988): 1.

27. *Africa Recovery* 3, no. 3 (December 1989): 22.

28. Merrill J. Bateman, et al., *Ghana's Cocoa Pricing Policy* (Washington, D.C.: World Bank Working Paper WPS 429, June 1990).

29. *From Crisis to Sustainable Growth*, p. 8.

30. *Ibid.* p. 173.

31. Commander et al., "Senegal," p. 149.

32. Jurgen Wulf, "Zambia Under the IMF Regime," *African Affairs* 87 (October 1988): 589–590.

33. Kydd reported that the Zambian government's administrative controls over the economy enabled it to protect aggregate consumption levels while sacrificing investment. Jonathan Kydd, "Coffee After Copper? Structural Adjustment, Liberalisation, and Agriculture in Zambia," *Journal of Modern African Studies* 26, 2 (June 1988): 235. These findings reinforce those of the Bank itself which recorded in *Adjustment Lending* (p. 24) that "the burden of adjustment fell heavily on investment, as is shown by the relative worsening of the investment/GDP ratio for nearly two-thirds of the [adjusting] countries."

34. World Bank, *World Development Report 1991* (Washington, D.C.: World Bank, 1991), p. 121.

35. World Bank, *Report on Adjustment Lending II* (Washington, D.C., World Bank, 1990), p. 85.

36. Reginald Green, "The Long Road to Development," *Africa Recovery* 4, 1 (April-June 1990): 28.

37. Commander et al., "Senegal" p. 169.

38. E. Gyimah-Boadi, "State Enterprises Divestiture: Recent Ghanaian Experiences" in Rothchild ed., *Ghana: The Political Economy of Recovery*, p. 204.

39. Helena Ribe and Soniya Carvalho, *World Bank Treatment of the Social Impact of Adjustment Programs* (Washington, D.C.: World Bank Working Paper WPS 521, October 1990), p. 3.

40. Data from *Africa's Commodity Problems*; and Per Pinstrup-Andersen, "The Impact of Macroeconomic Adjustment " in Commander ed., *Structural Adjustment and Agriculture* pp. 90–104.

41. Ribe and Carvalho, *World Bank Treatment of the Social Impact of Adjustment Programs*, p. 7.

42. World Bank, *World Development Report 1990.*

43. Kraus, "The Political Economy of Stabilization and Structural Adjustment in Ghana," p. 133.

44. Structural adjustment loans must be repaid earlier than IDA project lending; these loans have thus contributed to an increase in debt service ratios.

45. Data from Matthew Martin, chapter 4 in this volume, and Martin, "Negotiating Adjustment and External Finance: Ghana and the International Community, 1982–1989," in Rothchild ed., *Ghana: The Political Economy of Recovery*, p. 253.

46. Kraus, "The Political Economy of Stabilization and Structural Adjustment in Ghana;" and Martin, "Negotiating Adjustment and External Finance."

47. World Bank, *Report on Adjustment Lending II*, pp. 11 and 22.

48. Jeffrey Sachs, "The Debt Overhang of Developing Countries" in G. Calvo, et al.,eds., *Debt, Stabilization and Development: Essays in Memory of Carlos Diaz-Alejandro* (Oxford: Basil Blackwell, 1989).

49. IMF, *World Economic Outlook May 1990* (Washington, D.C.: IMF, 1990), p. 195.

50. World Bank, *Annual Report 1989*, p. 112.

51. Joshua Greene, *The External Debt Problem of Sub-Saharan Africa* (Washington, D.C.: International Monetary Fund Working Paper 89/23, 1989), p. 9.

52. Data from *Sub-Saharan Africa: From Crisis to Sustainable Growth* Table 20, p. 235; and *Africa's Commodity Problems*, Table 10, p. 129.

53. Asli Demirguc-Kunt and Refik Erzan, *The Role of Officially Supported Export Credits in Sub-Saharan Africa's External Financing* (Washington, D.C.: World Bank Working Paper WPS603, February 1991), p. 12.

54. More than $2.1 billion in arrears to the Fund is owed by five African countries—Liberia ($308m), Sierra Leone ($103m), Sudan ($889m) and Zambia ($801m). International Monetary Fund, *Annual Report, 1990* (Washington, D.C.: IMF, 1990), p. 57.

55. In April 1991, seven African countries—Benin, Burkina Faso, Equatorial Guinea, Lesotho, Mali, Rwanda, and São Tomé and Príncipe had SAF arrangements with the Fund with loans totaling SDR137 million. A further eleven countries—Gambia, Ghana, Kenya, Madagascar, Malawi, Mauritania, Mozambique, Niger, Senegal, Togo, and Uganda—had ESAF arrangements totaling SDR1.3 billion. *IMF Survey* (June 10, 1991), p. 188.

56. Greene, *The External Debt Problem*, p. 3.

57. World Bank, *Annual Report 1989*, p. 106.

58. Data from *Financial Times* (London) May 29, 1990, p. 19.

59. Joan M. Nelson, ed., *Fragile Coalitions: The Politics of Economic Adjustment* (New Brunswick, N.J.: Transaction Books, 1989).

60. Naomi Chazan, "The Political Transformation of Ghana Under the PNDC" in Rothchild, ed., *Ghana: The Political Economy of Recovery*, p. 30.

61. Henry Bienen, "The Politics of Trade Liberalization in Africa," *passim*.

62. Stephan Haggard and Robert R. Kaufman, "Economic Adjustment in New Democracies" in Nelson ed., *Fragile Coalitions*, pp. 57–77.

63. Samuel P. Huntington, *Political Order in Changing Societies* (New Haven: Yale University Press, 1969).

64. Ravi Gulhati, *Malawi: Promising Reforms, Bad Luck* (Washington, D.C.: World Bank, EDI Development Policy Case Series, Analytical Case Studies, No. 3, 1989).

65. Thomas M. Callaghy, "The Political Economy of African Debt: The Case of Zaire" in Ravenhill ed., *Africa in Economic Crisis*, pp. 307–346.

66. *Report on Adjustment Lending II*, p. 2.

67. Thomas M. Callaghy, "Lost Between State and Market: The Politics of Economic Adjustment in Ghana, Zambia, and Nigeria," in Joan M. Nelson, ed., *Economic Crisis and Policy Choice* (Princeton: Princeton University Press, 1990), pp. 257–319.

68. See the comments reported in Cadman Atta Mills, *Structural Adjustment in Sub-Saharan Africa: Report on a Series of Five Senior Policy Seminars Held in Africa 1987–88*, (Washington, D.C.: World Bank, EDI Policy Seminar Report No. 18, 1989).

69. Ravi Gulhati, "Response" in Kjell J. Havnevik ed., *The IMF and the World Bank in Africa* (Uppsala: Scandinavian Institute of African Studies, 1987), p. 91.

70. Peter Drucker, "The Changed World Economy," *Foreign Affairs*, 64 no. 4 (Spring 1986): 786–791.

71. *From Crisis to Sustainable Growth* p. 23.

Chapter Two

The IMF and the World Bank in Africa: How Much Learning?

REGINALD HERBOLD GREEN

> The small boy breaks a pot [and] goes to tell his mother "It got broken," not "I broke the pot" but "It got broken." And who did this? We did. We broke the pot.
>
> —Jerry John Rawlings, Head of State, Ghana

> Adjustment programmes which rend the Fabric of Society cannot be sustained.
>
> —E.V.K. Jaycox, Vice President (Africa), World Bank

> We cannot get into the habit of living on handouts.
>
> —President Joaquim Chissano, Mozambique

The Road to Stabs and SAPS

In 1993, one may be forgiven for thinking that trends in development, growth, food supply, and the human condition in Sub-Saharan Africa (SSA), both continentally and nationally, have always been perceived as disasters. One might also suppose that external involvement and, consequently, national economic policy and strategy have been formed in the context of highly conditional, basically (if unevenly) neoliberal Stabilization Programs (Stabs) and Structural Adjustment Programs (SAPS). This is in fact an example of "always" being a very short period—one decade. Hence a historical perspective is needed, not least because, by their previous policies, the Bank, and to a lesser degree the Fund, are among Chairman Rawlings's "we" who broke the pot.

In the 1960s, growth of output and exports was above population growth both regionally and for most countries in SSA.[1] After about 1965, food production probably lagged behind population growth.[2] But this was not truly realized as a trend, as opposed to a crisis period, until the 1980s.[3] Deficiencies in human conditions (income distribution, health, education, malnutrition, employment) were perceived as severe but improving, being supposedly closely correlated with, and resulting from, growth. Broadening the colonial policy of state intervention and strengthening the colonial pattern of top-down technical and administrative structures were widely viewed as a matter of course by capitalist as well as socialist decisionmakers, analysts, and aid agencies.

The period 1970–79 was a poor one for most Sub-Saharan economies, especially in overall growth.[4] The reason is unclear because focusing on the 1970s as a whole obscures the presence of three distinct average periods: 1970–73, 1974–75, 1978–79. The period 1974–75 was a period of short-term crises (drought, import prices—far more broadly than just petroleum, fiscal imbalance, and threats to public service maintenance) for most SSA economies. But a majority of countries were able to cope well because external bridging aid and low conditionality IMF funding (plus import support from the World Bank) rose; the drought cycle turned; terms of trade improved as industrial economies and world trade returned to rapid growth; and guaranteed export credits and commercial finance became available on an unprecedented scale (albeit unequally by country).[5] As a result, 1976–79 were years of rapid (on average over 5%) output growth, public service revival, and the formulation of ambitious new targets. The negative export volume and low food production growth rates, as well as rising ratios of debt service to exports and of external to total investment finance, were not fully recognized. When noted, they were viewed as correctable trends.

Concern for human welfare (then styled "employment" or "basic needs") began to grow.[6] Growth was bypassing majorities and basic service access was very uneven (by country and within countries), which came to be widely accepted as a basic problem of most national development strategies. But, with a few exceptions (such as Tanzania whose 1967 Arusha *Declaration 7* did mark a strategic shift toward basic needs production and provision), little coherent program formulation, let alone implementation, emerged before the crises of the 1980s, which engulfed all but a handful of SSA economies. The year 1980, unlike 1970 or even 1973–74, does appear to mark a turning point. Terms of trade (measured on a 1975–79 base) fell precipitously; commercial[8] and export credit dried up; and the full impact of slow food production growth on urban provisioning in drought years became brutally clear. Import compression (often strangulation) had a negative multiplier effect on output (and even on exports); fiscal crises led to a deterioration of basic services (in some cases to the point of virtual collapse); and government policy became a series of exercises in crisis management. Attempts to cope in the basically successful 1974–75 manner now failed. Persistence with these strategies can be seen, in retrospect, to have aggravated the underlying problems. Thus 1980–81 marked continued decline for economies already in decline (e.g. Ghana), failure for those attempting to break out of stagnation through massive increases in investment financed by external debt (e.g. Togo, Malagasy Republic), and a false start for those seeking to rerun 1974–75 type bridging programs (e.g. Tanzania).

In the late 1970s, SSA states had requested a World Bank study on the reasons why their growth (then running at about 5% a year,[9] albeit unevenly by country, and after a poor 1970–73 and depressed 1974–75) was so slow. Late in 1981, the *Accelerated Development* (AD) report appeared.[10] It had the impact of a bombshell. As a senior official of a highly successful African economy put it, "We asked for bread and they chucked a stone at us."

In brief, AD argued:

- SA growth had been low throughout the 1970s (about 2%).
- the underlying cause lay in low agricultural (and especially agricultural export) growth (under 1.5% overall, somewhat below 2% for domestic food, 0% for exports).
- the basic reason for the poor performance was that SSA states had the prices wrong and restricted imports, as well as trying to do too much and interfering with markets and private enterprises.
- getting the prices right and securing a doubling of net resource inflows should yield a 3.5% GDP (and agricultural export) growth rate, especially because primary product terms of trade were set to improve (a projection the Bank reversed a few weeks before AD appeared).

In detail, AD was less stark. It did cite historical and external problems; listed dozens of other agricultural issues; praised a few government departments and public enterprises; and devoted some attention to health and education as human investments. But these were tack-ons, the result of bargaining within a committee written document. The core was hard neo-liberalism and was put bluntly as the authorized version of what to do. SSA countries would have to follow this agenda in order to get significant Bank finance beyond a decreasing number of project loans. This would be especially true if one wanted Bank support (via a Consultative Group) in mobilizing the doubled external resource inflows which the Bank, in AD, and subsequently, viewed as essential if SSA growth in the 1980s was to be as high as that of the population.

African terms of trade—excluding oil—declined through the 1980s with limited and brief exceptions. Even oil (the largest single export) fared very badly on a trend basis.[11] Furthermore, when emergency food aid (no one, reasonably enough, predicted the drought cycles) is excluded, net resource transfers to SSA divided by import prices stagnated after 1982 at levels little above those of 1981.[12] This is a far cry from AD's call for doubling. Therefore, on AD's own projections SSA should have enjoyed a falling *per capita* output in the 1980s (as it did) even if every country had adopted staunchly neo-liberal strategies in 1982 (as they did not).

Continuity in Adversity: The IMF in Sub-Saharan Africa

The IMF operates on a model projecting and seeking to regulate aggregates like output, exports, imports, government revenue, and expenditure and credit in monetary (not real volume) terms.[13] In this model there is no formal analytical connection between monetary and real volume magnitudes. There are no production functions. Indeed, the model virtually assumes no change in real output over a one- to three-year standby (SBA) period. Growth is plugged in as an estimate from outside the model in Extended Facility projections.

Therefore, the Fund is in the stabilization business: reducing external, fiscal, banking, exchange rate, and price imbalances, and doing so by cutting absorption of domestic production and imports into private consumption, public services, and investment. Drops in real wages, cuts in real public spending (except on external debt service), lower real credit for enterprise working capital (a de facto result, not an explicit goal), sharp devaluation, and high real interest rates are the main instruments sought in practice. Import liberalization, formerly a Fund theme, is now more a Bank than a Fund operational priority.

The IMF, by its own assertion, is not in the development or growth business, although it is in the business of lending (typically at about 8% with six years to repay, including three years of grace) relatively small bridging or external arrears reduction financing. It urges demand reduction to create a new, lower but stable base from which growth/development can then be resumed.

The performance checks ("trigger clauses"), default on which halts disbursements, relate to total bank credit, bank credit to the government (and often selected enterprises), and external arrears and/or reserves. Caps on nominal wage increases, and floors on real interest rates are often only slightly less explicit conditions.

The Fund's power does not depend on its net lendings (drawings), which have been quite low over 1980–88 and negative to SSA from 1987. It arises because a highly conditional agreement with the Fund is a precondition for a Bank structural adjustment program, a Paris Club (official creditors) debt rescheduling and for enhanced bilateral assistance.

From 1985, the Fund has moved to low interest, medium term (up to 10 years to repay), Structural Adjustment and Extended Structural Adjustment Facilities.[14] In practice, these roll over earlier standby and extended facilities.

The problems with the Fund's approach are well researched:[15]

- "trigger clauses" are likely to be broken because projections are based on weak data and imperfect foresight. Renegotiation takes time even when the Fund agrees that the country is not "at fault."
- despite willingness to include grant aid increases as analogous to exports and output (which, in the short run, they are), the Fund model is highly contractionist in thrust.
- the effects of the drop in the real wage and increases in real producer prices required, or at least strongly pushed, cannot be determined from the model in terms of real (supply) response, as opposed to monetary (demand) impact.
- projections of exports and of domestic inflation are systematically too optimistic, leading to an even greater probability of pulling "trigger clauses."
- credit ceilings are not built up from enterprise working capital needs for projected output levels (or for possible government real expenditure levels), but solely from a somewhat simplified de-

mand set of equations of the *(Money) (Velocity) = (Price) (Real Output)* variety, with velocity (unrealistically) and output (fatalistically) being held constant. As a result, credit ceilings frequently prevent viable firms from restoring or even maintaining output levels despite availability of real resources (including import support loan or grant imported inputs). Contraction of imports, public services, household incomes and consumption, and (in practice) fixed capital rehabilitation and investment is not an economically self-evident high road to resuming growth, especially in structurally weak, seriously debilitated economies with poor export prospects. Socially and politically, it is very likely to be a high road to disaster and instability.

- the Fund has dropped its "real devaluation" approach (adjusting the exchange rate against the trade-weighted average of those of commercial partners) to offset excess inflation since the late 1970s, or the last period of a relative balance approach, to setting parities in favor of shadowing the parallel market rate. In comparison with the comparative inflation approach, the worsening of terms of trade does militate for higher foreign exchange prices. But no logical basis for using a partly capital flight, highly imperfect, nonuniform rate as a target exists.

The Fund is by no means unaware of these criticisms. Nor is it totally unsympathetic. For example, it now agrees that for real interest rates of +5% to -5%, there is little empirical evidence that savings are much affected.[16] In fact, its data for SSA over 1974–85 show three countries with slightly above trend line Capital Formation/Growth ratios and four below. The four below include two with somewhat negative rates. This casts doubt on the short and medium term allocative efficiency argument for positive real interest rates, more so than the Fund's somewhat grudging admission that it may be small. Indeed, the Fund agrees in principle that slower devaluation, higher credit ceilings, and rising personal and government consumption would be desirable during adjustment. But it argues (correctly) that this would require much higher levels of interim grant or very soft loan finance, and that this is not available (to date, usually also correctly). With respect to constructing estimates of credit needs, it argues that this would be difficult (true) and would prevent credit control (less evident), while admitting that certain productive sectors in some SSA countries have had real output needlessly constrained by credit ceilings.

Increasingly, Fund stabilization is being seen as not merely less than complementary to Bank adjustment with growth, but in antagonistic contradiction to it (a view that Bank officials dare not state overtly but rather implicitly confirm by referring to conflicts, and in some cases leaning on the Fund when the country and the Bank have agreed on a structural adjustment framework).[17]

Furthermore, before the emergence in 1986–89 of the Structural Adjustment Facility (SAF) and Extended Structural Adjustment Facility (ESAF), Fund finance had been too short term and at too high an interest rate for countries needing prudent structural adjustment (as several of them and the Bank have explicitly stated). The problem is that SBAs or Extended Fund Facilities (EFFs) provide bridging finance for external and fiscal imbalances assured to be correctable in 18 to 36 months. However, no one now seriously supposes that this applies to most SSA economies. Indeed, even the Structural Adjustment Report did not make any such claim: witness its call for doubled external resource inflows and thus acknowledgment of a broadening trade imbalance.[18] Therefore, one may argue that the IMF has lent to SSA far too much and for the wrong purposes. That criticism is reinforced in cases such as the Sudan, Zambia and Ghana where hundreds of millions in IMF drawings have been used basically to reduce or hold down (temporarily in the first two instances) commercial arrears and arrears to other debt holders.

It is possible to sketch the IMF approach in fairly broad brush and static (or stable, continuous) terms because the IMF has not structurally adjusted its approach to stabilization in SSA or elsewhere since 1980, except to increase conditionality and to create special financing through the SAF and the ESAF. But these were undertaken to bail the Fund out of more defaults and to avert disaster for countries whose structural adjustment programs (including external finance) were on course if, and only if, they could avoid having to make large net repurchases from (i.e. repayments to) the Fund. They are thus reactive and limited, not proactive and general.

The results are only slightly less difficult to characterize. No Fund program without a parallel Bank/bilateral structural adjustment program has succeeded since the late 1970s, if success means just restored external balance and resumed growth of GDP above that of output. In some stabilization/structural adjustment contexts (e.g. Ghana and Gambia), Fund finance has played a useful bridging role.[19] But this role has served to secure higher Bank/bilateral flows rather than to restore trade balances. And, in these cases, SAF/ESAF have come just in time to roll the bridge into longer term, lower interest funding before repayment would have capsized the programs. In other cases (e.g. Tanzania, Nigeria, and Rwanda), little Fund money has been used because these countries (and the Bank) deemed this too costly and, moreover, too short term to be any large part of the answer, rather than exacerbating the debt problem.

Accelerated Development to Structural Transformation with Sustainable Growth

The Bank's record is much harder to summarize. The Bank shapes its programs to the local context more, and is less monolithic—and even, at times, less internally consistent—in approach than the Fund. It does learn from experience and change course, even if rarely admitting it makes mistakes (a reticence damaging to its credibility). It has, in fact, engaged in a thoroughgoing structural adjustment of structural adjustment.

With respect to privatization of enterprises, the Bank has de facto retreated[20] to a pragmatic line. Efficiency (in real output and real resource costs as well as profits) is the key and is acceptable through better public enterprise management, autonomy, and accountability or joint ventures, as well as by closure or sale. But it contends (correctly) that many SSA public enterprises are very inefficient and/or have investment requirements that the state cannot meet. Therefore, doing fewer things but doing them better would be preferable. The problem of overoptimism as to the availability of foreign and domestic entrepreneurs remains, as does a certain insensitivity to the economic costs (surplus outflow and reinvestment abroad) as well as political costs of foreign and domestic minority (e.g. Mauritanian, Lebano-Syrian, Indian, Somali) takeovers.

In the case of user fees, the Bank is much more open to the charge of gross ideological bias; one, incidentally, that dates at least to the early 1970s. Indeed, its enthusiasm for universal primary health care and universal basic education, taken with its own findings that many (up to 50% in some countries) users cannot pay substantial amounts, are hard to square with its resolute championing of charges. These do deny access to poor people (even if cap and waiver schemes exist in principle); have high cost-revenue ratios; are unlikely in most cases to cover more than 10 percent of costs of services; are less progressive (and less oriented to vulnerability reduction) than would be higher import or manufacture multirate sales taxes as long as these exempted basic foods and artisanal products. (For such taxes administrative reality forces progressivity and provides an incentive to the informal sector.)

In practice, the greatest cost may be the diversion of large amounts of technicians' and decisionmakers' time to a fairly trivial issue. Some fees (e.g. Zimbabwe's health charges for those in receipt of above twice the minimum wage, and for "above normal" room and board services) do make sense and yield some revenue at low access cost. But they are no more significant to revenue or budget balancing than any other 1 to 2% of total recurrent revenue taxes or charges, and should receive no more attention. The Bank may need a shift to downgrade fees. In Mozambique, it agreed that a system devised according to its principles had drastically reduced attendance at health posts, yielded little revenue, created serious administrative and financial probity problems, and thus perhaps needed revision or even partial withdrawal. In practice, inflation is being allowed to erode it into insignificance.

On government expenditure, the Bank has reversed course. It now seeks to target real increases—up to 15 to 18% of GDP for recurrent budgets and 30% overall[21]—and to mobilize external soft funding where domestic revenue cannot reach these levels for some years. Human investment, infrastructure maintenance, and economic services are back in fashion. Government (civil service) reform is no longer merely a euphemism for "redeployment" (i.e. sacking). It now also refers to raising real wages of a smaller number of civil servants, improving skills and institutional capacity, and decreasing the number of services in order to improve performance.

Overall employment/self-employment expansion is now stress-ed as a goal, as a means to, as well as a consequence of higher output.[22] Precisely how it is to come about is less clear. In practice, actual programs to permit small-scale farmers to produce, sell, and buy more are thin on the ground, while private enterprise growth is as much an article of faith as an empirically researched projection (much less one with Korean-style support and incentive measures attached).

The Bank's faith in markets and liberalization remains undimmed in principle but has been amended to include non-price factors, and greater flexibility as to timing and modalities of liberalization. For example, the Bank's own studies suggest that only 10% of variations in agricultural[23] growth appear to relate to (official) price variations. Hence infrastructure, transport, inputs, and research and extension now feature more prominently. While the Bank still believes that much state intervention in African markets creates worse failures than non-state inspired market imperfections, the AD Report's virtual categorical opposition to selective interventions has been tempered. On trade liberalization, reality has again shifted. Efficient import substitution is now Bank-endorsed; given present primary product export prospects and food import trends, it has to be![24] Calculated, targeted protection therefore is sometimes accepted, as is step by step liberalization. On exchange rates, the Bank tends, in public, to follow the Fund and has not really worked out when a devaluation below comparative purchasing power restoration would raise exports more than inflation.

"Shock cures" are now almost out of Bank terminology and the pace of adjustment is targeted on a balance between the dangers of institutional, social, and market damage from overly quick shifts and the difficulties of gaining large enough soft external funding for long enough to allow a less compressed time scale. With evidence of increased debilitation, more sluggish responses, and a worse than anticipated external economic environment (trade, drought, and war), there has been a steady "lengthening" of structural adjustment programs. In 1983, it was generally a three-year process, including the stabilization phase. It has gradually crept up to five to seven years after stabilization, i.e. up to ten years. This has mirrored the effort to keep the Ghana flagship program going. The program, which was to have run out in 1986, is now to expire in 1993. In fact, on this long running SAP, external balance projections do not show a closing of the current account deficit (excluding grants) until the mid-1990s. *Au contraire*. Thus, further lengthening can be expected, with resultant rises in "aid fatigue" by donors (who have not raised aid as much as shifted it from non-SAP to SAP countries), and "adjustment fatigue" by recipients who sometimes see GDP per capita rising slowly but at the price of massive social political and economic efforts and tensions.

But, in 1991, the Bank negotiated Zimbabwe into an SAP focused on import liberalization and a float of the exchange rate, with much more rapid changes than Zimbabwe had thought prudent. Growth collapsed, inflation spiralled, the exchange rate fell like a rock with a widening trade gap, and mounting inflation and the breakthrough on capital inflows (Zimbabwe's reason for seeking to get World Bank blessing for continuation of its own 1984–89 "in-house" SAP).

Since 1985, the Bank has been quite clear that structural adjustment is feasible only with growth. That is to say, if by the second or third year of the program GDP growth is not sustainably above that of population, it will probably be impossible to make a later breakthrough without major increases in funding. Program collapse is thus likely. Similarly, for the period 1986–89, the Bank has come (in Vice President Jaycox's words) to accept that structural adjustment programs which rend the fabric of society are not sustainable. Furthermore, the Bank has quietly resuscitated President MacNamara's thrust against absolute poverty and for human investment more generally, although it still has not internalized or programed enhanced production by poor people as a significant strategic element.

Certain procedural problems appear endemic to Bank SAPery. First, the priority public investment (PI) program is a very odd framework for government or Consultative Group action. By nature, it does not focus on policy or overall investment. Nor does it give a guide to resource inflow needs. Projections showing external needs and sources articulated by government and enterprise, and by recurrent operations and capital rehabilitation, or new investment (as used by Tanzania and, to a degree, Mozambique), would seem a more serviceable tool for Consultative Groups.

The overall Fund/Bank policy framework papers (PFPs) also pose problems. Countries have rarely taken adequate initiatives in submitting their own drafts as a basis for discussion. Too much initiative is thus left in the hands of the international financial institutions although, in fairness, some of their drafts clearly do draw on government strategy papers. The latter, in turn, have such lengthy internal negotiation and decision-making processes that little time is allocated to country study, analysis, counterproposal, and dialogue.

Most programs remain underfunded (by Bank estimates). Some have been doomed from the start for that very reason (Zambia is a clear example, and—at least for some programs—is accepted as such by the Bank). Others have had very serious lags. Luck has enabled some to survive: in Ghana in 1983, the culmination of the worst drought in recorded history, coupled with massive forced repatriation of Ghanaians from Nigeria, served as a *diabolus ex machina* to deflect criticism from policy.[25] In Tanzania, there had been more modest but real growth. But lags in certain key sectors—e.g. transport rehabilitation in Tanzania, industry in Ghana and Tanzania, food production in Ghana, and rather ill-managed marketing privatization to co-ops in Tanzania—are leading to new structural distortions.

A related point is "creeping conditionality." This is not so much a matter of new ultimate goals—if anything, the Bank has become less neo-liberal. Rather, it relates to shifts from down the road goals to new instant requirements (as in the case of import liberalization in Ghana in 1985–86) and the disastrous instant liberalization in Zimbabwe's 1991 SAP, which sent a previously moderately successful economy into free-fall. Just as one can argue that the longer a program enjoys some success the greater the cost to the country and to the international finance institutions of its collapse, it is arguable that this will provide countries with more negotiating power than they have utilized to date. In fact, this power has been used in Ghana and Tanzania (as well as in Mozambique, which is a rather special case because of war destruction) to considerable, if considerably unpublicized, effect.

On external factors, the Bank has adopted what could be called a "two faced," or "realistic," approach. It accepts that, whatever the causes of economic debilitation in SSA, 1980s terms of trade and primary product quantity growth trends, industrial economy protectionism, and the heaviest (relative to exports) debt overhang of any region, threaten to destroy structural adjustment efforts—as does underfunding. The Bank makes these points quite strongly to the North, especially with respect to debt relief and soft finance. This has helped change the climate so that "creeping debt write-off" is moving fairly quickly for low-income countries, a breakthrough the Bank hopes to extend to lower middle-income countries. On soft resource inflows, the Bank has raised flows to SAP countries via IDA reallocations and its Special Programme to about 8% a year since the mid-1980s. But, excluding food aid, this is primarily a reallocation from non-SAP countries. Since the Bank wishes to see adequately financed SAPs on a sustained basis in most of SSA, it is reverting back to the AD Report's call for doubled resource inflows, but this time for the 1990s as opposed to the 1980s.[26]

When speaking to SSA countries, the Bank argues first that domestic reform is necessary and desirable whatever the external context and, second, that it is unsound to budget export price improvements, reductions in barriers to market access, debt write-off or aid flows until and unless they are ensured. These points are sensible, but have left SSA countries with the perception that the Bank is doing less than it actually is to make these conditions a reality. There is also the unwarranted suspicion that external debt repayment is a Bank priority when, except for its own debt, it advocates the opposite for the SAP countries.[27]

The results of SAPs are, overall, predictably, unclear. There have not been enough programs running long enough and seriously enough for cross country data at one point in time, or over time, to yield clear answers. The program is aggravated by the fact that pre-SAP economic trends were in most cases both downward and below average. The Bank-UN Economic Commission for Africa (ECA) statistical war is waged from both sides with highly selective and less than appropriate data. On the Bank's part, category choices and shock adjustments in *Africa's Adjustment and Growth in the 1980s*[28] are hard to perceive as anything but rigged. That document does not serve the Bank nor SSA well. It was evidently an ill-digested or rushed review draft, devised not to preempt ECA's *African Alternative Framework*[29] (as many in SSA suspect), but to prove to donors that "structural adjustment works" as well as to reduce "aid fatigue" at the Spring 1989 Bank/Fund Development Committee Meeting.

A recent study suggests positive overall results on what appear to be reasonable projections of likely economic trajectories without SAPS.[30] However, it shows poor results on fixed investment and high social and economic costs of certain measures—e.g. mass firings, fees for basic services—with no discernible offsetting macroeconomic gains.

Looking at country cases, there are several successes: Ghana, Tanzania, Mozambique, Rwanda; perhaps Kenya, Gambia, and Senegal. There is one partial success reversed by war—Malawi. But, here, it is hard to separate out the policy shift gains from those caused by increases in net external resource inflows. Probably both have been relevant.

But there are failures: Zaire, Zambia, the Sudan, Somalia, Togo, and most recently Zimbabwe. And other cases (e.g. Uganda) are unclear because both the policies and inflows are still in an extended infancy or have been recast after years of nonsuccess, e.g. Malagasy Republic.

Modernization, Mimicry, Self-Reliance: From Lagos to African Alternatives

SSA has been slow to shift away from approaches to modernization and growth that rely merely on the intensification of investment in physical and human capital. Equally, self-reliance formulations often seem to be smudged copies of models associated with the United Nations Economic Commission for Latin America (ECLA) of the 1950s. Such models are oddly blended with copying out the Treaty of Rome as a guide to economic cooperation based on managed markets and planned economic cooperation. At least at the official level, this was true from the 1980 *Lagos Plan of Action* (Lagos) through the 1986[31] *African Priority Programme for Economic Recovery* (APPER).[32] This is, in one sense, an unfair criticism. Lagos was a start toward a strategy designed for a world context similar to the 1970s, and APPER had a chance of success assuming, first, that it had actually received the aid and debt relief estimated as needed and that, second, the 1986–88 terms of trade evolution had been positive or neutral instead of negative.

Academic and journalistic thought has had more radical (or strategy adjusting) elements, as exemplified in the work centered loosely around the Institute for African Alternatives. The problem here, however, is of another order. First, the Fund's stabilization model is equated in much of this work with the Bank's Structural Adjustment model. As this is simply not accurate, it does not advance analysis. Second, the pre-SAP declines are ignored and the whole blame for post-1980 economic debilitation is put on SAPs and Stabs—with little effort to project what would have happened had previous policies continued. Third, errors of program design and of poor negotiations by African governments are conflated with more basic analytical issues (e.g. the role of industry, optimal market intervention) in a way that often obscures rather than illuminates. Thus a dialogue of the mutually deaf (or of two prophets speaking at each other in tongues) has ensued.[33] The Bank is not unamenable to reasoned critique—both UNICEF and IDS (Sussex) obtain hearings and have some influence on thinking because the Bank perceives these agencies as putting forth serious and hard-headed analyses of Bank aims, failures, and limitations. That it does not see most SSA critics in this light is unfortunate, especially because it tends to cause SSA contacts, no matter how independent and privately critical, to be viewed as "sell-outs" or, at best, premature surrenderers ("hand uppers") who give up their principles for only marginal influence on Bank practice.

ECA's *African Alternatives*[34] is a step toward molding official and academic African analysis toward an African based strategic framework and, perhaps, toward setting the foundations for more serious strategic and conceptual dialogue between the Bank and SSA. It does:

- clearly set out the need to alter strategy to reduce imbalances and restore growth.
- focus on the need to reduce import intensity and to raise exports to erode the present massive dependence on external finance.
- help to develop sound industrial and interstate economic cooperation policies; and
- help to identify ways to build up effective market management and intervention without creating costly distortions or blocking the creative potentials of the public and private enterprise sector.
- reduce defense budgets to the benefit of basic services, and increase popular participation both to increase productive efficiency and to redress the bias in allocations against absolutely poor households and women.

Two of three post-1989 Bank priorities[35] are stressed by ECA:

- improving the quality of governance as to accountability, competence and regular, competitive choice of leaders.
- basic services/human investment as a key part of transforming African economies' dynamism (or lack of it).

The third is cited but in little concrete detail:

- treating poverty reduction (primarily by enhanced production by poor households) as one of the bottom line goals to be pursued.

It seeks to achieve the above via increased domestic resource mobilization, better terms of trade and market access, and massive debt write-offs. As to instruments, it has less faith in macro monetary tools, especially in across the board devaluation (for which, rather oddly, it would substitute multiple exchange rates as opposed to a fiscal pattern of differential export subsidies and import taxes à la South Korea or Brazil).

Despite having outlined the Fund model in some detail and mistakenly calling it the Bank's model, the ECA's document[36] does raise key issues and, in some respects, is "harder" on SSA than the Bank. But is it an alternative? Except for the third, fourth, and last of these points, about which ECA is very vague, there is not much divergence on aims from the Bank's actual model. And in these cases, the practical difference in actual programs requires (and deserves) more dialogue to elucidate how wide the gap actually is. On the external front, ECA proposes no more than the Bank does; the apparent alternative is to urge SSA to act as if the changes are happening now instead of acting when (if) they take place. In short, ECA's "structural adjustment" seems to be a variant of the Bank's "structural adjustment," not a radical alternative. It does raise certain key issues for examination. Furthermore, it squarely makes the case that, as SSA moves from a three year to a ten year and maybe even a fifteen to twenty year exercise, rethinking what the strategy must include is necessary for a long term, as opposed to a short-to-medium term restructuring form of development.

Social Fabric, Human Condition: Critique or Complement?

Initially, structural adjustment—perhaps because it was seen as short-to-medium term—did not address income distribution, absolute poverty, or losers from stabilization and adjustment measures with any seriousness. Claims that poor farmers would gain and rich city dwellers would lose were, at best, pious hopes and, at worst, decorative rhetoric.[37]

This, in part, flowed from political ingenuousness and little analysis of poverty. The Bank seems to find it difficult to realize that powerful and wealthy groups can protect their interests and shift themselves to benefit from new policies while unloading costs on the poor. Furthermore, it is by no means clear that the bulk of SSA agricultural exports are produced by households with below average incomes. *Au contraire.* A core of above-average income producers usually provide the lion's share, with a penumbra of many small low income producers furnishing the rest. And urban wage earner/informal sector real incomes fell draconically after the mid-1970s so that, by the 1980s, urban absolute poverty was an empirically and humanly (as well as perhaps politically) significant reality.[38]

Ill-considered early efforts to balance recurrent budgets by cutting services, as opposed to raising taxes or grant aid, exacerbated the poverty problems, as did wholesale cuts in government/public enterprise employment. Such cuts were less common than supposed, given natural turnover and the presence of "ghost workers" to be exorcised rather than fired.

From 1985, social criticism was emphasized by—rather improbably—UNICEF. In *Within Human Reach*, UNICEF reasserted the human and productive[39] importance of basic services and of production by poor people. It demonstrated that they could be cost efficient, consistent with growth, and complementary to macroeconomic structural adjustment policies. *Adjustment with a Human Face*[40] developed these hypotheses with reference to specific structural adjustment programs, most of which showed serious avoidable deficiencies from this perspective.

The Bank—partly in response, partly as an outcome of reflection or experience, partly as a result of its own research on health, education and water units—began in 1985 to alter policy and, to a lesser extent, resource allocation:

- primary health care, basic education, and, less uniformly, pure water and urban infrastructure were restored to the agenda as priorities in order to increase equity and the ability to produce.
- increasing attention was paid to programs directly aimed at small farmers (including female-headed households) and informal sector artisans—albeit with weak articulation.
- labor intensive public works were seen as the way to reduce poverty without raising costs; and
- providing some compensation to losers who could otherwise impede program implementation (by no means necessarily the poorest) was accepted as a necessary cost of adjustment and was financeable via Consultative Groups.

This led to the Bank's creation of a Social Dimensions of Adjustment (SDA) unit to build a data base in order to conceptualize poverty in SSA countries, identify pressure points for reducing it, and implement minor poverty-alleviation funding. And by 1987–88, Ghana secured $75 million to set up PAMSCAD (Programme to Mitigate the Social Costs of Adjustment). By this time, however, the focus was shifting:

- absolutely poor households as a whole had become the priority group—not just (especially in many PAMSCAD projects) those adversely affected by structural adjustment.
- production by poor people was seen as (potentially) the basic way forward, complemented and sustained by basic service access.
- women were identified as a group (especially female-headed households) who were disproportionately poor, overworked, and unlikely to benefit from macro policies that did not specifically address gender issues.
- the urban poor were accepted to be a large group with absolute poverty comparable to (if diffusing in patterns and ways out from) the rural poor.

Tanzania and, more explicitly, Mozambique, put restoration of basic services and minimum wage protection into their strategic frameworks, thus eschewing the subsequent need to add PAMSCAD-type supplements.

At the ECA's Khartoum Conference on the Human Dimension, and in its *Declaration*[41] human condition improvement and especially absolute poverty reduction were analyzed seriously by African officials. Production by poor people, universal access to basic services, nutrition, women's workload, participation, and war costs were prominent themes in conference papers[42] and in the *Declaration*, which was later endorsed by African ministers and heads of state. In practice, MacNamara's "eradication of absolute poverty" and the ILO's "basic needs" themes had been relaunched with more emphasis on production, new language and, for the first time, serious African participation and support.

Khartoum was sharply critical of the failure of Stabs and SAPs to treat poverty, nutrition, health care, and education imbalances as just as important as fiscal and external imbalances, and their consequential failure to place redressing these imbalances at the center of strategy and resource allocation. In all fairness, the Bank could have pointed out that few SSA governments had done so either, and that PAMSCAD, for example, had been the subject of just as intense a dialogue in Ghana as with (and in) the Bank.

By 1989, the Bank, the Fund, and most bilateral donors endorsed SDA and Human Condition approaches. However, actual program articulation and resource allocations (while beginning to change) lagged well behind. How much of this is technical, how much inertial, and how much the lack of full commitment by many decisionmakers (including that of SSA proposal representatives) is still difficult to evaluate.

In 1990,[43] the Bank made poverty the theme of its annual *World Development Report*, and in 1991 it issued an operational directive[44] on poverty reduction, followed by a 1992 handbook[45] on how to do it—both directed to Bank staff. In Bank procedures this does represent a high level of commitment/prioritization. On the other hand it remains rather unevenly visible in many SAPs.

Brave New Worlds or Roads to New Debacles?

As noted, SSA has some successful SAPs moving into their sixth to tenth years, and has several promising younger ones. But it also has a catalogue of failures and doubtful cases. As yet, no programs other than Mauritius have made breakthroughs into rebalancing external accounts or toward restarting industrial development. The trend rate of growth of agricultural production in SSA remains at 2%—now for exports and domestic food alike—whereas both external balance and nutrition demands require 4%.[46] Even if (as seems plausible) the SAP country average is 3%, that is only about 60% of the distance to be traveled from 1970s growth to requisite trends. Non-price structural constraints (including lack of relevant knowledge, market access, adapted, tested, economically viable, and user friendly new technologies), seem harder to overcome than grossly manipulated prices or one channel marketing.

The brave new world's hopes of the AD Report have not been realized. And, in all fairness, even AD did not posit much of an increase in GDP per capita, and that only after a doubling of aid and terms of trade improvement that never took place. Overall, SSA's decline appeared to be bottoming out in the late 1980s and those countries with serious, sustained strategies (including Zimbabwe, Cape Verde and Botswana in the non-SAP group) had begun to achieve growth trends above population growth and restoration of basic services. But, except for Botswana—which has had unique advantages on the export front on which to capitalize by good policy—each of these cases was either dependent on very high, not soft, external resource inflows or in danger of its recovery being strangled by lack of access to them (e.g. Zimbabwe). Even so, the successes, limited and fragile as they were, suggest that at least several countries both within and without the SAP intensive care ward, were not necessarily on the path to new debacles.

Some guideposts to successful versus failed SAPs can be identified even though not one of them applies to all successes (or is absent in all failures):

- a national strategic shift prior to Stab/SAP adoption and an ongoing dialogue allowing the program to be seen as either "owned by" the African state or at least as a negotiated, not imposed one.
- enough discipline in the dominant decision-making group so as to avoid having many of its members publicly bad-mouthing what was set out as their program (never solved in Zambia and, in Ghana, solved by excluding dissenting leaders).
- accessibility of leaders to dialogue on strategic adjustments (e.g. PAMSCAD in Ghana) presented as such, not as a repudiation of the program.
- either a first year so bedeviled by calamities not related to structural adjustment so as to give it a free ride (e.g. Ghana), or a pre-SAP recovery that could be built upon (e.g. Tanzania).
- finance near the minimum levels posited by the Bank and country with fairly fast initial disbursements, and no more than normal subsequent "pipeline" bottlenecks.
- visible results (or supposed results) of structural adjustment such as strengthened health and education, more affordable food, more goods in shops (oddly enough, even at prices few could rarely afford).
- no major worsening of war costs (Zimbabwe and Tanzania in 1987–88 are exceptions) and, more particularly, no worsening of basic security conditions. (Worsening is the key word; slow improvement in appalling initial conditions was consistent with initial SAP success in Mozambique); and
- flexibility on the part of the Bank and (at least compared with its general role) the Fund with respect to targets, priorities, phasing, and specific program content.

If these are checked against successes and failures (viewed dispassionately, excluding Zaire from successes, and recognizing that some applications were gambits without any serious purpose beyond grabbing some cash and running—e.g. Sierra Leone and Liberia), most cases are explicable in these terms. This may suggest that countries should sort out strategic priorities and begin price and fiscal reforms before Stab/SAP negotiations. They do suggest that Tanzania's tactic of having its initial Consultative Group and Paris Club agreements before a final Fund standby agreement (though conditional on the latter being reached) was useful in cutting the lag from initial measures incurring costs, and the arrival of external resource flows allowing gains.

Early 1990s progress and prospects again appear more problematic with at least five at best ambiguous (or in one case clearly negative) factors:

1. The speed and volume with which peace dividends from reduced military spending can be tapped.
2. The recurrence of drought in the Horn and Southern Africa from 1989–90 on.
3. The external race between aid fatigue (high transfer with low results) and aid rejuvenation based on perceptible progress.
4. The parallel domestic race between adjustment fatigue (all the running one can do to stay in more or less the same place) and transformation trajectory support from clearly visible benefits.
5. Whether competitive elections are likely to "reward" sound, and "punish" unwise economic policies or—given general economic unsuccess levels—to result in populist competitive bidding and regular rejection of governments seeking re-election, whatever the merits or demerits of their policies.

Most SSA governments (and economies) have few degrees of freedom left. They are hemmed in by present resource levels, by poor external economic environment prospects and limited probability of any large increases in the inflow of net resources—as well as by the need to deliver perceived benefits to voters.

Learning by Doing: Lessons of Experience

What the Fund, the Bank, and individual SSA governments have learned over the period 1983–92 varies widely. There have been no sudden conversions. Ghana had tried a fairly tough bootstrap stabilization program in 1982 that restored domestic government credibility but failed to attract external support because, during the period 1972–81, external credibility was totally destroyed and the image of the new government put off many potential resource providers. Nor is it clear that long term objective divergences have narrowed all that much as yet. Tanzania and Mozambique are still basically human condition/radical social democratic in orientation, and Angola's Stab/SAP bid is actually an African Leninist or Stolypinist (to cite the earlier Czarist capitalist analogue) New Economic Policy. The Bank is very clearly devoted (as in 1981) to hard-headed capitalist development, albeit modified to seek to include poor people by overt state interventions.[47] But on short-term targets, modalities, and flexibility there has been some convergence springing from and strengthening an increasingly serious dialogue and, in some cases, allowing for fairly long-running, moderately successful programs.

The Fund has learned least, or has altered its basic thrust least. It has learned that high-cost, short-term credits are, in a structural adjustment context, part of the problem, not the solution. But, arguably, it was always aware of that; the aberration was the huge (relative to country size) drawings it advanced in several cases. Hence the Fund is now making the best of being locked in through softer, longer, more easily rolled-over SAF and ESAFs.[48]

Apparently, the Fund's faith in its model is unshaken (at least institutionally; not all of its African country based officials would agree). The evident shifts include accepting that grant and soft loan finance to close trade and fiscal gaps is better than nothing and is thus acceptable. Also, in some cases, (e.g. Tanzania, Mozambique, and Angola), it accepts that standard credit ceilings run into structural constraints even if government bank borrowing is reduced to the vanishing point, although neither it nor the Bank has constructed an operational route to bypass this bottleneck. What it has not learned is that the economies in which stabilization based on the Fund model works (e.g. semi-industrialized Southern Europe) are so different from SSA that the model itself may be inapplicable in anything like its present form.

The Fund has relearned that it is not a development agency. It deploys this rather well (in its own terms) to escape responsibility for results in human, and especially women's conditions, even while advocating that countries do pay more attention to them. But it does not accept that it should retreat to refinancing old drawings through new SAFs and ESAFs and providing genuinely short term, low conditionality, fast drawings for genuinely cyclical shocks that regularly threaten basically viable structural adjustment programs. That would mean reducing itself to a marginal role in Africa and turning over most of its present macro policy functions there to the Bank.[49]

The Bank, as outlined above, has learned much more. This is obscured by its habit of adding in new elements and shifting course without ever quite admitting that it has learned something or made a mistake.

Where the Bank is now most unclear is on how to transform "3 to 10 year Structural Adjustment with Growth" to "10 to 20 year Structural Transformation with Development." The long gestation of its 1989 *Sub-Saharan Africa: From Crisis to Sustainable Growth*[50] exemplifies this problem. Industrial strategy, regionalism, production by poor people, and the uses or limits of efficient market intervention are among the areas in which it has learned that simplistic neo-liberal answers will not do. But it has not sorted out new, more Africa-oriented approaches.

With respect to exports, the Bank now half accepts that increasing exports of traditional primary products is a route with "no through road" and "bridge out" signs posted. It half realizes that a war to regain market share would reduce SSA export earnings while it endured, and would probably be won by exporters with financial resources to hold out (i.e. the Brazils and Malaysias, not the Ghanas and Tanzanias). But the Bank has not even begun serious research on what alternative export development strategies might work in which countries. This is perhaps the case because that route requires "picking winners" and using selective market intervention.

Ideologically, the Bank is suspicious of those routes and, pragmatically, it believes (probably correctly) that most SSA governments have little capacity to articulate or implement them competently or without massive distortions from corruption.

Oddly, the Bank has learned about the need for emergency finance better than the Fund has. But it has few means to provide it. It hopes that food aid can be used in this way and, in 1989, added $100 million to the Ghana Consultative Group target to offset cocoa price falls. Neither is as effective nor as fast as restored availability of low cost, low conditionality facilities (on the lines of the 1974 Oil Facility and the old, low conditionality use of the Compensatory Finance Facility) would be.

In the case of SSA governments, a majority have not yet transformed structural adjustment strategies as now articulated into policies and resource allocation on a multiyear basis. Most appear to have learned the following:

- the late 1970s will not come again; thus, in a more hostile economic world, better management and tighter resource allocation is essential.
- if exchange rates, interest rates, and crop prices are wildly out of line with other prices and market forces, they can gravely hamper growth.
- price controls cannot work if supply is less than 80% to 90% of demand at set prices, or if the prices bankrupt producers (usually to the benefit of merchants, not end users).
- fiscal discipline matters, but within a context in which both real service cutting and real resource enhancement have cruelly real and tight limits.
- export reserves matter because economic transformation requires more, not less, imports and because dependence on creditors or donors is much less consonant with self-reliance and self-determination than dependence on exports.
- attempting to provide too many services and to operate too many enterprises relative to available resources produces worse results than concentrating on more limited ranges.
- subsidies that are adequate to avert absolute poverty cannot be financed and are very likely to serve the not-so-poor better than they do the very poor; therefore,
- more production by poor households needs to be facilitated (albeit precisely how is usually less elaborated).
- market intervention, if badly designed or mismanaged, can aggravate market imperfections and failures.
- prolonged economic unsuccess (whatever the cause) leads to social unrest and pressure for competitive elections the incumbents are unlikely to win.

While many SSA governments were aware of all of the above in principle in the 1970s, at least a score, and perhaps more, know it much more acutely now from bitter experience.

Platonic Guardians or Pragmatic Partners?

The Fund, and especially the Bank, have a built-in tendency to view themselves as "Platonic Guardians" with SSA governments, other institutions, businessmen, and select academics as, at most, junior warriors (to advise marginally and implement unqualifiedly) and the rest of the Africans (and academics) as workers who are to do as told for their own good.

The Fund, full of faith in its overall monetary demand management model, is the pure Guardian. It knows best. But it is less intrusive as to details than the Bank. And if a state maintains reasonable external balance (and thus does not use Fund resources on a large scale or for extended periods), the Fund is moderately relaxed in its dialogue with it. Unfortunately, few SSA states now meet that test.

The Bank is less certain as to how much it knows, how fully, in what contexts, and with what rate of depreciation or obsolescence of knowledge stuck. It does wish to look at new data, new proposals, and new phasings, albeit subject to some acceptance of its lead role and of the need to act promptly. But its knowledge and concerns are far more extensive in scope and intensive in sectoral and micro articulation than those of the Fund. Therefore, if it faces a government in desperate need of finance with little data, limited analytical expertise, weak negotiators, and no strategy that is both plausible and backed by key national decision-makers, it becomes a far more intrusive Platonic Guardian than the Fund.

Arguably, this is SSA governments' fault as much as that of the Bank. Consensus built on analysis and data can be created—even if at a real cost in lost time, as in Tanzania over 1981–84. Many, though by no means all, SSA governments can field teams with as much expertise and intelligence as the Bank can deploy with respect to any one country. "No, but" and "yes, except" negotiating stances (or preparing overall program discussion drafts) do yield results.

But the Bank does, even then, have two rather counterproductive habits. The first is to send a large number of sectoral program and review missions, all of which demand to see very senior people so that a wholly inefficient share of their time is allocated to meeting Bank functionaries as opposed to getting on with the job. Furthermore, the Bank has a tendency to view what it has accepted in negotiations as temporary necessities or local peculiarities to be ironed out over time in what seems to many in SSA to be creeping conditionality, not partnership.

Also, the Bank's call on SSA countries to broaden participation is both ambiguous and wildly at variance with its own patterns of operation. If participation is to mean something more than implementing policies set by someone else, it must involve representation (in both senses) before decisions are taken and accountability afterward.[51] Otherwise, it is participation in the sense of Lord Malvern's definition of partnership in Rhodesia's Nyasaland: that of horse and rider.

The Bank does not hold itself accountable to member states for bad advice, botched projects, or failure to mobilize agreed-upon, necessary funding. Nor is its tendency to seek a broad-based dialogue and information exchange in client countries manifest in the time it provides for reply to its draft documents or the restrictions it imposes on their distribution (although some progress is evident in this respect over the past few years). Finally, it is hard to see how local groups of peasants, federations of women, or trade unions can be involved in negotiations with the Bank, much less hold it accountable. As a Platonic Guardian for the poor (which the Bank on occasion seriously tries to be), it is hard to see how it can function, except by converting governments to human condition-focused strategies which, the Bank, in practice, finds hard to accept as core program components.

Yet, as the Bank stresses, SAPs must be domesticated, internalized and Africanized if they are to survive, let alone function effectively. This is possible only if the Bank accepts that there can be disagreement among informed persons of goodwill on goals as well as on specific program content. This further requires recognizing that Africans can be, and often are, experts on their own countries' economies and social and political realities. They are thus complementary or, on occasion, superior to the Bank. In principle, and with at least half its mind, the Bank would give its assent to these propositions. In practice, and emotionally, it still too often recoils from them. Partnership cannot mean total conversion of one partner to the other's views. With respect to structural adjustment in SSA, building enduring partnerships between the Bank and governments is, with few exceptions, a continuing struggle for both parties (or would-be partners).

What Is To Be Done?

If SSA economies, polities and persons are to survive, much less prosper, several key barriers must soon be addressed more effectively than they have been in structural adjustment to date:

1. Export expansion through diversification based on empirical studies and analysis of what the least bad options are on a country-by-country basis.
2. Industrial transformation to reduce imports necessary at any level of output, and to augment exports.
3. Finding interim and long-term means to raise the agricultural growth trend to 4% and keep it there.
4. Focusing strategy on empowering poor people to produce more and to have access to the basic services (health, education, pure water, extension, and fuel) necessary to do so.
5. Building up participation of and accountability to people in the economic and social processes as well as the political.
6. Restoring directly productive fixed investment—an aspect in which SAPs have been notably weak perhaps because their pushing out of inefficient public sector investment has been much more effective than their pulling in of efficient private investment.
7. Paying serious attention to the pervasive economic and human consequences of war (as illustrated in UNICEF's *Children On The Front Line*[52]) as well as how "peace dividend" installments, which now seem potentially available at least in Southern Africa, could be allocated to develop as well as to rehabilitate.[53]
8. Paying equally serious attention to the needs and capabilities of women with specific focus on women's extraordinary workload and female-headed households.
9. Develop rehabilitation of livelihood programs (as well as more effective disaster relief) to enable households whose incomes and assets have been wiped out by drought or war to regain a livelihood base that allows them access to more "standard" development programs.[54]
10. Build up safety nets for households who cannot (during calamities or permanently) be empowered to produce enough to climb out of absolute poverty;[55]
11. Building viable regional economic coordination based on agreed common interests (including but not limited to trade to validate increased production), more efficiently pursued on a joint basis, rather than severally; and

12. Recognizing that 3% population growth rates spring from and entrench absolute poverty so that the bulk of population policy needs to focus on reducing infant and under five mortality rates, raising household food security and adequacy, popularizing child spacing to enhance child and maternal health, and moving to universal primary and applied education (especially for women). Technical and material support services in the health system are an important, but secondary, area of activity.

In one sense, this agenda confirms ECA's assertion that structural adjustment must be transformed (not merely adjusted) into structural transformation by broadening its scope and lengthening its time horizon to become an overarching political and economic strategy. This contrasts with a 1981-style foundation-relaying exercise that was inherently limited in scope and duration.

It is not clear whether the World Bank's long-term policy study, *From Crisis to Sustainable Growth*, is a major step in this direction because the link between such documents and the Bank's operational programs is never simple and direct and may be very weak. There is also an urgent need to refine and strengthen the analytical base of ECA's *African Alternatives* and of the *Khartoum Declaration*, preferably with supporting review and input from international financial institution personnel. To date, however, the Bank side seems unlikely to demonstrate sufficient ambition, and the Africans seem to be less than adequate on the analytical front and too prone to conflate the international economic environment that would prevail in a just world with that which one might reasonably expect to obtain in the 1990s.

Breakdown, Breakout or Breakthrough?

In one sense, there is no alternative to structural adjustment. If governments do not structurally adjust their economies by planned strategic and programmatic interventions, market forces will adjust them just as structurally but at a higher cost. By December 1981, Ghana had structurally adjusted with a vengeance from December 1972 precisely because there had been no coherent economic policy for nearly a decade and an inherently wildly overdetermined one (resources overallocated) for at least three years. The period 1982–91 represents, in a basic sense, the use of a coherent strategy (albeit one amended from and by experience) to reverse much of the earlier adjustment.

However, there are possible alternative paces, instruments, sectoral emphases, and social priorities within structural adjustment. Ghana is not the Côte d'Ivoire; nor is it Kenya, Tanzania, or Mozambique, although all have serious adjustment programs. In part, this relates to historic and contextual differences, but it also involves willed choice.

An overall breakdown of structural adjustment in SSA is unlikely. Too many programs have achieved too much and, moreover, represent too much sunk capital for SSA governments and societies, international financial institutions, and donors for them to be easily scrapped or reversed.

But breakdowns—from mistakes, exogenous shocks, and underfunding—are likely to continue and competitive elections to add a new risk. That is hardly surprising. However, another category needs to be faced squarely. In some SSA countries, economic policy failure is a mirror of social and political pathology. International financial institutions and bilaterals alike have shored up these regimes by attempting (unsuccessfully) to buy economic reform while predictably failing (as in the Philippines under Marcos) to get it. A strong case exists for halting structural adjustment-type support to these governments and deploying what resource flows do go to their territories to humanitarian and survival assistance for the poor until basic political change takes place. The Fund does not operate on that logic. The Bank does if the dictatorial regime is clearly inefficient in use of resources but will not (cannot) take a lead if the economic policies practiced, narrowly defined are plausible. For example, it has dropped Zaire largely on its own initiative (as it did pre-1983 for Ghana) but has been much less operationally negative in respect to Malawi.

The chances of SSA breaking out into Asian NIC-type economic dynamism by the year 2000 are nil. Even one such case would be surprising. Neither the unlimited cheap capital, easy access to export markets for newcomers, nor the human capital bases for such a transformation exist now or can be foreseen for the coming decade. The least inconceivable contenders are Zimbabwe (given peace and rapid adjustment of the disastrous initial SAP package) and Mauritius (given deepening of its export manufacturing sector and continued/enhanced EEC market access).

A breakout on the human condition side is conceivable for perhaps a dozen countries. This requires taking seriously Adam

Smith's dictum that no nation can be great and prosperous the majority of whose people are poor and miserable. The resources needed to cut absolute poverty in half and to achieve universal basic service access by the year 2000 do exist (or could exist) in up to half of the SSA states.[56]

As that point illustrates, what is possible is a series of breakthroughs, some sector or target—and some country—specific. Fragility and fatigue result from steadily pushing the boulder uphill—even if, unlike that of Sisyphus in Greek mythology, the rock can, with luck, be prevented from regularly rolling all the way back to the base of the hill. That outlook is cause for limited optimism, not triumphalism, nor yet despair.

The realistic slogan for Africans—who must try to regain control over their economic destinies is the Lusophone African one:

"A lutta continua" (the struggle continues).

The optimistic one is from Pliny: "Out of Africa, there is always something new."

NOTES

1. See R. H. Green, "From Deepening Economic Malaise Toward Renewed Development: Notes Toward African Agendas for Action," *Journal of Development Planning* 15 (April 1985).

2. *Ibid* and World Bank, *Africa's Adjustment and Growth in the 1980s* (Washington, D.C.: World Bank, 1989).

3. See C. Allison and R. H. Green, eds., "Accelerated Development in Sub-Saharan Africa: What agendas for action?" IDS *Bulletin* 14, no. 1 (January 1983) and see also C. Allison and R. H. Green, eds., "Sub-Saharan Africa: getting the facts straight," IDS *Bulletin* 16, no. 3 (July 1985).

4. See World Bank, *Accelerated Development in Sub-Saharan Africa: An Agenda For Action* (Washington, D.C.: World Bank, 1981); Green, "From Deepening Economic Malaise;" T. Rose, ed., *Crisis and Recovery in Sub-Saharan Africa* (Paris: OECD Development Centre, 1986).

5. See Green, "From Deepening Economic Malaise;" and R. H. Green, B. Van Arkadie and D. Rwegasira, *Economic Shocks and National Policy Making: Tanzania in the 1970s* (The Hague: Institute of Social Studies, 1981).

6. See International Labor Organization, *Employment, Growth and Basic Needs: A One World Problem* (Geneva: ILO, 1975).

7. (Dar es Salaam: Government Printer, 1977).

8. See World Bank, *Toward Sustained Development in Sub-Saharan Africa: A Joint Program of Action* (Washington, D.C.: World Bank, 1984); World Bank, *Africa's Adjustment and Growth*; and Economic Commission for Africa, *Africa's Submission to the Special Session of the United Nations General*

Assembly on Africa's Economic and Social Crisis (New York, Addis Ababa: 1986); and UNCTAD, *Trade and Development Reports* (1980–1992).

9. See Green, "From Deepening Economic Malaise."

10. World Bank, *Accelerated Development in Sub-Saharan Africa.*

11. See UNCTAD, *Trade and Development Reports.*

12. See World Bank, *Sub-Saharan Africa: From Crisis to Sustainable Growth* (Washington, D.C.: World Bank, 1989); R. H. Green, "Africa 1975–95: The Political Boom, Decline, Conflict, Survival—and Rivalry?," UN Non-Governmental Liaison Service *Occasional Paper* (July 1991); UNICEF/OAU, *Investing in Africa's Children* (New York, Addis Ababa: UNICEF/OAU, 1992).

13. See J. J. Polak, "Monetary analysis of income formation and payments problems," *IMF Staff Papers* 6 (June 1957); J. de Laroisière, *Does the Fund Impose Austerity?* (Washington, D.C.: IMF, 1984); R. H. Green, "The IMF and Stabilisation in Sub-Saharan Africa: a critical review," IDS *Discussion Paper* 216 (June 1986); S. Please, "Structural Adjustment, IMF Conditionality, and the World Bank" in *The Hobbled Giant: Essays on the World Bank,* (Boulder/London: Westview, 1984) for fuller explanation.

14. See P. Mistry, *African Debt Revisited: Procrastination or Progress?,* (The Hague: Forum on Debt and Development (FONDAD), 1991).

15. E.g. Mistry, *African Debt Revisited;* Please, "Structural Adjustment"; R. H. Green, "Political-Economic Adjustment and IMF Conditionality," in J. Williamson ed. *IMF Conditionality* (Washington, D.C.: Institute for International Economics, 1983), and Green, "The IMF and Stabilisation in Sub-Saharan Africa."

16. Indeed IMF *Staff Papers* based on its Research Department's work find limited correlations in Africa between most of its policy prescriptions (other than avoiding severe exchange rate overvaluation) and most economic or social outcome indicators.

17. See Please, "Structural Adjustment"; Green, "The IMF and Stabilization in Sub-Saharan Africa."

18. From World Bank, *Accelerated Development in Sub-Saharan Africa* through World Bank, *Sub-Saharan Africa.*

19. See on Ghana, R. H. Green, "Stabilisation and Adjustment Policies and Programmes," *Country Study 1 Ghana* (Helsinki: World Institute for Development Economics Research (WIDER), 1987) and on Tanzania during the 1984/85 crisis, Green, Van Arkadie and Rwegasira, *Economic Shocks and National Policy Making.*

20. E.g. World Bank, *World Development Report* (Washington, D.C.: World Bank, 1983–1992); and World Bank, *Reducing Poverty: Handbook and Operational Directive* (Washington, D.C.: World Bank, 1992).

21. World Bank, *Sub-Saharan Africa.*

22. World Bank, *Reducing Poverty;* R. H. Green, "Towards Livelihoods, Services and Infrastructure: The Struggle to Overcome Absolute Poverty," paper at conference on the *Eradication of Poverty in Africa* (Ota, Nigeria: Africa Leadership Forum, July 27–29, 1992).

23. See K. M. Cleaver, "The Impact of Price and Exchange Rate Policies on Agriculture in Sub-Saharan Africa," *World Bank Staff Working Papers* 728

(Washington, D.C.: World Bank, 1985); World Bank, *Africa's Adjustment and Growth.*

24. See World Bank, *Sub-Saharan Africa.*

25. See Green, "Stabilisation and Adjustment Policies and Programmes;" and R. H. Green "Articulating IMF Stabilisation with Structural Adjustment in SSA Agriculture" in S. Commander ed., *Structural Adjustment and Agriculture* (London: ODI, 1989).

26. World Bank, *Sub-Saharan Africa.*

27. See Mistry, *African Debt Revisited;* B. Onimode ed., *The IMF, The World Bank and the African Debt: the Social and Political Perspectives* (London: Institute for African Alternatives/Zed Books, 1989) and B. Onimode ed., *The IMF, The World Bank and the African Debt,* Vol.I: *The Economic Impact,* Vol.II *The Social and Political Impact* (London/New York: Zed Books, 1990); but also E.V.K. Jaycox et al, "The Nature of the Debt Problem in Eastern and Southern Africa" in C. Lancaster and J. Williamson eds., *African Debt and Financing* (Washington, D.C.: Institute of International Economics, 1989); World Bank, *Sub-Saharan Africa.*

28. World Bank, *Africa's Adjustment and Growth.*

29. ECA, *African Alternative Framework to Structural Adjustment Programmes for Socio-Economic Recovery and Transformation* (New York Addis Ababa: United Nations, 1989).

30. F. Bourguignon and C. Morrison, *Adjustment and Equity in Developing Countries: A New Approach* (Paris: OECD, 1992).

31. OAU, *Africa's Priority Programme for Economic Recovery, 1986–1990* (New York Addis Ababa: FAO for OAU, 1988).

32. ECA, *African Alternative Framework.*

33. See Onimode, *The IMF, The World Bank and the African Debt* for a fairly representative selection of proponents of this outlook (and a few dissenters from it).

34. ECA, *African Alternative Framework.*

35. World Bank, *Sub-Saharan Africa;* World Bank, *Reducing Poverty;* and *World Development Report* (1990).

36. ECA, *African Alternative Framework.*

37. E.g. in World Bank, *Accelerated Development in Sub-Saharan Africa.*

38. See World Bank, *Reducing Poverty.*

39. UNICEF, *Within Human Reach: A Future for Africa's Children* (New York: 1985).

40. G.A. Cornia, et al., eds., *Adjustment with a Human Face: Protecting the Vulnerable and Promoting Growth,* (Cambridge: Cambridge University Press, 1987).

41. ECA, *The Khartoum Declaration.*

42. See R. H. Green, "The Human Dimension as the Test of and a Means of Achieving Africa's Economic Recovery and Development: Reweaving the Social Fabric, Restoring the Broken Pot," paper for the UN ECA *International Conference on the Human Dimension of Africa's Economic Recovery and Development* (Khartoum, Sudan: March 5–8, 1988).

43. *World Development Report,* 1990.

44. World Bank, *Reducing Poverty.*

45. *Ibid.*

46. World Bank, *Africa's Adjustment and Growth*; S. Commander ed., *Structural Adjustment and Agriculture.*

47. World Bank, *Reducing Poverty.*

48. See Mistry, *African Debt Revisited.*

49. *Ibid*; Please, "Structural Adjustment."

50. World Bank, *Sub-Saharan Africa.*

51. World Bank, *Sub-Saharan Africa*; and World Bank, *Reducing Poverty* accept this. But World Bank, *Reducing Poverty* clearly takes a relatively narrow functionalist view of participation and, indeed, suggests it is inappropriate even in some (many?) poverty reduction programs.

52. UNICEF, *The State of the World's Children* (New York: 1987, 1989, 1992); R. H. Green, "Killing the Dream: The Political and Human Economy of War in Sub-Saharan Africa," IDS *Discussion Paper* 238 (November, 1987).

53. UNICEF, *The State of the World's Children*; UNICEF/OAU, *Investing in Africa's Children.*

54. See Green, "Towards Livelihoods, Services and Infrastructure."

55. *Ibid*; World Bank, *Reducing Poverty.*

56. See UNICEF/OAU, *Investing in Africa's Children.*

SOURCES

Allison, C. and R. H. Green eds. "Accelerated Development in Sub-Saharan Africa: What agendas for action?" IDS *Bulletin* 14, no. 1 (January 1983).

———. "Sub-Saharan Africa: Getting the Facts Straight." IDS *Bulletin* 16, no. 3 (July 1985).

Bourguignon, F. and C. Morrison. *Adjustment and Equity in Developing Countries: A New Approach.* Paris: OECD, 1992.

Cleaver, K. M. "The Impact of Price and Exchange Rate Policies on Agriculture in Sub-Saharan Africa." *World Bank Staff Working Papers* 728. Washington, D.C.: 1985.

Colclough, C.L. and R. H. Green eds. "Stabilisation—For Growth or Decay? Short Run Costs and Long Run Uncertainties in Africa." IDS *Bulletin* 19, no. 1 (January, 1988).

Commander, S. ed. *Structural Adjustment and Agriculture.* London: ODI, 1989.

Cornia, G. A., R. Jolly, F. Stewart eds. *Adjustment with A Human Face: Protecting The Vulnerable And Promoting Growth.* Cambridge: Cambridge University Press, 1987.

Daniel, P., R. H. Green and M. Lipton. "A Strategy for the Rural Poor in Sub-Saharan Africa: Towards oblivion or reconstruction." *JDP*, 15 (1985).

Davies, R. and D. Saunders. "Stabilisation Policies and the Effects on Child Health in Zimbabwe." *Review of African Political Economy* 38 (April, 1987).

Dell, S. S. and R. Lawrence. *Balance-of-Payment Adjustment in the 1980s.* Special issue of *World Development* 14, no. 8 (1987).

Dervis, K., J. de Melo and S. Robinson. *General Equilibrium Models for Development Policy*. Cambridge: Cambridge University Press for the World Bank, 1982.

de Vries, R. and C. Porzecanski. "Comments" in J. Williamson ed. *IMF Conditionality*. Washington, D.C.: Institute for International Economics, 1983.

Economic Commission for Africa (UN ECA). *The Khartoum Declaration: Towards a Human-Focused Approach To Socio-Economic Recovery and Development in Africa*. Khartoum: The International Conference on the Human Dimension of Africa's Economic Recovery and Development, Economic Commission for Africa, March 1988.

Godfrey, M. "Trade and Exchange Rate Policy in Sub-Saharan Africa," in C. Allison and R. H. Green eds. "Sub-Saharan Africa: Getting the Facts Straight." .

Green, R. H. with D. Rwegasira and B. van Arkadie. *Economic Shocks and National Policy Making: Tanzania in the 1970s*. The Hague: Institute of Social Studies, 1981.

——— "Political-Economic Adjustment and IMF Conditionality," in J. Williamson ed. *IMF Conditionality*.

——— "From Deepening Economic Malaise Toward Renewed Development: Notes Toward African Agendas For Action." *Journal of Development Planning* 15 (April, 1985).

——— "The IMF and Stabilisation in Sub-Saharan Africa: A Critical Review." IDS *Discussion Paper* 216 (June, 1986).

——— "Stabilisation and Adjustment Policies and Programmes." L. Taylor ed. *Country Study 1 Ghana*. Helsinki: World Institute for Development Economics Research (WIDER).

——— "Killing The Dream: The Political and Human Economy of War in Sub-Saharan Africa." IDS *Discussion Paper* 238 (November, 1987).

——— "The Human Dimension as the Test of and a Means of Achieving Africa's Economic Recovery and Development: Reweaving the social fabric, restoring the broken pot." Paper for the UN ECA International Conference on the Human Dimension of Africa's Economic Recovery and Development. Khartoum, Sudan: March 5–8, 1988, ECA/ICHD/88/3 and Executive Summary ECA/ICHD/88/3/Add.18.

——— "Articulating IMF Stabilisation With Structural Adjustment in SSA Agriculture." In S. Commander ed. *Structural Adjustment and Agriculture*.

Green, R. H., with D. Asrat, M. Mauras and R. Morgan. "Children in Southern Africa." In *Children on the Front Line: The Impact of Apartheid, Destabilisation and Warfare on Children in Southern and South Africa*. New York: UNICEF, 1987 and 1989.

——— "Africa 1975–95: The Political Boom, Decline, Conflict, Survival—and Revival?.'" UN Non-Governmental Liaison Service *Occasional Paper* (July 1991).

Green, R. H., with C. Broad and R. Morgan. *Children on the Front Line*. Windhoek/New York: UNICEF, 1992.

——— "Toward Livelihoods, Services and Infrastructure: The Struggle to Overcome Absolute Poverty." Ota, Nigeria: Africa Leadership Forum conference on the *Eradication of Poverty in Africa*, July 27–29, 1992.

Griffith-Jones, S. and Green, R. H. "External Debt: Sub-Saharan Africa's emerging iceberg." In T. Rose ed. *Crisis and Recovery in Sub-Saharan Africa.*

Harvey, C. "Successful Adjustment in Botswana." In C. Allison and R. H. Green eds. "Sub-Saharan Africa: Getting the Facts Straight." IDS *Bulletin* 16, no. 3 (July, 1985).

Hugon, P. "The Impact of Adjustment Policy in Madagascar." In C. L. Colclough and R. H. Green eds. "Stabilisation—For Growth or Decay?"

Iliffe, J. *The African Poor.* African Studies Series 58. Cambridge: Cambridge University Press, 1987.

IMF. *World Economic Outlook,* Washington: 1982–1992.

International Labour Organisation. *Employment, Growth and Basic Needs: A One World Problem.* Geneva: ILO, 1975.

Jaycox, E.V.K., R.I. Gulhati, S. Lall and S. Yalamanchili. "The Nature of the Debt Problem in Eastern and Southern Africa." In C. Lancaster and J. Williamson eds. *African Debt and Financing.*

Johnson, O. E. G. "The Agricultural Sector and Adjustment Programmes Supported by IMF Stand-By Arrangements." In S. Commander ed. *Structural Adjustment and Agriculture.*

Kadhani, X. and R. H. Green. "Parameters as Warnings and Guide Posts: The Case of Zimbabwe." *Journal of Development Planning* (1985).

Khan, M. "Macroeconomic Adjustment in Developing Countries: A Policy Perspective." *World Bank Research Observer* 1, no. 2 (January 1984).

Khan, M., and M. Knight. "Stabilisation Programs in Developing Countries." *IMF Staff Papers* 28 (March, 1981).

Killick, T. "Unsettled Questions About Adjustment With Growth.' *International Monetary and Financial Issues for the Developing Countries.* Geneva: UNCTAD, 1987.

Lancaster, C. and J. Williamson eds. *African Debt and Financing.* Washington, D.C.: Institute of International Economics, 1986.

Laroisière, J. de. *Does the Fund Impose Austerity?* Washington, D.C.: IMF, 1984.

Lipton, M. "The Place of Agricultural Research in the Development of Sub-Saharan Africa." IDS *Discussion Paper* 202 (1985).

Longhurst, R. "Structural Adjustment and Vulnerable Groups in Sierra Leone." In C. L. Colclough and R. H. Green eds. "Stabilisation—For Growth or Decay?."

Mistry, P. *African Debt Revisited: Procrastination or Progress?* Forum On Debt And Development (FONDAD). The Hague: 1991.

Ndegwa, P., L. Mureithi and R. H. Green eds. *Development Options for Africa in the 1980s and Beyond,* Nairobi: Oxford University Press, 1985.

Onimode, B. ed. *The IMF, The World Bank and The African Debt: The Social and Political Perspectives,* London: Institute for African Alternatives/Zed Books, 1989.

——— *The IMF, The World Bank and The African Debt,* Vol I *The Economic Impact,* Vol II *The Social and Political Impact.* London and New York: Zed Books, 1990.

OAU. *Africa's Priority Programme For Economic Recovery, 1986–1990.* New York, Addis Ababa: FAO for OAU, 1985.

OAU/ECA. *Africa's Submission to the Special Session of the United Nations General Assembly on Africa's Economic And Social Crisis.* New York Addis Ababa: 1986.

Please, S. *The Hobbled Giant: Essays on the World Bank.* Boulder/London: Westview, 1984.

Polak, J. J. "Monetary Analysis of Income Formation and Payments Problems." *IMF Staff Papers* 6 (June, 1957).

Rose, T. ed. *Crisis and Recovery In Sub-Saharan Africa,* Paris: OECD Development Centre, 1985.

Topolski, J. "Togo: A Structural Adjustment That Destabilizes Economic Growth." In C.L. Colclough and R. H. Green. "Stabilisation—For Growth or Decay?"

UNECA. *African Alternative Framework to Structural Adjustment Programmes for Socio-Economic Recovery and Transformation.* New York, Addis Ababa: 1989.

UNICEF. *Within Human Reach: A Future for Africa's Children,* New York, Addis Ababa: 1985.

——— *The State Of The World's Children.* New York, Addis Ababa: 1986–1992.

UNICEF, with OAU. *Investing In Africa's Children.* New York, Addis Ababa: 1992.

United Nations, General Assembly. *United Nations Programme of Action for African Economic Recovery and Development 1986–1990,* Resolution Adopted by the General Assembly, New York (June, 13 1986).

Wheeler, D. "Sources of stagnation in Sub-Saharan Africa." *World Development* 12, no. 1 (1984).

Williamson, J. *IMF Conditionality,* Washington, D.C.: Institute for International Economics, 1983.

——— "Prospects for the Flow of IMF Finance to Sub-Saharan Africa." In C. Lancaster and J. Williamson ed., *African Debt and Financing.*

World Bank. *Accelerated Development in Sub-Saharan Africa: An Agenda For Action.* Washington, D.C., 1981.

——— *Sub-Saharan Africa: Progress Report on Development Prospects and Programs.* Washington, D.C., 1983.

——— *World Development Report.* Washington, D.C., 1983–1992.

——— *Toward Sustained Development in Sub-Saharan Africa: A Joint Programme of Action.* Washington, D.C., 1984.

——— *Financing Adjustment with Growth in Sub-Saharan Africa, 1986–90.* Washington, D.C., 1986.

——— *Africa's Adjustment and Growth in the 1980s.* Washington, D.C., 1989.

——— *Sub-Saharan Africa from Crisis to Sustainable Growth: Long Term Perspective Study.* Washington, D.C., 1989.

——— *Reducing Poverty: Handbook and Operational Directive.* Washington, D.C., 1992

Chapter Three

Debt, Conditionality, and Reform: The International Relations of Economic Restructuring in Sub-Saharan Africa

DAVID F. GORDON

My purpose is to explore the dynamics of debt, conditionality, and reform in Sub-Saharan Africa as they evolved in the 1980s. Although my perspective is regional, I nevertheless draw on specific examples to illustrate the analytical themes and empirical trends. While each of the topics under consideration has generated what is by now a fairly substantial literature, there have been surprisingly few attempts to examine them together. In particular, the discussion of African debt has generally been divorced from the issues of conditionality and reform. But, debt issues are not usefully addressed in isolation. The debt crisis is, at the same time, both a source of reform and a constraint to reform's having its desired impact of restoring economic health. I will argue that the debt crisis grew out of the very same policies that generated Africa's broader economic crisis, which is the rationale for both reform and the use of conditionality. Moreover, the external agencies that have been most active in promoting reform through conditionality—the international financial institutions (IFIs)—are, at the same time, the most important creditors in the debt crisis and have been given the task of providing further financial resources to the continent. While the IMF and World Bank almost always attempt to separate their roles as creditors and financiers from their role as promoters of reform, I will argue that the evolution of IFI conditionality in Africa has been linked to the evolving creditor and financier positions of the Bank and the Fund.

Debt

It is now generally accepted that Africa cannot grow out of its debt: despite the continually rising volume of total debt and debt service, the actual level of debt repayment is declining, and rapidly. While debt repayment levels had reached $12 billion in 1985, they had fallen to $9.5 billion in 1987 and have continued to diminish.[1]

While African debt has been the focus of special international attention since 1987, the crisis is unlikely to be speedily resolved. There has already been a great deal of de facto debt relief and many of the debt reduction plans under consideration will do little more than give this de facto relief de jure recognition. In addition, a very large, and increasing, proportion of African "problem" debt (that is, debt in countries with the least capacity to repay) is with the IFIs, who are, for reasons we will explore, loath to reschedule let alone reduce the debt. But if resolution is unlikely, improved management is both possible and necessary if economic reform efforts in Africa are to be more successful.

Africa's debt crisis was originally the *result* of the larger and more fundamental economic malaise—in a real sense the product of a generation of misguided economic policies that were themselves part and parcel of "crony statism." According to Callaghy, Africa became dominated by "a crony statism consisting of three interrelated characteristics: clientelist networks used to build support through the extraction and distribution of rents, the expansion of the size of the state, including the creation of an extensive parastatal sector, and the purchase of primarily urban support via state welfare services and subsidies. . . . Most African states were transformed into highly personalistic, authoritarian, but weak, administrative states—lame Leviathans—in which crony statism and a subordinated crony capitalism prevailed."[2]

But, if Africa's debt crisis originated in "crony statism," in the past five years, the extent of the debt crisis has transformed it into an important *cause* of continuing economic distress. The debt crisis reinforces the economic crisis in several interrelated ways.

First, it absorbs a substantial proportion of crucially needed scarce foreign exchange in debt service payments. Second, it makes budgetary management more difficult by absorbing a large proportion of expenditures, especially in the context of needed exchange-rate devaluations. Finally, the imperative for reform is weakened when debt service acts as a high marginal tax rate on reform; that is, when the benefits of reform are accruing to external actors in the form of debt service payments.

Underlying the evolving issue of African debt has been the changing political relations between debtors and creditors. African governments tend to believe that, freed from the burden of debt, they would be able to achieve restored economic growth and development. Until recently, creditors in the IFIs believed that debt relief, by itself, would have limited effects in Africa. Similarly, the IFIs tended to be skeptical about the commitment of many African governments to fundamentally change the policies that created the debt crisis in the first place. For most of the 1980s, this sharp diversion in perceptions generated a conflictual atmosphere between African governments and the IFIs.

But, in the late 1980s, skepticism (often in the form of staff recommendations) took a back seat to other factors in determining IFI actions in Africa. Both the Fund and the Bank have been increasingly willing to undertake or maintain externally supported adjustment programs in the face of such skepticism because of their interest in a country's repaying existing obligations, political pressures from their shareholders, i.e. the leading Western governments, to continue to provide much-needed foreign exchange to financially strapped African governments, and their own desire to maintain the existing structural adjustment regime in which the IFIs continue to act as "financiers of last resort" to Africa in return for being excluded from debt reduction schemes. For example, in the final years of the Kaunda regime in Zambia, the IMF, which has substantial financial exposure in the country, heavily pressured the concessional donors to co-finance Zambia's adjustment program in the face of considerable skepticism (in retrospect, well-justified) about its viability.

The Origins of the Debt Crisis

Similar to other developing areas, the origins of the African debt crisis lie in the aftermath of the first oil crisis of 1973. But the effect of the oil shocks of the 1970s was somewhat different in Africa than the rest of the developing world.[3] The rapid increase in oil prices was part of a much broader commodity boom that affected many of Africa's other major commodity exports such as bauxite, cocoa, coffee, cotton, tea, groundnuts, and uranium.

The oil boom transformed the availability of credit in the international banking system while the commodity boom enhanced international perceptions of African credit-worthiness. Demand for financing was relatively stable in the industrialized countries, but the oil price hikes generated a demand for external borrowing in both the oil importing countries, to cover the additional cost of oil, and in the heavily populated oil exporting countries, which sought to use their enhanced credit-worthiness to promote industrialization. Banks lent to both sets of countries because the new additional liquidity had to be on-lended or be slowly eaten away by inflation, while the commodity boom had generated the optimistic expectation that future export revenues would rise commensurate with new obligations.

In Sub-Saharan Africa, the explosion in commercial bank lending never reached the poorest countries. But even in those countries there was a rapid run-up in debt originating from export credit agencies in Western countries (committed to boosting their own exports to compensate for the rising costs of oil imports) and the IFIs. Borrowing in the mid-1970s appeared to make sense given the low or negative real interest rates that were the outcome of high rates of inflation, rising commodity prices, and excess liquidity.

This process, commonly referred to as the recycling of petrodollars, was seen at the time as a sign of flexibility and maturity in the international financial system, precluding the need for drastic domestic adjustment in oil-importing developing countries. Between 1973 and 1977, Africa's total volume of debt increased from $9 billion to $27 billion. But was petrodollar recycling really effective?

Even as late as 1980, when debt to GNP ratios for oil-importing countries were significantly increasing, the IMF defended the system: "the question of whether a country should seek further credit should not be answered by reference to statistical measures . . . Higher foreign indebtedness is sound policy for both lender and borrower because the higher level of investment financed by foreign borrowing will eventually be reflected in additional net export capacity."[4]

But, in Africa, the resources were not being effectively utilized as productive investments. Rather than promoting development, the windfall resources that flowed to Africa created unrealistic expectations, facilitated budgetary mismanagement, and produced "white elephants"—hotels, steel mills, new capitals, and palaces. Strong commodity prices allowed governments to substantially increase public expenditures, which became difficult to compress when, in the late 1970s, commodity prices fell. The productivity of investment was declining. In retrospect, it was during the commodity boom years, during which time African growth data looked good, that the seeds of later disaster were laid.

Given rising commodity prices and a rapid rise in foreign financial flows, much higher rates of economic growth should have been achieved during this period. Much of the growth was simply an expansion of government services; most of the rest was the Keynesian effect of short-term stimulation. The basis for sustained productive expansion was not being laid. Most important, foreign borrowing was not financing additional export capacity. This is an important difference between Africa's debt build-up and that of Latin America. In the period before the oil crisis, Latin America's export performance had been particularly poor, in volume terms increasing at only one percent per year. But there is little doubt that petrodollar recycling in Latin America, despite leakage through capital flight, was financing the expansion of exports. Between 1977 and 1984, Latin American export volumes rose by more than 5% annually.[5] At the same time, African export volumes were stagnant.

When the commodity boom ended in the late 1970s, African countries continued to build up their volume of debt. Borrowing went to finance the second increase in oil costs (in 1979) and to avoid politically painful and socially disruptive cutbacks in public expenditure. The burden of domestic adjustment to declining terms of trade fell most heavily on investment as countries increased price subsidies and supports. The total volume of debt between 1978 and 1982—the commodity bust period—increased from $27 billion to $72 billion. Meanwhile, both the sources of financing and the recipients evolved. Commercial borrowing shifted almost solely to the oil-exporting countries; in the poorest countries, the IFIs, especially the IMF, became the major creditors.[6] The IFI's financial stake in Africa increased dramatically in the 1980s. In 1982, IMF credits made available to Sub-Saharan Africa already totaled $4 billion. By 1988, they were more than $7 billion. The multilateral banks' stake (of which the World Bank constitutes the bulk) increased from $14 billion in 1982 to more than $30 billion in 1989.[7]

During the commodity bust period, the accumulation of new debt financed a substantial run-up in the current account deficit in Africa. The current account deficit is the excess of import costs and invisible payments over the value of exported goods and services. It is, by definition, financed by capital inflows and by drawing-down foreign currency reserves. It is normal and appropriate for developing countries to run modest current account deficits that are then financed from abroad. For instance, in the decade prior to the 1973–74 oil shock Africa ran a current account deficit of slightly over 20% of exports and Latin America ran one of slightly under 20% of exports.

The trouble comes when the current account deficit increases to the point that it can be maintained only by unsupportable additional volumes of debt or by squeezing import levels. That is precisely what happened during the second phase of the emergence of Africa's debt crisis. A comparison here between Africa and Latin America is again instructive. In the four years after the end of the commodity boom, Africa's current account deficit as percent of exports more than doubled to 45%. At the same time, the percent deficit in Latin America (and this is just before the onset of the Latin debt crisis) was only 32%. More important, Latin America was able to rapidly reduce its current account deficit by a combination of export expansion and import contraction to only 4% in 1984. In Africa, the current account deficit as percent of exports also dropped, but much more slowly (to 32% in 1984), and the adjustment was totally on the import side.[8]

This analysis strongly suggests that what distinguishes the emergence of the debt crisis in Africa from that in Latin America is Africa's poor export performance. Was this a terms-of-trade problem, an access to market problem, or an international competitiveness problem? The short answer is a bit of the first, virtually none of the second, and a lot of the third. As regards terms of trade difficulties, economic rigidity and lack of responsiveness, especially in low-income countries, has created a particular vulnerability in Africa to the sharp vicissitudes of the international economy. In the 1980s this was exacerbated by low commodity prices and the vicious cycle of low import volume constraining export growth. A large part of Africa's export problem is due to the composition of its exports. Primary products are twice as important to Africa than to other developing regions and international demand for primary product exports has been much more sluggish than demand for manufactures. Many of these features are themselves the result of the policy regimes that have been followed in Africa.

But the main trade problem for Sub-Saharan Africa has been the loss of market share to other developing regions. During the 1970s, Africa's share of non-fuel exports of developing countries fell by more than half, from 19% to 9%. The World Bank has estimated that if Africa had maintained its 1970 share of non-oil primary commodity exports, its export earnings today would be $9 to $10 billion higher, a level that would cut its debt service ratio in half.[9] Jonathan Frimpong-Ansah, one of Africa's leading economists, in a study of trade issues in Africa, concluded, "the evidence showed that poor producer incentives were the principal factor in the decline of export production and that over-valued exchange rates and excess producer taxation were the principal adverse components. The general conclusion regarding the falls in export volume in Sub-Saharan African countries is that they are largely due to internal policy factors."[10]

Africa's loss of export market share was largely the result of a particular characteristic of "crony statism"—its import orientation. The origins of import orientation lie in both politics and in development strategies of the 1960s and 1970s. As mentioned by Callaghy, "crony statism" was based upon maintaining urban support. One mechanism to do so was to promote the availability of relatively inexpensive imported goods. Overvalued exchange rates do precisely this. At the level of development strategy, overvalued exchange rates were rationalized because they allowed relatively inexpensive purchase of capital and intermediate goods to promote import-substituting industrialization. Thus, the demand for imports was fostered by government policy. At the same time, since imports were only lightly taxed and the non-trade taxation capacity of African states was limited, taxation of exports became the predominant way to generate revenues. This reinforced the effect of exchange rate overvaluation in diminishing the incentives for export production.

Import orientation at the same time generated powerful opportunities for rent-seeking investments and corruption. A key feature of "crony statism" is state control of access to foreign exchange through trade licensing. As African currencies became overvalued, black markets for foreign exchange were generated. In many countries, the differential between the official and black market rate became very high. In Nigeria, for example, by the mid-1980s there was a roughly five-to-one ratio between the official and black market exchange rates for the naira. In that context, anyone having access to foreign exchange at the official rate, through a trade license, could immediately return to the black market and trade it for five times his original naira holding. The scope for personal gain by importers was enormous, creating powerful incentives for investment into this largely nonproductive sector. There was also tremendous scope for corruption among those responsible for the issuance of the licenses. The alliance of politicians, bureaucrats, and traders, not surprisingly, became a key component of the coalition behind "crony statism" in Nigeria and other countries.[11]

The point of this exercise is to demonstrate that not only is there a direct relationship between African politics and the general economic crisis, but also that the "political origins" thesis applies equally to Africa's debt crisis. Africa's debt crisis, while immediately precipitated by the second oil shock, is the long-term result of its poor export performance; that poor export performance is a function of import orientation, which, in turn, is an important characteristic of "crony statism." Africa's economic crisis was not initially the result of debt; rather the debt crisis was the inevitable outcome of Africa's economic crisis interacting with key trends in the international economy.

This is not to suggest that the debt crisis is solely the "fault" of African governments. As discussed, high levels of borrowing made some sense, especially before 1978. Furthermore, creditors share the blame for the rapid rise in the volume of debt due to their aggressive marketing of both loans and export credits and their participation in "white elephant" schemes. Fluctuations in interest rates and the sharp decrease in international liquidity, which turned the high volume of debt into a crisis of unsustainable debt service levels were, of course, completely beyond the control of African governments. In the period of the commodity bust, it was almost inevitable that African governments would seek to avoid difficult domestic adjustment through continued external borrowing justified by the hope that commodity price levels would again turn upward. But the fact remains that had export performance been better, all of these factors would have been much more manageable.

Once the burden of debt became overwhelming, by the early 1980s, both international market forces (weakening terms of trade and the depreciation of the dollar) and the very efforts undertaken to manage the debt crisis (IFI programs and debt reschedulings) served to continually increase the volume of debt. By 1987, African debt totaled roughly $130 billion, with very little of the new debt incurred in the previous five years going to productive investment that could break the vicious cycle syndrome described earlier.[12] Unfortunately, at the very time when African governments began to become sensitive to the "policy" origins of their difficulties, the evolution of the debt crisis moved increasingly beyond their control.

Structure of Debt, Debt Service, and Debt Reform Initiatives

The overall volume of African debt pales in comparison to that of Latin America or to the so-called heavily indebted countries (HICs) that have been the object of most international debt schemes. However, for Africa, the burden of debt is greater than that in Latin America and the HICs. Debt and debt-service levels have risen more rapidly for Sub-Saharan Africa since 1982 than for any other set of countries. Only 12 Sub-Saharan African countries have serviced their debts regularly since 1982. The World Bank now characterizes 31 African countries as debt-distressed. Moreover, the social impact of debt and recession in Africa, especially low-income Africa, has been substantially more severe (although it has probably been politically less destabilizing) than in Latin America.

Africa's debt, unlike that of Latin America and the HICs, never posed a threat to the international financial system. The volume is small and the proportion owed to commercial banks is much smaller (35% of African debt) than that of the HICs (70%).[13] But the large debt overhang does threaten the viability of economic reform, both by making the benefits of reform (enhanced external balances) appear to accrue substantially to foreigners and by limiting the likelihood that reforms will have their desired impact of stimulating growth. The modest size of African debt (and its public character) and the threat it poses to economic reform appear to offer incentives for creative management. This is especially so given that, as discussed above, the overall level of debt repayment has been declining for several years and there is almost universal agreement that even current levels of debt service will not be sustainable.

But the modesty of the debt volume and Africa's insignificance to the overall international system limit the impetus for more concerted debt relief. For most of the 1980s, the main instrument for managing Africa's debt crisis has been reschedulings through the Paris Club (for public debt) and the London Club (for commercial debt). By 1990, thirty Sub-Saharan African countries had negotiated some 120 reschedulings for debt totaling close to $30 billion.[14] This figure substantially overstates the actual debt relief, since for many countries it includes successive rescheduling of already rescheduled debt. Generally, an IMF program was a precondition for participation in formal debt rescheduling. The lack of realism in this method of debt management is reflected in the declining proportion of debt service that was being repaid even after rescheduling. Nonetheless, broader measures will not be easy to generate.

Negotiating more effective debt relief will be analytically complicated, time-consuming, and inevitably raise difficult issues of burden-sharing. Burden-sharing problems among the commercial banks held up implementation of the Brady Plan of modest debt reduction for the HICs. Put quite simply, each individual bank has an incentive to hold back from offering debt reduction in the hope that the reduction offered by other banks will restore the debtors' capacity to fully repay its remaining obligations. For African debt, the burden-sharing problems are quite different and occur among the three different types of creditors—bilateral donors, IFIs, and commercial lenders.

In order to better understand the burden-sharing problem and the limited possibilities for a radical reduction of Africa's debt service burden, let us examine the debt service and debt repayment experiences of the three types of creditors and how each has responded to calls for more radical options.[15] Total debt service payments in Africa rose from $7 billion in 1981 to $12.2 billion in 1985. Despite the increase in the amount of debt service, the proportion of debt service owed (after rescheduling) that was actually paid decreased from over 80% to under 75%. After 1985, both actual debt service and proportion of obligated debt service paid sharply decreased. In 1989, out of a totaled scheduled debt service of $18 billion, only slightly more than $7 billion (about 40%) was actually repaid.

In 1990, bilateral debt constituted 39% of total debt and accounted for 33% of *scheduled* debt service. For low-income countries these figures are even higher. But, at least since 1985, bilateral debt repayment has comprised less than 15% of actual debt service paid. In 1989, even after rescheduling, only 20% of the amount due on bilateral debt was actually repaid. Bilateral debt is the largest single component of African debt and is most amenable to debt reduction. For several years, the IMF and the World Bank have recognized that the conventional approach to African debt was insufficient and have urged bilateral donors to provide debt reduction or cancellation. This is in fact occurring. A number of bilateral donors, especially the Scandinavian countries, began in the mid-1980s to convert concessional loans to grants. At the Toronto Summit of the industrialized nations, in 1988, the United States and West Germany, holdout nations, agreed to the principle of relief for non-aid debt in Africa. While the bilateral debt relief programs were slow to get off the ground, by 1990 the pace of implementation had increased substantially, with the U.S., France and West Germany all putting very substantial debt reduction programs in place. Unfortunately, bilateral debt relief, while having made the important conceptual breakthrough of legitimizing the principle of debt reduction, has not had a large cash-flow impact, since it focuses on that portion of African debt which already had the lowest ratio of repayment.

The IFIs comprise a little over one-quarter of Africa's total debt volume, but represent an ever-increasing percentage of actual debt service paid. In 1987, one-third of debt service paid went to multilateral creditors; by 1990, the share had risen to over one-half. Even though the World Bank and the IMF have steadfastly refused to formally reschedule their obligations, let alone reduce them, arrears to the two institutions are building up. In 1989, the IMF and the

World Bank received only 85% of payments due to them. For a large number of low-income African countries, IFI debt constitutes more than half of their total obligations.

The Fund and the Bank have not accepted any obligation to share in the burden of debt relief, arguing that internationally mandated guidelines in their charters, their revolving character (in the case of the IMF), and their special role as a source of liquidity for Africa (in the case of the Bank) must exempt them from any overt debt relief. Beneath these public explanations are the two institutions' fears that debt relief in Africa might be the thin end of the wedge that would legitimize similar actions for Latin America, Eastern Europe and the other HICs.

The IFIs have, however, generated mechanisms to increase their flows to Africa and to increase the concessionality of such lending. As discussed, the IMF became heavily involved in lending to Africa in the early 1980s. Because of repayment schedules, by 1986 there was a substantial negative flow (about SDR 1 billion) from the region to the IMF. To balance this, the Fund created the Structural Adjustment Facility and Enhanced Structural Adjustment Facility to recycle repayments from governments to the IMF back to Africa on highly concessional terms. By the end of 1990, SDR 2.5 billion had been committed under SAF and ESAF, but disbursement has been slow, and through 1991 the negative financial flows from Africa to the IMF continued.[16] In response to the desperate financing needs of Zambia, the Fund also created the Rights Accumulation Program, which, while not an explicit form of debt relief, allows the Fund to engage in operations in countries in which they are heavily exposed.

The World Bank, at about the same time, inaugurated the Special Program of Assistance, which, among other things, seeks to devise approaches to rescheduling nonconcessional debt without accelerating the growth of total debt volume. In 1988, the Bank began to grant interest payment relief to 13 low-income African states on loans received years earlier. The Bank has also committed an ever-expanding volume of its concessional IDA loans to low-income Africa. Net transfers from the World Bank to Africa reached $2 billion in 1990.

Nonetheless, if a more concerted approach to debt reduction in Africa is to be developed, it will inevitably have to involve some form of action on IFI debt. Several options are possible for this, but none appear feasible or likely. One option would be to replace existing loans with ones offering more concessional terms. Another would be the creation of a new international facility to buy out the debt owed to the IFIs, replacing it with new loans on more concessional terms. A third would be for bilateral donors to directly pay some of the debt obligations of African states to the IFIs. Each of these options would demand substantial new resources from the bilateral donors during a time of severe budget limitations, new commitments to Eastern Europe, and the apparent decision by the donors that bilateral debt relief is the appropriate tack for them to take on the African debt problem.

Commercial creditors account for some 35% of the total debt volume. Not surprisingly, this is concentrated among oil-exporting and other middle-income countries. Nigeria alone constitutes one-third of all long-term commercial debt in Africa. Private creditors absorbed less than 50% of Africa's debt service in 1989, down from 68% in 1983–85. Commercial credits can be divided into long-term and short-term debt. Short-term debt is basically trade finance for which, despite arrearages, debt reduction is not feasible. For long-term debt, middle-income and oil-exporting countries have kept up fairly high levels of repayment, while low-income countries are building up substantial arrearages. The arrearages on commercial debt that Africa has generated have further damaged African trade performance by necessitating cash payments, externally confirmed letters of credit, or price premiums for goods sent on credit because of delays in payment. Those countries keeping up payment of their long-term commercial debt have every reason to keep doing so, since it allows them continuing access to international capital markets. For low-income countries, the levels of long-term commercial debt are so modest as to not engage the attention of commercial banks in formal debt reduction schemes, though there has been some swapping of these assets. The World Bank has set up a debt reduction facility to expedite the use of swaps to reduce commercial bank debt. Nevertheless, African debt to commercial creditors does not appear to offer much scope for reduction.

While in the late 1980s there was a plethora of proposals for additional debt reduction in Africa, my analysis helps explain why there has been, in fact, so little scope for radical new initiatives. Such initiatives would have demanded the new commitment of donor resources and shared agreement among all of the key creditors. Neither has been or is likely to be forthcoming. Except for bilateral debt reduction, the financial resources involved would have to be up-front payments to create the facilities to finance the reductions. Thus, Africa's debt crisis is unlikely to be fundamentally resolved in the near future. The most likely scenario is a continuation of reduced actual debt service prompting increased official debt forgiveness. While widespread bilateral debt relief is on the agenda, it cannot by itself address the continuing squeeze that the debt crisis places on cash flow.

Ironically, at a time when responses to Latin American debt have moved away from the "liquidity" approach focusing on new financing, a liquidity approach to Africa's financial problems may be the only politically viable route. This approach will necessitate a continued rise in the levels of bilateral assistance and enhanced funding from the IFIs. For the IMF, disbursements of ESAF funds can be sped up to reverse the net flows back to the IMF. For the World Bank, IDA funding can be enhanced and directed ever more strongly to Africa. For this approach to play a positive role, the increased transfers need to be highly concessional so as not to add to the debt service burden and they must be directed to reviving Africa's productive capacity, especially in the export and import-substituting sectors.

But the liquidity approach is not without its drawbacks. It does little to lower the debt overhang that countries face and might, in fact, increase the debt service obligations that countries face in the medium term. In addition, while more politically manageable at the international level, the liquidity approach will reinforce the domestic linkage between policy reform and debt, thus maintaining the politically unsustainable impression that economic reform is being undertaken to placate external creditors rather than to promote national development interests. This leads us directly to the issues of the viability of conditionality and the outlook for economic reform in Africa.

Conditionality and Reform

In Africa, the international financial institutions and the donor community have been at the forefront of efforts to promote economic restructuring in order to restore sustainable economic growth. Controversy about the role of the IFIs has focused on their use of conditionality to leverage policy change. The use of conditionality expanded in scope after the first few years of the 1980s, following the failure of the IMF's efforts to reverse Africa's economic decline through its traditional instrument of the short-term "standby" arrangement. In the aftermath of this failure, the World Bank, as well as some of the bilateral donors (especially USAID), took the lead in what in fact has been a much more ambitious attempt to restructure African economies through conditional programs.

The predominance of conditionality in Africa in the 1980s generated the widespread misperception that external actors have been the major, if not the only, source of economic policy change. While the donor community has taken the leading role in setting the agenda within which African governments have responded to the continent's economic crisis, other factors have also motivated economic reform. The very fact of economic decline has weakened the political payoffs of "crony statism" in many nations, thus leading to some agreement on the need for reform if not full consensus on its content. Agreement about the need for reform has also been promoted by the general reorienting of global strategies for growth—a new belief in the efficiency of markets, a more open stance toward the international economy, a larger role for entrepreneurship—that has affected other areas of the developing world as well as Eastern Europe. Glasnost and perestroika in the former Soviet Union, the remarkable changes transpiring in Eastern Europe, and the rise of the "four tigers" of East Asia have energized a growing number of African intellectuals today, much as the Cuban revolution and the Chinese Cultural Revolution did a generation ago. Finally, Africa's debt burden, illustrating the need to generate a more viable policy framework, itself serves as an incentive to reform. A young generation of economic technocrats imbued with the belief in economic reform is emerging all over the continent. So while the role of conditionality in promoting reform has been substantial, it has hardly been the only factor at work.

By the late 1980s, within Africa there was a broad consensus about the necessity for economic reform. But, while the need for economic reform in Africa has been almost universally proclaimed (even by the architects and beneficiaries of "crony statism"!), it remains a bitterly contested terrain of public policy. The economic and technical problems of reform are far more complicated than many thought. Almost invariably, the specifics of reform programs lie firmly in the intellectually sticky realm of "second-best" solutions. A 1990 World Bank Working Paper by Harvard economist Dani Rodrik argues that the economic theory behind liberalization efforts in developing countries is embarrassingly weak.[17] Similarly, Toronto economist G. K. Helleiner, a long-time observer of Africa, has argued that there is little common meaning attached to "structural adjustment."[18] Equally problematic are the social and political ramifications of reform, touching as they often do basic elements of the social fiber of African societies. These ambiguities about the nature and impact of economic reform lie at the root of the debates concerning conditionality.

It is not easy to define conditionality precisely. In general, it refers to the agreements between donors and recipients that exchange financial transfers (either grants or loans) by the donors for policy changes by the recipients. But the specific relationship between the resource transfers and the policy changes is a source of disagreement among observers of conditionality. Donors themselves tend to portray this relationship as *reinforcement*, i.e. that the resource transfer provides an added incentive for the recipient government to implement policy changes to which it is already committed. Critics of the IFIs have viewed the relationship as *imposition*, i.e. that the donors utilize financial transfers to enforce inappropriate policy changes on otherwise unwilling governments. Academic analysts have tended to conceptualize the relationship as one of *purchase*, i.e. that the donors "buy" reforms that governments, for one reason or another, would otherwise hesitate to make.[19]

Conditionality in Africa presents the following paradox: while in the course of the 1980s there was an ever-expanding set of conditions placed upon donor resource flows to Africa, evidence suggests that there has been increasingly less donor influence over policy outcomes. In other words, we have witnessed ever more conditions, but less and less effective conditionality. While the IMF has sometimes been able to generate policy reform on narrow stabilization measures, including devaluation, the use of the financial leverage of conditionality on the part of the Fund, World Bank, and the bilateral donors has proven too blunt an instrument and a wasting asset for promoting broader economic reform. While it has been effective in placing the issue of policy reform on the agenda of many African governments and in *initiating* some reform efforts, it has played a far less positive role in *sustaining* reform.

It is useful to make a distinction between the financial leverage of "pure" conditionality and the broader instruments of influence that, in practice, have accompanied IFI and other donor policy-based loans and grants in Africa. Financial leverage, while the most visible element within conditionality, is part of a much broader pattern of donor influence on economic reform in Africa. Where conditional programs have been effective, the effective wielding of intellectual and political influence has also played an important role.[20]

The IFIs have been the main conduit of the diffusion of the ideas of economic liberalism in Africa. This has taken place through a number of mechanisms, some linked to conditionality, others independent of it. Directly linked to conditionality are the formal "policy dialogues" that the IFIs engage in with all recipient governments both over individual programs and concerning the broader overall economic policy context. Extensive training programs that the IFIs conduct are attended by both middle- and senior-level government technocrats. In addition, many senior African policymakers have actually worked in the IFIs. Finally, the IFIs and the other donors involved in policy reform have provided extensive technical assistance support, especially to core economic ministries such as central banks, ministries of finance, and ministries of planning. Taken together, these sum to a tremendous intellectual impact on the way economic policy is perceived, especially by technocrats.

This influence has been particularly important given the breakdown of Africa's traditional public-sector led and inward-looking development strategy. In the context of Africa's economic decline, government technocrats have been forced to consider alternative models and strategies. The financial dependence of African governments on the IFIs gave these agencies unusual access to economic policymakers. Over time, the range of interactions described in the previous paragraph helped to substantially change the terms of the policy debate in a large number of African states. Consider Nigeria and Tanzania as examples. A decade ago, the economic discourse in both countries were conducted in categories (Marxist-socialist for Tanzania; nationalist for Nigeria) far different than those (neoclassical economics) that dominate in the IFIs. Today, the terms of the economic debates, both domestically and between those governments and the IFIs, has evolved dramatically in the direction of the categories propounded by the IFIs. These changes would not have come about without the ongoing interactions with the IFIs.

Another, and more sensitive, form of influence by the IFIs and donors is political influence. According to their charters, the IFIs are supposed to be strictly apolitical. They have never really been apolitical, but the rise of conditionality in Africa forced them inexorably into an even more active political stance. Increasingly, as the 1980s wore on, the donors most directly engaged in policy reform coordinated closely with individuals at the highest technical levels of the bureaucracy. In many policy reform efforts, a key political role was played by "credible technocrats," individuals having the ear of both senior government officials and respected by the donor agencies as well. Such technocrats have been crucial to reform efforts in Tanzania, Madagascar, Kenya, and Nigeria among other countries. In several countries, the most prominent being Nigeria, IFI representatives have played an important role in coordinating and enhancing the political influence of these technocrats. In other countries, such as Malawi, while the IFI political role was less direct, a central aim of policy reforms proposed was to enhance the political influence of senior technocrats.

Thus, while *financial* influence is the most tangible form of IFI and donor influence, *intellectual* and *political* influence have also been important components of donor efforts to promote economic restructuring through conditionality. While in theory conditionality is generally analyzed as the exertion of financial leverage, in practice it has involved varying mixes of financial, intellectual, and political influence. In fact, I will argue that, for a number of reasons, the influence that derives to donors from the financial leverage of "pure" conditionality is quite limited and is highly unlikely to form the basis for successful efforts to promote economic reform. As the 1980s drew to a close, the IFIs appeared increasingly aware of the limits of financial leverage, arguing that country "ownership" was necessary for successful reform.[21]

What donors involved in conditionality have been less willing to concede are the inherent problems that the process entails. In general, the entire conditionality "game," whereby donors attempt to "buy" as much reform as they can while recipient governments attempt to get as much money from the donors as they can with as little reform as possible, draws government attention away from the serious need for economic restructuring by creating a context in which the benefits of reform became identified as increased donor resources rather than improved economic performance. Decisions concerning economic reform too often become responses to external pressures and attempts to maximize external resource flows rather than efforts to grapple with imperative domestic problems.[22]

Furthermore, the financial leverage of conditionality becomes vulnerable to manipulation as donor interests expand beyond the single goal of promoting economic reform. Once would-be promoters of reform develop large stakes as creditors in a situation in which repayment is problematic, their reform goals are in danger of becoming subordinated to their creditor interests. Similarly, since the IFIs and the donor agencies have assumed the task of providing a financial cushion for Africa in the context of an unsustainable debt situation, the conditionality that is attached to their financial transfers over time has lost much of its credibility. The evidence suggests that external finance can either be an instrument for cushioning the debt burden or a lever for promoting economic restructuring; it is very difficult to do both simultaneously.

In rest of this section, I will explore the origins of conditionality in Africa, dissect the mechanics of conditionality, and offer some explanations for why its influence has been more apparent than real. I will also examine the validity of the critiques of conditionality made from the left, i.e. that it threatens the sovereignty of African states, and from the right, i.e. that it actually impedes adjustment by providing African governments the leeway to continue "business as usual." Finally, I will explore some of the reasons why conditionality in general has been a frustrating experience for both the donors and the recipients.

The Rise of World Bank and Bilateral Conditionality

The use of conditionality in Africa by the World Bank and some of the bilateral donors has been driven by a range of factors. The World Bank's 1981 Berg Report paid special attention to policy problems as a source of economic distress. Critical among these problems were poor public sector management, a bias against agriculture, and trade and exchange rate biases against exports.[23] The Berg Report's focus on the policy roots of Africa's economic crisis was consistent with several large cross-national studies that appeared at about the same time, all of which argued that a country's international trade regime was an important source of differential growth in the Third World. Countries with "open" trade regimes consistently outperformed those with more "closed" regimes, both in times of international economic stability and in times of international shocks. Africa was seen as the prime example of a region where efforts to promote import-substituting industrialization led to adverse economic outcomes.[24] Within the World Bank, a series of project assessment reports concluded that the relatively poor outcome of Bank projects, particularly in the agricultural sector, had been due to inappropriate overall economic policies that thwarted even the best designed projects.

The Berg Report argued that growth and development in Africa could be reignited only through a process of "structural adjustment" centered on realigning overvalued exchange rates, improving price incentives (especially in agriculture), limiting the role and improving the performance of the public sector, and energizing entrepreneurship in the private sector. The implication of all of this for the World Bank was the need to design lending instruments that could improve the quality of projects by giving the Bank a larger influence over the general policy environments in African countries.

Many of the bilateral donors, for their part, were concerned that traditional foreign assistance activities (focusing on projects) were not working. A series of empirical studies suggested that foreign assistance, in theory intended to supplement investment, was slipping over to support increased consumption.[25] This, combined with a more generalized "aid fatigue," led several of the bilateral donors also to be interested in new forms of assistance.

Coincidentally, the onset of the economic crisis led African governments to also seek different forms of funding from the World Bank and the bilateral donors. Countries sought resources that were flexible, not tied to particular projects, were fast-dispersing, and could be used to maintain import capacity. They sought nonproject assistance. Thus, at the same time as recipients sought more flexible resources, donors sought influence over policy. The basis was laid for a new instrument: the non-project, policy-based loan or grant.

The World Bank's use of conditionality in Africa was also influenced by critics of the IMF "demand management" approach to Africa's external payments crisis. Critics argued that Fund programs were inappropriate to the problems of African countries for two reasons: first, their time scale was unrealistically short; second, their approach was too narrowly focused on the financial sector rather than the "real economy," the supply-side issues of enhancing responsiveness and growth.[26] The failure of IMF programs in the early 1980s lent weight to the critics. While these views never gained full support at the IMF, (despite the stretching of IMF programs to include "supply-side" issues), they did find a sympathetic ear among policy-makers at the World Bank. Rather than propose an alternative to IMF programs, the Bank developed an instrument to supplement the demand-restraint and external balance-oriented IMF programs with "supply-side" measures.

Conditionality-based non-project instruments were the outcome of the confluence of donor assessments of the sources of Africa's economic malaise, recipient demands for more flexible non-project funding, and the influence of alternative stabilization strategies. The most prominent of these instruments was the World Bank's Structural Adjustment Loan (SAL). The typical SAL sought a range of policy changes: improvement in producer prices, especially in agriculture; the reduction or elimination of consumer subsidies; the liberalization of international trade through quota and tariff reduction; the liberalization of domestic trade through reducing licensing and price controls; the reorganization and streamlining of government agencies, including reducing the size of the public service; the restructuring of education and health services and the introduction of cost-recovery schemes; the restructuring and sometimes privatization of state-owned enterprises; and the development of multi-year investment plans.

In return for agreement to a set of mutually developed policy reforms by the recipient country, SALs offered non-project "free" foreign exchange: that is, a direct infusion into the central bank, whose local currency counterpart directly augmented the government's budgetary revenues. Conditionality in SALs concerned implementation of the policy changes themselves, rather than meeting aggregate targets (such as reducing the rate of inflation) as in IMF programs. The World Bank later initiated Sector Adjustment Loans (SECALs), a similar instrument targeted at sectoral (agriculture, industry, education, export) rather than macro-level adjustment. At the same time, it encouraged bilateral donors to co-finance Bank programs by pledging their own resources, which are added to the total financial package. A number of major donors have done this, while the U.S., U.K., and France have, in addition, undertaken their own conditionality-based policy programs.

Conditionality-based lending is designed to enhance growth in three ways: by improving the policy environment, by directly increasing the availability of foreign exchange, and by catalyzing other foreign exchange flows, both private and public, concessional and nonconcessional. These increased foreign exchange flows ease the import constraint which, in turn, is supposed to facilitate a quickened response to the reforms undertaken. Conditionality was seen by the IFIs as particularly important in Sub-Saharan Africa, since the drying up of commercial flows signaled that international capital markets had essentially declared the region non-creditworthy. Conditionality was intended to decrease the likelihood that external finance would play the role that so much of it had in the 1970s: allowing countries to escape the imperatives of adjustment, providing "rents" for privileged groups, and ending up as capital flight. Unfortunately, it does not appear that the architects of conditionality seriously explored the question of how reform would work domestically, how donor influence would have its desired effect, and whether the leverage offered by conditionality would be practical. It is to these issues we now turn.

The Analytics of Pure Conditionality

To better understand how conditionality works, let us begin by presenting a simplified economic model of pure conditionality.[27] In the model, economic growth is constrained by a lack of efficient investment, which in turn is a result of government policy. The indirect, but primary, goal of conditionality is to catalyze the restoration of external investment flows from private sources. Foreign investors refuse to lend because they fear that their loans will not be repaid. They believe this because they recognize (correctly) that governments have a strong preference for present consumption (including, for the purpose of simplicity, rent-seeking investment) over future consumption. Thus, financial inflows will inevitably go to consumption rather than investment. The direct goal of conditionality is to bind the recipient government to alter its consumption/investment preference function toward investment. Thus, conditionality functions not only to enhance the viability of the loans to which it is attached, but also to improve the investment climate for all creditors, thus catalyzing restored external private flows. Similarly, conditionality promotes a context in which assumptions about foreign aid as additional to domestic savings become realistic, thus promoting increased foreign assistance.

This economic model is consistent with a range of real-world perceptions of conditionality. It provides a basis for the widely held belief that conditionality involves ceding sovereignty to the IFIs. It also provides the theoretical underpinning for the widespread notion that an IMF agreement is akin to the Good Housekeeping Seal of Approval for government policy, increasing the attractiveness of a country to foreign investors. It can explain IFI optimism about the potential for policy reform in Africa and IFI frustration that recipient countries generally didn't believe that conditionality was in their interests. The model is consistent with IFI and donor beliefs that conditionality enhances the creditworthiness of countries.

But, as the 1980s evolved, conditional agreements became separated from increases in private external flows, especially in Africa. This suggests that conditionality has become less credible in the eyes of international capital markets, and that there might be flaws in the economic model of conditionality presented above. In fact, the model sinks or swims on the assumption that conditionality is, in practice, binding: that is, that governments will implement conditional agreements. How valid is that assumption?

While African states have had a powerful incentive to *enter into* conditionality-based agreements—their desperate need for the foreign exchange that accompanies such agreements—they have much weaker incentives to *implement* the conditions that they have agreed to; nor do they always have the technical or political capacity to do so.[28] The weakness of these incentives derives from several different sources: characteristics of the international system, incentives in the IFIs and donor agencies, and politics in African countries.

The conditionality process is weakened by the fact that governments often believe that noncompliance will go unpunished. In the "anarchic" international system, the legal constraints upon sovereign nation-states are minimal. In theory, the IMF and the World Bank should be able to ensure compliance with programs by threatening to withhold *future* funding if the conditionality attached to existing programs is not implemented. But, are the IMF and the World Bank really the tough financial "cops" they are often made out to be?

Here is where the multiple roles of the IFIs—promoters of reform, major creditors, and "financiers of last resort"—come into conflict. The international pressures on the IFIs to continue to supply liquidity to African states, largely growing out of humanitarian concerns about African poverty and that Africa not fall further behind the rest of the world, undermine the IFI's ability to sanction noncompliance with conditional agreements. The situation is worse for bilateral donors such as USAID who often have more obvious political stakes that preclude sanctioning. For instance, the U.S. strategic commitment to President Mobutu of Zaire limited its ability to exert leverage in favor of economic reform. Moreover, given that debt repayments may be put at risk if programs are canceled, the IFIs themselves had a growing disincentive to enforce conditionality as their financial exposure in Africa increased throughout the 1980s.

This bias against sanctioning noncompliance is reinforced both by the difficulty in monitoring compliance and by the bureaucratic incentives within donor agencies. SAL conditionality is often very difficult to monitor, with the possibility that reforms enacted might be countermanded by other policy initiatives outside of the scope of programs. The resources provided for monitoring and evaluation of conditional programs are minuscule compared to the task involved. It is no exaggeration to say that the Bank often does not really know if governments are complying with its conditions. Partially for this reason, Fund staff are often openly disdainful of the World Bank's claim to be effective in applying conditionality.

Staff members of the IFIs have seen that their path to a successful career is through participating in the design and implementation of successful policy reform programs. They thus have a strong incentive to portray the conditional lending activities in which they have been involved in the best light possible. Similarly, at an institutional level, given the controversy attached to conditionality, the IFIs have a broad institutional interest in enunciating the positive. This is particularly true for countries that have good relations with the IFIs, repay their debts, and have been described as successful adjusters, such as Kenya (until 1990) or Ghana. In such contexts, recipient governments have gained a good deal of flexibility in how (or whether) they implement conditionality-based programs.

Evidence from recent studies supports this interpretation. Several comparative studies agree with Tony Killick's finding that the IMF has experienced considerable difficulty in ensuring that its programs are implemented.[29] A major reason for this is, as noted by Bienen and Gersovitz, that the penalties for partial compliance are not great.[30] If anything, the World Bank and the bilateral donors are even more flexible. Gates, in a study of Bank and USAID conditionality, found minimal risks for noncompliance.[31] IMF, World Bank, and bilateral programs are continually renegotiated.

Of course, sometimes there are sanctions for nonimplementation; the IFIs are hardly "paper tigers." When a government publicly repudiates a program, as Zambia did in 1987, IFI funding does get cut off. Also, governments do have to show some real efforts in order to qualify even for policy-based programs. IMF programs are sometimes discontinued, and World Bank SALs generally are undertaken only in the context of an IMF program. But discontinuance, in and of itself, has not heavily damaged a country's ability to reapproach the IMF and the World Bank and renegotiate a new program. The World Bank's main form of sanction in adjustment lending is to delay dispersal of funds, not a particularly powerful lever of influence. The point of this discussion is that recipient governments are aware of the very limited sanctions for nonimplementation and are thus less likely to implement the agreed-upon conditions. The stop-go nature of the implementation of conditional agreements presents a picture quite different from the theoretical model of conditionality, in which it is assumed to be binding. It is thus not surprising that conditionality has lost credence with global financial markets and has not had the "catalytic" role of generating additional private investment it was designed to have.

Within the IFIs, there has been a growing recognition that the limited likelihood of sanctioning noncompliance substantially weakens the financial leverage of conditionality. This is expressed empirically in the growing emphasis in donor discussions of economic reform on ascertaining recipient government "commitment" *before* initiating policy-based programs.[32] If conditionality was more binding, this would not have arisen as a concern. The World Bank and USAID have begun to engage political scientists as staff members and consultants to work on policy-based programs. But judging commitment is very difficult indeed, largely because of the incentives generated by the very lack of sanctioning. "Commitment" is likely to be susceptible to the "game" aspects of conditionality, and to be very difficult to predict with much confidence.

The limited likelihood of sanctioning creates a context where elites have an interest in expressing a commitment to reform even where one does not exist. Generally, the policies attached to conditional financing challenge the interests of key components of the coalition behind "crony statism." For example, devaluation hurts anyone who has had privileged access to undervalued foreign exchange. This gives rise to what Miles Kahler has labeled the "orthodox paradox" of conditionality: how can external actors convince governments to change policies that are economically damaging but politically rational? While state policy and political coalitions produce many of the distortions that conditionality seeks to change, external actors must nonetheless work through the instruments of the state.[33] A growing literature has argued that economic restructuring programs have not been more effective because the dominant elites have a vested interest in the status quo and thus don't want them to work.[34] In the 1980s, in Africa, the cases of aborted adjustment in Liberia, Zaire, and Somalia are examples in which entrenched elites gained access to considerable conditionality-based external resources without moving beyond the initial stages of implementation of reform packages.

But the influence of entrenched interests is not the only political factor that limits the likelihood of effective implementation of structural adjustment programs. Even those leaders who are committed to reform face severe political difficulties. Recall the "time consistency" problem—the preference for consumption over investment—that is the rationale for conditionality. The root of African governments' preference for immediate consumption over investment is the political fragility of African states. The imperative of regime maintenance often clashes with conditionality's effort to shift government expenditure (and societal incentives) from consumption to production. The classic empirical example of this is risks attached to removal of consumer subsidies on basic goods, such as bread or flour. African politicians, like all others, have difficulty looking beyond the short term. Parallel to the "time consistency" problem is the "coalition" problem, the fact that while the benefits of adjustment tend to be marginal but broad-based, the costs are sharp and focused. The theory of collective action suggests that, in such circumstances, "losers" will politically mobilize against the reform to a much greater degree than "winners" will mobilize in its favor. Unsurprisingly, it has therefore been extremely difficult in Africa to gain political momentum for economic restructuring.[35]

Even those elites who want economic restructuring to work—and their numbers are increasing in the face of the collapse of alternative Marxist models and the success of the East Asian NICs—do not always have the ability to ensure implementation nor do they wish to pay the inevitable cost of implementing such programs.[36] In several instances, conditionality-based agreements entered into in good faith by governments were not implemented because of a combination of limited technical skills and bureaucratic blockage. This is an especially difficult problem in complex institutional reform efforts such as privatization and budget and tax reform. Implementing structural adjustment is an inherently difficult task; it involves changing standard operating procedures, challenging vested interests in the bureaucracy, and establishing new relations with the private sector and nongovernmental organizations.

Finally, ruling elites do not necessarily accept the technical analysis upon which the policy conditionality is based. They may not believe that their undertaking the policy changes indicated will achieve the intended outcomes. The record of IFI programs in Africa during the economic crisis suggests that this analytical skepticism is justified. Many governments have completed one stabilization program only to have to return to the IMF in a year or two to undertake a new program, having failed to achieve balance-of-payments stability that is the goal of Fund programs. If anything, the technical analysis behind World Bank and bilateral donor "structural adjustment" programs is weaker still; and the

Bank can only point to Ghana as the single example of sustained, effective "structural adjustment" in Africa.

This entire analysis suggests that the incentives for fully implementing conditionality-based agreements are not particularly strong, and that the ability of IFIs and other donors to "buy" economic reform through the instrument of pure conditionality is very limited. At the same time, it challenges the notion that donor conditionality has diminished the sovereignty of African states by allowing the IFIs to assume control over economic policy. While donor financial leverage, in the context of Africa's economic deterioration, could put the issue of economic restructuring on the agenda of African governments, it was capable, by itself, only of generating initial stabilization measures.

Nonetheless, in a limited number of African countries, economic reform activities have been quite substantial. How can we explain the extent of reform initiatives in these countries in recent years despite the narrow political base of support for such activities? The primary explanation for this is domestic. When substantial economic reform has taken place it has been because political leaders have seen the consequences of failing to undertake reform, i.e. the continuation of a downward economic spiral, as being more risky than those of undertaking it. But, in almost every case where this process has been at work, there has also been a dimension of external influence. To understand this, we need to return to the distinction among different forms of donor influence. While the role of financial leverage as an instrument of donor influence is indeed limited, when combined with intellectual leverage, it has played a significant role. A more satisfying model of conditionality in Africa would focus on the interplay between the three levels of influence: financial, intellectual, and political.

A rough "ideal type" of how conditionality in Africa, when successful, has worked in practice is as follows: policy dialogue, both formal and informal, and joint technical analyses form the basis for establishing consensus and commitment on the part of senior technocrats for particular economic reform endeavors. These technocrats then persuade their political mentors of both the costs of the status quo and the need for such changes; their position reinforced, either directly or indirectly, by their relations with the donors and the knowledge of availability of donor resources. While the ultimate weight of donor influence is financial, it is wielded through the intermediate steps of intellectual influences, especially on key technocrats, and through generating "transnational coalitions" with those technocrats that enhance their political weight in policy decision-making.

Conclusion: The Impact of Conditionality on Economic Restructuring

What, then, has been the impact of conditionality on economic restructuring programs in Africa? The impact can usefully be divided into themes involving economic outcomes and those involving political process. There is a large and growing literature that tries to calculate the impact of policy-based operations on economic trends.[37] This is a methodologically challenging issue. Conditionality agreements involve both policy changes *and* resource transfers. Disentangling the impact of these two elements is very difficult, involving the use of sophisticated models of individual economies. Ideally, one would wish to answer three questions: first, what has been the impact of conditionality on a country's policy environment; second, what has been the impact of these policy changes on economic outcomes; and third, what has been the impact of the financial resources transferred. On none of these issues is there a broad consensus.

One approach to these questions is to ask what would have happened in the absence of conditionality. This is a tough question to answer because it necessitates the construction of several counterfactual scenarios. The first is an international counterfactual. What would have happened in Africa had the international financial resources that went along with the conditionality agreements not been forthcoming? A simple approach to this is to subtract the value of conditionality-based external resources from total external resources and then calculate the further import contraction this would generate and its impact on levels of GDP. But this assumes that conditionality-based flows were completely additional to other external flows, which is almost certainly not the case in aggregate terms though it may be a good way to think about each specific loan or grant. This method also assumes that debt service payment is not higher under conditionality-based programs. That has certainly not been the case. In numerous countries that have, for one reason or another, ended conditionality-based programs with the IFIs, among the first changes is a lowering of debt service payment.

A number of World Bank reports on adjustment in Africa make the strong case that those countries engaged in sustained, externally supported adjustment programs have performed better than those without them. But, the Bank has been criticized for not analyzing the independent effect of higher resource flows to "adjusting" countries. Better performance might be a result of enhanced resource flows rather than policy changes. The Bank itself accepts that improved external flows are important to the success of policy reform efforts. But, a recent econometric exercise undertaken by British researchers concluded that there was not strong evidence that the finance accompanying policy-based agreements caused improved growth performance in countries implementing such agreements.[38]

The second counterfactual, a domestic policy one, is even more challenging. This explores what the policy actions of a government would have been in the absence of conditionality. To what degree does conditionality drive policy? This is a question that can be posed both for policy formulation and policy implementation. In principle, one can conceive of a situation in which conditionality agreements embody nothing beyond government's own policy preferences. Officially, the IFIs contend that conditionality is merely an instrument of discipline in the implementation of government-generated policy goals. This appears to be contradicted by the active role that IMF and World Bank officials have personally played in drawing up the economic restructuring programs in numerous African countries. The degree of variance between a government's own preferences and what is embodied in conditional agreements is probably quite high between countries.

The third counterfactual derives directly from the second; that is, what would have been economic outcomes in the absence of the policy-changes that were engendered by the conditionality-based agreement?

The difficulty of constructing realistic counterfactuals makes the systematic assessment of the impact of conditionality on economic outcomes problematic. What is more amenable to systematic assessment is the extent and nature of economic restructuring that has actually taken place. There is now a large literature of case studies on economic restructuring in Africa, as well as a number of comparative and aggregate assessments, some from the World Bank and others from academic researchers.

In examining the 1980s economic restructuring efforts of ten representative African countries, David Sahn and his colleagues at Cornell University found that, "Measured against the failed policies that predated the reforms, considerable progress has been made . . . Both in terms of policy change and performance outcomes."[39] This finding is consistent with that of the World Bank's recent Third Report on Adjustment Lending, which concludes that policy reform and adjustment support has restored growth in actively adjusting African countries to the "moderate levels" of the 1970s.[40] Both the Cornell and the World Bank study agree that two elements of structural adjustment that appear to show considerable, and sustained, success in a number of African countries are exchange rate reform and pricing and marketing reform for food crops.

Outside of the CFA zone, virtually all countries that have undertaken donor-supported adjustment programs have succeeded in lowering the spread between official and parallel exchange rates, and, indeed, in depreciating the real effective exchange rate. This is significant since many critics of adjustment had argued that it would not be possible to depreciate the real exchange rate in African circumstances. More recently, there has been a growing trend for countries to go beyond periodic devaluations to establish market-oriented exchange rate regimes, either through legalizing foreign currency trading or through some form of foreign exchange auction.

The importance, both economic and political, of exchange rate reform should not be minimized. The exchange rate is the single most important price in any economy, and over-valued exchange rates distort all other prices. Experience in a range of developing countries has emphasized the importance of exchange rate depreciation to the success of associated trade reform efforts, especially tariff reduction. Politically, exchange rate depreciation and the ending of official monopolies over the allocation of foreign exchange restrict what was one of the most important sources of rent-seeking behavior. The ultimate sustainability of exchange rate reform is yet to be secured, however, given that, in virtually all cases, the existing exchange rates are maintained by very high levels of foreign aid, while export responses have generally been less than expected.

Given the centrality of agriculture in most African countries, the incidence of success in food pricing and marketing reform is also very significant. The impetus to reform of food pricing and marketing policy was the practical breakdown of the state-dominated marketing channels and the shift of both production and trade into the informal sector. Thus, in many countries, the political benefits of the old system had already largely worn away. One of the most interesting findings of recent studies is that the cost of raising incentives for farmers has generally not been at the expense of consumers. Part of the reason is that, in many countries, few consumers in practice had access to officially priced food. Part of the reason is that lower marketing margins generated by increased efficiency throughout the marketing chain has allowed both producers and consumers to gain. It is not surprising, then, that food policy reforms have tended to be sustained.

While the successes of structural adjustment in Africa are important, the fact remains that, in many ways, the overall results of economic reform in Africa have been less than encouraging; and the sustainability of reform efforts remains tenuous, especially given the new environments of political liberalization. The World Bank concedes that the growth rates achieved for the actively adjusting countries of Sub-Saharan Africa (around 3.5% per annum) lag well-behind those for adjusting countries in other regions. Export and savings responses have been weak and, not counting donor-provided resources, investment levels are still exceedingly low. In particular, the private investment supply response that will be needed to sustain economic recovery and growth has not been forthcoming. A group of "adjustment stars" has yet to emerge in Sub-Saharan Africa, and adjustment efforts in the best performing countries remain dependent upon extraordinarily large donor transfers (for instance, donor resources constitute between 15 and 20 percent of Ghana's GDP).

A major explanation for the limited impact of adjustment is that existing programs have not been very successful in promoting reform in several crucial areas such as fiscal policy and the public service, the regulatory environment affecting private investment, and export crop pricing and marketing. David Sahn concludes that "In many instances, policy change has lagged behind rhetoric as implementation of reforms has often proved more perilous than planning them."[41]

Fiscal deficits have proved very difficult to attack, on both the revenue and the expenditure side. Even those countries that have had some success in reducing budget deficits have tended to do so in ways that negatively affect medium and longer-term development potential. In virtually no country has fiscal reform enabled the budget to become a real tool for effectively managing the development process. Budget cutbacks have tended to target investment rather than consumption, with maintenance being especially neglected. Civil service reform programs have tended to lag far behind schedule, with virtually no success in either cutting the public sector wage bill nor in providing senior technical staff with competitive wage packages.

Reform of the regulatory environment affecting private investment has also been lagging. In many African countries, the lack of complementary reform measures in the regulatory environment have limited the impact of trade reform and industrial sector reform initiatives. In many donor-supported reform programs, there has been detailed conditionality for exchange rate reform and for trade liberalization, while the conditionality for regulatory reform has been limited and fuzzy.

The experience of substantial reform in food crops contrasts with that of limited reform in export crops. The roots of this difference lie in export crops' continuing role as a major source of taxation revenue for African governments. While the incidence of export taxation has diminished in many countries, governments have generally seen this as all the more reason to maintain their ability to tax what they can. Thus, the reform imperative has been much weaker in the export crop sector than it has been in the food crop sector. As a result, the export response to adjustment has been limited. The lack of success in export crop policy reform thus has quite serious implications for the overall sustainability of the reform process.

Taken together, the limited extent of reform in the budget and overall public management, in the regulatory regime facing private investors, and in export crop pricing and marketing, present a picture of reform outcomes substantially less successful than that discussed earlier for exchange rate and food crop policy. The reform cup in Africa can be thought of as either half full or half empty. But, either way one looks at it, the cup has not been full enough to provide an enabling environment for private investment.

What has transpired under conditionality-driven structural adjustment programs in Africa is thus not fundamental economic restructuring but "partial reform." In most Sub-Saharan countries that have initiated reform, the dynamics of the reform process in the 1980s led to neither a collapse of adjustment efforts nor to fundamental transformation and dynamic economic growth, but rather to a suboptimal mix of partial measures. In a typical "partial reform" syndrome, a willingness to initiate adjustment measures is not supplemented by the basic institutional and attitudinal changes needed to carry through a transformation to market-oriented and private sector-led growth. Adjustment efforts have some success in eliminating the worst distortions and in restoring low-level economic growth, but do not really transform either policy-making or the overall economic environment. The "partial reform" outcome is consistent with what most African incumbent regimes desired from donor-supported reform programs. Robert Bates has argued that, from a recipient perspective, structural adjustment is a last-ditch effort to reform a regime from within, while minimizing political costs, in order to restore its viability in a new economic environment.[42] In other words, for governments, the goal of adjustment was "partial reform."

Donor conditionality has played an important role in the "partial reform" syndrome. On the one hand, conditionality, broadly defined, has played a predominant role in *initiating* economic restructuring in Africa. Donor pressures have been successful in promoting reform in areas that are technically blunt, politically manageable, and institutionally non-complex. The exchange rate is a prime example of this. But donors have also had a tendency to sustain the "partial reform" syndrome, because of their strong incentives to maintain donor programs even in the absence of thorough and effective implementation, and the inability of conditionality to affect so many of the factors that determine the success of adjustment.

But the broader political impact of conditionality has been destabilizing to incumbent regimes and has played an important role in bringing about the demise of so-called "development dictatorships" in Africa. This impact has been felt in several different but often mutually reinforcing ways.

Conditionality-driven programs propelled the expansion of the nongovernmental sector. According to Naomi Chazan, "Many governments, cognizant of the role of the voluntary sector in the provision of essential services, relaxed some of the restrictions on organizational life in order to relieve them of direct responsibility for public welfare."[43] This led to flowering of both local-level voluntary development organizations and intermediate organizations all over the continent, breaking the organizational monopoly that most African"development dictatorships" had imposed, and creating the beginnings of an organizational counterpoint to the state.

Conditionality also facilitated the expansion of the informal sector by weakening, in practice if not always expressly, the ability of the state to restrict informal activities. The informal sectors became, in many countries, the most dynamic area of the economy. The political impact of this, in turn, was the development of a significant resource base outside of the control of the state.

Donor programs, even when not fully implemented, reinforced the effect of the economic crisis in reducing the patronage available to rulers and the amount of rent-seeking in most African political systems. This threatened the control mechanisms in most African states. As van de Walle explains, "The essential problem for state leaders during the reform process is to maintain control of the clientelist networks on which they have based their power, even as they decrease the cost of those networks by ousting old clients or curtailing their access to rent-seeking."[44]

Paradoxically, in most African states, even as structural adjustment programs were initiated to limit patronage and to restore the fiscal balance, corruption increased and budget deficits worsened. Two processes appear to be at work. First, the state's internal discipline collapsed as the system of rewards and loyalty that previously held the system together frayed. This is particularly evident in the growing inability of many African states to raise taxation revenues, even in the context of donor-supported revenue-enhancement projects. Second, the threat of major policy changes gave a powerful incentive for those administering the systems to get as much as they could in the fear that the tap would soon run dry. As the political crisis hit in the late 1980s, both of these trends were exacerbated as it became "every person for himself," in the expectation of imminent political change.

At the same time as the state began to fray from within, structural adjustment programs became the target of many of the urban middle-class protest movements that later became more deeply politicized. Protests generally attacked cuts in housing allowances, school stipends, and price increases for basic goods. But while this has often been interpreted as deep-seated opposition to adjustment, the reality seems somewhat more complex. The logic of economic reform efforts suggested to the same urban middle-class the need for deeper institutional and political change, and the protests quickly shifted from being against adjustment to being against incumbent regimes. This two-sided impact of reform is seen in the ambiguous attitude of many of the new political movements toward economic reform efforts. For example, while in opposition, the Movement for Multi-party Democracy (MMD) in Zambia criticized some of the government's stabilization initiatives as being too harsh, while at the same time calling for fuller implementation of structural adjustment measures! Since taking power, MMD has already implemented reforms that go far deeper than any envisioned by Kaunda's former regime.

Thus, the overall political impact of donor-supported structural adjustment was to interact with broader international trends to destabilize existing African regimes. This fact raises problems with the conservative critique of conditionality. This perspective charges that conditionality-based external resource transfers enable governments to continue to avoid necessary reforms by providing them with "breathing space" that they otherwise could not have.[45] Clearly, some elements of the analysis that I have presented, especially the limited sanctions for noncompliance and the counterproductive impact of large volumes of balance-of-payments financing are consistent with such an interpretation.[46] But what about the larger picture? Does conditionality lubricate reform or does it offer an escape from it?

The cumulative political impact of donor conditionality—destabilization—appears to be quite different from its immediate political impact—breathing space. The evidence from Africa suggests that, except in cases where conditionality-based agreements were really motivated by donor security interests and thus had almost no impact, it is difficult to argue that, in the longer term, conditionality-based resource transfers have effectively protected incumbent regimes from facing the imperatives of adjustment.

Nonetheless, given the high expectations of the early and mid-1980s, the record for externally supported economic restructuring efforts in Africa has been disappointing. But the fact is that nowhere in the world has fundamental reform ever been substantially driven by external actors. In both Asian and Latin American countries, fundamental reform took place only when domestic leaders put in place programs that went far beyond anything suggested by the IMF and the World Bank. This has not yet happened anywhere in Africa.

While the donor community generally has been well-motivated in assuming ever greater responsibility for responding to Africa's economic crisis, it may have been mistaken to do so. First of all, as the analysis presented in this chapter has shown, its ability to address such large issues is inherently limited. More importantly, taking on such responsibilities has had a serious downside—encouraging a growing "dependency syndrome" in which Africans assume that their problems can and will be addressed by outsiders.

In the 1990s, with the end of the Cold War, the increasing demand for resources from Eastern Europe and the former Soviet Union, and the growing "aid fatigue" in Western capitals, the likelihood of the donor community continuing to expand its role in Africa is limited. This is not necessarily a bad thing. For the donors, and donor conditionality, have "hemmed in" Africa in a very peculiar way; not by imposing inappropriate strategies or policies, but by substituting external pressure and financial resources for domestic leadership and an indigenous process. In the 1990s, with luck, the processes of African democratization and relative external disengagement may provide a more conducive environment for a development breakthrough than did the 1980s pattern of massive external financial involvement and omnipresent donor conditionality. This is not to say that African economies can recover without external support, but that such support can, at most, play a supportive role in Africa's development efforts. The main initiatives for African development must come from Africans themselves.

NOTES

1. Percy S. Mistry, *African Debt: The Case For Relief For Sub-Saharan Africa* (Oxford: Oxford International Associates, 1988), p. 4.

2. Thomas Callaghy, "Lost Between State and Market," in J. Nelson, ed., *Economic Crisis and Policy Choice: The Politics of Adjustment in the Third World* (Princeton: Princeton University Press, 1990), p. 258.

3. For an excellent survey of debt-related issues in the Third World see Jeffrey Sachs, ed., *Developing Country Debt and Economic Performance* (Chicago: University of Chicago Press, 1989).

4. International Monetary Fund, *World Economic Outlook 1980* (Washington: International Monetary Fund, 1980) p. 76.

5. Rupert Pennant-Rea, *The African Burden* (New York: Twentieth Century Fund, 1986), pp. 13–16.

6. For an excellent discussion of African debt issues by two senior World Bank staff members, see Charles Humphreys and John Underwood, "The External Debt Difficulties of Low-Income Africa," in I. Husain and I. Diwan, eds., *Dealing With the Debt Crisis* (Washington: The World Bank, 1989).

7. Mistry, *African Debt*, p. 16.

8. Pennant-Rea, *The African Burden*, p. 14.

9. Humphreys and Underwood, "The External Debt Difficulties."

10. Jonathan Frimpong-Ansah, "Sub-Saharan Africa and the International Trade System," unpublished manuscript, 1988, p. 44.

11. See Callaghy: "Lost Between State and Market," for a discussion of the politics of adjustment in Nigeria.

12. Joshua Greene, "The External Debt Problem of Sub-Saharan Africa," *IMF Staff Papers*, Washington, D.C., December 1989.

13. Mistry, *African Debt*, p. 8.

14. World Bank, *World Debt Tables 1990–1991* (Washington: World Bank, 1991).

15. The data used in the following section are primarily drawn from Percy Mistry's excellent study that is cited earlier and supplemented by recent IMF and World Bank figures. Some of the calculations are my own.

16. World Bank, *World Debt Tables*, p. 92.

17. This working paper was later published. See Dani Rodrik, "How Should Structural Adjustment Programs Be Designed?," *World Development* (July 1990).

18. G. K. Helleiner: "Structural Adjustment and Long-Term Development in Sub-Saharan Africa," unpublished paper, 1989.

19. For a recent restatement of the "reinforcement" position by senior World Bank staff see Vittorio Corbo and Stanley Fischer, "Adjustment Programs and Bank Support: Rationale and Main Results," unpublished manuscript, August, 1990. For an example of the "imposition" perspective, see Robert Browne, "Conditionality: A New Form of Colonialism" in *Africa Report*, September 1984. For the "purchase" argument, see Paul Mosley, *Conditionality as Bargaining Process: Structural Adjustment Lending 1980–1986* (Princeton: International Finance Section, Princeton University, 1987).

20. For a similar argument see, M. Kahler, "International Financial Institutions and the Politics of Adjustment," in J. Nelson, ed., *Fragile Coalitions: The Politics of Economic Adjustment* (New Brunswick: Transaction Books, 1989).

21. See the World Bank's Long-Term Perspective Study on Africa, *Sub-Saharan Africa: From Crisis to Sustainable Growth* (Washington: World Bank, 1989).

22. For examples of this syndrome, see the country case material presented

in P. Mosley, J. Harrigan, J. Toye, *Aid and Power: The World Bank and Policy-Based Lending in the 1980s* (London: Routledge, 1990).

23. World Bank, *Accelerated Development in Sub-Saharan Africa* (Washington: World Bank, 1981).

24. Ibid. Also see Michael Roemer, "Economic Development in Africa: Performance Since Independence and a Strategy For the Future," *Daedalus* (Spring 1982).

25. For the original economic theory of development assistance see H. Chenery and A. Strout, "Foreign Assistance and Economic Development," *American Economic Review* 56, 4 (1966). For a review of the empirical studies on the impact of aid see Paul Mosley, "Aid, Savings and Growth Revisited," *Oxford Bulletin of Economics and Statistics*, 42 (1980). For a recent overview see A. Krueger, C. Michalopoulos, V. Ruttan, *Aid and Development* (Baltimore: Johns Hopkins University Press, 1989).

26. See Tony Killick, et. al., *The Quest for Economic Stabilization: The IMF and the Third World* (London: Heinemann Books, 1984).

27. This model is heavily influenced by the recent work of Jeffrey Sachs, published both by the National Bureau of Economic Research and the World Bank. See, for example, "Conditionality and the Debt Crisis: Some Thoughts for the World Bank," unpublished manuscript, 1986; and *Efficient Debt Reduction* (Washington: World Bank, 1989).

28. For a theoretical discussion of the broader issue of which this is a subset see Robert Putnam, "Diplomacy and Domestic Politics: The Logic of Two-level Games," *International Organization* (Summer 1988).

29. Killick, *The Quest for Economic Stabilization*, pp 251–255. Comparative studies include K. Remmer, "The Politics of Stabilization: IMF Standby Programs in Latin America, 1954–1984," *Comparative Politics* (1986); S. Haggard, "The Politics of Adjustment: Lessons From the IMF's Extended Fund Facility," in M. Kahler, ed., *The Politics of International Debt* (Ithaca: Cornell University Press, 1986); and J. Zulu and S. Nsouli, *Adjustment Programs in Africa: The Recent Experience* (Washington: Occasional Paper No. 34, IMF, 1985).

30. Henry Bienen and Mark Gersovitz, "Economic Stabilization, Conditionality and Political Stability," *International Organization* 39, 4 (1985).

31. Scott Gates, "Micro Incentives and Macro Constraints on Development Assistance Conditionality," unpublished Ph.D. dissertation, University of Michigan, 1989.

32. Vittorio Corbo and Steven Webb, "Adjustment Lending and the Restoration of Sustainable Growth" (Washington: World Bank, 1990).

33. Kahler, "International Financial Institutions and the Politics of Adjustment."

34. Callaghy, "Lost Between State and Market"; and Gates, *Micro Incentives and Macro Constraints*. For a discussion or the Zambia case see Kenneth Good, "Debt and the One-party State in Zambia," *Journal of Modern African Studies* 27, 2 (1989).

35. See Center for Strategic and International Studies, *The Politics of Economic Reform in Sub-Saharan Africa* (Washington: CSIS, 1992).

36. Within the World Bank there is an increasing focus on the problems of implementing policy reform programs. For discussions of the issues involved see John Nellis, *Public Enterprise Reform in Adjustment Lending* (Washington: World Bank, August, 1989); and Barbara Nunberg, *Public Sector Pay and Employment Reform* (Washington: World Bank, October, 1988).

37. *Ibid.*, Mosley, Harrigan and Toye. Also, Mohsin Khan, "The Macroeconomic Effects of Fund-Supported Adjustment Programs, *IMF Staff Papers*, 1990. For Latin America, see M. Pastor, "The Effects of IMF Programs in the Third World: Debate and Evidence from Latin America," *World Development* (February 1987). For Africa, see B. Ndulu, "Growth and Adjustment in Sub-Saharan Africa," unpublished manuscript, 1990.

38. Jane Harrigan and Paul Mosley, *World Bank Policy-Based Lending 1980–1987: An Evaluation* (Manchester: Institute for Development Policy and Management Paper, 1989).

39. David E. Sahn, "Economic Crisis and Reform in Africa: Lessons Learned and Implications for Policy," in D. Sahn, *Adjusting to Policy Failure in African Economies* (Washington: Cornell University Food and Nutrition Policy Program, 1992).

40. World Bank, *Third Report on Adjustment Lending* (Washington: World Bank, 1992).

41. Sahn, "Economic Crisis and Reform in Africa."

42. Robert Bates, "The Reality of Structural Adjustment: A Skeptical View," in Simon Commander, *Structural Adjustment and Agriculture* (Portsmouth: Heinemann Educational Books, 1989).

43. Naomi Chazan, "Africa's Democratic Challenge," *World Policy Journal* (1992).

44. Nicolas van de Walle, "Rent Seeking and Democracy in Africa," unpublished MS, 1992.

45. James Bovard, *The Continuing Failure of Foreign Aid* (Washington: Cato Institute, 1986). Doug Bandow, "What's Still Wrong With the World Bank," *Orbis* (Winter, 1989).

46. An earlier essay that agrees with some elements of the conservative critique while rejecting its ultimate validity is E. Berg and A. Batchelder, "Structural Adjustment Lending: A Critical View" (Washington: World Bank, Country Policy Department, January 1985).

Chapter Four

Neither Phoenix nor Icarus: Negotiating Economic Reform in Ghana and Zambia, 1983–1992

MATTHEW MARTIN

Mr. Kaunda has never known the first thing about economics . . . the IMF's liberalism-plus-austerity is the right remedy.

Ghana, which led the revolt against economic reason, now gets full marks for trying to restore it. . . . Ghana has done well because its disaster was complete.[1]

These quotations typify the opinion of IMF-sponsored economic reform programs in Ghana and Zambia held by many in the international financial community.[2] Ghana's post-1983 program is seen as the major Sub-Saharan success story, as the country rose, like the phoenix, from the ashes of 15 years of economic and political turmoil, thanks mainly to its "political will" to implement IMF-style policies. Zambia is a "bad boy": the collapse of its Economic Recovery Program (ERP) in May 1987 is often ascribed to poor implementation or "lack of political will" by the Zambian government. It is believed, like Icarus, to have ignored advice from those who knew better—the IMF and World Bank—and strayed from the path of economic righteousness.

That view, I argue, is simplistic. Overall, Ghana has implemented far more economic policy reforms than Zambia, and with more positive results for the economy.[3] However, this outcome was not determined by "political will." It depended on the degree of domestic political support for reform; economically and administratively appropriate design, and flexible implementation of reform; and availablity of foreign exchange. In turn these factors depended on how reform and external finance were negotiated between Ghanaian and Zambian governments and external actors. The negotiating procedures of the 1980s did not guarantee any of the above factors in a predictable or sustainable way, and was not in the interest of any party to the talks. However, it began to change in 1986, and such change must continue if Ghana and Zambia are to sustain "adjustment with growth" in the rest of the 1990s. The following sections will deal with each of these issues in turn.

Programs, Successes, and Failures

Ghana and Zambia had IMF programs before 1983, but in 1983 both embarked on new periods of reform. In 1983–92, Ghana had six IMF programs: three standbys, followed by an Extended Fund Facility (EFF) combined with a Structural Adjustment Facility (SAF) in 1987, an Enhanced SAF in 1988–91, and a "Fund-Monitored Program" (without a loan) from 1992. Zambia also had six programs: three standbys during 1983–87 before abandoning the IMF for its own Interim National Development Plan (INDP) in 1987–89, and since 1989 a Policy Framework Paper in 1989–90, a Fund-Monitored Program in 1990–91, and a Rights Accumulation program in 1991–92.[4]

Several excellent studies of adjustment in each country[5] conclude that Ghana has implemented much more adjustment than Zambia. This is certainly true in terms of continuing with adjustment programs. None of Zambia's programs before 1987 were completed, formal talks were abandoned in 1987–88, and the renewed program had to be suspended in the second half of 1991. All of Ghana's programs were finished as planned, and during a nine-year period there was no breakdown in talks.

More detailed analysis of whether program targets and objectives were implemented during 1983–90 shows that Ghana's record was not as perfect—and Zambia's not as appalling—as the progress of talks indicates. Ghana breached many of its monetary and reserves targets, and often fell short of its inflation and real GDP growth objectives. Zambia met many of its fiscal targets, and most of its current account objectives.[6] However, in general, Ghana breached conditions by far smaller margins than Zambia. In addition, as discussed below, the Ghanaian government was much more capable of explaining the reasons for breaches, and the Fund reacted more flexibly to them partly because economic indicators and policy were moving in the right direction. These vital additional factors decided that Ghana's programs continued while Zambia's did not.

Ghana's policies have produced positive economic trends, as shown in table 4.1, below. Per capita GDP and consumption have risen substantially (as have real wages). Budget revenue has trebled as a proportion of GDP, producing a surplus in spite of higher spending. Exports and imports have grown in value and volume. In the early years of adjustment, the programs failed in several ways. Inflation and money supply growth were high. Debt and debt service rose rapidly, requiring large new aid to allow debt to be paid on schedule, and arrears of US$440m to be cleared. Export earnings had a narrow commodity base of cocoa, gold, and timber, because agricultural and manufacturing supply response was disappointing. Food self-sufficiency was elusive, and soaring timber exports caused environmental damage. Savings and investment were worryingly low. However, most of these faults have been remedied (see below). Inflation, money supply growth, debt, and debt service are falling. Nontraditional exports are growing as supply response improves. More attention is being given to food and the environment. Savings and investment have risen. Yet budget revenue, savings, investment, and imports remain dependent on large aid flows and, excluding aid grants and interest payments, the current account deficit has risen considerably. Stabilization and recovery have almost been achieved, but self-sustaining domestically financed development is a long way off.

In contrast, most of Zambia's economic indicators have moved in the wrong direction. Per capita GDP and consumption have fallen almost as fast as before 1983. Savings and investment are barely above the levels of 1983–84. Budget revenue and expenditure have both fallen by 4% of GDP, leaving the fiscal deficit unchanged. Money supply growth and especially inflation are far higher than at the start of adjustment. Exports and imports collapsed until 1987, and by 1990 exports were only 10% above the value of 1983, and imports were 25% lower. Debt and scheduled debt service grew rapidly, payments were less reliable, and arrears mounted; though scheduled debt service apparently fell back at the end of the decade, amounts due to clear arrears meant that even large new aid flows could not prevent negative net transfers. Real wages fell, social services were hit and income inequalities grew; food self sufficiency occurred only in 1986. Agriculture and manufacturing failed to grow as hoped. In mid-1992, the Zambian economy still relied on copper exports and aid for imports; neither stabilization, recovery nor self-sustaining growth were in sight.

Overall, Ghana's adjustment was much more successful than Zambia's. Three factors explain this: domestic political support; the design and implementation of programs; and availability of foreign exchange. It is impossible to separate them or apportion responsibility, because they interact; nor is it necessary in order to show that all three should be (and are usually not) considered when negotiating reform.

Domestic Political Support[7]

The successes or failures of the programs cannot be ascribed to blunt factors such as the "political will" of either the government or the broad type of regime. Until 1990, the government of the Republic of Zambia (GRZ) was one-party civilian, under President Kaunda, with periodic elections; in 1991, multiparty elections resulted in a new government under President Federick Chiluba. Throughout 1983–92, Ghana was ruled by the unelected Provisional National Defence Council (PNDC), headed by President Rawlings; but by mid-1992 the PNDC had made rapid progress toward multiparty democracy, with presidential elections planned for November. More specific political characteristics of each country affected support for IMF programs over time: the motivations, cohesion, and power of each government; and the interests, beliefs, and power of extra-governmental forces.

Government Motivations, Cohesion, and Power

The ideologies of Kaunda and Rawlings could theoretically have opposed IMF policies. Kaunda was "humanist," welfarist, and statist, and the PNDC proclaimed itself Marxist revolutionary. "Humanist" concern for growing social problems (malnutrition, poverty) did reduce Kaunda's commitment to IMF-style policy, but Marxism had no influence on Ghanaian policy after 1983. The Chiluba government had no ideology opposed to adjustment.

Table 4.1

Comparative Economic Indicators, 1983–90

	Ghana								Zambia							
Domestic Economy (annual % change)	1983	1984	1985	1986	1987	1988	1989	1990[e]	1983	1984	1985	1986	1987	1988	1989	1990
Real Per Capita GDP	-7.0	6.0	2.5	2.6	2.1	3.5	3.0	2.8	-4.8	-4.4	-1.6	-2.9	-0.9	2.6	-3.6	-3.2
Real P.C. Consumption	-1.5	5.2	2.6	0.5	4.0	3.9	2.1	2.7	-7.8	-0.9	-1.3	-12.0	-8.9	2.4	-0.7	-4.3
Inflation (year end)	121.9	40.2	19.5	33.3	34.2	26.6	30.5	21.1	19.4	20.1	58.3	34.6	50.4	64.1	161.8	105.2
Money Supply (M2)	37.0	60.5	59.5	53.7	53.0	43.0	26.9	27.8	11.2	18.0	23.5	93.1	54.3	61.6	65.3	45.8
(ratio as % of GDP)																
Savings	3.6	9.0	8.1	7.9	9.0	10.6	12.0	12.3	12.9	14.2	14.7	27.8	18.5	18.8	14.1	17.3
Investment	3.7	7.6	9.6	9.7	10.8	12.3	14.1	14.5	13.7	14.7	14.9	23.8	13.9	12.3	8.7	14.7
Budget Revenue	5.6	8.4	11.8	14.4	14.9	14.5	15.9	na	25.6	22.6	22.3	24.7	22.1	18.3	17.6	21.9
Budget Expenditure	8.2	10.2	14.0	14.3	14.3	14.2	15.2	na	33.8	30.0	36.7	53.2	32.9	30.4	27.0	29.8
Budget Deficit or Surplus	-2.7	-2.1	-2.2	0.1	0.5	0.4	0.8	na	-8.3	-7.4	-14.4	-28.5	-10.8	-12.1	-9.4	-7.9
External Indicators (annual % change)																
Export Value	-27.1	29.1	11.6	18.5	10.0	6.9	-5.8	na	11.2	-7.2	-0.4	-30.6	12.7	28.1	27.8	-15.5
Volume	-27.9	2.0	21.1	10.8	7.7	12.3	16.1	na	-2.5	-0.9	-4.0	-8.3	7.9	-12.5	15.8[e]	na
Import Value	-15.1	23.3	9.0	9.2	27.4	6.1	6.2	na	-23.7	-6.4	12.3	-29.3	2.8	10.7	20.4	3.8
Volume	-9.7	27.0	11.2	14.3	12.9	4.7	7.3	na	-28.7	10.8	6.5	-27.7	1.1	7.7	17.8[e]	na
Terms of Trade	6.8	30.2	-5.9	12.5	-8.3	-3.9	-22.2	na	15.2	0.0	-8.9	-12.7	10.9	51.0	9.2	-10.4
Total Debt (US$m)	1650.0	1941.0	2229.0	2732.0	3271.0	3058.0	3151.0	3498.0	3799.0	3811.0	4637.0	5707.0	6599.0	6832.0	6739.0	7223.0
Debt Service (US$m)*	152.0	248.0	366.0	385.0	526.0	651.0	535.0	469.0	577.0	642.0	706.0	709.0	715.0	707.0	801.0	780.0
Debt Service/Exports of Goods and Services	31.8	40.3	54.5	47.8	58.3	68.0	56.7	48.5	60.2	67.6	74.9	109.9	99.7	79.2	56.5	66.0
Net External Financial Flows (US$m)**	131.0	135.0	117.0	54.0	137.0	180.0	356.0	na	16.0	-43.0	185.0	-81.0	-1.0	-102.0	-159.0	35.0

*-excluding arrears reduction

**-calculated according to the usual World Bank menthod: as a residual based on current account deficit less interest payments and grants + changes in gross reserves.

na-not available

[e]-estimated

SOURCES: Confidential IMF and World Bank program, Article IV and Recent Economic Developments documents.

In practice, both governments and the IMF agreed on the long-term aim of self-sustaining growth through adjustment, by rehabilitating and diversifying exports. The PNDC negotiating positions agreed with the principles of many IMF proposals, but disagreed on their speed, sequencing, and severity. The GRZ under Kaunda often opposed both the principles and the details, but under Chiluba it was closer to the position of the PNDC.

In both countries, the most powerful motivation for agreements with the IMF was a longstanding economic decline that had recently accelerated and was not projected to go away (a "trough" factor). By 1983, both countries had a decade of falling GDP, real wages at 20% of 1975 levels, and real imports 80% below 1980s peaks. Both faced economic collapse just before agreement. By mid-1982, drought in Ghana brought a food shortage (requiring imports), a power shortage (reducing manufacturing), and fires (cutting timber and cocoa exports). Foreign exchange and gasoline supplies were drying up, and a million migrant workers returned after expulsion by Nigeria. By the end of 1982, Zambia's reserves covered only seven weeks of imports, debt arrears were mounting, and food and foreign exchange were short; by mid-1985, foreign exchange and gasoline were vanishing. Similarly, the Chiluba government inherited an economic mess from Kaunda in 1991.

Both countries' governments publicly announced a need for policy change in 1983. The PNDC had taken drastic measures in early 1982, but they did not produce major economic benefits, largely because of a shortage of foreign exchange. The GRZ equally believed that only the IMF could mobilize foreign exchange. Both governments tried to find other funds, but in 1982, Eastern Bloc countries gave Ghana only token loans, and Arab and Indian central and commercial bank bridge loans to Zambia became prohibitively expensive by 1983. Most Organization for Economic Cooperation and Development (OECD) governments and commercial lenders were making new funds conditional on IMF agreement. Zambia's commercial bank oil import loans were suspended in 1985, and Nigeria and Libya refused to give Ghana cheap oil in 1982–83.

Many proponents of reforms in the GRZ used a "no alternative" argument in 1983, and prevailed for long enough to achieve agreement. However, many Zambian leaders continued to believe until 1987 that the "trough" was due to a temporary fall in world copper prices, rather than their own past economic policies, and lobbied for abandoning the IMF because it did not bring economic results. After Zambia's independent recovery program ran out of steam in 1989, the "no alternative" argument became even stronger, creating virtual unanimity behind a new Fund program by mid-1989. Ghana's leaders—and Chiluba's government in Zambia—were free to blame past governments' policies for the "trough," admit its seriousness, and dismiss alternatives; this gave them a "honeymoon period" with the electorate and reinforced their commitment to reform.

Some officials and politicians in each country (more in Ghana) had higher expectations, due partly to Fund, World Bank, and OECD government salesmanship. They believed IMF measures would produce economic recovery, and mobilize huge net flows of aid, bank loans, and foreign investment. This was also true of many in the Chiluba government, who believed that they would implement the measures more coherently than their predecessors. But such expectations could breed rapid disillusion. One previously pro-reform Zambian official said in March 1987: "The Fund doesn't care why or how we are adjusting: it just thinks our previous policies were wrong. The means have become the ends."[8]

As is already apparent, neither country's governments had a united "political will"; all were to some extent unstable and divided. In Ghana, political instability delayed the initial agreement in 1983. The previous government had been too unstable to agree. The PNDC took 6 months to resolve internal divisions. Negotiations with the IMF (from April 1982) prompted IMF opponents to attempt coups in October-November 1982. These gave Rawlings the excuse to push them out of government. By the end of 1983, the PNDC had lost almost all anti-IMF members. Many backed coup attempts in 1983–85, but had no influence on economic policy.[9] Most political leaders believed there was no alternative to the IMF, and that the economic benefits outweighed the political problems. In 1986, popular protest and foreign exchange shortfalls increased internal division, but this receded with the changes to the program in 1987–88. Rawlings was able to keep the same senior economic team throughout, enhancing policy continuity, implementation experience, and public credibility.

During 1983–87, Zambia's top policy-making body, the National Council, opposed the IMF by growing majorities. Many IMF opponents were the GRZ's strongest supporters, preventing greater potential threats to political stability (e.g. ethnic tensions). They could not be removed, and remained to speak against the IMF.[10] Their dominance peaked in 1986–87, after IMF opponents replaced Finance Minister Mwananshiku, Central Bank Governor Phiri, and Presidential Economic Advisor Mulaisho in April 1986. After the relative failure of Zambia's home-grown adjustment program in 1987–88, the National Council supported a new program with the Fund, but in 1991 internal opposition grew again in advance of the elections.

In Ghana, a clear, simple policy-making structure eased agreement and implementation. A few pragmatic military leaders made the decisions, advised by a small group of united and extremely competent economic officials (who also negotiated with the IMF). Senior military leaders were also united in supporting Rawlings and most IMF policies. In Zambia, complexity exacerbated division. The National Council, party central committee, cabinet, ministries, and parastatals had a say, reflecting decision-making processes institutionalized since independence and Kaunda's need to balance all groups. Final decisions rested largely with Kaunda, advised by confidants and economic officials. But economic officials were less powerful or united in supporting the program. By 1986–87, as the program failed to produce major economic benefits, their cohesion waned, and opponents of the IMF became more vociferous. In 1989–90, structures were simplified, with the cabinet and the National Economic Monitoring and Implementation Committee (NEMIC) taking almost all decisions. With the arrival of Chiluba's government in late 1991, the new governing party (MMD) lost all formal involvement in economic decision-making: decisions became more centralized in a small group of economic officials around the president.

Division within both governments continued in the mid 1980s while they implemented the measures. There were disputes over many measures at four stages: approving measures in principle; approving timetables and implementation details in principle; announcing measures; and actual implementation. These were more common in Zambia: for example, disputes delayed the ending of consumer maize subsidies for almost two years. They also led the PNDC to reverse civil service benefit cuts in 1986. Implementation exacerbated intra-government division, especially in Ghana in 1983–84 and in Zambia in 1985–87.

Heads of government resolved or overrode division. Rawlings and Kaunda were both politically shrewd, and cared about the economic future of the country; but neither was a trained economist. The main differences were their beliefs, their freedom to exercise absolute power, and their will to be ruthless when necessary. Rawlings was pragmatic, and saw no alternative to IMF-mobilized money and measures; Kaunda was constrained by humanism and wavered in his belief in the efficacy of IMF reforms or the ability of the IMF to mobilize foreign exchange. Rawlings was able to take rapid decisions; Kaunda arbitrated among sectional groups. When necessary, Rawlings was more willing to detain trade union and student leaders, and overrule or remove anti-IMF politicians. Kaunda initially overrode GRZ opposition to the IMF, but in January–May 1987 gradually decided not to expend political capital, pushing implementation past the GRZ and popular dissent, because the program was not producing large economic gains and the IMF did not soften conditions sufficiently. He believed the political and social costs of the program outweighed its economic benefits, and ended talks.[11] In 1989, Kaunda saw that the independent New Economic Reform Program had failed, as foreign exchange shortage and inflation increased rapidly, and agreed to another formal Fund program; but in 1991 he decided to suspend it as elections approached. After the elections, Chiluba played a crucial role in rapidly uniting the new government behind a new program.

Extra-Governmental Influences

Government division often reflected extra-governmental pressure. Both societies contained similar groups that supported or opposed the IMF depending on their interests and belief in IMF measures (or the lack of an alternative).[12] No group was unanimous or favored/opposed all adjustment measures. However, in Ghana, all groups were disorganized, leaderless, and disunited, and the many changes of government in the 1970s and 1980s disrupted lobbying channels. On the other hand, in Zambia, until 1991 opponents were well-organized, well-led, and united, and had well-established channels through which to lobby the GRZ. In contrast, with the arrival of the new Chiluba government in 1991, lobbying channels had to be rebuilt.

Politicians and civil servants were the most powerful group in both countries. They resisted or delayed changes not only because they believed they would not work, but also because the innovations damaged their interests by reducing their living standards, bringing layoffs, depriving them of "rents" from existing policies, or reducing their prestige and status. This applied especially to reforms in major parastatals, with delay in reform of the Cocoa Board in Ghana, and in restructuring Zambia's copper mining, maize harvesting, and agricultural marketing policies. It also delayed budget reform in Zambia and reversed civil service benefit cuts in Ghana in 1986. Many interviewees saw resistance by such groups as a major barrier to reform in Zambia; but after the 1991 elections, a gradual replacement of most senior civil servants relaxed this constraint on adjustment.[13]

The other "semi-governmental" group was the armed forces. In both countries, the higher ranks could be relied upon to support the government; they were replaced when they did not. The support of the lower ranks was also crucial in Ghana: though opposed in principle to many adjustment measures, they were convinced by consistent large real wage and benefit increases, and new equipment purchases which maintained their prestige. The lower ranks were much less well-rewarded in Zambia: planned cuts in military spending partly precipitated the coup attempt in 1990—but after the 1991 elections the new Chiluba government had sufficient mandate to ignore them.

Multinationals, white and expatriate businessmen, and large-scale farmers were consistent public supporters in both countries. They gained more access to foreign exchange for imports, and increased production and profits; but their economic gains were resented by other groups. Most local businessmen initially backed reform, but (notably in Zambia) many were disillusioned by 1986–87, because of inflation, lack of credit for working capital, rapid devaluation, and foreign competition from trade liberalization.[14] Farmers were potential supporters of measures that increased their income, but in both countries smallholders were unorganized. The PNDC initially tried to mobilize their support for the 1987–88 local government elections, but eventually fell back on large farmers and migrant workers. In Zambia the influence and organization of the minority of commercial farmers led agricultural reform to concentrate on providing foreign exchange and raising producer prices rather than structural problems.[15]

Trade unions, students, academics, the urban poor, and many in the middle class generally opposed IMF agreement in both countries, becoming more vociferous when they perceived no short-term economic benefits or when measures were hastily implemented. Trade unions were largely ineffectual in Ghana, but had more power in Zambia, especially in the copper industry—the country's key foreign exchange earner. They resisted wage and staff cuts and mine closures. Their power determined government reaction (which in turn determined the effect of the opposition): this combined consultation and repression in varying degrees. After mid-1983, the GRZ negotiated with them, pushed the IMF for higher wage rises, and tried to involve them in designing reform; but over time union protest grew, often led by Chiluba who was then head of the largest union federation, culminating in major strikes in January–May 1987. The PNDC combined some concessions while ignoring, detaining, or expelling union leaders.[16] Equally, it closed the universities to quell student protest more readily than the GRZ. Only in 1986, when civil servants, the army, trade unions, and students united, did the PNDC take notice and adapt the program. In 1991, the elections in Zambia brought into government many former trade union and university leaders; as a result, strikes and protests were less well-organized, united, and led—and had less effect on government policy.

In Zambia, 53% of the population was urbanized by 1987, compared to only 32% in Ghana.[17] Urban popular protest in Zambia was the main reason for abandoning the program. In 1983–84 it led to some backtracking on reform, but the December 1986 maize riots were a profound shock to GRZ's (especially Kaunda's) commitment to rapid and dramatic adjustment; they changed the political climate in Zambia far more fundamentally than the IMF realized. They reflected the accelerating collapse of urban real incomes due to rising inflation, and the inept introduction of the maize price increase.[18] The final straws in Kaunda's decision to abandon the IMF were an escalating strike wave in January–May and Lusaka riots over gasoline price increases in April.[19] Again in mid-1990, maize price increases led to riots, but this time their impact was offset by the government's more unified stance behind the program.

In the context of divided societies, the governments' public explanation of policy was vital to successful reform. In Ghana, division was kept private by policymakers' restraint, government control of the media, and PNDC proclamation that the program was its own. The PNDC united in presenting the IMF program as pursuing the revolution and, insofar as ideology mobilized support for the government, it also helped the program in 1983–84. On the other hand, the GRZ was divided in public over whether the IMF reforms were humanist. Ministers publicly criticized reforms and the IMF throughout 1983–87, reflecting a freer press, Kaunda's reluctance to suppress dissent, and the identification of the program with the IMF. This division undermined the credibility of reform. Changing the economic team in 1986 shook donor and business confidence, and accelerated the fall of the currency in the foreign exchange auction.[20] Changes of policy direction also damaged government credibility. This was particularly true when Zambia's IMF talks broke down in May 1987, and when it later returned to the IMF—but it also applied to the PNDC's reversal of civil service benefit cuts in 1986.

Consulting interest groups did little to reduce opposition. The GRZ held a National Economic Convention in July 1984 to increase consensus behind reform and sent out leaders to explain the 1985–86 program. But many were unenthusiastic proponents, or oversold potential benefits, damaging GRZ credibility when they did not materialize. The PNDC allowed less public debate, instead launching a campaign to convince people that reform was the only viable and revolutionary route to recovery, and that it was Ghanaian-designed. This became less effective as memories of the "trough" faded and interest groups did not reap benefits of GDP growth—but after 1987 genuine benefits arrived for most groups. As one IFI official said: "Attempts to convince people inside and outside governments are counteracted if programs fail to produce short-term economic benefits. Consultation exercises only identify the government more closely with the program and increase its instability."[21]

The ultimate form of consultation was election. Zambia's one-party elections delayed agreement in 1983 and influenced the decision to end the IMF link in 1987. The multiparty elections of 1991 led to the suspension of the adjustment program by the government, to allow the GRZ more room to increase budget expenditure and imports. Ghana's 1987–88 local elections led the PNDC to slow the pace of adjustment and boost social spending; but even so, economic benefits for the voters did not materialize, and the PNDC had to resort to administrative manipulation of the election results. By mid-1992 it was still difficult to judge the possible effects of the approaching multiparty presidential and parliamentary elections on adjustment implementation, but it is striking that no major party formally declared itself opposed to the PNDC's economic policies, although major political figures did speak against them.[22] Indeed, economic policies seemed to be a relatively minor issue compared with the proliferation of parties and whether Rawlings would stand for the presidency. In September 1992 he announced that he would do so. Some IFI staff saw elections as "a major barrier" to implementation,[23] though post-election honeymoon periods can give new governments more leeway. Rawlings won the November presidential election with about 60% of the vote, and the opposition boycotted the late December parliamentary elections, allowing Rawlings to maintain complete control of the government. The PNDC may have shown that growth-oriented adjustment can facilitate at least partial political liberalization, particularly when substantial economic reform comes first and the opposition is badly fragmented.

A failure to improve conditions can also be a powerful contributory factor in government instability. Yet the relationship between reform and instability is much more complex. In Ghana, prior government instability speeded agreement because the PNDC needed to produce economic results, and enhanced implementation because it allowed the PNDC to blame economic problems on predecessors, and made coup attempts unpopular. This "honeymoon period," the disorganization of opposition and the "trough" effect produced a "culture of silence" in Ghana, which allowed the government to implement adjustment with relatively little instability until 1986. In Zambia, prior stability speeded agreement by enabling Kaunda to override the National Council. However, it weakened implementation because of discontent with past economic performance, and a legacy of GRZ internal disagreements on other issues. Each period of instability (the strikes of 1985, the riots of 1987 and 1990, and the coup attempt of 1990) directly reflected the introduction of new adjustment measures, and was in turn followed by slippage in implementation. The ultimate instability of a pre-election period led to the suspension of the adjustment program in mid-1991.

There was nothing in the state or society of Ghana or Zambia that necessarily precluded reform. They shared political and social characteristics that made reform more difficult, but these were more prevalent in Zambia. In particular, Ghana had a stable team of military leaders who supported extremely competent economic officials, which was one major reason why Ghana achieved more reform. Members of governments and the population acted according to their beliefs, interests, and power. Reconciling these to support reform depended on "carrot" (perceived economic benefits from programs) and "stick" (the government's will and ability to force measures through). Ghana's programs produced more carrot (imports, budget expenditure increases, real wage rises) than Zambia's, and the GRZ was not prepared or able to use as much stick against more formidable opposition. Zambian politics could tolerate the rapid pace of adjustment demanded by the IMF only for short periods, leading to the repeated suspension of programs, the suspension of talks in 1987, and ultimately the fall of Kaunda's government. As one World Bank official involved in Ghana's 1982–84 talks has said, "While the Zambian authorities concluded that the adversity caused by the economic reforms was clearly unsustainable, the leadership in Ghana remains undeterred in undertaking reforms."[24] It remains to be seen whether the new Zambian government will be any more resilient, and whether the post-election government in Ghana will be as successful in designing and implementing reform.

Program Design and Implementation

The second factor in success was whether the program was correctly designed, appropriate to the country's economic and administrative capacity for reform, and implemented flexibly to overcome design faults (a section below explains why programs had design faults). Nobody, including the IMF, knew the exact policies needed to produce "adjustment with growth" in Ghana or Zambia, given limited data and previous research.

Yet three types of design faults could have been remedied regardless of country context:

- *Experimentation*. Programs often "learned by doing," using countries as "guinea pigs" for untried ideas, but did not build in safeguards in case experiments went wrong. Zambia's foreign exchange auction was experimental in having a single exchange rate; and Ghana's in putting pharmaceutical imports and cocoa exports at a preferential rate.[25]
- *Incorrect sequencing*. Failure to control fiscal policy or monetary growth, or to establish efficient systems to channel foreign exchange to the Zambian auction before it began, helped to cause rapid devaluation and inflation, by increasing demand for foreign exchange and reducing its supply. The capital and current accounts, and exchange and interest rates, were liberalized before fiscal and monetary stability had been achieved, sectoral distortions corrected, or the credibility of a sustained reform program established. This accelerated speculative demand for foreign exchange.[26]
- *Conflicting conditions* (either within IMF programs or between Fund and Bank). Devaluation in Ghana and Zambia pushed up the cost of debt service and other foreign exchange-denominated payments in budgets, helping to breach expenditure ceilings in both countries in 1986. It created gasoline price (and increased maize price) subsidies compared to world prices, breaching IMF conditions on reducing or eliminating subsidies—and making the IMF insist on further price rises. Finally, devaluation and high interest rates made small farmers and small businesses (who were supposed to be leading sources of growth) unable to find or borrow enough local currency to purchase foreign exchange in the auction and import capital goods to raise productivity.[27]

Four other faults made programs inappropriate to the economic and administrative capacity of Ghana and Zambia:[28]

- *Proliferating conditions*. Zambian programs in the 1970s averaged 10–15 conditions, but the 1986 standby included 29, and the 1989 PFP contained 9 pages of conditions! Ghana's conditions rose from fewer than 20 in 1983 to more than 40 for the Enhanced Structural Adjustment Facility.
- *Tighter conditions*. Until the mid-1980s, conditions in most new programs became "tighter," requiring more rapid or sharper adjustment. This was particularly true of the 1984 standby in Ghana and Zambia's mid-1986 resumption talks. Later in the decade they began to react more closely to actual developments,

requiring greater adjustment from Zambia but less from Ghana because its macroeconomic situation improved.

- *Deeper conditions.* Throughout 1983–92, conditions also became more specific or "deep," as broader targets did not produce expected results or were not implemented. For example, both Ghana's civil service benefit cuts of April 1986 and the Zambian maize price rise of December 1986 were conditions exactly specified and timetabled by the IMF.[29]
- *Preconditions.* Conditions which had to be implemented before the IMF would begin disbursing a new loan also proliferated and became tighter and deeper for both countries during 1983–88. They included action on exchange rates, interest rates, budget cuts, arrears clearance, and import liberalization. However, by the end of the decade, the relationship of growing trust between the IMF and Ghana led to reduction of preconditions.

These four trends increased strain on the economy, and political and administrative demands on both governments, and decreased their freedom to implement overall reform targets in ways they chose, without any extra disbursement of external finance. They also strained IMF and World Bank administrative capacity to design conditions appropriate to Ghanaian and Zambian circumstances; to avoid or reduce experimentation, incorrect sequencing, and conflicting conditions; and to monitor compliance or suggest ways of fine-tuning implementation.

Both countries had low *economic capacity to adjust.* This was due to imperfections in capital, factor, and product markets, including poor communications and incomplete or delayed information flows, an inadequate transport system, declining provision of education and training, low social and labor mobility, dualistic capital markets, and private and public sector monopolies and monopsonies. In addition, protracted recession and import strangulation cut availability of capital and consumer goods; massive excess demand for foreign exchange caused rapid devaluation in an auction; capacity underutilization and decay of capital equipment reduced manufacturing supply response; and low living standards and unemployment cut the tax base and propensity to save. There were also sectoral, distributional, and seasonal constraints on adjustment. These caused "lags" and shortfalls, and unexpected results from reform policies, reducing political support.

However, there were six factors that explained differences in economic capacity between the two countries:

- *Skill and supply of labor*. Ghana had a much better-educated and trained labor force than Zambia, with ample supplies of the skills needed in all sectors of the economy. Ghana also benefitted from an influx of mobile and cheap labor in 1983–84, when Ghanaian workers were expelled from Nigeria. In contrast, Zambia suffered shortages of skilled labor.[30]
- *Supply response of main export commodities*. Trebling local currency producer prices for Ghana's main export, cocoa, between 1983 and 1987 produced a rapid export rise after 1984, partly by reducing smuggling through neighboring countries. Such price incentives could not increase Zambia's main export, copper: it was not smuggled and was purchased in foreign exchange at world prices (which fell during 1983–86). Ghana was also able to achieve rapid export diversification into other "traditional commodities," particularly gold and timber, reflecting underexploited and easily accessible natural resources.
- *Sectoral composition of GDP*. In 1986, 45% of Ghana's GDP came from agriculture, compared to 11% in Zambia. This implied that a given percentage increase in Ghana's agricultural output would have a greater effect on overall GDP growth, while Zambia required spectacular agricultural growth to boost overall GDP.
- *Size of informal sector*. Because Ghana's was larger, its prices had adjusted to much higher parallel market levels (and its import prices to higher parallel market exchange rates) before 1983. This weakened the impact of the official inflation rate and devaluation on purchasing power, and gave workers more chance to hold simultaneous jobs in formal and informal sectors to reduce income losses, or to switch to informal sector jobs when laid off from formal jobs.
- *Food subsidies*. Ghana had no food subsidies before 1983, but Zambia's gave substantial income support to urban households. Thus measures to cut subsidies, when implemented repeatedly and hamfistedly, were the beginning of the end for the Zambian program in 1987. The failure to introduce further cuts was largely responsible for suspending the 1991 program.
- Ghana's changing *weather* first constrained and later boosted capacity. In 1983–84, drought prevented agricultural growth and brought high food-price inflation. Good rains in 1984 explained 50% of the fall in inflation (which occurred in spite of rapid mon-

etary growth) in 1984–85 and, together with policy changes, boosted noncocoa agriculture, which accounted for all GDP growth in 1984. In 1987–88, partial drought helped depress growth and push inflation to 40–50%.[31] In contrast, Zambia's rains were good enough to boost economic activity only in 1988, when there was no IMF program, and in 1989–90 and 1992 drought cut agricultural production and GDP growth.

Such major differences in economic capacity required tailoring programs to country circumstances. Yet programs often implemented lessons of one country in another regardless of different circumstances: Zambia's foreign exchange auction was an idea copied from Uganda's 1983–84 program, though the two economies were fundamentally different. However, learning lessons could be positive when they led to caution. Ghana's (and Nigeria's) auctions learned from Zambia's problems: they ensured prior monetary and fiscal stability to reduce demand for foreign exchange, and adequate prior supply of foreign exchange.

On the other hand, important differences of design between the two countries' programs also explain much of their success and failure. Ghana's greater economic and administrative capacity led the PNDC and IMF to have higher expectations of output and supply response in Ghana. Together with rising net foreign exchange inflows, this encouraged them to design a more growth-oriented program after 1984. In turn this design enhanced Ghana's capacity to adjust, with several measures that increased supply—instead of compressing demand, the main focus in Zambia.

- Ghana's budget deficit was eliminated after 1985 by trebling revenue as a proportion of GDP (partly due to tax receipts from rising imports). This enabled the expenditure/GDP ratio to rise from 8% in 1983 to 15% in 1989.[32] In Zambia, the slight reduction in the deficit between 1983 and 1989 was due to rapid falls in both revenue/GDP (especially from import tax and sales duty) and expenditure/GDP. Expenditure cuts in Zambia were swinging in real terms, especially if interest payments are excluded.
- Fiscal stability in Ghana reduced the government share of borrowing, freeing more resources for private sector investment and gradually reducing money supply growth and inflation. Higher Ghanaian government capital expenditure (helped by large aid flows) and private sector investment boosted gross fixed capital

formation, and savings/GDP and investment/GDP ratios in Ghana, in contrast to trends in Zambia.

- Nominal wages were allowed to rise faster in Ghana than in Zambia, partly because recurrent budget expenditure was protected. With lower inflation, real minimum wages rose by 120% in Ghana during 1983–87, reducing urban discontent and trade union protest. In Zambia, they fell substantially during the same period, increasing protest.[33]

As nobody was sure whether measures would work, they often needed *fine-tuning through flexible implementation*. Proliferating, tighter and deeper conditions and preconditions strained Ghanaian and Zambian administrative capacity to implement them, even with committed reformists in power. This capacity also varied with the number, training, experience, commitment, and morale of the staff involved; the complexity of the decision-making structure; and above all the speed of economic collapse during the program. One pro-reform GRZ official said: "In order to meet monetary and fiscal targets (let alone the others), negotiate external finance, and incidentally run the economy, we needed to be in five places at once and have 36 hours in a day."[34]

Monetary and fiscal targets caused the greatest administrative problems for both countries. Both foreign exchange auctions were administrative nightmares, requiring complex documentation and monitoring procedures, and reports to aid donors to gain more aid. Administrative incapacity was due to poor organization, coordination, delegation, monitoring systems, and technical understanding of the wide range of new measures. To the extent that the IMF and World Bank ignored these, or implemented unsuccessful administrative reform, they were partly responsible. It was particularly acute in Zambia, where skilled or experienced professional staff were scarce; conditions like the import tax for the 1986 standby, which needed complex constitutional approval, took 14 months to implement. In contrast, Ghana achieved remarkable improvements in fiscal and monetary monitoring and aid processing by 1988; but lack of permanent institutional mechanisms to adjust agricultural, fertilizer and gasoline prices caused delay.[35]

The Ghanaians proved much more capable at fine-tuning—and, by sustaining adjustment, at convincing the IMF to allow changes in mid-program—as emerges from comparison of the two foreign exchange auctions.[36] Both governments managed the auctions, but in different ways. Both initially excluded some foreign exchange transactions (debt service and oil/fertilizer imports); Ghana also excluded pharmaceutical imports and cocoa exports, and Zambia imports for the copper mines. But Ghana initially used a lower exchange rate for excluded items, which reduced the negative impact of devaluation on budget expenditure, whereas Zambia had a single rate. The Fund agreed to Ghana changing auction rules in order to limit speculative bidding and reduce demand for foreign exchange. The PNDC used "Dutch" bidding (where the successful bidder paid the rate bid), 100% prior deposit of local currency by bidders, strict and changing eligibility and documentation requirements which reduced the number of bids accepted (and excluded consumer goods imports in 1986–87).

On the other hand, the IMF opposed rule changes in Zambia, because it did not trust the GRZ to devalue in a managed auction. Though the Zambian pro-reform team asked the IMF to allow rule changes early in 1986, IMF "theologians" refused. This was a major cause of the ensuing depreciation below what the GRZ—including the pro-reform team—saw as an acceptable level, which gave opponents powerful ammunition for the removal of that team. This was then followed by hamfisted GRZ management of the auction, including large changes in the amount of foreign exchange supplied, tighter documentation requirements, Dutch bidding, and a 30% deposit—all without IMF approval. In addition, Ghana satisfied auction demand for foreign exchange at key stages by borrowing from Standard Chartered Bank, while Zambia's auction faced inadequate foreign exchange supply throughout.[37]

There were also negative examples of implementation by both governments, announcing or reversing measures before details had been finalized. Sometimes this was done against Fund and World Bank advice. Due to the collapse of the currency, rising inflation and growing political opposition, the GRZ first changed the rules of the foreign exchange auction, then pumped large amounts of foreign exchange into it, and then suspended it in January 1987 with no clear idea of how to replace it. The announcement of an interim fixed exchange rate with two days of warning allowed speculators to make a killing. The PNDC reversed cuts in civil service wages and benefits rapidly in April 1986, in order to dampen popular protest, without sufficient time to assess the implications for fiscal and monetary targets. The IMF suspended the program and insisted on compensating cuts in other government expenditure. Its inflexibility almost led a government wholly committed to adjustment, with remarkable economic and administrative capacity and little political instability, to suspend talks with the IMF. Though (as discussed more below) the Fund soon softened its position, this incident showed how vital careful implementation was to successful adjustment.

However, poor implementation often followed IMF or World Bank advice. The Zambian auction was restored in March 1987 without a complete relaunch of the reform program to boost its credibility, or huge inflows of foreign exchange to pay off arrears. The rate was bound to collapse, and did. In December 1986, Zambia's 120% price rise for the expensive grade of maize meal was announced without properly informing the private maize millers of how they would be compensated for loss on the cheaper grade. They reduced production of cheaper meal (the GRZ argues that they were acting irresponsibly, and should have requested more information), and resulting shortages were the true cause of riots in which 17 people were killed. The fault lay on both sides. The GRZ had delayed price rises for 2 years. The IMF and World Bank were exasperated at this delay, and insisted on a price increase by the exact amount immediately as a precondition for standby resumption, in order to close the budget deficit. Pushing this rapidly through a divided GRZ meant that neither the IFIs nor the GRZ had time to monitor maize availability.[38]

There were design faults in both countries' programs. Yet the faults were greater in Zambia, affecting key measures (the foreign exchange auction and maize price). Given Zambia's lower economic and administrative capacity, they made a key contribution to the stop-go nature of reform. Because the Fund and the GRZ had lower expectations of output or export supply response in Zambia, they decided that aggregate demand had to be cut sharply, reducing budget expenditure, imports, and real wages.[39] When compounded by inflexible implementation and inadequate fine-tuning, it was not surprising that the program lacked political support. In contrast, Ghana's program was designed as more growth-oriented and supply-enhancing, increasing budget expenditure, imports, and real wages. Greater economic and administrative capacity, and flexible implementation, produced economic and political benefits which sustained the program.

Foreign Exchange Availability[40]

The amount of foreign exchange mobilized by reform was a third crucial factor in the relative success of the programs. Most importantly (as already discussed), it influenced the design and implementation of the program—indeed it often prevented governments from meeting specific program targets. In addition, the extra amount of aid and debt relief pledged helped to reinforce government commitment to reform.

Zambia's inflows of new foreign exchange fluctuated wildly, but exceeded pre-1983 levels only in 1986 and 1991. The IMF and multilateral lenders provided an annual average of 70% of the total (though World Bank lending rose more slowly than in Ghana). Bilateral donors did not believe until 1985 that reform would be sustained, and then lost faith early in 1986; they provided much lower gross flows than in 1980–81, and commercial flows collapsed.[41] Many in the GRZ and World Bank argued that the international community was not responding sufficiently to Zambia's reform efforts.[42]

However, Ghana's gross inflows rose sharply, doubling between 1982 and 1989. In 1983–86 the IMF (average US$200mpa) and other multilateral lenders (US$200mpa) led the way, financing 70–80% of imports in 1983–84. Bilateral donors increased commitments only by limited amounts, through antagonism to the PNDC and uncertainty that the program would continue. By 1987–88, encouraged by large new World Bank adjustment loans and the PNDC's ability to sustain adjustment, they were disbursing US$250mpa. Gross inflows rose fast in 1984–5, providing substantial demonstration of the international community's support. A slower rise in 1986 coincided with adjustment problems, but thereafter gross flows rose much faster.

The more important figure for each country was net inflows, after debt service, debt relief and arrears accumulation or reduction. This was the key difference between Ghana and Zambia. Ghana's debt rose from US$1.65bn in 1983 to US$3.50bn in 1990, by a higher percentage but a lower actual amount than Zambia. Its debt service-export earnings ratio rose from 32% in 1983 to 49% in 1990, peaking above 55% in 1987–89. Because most of its debt to governments had been rescheduled in the 1970s, and it owed negligible amounts to commercial creditors, only about US$250m of oil import payment arrears to Nigeria and Standard Chartered

Bank were rescheduled (reducing the debt service ratio by only 6–8%pa). Service to the IMF was 40% of the total in 1987–88, because of the short repayment periods of IMF loans. Until 1986, debt service rose even faster than gross inflows, leading to a fall in net inflows from US$131m in 1983 to US$54m in 1986. The falls in net inflows were in 1985 and 1986, which was also the most difficult time for adjustment.[43]

Between 1983 and 1990, Zambia's debt rose from US$3.80bn to US$7.22bn, and its scheduled debt service-export earnings ratio from 60% to 66%; however, it peaked in 1986–87 at 100% or higher.[44] Most service due in 1983–86 on medium and long-term debt to governments and commercial creditors was rescheduled or fell into arrears, reducing the actual debt service ratio by 20–30%. But the low and stagnant gross inflows meant that net financial inflows were positive only in 1983, 1985 and 1990–91, and were highly negative in 1986, 1988 and 1989, because of rising debt service and (in 1986) net outflows to the IMF of US$141m. In April 1987, the GRZ faced a 1987 scheduled debt service ratio of 190% including arrears, and a projected net financial outflow of SDR25m.[45] This gave supporters of adjustment little basis for arguing in 1986–87 that it mobilized additional external finance.

In turn net inflows largely determined the volume of imports financed by available foreign exchange, which was a key element in growth and government commitment to adjustment; this also depended on export earnings and terms of trade. Ghana's export earnings rose 89% between 1984 and 1989, because of successful reform, local currency price incentives and foreign investment, while Zambia's fell 29% between 1983 and 1986. In the crucial early reform period, Ghana's terms of trade improved by 47%, while Zambia's fell. Higher net financial inflows in Ghana widened the disparity in import volumes: Zambia's fell by 51% in 1983–86; Ghana's rose by 46% in the same period.[46] Slower import growth in 1985–86, caused by lower net financial flows and export growth rates, coincided with adjustment problems, as the PNDC questioned whether enough growth was being allowed. Similar questions in the GRZ contributed to the abandonment of talks with the IMF in 1987.

Expectations were also important: both countries had large shortfalls of foreign exchange compared to program targets. By 1986, slow disbursement of aid by bilateral donors had created a backlog of US$950m for Ghana. Zambia had even larger shortfalls: gross flows were US$302m less than projected in 1986 alone. In both countries, this reflected donor and technical problems in processing funds; but in Zambia the problem was compounded by suspension of IMF and donor disbursements while adjustment programs were renegotiated.[47]

Programs also consistently underestimated scheduled debt service for Zambia (in five of seven program years). This reflected underestimates of short-term debt and arrears, and overestimates of the amount of relief creditors would provide (especially the amount the Paris Club of creditor governments gave Zambia in 1984[48]). On the other hand, better debt records meant that overestimates of debt service were the norm for Ghana after 1984.

Projections of other balance of payments variables were also wildly optimistic.[49] Prices and production fell short for copper and cobalt in each program year for Zambia, and prices for cocoa in 1986 for Ghana. Zambian copper earnings shortfalls, due largely to price falls, were the largest single cause of collapse in all three programs. They were compounded by SDR-US$ and UK£-US$ exchange rate changes: as the dollar fell, copper earnings were worth less.[50] Import volumes were lower than projected in every year of both countries' programs during 1983–87, but to a lesser degree for Ghana after 1984.

As with macroeconomic policy, Ghana was more successful at fine-tuning external finance availability, by filling temporary shortfalls with short-term bridging loans. Its loans paid for oil imports in 1983 and 1986, supported the foreign exchange auction, and prevented arrears to the IMF. They were a vital source of stability in IMF programs, covering delays in foreign exchange receipts and enabling more long-term planning of imports and debt service. In addition, in the context of growing foreign exchange and import availability, Ghana was able to repay them all on time, usually out of IMF funds, and new loans remained available in 1987–88. On the other hand, Zambia had to juggle larger and more persistent shortfalls of imports and foreign exchange day-to-day, with increasing desperation. It borrowed more than US$400m of bridging loans in 1983–86, but because shortfalls were much larger than in Ghana, these went immediately to pay growing IMF or World Bank arrears. By 1986, Zambia had insufficient foreign exchange to repay the bridging loans. It took out new loans to repay them, but in late 1986 and early 1987, banks refused to lend.

Overall, optimistic balance of payments projections and external finance shortfalls had crucial effects on the different abilities of each country to implement adjustment targets, and on government and donor commitment to the adjustment program. Higher gross financial inflows and export earnings allowed Ghana to pay most debt service on schedule, and to reduce its arrears. They helped it to implement IMF fiscal and current account targets, thereby increasing donor faith in the program and beginning to restore commercial lender confidence. It also allowed imports, investment, and budget expenditure to grow, with knock-on positive effects on GDP and per capita consumption. This dampened political opposition and reinforced government commitment to adjustment, but even so, persistent shortfalls of aid were one reason for the acrimonious IMF-Ghana negotiations in 1986.

In contrast, Zambia's gross financial inflows stagnated and exports fell sharply. In spite of rescheduling, debt service arrears grew, donor commitment wavered, and commercial lender confidence collapsed. Imports halved, and except in 1986, investment and budget expenditure stagnated. This "undermined many of the production and export benefits of courageous economic reforms," as one World Bank staff member has said. Political opposition grew and GRZ commitment to reform wavered. Persistent shortfalls undermined GRZ belief in the international community's ability to mobilize enough finance to support "adjustment with growth," and gave program opponents powerful arguments to use against reform supporters. By April 1987, most in the GRZ (using data agreed by the IMF) believed Zambia would have higher import and GDP growth if they abandoned the IMF program and limited debt service to 10% of export earnings.[51]

The Faults of the Negotiation Process[52]

Because of the way reform and external finance were negotiated between the PNDC and GRZ and external actors, both countries' programs had political problems: economically or administratively inappropriate measures, which were inflexibly implemented; and foreign exchange shortfalls.[53] There were four stages in IMF talks—preparation, negotiation, approval and renegotiation—which overlapped in practice.

Preparation: neither PNDC nor GRZ had time to design a complete program independently. The PNDC at least prepared its own Economic Recovery Programs, but with IMF and especially World Bank advice. The GRZ prepared only positions on negotiating issues, though it drafted a program in February 1987. Both spent half their preparation time compiling fiscal, monetary, and balance of payments data requested by the IMF. This left them little time to construct detailed arguments about the political, administrative, and economic feasibility of measures. The GRZ was also delayed by internal negotiations and staff changes; but PNDC preparation improved substantially with staff continuity and experience, helping it to gain marginal concessions by 1985–86.

The IMF prepared a draft program or "letter of intent," containing precise measures and targets, based on IMF staff analysis and calculations of the "distortion" of the economy. These were often based on faulty data provided by the GRZ/PNDC or estimated by Fund staff: notably on inflation, budget expenditure/revenue, and external financing.[54] Some draft letters of intent were "mere intellectual exercises," abstracted from Ghanaian or Zambian circumstances;[55] others took some account of World Bank or PNDC/GRZ views, depending on the flexibility of individual IMF staff. Nevertheless, they tended to define the negotiating agenda, especially in Zambia's talks.

Both sides also concentrated on targets, dates and wording of measures rather than implementation methods. Given the need for rapid agreement to prevent further economic collapse, neither IMF nor PNDC/GRZ had enough administrative capacity to prepare for negotiations by determining domestic political support for measures or their economic or administrative appropriateness; or by preparing accurate data on likely foreign exchange available.

Negotiation: comparing documents on IMF initial negotiating positions with final agreements shows that until 1986 the initial position of the IMF determined 90–95% of Zambia's programs, but only 80–85% in Ghana's.

The IMF position was decided by negotiations within the IMF, between missions, resident representatives, departments and senior management, as well as the strength and views of individual staff and departments, and the backing they received from top management; the Fund's "institutional memory" of Ghanaian and Zambian compliance with past programs; and the views of major creditor governments on the IMF Executive Board.

IMF staff working on both countries varied considerably in their views and flexibility in negotiations, but those on Ghana were in general more flexible (in IMF parlance were more "pragmatists" than "theologians").[56] Resident representatives and African department staff were usually more flexible than technical departments. Actions of individual staff had considerable influence on talks, largely because the IMF had overwhelming power. Theologians caused GRZ (and occasionally PNDC) resentment by "take it or leave it" presentation of draft letters of intent; this delayed new standbys and weakened the position of pro-agreement GRZ officials. They also rejected changes to Zambia's foreign exchange auction during February-June 1986, pushing the GRZ to take unilateral action. In intra-IMF disputes, senior IMF management tended to back theologians, especially on Zambia; this reflected the IMF's institutional view of government "political will" to implement programs and the views of Board members.

On the whole, Fund staff and management had negative memories of both countries' implementation before 1983, but while Zambia's image stayed negative (due largely to continued implementation problems, but partly to some IMF staff views), Ghana's fulfillment of successive programs improved its image. Meanwhile, powerful IMF Board members became more hostile to Zambia, not only because of implementation problems, but also because Kaunda abandoned mediation in Southern Africa and vociferously supported sanctions against South Africa. The U.S. and U.K. did not intervene to soften conditions on Zambia's behalf in 1986, as they had done in 1983–84. In contrast, by 1986 Canada and the U.K. backed concessions for Ghana, because of Ghana's adjustment record and Canada's and the U.K.'s trading and investment interests, and U.S. and FRG hostility to the PNDC had waned. Due largely to its good performance, Ghana became a "test case" for IMF-style reform in Sub-Saharan Africa by 1985–86; Zambia held that status only briefly in 1986.

Such views of individual countries were largely overruled by a hardening of Board attitude to Sub-Saharan Africa as a whole in 1982–86 because of program breakdowns and growing arrears to the IMF. This produced many of the problems described in earlier sections. Net foreign exchange inflows fell as IMF loan amounts were reduced compared to the period before 1981, and implementation capacity was strained as conditions or preconditions tightened, proliferated, and deepened. The Board attitude also supported "theologians" in intra-IMF disputes. Even Ghana gained few major concessions by 1986, producing "adjustment fatigue."[57]

Meanwhile, as discussed previously, domestic political factors explained the different negotiating abilities of the two governments, and thereby their success in adapting the IMF's initial positions. PNDC negotiating ability improved considerably in 1983–86, due to less division, a simpler policy-making structure and staff continuity. Its credibility with the IMF also improved, thanks to sustained adjustment and the persuasiveness, experience, politico-economic skills, preparedness, and IMF knowledge of its officials. Several GRZ negotiators also had these qualities but, because of greater division and extra-governmental pressure, complex policy-making structures, and staff changes, they were less well-prepared for negotiations. Their credibility with the Fund was also undermined by Zambia's poor record of implementing programs.

Yet negotiators from both countries faced acute strain and overwork from talks within government and with the IMF and other creditors, and day-to-day economic management. They were also short of support staff, as well as financial and technological resources. In addition, even when debtor negotiating capacity improved, superior IMF power generally made domestic political support for prospective measures an insignificant consideration in IMF positions. The IMF and most OECD governments took a simplistic view, relying on a fragile coalition of support from Kaunda and a few economic officials; and, fortunately, a less fragile coalition of Rawlings, the army, and economic officials.[58] Politicians were often pigeonholed as "opponents," to be talked into seeing the light, bypassed, or replaced; or "proponents" who were given no major concessions to help them convince opponents or keep their jobs.[59]

With the IMF Board's hardening attitude to Sub-Saharan Africa, and past breakdowns seen as due to insufficiently "deep" conditions, many IMF staff saw economic and administrative feasibility as a matter of a "comprehensive" program (i.e. as many "deep" conditions as possible). This imperative took precedence over designing conditions appropriate to the Ghanaian or Zambian economy, especially because data were so unreliable. Data were often disputed, with the IMF overruling GRZ and PNDC calculations of budget expenditure or monetary growth as "optimistic," or balance of payments figures as "pessimistic."[60]

World Bank influence on IMF programs was limited. In both countries the Bank, especially its resident mission, played a key role in convincing governments to initiate reform. On some issues, Bank and Fund staff agreed; where they disagreed, Bank staff were often divided. The Fund and Bank agreed to an informal division of labor: the Bank left monetary and exchange rate policy largely to the Fund, and concentrated on sectoral reforms. However, they had severe disputes over both countries, notably on fiscal policy and import levels. The Bank also suggested key compromises, including a foreign exchange auction for Zambia in 1984 (instead of devaluation), a dual exchange rate for Ghana in 1983, and the more flexible form of (and changes in) the Ghanaian auction in 1985–86. However, in general the Fund was not seeking compromise, and Fund views prevailed in Fund-Bank disputes.[61]

The dominance of IMF and OECD government views over the outcome of talks reduced GRZ and PNDC commitment to reform. GRZ officials (whether broadly pro- or anti-agreement) felt they had virtually no say, and the IMF made significant concessions only in March 1987. Most PNDC officials felt somewhat exasperated at IMF inflexibility, especially in 1985–86. This had a negative effect on implementation, especially if opponents of measures were unconvinced. When it made negotiations acrimonious (as for Zambia in 1984–85 and Ghana in 1986), it delayed agreement and reduced attention to political, economic, or administrative feasibility. All sides knew this made programs more vulnerable to political problems and misdesigned or misimplemented measures, but the IMF saw no other option and decided to "hope for the best."[62]

Approval and Calculation of External Finance Needs: negotiating procedure also left less time to ensure adequate foreign exchange, to arrange repayment of arrears to the IMF, and for the PNDC and GRZ to fulfil any "preconditions," all necessary before formal approval of the program by the Board. Above all, IMF staff often believed there was little additional last-minute foreign exchange to support the program. Thus, instead of calculating a "financing gap" (tailoring external financing to a model of how much was needed to provide a target level of growth), they tended to calculate an "adjustment gap," tailoring balance of payments projections to an estimate of the amount of external finance available.

As a result, export prices and production had to be overprojected—one Fund staff member said of Zambia: "we had to close the gap, and copper projections were the largest variable, so we made them look as good as possible." They restrained projected rises of imports and reserves, which caused acrimonious disputes with the Bank and PNDC/GRZ, who generally wanted higher imports to boost growth and higher reserves to guard against foreign exchange shortfalls. In addition, projections of external finance were often wildly inaccurate, due partly to faulty data on debt and new finance, and partly to optimism needed to close the gap. They took aid disbursement pledges at face value, in spite of a history of disbursement shortfalls throughout Africa. They overestimated debt relief that would be (or had been) provided, by not allowing for downpayments on arrears and short-term debt; this made Zambia's 1984 program underfinanced before it started. Finally, balance of payments projections were juggled at the last minute, especially for Zambia in early 1987, without changing the adjustment program targets to ensure overall coherence.[63]

The "adjustment gap" calculation also allowed creditors to pretend that programs were sustainable without any major concessions on debt relief or new funds.[64] Finally, import cuts and optimistic export projections were sometimes forced past PNDC and GRZ opposition; this reduced their commitment to programs. Many authors use the term "external shocks" to imply that foreign exchange shortfalls are external to the program and cannot be predicted or guarded against. This description of the procedure used to calculate external finance needs shows that this is not true: the procedure made programs vulnerable to foreign exchange shortfalls.[65]

Implementation and Renegotiation: IMF reaction to noncompliance with program conditions was inconsistent. There were no formal rules on when the IMF could waive conditions or had to negotiate a new program. There was only a limited correlation between the number of conditions missed by the GRZ or PNDC (or the amount by which they were missed) and suspension of disbursements, waiver of conditions, or cancellation of programs.

The Fund took note of political problems, administrative or economic capacity to implement conditions, misdesign of conditions, and foreign exchange shortfalls. However, it usually downplayed administrative or economic incapacity, added new conditions to reform administrative procedure or institutions, or insisted on more technical assistance. It saw foreign exchange shortfalls as "external shocks," which could be only partly compensated by more external finance and therefore demanded more adjustment. It denied that the programs were misdesigned, and blamed most problems on the "low political will" of senior politicians (ignoring complex political factors) or misimplementation by the PNDC or GRZ. It therefore continued to insist on the same conditions (including reintroducing Zambia's foreign exchange auction), or added conditions to make programs "comprehensive."

Yet the Fund did not assess which factors were responsible for noncompliance with programs, or vary its response accordingly. Zambia's 1983–84 standby was canceled because of debt service arrears and an excessive budget deficit/GDP ratio. These were due respectively to a foreign exchange shortfall and a budget revenue shortfall, both caused by copper price and production shortfalls; the budget deficit also caused the third breach of central bank credit to the GRZ. In 1986, almost all conditions were breached, but again partly as a result of foreign exchange shortfalls. Fiscal and monetary breaches were due to exceptional extra expenditure through devaluation, higher debt interest payments than expected, and revenue shortfalls. IMF documents for December 1986 showed that excluding unforeseen foreign exchange shortfalls, the GRZ easily met its budget deficit and current account targets—but recommended further budget and import cuts. Other issues causing cancellation (further devaluation in 1983–84 and 1984–85, and disagreements over future budget expenditure in 1984–85) were due to political and technical disagreements.

The IMF did not distinguish causes partly because the key factor in decisions was the subjective view of powerful governments on the Board, and of IMF staff and management. Zambia's 1983 and 1984 standbys were canceled partly because staff and Board saw Zambia as having a poor implementation record, and wanted to have new standbys to make conditions "deeper" and "tighter."

Ghana's 1985–86 standby ended not because Ghana had breached conditions, but because the Board wanted softer conditions.

GRZ-IMF negotiations in 1986–87 are an excellent illustration of inadequate negotiation procedure during programs. In February–April 1986, GRZ officials and some Fund and Bank staff argued strongly for more flexible implementation of the foreign exchange auction and maize price increases, partly to keep the pro-reform economic team in place. They were overruled by IMF "theologians" and the Board. The GRZ, facing rising inflation and devaluation greater than the IMF had projected in March, replaced the pro-reform team, introduced auction changes, and delayed the maize price increase without IMF approval. The IMF then suspended disbursements and insisted on tighter conditions for resuming the standby. By December, the GRZ agreed, but one of the tighter conditions was the maize price increase. When riots resulted, the talks collapsed. By March–April 1987, several Fund and Bank staff knew the GRZ was edging away from a program; they felt that IMF concessions in April came "too little and too late," due to failures of communication between IMF and GRZ, and internal disputes within both.[66]

The method of treating noncompliance made programs more vulnerable to the causes of noncompliance. It undermined debtor commitment to reform by its subjectivity, inflexibility, and simplistic analysis of political problems. It increased foreign exchange shortfalls by suspending disbursements and further "juggling" adjustment gap data. It cut administrative capacity to implement by distracting all sides in new talks. Finally, the greater pressure for rapid agreement increased program misdesign and misimplementation.

Faults in the procedure of IMF negotiations exacerbated political opposition to economic reform, and encouraged foreign exchange shortfalls and economically or administratively inappropriate (or otherwise misdesigned or misimplemented) programs. They did not create these problems: similar difficulties arose in implementing programs independent of the IMF (Ghana in 1981–82; Zambia in 1987–88). However, to the extent that the procedure did little to overcome them, the problems were symptoms of its faults.

Negotiating procedure was therefore not in the interest of any party to the talks. By 1986, it was damaging the credibility of IMF-sponsored reform even in "good" countries like Ghana: it was amazing that the Ghanaians achieved as much adjustment as they did. Even so, after the IMF and World Bank suspended their loans in 1986, Ghana's Finance Secretary Botchwey (a reform supporter) declared the economy "dead in the water," and adjustment "in danger."[67] By 1987, by exacerbating political problems, economic and administrative incapacity, and foreign exchange shortfalls, it had led Zambia to abandon IMF talks.

Reforms During 1986–92[68]

Many other developing countries, particularly in Sub-Saharan Africa, were experiencing similar problems. From 1986, the IMF, World Bank, and OECD governments acknowledged that the negotiating process did not fulfill their interests, and began to reform it. Having persisted with adjustment, Ghana could take advantage of these reforms. Zambia's talks collapsed just as reforms were being introduced; until it agreed to an IMF program in September 1989, it did not benefit.[69]

Economic Reform

Between 1986 and the present, there has been growing flexibility in the design and implementation of adjustment programs. Ghana's program was one of the pace-setters for this flexibility, which came at a key time. In 1986, PNDC commitment to adjustment was waning and extragovernmental opposition growing. In protracted negotiations, Ghana (backed by the World Bank) argued for a more growth-oriented program, and achieved it. The growth, investment, savings, and import objectives were increased, higher budget expenditure and a larger deficit were allowed, and the Fund relaxed conditions on gasoline price increases and domestic credit cuts.

In addition, the program gradually concentrated more on social and environmental effects. The World Bank joined UNICEF in 1987 in promoting a Program of Action to Mitigate the Social Costs of Adjustment (PAMSCAD), a program of social sector projects to be funded separately by aid donors. Though it was small (US$80m) and took a long time to get started, it was the first such program in Africa and a major step to combatting the social costs of adjustment. In particular, it reduced the potential negative political results of reducing civil service employment. Ghana has also benefited from studies on how to incorporate antipoverty measures in adjustment programs, under the World Bank-United Nations Development Program-African Development Bank Social Dimensions of Adjustment (SDA) program, and from World Bank studies on how to increase its food security. From 1990, the government banned exports of certain types of timber, to reduce environmental damage.[70]

This flexible design and implementation persisted until 1992. Design conditions became gradually less tight (in the sense of additional adjustment required), and preconditions diminished as trust grew between the PNDC and IMF. Thanks in part to larger flows of external finance, programs became increasingly growth-oriented. As an example on implementation, when the PNDC ended the auction and unified the auction rate with that of private foreign exchange bureaus in 1990, it convinced the IMF to allow continued surrender of 60% of foreign exchange to the Bank of Ghana, and other measures to limit speculation.

Greater flexibility came too late to save Zambia's program in 1987. The Policy Framework Paper (PFP) signed in December 1986 contained conditions that were tighter and more detailed than before, and it was abandoned after the maize riots. Concessions on conditions in April 1987, notably a larger budget deficit and slower rises in maize consumer prices, prompted partly by World Bank and OECD government mediation, were insufficient to enable a new PFP.

However, since negotiations reopened in 1988, program design and implementation have been slightly more flexible. In preparing the PFP in 1989, Zambia and the IMF compromised on maize prices, devaluation, and budget expenditure, with help from independent advisers and the World Bank and pressure from OECD governments. In 1990–91, a Social Action Program was designed and added to the program. There was also some leeway in implementation, allowing import liberalization and maize meal price rises to be delayed during 1990–91, but this was very limited and the Fund and GRZ formally suspended the program before the elections of 1991. In addition, the IMF has insisted on continued rapid adjustment, with tight and proliferating conditions and preconditions. The program has remained broadly deflationary and marginally growth-oriented; falls in per capita GDP, per capita consumption, import volume, and budget expenditure as a percentage of GDP were projected in 1991 and 1992 programs.

The changes in programs reflected general trends in IMF procedure: more effort to tailor conditions to national capacity, more thorough preparation and data compilation, and more support from senior management for Africa department staff and resident representatives. The greater flexibility for Ghana resulted from IMF appreciation of Ghana's past adjustment, its wish to maintain the Ghanaian program, pressure from OECD governments and the World Bank, the collapse of other Sub-Saharan programs (which was ruining the Fund's reputation in Africa in the mid-1980s); more effective negotiation by the Ghanaians; and the greater leeway provided by higher external finance inflows. Less flexibility for Zambia partly reflects the need to counteract what the Fund perceives as the "backward steps" taken during 1987–89; the historically based IMF mistrust of the Kaunda government until its fall in 1991; the Chiluba government's anxiety to hasten adjustment; and lower net external finance. The changes therefore produced a program more appropriate to Ghana's political, administrative, and economic capacity, which avoided major implementation problems, but have not had the same effect on the Zambian program.

Calculating and Fulfilling External Finance Needs

There have also been changes in the calculation and provision of external finance needs. Zambia's program in 1990 introduced a "contingency mechanism" to reduce the risk of balance of payments or external finance shortfalls compared to program projections. Copper export earnings were projected in the program at much lower levels than actually expected: any excess earnings were to offset aid disbursement shortfalls, with the remainder used to boost reserves or repay the IMF faster. In 1991 the mechanism was refined and expanded to allow for possible higher oil prices. This mechanism reflected a genuine learning process within the Fund, based on internal study and debate, because many earlier programs (especially in Zambia) had been derailed by such shortfalls. Throughout 1990–91, it kept import levels approximately as projected, and donor and GRZ staff see it as a major reason why a number of programs have not broken down.

Less formal methods have been used for Ghana. Since 1987, the IMF has agreed to less optimistic balance of payments projections to guard against probable cocoa price falls. Unfortunately, extremely low cocoa prices in 1987–88 led to the suspension of SAF and EFF disbursements because they directly caused breaches of budget and external sector conditions. They also led to shortfalls in import volume in 1987–89. Since then they have been offset informally by excess aid disbursements.

The more growth-oriented design of the Ghanaian adjustment program, and the artificial pessimism of the Zambian balance of payments projections under the contingency mechanism, both demanded greater efforts by donors and creditors to provide external finance.

The IMF seemed to be making these efforts. In November 1987, it granted Ghana a huge package of loans on softer terms: SDR143m through the Structural Adjustment Facility (SAF); and SDR245m through the Extended Fund Facility (EFF)—the first EFF loan to Sub-Saharan Africa for four years. In November 1988, Ghana gained an Enhanced Structural Adjustment Facility (ESAF) loan of SDR368m, but the amount of new money was less than it seemed, because SDR250m undisbursed from the SAF and EFF were included. These loans did not prevent net repayments to the IMF throughout 1987–92, and will not prevent net repayments in 1993–97. However, they reduced net flows to the IMF (and with other measures increased net inflows to Ghana) enough to reinforce Ghana's commitment.

Zambia was about to be granted a SAF loan in December 1986, but since then arrears to the IMF have prevented it from borrowing. It failed to mobilize enough additional aid to clear them at a donor "support group" in 1989. In May 1990, prompted largely by the Zambian case, the IMF Board introduced the "rights approach," which allowed the GRZ to accumulate rights to IMF loans, without ever receiving the funds. The "rights" were credited to the IMF, to offset arrears. Once all arrears were cleared, Zambia could draw new IMF loans. In addition, it had to pay all current IMF debt service. This combined burden of arrears clearance, current service to the Fund, and no new IMF loans implied underfunded (and therefore less growth-oriented) adjustment programs, and contributed directly to the suspension of the program in 1991. In June 1992, Zambia started the second year of its rights program, postponing the date for resuming normal relations with the Fund—and continuing underfunded adjustment—until June 1994.

The World Bank has dramatically increased its IDA commitments and disbursements to both countries (though Zambia had first to use an expensive Bank of England bridging loan to clear arrears to the World Bank). In addition, the "fifth window" initiative has given both countries relief from interest payments due on IBRD loans they received when they were middle-income countries. This has reduced Ghana's debt service by a total of US$20m in 1988-92; and Zambia's by US$70m in 1991–92.

Bilateral and multilateral aid to Ghana continued to rise sharply, as donors tried to compensate for cocoa price falls and allow more import growth: pledges at Consultative Group meetings were of US$800m a year for 1987 and 1988, US$900m for 1989–90, and more than US$1bn for 1991–92. Donors also responded for Zambia, making pledges exceeding US$700m in 1990 and US$900m in 1991. These pledges demonstrated donors' commitment, and reinforced PNDC and GRZ determination to persist with reform.

Both countries have also gained from the World Bank's Special Program of Assistance (SPA). This has mobilized additional bilateral aid, enabled the Bank to monitor bilateral aid disbursements and foreign exchange availability more closely, concentrated aid on cofinancing economically viable projects and reform programs, and reduced demands on recipient and donor staff by streamlining conditions attached to the aid. However, disbursement has remained behind schedule, largely because of delays in bilateral aid. At the end of 1991, Ghana's "pipeline" of undisbursed aid exceeded US$2.5bn. Zambia had disbursement shortfalls estimated at more than US$160m in 1990 alone. The delay is slightly greater in Zambia, reflecting both donor uncertainty that adjustment will be sustained, and GRZ problems coping with processing the complex conditions attached to aid. Aid shortfalls have been largely responsible for foreign exchange shortfalls in Ghana since 1988, and have offset most of Zambia's excess copper earnings under the contingency mechanism in 1990–91.

In addition, gross flows continue to be almost outweighed by debt service in Zambia, while net flows have risen sharply in

Ghana. This reflects the end of the debt service "hump" in Ghana, and accelerated efforts to cancel Ghana's debt service by Canada, Denmark, FRG, France, the U.K. and the U.S.. Almost all aid debt was canceled, amounting to US$440m or 15% of total debt, and reducing debt service payments by US$55m a year in 1990–91 (7–8% of export earnings). Canada, Denmark, the Netherlands, and Sweden canceled loans owed by Zambia in 1986, but others (the U.K. and U.S.) held back until 1990–91 because it had no IMF program. In 1990, Zambia received the highly concessional Toronto terms from the Paris Club. But this reduced annual service by only US$14m compared to previous terms, so creditors had to go further, by deferring 30% of the interest due on the agreement, in order to provide the external finance needed to support the program. In 1992, Zambia received the "Enhanced Toronto" terms, but these saved only US$17m, and interest on the 1990 agreement had to be deferred again.[71]

Commercial creditors took no initiatives. Ghana's commercial debt arrears were cleared by 1990. Though Zambia applied to use World Bank money to buy back its commercial debt, there had been little progress on this by mid-1992. The only contribution to relief by commercial creditors was to reduce debt through debt-equity swaps, which cost them nothing as they had already set money aside against bad debts.

The contrast between Ghana and Zambia is stark: in Ghana, rises in new aid are leading to larger net flows, allowing larger current account deficits and import volumes. In Zambia, aid increases are being mostly offset by rising debt service, particularly for arrears to the IMF and World Bank. Clearing these arrears forced Zambia to cut reserves temporarily, and donors to disburse aid faster, in 1991. These added to the cost of the bridging loan to clear World Bank arrears, and underfinancing caused by the IMF's "rights approach." They have prevented a substantial rise in net inflows or import volumes, which would be needed to make Zambia's program genuinely growth-oriented.

Conclusion: The Need for Further Reform[72]

While initiatives since 1986 have reduced some faults in negotiating procedure, they have not gone far enough. The lesson of economic reform in Ghana and Zambia in 1983–92 is that further reforms are required in the procedure for negotiating economic policies and external finance.

Economic Policy Reform

Recent negotiations, notably those of Ghana, have taken more notice of political, administrative, and economic constraints on reform, but have not systematically assessed them. Successful and sustained reform in both countries will require basing programs on three aims: maximizing domestic political support; increasing economic capacity to adjust; and increasing administrative capacity to adjust.

The first step is to improve preparation for talks. To make data as impartial and accurate as possible, joint preparation by teams of IMF, Bank, PNDC, or GRZ and independent experts should precede formal talks. It is vitally important that both IMF and PNDC/GRZ staff write their own independent draft programs, concentrating on details and implementation methods, but leaving room for concessions by suggesting broad ranges instead of precise targets and by offering several ways to achieve them. Severe disputes on programs or individual policies in either country might be resolved by using such teams or independent advisers to report on past incapacity or program misdesign and misimplementation, and suggest broad outlines of a program or compromises on individual measures.

As to the outcome of talks, tailoring policies to Ghanaian and Zambian circumstances requires more stress on certain largely neglected policy areas. To some degree, as judged by the failures of programs described previously, these are similar in both countries: export diversification; reducing budgetary and import dependence on external finance; reducing debt stock and debt service payments; food production, social sector, income distribution, and environmental issues; and improving supply response, especially in manufacturing. More stress on these wider, longer-term and structural issues implies World Bank influence and representation equal to that of the Fund in SAF and ESAF talks, because it has more expertise and experience on these issues—and the involvement of more independent expertise from within and outside Africa.

The two economies are at different stages: while Ghana needs continued recovery and long-term self-sustaining growth, Zambia also faces enormous short-term problems of stabilization and recovery. Short- and long-term, stabilization and self-sustaining growth cannot be separated because similar political, economic, and administrative incapacity affects policies designed to achieve them. Yet for countries like Ghana, which have undertaken initial periods of stabilization, the World Bank could assume program leadership, to demonstrate the focus on longer-term issues.

The political coalition behind reform in both countries remains narrowly based, and especially fragile in Zambia. To maximize political support, governments must have a larger part in program design. To the extent that they prepare their own draft programs and negotiations are marked by genuine compromise, policies will be genuinely "domestically designed," and intragovernmental discontent reduced. During preparation, negotiation and implementation, PNDC, GRZ, and IMF/World Bank representatives should consult constantly with all parts of government and extragovernmental interest groups (especially civil service, parastatals, trade unions, and business) to take account of their views and explain proposed measures. Such consultation should concentrate on measures that have caused past political problems (devaluation, maize and gasoline price rises, civil service retrenchment in Zambia; civil service wage and benefit changes and gasoline price rises in Ghana). It would aim to gain intra- and extra-governmental support for measures that were more gradual, in order to minimize the risks of negative short-term effects. One major lesson of the fate of adjustment in Ghana and Zambia is that short-term economic gains help to improve prospects for adjustment: that economic reform is more likely to persist if it is genuinely "growth-oriented."

Even with such changes in procedure, programs would not be foolproof. Thus negotiations must leave more room for flexible *implementation*, and reactions to problems must be more flexible. Continuing detailed analysis of causes (by both IMF and PNDC/GRZ, or by advisers) and consultation within Ghana and Zambia will help, as will implementing measures only after GRZ/PNDC officials have been fully trained; and, where possible, without encouraging speculative activity by extragovernmental interest groups involved in or affected by implementation.

This new negotiating procedure will require internal changes on both sides, to simplify and maximize communication within and between them. Within the IMF, to encourage sensitivity to national constraints, more staff should be assigned to the African Department on each country. They should regularly review experience on political, administrative, environmental, and social issues, assessing the causes of implementation problems more precisely to ensure that the IMF's "institutional memory" of the countries is accurate. Resident representatives in Accra and Lusaka should have immediate access to (and support from) top IMF management and, together with staff of the Bank and donors in Accra and Lusaka, be responsible for warning of political or administrative problems.

Changes in debtor government negotiating procedure are also needed, particularly in Zambia, which requires continuity of experienced staff and more trained support staff, to improve administrative capacity to design, negotiate, and implement policies; a simpler policy-making structure, with a lead agency or stable small team to conduct negotiations and supervise implementation; and a mechanism for reporting to a wider coordinating group of interested agencies, to maximize political support. Ghanaian negotiating procedure needs far fewer changes, though there is room for continued training and expansion of support staff and more consultation of interested government agencies.

External Finance

Recent initiatives will increase net flows to Ghana and Zambia. However, the problem is much more fundamental: after a decade of adjustment, the international community still has no idea how much external finance any country needs to support economic reform. In order to maximize the effectiveness of future external finance for Ghana and Zambia (and minimize the additional amounts needed), the faults of gap calculations and methods used to fill them must be remedied.

The volatility of export earnings and external finance flows argues that the top priority should be to apply a version of the contingency mechanism used in Zambia to the Ghanaian program. The amount of debt reduction and new money should be based on worst case projections of the balance of payments. This should spring from much more detailed study of all components of the balance of payments, especially of how to prevent growing import dependence, which was a major failure of earlier programs;[73] and on comprehensive analysis of the relationship between external finance and development, to ensure that "gap" calculations are tailored to each country's "financing needs" (rather than the procedures and practices of creditors and donors).

Filling this genuine gap will imply comprehensive debt relief and new finance from all creditors, including OPEC governments and commercial creditors. The best way to achieve this will be by greater synchronization and *coordination* of decisions on debt relief and new flows by different groups of creditors (and within creditor governments). Ghana's decisions already center on Consultative Groups, because it has so little rescheduling. This saves considerable staff time on all sides, leaving more for design and implementation of adjustment. Zambia faces separate Paris Club, London Club, and other rescheduling negotiations, all of which could be combined in one meeting, maintaining confidentiality and separate decision-making by separate caucuses for different creditor groups. Joint creditor-debtor preparation of such a meeting and monitoring of its implementation would reduce delay and duplication for all sides.

For Zambia, the most crucial gap-filling issue remains reducing debt stock and service—but it is also important for Ghana. Creditor governments are the main potential source of reduction. For Zambia, they can cancel 100% of aid debt (which would reduce annual debt service by US$10–12m compared to current rescheduling terms). They can also move further than the Enhanced Toronto terms on nonconcessional debt, toward Trinidad terms (66% cancellation) or even Pronk terms (100% cancellation). Trinidad terms would save Zambia US$15m annually, and Pronk terms another US$35m. They could also reschedule debt service due during a three-year period, to match the rights accumulation program period. This would avoid expensive and time-consuming annual negotiation and enhance long-term planning.

Ghana is intent on avoiding rescheduling, in order to maintain its access to new export credit loans. Even so, cancellation of all aid debt could save it US$30–40m a year (because it is not currently rescheduling), and canceling 100% of nonconcessional debt contracted before 1986 would save US$50m a year.

Both countries would also benefit if creditor governments refinanced debt service with additional grants; accepted payment in local currency; or converted their debt into equity, development or environmental projects. These measures would not necessarily imply cancellation, and could therefore be undertaken without damaging Ghana's creditworthiness. Several bilateral donors, however, are suggesting that providing such large amounts of aid (especially if it means diverting aid from other nations) may be unsustainable in the longer-term.

Ghana's commercial creditors could also undertake debt-equity swaps, but this is unlikely given Ghana's good repayment record. Zambia needs to finalize as soon as possible its use of World Bank money to reduce commercial debt or debt service by bonds or buybacks.

Both nations have large debt service burdens to multilateral institutions at least until 1997: US$250–300m pa (not including arrears) for Zambia, and US$150–200m pa for Ghana. These institutions should provide net inflows, on softer terms, to refinance current (and reduce future) debt service. For the IMF, this would imply faster and larger disbursement of ESAF loans, with repayment periods lengthened to match IDA; for the World Bank, it will require a larger replenishment for IDA IX in real terms than IDA VIII. In addition, both the Fund and the Bank could use more of their resources to subsidize repayments of principal and interest on past expensive loans to low-income Africa, and the Fund could soften the rights approach to allow the debtor country to receive a proportion of the rights as new disbursements during the rights accumulation period. These measures need not imply cost to governments: using the undisbursed portion of SAF and ESAF resources, a small part of the IMF gold reserves, the investment income from those reserves, a small issue of SDRs, and 100% of IDA repayments due in 1990-95, would provide ample funds.

Like most other African countries, Ghana and Zambia found themselves "hemmed in" in the mid-1980s, by collapsing economies and flows of external finance. At the present time, Ghana is much less "hemmed in," because of its economic policy reforms, although these remain dependent on large volumes of aid and imports. Zambia is if anything more "hemmed in," because of a combination of intermittent reform and foreign exchange shortage. The past experience of both countries is that political liberalization has tended to undermine economic reform, by increasing the demands on government for expansionary policies. At the moment, both countries are well-placed to sever this connection.

Having survived both the presidential and parliamentary elections, the Rawlings government is likely to continue to pursue vigorous economic reform, and Zambia's democratically elected government is still in a post-election honeymoon period when reform may be easier to introduce. Yet this is no reason for complacency: it will be impossible to sustain this combination of economic and political liberalization without major changes in the way reform programs and external finance are negotiated.

The lesson of the Ghanaian and Zambian experience is not that a country can escape by just maintaining its "political will" to implement incontrovertible "economic reason." It is that economic reform programs succeed insofar as they increase domestic political support; administrative and economic capacity; careful design and implementation; and foreign exchange availability. If further changes in procedure ensure that programs take full account of these factors, they will make programs much less likely to break down in all African countries. They will reinforce the political liberalization and self-sustaining development Africa needs, by showing that the international financial community realizes the complexity of negotiating economic reform in Sub-Saharan Africa and that "A once and for all judgement of the 'readiness for reform' of a government and its leaders, or a nation, is unfair to the millions of people living in poverty and seeking progress now."[74]

Notes

1. *The Economist*, May 9, 1987, p. 15 and August 20, 1988.

2. For an extension of this argument to all of Sub-Saharan Africa, see my book *The Crumbling Facade of Africa's Debt Negotiations: No Winners* (MacMillan Press, 1991). I am grateful to the Economic and Social Research Committee for funding the research. I would also like to thank the many people who helped me, particularly James Mayall, Tony Killick, Gerald Helleiner, Percy Mistry, Susan Strange, and all those who allowed me to interview them and to look at their papers or those of their institutions. In what follows, any details not sourced are from confidential documents.

3. My aim is to compare the two sets of IMF programs to draw lessons for future IMF negotiations. Thus this chapter does not discuss Zambia's 1987–88 Interim National Development Program, because it did not involve the IMF.

4. Both countries also negotiated reform programs with the World Bank. This chapter largely omits them (to avoid excessive length and complexity), but discusses the Bank's role in IMF talks.

5. This section is based primarily on confidential IMF and World Bank documents, and interviews with all sides in the talks. See, in addition, the the following literature:

For Ghana: Sheetal K. Chand and Reinold van Til, "Ghana: Towards Successful Stabilisation and Recovery," *Finance and Development* 25, 1 (March 1988): 32–35; Reginald Herbold Green, "Ghana: Progress, Problematics and Limitations of the Success Story," *IDS Bulletin* 19, 1 (January 1988): 7–15; Reginald Herbold Green, *Stabilization and Adjustment Policies and Programs: Country Study 1—Ghana* (Helsinki: World Institute for Development Economics Research, 1987); Tony Hodges, "Ghana's Strategy for Adjustment with Growth," *Africa Recovery* 2, 3 (August 1988): 16–20, 27; John Loxley, *Ghana: Economic Crisis and the Long Road to Recovery* (Ottawa: North-South Institute, 1988), and Matthew Martin, "Negotiating Adjustment and External Finance: Ghana and the International Community, 1982–89," in Donald Rothchild, ed., *Ghana: The Political Economy of Recovery* (Baltimore: Johns Hopkins University Press, 1991).

For Zambia: Christopher Colclough, "Zambian Adjustment Strategy—With and Without the IMF," *IDS Bulletin* 19, 1 (January 1988): 51–60; Christopher Colclough, "The Labor Market and Economic Stabilisation in Zambia" (Washington: World Bank PPR Working Paper No. 272, November 1989); Ravi Gulhati, *Impasse in Zambia: the Economics and Politics of Reform* (Washington: World Bank Economic Development Institute Analytical Case Study No.2, July 1989); Tony Hodges, "Zambia's Autonomous Adjustment," *Africa Recovery* 2, 4 (December 1988): 6–13; Igor Karmiloff, *Industrialisation in sub-Saharan Africa: Country Case Study—Africa*, ODI Working Paper 26 (London: Overseas Development Institute, 1988); Jonathan Kydd, "Coffee After Copper ? Structural Adjustment, Liberalisation and Agriculture in Zambia," *Journal of Modern African Studies* 26, 2 (June 1988): 227–251; Martin Sakala and Manenga Ndulo, "The International Monetary Fund and the Zambian Economy," in K. J. Havnevik, ed., *The IMF and the World Bank in Africa* (Uppsala: Scandinavian Institute for African Studies, 1987); Hans-Otto Sano, "The IMF and Zambia: the Contradictions of Exchange Rate Auctioning and De-Subsidisation of Agriculture," *African Affairs* 87, 349 (October 1988): 563–577; Jurgen Wulf, "Zambia Under the IMF Regime," *African Affairs* 87, 349 (October 1988): 579–594; and Roger Young, *Zambia: Adjusting to Poverty* (Ottawa: North-South Institute, 1988).

It also draws on Thomas M. Callaghy, "Lost Between State and Market: The Politics of Economic Adjustment in Ghana, Zambia and Nigeria," Joan M. Nelson, ed., *Economic Crisis and Policy Choice* (Princeton: Princeton University Press, 1990), pp. 257–319; the *Country Economic Review* and *Country Economic Profile* (1983–June 1992) of the Economist Intelligence Unit, London for both countries, and many periodicals.

6. For a comprehensive analysis of compliance with these targets, and the effects of external finance shortfalls on adjustment, see Matthew Martin and Percy Mistry, eds., *How Much Aid Does Africa Need?* (forthcoming).

7. In addition to the sources cited in note 5, political developments in Ghana are discussed by Kwame A. Ninsin, "Ghanaian Politics after 1981:

Revolution or Evolution ?" *Canadian Journal of African Studies* 21, 1 (1987): 17–37; Donald I. Ray, *Ghana: Politics, Economics and Society* (Boulder: Lynne Rienner, 1986); Donald Rothchild, and E. Gyimah-Boadi, "Ghana's Decline and Development Strategies," in John Ravenhill, ed., *Africa in Economic Crisis* (New York: Columbia University Press, 1986). There is no comparable recent source on Zambia's politics since 1983.

8. Interview, Lusaka, February 1987.

9. Rothchild and Gyimah-Boadi, "Ghana's Decline," pp. 270, 273–274 and confidential interviews.

10. In January 1983 only 11 of 28 members of the Central Committee voted for an IMF program, and in June–September 1985, only 5. *South*, February 1987, p. 20. More precise figures from interviews in Lusaka, March 1987.

11. International financial institution (IFI) documents and interviews in Lusaka and Washington show that in December–January 1986 he was shaken by the maize riots, the death of his eldest son and regional problems, but by February 1987 he was back in control, deciding to end talks unless the IMF made concessions by April–May.

12. This description is simplified for the sake of brevity: for an excellent analysis of the complex effects on income patterns of different social groups in Ghana, see Green, *Stabilization*, pp. 12–21.

13. On Ghana, see Green, "Ghana" on the Cocoa Board and Rothchild and Gyimah-Boadi, "Ghana's Decline" on the civil service; on Zambia, Gulhati, *Impasse*, pp. 37–46.

14. Interviews with 14 prominent business leaders, Lusaka, February-March 1987.

15. Callaghy, "Lost"; Gulhati, *Impasse*, pp. 43–46.

16. On Ghana, see Nicholas Van Hear, "Labour and Structural Adjustment in Nigeria and Ghana" (paper to ASAUK conference, September 1988, mimeo).

17. World Bank, *World Development Report* 1989, p. 224, Table 31.

18. The precise political cause of the riots is disputed—Sano, *IMF*, p. 572, note 11, says World Bank staff blamed politicians opposed to reform for stirring them up. However, they were able to stir up opposition because of the collapse in urban real incomes, especially in the Copperbelt. See Colclough, "Zambian," p. 59. See also below for how misimplementation contributed to the riots.

19. Interviews, London and Washington, May–July 1987.

20. See especially Kydd, "Coffee"; and Murray Sanderson, "Why Zambia's Auction Failed" (paper to Economics Association of Zambia Conference on the Zambian Auction System, Lusaka, June 1987, mimeo). The replacement of the expatriate governor of the Central Bank did not have the same negative effect in 1992 as it did in 1986, even though he had been regarded as a key supporter of reform, because he was replaced by Dominique Mulaisho, another supporter (and Kaunda's former economic adviser).

21. Interview, Washington, July 1987.

22. See for example the endorsement of PNDC policies and promise of continuity by one presidential candidate, Jonathan Frimpong-Ansah, in *West Africa*, May 25–31, 1992, p. 876.

23. A view expressed by two IMF staff interviewed.

24. Young, *Zambia*, p. x. See also Colclough, "Zambian" and Gulhati, *Impasse*, for the view that Zambian politics could not tolerate the speed of adjustment. The view that there is nothing in states or societies which necessarily prevents reform is supported by Henry S. Gersovitz and Mark Bienen, "Economic Stabilization, Conditionality and Political Stability," *International Organization* 39, 4 (Autumn 1985): 729–754; J. D. Fearon, "International Financial Institutions and Economic Policy Reform," *Journal of Modern African Studies* 26, 1 (March 1988): 113–137; Ravi Gulhati, *The Political Economy of Reform in Sub-Saharan Africa: Report of the Workshops on the Political Economy of Structural Adjustment and the Sustainability of Reform* (Economic Development Institute Policy Seminar Report No.8, World Bank, Washington, D.C., 1988); Stephan Haggard, "The Politics of Adjustment: Lessons from the IMF's Extended Fund Facility," *International Organization* 39, 3 (Summer 1985): 505–534; and Joan M. Nelson, *The Politics of Economic Adjustment in Developing Nations* (Princeton: Princeton University Press, 1989).

25. See *Africa Analysis*, August 8, 1986, p. 5.

26. See Kydd, "Coffee", pp. 242–243; and Gulhati, *Impasse*. It also went against the conventional wisdom on sequencing—see Sebastian Edwards, "Sequencing Economic Liberalization in Developing Countries," *Finance and Development* (March 1987): 26–29; Michael Mussa, "Macroeconomic Policy and Trade Liberalization: Some Guidelines," *World Bank Research Observer* 2, 1 (January 1987): 61–77; Martin Wolf, "Timing and Sequencing of Trade Liberalisation in Developing Countries," *Asian Development Review* 4, 2 (1986): 1–24.

27. See *Africa Analysis*, on Zambia; Green, "Ghana," p. 8 on Ghana; and Gulhati, *Political*, p. 24 and *Impasse*, pp. 35 and 44–45. Other sources are confidential IMF and World Bank documents.

28. It is also possible to argue that certain measures were inappropriate to the political context of Ghana and Zambia: such measures have been discussed under political support.

29. Confidential IMF documents, including the PFP document for December 9, 1986, supported by interviews, and by UNECA Secretary-General Adedeji (BBC World Service, *The World Today*, June 24, 1988) and UNICEF's Richard Jolly, *IDS Bulletin*, January 1988, p. 75.

30. For more details of labor shortages, see Colclough, *The Labour Market*, pp. 32–33.

31. The role of weather is acknowledged by Chand and van Til, *Ghana*, p. 34, as well as Green, *Stabilization*, and Loxley, *Ghana*.

32. See Chand and van Til, "Ghana," p. 34, and Green, "Ghana."

33. On Ghana, see Green, *Stabilization* and Loxley, *Ghana*; on Zambia, Colclough, "Zambian."

34. Interview, Lusaka, March 1987. See also Kydd, "Coffee," p. 243 and Young, *Zambia*, p. ix, for the view that Zambia's 1985–86 program was too comprehensive.

35. Sources for administrative problems are IMF documents. On auctions,

see also Charles Harvey, "Non-Marginal Price Changes: Conditions for the Success of Floating Exchange Rate Systems in Sub-Saharan Africa," *IDS Bulletin* 19, 1 (January 1988): 67–74; and Martin Sakala and Manenga Ndulo, "The Zambian Foreign Exchange Auction" (Lusaka: University of Zambia/Bank of Zambia, 1987, mimeo). Tony Killick, ed., *The Quest for Economic Stabilisation: the IMF and the Third World* (London: Overseas Development Institute and Gower Press, 1984), pp. 193–194, 211 and note 38 show administrative problems of fiscal and monetary measures. Justin Zulu and Saleh Nsouli, *Adjustment Programs in Africa* (IMF Occasional Paper No. 34, Washington, April 1985), pp. 14–16, show impracticable fiscal and debt management reforms.

36. This description of the auctions is based on Loxley, *Ghana*, pp. 12–13; Young, *Zambia*, pp. 30–33; Sakala, *Zambian*; 1986–89 issues of *Africa Economic Digest* and *West Africa*; and confidential IMF documents.

37. For more examples of fine-tuning, see Martin, *Negotiating Adjustment*.

38. See sources in note 26, and John Clark, *Debt and Poverty: A Case Study of Zambia* (Oxford: Oxfam, 1987); and Joan M. Nelson, "Poverty, Equity and the Politics of Adjustment" (paper to the International Studies Association annual conference, London, March 1989, mimeo). This account is confirmed by confidential IMF documents, including the IMF PFP document for December 9, 1986.

39. See also Gulhati, *Impasse*, p. 49.

40. Much of this section is based on Matthew Martin and Mistry Percy, eds., *How Much Aid Does Africa Need*? (forthcoming, 1993).

41. See also Young, *Zambia*, p. 2. These figures are from confidential 1987–88 IMF and World Bank documents.

42. See also Gulhati, *Impasse*, p. 49; and Edward K. Jaycox, et al., "The Nature of the Debt Problem in Eastern and Southern Africa," in Carol Lancaster, and John Williamson, eds, *African Debt and Financing* (Washington, D.C., Institute for International Economics, 1986).

43. Details on bridges and refinancings are from confidential interviews and documents. Joe Abbey has correctly shown that the net inflows to Ghana were modest compared to export earnings or GDP: the intention here is rather to point out that there were net inflows, while in Zambia there were not; see Joseph Abbey, "On Promoting Successful Adjustment: Some Lessons from Ghana," The 1989 Pere Jacobsson Lecture, International Monetary Fund, 1989.

44. Figures for debt service are author's calculations, based on confidential World Bank and IMF documents.

45. Figures calculated from balance of payments data given in confidential IMF 1987–88 documents.

46. Ghanaian figures from Loxley, *Ghana*, p. 24 and *Africa Economic Digest*, January 30, 1989; Zambian from Colclough, *Zambian*, and confidential 1988 IMF documents.

47. These figures and explanations are from confidential 1987–89 IMF documents. See also Gulhati, *Impasse*, p. 49, for discussion of incorrect projections.

48. See Jaycox, "Nature," pp. 60–62.

49. For a comprehensive analysis of balance of payments projections, and of the relationship between external finance and adjustment in Africa, see Martin and Mistry, *How Much Aid.*

50. Abdalla of the IMF admitted IMF "serious miscalculation" in June 1987 (*Times of Zambia*, June 19, 1987). Green, *Stabilization*, p. 53, comments on cocoa projections.

51. Quotation from Gulhati, *Impasse*, p. 50. World Bank Vice President for Africa, Edward Jaycox, expressed similar views in *Africa Report*, November-December 1987. Callaghy, "Lost"; Chand and Van Til, "Ghana"; Green, *Stabilization*; Loxley, *Ghana*; and Young, *Zambia*, also see net financial flows as a key factor in program success.

52. It is impossible to do full justice to these faults in a brief article: see Martin, *No Winners* (chapter 2 on the IMF, chapters 3–6 on debt rescheduling negotiations).

53. Because details of IMF and debt rescheduling negotiations are confidential, sources for this section are confidential documents and interviews unless otherwise stated.

54. This faulty data caused frequent revisions of data in later IMF documents, and severe disputes over data during negotiation. On external financing, see below.

55. Former Bank of Zambia Governor Phiri, in Gerald K. Helleiner, ed, *The IMF and Africa* (IMF, 1986), p. 95, confirmed by documents and interviews for Ghana and Zambia.

56. Terms used in interviews with three IMF staff. Callaghy, "Lost," says some Ghanaian officials gained the impression that some IMF staff were acting tough to try to get promotion: this was also suggested in my interviews with Ghanaian and Zambian officials, but cannot be verified. Other reasons suggested were unquestioning belief in IMF conditions, and overwork.

57. This view is confirmed by Callaghy, "Lost"; Green, *Stabilization*; and Young, *Zambia.*

58. This view was expressed in interviews with both sides, and is also expressed by Callaghy, "Lost."

59. On simplistic IMF views, the sources are confidential IMF documents and interviews. See also *Africa Confidential*, December 12, 1984, p. 3 on Ghana; on the failure to help "proponents," see below on implementation.

60. Sources are confidential IMF documents and interviews.

61. This paragraph is based on Fund and Bank documents and interviews.

62. Quotation from an interview with an IMF official, confirmed by interviews with all sides.

63. Evidence for this paragraph is confidential IMF and World Bank documents, and interviews with all sides.

64. For this attitude, see Martin, *No Winners*, chapters 3–6.

65. For much more detail, see Martin and Mistry, *How Much Aid*, chapters 4 and 5.

66. This account is based on interviews with IMF and World Bank staff, and is confirmed by documents which show failures of communication, especially in March-April 1986 and February-April 1987.

67. Green, *Stabilization*, p. 52, confirmed in interviews with Ghanaian and IFI officials.

68. These reforms and the reasons behind them are discussed briefly in Tony Killick and Matthew Martin, *African Debt: the Search for Solutions* (UN Africa Recovery Program Briefing Paper No.1, New York, June 1989), reprinted in *Africa Recovery*, August 1989; and at greater length in Martin, *No Winners*, chapter 7.

69. Therefore it is ironic that many of those arguing for reform in 1986–87 within the Fund, Bank and creditor governments used Zambia as their example.

70. On the design faults, Andrew Norton, "Ghana Social Profile" (London: Overseas Development Administration, 1988, mimeo); on the slow implementation, *African Economic Digest*, January 30, 1989.

71. Toronto terms offered creditors three options: cancel 33% of debt service and reschedule the rest with 8-year grace and 14-year maturity; extend grace to 14 years and maturity to 25 years; or cut interest rates by 3.5 percentage points or 50% and reschedule over 8 and 14 years. Enhanced Toronto terms retain the second option, but enhance the first and third options to the equivalent of 50% cancellation or 50% reduction of service payments due in net present value terms. Figures on the effects of Zambia's agreements are from IMF and World Bank calculations.

72. For more details and explanation of these reforms, see Martin, *No Winners*, chapter 8; and Martin and Mistry, *How Much*, chapter 10.

73. How to reduce import and aid dependence by changing import liberalization and aid provision is the subject of a project being conducted by Percy Mistry, myself, and government officials from six African countries.

74. Gulhati, *Political*, p. 12.

Chapter Five

The Political Repercussions of Economic Malaise

NAOMI CHAZAN AND DONALD ROTHCHILD

Economics, Politics, and the Dynamics of Change

The beginning of the third decade of African independence was marked by a retrogressive cycle of economic recession and political enfeeblement.[1] Explanations for the continental crisis of the early 1980s highlighted the close connection between state incapacity and economic deterioration. While some observers stress neo-orthodox interpretations (such as the deleterious economic effects of policy distortions, untethered bureaucratic expansion, and poor implementation) and others emphasize structural concerns centering on the adverse consequences of external dependence, socioeconomic inequality, and limited access to resources, most analysts today concur on the centrality of political factors underlying the contemporary African predicament.[2] Yet equally important has been the growing realization that economic decline undermined state structures and exacerbated political unrest. "There is a crisis of political authority that is just as severe as the well-known crisis of economic production. These two crises are intimately interrelated, each being both a cause and an effect of the other."[3]

The 1980s were punctuated by diverse attempts to overcome

the debilitating effects of the postcolonial syndrome by replacing the destructive link between scarcity and political impotence with a reinforcing dynamic of economic growth and political stability.[4] The food shortages of the early part of the decade, however, coupled with growing financial distress, compelled African governments to address pressing economic problems first. The adoption of externally devised economic reforms inevitably impinged on the relationship between politics and economics. If political rationales for economic measures predominated in the past, economic initiatives assumed center stage during the 1980s. What are the political effects of reversing the sequence of economic and political priorities? How has economic liberalization affected the nature and direction of political life? What will the political repercussions be if measures of political and economic liberalization do not yield palpable economic gains, or if these changes prove ephemeral?

This chapter explores the political impact of economic malaise and reform. First, it examines the postcolonial structure of power in Africa and its relationship to the economic deterioration of the late 1970s. Second, it analyzes the various manifestations of the accompanying crisis of the state. On this basis, it delves into the impact of economic and political reforms and the concomitant constraints imposed by the international community on the construction of the social order, state agencies, and regime forms. And third, it considers the relationship between economic crisis, the reorganization of civil society, and the nature of social demands that proliferated in 1989 and the early 1990s. Finally, it assesses the possible political consequences of the failure of economic adjustment policies.

In order to grasp the nature of change in the contemporary African political world, it is necessary to look beyond the formal realm of official institutions and policies and to delve into the informal arena of hidden politics at the societal, state, and international levels. Formal politics is manifest in political practice and especially in the various uses of political exchange, reciprocity, coalition, cooptation, persuasion, coercion, and repression that illuminate the main features of state power. Informal politics is traced through forms of societal construction as expressed in patterns of incorporation, collaboration, resistance, and withdrawal from state involvement.[5] Since the locus of effective authority in Africa is still fluid, the study of the interaction between these spheres is vital to understanding the structure of power relations in particular contexts.[6]

Power configurations are therefore determined by the connection between three main components: the social order (the organization of social groups, the resources at their disposal, the norms that bind them, the interests they pursue, and their relations with other social networks); the state (specifically the organizing framework, the official administrative, coercive, and political apparatuses, the composition of ruling elites, and the spheres of formal action); and the regime (the principles, rules, and mechanisms that govern the interaction between the state and its society). The relationship between political processes and economic growth and development is an outgrowth of shifts in the concentration and distribution of power among these elements over time.

Different patterns of power construction and allocation have developed in Africa since the beginning of the colonial period. Formal and informal political institutions reflect changing foci of economic and social interchange in particular contexts. Political trends in the 1980s are a manifestation of the dynamic combination of these historical socioeconomic processes, immediate responses to particular circumstances, and the impact of adjustments in social structures and economic orientations. Thus specific power constellations have influenced policy choices and generated power realignments that themselves constitute constraints on the range of choice open to political actors. "If the consequences of policy become sources of new policy, there is a strong argument for considering the sources and systemic consequences of policy together."[7] In these circumstances, the political repercussions of economic reform are not only a direct result of particular measures but also the unintended outcome of the conditions that induced new policy initiatives.[8]

The quest for authoritative structures has been the dominant theme of modern African politics. During the first phase of independence, authoritarian forms prevailed throughout much of the continent largely because the authority of official agencies was so tenuous.[9] Despite the diversity of types of authoritarian rule,[10] most African governing elites evinced statist propensities. Statism accentuates the domination of the state as an autonomous actor, in contrast to stateness, which highlights the capacity to entrench the authority of the central state and to regularize its relations with society.[11] In weak state circumstances, exclusionary and coercive arrangements encouraged clientelism, thereby introducing a political logic that often hindered economic growth and gradually undermined organizational capacity.

The second postindependence phase was marked by economic decline and state decay. Political instability was pronounced, and individuals and groups developed elaborate coping mechanisms to deal with the exigencies of profound scarcity. The foundation was prepared at this juncture for a more fundamental reordering of power relations between state and society.[12]

The adoption of structural adjustment programs by some African countries (which frequently accompanied a third and ongoing phase) has contributed significantly to the direction of this reorientation. By reducing the amounts of resources at the disposal of the state and limiting the size of state agencies, reform measures have had the effect of curtailing the scope of state activities. At the same time, social groups have been able to take advantage of local initiatives to expand the informal economy, generate a new breed of entrepreneurs, and enrich associational life. The creation of discrete political spaces at the state and societal levels has begun to alter the distribution of power in many African countries. A revised logic linking political survival more directly to economic rationality is beginning to emerge.[13]

The fourth phase consists of experiments with political liberalization in the 1990s. Partial and hesitant though they may be in many countries, they represent an awareness of the need to create an enabling political environment in which economic development can occur. Such political reform measures may have the effect of reformulating the rules of postcolonial politics, linking a strong and legitimate state with a strong and active society. By developing new norms and types of regime, these emergent democratic orders hold out a significant potential for "getting politics right."[14] State leaders, determined to remain in office, have an incentive to be responsive to the legitimate demands of society, encouraging a sense of public involvement in civic affairs that promotes stability and coherent state-society relations. In principle, responsive government and economic efficiency become intertwined with the development of organizing principles of state and of effective mechanisms of political exchange. As a consequence, ongoing efforts in a number of African countries to design innovative forms of democratic rule may replace the statist schemes of the past with more open and interactive forms of governance in the years ahead.

State Construction in Postcolonial Africa

Africa's political configurations on the eve of independence resulted from varying combinations of precolonial and colonial influences and specific arrangements negotiated during the process of decolonization. Colonial rulers imposed a functional state structure on diverse African societies lacking a common tradition of centralized authority.[15] The efficacy of the colonial state was derived from its superior coercive capabilities and was cemented, albeit in different ways, by the colonial powers, through, for example, pacts with local leaders who frequently continued to administer indigenous law under external supervision.

Although nationalist movements challenged the authority of the colonial state, they rarely created substitute sources of legitimacy acceptable to a broad gamut of their populations.[16] Confronted with heightened public expectations, competing group claims for scarce, state-controlled resources, and the limitations of dependent economies, the leaders of most newly independent African states hastily abandoned their independence constitutions for authoritarian and semi-authoritarian arrangements. The new ruling elites hoped that state-controlled exclusionary regimes would facilitate their quest for state hardness.[17]

The process of state reorganization during the first years of independence resulted in the creation of neopatrimonial, centralized bureaucratic structures which, while lacking a clear conception of the general interest, worked to promote the concerns of their office-holders and clients.[18] Even though the state was detached from key social groups, it was not necessarily autonomous. Nor was it able to penetrate society and extract sufficient resources to implement its own policies.[19] The political logic of postcolonial regimes thus tended to accentuate extractive and instrumental norms at the expense of broader developmental concerns. This syndrome had several important consequences. It exposed the political leadership to pressures from powerful patrons, thus limiting its autonomy and contributing to the erosion of the state's organizational capacity. It also affected policy direction, encouraging the lowering of prices paid to rural producers and the allocation of subsidies granted to urban consumers. The growth of parastatal corporations and marketing boards that gained a monopoly over the extractive and distributive systems also led to reduced incentives in the agricultural sector. The effect was to deepen the countries' dependence on foreign food sources,[20] while the utilitarian nature of patronage tended to reinforce elite politics, especially in party regimes where the ritual of elections was sustained. In these instances (Cameroon, Zambia, Côte d'Ivoire, Kenya) elitism was accompanied by some proportionality in official allocations. In countries where the elites were fractionalized (Nigeria, Ghana, Benin, Uganda), however, the military intervened, setting in motion a cycle of regime changes that magnified the extent of unpredictability in the official realm.

In each African country, societal organization underwent certain modifications to adapt to the political realities of postcolonial times. Society had been organized during the first independence decade primarily along ethnic, religious, and occupational lines. The associational vibrancy that characterized many African cities in the latter part of the colonial period was subdued in most places, however, as the new ruling elite placed limitations on organizational freedoms.[21] Even so, some groups had been incorporated directly into ruling circles, and others, particularly those controlled by powerful patrons, collaborated openly with state officials (the leaders of the Muslim brotherhoods in Senegal are one case in point). Because of their geographical location near the seat of government, these urban-based organizations were also among the first to voice dissatisfaction with governmental policies and to question the uses and abuses of state power. Their reluctance to extend support usually presaged political unrest; consequently, it was imprudent for ruling elites to dismiss their concerns summarily.[22]

The stability of these arrangements varied substantially. The most resilient patterns of power construction were those in which the boundaries between the formal and the informal were well demarcated and respected. The greatest amount of instability occurred where these frontiers were violated, either through the infiltration of informal factions into the formal realm (especially in cases of personalistic takeovers) or through attempts at total control, measures that quickly brought on intense opposition, including armed resistance (Angola, Ethiopia).[23]

Two common features of these heterogeneous patterns stand out: the incomplete institutionalization of the state apparatus and the tendency for administrative-bureaucratic propensities to exceed the actual degree of state consolidation. The political experience of independent African countries has highlighted the risks attendant upon the expansion of administrative devices at the expense of participatory mechanisms. In terms of effective governance, therefore, the initial frameworks of public life in Africa, with all their unique and distinguishable features, appear too detached from social concerns, economic exigencies, and local processes.

Crisis and Response

The 1970s witnessed the entrenchment of postcolonial political structures and the first signs of the harmful effects of authoritarian systems on Africa's economies. The rise of world oil prices and the concomitant economic recession reduced the profits gleaned from an already stagnant agricultural export sector. At the same time that fiscal reserves were largely depleted, state officials artificially propped up expensive food imports, overvaluing local currencies and increasing price supports. Incentives for production diminished substantially and efficiency suffered.

By the close of the second independence decade, governments were barely supported by weak, overextended, costly, and increasingly inefficient state structures. The state continued to expand central functions while accomplishing less. At this juncture, state capacity was constrained in three ways. First, economic difficulties in the industrialized world coupled with an apparent donor fatigue to create increasing immobility. Second, internal discontent mounted as agricultural production declined, population pressures intensified, and inflation soared. Clientelistic politics remained in evidence but no longer provided an adequate response, especially in the major urban areas. Third, as structural imbalances became more pronounced, much of the continent was subjected to environmental threats: desertification, soil erosion, and the absence of rainfall.[24]

Such external and internal factors imposed severe constraints on all political actors, drastically limiting their range of choices. State leaders strove to mitigate the adverse political effects of economic deterioration and to appease their urban support groups. To this end, they adopted a package of policies, including the imposition of price controls, the overvaluation of exchange rates, and the borrowing of extensive funds from foreign sources.[25] Despite these efforts, the circle of beneficiaries of state handouts contracted in most countries. To cope with the shortfall, state elites frequently reduced allocations for education, health, and welfare, bringing on civilian unrest.

Not surprisingly, therefore, the late 1970s and early 1980s were characterized by a dramatic rise in strikes, demonstrations, riots, military takeovers, and civil strife. In Kenya, Zaire, Ghana, Sierra Leone, Zambia, and Uganda urban wage-earners organized strikes to protest rising prices and growing economic hardships. Food riots broke out in Liberia, Tanzania, and Sudan, generally as spontaneous reactions to the high cost and decreasing availability of basic commodities. Between 1979 and 1985, 22 successful *coups d'état* occurred; moreover, aborted coups were recorded throughout the continent, notably in Tanzania, Niger, Angola, Zimbabwe, and Kenya.[26] Personal security deteriorated and massive dislocations became commonplace in areas prone to protracted civil wars. Thus in the Western Sahara, Chad, Sudan, Ethiopia, Angola, Mozambique, and Zaire intense poverty and civil wars proved to be adversely intertwined. The proportion of military expenditures to GNP was highest in the poorest countries on the continent, whose governments diverted scarce resources to military spending, thus further aggravating the conditions that necessitated these expenditures.[27]

Economic discontent was also a factor in the rapid turnover that took place in the top leadership of the African states. Some heads of state were ousted by military interventions, putsches, or, in the case of Idi Amin, by armed invasions. In five countries (Kenya, Angola, Botswana, Guinea, and Mozambique), the founding fathers died in office and peaceful successions occurred. And in four countries (Senegal, Cameroon, Sierra Leone, and Tanzania), the first generation of independent leaders stepped down from their positions, transferring power to hand-picked successors. By the middle of the 1980s, only three of the original founding fathers remained in office in sub-Saharan Africa—Félix Houphouët-

Boigny in Côte d'Ivoire, Kenneth Kaunda in Zambia, and Hastings Kamuzu Banda in Malawi.[28]

Political upheavals varied considerably in intensity. In some countries the elites maintained their unity while factionalism was held in check, social and ideological cleavages were contained, mediations were regularized between the state and key constituencies, and some administrative capabilities were maintained. In those countries (Zambia, Gabon, Côte d'Ivoire, Cameroon) political unrest did not lead to major disjunctures.[29] In others (Ghana, Burkina Faso, Uganda), however, the absence of such cushioning factors increased the degree of political disruption. Most African states stood somewhere in the middle: political enfeeblement further strained the capacities of overextended state institutions; performance levels diminished; and economic progress, where it had occurred, declined significantly.

Throughout the continent the fall in economic production was compounded by the shortcomings of political and economic management.[30] Immiserization spread as smaller and more coercive ruling cliques monopolized entitlements, limited opportunities in the formal economy, and relinquished responsibility for the welfare of their citizens. Increasingly, state officials "de-linked" public institutions from their social groups.[31] The contraction of the formal political arena may have accentuated the autonomy of ruling coalitions; it did not, however, harden state institutions.[32]

In the early 1980s, the antidevelopmental character of bureaucratic-centralist arrangements became exposed in sharp relief. Authoritarianism, in its multiple institutional and ideological manifestations, encouraged the dissipation of public resources and the continuance of external dependency. Public institutions, increasingly unable to implement their own regulations, contributed to policy failure. As economic conditions deteriorated and famine set in, overburdened state institutions became progressively less responsive to public demands. The effect was to accelerate the process of societal disengagement by the latter part of the decade. As one observer put it: "Neo-colonial economic structures decayed while state power could not be used decisively to transcend them."[33] Statism thus helped to bring on economic decline which in turn further undermined state capacities.

In the context of economic failure, renewed attention to issues of political and economic power—its concentration, its dispersion, and its possible redistribution—became essential. The initial reaction of many Africans to the disappointments of the early 1980s was to attempt as far as possible to enclose themselves in the informal domain. In doing this, they sought to insulate themselves from an unpredictable state bureaucracy, and to ensure a modicum of survival in conditions of great adversity. Unlike previous activities in the informal sector, societal adaptations to the economic constraints of this period were not merely a continuation of past patterns or a response to the withdrawal of official services, but attempts to fulfill basic needs under dire circumstances.[34]

By the late 1980s, public disillusionment with state and public sector performance became widespread. Hence the rapid expansion of the informal sector became directly linked to economic scarcity, to blocked access, and to the inability to influence formal state institutions.[35] Stringent state controls accelerated its spread. "Every increase in centralization and every additional attempt to control the economy increase[d] the losses and delays due to inefficiency and thus stimulate[d] the growth of informality as a palliative to scarcity."[36]

Societal groups honed a variety of survival techniques.[37] The first strategy, primarily employed by urban dwellers, involved finding ways of accommodating to reduced circumstances. They ignored some laws and flouted others. In addition, social groups used silent means to resist perceived exploitation.[38] A second coping technique revolved around the parallel market. The underground economy burgeoned in the 1980s, frequently accounting for well over half of the productive activity.[39] The elaborate (and often illegal) informal economy became the most important funnel for the distribution of goods and services as well as a significant setting for petty manufacturing and small-scale food production, particularly in the urban areas.[40] Effectively organized, the informal sector developed norms of interchange that were carefully enforced by popularly backed arbiters. These activities progressively became the mainstay of economic life in many parts of Africa.

A third survival mechanism, employed mostly in the first part of the 1980s, consisted of self-encapsulation, primarily in the rural areas. A shift from the production of commodities for export to food crops was one expression of this trend.[41] In many villages self-provisioning and bartering relations were nurtured. Local communities began to make farm and household implements from available materials, organize their own schools and clinics, construct substitute marketing networks, and, above all, enunciate an ethic of self-reliance.[42] The deliberate disengagement from state channels was not feasible everywhere. Where it did take place, however, it was usually accompanied by the adaptation of new technologies to local conditions.

Finally, some individuals turned to emigration as a mode of survival. The escape option, which required considerable initiative, was used by unemployed laborers as well as by highly skilled professionals. In the 1980s, Africa had the highest proportion of refugees in the world. Millions of Africans migrated to neighboring countries or abroad in an effort to gain safe sanctuary, avert starvation and seek gainful employment. In escaping civil wars and government repression, however, such population movements often placed heavy constraints upon the efforts of receiving countries to achieve their own developmental objectives. For example, the military destabilization of Mozambique by South African-backed Renamo insurgents pushed hundreds of thousands of rural dwellers into neighboring Malawi; similarly, the protracted war in Eritrea created a heavy burden on Sudan.

Survival mechanisms were apparent in other spheres as well. Social groups and village communities engaged in educational activities, developed apprenticeship programs, organized work groups, and periodically staged performances. Songs, jokes, music, and an informal market literature became part and parcel of the quest for survival.[43] Through these channels disaffection with official policies was voiced, leaders berated, standards of accountability defined, alienation articulated, and avoidance advocated.[44] Religious movements, and especially spiritualist churches and fundamentalist Islamic sects, provided vehicles for other forms of exit. In extreme cases, outlets for survival were found in organized crime—armed robbery, banditry, smuggling, and drug-dealing.

These activities were conducted by a variety of organized social interests. Some of these groups date back to the precolonial and colonial periods; others are relatively new constructs. These groups consisted of primary associations (households, villages, kinship units, and local development societies); occupational societies (traders, teachers, farmers); youth and women's organizations;[45] religious communities; and a variety of voluntary associations. These evolving social networks provided alternative frameworks for communal identification and social interaction. Specific social formations served as vehicles for self-preservation, and in some instances they provided a means for growth independent of the state.

Such survival mechanisms displayed several common features. They required a framework for conflict resolution, a credit and finance system, a means of enforcement, a measure of secretiveness, strong bonds of friendship or trust, a modicum of security, and some durability over time.[46] During the turmoil of the early 1980s, most people kept their options open. They sought flexibility as well as continuity and tended, in ingenious ways, to maximize their opportunities within a context of substantial constraint.[47]

No consensus exists as to the significance of this informal response to Africa's economic and political crisis. Some observers have insisted that these activities represented necessary yet ephemeral strategies for coping with economic contingencies, and that they did not obviate the ongoing centrality of patronage ties, cancel the paramountcy of the ruling classes, or reduce the key position of the state in providing economic leadership or in shaping social relations. Others have argued forcefully that local initiatives and institutions were evidence of counter-centralizing processes at work and that they provided a critically needed incentive for the designing of novel forms of development.[48] These debates have centered primarily on the activities of rural producers and have largely overlooked significant processes taking place in the urban areas. More to the point, they have tended to focus on the origins of survival strategies rather than on the outcome of these endeavors.[49] Actually both interpretations may be correct.

These conflicting interpretations aside, there is broad agreement at this juncture as to the extensiveness of group and individual initiatives outside the state arena. As economic conditions worsened in the early 1980s, the pace of migration to the cities subsided in many countries. The percentage of GDP contributed by agriculture rose, and urban residents suffered far greater reductions in incomes at this time than did their rural counterparts.[50] The immediate political significance of an expanded informal sphere was to circumscribe the reach of the African state, to further curtail the state's penetrative capacities, and to create organized pockets of resistance to official repression. Informal activities had the effect of chipping away at the state from below. They defied statist pretensions by limiting the extent of state penetration within the periphery.[51] Whether these activities possessed the organizational, material, and normative attributes necessary to promote the emergence of alternative political entities was another question. Informal coping mechanisms were fragmented and frequently highly particularistic and parochial. They accentuated protest but did not usually point to any non-statist models of power restructuring.[52]

The multifaceted African crisis of the early 1980s helped to illuminate the organization and structure of social systems at large.[53] It accentuated struggles for social control and highlighted contending strategies that vied with each other for moral as well as instrumental supremacy. The decisions and actions of public officials and societal interests clearly diverged. Formal policies often widened the gap between enfeebled state organs and social groups; survival strategies magnified the fragility of the social order. Hence the disengagement of society from the state became the overriding feature of initial societal responses to the crisis in the early 1980s. Both local rebellions and official repression were expressive of this confrontation.[54] The contraction of the formal political arena and the social enclosure that ensued varied in intensity. But as political structures became embedded in increasingly narrow social segments, no state was spared at least some loss of capacity.

The crisis and its immediate responses revealed several core political constraints on effective economic management: the unwieldy character of the bureaucratic apparatus and its ambiguous relationship to political institutions; the problematic correlation between state power and the amassing of personal wealth; the contradiction between extractive practices and the fundamental norms of public responsibility and accountability; the ironic link between state maintenance and external dependence;[55] and, above all, the weakening of state structures in light of the strained nature of state-society relations. It became increasingly evident that the unintended consequences of administrative-centralizing and exclusionary rule could not be overcome without a fundamental reassessment of power configurations.[56]

Reform and Restructuring

By the mid-1980s African leaders, faced with economic decline, increasing balance of payments problems, and heightened unrest, could no longer avoid confronting the ramifications of their policies. They began to investigate ways of strengthening the capacity of the state and its institutions. In doing this, they faced a threefold challenge: to devise appropriate methods of reviving public institutions, to reorganize their relationship with disenchanted societal groups, and, above all, to restore control over the economy.

Given the alarming conditions prevailing at the time, the reassessment process focused mainly on the economic dimensions of the challenge. With only a limited ability to extract resources from domestic sources and with state treasuries near empty, leaders found themselves "hemmed in," with little recourse but to seek foreign assistance. Country after country acceded, formally at least, to the International Monetary Fund's and the World Bank's reform packages. Formal acceptance of IMF conditionalities regarding a stabilization regimen entailed additional constraints on African policymakers. First, the difficulties arising from the dependence of the African governments on external sources for operating budgets was compounded by the establishment of new mechanisms for an ongoing monitoring by international agencies. Second, formal agreement to the substantive provisions on structural adjustment implied a reduction in resources available for political allocations. And third, the stress on the economic as opposed to the political dimensions of the African crisis fostered an element of ambiguity about the role of the state in the development process. These limitations, coupled with existing constraints, had an important influence on the political byproducts of economic reform. Because of such factors, compounded by the increasing limitations of exit options, societal responses to the crisis have in recent years taken on qualitatively different forms than those of the early and mid-1980s.

Societal Readjustment

International demands for structural adjustment and the effort by Africa's state elite to accommodate them had an extensive impact on African economic and societal relations. In terms of burgeoning informal sector activities, the new pricing policies, the reduction of subsidies, and the deregulation of many markets encouraged the refinement and institutionalization of local initiatives. In particular, parallel market activity was allowed to expand as employment prospects in the formal sector contracted, opportunities for migration decreased, and withdrawal to local-level self-sufficiency occurred.[57] Microindustries in the rural and urban areas became increasingly important foci of domestic production. Manufacturing cooperatives emerged and produced goods for growing local markets—now revived after a long hiatus. New distribution networks were created and transportation channels improved.

Economic reform contributed to a process of straddling between the formal and informal sectors. Thus initial investments in the informal economy were frequently funded by capital derived from formal sources; informal activities were bolstered by wages earned in the formal sector; and, most notably, the profitability of the second economy depended upon its forward and backward linkages with the official one.

Governmental reactions to proliferating parallel market activities varied from country to country. At first, governments attempted to control informal initiatives and, where possible, to eradicate them (particularly in the urban areas).[58] Next, some governments tried to tax revenue derived from informal activity. Most recently, and sometimes in tandem, there has been a growing awareness of the need to strengthen and expand the informal economy and to integrate it more fully into the formal sphere.[59] This integrative approach reflects a recognition of the essential interlocking of the two economic networks. Politically, a greater acceptance of the parallel market came together with enhanced bargaining possibilities for local communities and social groups.

Another effect economic recovery programs had on the informal sphere was to facilitate the growth of entrepreneurs who possessed sources of accumulation independent of the state. This group flourished in the latter part of the 1980s because a number of diverse processes converged: office-holders continued to exploit state resources, translating their power into private wealth; local businessmen and women emerged in numbers, deriving their income and their status from their positions in the informal sector; and privatization measures were carried out through the sale of state corporations and marketing boards.[60] In some cases, a new set of entrepreneurs came to control indigenous markets; establish manufacturing, construction and trading firms; engage in external trade; and, some times even help subsidize social services, sanitation, health, and private education. Economic recovery programs thus exacerbated income differentials and accentuated the enormous social inequalities that accompanied the growth of the parallel economy. Entrepreneurs in Nigeria, Kenya, Zaire, Cameroon, and elsewhere formed a nouveau riche stratum whose lifestyle diverged from the bulk of the population.

Inevitably, the emergence of this group had considerable political ramifications. It suggested the beginning of the alteration of patronage structures away from an exclusive focus on the state,[61] and set in motion processes of class formation based on material rather than political criteria for social stratification. In this respect, alternative channels for accumulation constituted the first signs of a potentially fundamental process of power redistribution. Moreover, in countries where a distance developed between state power and capital accumulation (Nigeria, Kenya, Senegal, and Cameroon), business groups could play a vital role in the coalescence of civil society (that part of society that interacts with the state).[62] Yet the discrepancies in income and wealth could not but fuel populist sentiments, especially where access to resources for weaker groups continued to be blocked (particularly evident in parts of Kenya, Nigeria, and Côte d'Ivoire).

Still another key repercussion of economic reform has been to broaden the space available for associational life. Networks of occupational, service, local community, religious, and voluntary organizations have blossomed in recent years. Some of these groups have been concerned primarily with the welfare of their members, offering goods and services on a regular basis. Others have concentrated on development efforts (local self-improvement associations, neighborhood development committees, self-help cooperatives, credit unions). And another set has dealt with issues of empowerment.[63] All these organizations have evinced a special interest in group maintenance. Within their frameworks they have evolved specific notions of authority, community, and distributive justice. They have stressed norms of reciprocity, trust, leadership responsibility, and accountability. Perhaps most significantly, they have nurtured group identification and endowed membership with consciousness and meaning.[64]

Social organizations sometimes developed an intricate relationship with state agencies and with the international community. Within individual countries, the operational space of associational networks was repeatedly redefined by the interaction of governments with NGO's, and particularly by the economic strategy and administrative capacities of formal institutions on the one hand and the geographical locations and contents of group activities on the other.[65] To avoid dissolution, as in the early years of independence, voluntary groups tended to maintain a low profile and to engage in selective collaboration with other groups and with the government. In turn, governments permitted the expansion of voluntary agencies and, when unable to coopt them, tried to coordinate and direct their activities.[66] An intermediate level of social organization began to emerge at this juncture which had important transnational and international linkages.

Structural adjustment programs thus had a direct influence on the organization of Africa's social life, creating a variety of new opportunities for civil associations in the late 1980s. By cutting back on the size of the civil service, marketing boards, and parastatal bodies, and by adopting a series of privatization measures (for example, the Ghana government indicated that it was prepared to accept bids on all but eighteen of its 185 state-owned enterprises), the state inevitably enlarged the space available for associatiational activities.[67] Moreover, in response to donor preferences for greater public involvement in decision-making, governments decentralized responsibilities to local councils and relaxed some restrictions on the endeavors of civil associations. The effect was to relieve central authorities of certain responsibilities for public welfare while opening the way for a significant increase in the variety and range of associational activities.

At times, however, this process led to the emergence of conflicts of interests among groups and their representatives. The reversal in rural-urban terms of trade, encouraged in part by donor support for increased producer prices for cash crops and agricultural productivity generally, exacerbated tensions and rivalries among their respective elite representatives.[68] In certain countries—Ghana is a notable example—the urban bias of the past was largely reversed, as the population of the countryside benefited substantially while key urban groups shouldered a large share of the cost of the country's infrastructural improvements. As a consequence, powerful urban groups—trade unions, middle class professionals, and students—came to form the main opposition to certain reform policies and programs. Leaders now had to devise methods of capitalizing on diffuse rural support without further antagonizing better organized urban populations.[69]

By the late 1980s, a number of associations, particularly at the middle rung, had seized the opportunity to expand their roles and objectives. Thus civil associations—such as professional, worker, student, and women's groups—displayed a new vigor. In other cases (human rights associations, consumer protection groups, political clubs, and civil liberty unions) new intermediate groups emerged and, in a process reminiscent of the spurt of associational activity at the time of decolonization, made a variety of demands upon state officials.[70] At the local level, voluntary development organizations surfaced throughout the continent, creating a constituency for welfare and self-help projects on a countrywide scale.

Within these social groups, participatory values were inculcated on a small scale. These groups opened new channels to economic and political opportunities and set out citizen rights and duties. Most significantly, they had the potential to bring scattered groups into overarching networks, pluralizing Africa's institutional terrain during the latter part of the 1980s.[71] In many respects, social groupings carved out their own political spaces; by asserting niches of autonomous action, they substantially strengthened civil society.[72]

The variety evident in the formal sector facilitated a restructuring of social life. As specific groups affirmed their separate spheres of activity, wider communication networks based on lateral transactions became possible. In many countries horizontal channels of group interaction evolved alongside vertical political links, laying the groundwork for a reorientation of the direction of societal interaction. Therefore, the development of new forms of pluralism through the growth of informal frameworks buttressed by distinctive rules and binding values led to a greater degree of societal interlocking.

By the end of the 1980s, Africa's informal system was so rich and so pervasive that it constituted a network of horizontal and vertical exchange relations that paralleled the formal hierarchy.[73] The broadening scope and shifting boundaries of informal politics served notice that politics no longer coincided fully with state structures and that state-led initiatives would be met with overt or increasingly sophisticated covert resistance. But if patterns of social interaction began to coalesce separately from the state, they neither ignored its presence nor rejected its significance. Changes in informal politics in the aftermath of the introduction of economic reforms highlighted the extent of interchange between the two realms. Not only were the boundaries of the state recognized and internalized by informal actors, but also much informal economic, associational and entrepreneurial activity depended on various forms of linkage with official agencies. New forms of interaction between the formal and informal systems began to replace the dynamic of state-society confrontation that had marked the first decades of independence.[74]

Thus market orientations and liberalization measures introduced by structural adjustment had the effect of reinforcing and entrenching patterns of societal self-reliance.[75] The impact of economic reform on informal politics underlines the changing location of decision-making authority, highlighting, with renewed intensity, basic questions about the balance of power between state organs and society in many parts of Africa.[76]

The political significance of readjustments in the informal sector was directly related to shifts in the form and nature of official state institutions. The most apparent changes took place in the organization and scope of the state apparatus. In most countries, at least on the declaratory level, state agencies were revamped in three major ways: the freezing and, in some cases, retrenchment of the civil service; the reorganization, sale, or closing of a number of unprofitable state corporations and the dismantling of some marketing boards; and the exploration of possible decentralization measures. The net result of these programs has been to pare down the size of the state apparatus and limit the institutional pervasiveness of state agencies. However, economic recovery measures achieved success only where political and administrative patterns of decision-making were altered, administrative institutions were insulated more carefully from political interference than in the past, bureaucratic norms of accountability and probity were enforced, and bureaucrats were protected from direct pressures applied by vocal social groups. In short, the capacity of the formal sector was improved only where officials were able to detach themselves from the postcolonial syndrome at the heart of the current development crisis.[77]

For example, countries such as Ghana and Uganda were able to revise administrative practices precisely because they had experienced severe economic and political upheavals. Other states (Côte d'Ivoire, Cameroon) operated reasonably efficiently in the 1980s, because they had earlier avoided some of the more problematic manifestations of the postcolonial administrative predicament. Either way, the economic reform programs of the late 1980s were implemented top-down by authoritarian regimes that imposed a variety of austerity measures in the face of intense opposition from urban workers and their allies.

In general, structural adjustment did not accomplish the political reforms necessary for the creation of an enabling environment in which the economic reforms could succeed over the long term. Sustainable development required the creation and maintenance of legitimate political structures, something that we turn to in the next section.

The Moves Toward Political Liberalization

If structural adjustment initiatives were launched by the state to comply with the demands of external donor agencies, political reforms were conceded by state elites, often reluctantly, in order to fulfill long pent-up societal claims for public participation and governmental responsiveness and accountability. The bureaucratic-centralizing state had come to seem remote from the citizenry, an alien institutution "suspended . . . in mid-air above society."[78] The authoritarian one-party regimes, moreover, had not proved to be a short cut to economic development—a major explanation put forth by some to justify the limitations they imposed on partisan contestation and civil liberties. By 1989, various regime opponents, and particularly such urban middle-class spokespersons as church leaders, lawyers and other professionals, lecturers and students, businessmen, trade union officials, and some elements within the dominant political party itself, evinced a new spirit of dissatisfaction with the political status quo, calling for an end to state repression and an acceptance of increased political openness.[79] Political repression became identified with poor economic performance.[80] As Frederick Chiluba, the newly elected President of Zambia, put it following his inauguration: "We know how to secure a more just and prosperous life for man on earth—through the freedom to work, the freedom to toil, through free speech, free elections and the exercise of free will unhampered by the state. . . . The great nations, the prosperous nations, are the free nations."[81]

Certainly the call by many Africans for democratic reforms has been manifest throughout the postcolonial period. The revolt against arbitrariness and erratic personal rule, observes Colin Legum, is rooted not in external pressure for change, but is "initiated by Africans who have become increasingly resentful of the abuse of human rights, denial of effective representation in government, corruption, and the economic inefficiency of governments not accountable to an electorate."[82] To be sure, events in Eastern Europe and elsewhere did influence the process of change, but for the most part it was internally generated.[83] It reflected "long harbored deep-seated dissatisfactions with the single-party system as a device for arbitrary rule and private enrichment."[84] In Ghana, for example, a group of courageous leaders, including B. B. Asamoah, Adu Boahen, and Hilla Limann, broke the "culture of silence" prevailing under the Rawlings regime and called for the implementation of a process of transition to constitutional government. Firmly rejecting the description of Ghanaians as "passive," Boahen asserted: "We have not protested or staged riots because we trust the PNDC but because we fear the PNDC!"[85] The middle-class elite was fighting back, seeking to secure the liberal promise of the independence struggle.

Even during the heyday of authoritarianism in Africa, some countries were careful to maintain the bargains they struck at the time of independence or to launch new experiments. Politics was structured to promote two- or multiparty systems in Botswana, Mauritius, Gambia, and Senegal (since 1976). To those countries' credit, elections have occurred regularly and governments have remained reasonably responsive to societal demands. And in something of a high point for the democratic process in the 1980s, the government in power in Mauritius was replaced peacefully by another following a national election.

Although they successfully bucked the authoritarian trend of the times, these were unique country situations in Africa. All of them are relatively small in size and/or population and display special features which tend to be supportive of a democratic experience: Senegal's ruling *Parti Socialiste*, largely backed by the *marabouts*, managed to win convincing electoral victories in 1983 and 1988; the stability of constitutionalism and multiparty electoral processes in Gambia and Botswana are bolstered by the presence of a preponderant ethnic core group—the Mandinka in Gambia and the Tswana in Botswana; and in Mauritius, despite the ethnic appeals of several of the major parties, a broad consensus on democratic norms and values appears to have gained widespread acceptance.[86] In all four countries, then, democratic forms of governance could be said to have prevailed over a significant period of time but on the whole their systems "legitimate[d] the rule of the powerholders without endangering their continued supremacy."[87]

With the urban protests of the late 1980s and early 1990s, the leaders of voluntary groups in much of Africa escalated their demands for decisive moves of political liberalization. Associational activity increased markedly in range and intensity, as trade union, professional organization, student, and disaffected political leaders, among others, expressed their disapproval of the repressive tactics, corruption, and inefficiency of the authoritarian regimes then in power. The impact of this internally generated opposition was enormous, for by the end of 1991 a large proportion of the countries in Sub-Saharan Africa were either scheduled for or had already pledged themselves to some form of democratic governance. In Namibia, where the leadership has voiced a strong commitment to democratic values, a still-to-be-tested constitution grants all citizens the right to form or join political parties.[88] Moreover, as noted above, Zambia has seen one president replaced by another in a hotly contested but peaceful election, and the ballot box has been used to bring about regime changes in Benin, Cape Verde, and São Tomé and Príncipe.

In light of its influence and size in the region, Nigeria's process of regime change is currently being closely watched. If that country's transition to constitutional rule can remain on track despite the eruption of economic, regional, and ethnic confrontations and violence of 1992, it will signal a major move toward the acceptance of political liberalization on the continent. Certainly Nigeria's constitution framers have been most careful in preparing the ground for a resumption of civilian rule. Nigeria's Political Bureau, using the U.S. constitution as a model, recommended the continuation of a federal system of governance. It also proposed a federal executive branch composed of a directly elected president and vice president, assisted by appointed cabinet ministers. To be elected to the presidency, a candidate would have to gain a simple majority of the total national vote cast as well as 25 percent of the total votes in at least 230 (out of 302) local government areas. If no candidate met these requirements, an electoral college consisting of the national and state assemblies would be convoked, and this body would elect a president on the basis of a simple majority of those present and voting.[89] As a check on the executive branch, the Political Bureau suggested adopting a unicameral federal legislature; its 302 members would be elected from the 302 local government areas on the basis of a first-past-the-post system, although some seats would be reserved for women and minorities.

Nigeria's constitution framers also took pains to recommend a number of institutions intended to promote societal participation and inclusiveness. Continuity with the past was assured by the maintenance of federalism; however, the form of this federal system was altered when the military government of President Ibrahim Babangida, in part responding to societal pressures, decreed the creation of additional states. Moreover, the Political Bureau encouraged the establishment of such institutions as a two-party political system, the use of the "federal character" principle when making appointments to the federal cabinet, and the continuance, with minor modifications, of the revenue allocation formula hammered out under the administration of President Shehu Shagari in the early 1980s.

With the launching of the new constitution and the entrance into the transition period, the Nigerian government modified a number of these provisions. President Babangida, refusing to allow the registration of the political parties that initially had put themselves forward, designated his own political parties—the left-of-center Social Democratic Party and the right-of-center National Republican Convention. In addition, the 1992 constitution provided that the federal character principle would apply at every level of government, and not, as before, in appointments to federal positions only;[90] moreover, it raised the requirement for electing the president to one-third of the votes in at least two-thirds of the states. Nigerians were making significant efforts to reformulate the rules of the game, seeking to provide the basis for both societal participation and state efficacy for the years ahead.

Certainly if future governments in Africa can implement these political liberalization measures, they will greatly enhance the capacity of the state to establish the routines and institutions for sustained economic reform.[91] Such political liberalization measures appear to hold out the greatest possibilities for channeling state-society conflict along constructive lines, encouraging the development of learned patterns of relationship over time. And by buttressing practices of reciprocity and political exchange between state and societal elites, these political reforms help to firm up an environment that will promote economic growth and development.

The Fragility of Political Reforms

Political liberalization is occurring alongside economic liberalization efforts throughout much of Africa at the present time. A notable increase in the activities of voluntary associations has occurred, inhibiting a relapse into authoritarian practices as well as contributing substantially to processes of political reform. Even though the political mood on the continent is far more optimistic than at any point since the early years of independence, however, the recent wave of political liberalization should not be confused with democratization. It is important not to overstate the extent of the political change that has occurred, for in many countries the reform process has been a limited one, leaving many of the ruling elites firmly in control of their polities. In Bratton and van de Walle's words, "the partial liberalization of authoritarian regimes does not amount to a transition to democracy."[92]

If the political liberalization seems partial and somewhat brittle, this can be explained in part by the constraints facing these overburdened regimes: the inadequacy of the channels of political communication, the difficulty of establishing responsive political institutions, the problems associated with too many competitors and too intense a conflict (involving religious fundamentalism, ethnic nationalism, and class antagonism), the obstacles in the way of maintaining a dynamic civil society, and the complications in the way of reversing Africa's economic and social decline over the last 25 years. The relationships between newly empowered groups at the local level, civil society, and voluntary associations remain extremely tenuous.[93]

In this respect, external donor pressures for a restructuring of regimes impose costs on many sections of the population (austerity measures, provocation of resentment over privatization, exacerbation of existing interregional differences) that are likely to provoke determined resistance on the part of class, regional, and ethnic groups to change. "The winners of economic reform in Africa," warns Thomas Callaghy, "are few; they appear only slowly over time and are difficult to organize politically."[94] Given such a mix of economic and political constraints, sustained efforts to put democratic reforms into effect are likely to prove difficult. As a consequence, alternative forms of governance, which seek to facilitate the processes of economic reform by combining societal participation and (short-term) state capacity in various ways can be anticipated. The sequencing of reforms, possibly placing economic reforms before political reforms or vice-versa, may be utilized by hard-pressed ruling elites intent on enhancing their ability to deal effectively with multiple challenges in a difficult world environment.

In brief, current experiments with democratic forms of governance remain uncertain and somewhat fragile, especially in light of the tensions between societal demands and the capacity of the state to accommodate these demands. To reduce the burden on governments, it seems likely that many countries will attempt to rechannel popular demands. Hence in the next section we look briefly at the options open to Africa in the event that the present course of political and economic reforms proves beyond the grasp of current regimes and new political formulas for combining substantial societal participation with considerable state capacity to guide the process of economic change become necessary.

Trends and Prospects

The interrelationship between Africa's economic and political processes has been reconfirmed during the course of the 1980s and early 1990s—a period during which the momentum of economic change has been hampered by the lack of political measures necessary to buttress state authority and by changing conditions on the domestic and international fronts. The momentum of political change, constrained by economic deterioration and lack of economic resources to satisfy legitimate societal demands, has also stalled in some instances, pulling back from a full reorganization of the rules of political relations and reviving some of the old practices of heavy-handed administrative centralization and exclusion.

Within African states, some of the benefits accruing from economic reform have tended to diminish over time. As IMF and World Bank programs took hold, income and regional inequalities were exacerbated and social discrepancies became pronounced. In addition, the reforms entailed rising debt burdens and shrinking operating budgets. The political stabilization achieved by the recovery programs was itself dependent on continuing aggregate gains in economic performance. Given some of the negative byproducts of the new plans, the will, let alone the capacity, to implement policy changes was frequently lacking.

These difficulties were compounded by the end of the Cold War and the reluctance of the developed countries to make the kind of long-term aid commitments necessary to lift Africa from its present economic impasse. By the mid-1980s, there were signs that Western and Soviet assistance might decline, reflecting domestic budgetary difficulties, rising internal demands, the pressures of competition with other industrialized countries, donor fatigue, and disenchantment with Africa's progress. For John Ravenhill, there is a link between Africa's decline in importance as an economic partner with West Europe and "the growing disinterest of many European countries in Africa."[95] Thus, even if African debts are significantly rescheduled and credit lines extended, the possibilities of reversing stagnant growth rates do not appear encouraging.

To the extent that structural adjustment plans fail to measure up to current expectations, such occurrences are likely to have diverse political consequences. African states, already heavily constrained and lacking in meaningful choices, will then find themselves more hemmed in than ever. Although it is difficult to foresee the likely possibilities under these circumstances, we feel it necessary to point to a few of these trends and prospects.

One possibility is a kind of "enforced self-reliance," where a number of African countries, locked helplessly in situations of destructive civil wars or unable to produce substantial marketable exports, are involuntarily de-linked for all intents and purposes from the international community. The kind of destructive internal conflict that currently holds Somalia and Liberia in its grips could be a foretaste of similar developments on the horizon. Moreover, in other situations, exports and imports may decline further, indebtedness mount, and major agricultural and industrialization programs grind to a halt. In extreme cases, it is not inconceivable that civilian groups would launch autonomy movements against state domination, yielding anarchy; clearly this latter scenario could lead to a breakdown of authority and to worsening poverty and despair, furthering pockets of hopelessness. In other cases, some kind of autarchic development may be possible.

More constructively, but not very likely, is the prospect of some form of trans-state collective action. Certainly regional harmonization has considerable appeal for many African leaders and others. In principle, such strategies offer prospects for economies of scale, administrative economies, better coordination of planning, and enhanced international status. Yet efforts to develop regional organizations—the Economic Community of West African States, the Southern African Development Cooperation Conference, the Preferential Trade Area of East and Southern Africa, and the Economic Community of Central African States—point up the strength of political forces working against effective regional integration. Economic integration without political will lacks a dynamic of change; political integration linked to economic union appears threatening to the interests, and even the identity, of the constituent units. Although a logical aim, regional integration schemes are clearly constrained for the time being by a web of political anxieties and uncertainties.

The most likely eventuality would be a continuation of the processes evident in the 1980s and early 1990s. At the state level, this would mean combining efforts at political liberalization with the continuation of clientelistic practices, attempts to coopt oppositional elements at the margins, and the perpetuation of political and economic uncertainties. Soft states would still be unable to extend their regulations throughout the society under their control. At the societal level, the burst in civil society activity that took place in the early 1990s might recede slightly; growing alienation from the state and state institutions, however, would likely lead to a continuing expansion of informal social and economic activities at the expense of the political center.

A more promising option points in the direction of increased experimentation with regime change. Certainly the domestic and international constraints upon a thoroughgoing reformulation of political norms and practices are weighty. Yet even within current parameters, some intriguing explorations in the area of regime change will likely occur, revolving around attempts to consolidate new, more responsive orders on the continent. Such efforts might range from the establishment of authentic populist regimes to the creation or resurrection of democratic systems. If political liberalization is conceived of as the institutionalization of power sharing and the injection of new forms of reciprocity and political exchange, then the recent African experience contains components for building diverse and self-fulfilling forms of participatory rule.

Some African lands (Ghana and Burkina Faso), despairing over the poverty and inequality evident in their countries, determined that leftist-oriented populist regimes would be an appropriate response to their situations. Such regimes avoided the vanguard party associated with the classical Marxist-Leninist regime (although they used the rhetoric of Afro-Marxism) and rejected the individualism and acquisitiveness they associated with capitalism. Instead, they searched for their own genuine African forms of governance, emphasizing the values of social inclusiveness and broad citizen participation in political and economic decision-making as well as in the juridical proceedings of government. These populist regimes reorganized the institutions of state to rid the civil service of officials deemed corrupt or unsympathetic with the goals of the new rulers. They also sought to build new, cohesive social orders, linking the rural areas more closely with the lives and opportunities of the urban centers. In those contexts where the constraints of the domestic and international environments seem overwhelming, and leaders come to despair over the possibility of eliminating inequality and external dependence or achieving reasonable economic and social well-being for their people, some form of state populism may well be envisioned by some champions of the general public as the best of a series of stark political choices under the circumstances.[96]

The challenge of creating more democratic forms of rule in Africa hinges on finding ways to put existing democratic features together in a workable fashion. Economic development requires an enabling political environment, but the form that this political liberalization takes depends very much on the circumstances in each country—its norms, values, and configurations of power. If democracy is a developing idea whose meaning is enriched by contributions from all cultures and countries, as Richard Sklar has posited, then it might not be too far-fetched to suggest that new adaptations and models of democracy could emanate from Africa in years to come.[97] Clearly, the economic as well as the political future of Africa's societies may well rest on the outcome of these efforts to move toward more open political systems.

This chapter has argued that the ability to pursue extensive economic reforms, enhance the quality of life, and achieve social equality is constrained by internal and external influences beyond the control of Africa's contemporary regimes and depends in no small part on the institutionalization of participatory alternatives to the bureaucratic-centralist and exclusionary propensities that have largely prevailed in postcolonial times. Sustained economic development requires the institutionalization of norms and practices that ensures the process of state-society relationships will be regularized and predictable. Such recurrent patterns of relations will promote coherency and stability, thereby setting a firm foundation on which economic activity can take place. Whatever course is followed in the years immediately ahead, it seems clear from the preceding discussion that the key to establishing a productive dynamic of economic progress and state reform lies in the transformation of regimes toward greater and more regularized responsiveness to the demands of civil society.

NOTES

1. Special thanks are due to Letitia Lawson for her valuable suggestions on the second draft of this chapter.

2. The terminology, as well as the conclusion, draws on Thomas Callaghy, "Lost Between State and Market: The Politics of Economic Adjustment in Ghana, Zambia and Nigeria," in Joan Nelson, ed., *The Politics of Economic Adjustment in Developing Nations* (Princeton: Princeton University Press, 1990), pp. 257–319.

3. Michael Bratton, "The State, Civil Society and Associational Life in Africa," *World Politics* 41, 3 (1989): 409.

4. Richard Crook, "Patrimonialism, Administrative Effectiveness and Economic Development in Côte d'Ivoire," *African Affairs* 88, 351 (1989): 227–228.

5. Victor T. Le Vine, "Parapolitics: Notes for a Theory" (Jerusalem, July

1989). Our thanks to Professor Le Vine for permission to quote from his draft ms. This formulation may also be found in various communications with Catherine Boone of the University of Texas, Austin, whose insights are appreciated.

6. This observation is at the core of Joel Migdal, *Strong Societies and Weak States: State-Society Relations and State Capabilities in the Third World* (Princeton: Princeton University Press, 1988). The importance of the two spheres was first highlighted in the seminal article by Peter Ekeh, "Colonialism and the Two Publics in Africa: A Theoretical Statement," *Comparative Studies in Society and History* 17, 1 (1975): 91–112.

7. Donald L. Horowitz, "Cause and Consequence of Public Policy Theory: The Malaysian System Transforming Itself" (Duke University Program in International Political Economy, Working Paper No. 32, January 1988), pp. 1–2.

8. Albert O. Hirschman, *Essays in Trespassing: Economics to Politics and Beyond* (London: Cambridge University Press, 1981), p. 298.

9. Thomas Callaghy, *The State-Society Struggle: Zaire in Comparative Perspective* (New York: Columbia University Press, 1984), p. 32 and elsewhere.

10. Richard Hodder-Williams, *An Introduction to the Politics of Tropical Africa* (London: George Allen and Unwin, 1984), pp. xxi-xxii.

11. Otwin Marenin, "The Managerial State in Africa: A Conflict Coalition Perspective," in Zaki Ergas, ed., *The African State in Transition* (London: Macmillan, 1987), p. 61; and Donald Rothchild, "Hegemony and State Softness: Some Variations in Elite Responses," *ibid.*, pp. 119–122.

12. On the relationship between scarcity and political reordering see John Kincaid, "Introduction," *International Political Science Review* 4, 3 (1983), pp. 275–278.

13. John Ravenhill, "Africa's Continuing Crisis: The Elusiveness of Development," in John Ravenhill, ed., *Africa in Economic Crisis* (New York: Columbia University Press, 1986), p. 13.

14. Goran Hyden, "Governance: A New Approach to Comparative Politics," a paper presented at the African Studies Association, Chicago, October 1988, p. 23.

15. Jean-François Bayart, *L'État en Afrique: La Politique du Ventre* (Paris: Fayard, 1989), p. 58. Bayart places contemporary political developments firmly within an African "historical sociology of action" (see pp. 19–31).

16. Richard Crook, "Legitimacy, Authority and the Transfer of Power in Ghana," *Political Studies* 35 (1987): 552–572.

17. Rothchild, "Hegemony and State Softness," pp. 141–134; and Joshua B. Forrest, "The Quest for State 'Hardness' in Africa," *Comparative Politics* 20, 4 (1988): 423–442.

18. This thesis is summarized in Thomas M. Callaghy, "The State as Lame Leviathan: The Patrimonial-Administrative State in Africa," in Ergas, *The African State in Transition*, pp. 87–116.

19. The controversy over the relative autonomy of the African state has not been resolved. Some researchers claim that postcolonial African states were overly autonomous. See, for example, Robert J. Fatton, "The State of African

Studies and Studies of the African State: The Theoretical Softness of the 'Soft State' " (Paper Presented at the Thirty-First Annual Meeting of the African Studies Association, Chicago, October, 1989). These analyses, however, tend to confuse the detachment of state structures and the creation of a state-based system of domination with autonomy. See John Lonsdale, "The State and Social Processes in Africa," *African Studies Review* 24, 3 (1981): 139–225.

20. Rolf Hanisch and Rainer Tetzlaff, "Agricultural Policy, Foreign Aid and the Rural Poor in the Third World," *Law and the State* 23 (1982): 120–143.

21. See Sandra T. Barnes and Margaret Peil, "Voluntary Association Membership in Five West African Cities," *Urban Anthropology* 6, 1 (1977): 83–106.

22. See Naomi Chazan, "The New Politics of Participation in Tropical Africa," *Comparative Politics* 14, 2 (1982): 169–189.

23. Le Vine, "Parapolitics," pp. 9–14.

24. John Iliffe, *The African Poor: A History* (London: Cambridge University Press, 1987), pp. 230–259.

25. Paul Streeten, "Food Prices as a Reflection of Political Power," *Ceres* 16, 2 (1983): 16–22.

26. Figures in this section are based on Naomi Chazan and Timothy Shaw, "The Political Economy of Food in Africa," in Naomi Chazan and Timothy M. Shaw, eds., *Coping with Africa's Food Crisis* (Boulder: Lynne Rienner Publishers, 1988), pp. 4–19, and Chazan et. al., *Politics and Society in Contemporary Africa*, pp. 423–435.

27. The World Bank, *Accelerated Development in Sub-Saharan Africa: An Agenda for Action* (Washington, D.C.: World Bank, 1981, mimeo.), p. 186.

28. In the Maghreb, Habib Bourguiba of Tunisia remained in office until ousted by the military in 1987.

29. See Joan Nelson, "The Political Capacity of Stabilization: Commitment, Capacity and Public Response," *World Development* 12 (1984): 983–1006. For a case study consult: Henry Bienen, "Populist Military Regimes in West Africa," *Armed Forces and Society* 11 (1985): 357–377.

30. Sara S. Berry, "The Food Crisis and Agrarian Change in Africa: A Review Essay," *African Studies Review* 27, 2 (1984): 59 and *passim*.

31. The notion of de-linkage is developed in Kwame Ninsin, "Three Levels of State Reordering: The Structural Aspects," in Rothchild and Chazan, *The Precarious Balance*, pp. 265–281. This idea is captured in the concept of prebends, as developed in Richard Joseph, *Democracy and Prebendal Politics in Nigeria: The Rise and Fall of the Second Republic* (Cambridge: Cambridge University Press, 1987).

32. The tendency to confuse the autonomy of ruling coalitions with the autonomy of the state may be seen in Fatton, "The State of African Studies and Studies of the African State."

33. Communication from Catherine Boone, May 1989, p. 11

34. Contrast with Jeffrey Herbst, "The Exit Option and the Politics of Protest in Africa" (Princeton University, Draft ms., 1988), pp. 15–16.

35. René Lemarchand, "The State, the Parallel Economy, and the Changing Structure of Patronage Systems," in Rothchild and Chazan, *The Precarious Balance*, pp. 149–170.

36. Lomnitz, "Informal Exchange Networks," p. 37.

37. The following analysis is based on Victor Azarya and Naomi Chazan, "Disengagement from the State in Africa: Reflections on the Experiences of Ghana and Guinea," *Comparative Studies in Society and History* 19, 1 (1987): 106–131.

38. Robin Cohen, "Resistance and Hidden Forms of Consciousness Amongst African Workers," *Review of African Political Economy* 19 (1980): 8–22.

39. Pierre Mettelin, "Activities Informelles et Economies Urbaine: Le Cas de l'Afrique Noire," *Mois en Afrique* 223/224 (1984): 57–71.

40. Richard Stren, "L'État au Risque de la Ville," *Politique Africaine* 17 (1985): 74–85.

41. For one example see Stephen G. Bunker, "Bagisu Agricultural Innovation and Political Organization in the Ugandan Crisis" (Paper Presented at the Twenty-Fourth Annual Meeting of the African Studies Association, Boston, December 1983). Also see Bayart, *L'État en Afrique*, esp. pp. 308–315.

42. Roy Preiswerk, "Self-Reliance in Unexpected Places," *Genève-Afrique* 20, 2 (1982): 56–64.

43. These processes are analyzed in depth in Karin Barber, "Popular Arts in Africa," *African Studies Review* 30, 3 (1987), esp. pp. 1–4.

44. For an excellent case study see Thomas M. Callaghy, "Culture and Politics in Zaire" (Washington, D.C.: Department of State, Bureau of Intelligence Research, 1987). These ideas are elaborated in Naomi Chazan, "African Political Cultures and Democracy: An Exploration" (Paper Presented at the Conference on Political Culture and Democracy, Stanford, September 1988).

45. For a general treatment of the role of women in the informal economy see Michele Hayman, "Female Participation in the Informal Economy: A Neglected Issue," *Annals, AAPSS* 493 (1987): 64–82.

46. Le Vine, "Parapolitics," pp. 4–9.

47. Sara Berry, *Fathers Work for their Sons: Accumulation, Mobility and Class Formation in an Extended Yoruba Community* (Berkeley: University of California Press, 1985), esp. p. 83. In this work Berry challenges the assumption of peasant resilience developed in Goran Hyden, *No Shortcuts to Progress: African Development Management in Perspective* (Berkeley: University of California Press, 1983).

48. This debate has been conducted in the pages of *Development and Change.* See Nelson Kasfir, "Are African Peasants Self-Sufficient?" *Development and Change* 17 (1986): 335–357, Goran Hyden's response, "The Anomaly of the African Peasantry," in the same volume, pp. 1677–705, and the exchange between Lionel Cliffe, Gavin Williams, and Goran Hyden in *Development and Change* 18 (1987).

49. For an analysis of various approaches to developments in the informal sector see Naomi Chazan, "State and Society in Africa: Images and Challenges," in Rothchild and Chazan, *The Precarious Balance*, pp. 325–341.

50. See the example of Ghana as documented in Republic of Ghana, *1984 Population Census of Ghana, Preliminary Report* (Accra: Central Bureau of Statistics, February 1985). Similar evidence for Tanzania is cited in Goran

Hyden, "Governance and Liberalization: Tanzania in Comparative Perspective" (Paper prepared for Presentation at the 1989 Annual Meeting of the American Political Science Association, Atlanta, August 1989), p. 13.

51. Jean-François Bayart, "Civil Society in Africa," in Patrick Chabal, ed. *Political Domination in Africa* (London: Cambridge University Press, 1986), p. 119.

52. Martin Kilson, "Anatomy of Class Consciousness: Agrarian Populism in Ghana from 1915 to the 1940s and Beyond," in I. L. Markovitz, ed., *Studies in Power and Class in Africa* (London: Oxford University Press, 1987), pp. 50–66.

53. Michael John Watts, "The Political Economy of Climatic Hazards: A Village Perspective on Drought and Peasant Economy in a Semi-Arid Region of West Africa," *Cahiers d'Études Africaines* 23, 1–2 (1983): 43.

54. John Dunn, "The Politics of Representation and Good Government in Post-Colonial Africa," in Chabal, *Political Domination in Africa*, pp. 158–174.

55. Robert Jackson and Carl Rosberg, "Why Africa's Weak States Persist: The Empirical and the Juridical in Statehood," *World Politics* 35, 1 (1982): 1–24.

56. Michael Ford and Frank Holmquist, "Crisis and State Reform," in Chazan and Shaw, *Coping with Africa's Food Crisis*, p. 229.

57. Most of the recent information on the informal sector is contained in case studies. For some notable examples see: Janet MacGaffey, "How to Survive and Become Rich Amidst Devastation: The Second Economy in Zaire," *African Affairs* 82, 328 (1983): 351–363, and Cyril Kofie Daddieh, "Economic Development and the Informal Sector in Ghana Reconsidered: Notes Towards a Reconceptualization" (Center for International Affairs, Harvard University: African Research Program, 1987). For a summary consult: Naomi Chazan, "Patterns of State-Society Incorporation and Disengagement in Africa," in Rothchild and Chazan, *The Precarious Balance*, esp. pp. 124–130.

58. For two examples see: Lillian Trager, "The Creation of an Illegal Urban Occupation: Street Trading in Nigeria" (Paper Prepared for Presentation at the Twelfth Congress of ICAES, Zaghreb, July 1988), and Claire Robertson, "The Death of Makola and Other Tragedies," *Canadian Journal of African Studies* 17, 3 (1983): 469–495.

59. This approach is advocated in The Economic Commission for Africa's "African Alternative Framework to Structural Adjustment Programmes for Socio-Economic Recovery and Transformation." See summary in Toby Shelley, "Answers to Solutions," *West Africa* 3752 (July 17, 1989): 1160–1162.

60. The best case study of these processes is Janet MacGaffey, *Entrepreneurs and Parasites: The Struggle for Indigenous Capitalism in Zaire* (London: Cambridge University Press, 1987).

61. Lemarchand, "The State, the Parallel Economy, and the Changing Structure of Patronage Systems."

62. Bayart, "Civil Society in Africa," p. 116.

63. This classification is the basis of the arrangement of the articles in the special supplement of *World Development* 15 (1987), edited by Anne Gordon Drabek, "Development Alternatives: The Challenge for NGOs."

64. This theme is developed in Catherine Newbury, "Survival Strategies in Rural Zaire," in Nzongola-Ntalaja, ed., *The Zaire Crisis: Myths and Realities* (Trenton: Third World Press, 1986), pp. 99–112.

65. Michael Bratton, "The Politics of Government-NGO Relations in Africa" (Draft ms., 1988), pp. 19–23.

66. Shelley, "Answers to Solutions," p. 1162.

67. Naomi Chazan, "Africa's Democratic Challenge," *World Policy Journal* 9, 2 (Spring 1992): 286, 296; and Donald Rothchild, "Introduction," *Ghana: The Political Economy of Recovery* (Boulder: Lynne Rienner Publishers, 1991), p. 9.

68. See Callaghy, "Lost Between State and Market," pp. 257–319.

69. See ibid., pp. 28–29.

70. Adebayo Olukoshi, "Associational Life During the Nigerian Transition to Civilian Rule," a paper presented at the Conference on "Democratic Transition and Structural Adjustment in Nigeria," Stanford, The Hoover Institution, 1990, p. 1.

71. Bratton, "The Politics of Government-NGO Relations in Africa," p. 49.

72. One of the first analysts to document this development was Frank Holmquist, "Defending Peasant Political Space in Independent Africa," *Canadian Journal of African Studies* 14, 1 (1980): 157–167.

73. Lomnitz, "Informal Exchange Networks in Formal Systems," p. 5.

74. This is the main thesis of Bratton, "The State, Civil Society, and Associational Life in Africa."

75. Ford and Holmquist, "Crisis and State Reform," pp. 231–232.

76. Bratton, "The Politics of Government-NGO Relations in Africa," p. 12.

77. This is the thrust of the argument in Callaghy, "Lost Between State and Market."

78. Goran Hyden, "Problems and Prospects of State Coherence," in Donald Rothchild and Victor A. Olorunsola, eds., *State Versus Ethnic Claims* (Boulder: Westview, 1983), p. 69.

79. On this process in Zambia, see Michael Bratton and Nicolas van de Walle, "Toward Governance in Africa: Popular Demands and State Responses," in Goran Hyden and Michael Bratton, eds., *Governance and Politics in Africa* (Boulder: Lynne Rienner Publishers, 1992), pp. 50–51; and National Democratic Institute for International Affairs, *The October 31, 1991 National Elections in Zambia* (Atlanta: Carter Center, 1992), p. 26.

80. P. Anyang' Nyong'o, "Democratization Processes in Africa," *Codesria Bulletin*, No. 2 (1991): 3.

81. Quoted in *The October 31, 1991 National Elections in Zambia*, p. 8.

82. Colin Legum, "Africa: Who is Behind the Demand for Multi-Party Democracy?" *Third World Reports* (July 18, 1990): 2.

83. On the processes of diffusion, see Stuart Hill and Donald Rothchild, "The Contagion of Political Conflict in Africa and the World," *Journal of Conflict Resolution* 30, 4 (December 1986): 716–735.

84. Bratton and van de Walle, "Toward Governance," p. 42.

85. Albert Adu Boahen, *The Ghanaian Sphinx* (Accra: Ghana Academy of Arts and Sciences, 1989), pp. 51–52. Also see his manuscript, "Governance as

Conflict Management in West Africa: Ghana since Independence, 1957–1991," April 1992, pp. 120–123. (Typescript copy.)

86. This section draws on Donald Rothchild and Letitia Lawson, "The Interactions between State and Civil Society in Africa: From Deadlock to New Routines," in Naomi Chazan, John W. Harbeson, and Donald Rothchild, eds., *Civil Society and the State in Africa* (Boulder: Lynne Rienner Publishers, forthcoming).

87. Robert Fatton, Jr., *The Making of a Liberal Democracy: Senegal's Passive Revolution, 1975–1985* (Boulder: Lynne Rienner Publishers, 1987), p. 169.

88. Constitution of the Republic of Namibia, Article 17 (1).

89. Federal Republic of Nigeria, *Report of the Political Bureau* (Lagos: Government Printer, 1987), p. 137.

90. Federal Republic of Nigeria, *Official Gazette* 76, 29 (May 3, 1989), Sects. 15 (3), 144 (3).

91. These ideas are developed in greater detail in Donald Rothchild, "Structuring State- Society Relations in African States: Toward an Enabling Political Environment," a paper presented at the Colloquium on the Economics of Political Liberalization in Africa, Harvard University, Center for International Affairs, March 6–7, 1992.

92. Bratton and van de Walle, "Toward Governance in Africa," p. 51.

93. On the critical link between democracy and a viable and active civil society, see Naomi Chazan, "Africa's Democratic Challenge," pp. 222–224.

94. Thomas M. Callaghy, "Africa and the World Economy: Caught Between a Rock and a Hard Place," in John W. Harbeson and Donald Rothchild, eds., *Africa in World Politics* (Boulder: Westview, 1991), p. 60.

95. John Ravenhill, "Africa and Europe: The Dilution of a 'Special Relationship,' " in Harbeson and Rothchild, *Africa in World Politics*, p. 179.

96. Donald Rothchild and E. Gyimah-Boadi, "Populism in Ghana and Burkina Faso," *Current History* 88, 538 (May 1989): 221–224, 241–244.

97. Sklar, "Developmental Democracy," p. 691.

Chapter Six

The Future of the Manufacturing Sector in Sub-Saharan Africa

ROGER RIDDELL

> The most crucial structural change required in Sub-Saharan African countries is the one which brings about a minimum level of industrialization in those countries. In most of them, a genuine industrialization process has either yet to take hold or is still in a nascent stage.[1]

Introduction: Downgrading Manufacturing

Recent efforts to come to grips with and solve Africa's development crisis, particularly influential initiatives supported by Western donors and the international institutions, have tended to ignore or underplay the role of industry in general and of the manufacturing sector in particular.[2] In recent years, industrial development has increasingly been placed within a broad macroeconomic context, dominated by short-term, market-based structural adjustment programs, while no (or only minor) industry-specific policies have been proposed to encourage the expansion and diversification of the sector. This minor role given to industry is mirrored in aid priorities. Foreign aid to manufacturing industry, which constituted less than 12% of total official aid to Sub-Saharan Africa (SSA) at the start of the 1980s, fell to no more than 7% by 1989,[3] and this trend appears set to continue.

There are four reasons why this downgrading of the role of manufacturing in both short-term adjustment policies and in discussion of longer term development in Africa appears surprising. First, industry and industrial development were given pride of place in almost all former long-term strategies for African development drawn up by individual countries, often with the advice and consultation of the international agencies.

Second, and relatedly, the preeminence (or bias) given to industry in the development process did not arise from the whim of either African scholars or the newly independent governments of African countries: it was rooted in mainstream analyses and theoretical insights of the development literature, and has persisted down to the present day. In the early 1960s, the words "development" and "industrialization" were practically synonymous and, in the intervening period, that link has been preserved. More recently, accelerated industrial development aided by a range of industry-specific policies have been important elements in the successful development of the Newly Industrializing Countries (NICs); they have also featured prominently in the growing importance of what have been termed the new NICs.[4] As Hollis Chenery commented in the opening paragraphs of his seminal work on industrialization and growth: "Development is now conceived as the successful transformation of the structure of an economy. . . . Historically, the rise in the share of manufacturing in output and employment as per capita income increases, and the corresponding decline in agriculture, are among the best documented generalizations about development."[5]

Third, in the 1980s the emphasis placed on the role of manufacturing in debates and strategies for long term development *within* Africa continued. Indeed in parallel with a slowing down of manufacturing growth across a majority of African countries, the role of manufacturing industry appears to have been given a central place in policy statements emanating from African leaders, and from consensus statements from African regional organizations.[6]

Fourth and finally, one of the reasons why industry has increasingly been driven off the policy map is the belief that import-substituting industrialization has been such a failure in Africa. As we shall discuss below, in most cases the impact of import-substitution policies has been quite limited, and thus rather than the industrialization process being directed along the wrong path, it has scarcely even begun.

In the late 1980s, an increasing consensus appeared to be evolving over what course African development ought to take, manifested most strikingly in reaction to the World Bank's 1989 long-term perspective study *Sub-Saharan Africa: From Crisis to Sus-*

tainable Growth, which drew praise (or at least only minimal criticism) from both outside and within Africa.[7] Yet the consensus achieved remains predominantly related to *objectives*, and a wide gulf still exists over *methods* to marry long term objectives to short-term measures to address especially macroeconomic distortions, over what *precisely* to do and what *in practice* is likely to work. What is more, division, disagreement, and doubt over methods and execution would appear to be most visible in relation to industrial policy and strategy.

The strong contrasts between the emphasis given to the role of manufacturing within Africa by African governments and their advisers, its virtual absence in policy debate emanating from outside Africa, and the, at best, minimal treatment of manufacturing in structural adjustment programs (SAPs), all raise a series of questions for African development in the 1990s. Are these differing views on the role and place of the manufacturing sector in future African development merely differences in emphasis or do they also represent differences of substance? If the latter, is this a reflection of new theoretical insights into the process of development? If not, then the question arises whether the downgrading of the role of manufacturing in SAPs might leave SSA *more* underdeveloped and backward at the end of the 1990s than if an alternative pro-industry strategy were adapted.

As the 1990s opened it was becoming increasingly clear not only that industrial policy executed within the framework of orthodox structural adjustment packages was failing to lead to any form of industrial deepening, but also that the policies that were implemented had become the subject of growing opposition, not least from among industrialists. This has led to both resistance to and reversal of policies, a situation that appears likely to continue.

The purpose of this chapter is to look critically at the type of industrial policy the international financial institutions are promoting in Sub-Saharan Africa as a subelement of structural adjustment programs. We shall do so by looking at a group of countries on the subcontinent where the manufacturing sector has been most highly developed.[8] The conclusion drawn is not only that the approach is suboptimal, but also that there are risks that much industrial potential could be lost in the 1990s, if policies associated with the more orthodox approach to structural adjustment provides the dominant framework within which manufacturing sector development is placed. What is more, it appears that there are alternatives: the "hands-off" policy of neglect could well be altered to incorporate a more explicit package of policies to promote industrial expansion and deepening. Examination of what has been achieved by the manufacturing sector in Africa over the past 30 years, together with a dispassionate look at what will continue to restrain development in the 1990s, suggests that there is a range of benefits to be derived from focusing more attention on the promotion of manufacturing in Africa than is occurring at present under SAPs. This is not to argue that a greater focus on the manufacturing sector will "solve" the problem of African development, in either the short or medium term, or that a big blind push promoting the rapid expansion of manufacturing will short-cut the route to self-sustaining development. The benefits—if they do arise—are likely only to be seen in the longer term.

Alternative Approaches to Industrialization in the 1990s

Three Groups of Alternatives

For the purposes of the present discussion, we can classify the range of strategies on African manufacturing industry for the 1990s into three broad groupings, distinguished both by their general attitude to the market and by their more specific approach to industry. The three can be termed the "industrialize at all costs," the "benign interventionist," and the "harsh withdrawal" approach.

The Demise of the Radical Pro-Industry Approach

Briefly, the "industrialize at all costs" approach is for manufacturing and, more broadly, industrial development to be vigorously promoted—at almost all costs; it is clearly a "radical pro-industry" approach. The strategy is rooted in the view that "industry is the main lever of African development,"[9] and built upon the belief that African countries can short-circuit the "normal" process of development and leap into the stage of mature industrialization. This is to be achieved, most commonly, through the promotion of a range of new industries initially linked to import-substitution. The strategy involves the setting up of a range of, first, consumer-good, and then more complex industries, with production initially replacing imports, but then (hopefully) sustained by a mix of increased domestic and export demand. Thus linkages are seen as important in theory, even if, in practice, major gaps are apparent. Low on the agenda of priorities are the costs of importing the machinery required, the technical and managerial skills needed to operate factories, the technology used, the costs of production, the degree of protection needed, current and future levels of demand, and the degree of subsidy required for the products to be purchased.

In the history of postcolonial Africa, the radical pro-industry approach has had the longest run, and has been the most influential in relation to both policy-thrust and resource allocation, enduring from before the 1960s through the mid-1980s, if pronouncements in development plans are any guide to policy practice. Outside some academic ivory towers, however, the approach is now no longer taken seriously either outside Africa or, more significantly, by policymakers *within* Africa: there is little political support for it even among the ruling elites, while there are simply insufficient funds, either domestic or foreign, to return to such a strategy of economic engineering, blind to the limitations and costs of forever ignoring market and price signals.

The demise of this approach can be traced to a series of industry-specific as well as broader factors the importance of which have risen and become more influential as wider macroeconomic constraints began to bite especially during the 1980s. The most obvious problem is that in spite of channeling substantial resources to promote and establish manufacturing industry in Africa, the manufacturing base of most countries remains small, fragile, and predominantly high cost, linked predominantly to further processing of agricultural (and in some cases mineral) products but resulting largely in the manufacture of products of low quality internationally and thus not easily exportable. Surprisingly, too, while the strategy of industrialization was to establish a growing range of import substitutes, many countries have failed, in any marked degree, to achieve this. The fragility of the manufacturing base is also apparent from the low degree of interlinkage between manufacturing and other productive sectors of the economy, except through receipt of agricultural and/or mineral products for processing. The slowdown of overall economic growth in the 1980s, together with the rising shortage of foreign exchange and falling levels of investment, exposed these weaknesses as capacity utilization levels plummeted and what industry there was became increasingly affected by shortages of spare parts, exacerbated by failures to maintain plant and equipment. For the 1990s for most countries in SSA, the "industrialize at all costs" approach is a non-starter if for no other reason than it simply cannot be financed.

To Intervene or Not?

As the radical pro-industry approach appears for practical purposes to have been laid to rest, the key policy choice for the 1990s revolves around the question of whether to let the pace and pattern of industrialization take its course "naturally," within the context of wider macroeconomic policies, and guided exclusively by these signals and incentives, or whether some (a different and less prominent) sort of assistance should be given to promote manufacturing industry directly, and in so doing, to engineer a particular, and probably more rapid, form of industrial development than if its development was not the subject of such intervention. Herein lies the difference between the benign interventionist and the harsh withdrawal approaches.

Harsh withdrawal is the term used to encompass the approach linked most closely with the more orthodox type of structural adjustment programs promoted in SSA during the 1980s. Under this approach, manufacturing industry and its development are placed firmly within the broader macroeconomic framework: the shape and manner of manufacturing sector evolution are influenced predominantly by short-run market and price signals, as the state—in its various guises—stages a series of retreats from direct involvement in the manufacturing and other sectors, and as state marketing declines. Manufacturing is treated no differently from other productive sectors, and any special treatment historically accorded the sector is withdrawn. Thus, subsidies to and incentives for manufacturing are removed, protection through banning the import of competitive products ceases, and competitive imports are increasingly permitted at the same time as tariff levels are lowered. Consumer subsidies to stimulate demand for local manufactures are eliminated as any bias in the overall terms of trade is removed, while the likely fall in the external value of the currency results in increasing costs to manufacturers dependent on imported intermediate inputs and capital equipment, and foreign skills. The underlying objective of this approach is that the forces of supply and demand, and the increasingly market-determined price regime, increasingly determine the degree and pattern, and set the pace for change in the structure, of industrialization in the economy.

The most crucial question this raises is what effect such an approach is likely to have on African manufacturing sector development. Clearly what is not ruled out is a process of deindustrialization.[10] To the extent that manufacturing industry is unable to survive in the increasingly competitive world to which it is exposed, contraction of the manufacturing sector is to be expected, at least in the short term. There are few people who advocate deindustrialization; there are more who maintain that what is sometimes called "industrial restructuring" might well be a necessary precondition for a more viable form of industrial development to rise from the ashes of three decades of high-cost failure. At its best, the structural adjustment approach to manufacturing development anticipates not only restructuring of the manufacturing sector but also a type of restructuring that will in time result in industry being more cost-effective and, most importantly, enable the sector to turn outward and become more export-oriented.

Lying somewhere between the radical pro-industry- and the orthodox structural adjustment-type approaches lies a third one, whose characteristics are less easy to capture precisely. We have termed it the benign interventionist approach. Like the radical pro-industry model, two of its leading characteristics are interventionist and pro-industry. Yet, like the structural adjustment type, it is sensitive to the distortions and high costs that led to the adoption and influence of structural adjustment policies, and acknowledges that these are unsustainable. It is thus far from dismissive of the importance of responding to market and price signals, and of the need to attempt to eliminate macroeconomic distortions and imbalances. Thus its advocacy of industrial expansion and deepening is located within the context of a viable macroeconomic environment. The sharpest differences in the approach to macroeconomic policy-making between the benign neglect and harsh withdrawal approaches lie in the timing of the adjustment process, in the mechanisms to be used to promote a more efficient type of industry in the (longer) adjustment period envisaged, and in precisely how to respond to price signals.

Those who reject both the old "import-substitution" approach to industrialization (which is noted in SSA more by its absence than its failure) and the blind export-oriented approach, argue that the future prosperity of SSA is likely to be enhanced by a three-pronged type of industrialization. Policies to promote the expansion of manufactured exports and a more systematic approach to further import substitution need to be vigorously implemented, not in isolation but in conjunction with policies that seek to raise the efficiency of existing manufacturing enterprises.[11] Such an approach is likely not only to enhance the growth and deepening of the manufacturing sector, but also, in so doing, to assist rather than hinder attempts to solve Africa's longer term development problems. What is more, such an approach is finding increasing political support within Africa, which could well intensify as the current decade unfolds.

Few would quarrel with the objective of creating more industries which are internationally competitive or with the more general desire to increase the export-earning capacity of the manufacturing sector in Africa. The crucial question for policymakers is: what is the best method to achieve these aims? As the benign interventionist approach emerges from an examination of the performance of manufacturing in SSA over the recent past—in particular from attempting to isolate those factors which have inhibited industrial expansion and deepening, and those that have assisted it—the more detailed content of such an approach will follow a summary of analysis of the development of the manufacturing sector.

An Overview of Performance Trends[12]

A number of features of manufacturing industry in SSA reveal differences with other regions of the developing world. One is the smallness of manufacturing in SSA. In 1988, total manufacturing value added (MVA) of all the countries of the SSA region amounted to just over \$18 bn, \$1 bn less than the level reached in 1985. Excluding Nigeria, the MVA of the remaining countries of the SSA region in 1988 came to just over \$15 bn, lower than the individual levels of Turkey, Finland, or Indonesia.[13]

There are, however, differences other than size, most notably that the level and share of manufacturing in SSA remains extremely low compared with other parts of the developing world and there has been minimal growth in manufactured exports from the SSA region. Thus between 1965 and 1989, the ratio of MVA to GDP for SSA did not rise above 11%, compared with an increase from 20% to 30% for all developing countries, from 20% to 27% for all low-income countries, and from 20% to 23% for lower middle-income countries. From 1965 to 1984, the MVA/GDP ratio for low income economies of SSA rose from 9% to 10%; it fell from 9% to 7% for the middle-income countries of SSA.[14]

From 1965 to 1986, the ratio of manufactured exports from SSA to manufactured exports from all developing countries fell from 4.6% to 1.5%, while the ratio of the manufactured exports from developing economies to world manufactured exports rose from 8.4% to 15.6%.[15] Trends in the ratio of manufactured to total exports over time also reveal the poor performance of SSA. Thus from 1965 to 1984, this ratio fell from 7.8% to 5.9% for SSA; it rose from 3% to 8.2% in developing west Asia, from 28.3% to 58.5% in developing south and southeast Asia and from 5.2% to 18.6% in developing Latin America.[16]

If these were the only features of note, they might point to an approach to industrial policy different from that advocated and promoted in other parts of the developing world, and to similar policies being executed in all countries of the SSA region. Yet these trends provide only a partial picture. Thus in the decade of the 1960s, the average growth rate of MVA for SSA was *greater* than the average for all developing economies (8.3% to 6.5%), with this 1960s growth spurt contributing to a slightly higher than average performance for SSA over the entire period 1965 to 1980 (8.8% to 8%). It appears, too, to have been only in the 1970s that the performance of SSA began to lag behind other regions (except uniquely the Indian subcontinent), although these growth rate comparisons are clearly biased because of the low base from which SSA expansion is derived.

Perhaps of more significance is that the rate of growth of MVA for middle-income economies of SSA was higher than that achieved by all middle-income economies in both the 1960s and 1970s. It was only in the 1980s that the growth rate of MVA for the economies of SSA fell dramatically (to an annual average of 0.6% a year 1980 to 1987 compared with 4.9% in the 1970s); but not even this was unique, for the growth rate of MVA for Latin America fell equally sharply, from 5.5% in the 1970s to 1.1% for the period 1980 to 1987. Yet even these figures conceal differences. The average manufacturing growth rates of seven countries—Botswana, Cameroon, Côte d'Ivoire, Kenya, Nigeria, Zambia, and Zimbabwe—in the period 1980–87 *remained higher* than that achieved (on average) by all middle-income developing countries.

Of major importance is that aggregate trends for all the countries of the SSA region conceal some marked variations *between* countries over time. Thus, the performance of manufacturing exports when analyzed by numbers of countries has not been entirely adverse. For instance, the ratio of manufactured to total exports exceeded 15% for only three countries of SSA in 1966, for six countries by 1976, and 13 by 1986. Moreover, the contribution of a handful of countries to aggregate MVA growth has increased rapidly: in 1965, the combined MVA of Cameroon, Côte d'Ivoire, Ghana, Kenya, Nigeria, Zambia, and Zimbabwe came to 31% of the total MVA of SSA, but by 1985 it accounted for 66%. As for the pace of industrialization, the rate of growth of MVA exceeded 5% a year from 1963 to 1973 in 34 countries of SSA, from 1973 to 1979 in 13 countries, and in the difficult period from 1980 to 1986 in at least 10. For Botswana, Burundi, Mauritania, and Rwanda a sustained expansion of MVA of over 5% a year was recorded from 1963 to 1986.

Other trends highlight the *complexity* of performance. Thus out of the 20 countries that recorded a lower annual rate of growth of MVA from the period 1973–79 to 1979–86, eight had a higher MVA/GDP ratio in 1985 than they did in 1973. On the other hand, out of the 26 countries whose annual average MVA growth rate was higher in the period 1979–86 than in the period 1973–79, a full 15 recorded a fall in their MVA/GDP ratios.

Thus even a rapid overview of some of the aggregate data of manufacturing performance within SSA reveals that a view of African industrialization that suggests both progressively poor performance across all countries of the subregion and a record markedly different from other parts of the developing world is wrong. This should have implications for policy prescription and, in particular, should caution against two types of policy advocacy. First, the evidence provides few grounds for advocating policies for SSA industry that are markedly different from those followed in other regions. Second, differing performance between countries should make one extremely wary of policies that are applied willy-nilly to all countries of the subregion, especially if they are based on a premise of pessimism about the ability to embark on a process of industrialization. At minimum, blanket prescriptions for all countries of the subregion are bound to be suboptimal, they may also be counterproductive.

More worrying still is if the prevailing structural adjustment programs, which provide no role for direct intervention in industry to stimulate the growth of the sector, are advocated on the assumption that the interventionist policies of the past caused the problems and relative underdevelopment of manufacturing in SSA. This assumption can be challenged in at least three ways. First, as just noted, the record is not exclusively one of failure: there were and there continue to be successes. Second, some of these successes can be attributed in some (often large) measure to interventionist policies aimed at creating and stimulating the growth of manufacturing enterprises. Third, while much of African manufacturing industry is undoubtedly "high cost," it is too simplistic to attribute this to rising trade protectionism and restrictions on potential import substitutes. A closer look at the process of industrialization in a number of the more "successful" industrializers provides support for these conclusions.

Types and Patterns of Industrial Growth

Domestic Demand

Following approaches to industrial growth analysis utilized in other parts of the developing world,[17] it is possible to make a quantitative assessment of the manufacturing sector not merely by looking at trends such as growth in output and value added, but also by estimating the relative importance of domestic demand, import-substitution, and exports in explaining, or accounting for, the growth of manufacturing and its major sectors. Analysis of manufacturing in seven key countries—Botswana, Cameroon, Côte d'Ivoire, Kenya, Nigeria, Zambia, and Zimbabwe—produces the (unsurprising) conclusion that the predominant source of growth in manufacturing has been domestic demand (rather than either import-substitution or export growth).[18] For Botswana, 54%

of output growth was derived from domestic demand, for Cameroon, about 55%, for Kenya, 69%, Nigeria, 76%, and Zimbabwe, 72%,[19] while for Côte d'Ivoire and Zambia, domestic demand has been no less important.[20]

The dominance of domestic demand in aggregate growth could be interpreted either as caused predominantly by the growth of demand from within the sector itself, to which the wider (domestic) economy was able to and did respond favorably, or as a result of positive changes that occurred within the wider domestic economy with manufacturers supplying an increasing quantity of goods for the domestic market. There are a number of reasons why the latter explanation is likely to be of by far the greatest importance. First, the overall share of manufacturing in total output in the seven countries while significant is far from dominant. Furthermore, as subsectoral decomposition of the data reveals, manufacturing expansion has originated predominantly at the consumer-products end of the manufacturing process. Additionally, too, any substantial generation of domestic demand originating from within manufacturing would be confirmed if there had been both a high and rising level of import substitution in the different countries; the data, however, provide little support for such a conclusion to be drawn. Finally, the interpretation tends to be corroborated by comparing World Bank data for trends in MVA and trends in GDP growth rates: the four countries with average growth rates for MVA in the 1965 to 1980 period higher than the SSA average—Botswana, Côte d'Ivoire, Nigeria and Kenya—also had rates of growth of GDP higher than the SSA average.

We would thus seem to be able to make some important initial generalizations about manufacturing expansion. Not only does growth in manufacturing in these "successful" countries appear to have been predominantly dependent upon the growth of domestic demand, rather than upon either import substitution or export growth, but also the pace of growth of manufacturing seems to have been critically determined by the dynamics of the wider domestic economy. Relatedly, manufacturing growth has been dependent on access to sufficient amounts of foreign exchange required to finance both the purchase of plant and equipment and a significant proportion of inputs, which the manufacturing sector itself has in large measure been unable to earn. In the pre-1980s period, rapid growth of MVA was significantly enhanced by expansion of the more dominant productive sectors, led most frequently by agriculture.[21] In the 1980s, though, it was the policies adopted to address broad macroeconomic distortions (and therefore largely external to either agriculture or manufacturing) that played a major role in the slowdown in manufacturing growth in six of the seven countries, while, in the unique case of Botswana, it was a combination of a favorable macroeconomic climate and rapid expansion of the leading (nonmanufacturing) productive sectors that boosted manufacturing sector growth.

It would thus appear that a major cause of manufacturing growth in SSA has had its root in the establishment of an environment conducive to steady expansive growth outside the sector itself and principally primary product-related. As this conclusion seems to be confirmed for those countries in SSA with the most advanced manufacturing sectors, it would seem safe to add that for countries of the region with even smaller manufacturing sectors (the vast majority), substantial growth of manufacturing would be highly unlikely to take place unless their leading productive sectors were also experiencing sustained growth and expansion.

Import-substitution

The role of domestic demand in stimulating the expansion of manufacturing output should not be overemphasized. A far from insignificant part of manufacturing output growth for this cluster of countries originated in import substitution and/or export growth—ranging from 24% for Nigeria to 46% for Botswana. Of importance, too, in two countries for particular (albeit relatively short) periods of time, import substitution constituted the major source of growth: accounting for 55% of output growth in Zambia in the late 1960s and for 54% of output growth in manufacturing in next-door neighbor Zimbabwe from the period 1952–53 to 1964–65. Furthermore, doubts can certainly be raised about the ability of *sources of growth* analysis to convey the full extent of import substitution accurately, because it regards a reduction in the import ratio as import substitution only in the year in which the relevant fall in imports is recorded. Thereafter the import substitution effect is not explicitly considered and the change in output is allocated either to domestic demand or export, as appropriate.

The case-study evidence, however, reveals a second feature: while the degree of import substitution has varied from country to country, the overall impact appears in all but one of these countries (the exception being Zimbabwe) to have been minimal. It has resulted in neither a very significant degree of interlinkages with other subsectors of manufacturing or to other productive sectors of the economy (excepting, of course, further processing of primary products) nor to a significant fall in the importation of even simpler consumer goods. What this suggests is that the process of substituting for imports has tended to be rather haphazard. This is confirmed by other evidence, which also indicates that in many of the countries a large and, not unusually, a growing absolute quantity of manufactured imports still consist of consumer goods. Thus, even as late as the mid-1980s, almost exactly half of manufacturing in SSA was concentrated in the food, beverages, and textile branches, only 8% in chemicals and 10% in the manufacture of machinery and transport equipment. The dominance of consumer rather than intermediate or capital-oriented manufacture in present day SSA would suggest not only that manufacturing is relatively simple in technique but also that there has been little structural change in the postindependence period. Analysis of "apparent consumption" trends, shown in table 6.1, would tend to confirm this.[22]

Indeed the data suggest there has been a marked deterioration in the P/AC ratio of products within the foodstuffs subsector and those intermediate products for which SSA has had a relative high level of domestic production capacity. In the case of vegetable oil, there has been a decisive swing from aggregate surplus to overall deficit; for both soap, minimally, and for cement, more significantly, the P/AC ratios have been falling. Similarly there has been a deterioration in the relative production of other intermediary products and minimal production of more sophisticated products, including fertilizers crucial for agricultural development.[23] It is thus apparent that there is plenty of scope for further import substitution in SSA, placing in better perspective the view that future manufacturing policy should be dominated and determined by an expansion of domestic demand.

Complex rather than simple explanations appear to be the hallmark of the particular successes achieved in import-substitution. This can best be illustrated by the case of Zimbabwe where 30% of manufacturing sector growth was derived from import substitution activities for a period of more than 30 years. Its success came from a judicious mix of policies directed to the manufacturing sector and to events occurring, and incentives offered, in the wider economy.

The most important ingredients of this "success" would appear to have been the following:

- government support for industrial promotion and expansion;
- a sustained period without balance-of-payments problems;
- a long period of overall growth and continued diversification in the rest of the economy;
- a fairly developed and efficiently operating supporting physical, transport, and financial infrastructure;
- a developed capital market;
- high levels of local management and engineering skills, knowl-

TABLE 6.1
Production as a Percentage of Apparent Consumption, 1973–75 to 1981–83, Various Products

Selected Products	1973–75 No of SSA Countries	1973–75 % of SSA MVA in sample[a]	1973–75 P/AC %	1981–83 No of SSA Counties	1981–83 % of SSA MVA in sample	1981–83 P/AC %
Milk/Cream	22	22	36	17	11	26
Butter	27	74	82	25	68	64
Vegetable Oil	39	99	110	40	99	90
Cotton woven Fabric	25	73	86	25	79	91
Footwear	22	66	93	19	61	106
Soaps	23	48	91	22	71	90
Cement	29	92	79	25	90	74
Nitrogenous fertilizer	38	9	18	38	99	13
Phosphatic fertilizer	37	92	26	37	99	20
Pig iron	32	96	10	24	86	11
Angles, shapes sections	31	58	15	22	44	19

[a]This is the percentage share of total MVA of the respective product of all countries of SSA originating in the countries in the sample.

SOURCE: UNIDO, *Africa in Figures 1986*, (Vienna: UNIDO, 1986), Table 6; and UNECA, *Survey of Economic and Social Conditions in Africa 1985–1986* (Addis Ababa: United Nations, 1987).

edge of production processes, and ability to adapt machinery to local conditions;

- international confidence in the economy leading to inflows of foreign investment and technology (in the crucial pre-UDI period);
- trade agreements that ensured relatively captive neighboring and larger markets for goods;
- tariffs and quantitative restrictions, which provided protection to newly established firms and, in the case of some firms, the payment of subsidies.

What seems to have been important for Zimbabwe's success in import-substituting industrialization was not so much the dominance of one or other characteristic, but rather the convergence of so many supportive elements for long periods of time, together with the ability of both the government and manufacturers to adapt as circumstances, internal and externally induced, changed. This was shown most clearly in the period surrounding and just after the Unilateral Declaration of Independence (UDI) in 1965. Thus, prior to and during the Federal period (1952–53 to 1964–65), the economy was characterized by relatively low tariffs and few quantitative controls, the period of UDI (1964–65 to 1978–79) was dominated by almost all-embracing controls and regulations, including prohibition of a wide range of competing imports and limited access to foreign exchange. Yet in both periods the share of import substitution in overall growth exceeded 30%, a share equalled only by one other SSA country, Botswana.

While Botswana's manufacturing base remains minute, its importance lies in both its rapid and consistently high rates of manufacturing sector growth (in the world context surpassed only by China, South Korea, Singapore, Indonesia, and Libya) and in the very different policy environment from next-door neighbor Zimbabwe in which that growth took place. Botswana's open economic regime has been far more akin to that favored by the international financial institutions than that which prevailed not only in Zimbabwe but also in all our other case-study countries. Supporters of interventionist policies might wish to point to the uniqueness of Botswana—especially its lack of foreign exchange problems as well as its linkages both with South Africa and the rest of black Africa—as significant factors enabling it to pursue such an open policy. While this was undoubtedly important, perhaps a more critical conclusion to be derived from the differing experiences of

Botswana and Zimbabwe is surely the need to tailor policies to the particular circumstances of different countries. What is more, in their analysis of Botswanan manufacturing, Sharpely, Lewis and Harvey[24] end by questioning the wisdom of maintaining the present largely noninterventionist approach to manufacturing sector development into the 1990s, when traditional sources of foreign exchange are likely to be insufficient for growth, and an even greater acceleration of manufacturing growth appears increasingly necessary.

Manufacturing Export Growth

Not only has manufacturing export performance been poor for SSA countries in aggregate, but there has also been an absolute decline in manufactured exports in real terms for most countries—major exceptions include Botswana and, for a short period, Cameroon. Additionally, what are termed "manufactured" exports have tended to be dominated by the further processing of primary products (largely agriculturally linked) goods destined for markets outside SSA. In contrast, the (smaller) quantities of nontraditional manufactured exports have predominantly been destined for countries within SSA, usually near-neighbors. It is more than coincidence that the three countries with the largest value of manufactured exports over the post-1960s period—Côte d'Ivoire, Kenya, and Zimbabwe[25]—were initially the most industrially developed in their respective regions; in the early years, regional markets within Africa were often little more than extended domestic markets.[26]

The conventional and widely shared explanation for such a poor and deteriorating export performance runs along the following lines: manufacturing industry in SSA is not competitive internationally—probably because it never was and certainly because it has tended to become ever more high cost over the past two to three decades—because of, or significantly aggravated by, rising levels of protection, persistently overvalued exchange rates, and quantitative restrictions placed on competing imports.

The policy conclusions emanating from this assessment are that if the trends of the past two to three decades are to be reversed, priority should be given to reducing tariffs, eliminating quantitative restrictions, and ensuring that there is far closer alignment between nominal and real exchange rates. Does the evidence confirm or contradict this view? It appears at best to be ambiguous, as illustrated by examining the performance of a number of the industrial "frontrunners."

While for a range of industries in most of these countries, comparative price data indicate that domestic prices are higher (often considerably higher) than border prices, evidence from a number of countries, including Zimbabwe, Cameroon, Kenya, and Côte d'Ivoire, indicates some contradictory trends. Here international competitiveness across a range of industries appears to have been maintained in a climate of rising protectionism; what is more, there is strong evidence to show that indicators of competitiveness[27] between industries and, significantly, between firms in the same industry differ, often quite markedly, and that the degree of competitiveness has increased for certain firms over time.

Part of the reason for poor export performance lies in the prevailing policy environment. Until the mid to late-1980s, there was little if any concerted effort put into promoting manufactured exports, especially to destinations beyond SSA, excepting processed agricultural and mineral products. The principal role assigned to manufacturing in SSA was the establishment of factories in order to supply goods predominantly for the domestic (and regional) markets in the attempt to replace imports and hence reduce the overall import bill. While, as already noted, the effects were quite limited, one did occur: a climate encouraging manufacturers to look for, promote, and expand into markets beyond their borders or those of their near-neighbors was never established. Indeed a combination of the absence of trade promotion activities targeted to manufacturers and few or minimal export incentives reinforced each other and effectively dampened any ambitions manufacturers might have had to try to penetrate and obtain a foothold in overseas export markets. That this provides an important element in explaining the low level of manufacturing exports is confirmed by examining policy changes initiated in the 1980s, and monitoring their effects. In a number of African countries—Kenya, Zambia and Zimbabwe—the mid to late-1980s saw a significant expansion of nontraditional manufacturing exports. This occurred at a time when a series of explicit export promotion policies were introduced, including the establishment or extension of export incentives.[28]

Significant though these developments certainly have been, they need to be placed in a broader context. The overall effect on raising the export/output ratio has been modest at best. Additionally, in those countries where manufacturing industry has been relatively "long established"—Botswana is a notable exception here—and where some successes in expanding into the export field in recent years have occurred, there are only a few instances in which firms originally oriented to the domestic market switched in any significant degree to the export market.[29]

It is in the context of this discussion that the Botswana case needs to be considered. Botswana appears to be an exception to the general trends in three major ways. First, the growth of manufactured exports in the 1975–1985 period accounted for a higher share of output growth than for any of the other countries in the same period—and in some cases in any other one. Second, manufactured exports (excluding meat slaughtering) expanded at a rate of over 15% a year for much of the 1980s. Finally, the environment for the development of manufacturing in Botswana is characterized both by minimal external protection and by policies determining that the prices of manufactures domestically produced should be similar to the price of competing imports, all in the context of its membership of the South African Customs' Union. To conclude, however, that Botswana's manufacturing export successes have been due predominantly to its overall—and open—trade and tariff policies and to deduce that this liberal approach should be applied to other countries of SSA would be both premature and would ignore the advantages of alternative approaches in some of the other countries just noted.

There are also other factors. One is that, in contrast with the other countries, there has always been a climate of exporting in Botswana. Another is that Botswana's manufacturing base and, even more, its nontraditional exports constitute a tiny volume of goods. Most important, however, not even Botswana has managed to break out of its dependence on regional markets for its manufactured exports: less than 5% of its non-beef manufactured exports go to destinations other than Zimbabwe or South Africa, a share not dissimilar to most other countries of the region that have some manufactured exports.

What, overall, does the evidence suggest for future policies? If recent events are any guide to future policy decisions, it would appear that efforts to alter the structure of manufacturing and, in particular, attempts to raise both the level and share of exports in total output, are highly unlikely to succeed merely by tinkering with tariff levels and especially by rapidly opening up manufacturing to internationally competitive forces, unless and until changes are made to address the problems of what is often widespread comparative inefficiency at the enterprise level.[30] There is also little to suggest that, taken in isolation, attempts to create more domestic competition and to remove the power and control of large firms in particular industrial subsectors by encouraging "competition" will be likely to lead to a rapid expansion of manufactured exports. What is more, recent cross-sectional evidence with data from beyond Africa supports the view that such an approach is likely to be counterproductive,[31] while Botswana's experience would tend to confirm that a liberal trade and tariff regime on its own remains inadequate to induce the creation of a strong manufacturing sector capable of competing internationally.

Contemporary debate about African industrial policy does not seriously question the need for the countries of SSA to expand their manufacturing exports. What is in dispute is the approach to further this objective. The prevailing policy framework and trade and tariff regime in these countries does not provide anything like a sufficient explanation for the internal/external orientation or the cost structure of manufacturing enterprises. Clearly the macroeconomic framework is important, but it is not everything! Both the evidence from Africa and recent international research[32] suggest that what is needed is usually a range of policies aimed at raising productive efficiency, into which a set of broad macroeconomic policies need to be placed. To expand exports, what would appear to be needed, in general terms, is an overall commitment by the management, and supported by politicians and financial institutions, to improve efficiency through implementing a range of policies aimed at raising productive efficiency. Where African countries have managed to expand manufactured exports in recent years, the following factors have contributed to this expansion:

- more appropriate machinery,
- "new" management techniques,
- expanded research and technological capabilities,
- innovative ways of raising labor productivity,

- systematic attempts to enter new nondomestic markets with higher quality products packaged more attractively,
- attempts to reduce comparative transport disadvantages,
- the provision or extension of export credit guarantees and facilities to minimize foreign exchange risks.

Summary

In their various ways, the manufacturing performance of a number of countries (particularly of Zimbabwe, Kenya, Zambia, Côte d'Ivoire, Nigeria and Botswana) point to the following conclusions:

- that efficient manufacturing production can occur under a far from liberal trade regime (Kenya, Zimbabwe);
- that factors other than price play a major role in determining the extreme variations in efficiency occurring within different industrial subsectors; in particular, the role of management, machine design, and engineering skills play a critical role in explaining these differences (Nigeria, Kenya, Zambia, Zimbabwe, and Côte d'Ivoire);
- that sustained manufactured exports require far more than short-run cost advantages (Zimbabwe, Kenya);
- that questions regarding management and choice of machinery are vital to the creation of viable industries and that changes in the prevailing incentive system can play an important role in assisting the private sector to make decisions beneficial to both the firm and the economy as a whole (Kenya, Zambia, Côte d'Ivoire, Zimbabwe);
- that a sheltered regional market can assist the drive to create efficient manufacturing units (Botswana, Zimbabwe);
- that the development of manufacturing depends critically upon the presence and promotion of an adequate base of domestic skills (Zimbabwe, Kenya);
- that sustained import substitution and the development of linkages between subsectors of manufacturing and between manufacturing and other productive sectors are unlikely to be developed without recourse to specific incentives, (far from costless) industrial promotion activities, as part of a long-term perspective (Zimbabwe).

While analysis of the past can be only a guide to the future and it is clearly not possible to "prove" the merits of alternative future approaches, these various factors provide grounds for asserting that a policy framework more supportive of manufacturing industry—"benign intervention," rather than a "harsh withdrawal" approach, merits greater consideration.

Further Worries about Structural Adjustment Approaches

If an analysis of past manufacturing sector performance throws into question the wisdom of embarking on a policy for the future dominated by noninterventionism, a number of features and effects of contemporary structural adjustment policies provide additional worries. One is that in countries where such policies have been in place for the longest, such as Côte d'Ivoire, Nigeria and Ghana, there seems to be little indication of a rise in investment levels in manufacturing in general or of a rise in foreign investment in manufacturing, in spite of new investment codes and a whole panoply of new incentives offered to investors.

The long-term objective of structural adjustment programs is to raise the productive capacity of the economy through both macroeconomic and institutional intervention. Such intervention is intended to create an environment in which both domestic and foreign private investment can flourish. Yet in the short, or even medium term, the evidence suggests that it is unlikely that the typical SAP "package" will have an overall incentive effect on foreign direct investment (FDI), even if it may be positive in the longer term.

Concern about the short-term effects of SAPs on FDI has been reflected recently in the International Finance Corporation's (IFC's) Annual Report for 1989, which comments thus (p. 23):

> A number of African countries have embarked on economic and institutional reforms. These reform programs often make the business environment more difficult in the short to medium term by introducing the need to adapt to more competitive circumstances. Furthermore, measures aimed at reducing deficits often result in restrained overall demand and depressed local markets. Many businesses find it difficult to adjust to trade reforms and industrial restructuring measures and to absorb increased input and debt service costs caused by local currency devaluations. In this kind of environment, investors adopt a wait-and-see attitude

> before making new investments or expanding operations. In the long term, however, the success of such reforms should increase the scope for private sector activity.[33]

The question, of course, is whether the correct environment is being created for accelerated foreign investment inflow and for industrial expansion to occur. Recent studies in foreign investment in developing countries suggest that a low-wage regime is a far less important incentive for location in a developing country than in the past. As Lütkenhorst comments:

> Key factors in steering what has become a thinner flow of FDI to developing countries are skill levels, market size, the existence of an efficient industrial support network, the availability and quality of various support services as well as advanced telecommunication and information-processing facilities. Whereas previously a certain physical infrastructure (transport facilities, energy and water supply) was often sufficient to attract FDI, now a highly developed human and technological infrastructure would appear to be required.[34]

What this suggests is that the presence of a stable (and expanding) domestic industrial base together with access to, if not a domestic, than at least a reliable regional, market are becoming increasingly important factors in decisions of foreigners to relocate into developing countries. Not only does this provide a counter to the view that investors are likely to be attracted in significant numbers solely to invest in industries geared to the export market, but it also challenges the very assumptions of an industrialization strategy based on a trimming of the domestic industrial base and a shift to export-orientation.[35]

As for the hoped-for rise in manufactured exports flowing from adoption of SAPs, the (scattered)—albeit still rather early—evidence would tend to suggest that this has occurred if not to a greater then at least to an equal degree in countries like Zimbabwe and Zambia, where controls and interventionist policies have prevailed, than in those countries which have adopted structural adjustment policies. In Nigeria, the all-pervasive problem of smuggling is still a major factor inhibiting manufacturing export expansion, something untouched in practice by SAPs.

Another question is raised concerning the assumption of structural adjustment programs that the production should best be left to the private sector. In particular, recent work by Grosh[36] in Kenya suggests that "efficiency levels in public manufacturing are comparable with those in private sector manufacturing, and that quasi-public firms combining both private and public control substantially surpass efficiency levels in the private sector considered separately. Perhaps even more surprising, public firms are shown to be the recipients of less governmental trade protection than private firms when comparisons are made within industries."

Two final observations concern the impact on manufacturing attempts in Côte d'Ivoire and Nigeria to stabilize their economies. The first has been a quite marked contraction of production levels and employment in manufacturing, but little evidence of any other sort of "restructuring." What is uncertain is the extent to which this contraction is permanent or temporary. The second has been the level of resistance to tariff reductions from what are clearly politically influential groups of manufacturers. In both countries, tariff reductions were implemented and then reversed. Such effects raise the question of the extent to which these policies can be made to work in practice and over a period beyond the short term. It seems safe to assert that resistance is likely to stiffen if policies leading to substantial industrial contraction are indeed to be executed in the 1990s.

Alternatives to Contemporary Conventional Wisdom

The previous discussion brings us back to alternatives to the current structural adjustment approach. Having argued earlier that policies for the manufacturing sector for Africa for the 1990s need to be tailor-made to the particular circumstances of different countries, it would be inconsistent to propose any single alternative applicable across the African subcontinent. Yet it would appear that any alternative needs to be based on three criteria. First, it would seem sensible to build industrial strategies on the successes of the past, and on the methods that appear to have worked; second, they need to be based on a realistic assessment of the constraints that will continue to impede development in Africa in the 1990s; and third, they need to be capable of implementation.

As argued above, the days are already passed when a radical pro-industry policy presents a practical alternative for the 1990s, while the persistence of foreign exchange shortages argues strongly for a type of industrial restructuring that attempts to raise the level of manufacturing exports and their share in overall production. Further, it would appear that the last criterion listed in the previous paragraph—being capable of implementation—is likely to be addressed at all adequately only if far greater emphasis is given to the manufacturing sector than is occurring at present.

Shortages of foreign exchange, the fact of only minimal import substitution in the past, the need for greater overall efficiency in manufacturing, and contemporary evidence on the type of industrial structure foreign investors require point to an approach whereby the expansion of manufactured exports and a more systematic approach to further import substitution need to be implemented, not in isolation but in conjunction with policies that seek to raise the efficiency of existing manufacturing enterprises.

This perspective provides the context for articulating more precisely what the content of the *benign interventionist* approach might begin to look like. It clearly needs to be sensitive to both price and market signals, while not shunning either the explicit promotion of manufacturing industry or interventionist policies to enhance the expansion of manufacturing and the furthering of interlinkages with other subsectors of the economy.

Given the concerns expressed about the harsh withdrawal alternative, it might be helpful to articulate some of the main elements of the new approach by highlighting some of the differences between the two. Thus, the benign interventionist approach would tend to take a longer view of the adjustment process than the orthodox SAP approach. It would use the (longer) period of adjustment to implement policies that promote the diversification, strength and competitiveness of industry: industrial restructuring would therefore tend to take place behind the protection of controls rather than in the fuller face of international competition brought about by the rapid introduction of competitive imports and across-the-board tariff reductions. Likewise its approach to prices would be different. Noting current differences between domestic and border prices, the approach would attempt to assess why these differences occur. Instead of simply trying to accommodate to, and be guided by, short-run international (border) prices, consideration would be given either to postpone domestic price movements, if lower border prices are the result of short-run dumping, or to help industries or individual enterprises to reduce price differentials particularly by working to stimulate the competitiveness of domestic industry. It is in this context that the first of at least four broad areas of interventionism would be considered—though not all would apply to all countries or be applied with equal emphasis.

The first such area would embrace one or more of a whole series of potential measures aimed at improving the viability (competitiveness) of specific and currently operating industries. This would be likely to include activities to raise productivity at the plant level, through, for instance, reequipping the plant, altering machine-time and shift operations, enhancing skills, and even improving labor relations. Or it might embrace activities to improve product quality, adapt technologies, change packaging, streamline accountancy practices, or alter purchasing or final product stock practices. The second area would involve assistance in setting up new enterprises, perhaps even new industries. In contrast with the radical pro-industry approach, however, decisions to establish such industries would be informed by current price and market signals and (usually) by the need to produce products that could at least serve subregional markets. However they would also be guided by other factors, such as the need to save foreign exchange on importing final products, or the need to raise the value added of primary product exports and to reduce the cost of imported inputs to those sectors. The third area would involve support for industries that are unlikely, even in the medium term, to be competitive internationally, but that are judged to be crucial for long-term development, most likely (like a steel plant) because of their pivotal role in developing future industries.

A range of different forms of interventionism is envisaged in these different areas. These would include direct (mostly short-term) subsidies, a variety of forms of technical assistance, and subsidized loans and credit facilities. At the macrolevel, policies would be likely to include a slowdown in the pace of trade liberalization, and in the speed with which domestic industries are exposed to international competition in order that the more "sheltered" approach to adjustment be pursued. In some instances, quite high tariff levels might well be maintained for some time, and import bans continued; in other instances, for example where new industries are being developed, former policies of tariff reduction might be reversed, in line with orthodox infant-industry approaches. Additional interventionist measures would include a range of specific export incentives to stimulate the intended orientation of the sector to external markets, supplemented by the finance necessary to provide market intelligence and to help assess more medium to longer term comparative advantage.

Clearly, different types of interventionism proposed would incur different types of cost, and would set in train second round effects on what are already distorted markets. This brings us to the fourth area of intervention, which would consist of the establishment (and funding) of a facility to monitor the current viability and potential competitiveness of industry, and assess the impact, including the costs, of these different forms of interventionism. Clearly in different countries, the form of benign interventionism adopted will depend on the level of industrialization reached and the assessment of the future potential for further industrialization. The experience of Japan, the NICs, and other successful industrializers suggests that industry should be promoted and guided by means of a judicious balance of short-term price signals and interventionist policies aimed at striving to achieve longer term comparative advantage.

For such an approach to become a realistic alternative, it would clearly require both domestic and international support. Within Africa there are encouraging signs. There would appear to be sufficient overlap with strategies already on the table for support to be forthcoming: a policy that seeks deliberately to expand rather than lead to the contraction of the industrial base provides a far more politically attractive future than those peddled by the international institutions in the 1980s. What is more, there is little doubt that the Bank's policies for manufacturing industry in SSA have met with stiff resistance in a number of countries, therefore raising the important question of their feasibility. Thus in Nigeria, Kenya, Côte d'Ivoire, and Zimbabwe, opposition to manufacturing sector policies based on openness and liberalization have, in the past ten years, either significantly delayed or led to the watering down of such policies and proposals.

Of course, no approach to the further industrialization of countries in SSA is likely to work unless it also receives external stimulus and support. In particular for countries that still have a small and high-cost industrial base, there is considerable scope for foreign aid resources to supplement national efforts, in playing an important part in assisting the promotion, expansion, and restructuring of the manufacturing sector. Particular examples could include the following:

- funding and, perhaps helping to execute, sectoral and firm-based studies of inefficiencies particularly of intrafirm differences;
- helping to establish training assistance programs for manufacturing;
- assisting in expanding the technical skills base of the sector;
- identifying weaknesses in management and entrepreneurial skills and providing both stopgap replacement and the training of indigenous staff;
- providing help in building up a domestic competence to assess reinvestment needs and appropriate machinery purchase;
- assisting in promoting and sustaining manufacturing export programs including pinpointing gaps in product range, product quality and packaging;
- and monitoring current and anticipated trends in world trade in manufactures.

However if these resources are to be brought in from outside, it is equally important that they are used more to promote indigenous expertise at all levels, in both private sector enterprises and across the range of public sector institutions concerned with industrial policy and industrial promotion.

Conclusions

Today's environment provides little optimism that any policy to promote and accelerate the development of the manufacturing sector is going to be easy. In particular, most countries of the subregion are going to continue to be "hemmed in" by a range of factors that will dampen domestic demand, and thus limit the pace of industrial expansion and the scope for diversifying the manufacturing base. We have argued here that an approach to the manufacturing sector favoring benign intervention rather than neglect is likely to be more appropriate for helping to solve Africa's development problems. If such initiatives do occur, and especially if they are accompanied by new financial and technical assistance resources to the sector, the prospects will be enhanced for manufacturing to play a more prominent part in the development of a number of countries in SSA, thereby laying the base for a more diversified and sounder path of development than has characterized Africa over the past three decades.

We have been careful not to advocate a complete abandonment of structural adjustment-type initiatives. Not only would this ignore the contemporary political realities of African development, but also, given the distortions that affect many economies of the subregion, a series of adjustment measures clearly remain central to longer term development. We have instead suggested that they be adapted to particular circumstances, but within the context of more interventionist policies that seek to promote industrial growth and deepening.[37] The underlying assumption of the more orthodox structural adjustment package is that the forces of supply and demand, and the increasingly market-determined price regime, should increasingly determine the degree and pattern, and set the pace for change in the structure, of industrialization in the economy. On the basis of historical analysis of African industrial performance and the experience of the industrial process in other developing countries outside Africa, this perspective is rejected.

In the second half of the 1980s, structural adjustment policies increasingly took on a human face—and far more clearly needs to be done in this regard in the years ahead. The plea is that as the orthodoxy of structural adjustment approaches continues to change, it may also take on a new interventionist and industrial face.

NOTES

1. United Nations Industrial Development Organization (UNIDO), *Industry and Development Global Report* (Vienna: UNIDO, 1989), p. 20.

2. Although many publications use the terms "industry" and "manufacturing" interchangeably, this is confusing. According to the widely used United Nations *Systems of National Accounts (SNA)* series F. No. 2, revision 3, *industry* embraces extractive mining, construction, electricity, water and gas as well as the more narrowly focused sector, *manufacturing*. For the SSA region, the relative contributions of manufacturing and industry to GDP are very different, accounting respectively for 11% and 27% of GDP in 1989. World Bank, *World Bank Development Report 1991* (Washington: World Bank, 1991), p. 209.

3. This is especially true if one sets aside commodity import programs viewed more as balance of payments support.

4. For a discussion of the performance and prospects of some of the leading new NICs see S. A. B. Page, *Trade, Finance and Developing Countries: Strategies and Constraints in the 1990s* (London: Barnes and Noble, 1990).

5. H. Chenery, S. Robinson and M. Syrquin, *Industrialization and Growth: A Comparative Study* (New York: Oxford University Press, 1986), pp. ix, 1.

6. Indeed, the 1980s were termed the "Industrial Decade for Africa," with agreement that the 1990s should be called "The Second Industrial Decade for Africa." See also the texts of the two key initiatives proposed by African leaders in the 1980s: *The Lagos Plan of Action for the Economic Development of Africa, 1980–2000* and *A Programme for the Industrial Development Decade for Africa*, and reconfirmed, for instance, in the Economic Commission for Africa's July 1989 report *African Alternative Framework to Structural Adjustment Programmes for Socio-Economic Recovery and Transformation*.

7. This arose, in large measure, because of the method by which the final text was agreed, with considerable redrafting following from a range of meetings with scholars, politicians, and potential critics especially from within Africa.

8. See R. C. Riddell et al., *Manufacturing Africa: Performance and Prospects of Seven Countries in Sub-Saharan Africa* (London: James Currey, 1990) for an analysis of the development of manufacturing and future prospects of the sector in seven countries: Botswana, Cameroon, Côte d'Ivoire, Kenya, Nigeria, Zambia, and Zimbabwe. Criteria for country selection included the following: the absolute amount of manufacturing value added (MVA), the rate of growth of MVA and the MVA/GDP (gross domestic product) ratio.

9. A. F. Ewing, *Industry in Africa* (London: Oxford University Press, 1968), p. xiii.

10. A catch-all term by which is meant to convey a number of outcomes such as the closing down of enterprises and the contraction of particular industrial subsectors, a reduction in the importance of manufacturing in overall production resulting in both the need to allocate more foreign exchange to the purchase of imports that are no longer substituted and a reduction in the (albeit small) amounts of foreign exchange earned through manufactured exports.

11. Expanding manufactured exports is a constituent part of a strategy for the future growth and evolution of the manufacturing sector. It is not envisaged that manufacturing exports would replace primary product exports, at least not for some time: most countries in SSA are likely to continue to face foreign exchange shortages even if substantial manufacturing export expansion were to occur.

12. Because data may be inaccurate, and because different organizations use different groupings of countries to refer to the region "Sub-Saharan Africa," all discussion of quantitative data and trends in performance need to be treated with extreme caution.

13. World Bank, *World Development Report 1988* (Washington: World

Bank, 1988), pp. 236–237; World Bank, *World Development Report 1991* (Washington: World Bank, 1991), pp. 214–215.

14. World Bank, *World Bank Development Report 1986* (Washington: World Bank, 1986), pp. 184–185.

15. World Bank, *World bank Development Report 1988*, pp. 248–249.

16. United Nations Conference on Trade and Development (UNCTAD), *Handbook of International Trade and Development Statistics (supplement)* (New York: United Nations, 1983); United Nations Conference on Trade and Development (UNCTAD), *Handbook of International Trade and Development Statistics (supplement)* (New York: United Nations, 1987).

17. See, for instance, H.B. Chenery, "Patterns of Industrial growth," *American Economic Review* 50, (September 1960); S. R. Lewis, *Economic Policy and Industrial Growth in Pakistan* (London: Allen and Unwin, 1971); Chenery et al., *Industrialization.*

18. The approach to *sources of growth* analysis differs marginally from country to country. For Botswana and Kenya see J. Sharpley, S. Lewis and C. Harvey, "Botswana," in R. C. Riddell et al., *Manufacturing Africa*; J. Sharpley and S. Lewis, "Kenya: The Manufacturing Sector to the mid-1980s," in R. C. Riddell et al., *Manufacturing Africa*). O_i was the value of output of industry i, M_i the value of imports of the same industrial classification, Z_i the value of total domestic supply (Z_i=Oi_1+M_i), and X_i the value of exports from industry i; then by subtraction Di (=Z_i–X_i) is domestic demand for goods of the i'th industry; ui can be defined as the ratio of domestic production to total supply. All the values are at domestic market prices. The change in output (ΔO) for any industry between year 1 and year 2 can then be partitioned as follows:

$$\Delta O = u_1 (D_2 - D_1) + u_1 (X_2 - X_1) + (u_2 - u_1)Z_2$$

For the Zimbabwean *sources of growth* analysis, the equation used was:

$$\delta O = O_1 \times \delta DD/(O + M)_1 + O_1 \times \delta X/(O + M)_1 + \{ O_{2/}(O + M)_2 - O_{1/}/O + M_1\} \times (O + M)_2$$ where

O=Gross Output

DD=Domestic Demand

X=Exports

M=Imports.

19. The time periods for these figures are as follows: Botswana: 1973–74 to 1982–83; Kenya: 1970 to 1984; Nigeria:1963 to 1983; Zimbabwe: 1964–65 to 1982–83.

20. In the case of both Côte d'Ivoire and Zambia, however, it is apparent that import substitution was an important source of growth in the 1960s with, in the case of Zambia, import substitution exceeding domestic demand in the respective ratios of 55% and 44%.

21. Botswana would provide an exception here especially in the post-1980 period, where mining development has been a significant "motor" of development while in Zambia the importance of agriculture has been continually eclipsed by the vagaries of the copper mining industry.

22. Apparent consumption is the term used to describe domestic production plus imports less exports. A closely related ratio—production as a percentage of apparent consumption (P/AC)—indicates the degree to which con-

sumption of manufactured products is derived from domestic production as opposed to the importation of the products domestically consumed. Thus a P/AC score of 100 suggests that domestic consumption is the result entirely of domestic production and a score of 0 that domestic consumption occurs completely as a result of importing. A score in excess of 100 shows that the country is an exporter as more of the product in question is being produced than being consumed.

23. Data on fertilizer consumption and imports available from studies carried out by the Food and Agriculture Organization (FAO) of the UN show that in the years 1980 to 1985, SSA imported some 88% of its total fertilizer requirements, totaling 910,700 tons of nutrients, rising from 82% at the start of the period to an astounding 93% by 1985, most of which were obtained from the OECD countries and from Eastern Europe. Food and Agriculture Organization of the United Nations (FAO), *Supplement to the Report of the Feasibility Study on Expanding the Provision of Agricultural Inputs as Aid-in-Kind*, C.87/20-Sup. 1. September (Rome: FAO, 1987).

24. Sharpley et al., "Botswana."

25. The rise in manufactured exports from Mauritius has been a relatively recent phenomenon, and even by 1983 manufactured exports from Côte d'Ivoire, Kenya and Zimbabwe still exceeded those from Mauritius.

26. UNCTAD, *Handbook* (1987) trade data reveal that for developing Africa as a whole, 47% of manufacturing exports went to other African countries in 1970, but the share dropped to 24% by 1984. As Zehander, "Regional Cooperation in Perspective: Some Experiences in Sub-Saharan Africa," *The Courier*, 112 (November-December 1988): 57, comments in this context: "The relative export success of countries like Côte d'Ivoire, Cameroon, Kenya, Nigeria and Zimbabwe in their respective regions has less to do with the regional 'economic community' machinery (which at best has a strengthening role) than with the historical structure of their industrial sectors."

27. Such as measure of effective protection and the domestic resource cost.

28. For details of the Zimbabwe experience see R.C. Riddell, "Zimbabwe," in R. C. Riddell et al., *Manufacturing Africa* and R. C. Riddell, *ACP Export Diversification: The Case of Zimbabwe*, Working Paper No. 38 (London: Overseas Development Institute, 1990).

29. In Zimbabwe, Central African Cables (CAFCA) could be considered an example of a manufacturing company that in the 1980s changed from being domestically to export-oriented. It expanded exports fourfold to over $4.5 million from 1986 to 1988 and was expecting to raise the value by a further 16 percent in 1989; 35% of production was geared to export market in 1988. The company attributes its successes to a massive investment program, management commitment to exporting, and a sustained export drive among others. While almost all exports are to the regional market these markets have been secured both by overcoming South African and overseas competition.

30. These are discussed in the next section.

31. As C.D. Jebuni, J. Love and D.J.C. Forsyth, "Market Structure and LDCs' Manufactured Export Performance," *World Development* 16, 12 (December 1988): 1518, comment: "Where market power is positively related

to export performance, policy emphasis on eliminating monopolistic elements or creating small competitive establishments to promote exports of manufactured goods may be misplaced. Measures to restrict the development of large firms in favor of small competing firms may be counterproductive. The simultaneous positive influence on export performance of economies of scale suggests that export success may depend on having a concentrated domestic market structure which allows companies to enjoy scale economies domestically and thereby to achieve unit costs at which companies can compete abroad."

32. See, for instance, S. Caulkin, *The New Manufacturing: Minimal IT for Maximum Profit*, Economist Special Report (London: Economist Publications and Computer Weekly, 1989); and United Nations Industrial Development Organization (UNIDO), *New Technologies and Industrialization Prospects for Developing Countries, Main Policy Issues*, Issue Paper Prepared for Expert Group on Prospects for Industrialization Policies in Developing Countries Taking into Account the Impact of Developments in the Field of New and High Technologies (Vienna: UNIDO, April 1989).

33. In its 1990 Annual Report, the IFC makes similar comments about the negative effects of structural adjustment policies for investment in the short term, as well as the hoped-for revival in the longer term.

34. W. Lütkenhorst, "Challenges from New Trends in Foreign Direct Investment," *InterEconomics* (September/October 1988).

35. Some of the points raised here are derived from L. Cockcroft and R. C. Riddell, *Foreign Investment in Sub-Saharan Africa*, Working Paper WPS, No. 619 (Washington: World Bank, March 1991).

36. B. Grosh, "Public, Quasi-Public and Private Manufacturing Firms in Kenya: The Surprising Case of a Cliché Gone Astray," *Development Policy Review* 8, 1 (1990).

37. The details are spelled out in the previous section.

Chapter Seven

Coping with Confusion: African Farmers' Responses to Economic Instability in the 1970s and 1980s

SARA BERRY

For most countries in Sub-Saharan Africa, the 1980s were years of economic decline, marked by escalating levels of external debt and debt service obligations. In the short term, the crisis of the 1980s may be traced to a particularly unfavorable sequence of environmental and world market shocks in the 1970s, compounded by policies that reflected recently independent African governments' struggles to consolidate their power, rather than any consistent set of economic plans.[1] In addition to declining levels of income, output, basic services, and in some cases capital stock, African economies faced increasing instability in external markets, government policy, and domestic economic conditions. The impact of global and national instability on indicators of macroeconomic performance in Africa has been reviewed elsewhere.[2] In this chapter, I will look at how external shocks, together with shifts in government policies, have affected the conditions under which most Africans live and work; describe some of the strategies Africans have used to cope with instability; and explore their implications for understanding recent trends in economic performance, especially in agriculture.

My argument about how African farmers cope with instability, and how their strategies have affected recent trends in agricultural performance, derives partly from the general literature on how low-income farmers in developing economies cope with risk and uncertainty. Low-income farmers have trouble coping with risk not because they are innately conservative, but because they are poor. Because they have few assets (and hence little or no access to credit) to tide them over periods of poor harvest or shortfalls in income, they often choose crops, methods of production, or off-farm activities likely to yield some income (in cash or kind) at regular, short intervals, rather than those which might yield higher returns, but only at longer or less regular intervals. In this respect, African farmers are like poor farmers in other parts of the world.

In addition, African farmers' reactions to instability reflect the specific conditions under which they live and work. These have, in turn, been influenced not only by ecological and cultural conditions, which vary from one locality in Africa to another, but also by historical patterns of social and political change. In this chapter, I will examine the recent history of agrarian crisis in Sub-Saharan Africa in terms of the longer history of agrarian change since the beginning of colonial rule. I will argue that people's strategies for generating a livelihood and managing assets reflect the conditions under which they gain access to the means of production. Access to the means of production in rural areas of Africa has been subject to instability and struggle since colonial times. Accordingly, recent patterns of production and investment are best understood as outcomes of a conjuncture between long-term patterns of contested access to productive resources, and the increasing volatility of rural economic conditions since the 1970s.

The chapter is organized as follows. The first section describes recent patterns and sources of instability in rural income earning opportunities, including frequent shifts in government policies. This is followed by a brief discussion of the longer-term dynamic of struggle over access to the means of agricultural production in Sub-Saharan Africa; a section on farmers' strategies for coping with destabilization; and a concluding section on the implications of individuals' coping strategies for agricultural performance.

Recent Crises (1973–88)

Since the late 1960s, much of Sub-Saharan Africa has been subjected to a series of shocks, including major droughts, war, large increases in world oil prices, global recession, and declining export prices, which put severe strains on governments struggling to establish stable systems of self-government and launch sustained programs of economic development. The combination of world recession, mounting African debt, and increasingly depressed conditions within African economies undermined investors' confidence, contributing to a vicious cycle of declining private capital inflows which, together with stagnant or declining export earnings and purchasing power, forced African governments not only to borrow more from official sources in the 1980s but also to handle a large part of their mounting debt service obligations by rescheduling or accumulating arrears.[3]

In addition to declining levels of income and access to basic commodities and services, both world market conditions and many of the measures governments have taken to cope with them served to destabilize domestic markets and income-earning opportunities. In addition to the external shocks that helped to precipitate economic decline in Africa, since 1970, global commodity prices have fluctuated more widely than before.[4] Global commodity price instability and fluctuations in Sub-Saharan Africa's barter terms of trade made it difficult for governments to predict, let alone offset, the impact of world price shocks on their domestic economies. In a study of 58 developing economies, Guillaumont argued that the impact of unstable export volumes (as well as prices) on savings and growth was negative for all developing economies, but more so for low-income countries, many of which are in Sub-Saharan Africa.[5]

External instability was especially costly in Sub-Saharan Africa because of African economies' heavy dependence on imports. In a study of 24 African economies, Helleiner found significant negative relationships between (1) the annual rate of growth of GDP and instability of import volume, and (2) growth and the income terms of trade for the entire period from 1960 to 1980.[6] He concludes that, by the 1980s, there was little African governments could do to reverse the decline, without access to substantially larger flows of external resources than were currently available or projected.[7]

Volatile world market prices helped to destabilize agricultural prices and incomes within African economies both directly through fluctuations in farmers' earnings from export crops, and indirectly through fluctuations in the cost of imported foodstuffs and hence in demand for domestically produced substitutes. In attempting to maintain adequate supplies of imports and domestic foodstuffs, donor agencies and African governments sometimes adopted coping strategies that further destabilized domestic markets and conditions of production. Price and exchange controls drove an increasing volume of transactions into parallel markets, subjecting traders to added risks and the expense of concealment or bribery.[8] Crash programs in agricultural development such as Operation Feed the Nation (Nigeria) or Operation Feed Yourself (Ghana) were undertaken in the mid-70s, only to be abandoned within a few years for lack of funds or results. Cooperatives, planned villages, local development committees, etc., were created and dismantled, or sidelined, with bewildering frequency.[9]

In the 1980s, African governments found themselves unable to maintain basic infrastructure and services, such as transportation, education, and health.[10] Without money to maintain imports of crucial intermediate goods (gasoline, tires, vehicle parts, medicine, etc.) basic services declined, crippling the production and the marketing of agricultural as well as industrial goods.[11] In some countries (e.g., Zambia, Ghana, Tanzania) these developments compounded processes of decline that had been underway since the 1960s.

In the context of declining imports and mounting external debt, structural adjustment programs undertaken in the 1980s proved sharply contractionary.[12] Urban incomes fell, sometimes sharply. In a startling passage, which praises African governments for making progress in correcting urban-rural bias, the Bank noted some dramatic shifts in urban-rural income ratios: "In Tanzania, between 1980 and 1984, real farm incomes are estimated to have risen by 5%, while urban wage earners faced a decline of 50%. . . . In Ghana, during the same period, farm incomes stagnated but urban incomes fell by 40%. Such evidence leaves little doubt that the reforming governments have helped (sic) to raise the terms of trade between the countryside and the city"![13]

As expected, labor and capital did move back into agriculture after devaluation but, once there, faced volatile prices and unreliable transport and marketing services, which added to the uncertainty of returns to labor and working capital caused by weather, pest and disease attack, and the normal vicissitudes of domestic and local economic life.[14] The dilemmas of volatility were reflected in contradictory relations between agriculture and the nonagricultural sectors. At the same time that people were moving into agriculture to escape severe declines in urban incomes, studies of rural households found that household food security depended critically on access to income from non-farm activities, such as crafts, petty trade, and wage employment.[15] In Zambia, foreign exchange was so scarce that allocations were shifted unpredictably, as the government veered from one stopgap measure to another, in an effort to stave off pressures from foreign creditors, suppliers, and/or domestic interest groups. Good estimates that as much as one-third of the maize purchased from Zambian farmers in 1985 was never collected. While causes of this debacle were complex, it is significant that foreign exchange allotments for imports of diesel fuels, tires, and jute bags were inexplicably diverted at the last minute.[16]

Poor farmers suffered from unstable domestic markets for crops and basic consumer goods, but instability also posed problems for large-scale farms, the more so as they tend to be fully commercialized. In northern Ghana, large upland rice farms launched in the mid-70s with sizeable government subsidies declined when the subsidies were withdrawn a few years later.[17] In Nigeria, even multinational corporations found large-scale farming unprofitable because of uncertainties of labor supply and prices.[18]

In short, there is considerable evidence that conditions under which rural household members live and work have been extremely unstable in recent years. Not only have prices fluctuated widely, but access to off-farm employment, foodstuffs, basic consumer goods, agricultural inputs, transportation, health care, and education have also been subject to severe and unpredictable fluctuations.[19] To understand how rural household members have struggled to escape impoverishment and cope with instability, and how their struggles have shaped agricultural performance, we must look at the conditions under which farmers gain access to the means of production. These, as will be argued in the next section, have been subject to instability and tension since colonial times.

Contested Access to the Means of Production.

In recent years, there has been a growing interest among students of African rural development in understanding conditions of access to the means of production in rural economies. This interest has been sparked in part by the limited effectiveness of many rural development programs in Africa. Many observers have noted the persistence of traditional systems of land tenure, agricultural production, and labor and credit mobilization in rural African economies, but they do not agree on its implications for patterns of resource allocation and agricultural growth. On one hand, there is ample evidence that neither traditional land tenure practices nor the absence of formal credit institutions in rural areas blocked agricultural growth and commercialization in the past.[20] Market activity has been widespread in rural areas of Africa for a long time, and has encompassed commercial transactions in productive inputs and services, as well as in final goods.[21]

Nonetheless, the conviction remains that African rural factor markets are very imperfect.[22] Development experts frequently assert that communal tenure is widespread in Africa and results in serious misallocation of productive resources, over time as well as among crops and farms.[23] Hence, it is argued, sustained growth of agricultural output and productivity will require a radical transformation of the conditions under which African farmers gain access to the means of production.[24] It is less fashionable to criticize family labor and informal credit arrangements as inefficient, but they are presumed to be noncommercial and, hence, potentially inhibiting to rural development.

Part of the apparent contradiction between those who tout the prevalence of the market principle in rural Africa, and those who emphasize the crippling effects of market imperfections and/or precapitalist modes of production, arises from the conceptual framework of the debate. Actual changes in conditions of access over time cannot be accurately described in terms of dichotomies such as private vs. communal ownership, or commercial vs. social mechanisms of resource mobilization and management. Since precolonial times access to productive resources has been predicated on social identity defined by membership and/or status within social groups, including families, communities, political factions, religious brotherhoods, etc.[25]

However, it does not follow that rural African economies were characterized by communal property rights or collective modes of labor mobilization and management. Access to resources was contingent on membership in descent groups or communities, but the boundaries of such groups were overlapping and fluid. When a community or lineage incorporated new members, through marriage, slavery, fostering, etc., newcomers were assigned culturally sanctioned positions: wife, slave, child, client, disciple within the relevant group. However, the way culturally defined status was translated into specific rights to land and labor, obligations to work for or pay tribute to others, etc., varied from one individual or group to another, depending on relations among the particular people involved. In some cases, the process of absorbing new members into established groups could lead to the redefinition of criteria for membership, or of rules governing relations among group members. In some areas, for example, slaves were fully absorbed into the descent groups of their masters, even adopting new ethnic identities over the course of a generation or two[26], while in others, descendants of slaves retained separate and inferior status for generations.[27] Changing economic and political conditions gave rise both to new claims on land and labor and to new rounds of struggle over the definition of social identity and the meaning of status.

However, negotiations over the meaning of social identity or status could prove inconclusive, or be reopened when circumstances changed, creating tension and ambiguity rather than a clear reformulation of the rules. In such circumstances, exchanges of rights to land and labor were neither subordinated to the market principle nor exempt from it. Access to land, labor, and capital was acquired not through definitive transactions in rights of exclusive access and control, but through the negotiation of social identities which were themselves fluid and multifaceted. For example, in Asante, slaves who sought assimilation into local descent groups were aided by a taboo on speaking openly of anyone's slave origin, but hindered by their mothers' inability to trace legitimate descent from local matrilineages.[28] In central Kenya, the ritual of blood brotherhood was used to facilitate trade and migration by creating fictive kinship ties among trading partners, but it was sometimes repudiated by communities seeking to protect themselves from floods of immigrants in times of scarcity.[29] Similarly, in societies where bridewealth was paid in installments, sometimes completed after the death of the married couple, marriage was not a single event, but a lifetime process.[30]

Negotiations over social relations frequently involved exchanges of goods and/or money as gifts, bridewealth, or through ceremonies marking changes in status or social membership. In this way, the accelerating pace of rural commercialization in the twentieth century could act to reinforce traditional mechanisms of resource acquisition, rather than overthrowing them or rendering them obsolete. Bridewealth inflation, the monetization of older forms of tribute, which often accompanied the spread of cash cropping, and the ubiquity of rotating credit societies are all examples of this process. But commercialization also intensified the pace of renegotiation, rendering the specific meaning of traditional social status more changeable at the same time that it reinforced the salience of status in general as a means of defining access to productive resources.

If commercialization did not lead to a revolution in African rural factor markets, neither did the creation of colonial (later national) boundaries and systems of government. Colonial administrators brought European ideas about property, contract, and credit to Africa, but lacked the means to transform African systems of access along European lines. When they attempted to do this directly—e.g., through forced labor or by rounding up scattered, mobile peoples into permanent settlements—they succeeded mainly in disrupting indigenous methods of production and resource management. The decline of *citemene* agriculture in northeastern Zambia is a case in point.

Most colonial regimes in Africa were expected to pay their own way, raising revenue from their colonial subjects and employing Africans to supplement the often very limited numbers of European staff provided by their home governments.[31]

Elsewhere, colonial authorities tried to govern by indirect rule, mobilizing not only African labor, but also local collaborators—Africans in positions of traditional authority who could help collect taxes, mobilize labor, and keep order.[32] In addition to coopting or creating African chiefs as local agents of colonial rule, European administrators sought to maintain a stable social order in the colonies by coopting traditional systems of law and governance. Indirect rule, as this strategy was known, entailed the preservation of native law and custom, not just as a smokescreen for European extraction of Africa's resources, but also as a practical method of keeping down the costs of colonial administration.

When they were unable to find suitable traditional authorities, officials created them. Known as warrant chiefs, such individuals lacked traditional legitimacy, were exempt from established constraints on the abuse of power, and formed an unpopular and often destabilizing element in local systems of colonial government.[33] And, as with African chiefs, so with African cultures: when colonial officials did not find established, clearly bounded, homogeneous and mutually exclusive tribal polities on which to build the foundations of a stable, inexpensive system of government, they created them by carving out tribal reserves or demarcating large areas of social life to be governed according to native law and custom.

Neither warrant chiefs nor warrant cultures worked very well. Since precolonial lines of authority and social boundaries were often changing or contested, indirect rule meant, in practice, that conflict and instability were incorporated into the fabric of colonial administration.[34] To the extent that rules of access and/or processes of law enforcement and adjudication in African societies were already subject to contest and change, indirect rule tended to internalize struggle and instability, in the name of stable government and continuity with the past. Rights to land, labor, and capital goods (such as livestock or tree crops) continued to rest on social identity, but social identities were now subject not only to redefinition through shifting relations among Africans, but also to ambiguities arising from the colonizers' efforts to build a stable administration on inherently unstable or dynamic systems of customary rules and practices.

Conditions of access remained ambiguous and contested after independence. The policies of colonial regimes after 1945 were profoundly influenced by the global depression of the 1930s, and a growing concern among colonial officials with soil erosion, deforestation, and other signs of environmental degradation in Africa.[35] In Europe and the United States, the depression and the dust bowls of the 1930s stimulated the development of Keynesian economics and both public and scientific concern with conservation. Together, these developments generated a powerful rationale for increased state intervention in the management of productive resources and economic activity.

In Africa, they helped to legitimize what has been called the second colonial occupation.[36] After 1945, colonial regimes introduced comprehensive new programs of economic management in Africa, including large-scale development projects (the Tanganyika

Groundnut Scheme, the Niger Agricultural Project, an expanded Gezira Scheme, etc.); increased levels of public spending on infrastructure, amenities, and education; and legislation designed to rationalize land tenure or regulate conditions of labor supply on a national scale. At the local level, however, increased state intervention continued to be administered through Native Authorities, until the 1950s when, in many colonies, African nationalists' demands for self-government helped to sweep aside gradualist programs for economic and administrative reforms, in favor of rapid decolonization.[37]

To a large extent, independent African governments carried on the late colonial legacy of expanded state intervention in the management of national economies. Development schemes proliferated, government spending on infrastructure and administration increased, and government controls over prices and trade were greatly expanded.[38] All of this cost money, which was raised in large part through taxes on agriculture. State development programs also generated sharp increases in demand for imports, prompting governments to try to control import spending by expanding controls over foreign trade and payments, policies that were to continue in one form or another until the 1980s.[39]

Some independent African governments also launched ambitious schemes to transform conditions of access to the means of production. Land reform laws enacted in Kenya, Senegal, Côte d'Ivoire, and later Nigeria, were intended to rationalize the land tenure system in order to promote more productive patterns of resource use, and faster rates of agricultural growth. In the minds of their promulgators, influx controls and orders to expel aliens could be seen as logical (and therefore legitimate?) extensions of the idea that economic development requires massive state intervention into conditions of production and exchange.

In practice, increased state intervention did not lead to a dramatic transformation of conditions of access at the local level. Like their colonial predecessors, African governments have struggled to govern and promote expanded economic activity with limited funds and trained personnel, and have also sought to coopt local resources and authorities to strengthen their own administrative and fiscal capacity. Zambian chiefs, stripped of their prerogatives in the first flush of post-independence enthusiasm for modernization, regained them as government-created institutions failed to deliver promised services, solve disputes, or effectively regulate access to local resources. In Nigeria, chiefs' powers were reduced more gradually, but proved equally hard to eliminate even after several decades of independence.

For purposes of both administration and political mobilization, African leaders appealed to traditional rubrics of loyalty and legitimacy, often sharpening ethnic conflict in the process. If anything, independent African governments acted to increase the political salience of social identity, strengthening people's incentives to use them as channels of access to resources and opportunities. Accordingly, the panoply of increasingly comprehensive and costly government measures to regulate economic activity, which were initiated after 1945 and extended and elaborated after independence, enhanced and perpetuated struggles to use social identity to gain access to resources. In the process, they also reproduced the tendency for rules of access to be challenged repeatedly. Land-reform programs and development projects created new arenas of contest and introduced new resources to struggle over, rather than decisively redefining the rules of the game. Controls on prices, imports, and exchange rates erected new barriers to be lowered or evaded through negotiation, bribery, or the manipulation of political loyalties. In rural Zambia in the late 1970s, one observer found that access to land and labor was not so much shaped by development policies and their intended and unintended consequences as by arbitration sessions, which were chaired by the chief, in which land and headmanships were discussed and by local court sittings which dealt mostly with disputes between cowives. [40]

In short, access to resources was mediated through a complex process, in which income and wealth were used to influence social identities, and vice versa. Two consequences of the dynamic of resource access and control outlined here are of particular relevance to the present argument. The first was a tendency for claims on land or other forms of property to multiply over time. Because social identities and statuses were subject to change over time, claims on resources that hinged on social identity tended to change too. As one ethnographer put it, in discussing rights to tree crops in Cameroon, even when a farm was sold outright to a single individual in exchange for cash, that farm did not thereby become a piece of private property in the Western sense. Rather, over time, other members of social networks to which the purchaser belonged were likely to assert claims to the farm as relatives, heirs, former laborers, etc.[41] Similar patterns are described in studies of other rural economies across Africa.[42]

Second, since social identity and status could be achieved as well as ascribed, Africans also had strong incentives to invest time and money in acquiring or validating their membership in social networks, and/or advancing their status within them. Numerous studies of rural expenditure patterns have noted that farmers' outlays on ceremonies do not appear to wither away under the influence of rural commercialization or economic growth. On the contrary, in areas where expanding economic opportunities intensified competition for access to productive resources, farmers have often increased their investment in social relations through which they may assert or defend claims to the means of production.

As the foregoing discussion suggests, while both traditional and nontraditional social networks were important as channels of access to resources, they were not necessarily stable. By investing in social identity or status, farmers were not buying into closed, corporate, consensual communities, as Ranger describes the colonial stereotype of traditional African societies,[43] but rather into social arenas where people pursued influence and opportunity through shifting alliances or by contesting the boundaries or structures of the networks themselves. Boundaries of social networks have, accordingly, remained fluid and permeable, and institutions have tended to proliferate over time. It is within this context that farmers have organized their efforts to cope with increasing economic instability and decline since the early 1970s.

Coping with Instability

Literature on poor farmers' strategies for coping with risk often assumes that poor farmers are more averse to risk than prosperous or technically sophisticated ones and that, accordingly, they follow different strategies of resource use. This does not mean that poor farmers are inherently more conservative than wealthier ones. All farmers face unpredictable variations in yield (due to weather, disease, etc.) and price. Such uncertainties increase the cost of engaging in agricultural production: when yields or farm incomes are abnormally low, farmers must draw down assets or go into debt to provide for current needs. Prosperous farmers are no more indifferent to these problems than poor ones. They do, however, have more resources with which to cover the costs of providing insurance against sudden downturns in their revenues. Also, they are in a better position to take advantage of new opportunities and thereby strengthen their economic position over time. In the long run, the best way to increase one's economic security is to raise income or accumulate assets.

For poor farmers, however, access to opportunities to produce or earn more may be so limited that they provide little real protection against instability. At the least, increasing agricultural output or productivity is likely to take time, whereas the effects of sudden shifts in prices or output are immediate. Poor farmers are not, in other words, averse to maximizing profits; however, the concept of profit maximization conflates too many dimensions of farmers' strategies of resource acquisition and use to shed much light on behavior in specific contexts. In situations of unstable access to markets and resources, and/or unstable returns to productive activity, people are likely to make efforts to increase liquidity and to gain flexibility in the timing of labor inputs and other income-generating activities in order to be able to respond quickly to changes in economic conditions.

In this section I will describe some of the steps taken by African farmers to gain additional liquidity and flexibility in the face of fluctuations in output, prices, or access to input and commodity markets. In particular, I will discuss increased reliance on off-farm income, changes in cropping patterns and methods of cultivation, and patterns of investment. Few if any studies exist which trace precisely changes in the form and frequency of such activities in the wake of the world recession or the adoption of structural adjustment policies by African governments in the early 1980s. Instead, this discussion will draw on studies of farmers' methods of coping with instability in a variety of time periods to suggest some of the ways in which the recent destabilization of economic conditions in Africa may have altered or reinforced previous patterns of resource allocation and income use. The final section of the chapter will consider the implications of these effects for understanding the impact of recent destabilization on African agricultural performance.

Off-farm Income

Several recent studies have argued convincingly that access to off-farm income increases households' food security. Using data on household income and consumption from two villages in Burkina Faso, Reardon, et al. found that, in 1984 (a year of severe drought), the proportion of households with consumption security was higher in the Sahelian than in the Sudanic village, even though agricultural productivity is lower in the Sahel.[44] (Consumption security is defined as a level of food consumption at least 80% of FAO minimum calorie requirements for household members.) The Sahelians had an advantage: they earned a higher proportion of household income from off-farm sources. This enabled them to maintain consumption in the face of abnormally low yields more effectively than households in the Sudanic village, who derived a larger proportion of total real income from crop production and sales. The authors suggest, further, that farmers in the Sahelian village had come to rely on off-farm employment to a greater extent than those in the south, *because* their environment was generally poor and subject to frequent severe shortfalls in yield, leading them to spend more time and travel greater distances in search of opportunities for wage- or self-employment.

Although Reardon, et al., did not trace changes in households' income sources over time, their findings suggest that, if agricultural production and marketing become increasingly unstable, farmers may well increase their efforts to gain access to additional sources of off-farm income, in order to protect their levels of consumption and investment. Common sources of off-farm income are (a) working for other local farmers, (b) trade or other rural non-farm enterprises, and (c) migration in search of employment or opportunities for self-employment in more prosperous regions. Each has somewhat different implications for agricultural performance.

One way to supplement farm income is for members of farming households to hire themselves out to more prosperous neighbors. In addition, people who seek to increase their income security by hiring out may try to obtain shorter contracts, in order to gain greater flexibility in allocating their own time, or to reduce the time intervals between receipts of wages, in cash or in kind. Instability would therefore help to explain the trend, noted in a number of studies, toward daily or task contracts, as opposed to annual or permanent labor arrangements.[45]

Farmers may also seek off-farm income by engaging in trade. Diversification into trade often occurs as a result of agricultural growth. Farmers who have made some money from cash crop production invest part of their profits in local trade, either buying agricultural produce for sale to wholesalers or agents of marketing boards[46] or purchasing consumption goods or agricultural inputs to retail in rural markets.[47]

However, farmers may also move into trade in response to market destabilization. Unstable markets increase the risks and reduce the average returns to both trade and farming, but trade entails greater liquidity. Crops take weeks or months to mature, during which time prices of crops, labor, and other variable inputs may change dramatically, leaving the farmer exposed to considerable risk. Although traders may find themselves stuck with unsold inventories, they are not locked into biologically determined production periods of several weeks' or months' duration, as are farmers. A small stock of trade goods can usually be turned over fairly quickly, so that traders are in a better position than farmers to get out of a declining market and move into a more favorable one on short notice. The relative liquidity of trade compared to farming does not mean that trading profits are high: for many petty traders in both rural and urban areas in Africa they are miserably low. But for people who must cope with unstable markets in addition to poverty, trade may appear preferable to farming because of its liquidity.

The fact that farmers may be attempting to increase their involvement in off-farm employment (or self-employment) does not mean that employment opportunities will automatically increase to accommodate them. Opportunities depend on the level of demand in regional or even national economies, and on transportation facilities, etc., linking rural areas to centers of demand. Individual efforts to increase income or avert risk will reap higher returns in a prosperous economy than in a poor one. This does not mean, however, that people won't use similar strategies to cope with similar problems in both cases.

My point may be illustrated with a brief comparison of farmers' strategies in northeastern Zambia and western Nigeria during the 1970s. In both countries, national economic conditions were increasingly unstable during this decade, but Zambia was involved in a prolonged recession brought on by the collapse of the world copper price, whereas Nigeria was in the midst of the oil boom.

Once a flourishing labor reserve, which exported male labor to the copper belt and received substantial flows of remittances in return,[48] the Mambwe area in northeastern Zambia was badly hurt by the collapse of the world copper market in the early 1970s.[49] By 1978, the region was severely depressed, suffering from poor dietary variation and an unprecedented shortage of basic foodstuffs. [50] While many former miners and their relatives had returned to the rural areas,[51] Pottier found that many had not returned to farming, but were eking out a precarious living in petty trade. The preference for trade over farming was strikingly illustrated by the Mambwe response to high prices for beans. Although bean cropping was warmly recommended by local politicians and town planners, and sales increased, bean fever has not resulted in land development and higher levels of local agricultural production. Rather the opposite is true, for the Zambian grassland Mambwe prefer to buy up cheap beans, and millet, in villages across the border in Tanzania.[52] In this way, they shielded themselves against the possibility that the government would change its mind and reduce the price again before a full cropping season had passed leaving them with a harvest of beans that could be sold only at a loss.[53]

I encountered a similar response to destabilized markets in western Nigeria in the 1970s. In this case, aggregate demand was growing rapidly, due to Nigeria's booming petroleum exports. The effect of the oil boom on low-income households in western Nigeria was, in many ways, a mirror image of the impact of the copper recession in northeastern Zambia. Soaring foreign exchange earnings led to rapid growth in demand for imports, and considerable domestic inflation. Prices of food crops and other agricultural staples rose even faster than the general price index, but this apparently did not lead to significant growth in agricultural production. Instead, people devoted their energy and working capital to acquiring imported goods and reselling them in local markets. In Nigeria's booming petro-economy, where anyone who could buy a sack of rice or wheat flour could resell it at a profit in a few weeks or even days, there was little incentive to invest money or labor in cultivating crops that would require months to mature, might yield poorly, and whose price might decline relative to prices of other goods between planting and harvest time.[54]

In addition to trade and agricultural employment, rural household members also migrate out of rural areas in search of opportunities for off-farm employment or self-employment. Fluctuations in employment opportunities in urban areas are transmitted to rural communities through variations in the incomes and remittances of rural migrants, as well as in domestic and global demand for agricultural commodities. Both mechanisms contribute, in turn, to the destabilization of rural living conditions in the wake of fluctuations in global markets. In addition, whether or not migrants remit part of their earnings,[55] the withdrawal of labor from agriculture often induces changes in cropping patterns and methods of cultivation, which reinforce patterns of production that farmers use to cope with increasingly unstable markets.

Cropping Patterns

Faced with increasing economic instability, farmers may shift resources into the cultivation of crops (or combinations of crops) which increase their liquidity or allow them more flexibility in the allocation of labor time. Liquid crops include those which are readily saleable and/or mature relatively quickly. Flexible crops are those whose yields are relatively insensitive to the timing of labor inputs. In other words, the search for liquidity may lead farmers to sell a higher proportion of their output, contrary to the popular notion that risk aversion causes farmers to withdraw from markets and become self-sufficient. In a recent study of the famine of 1941 in Malawi, Vaughan questioned the view that increased tobacco cultivation by smallholders in the 1930s contributed to the famine.[56] In fact, tobacco growing households were better able to withstand the famine, since they could buy food when their own ran out. Similar points have been made in studies of households' strategies for coping with recent famines in Africa.

Faster maturing crops also increase liquidity by reducing the time farmers must wait for a return on their labor. Social scientists working on the design of technical improvements appropriate to African farming systems have suggested that maximizing yield may be less important than reducing time intervals between labor inputs and returns to them. In Rwanda, farmers interviewed by staff members from the International Potato Center were more interested in shorter maturing varieties of potatoes than in higher yielding ones.[57] Similar considerations help to explain the spread of cassava cultivation in many areas.[58]

In general, cassava and traditional varieties of swamp rice are two crops that have persisted (or spread) in recent years because they allow farmers considerable flexibility in allocating their labor time. Traditional swamp rice cultivation requires a fairly even flow of unskilled labor inputs over the growing season, whereas upland rice cultivation is characterized by seasonal peaks of labor input and requires a variety of specialized skills.[59] Swamp rice lends itself to cultivation by individuals working alone, or by unskilled hire labor. In contrast, upland rice cultivation is better suited to larger farming units, capable of mobilizing and coordinating activities of a number of people with different skills.[60] Also, yields are less dependent on the timing of labor inputs in swamp than in upland rice cultivation, another reason why swamp rice is easier to cultivate for individuals who lack access to others' labor.[61] Yields of improved rice grown on irrigated perimeters are, however, more sensitive to the timing of labor inputs, which has limited farmers' willingness to take up plots in irrigated schemes in some areas.[62]

A staple crop that allows farmers a great deal of flexibility in labor timing and income management is cassava, the cultivation of which is thought to have increased substantially in Africa in recent years.[63] Apart from planting, which must take place far enough in advance of the end of the rainy season for stakes to sprout properly, variations in the timing of inputs have little effect on yield. Mature cassava roots can remain underground without deteriorating for long periods (up to 24 months for some varieties). Thus, farmers have a great deal of leeway in managing the harvest and sale of cassava. The crop may be harvested little by little, for immediate consumption or for sale, or farmers may wait for a favorable price, then harvest the crop all at once. In other words, cassava has very flexible labor requirements and is well-suited to cultivation both by subsistence-oriented farmers and by fully commercialized ones, working with or without hired labor.

The advantages of particular crops in enhancing farmers' ability to cope with unstable markets and conditions of production depend not only on the biological characteristics of the crop and on local agroecological conditions, but also on who grows them. If, for example, married women grow wet rice on household fields, the output of which is controlled by the male head of the household, then they do not necessarily gain either flexibility or liquidity by allocating more of their labor to rice production. Studies of irrigated rice projects in West Africa suggest that new technology and resources may provoke domestic conflict and/or lead women to withdraw labor from rice growing on plots managed by their husbands or other male kin.[64] Cassava, on the other hand, is a crop women often grow on their own account, so that the advantages of flexibility accrue entirely to them. This may help to explain why women farmers have been found to rely increasingly on cassava in situations where their livelihoods are becoming increasingly precarious or subject to unpredictable changes.[65] Similarly, many swamp rice farmers are women, who have little access to extra labor and must fit cultivation into a daily schedule characterized by multiple, varying demands on their time.[66]

In short, whether or not farmers sell a larger proportion of crop output in the wake of market destabilization depends on their access to markets; on who grows what crops and on what terms; and on the availability of alternative sources of liquidity. Increasing reliance on cassava or swamp rice may be a means to increased commercialization, rather than an alternative. Similarly, more individualized cultivation can increase flexibility, by releasing farmers' time from uninterruptible tasks such as mobilizing and supervising labor for more liquid activities such as off-farm employment. I will return to this point below.

Methods of Production

Alternative techniques of cultivation also have different implications for liquidity and flexibility although, as in the case of cropping patterns, the flexibility associated with a particular technique varies from one socioeconomic context to another. For example, intercropping is frequently cited as a technique which not only saves labor and raises total yield per unit of cultivated land[67], but also stretches out the time over which a cultivated plot and the labor invested in it yield some return.[68]

However, in some localities farmers have increased monocropping in order to gain added flexibility or to reduce the waiting period between harvests. In the early 1980s, Fresco found that women in Kwango-Kwilu (Zaire) were not only cultivating more cassava, relative to other crops, but also staggering times of planting and harvest, reducing fallows, and monocropping more cassava than in the past. She concludes that "the remarkable flexibility of present farming systems . . . made . . . growth in food production possible for women with no access to labor other than their own."[69]

Similarly, Guyer found in 1988 that Yoruba women were more likely than men to specialize completely in cassava. In her sample, women's farms were smaller than men's, but more commercialized. Women hired a larger proportion of their labor and sold a larger share of their output. Guyer also found a marked increase since 1970 in the number of Yoruba women farming on their own account. Her findings are therefore consistent with my argument that instability does not necessarily lead farmers either to withdraw from markets or to diversify crop production per se.[70] On the contrary, economic instability may promote increased commercialization and specialization, even by very small-scale farm enterprises.

Patterns of Investment

Since the management of instability is, by definition, a matter of allocating resources over time, one would expect to find African farmers adjusting their strategies of investment as well as current production and income earning in the face of destabilization. I will limit my discussion to investment in stocks and social networks—two forms of investment which appear to be closely related to farmers' efforts to manage instability.[71] The argument made above about the advantages of trade relative to crop production in conditions of instability implies that farmers will invest in stocks, which can be rapidly turned over, in preference to capital goods with long gestation or payoff periods and/or limited resale markets. Such preferences are reflected in the behavior of farmers described by Pottier in northeast Zambia, by Shepherd in northern Ghana, and those I observed in western Nigeria.[72]

In addition, I would suggest that the destabilization of recent years has reinforced patterns of investment in social relations, which have had an important influence on the course of rural development in the long run. Previously in this chapter, I described a long-standing tendency for African farmers to invest in social relations as mechanisms of access to markets and the means of production, and argued that, while such investments certainly predate the colonial period, they were reinforced and expanded under colonial rule. Colonial administrators' efforts to build stable systems of government onto customary rules and structures generated unresolved debates over the meaning of custom. To protect or extend their access to productive resources in a world of contested rules and procedures, farmers were obliged to keep renewing (or, if possible, multiplying) their memberships in social networks through which access was negotiated. The resulting dynamic of struggle over resources and meanings, and investment in social status and identities, continued after independence. It has been reinforced, in recent years, by increasingly unstable conditions of resource mobilization and exchange.

For example, studies of rural expenditure patterns have shown no tendency for farmers to abandon (or even significantly reduce) expenditures on acquiring or reinforcing membership in social networks. Outlays on ceremonies, bridewealth payments, construction of family houses, or the education of close and distant kin figure as prominently in rural budgets in the 1970s and 1980s as in earlier times.[73]

In some areas, kin groups and other traditional institutions have been reorganized in an effort to keep abreast of changing economic conditions and practices. In western Nigeria in the late 1970s, descent groups were electing or appointing officers, opening bank accounts, and issuing circulars to announce annual meetings, at which kinsmen not only celebrated weddings, funerals, and naming ceremonies, or strategized over traditional title disputes, but also discussed scholarships, the management of family assets, or the launching of development projects to enrich themselves or their communities.[74]

An analogous process has been described in central Kenya, in relation to the land reform program initiated in the 1950s. Under the land reform laws, in order to register title to a piece of land, the individuals involved must first demonstrate the legitimacy of their claims. In many cases, the effect of the law legalizing private land ownership was to strengthen and enlarge descent groups (*mbari*). To raise money for litigation in order to establish claim to land titles, *mbari* not only rallied their members, but also accepted contributions from non-kin. In the event the litigation was successful, contributors would be rewarded with a piece of the land. In effect, the land reform law created a market for equity in extended families.[75]

The increased salience of social networks as means of access to productive resources does not mean either that traditional institutions provide a reliable safety net for impoverished or crisis-stricken rural households, or that corporate groups are gaining in size or importance with respect to rural resource management. For one thing, impoverishment and instability affect whole families and communities, undermining their ability to provide security for any of their members, let alone all. In declining (or unstable) economies, the returns to investment in social memberships are likely to be low (or uncertain).[76] Second, the meanings of social memberships are often contested, or redefined, as leaders compete for followers and people pursue resources and opportunities through social relationships.[77]

However, especially in rural areas, Africans do not appear to be losing interest in maintaining social networks, even if, as safety nets they tend to sag and tear. Rather, the reaction to economic decline or destabilization is often to diversify one's portfolio of social relations by proliferating memberships. Indeed, in some areas, the reproduction of extended family or community networks as mechanisms of access has gone hand in hand with a trend toward smaller units of agricultural production, as people seek flexibility in the management of their daily schedules together with diversification in their access to potential avenues of opportunity or the means of production.

For example, in Hausa communities in northern Nigeria and southern Niger, researchers have reported both a decline in the size of farming units[78] and an increase in the numbers of people asserting claims to land and other rural resources through their membership in extended families.[79] In central Kenya, farming units consist almost entirely of nuclear families[80] but, as we've seen, *mbari* have experienced a resurgence under the land reform. Similarly, observers have described simultaneous trends toward individualized cultivation and investment in extended family networks in rice-growing areas of the western humid zone and in tree crop growing areas in Nigeria, Ghana, and Côte d'Ivoire.[81]

Implications for Agricultural Performance

Instability tends to promote cropping patterns, methods of cultivation, and modes of organizing agricultural production which increase farmers' liquidity and/or permit them flexibility in the management of labor time. Cultivation of cassava and swamp rice has increased; production units have shrunk. Farmers do not withdraw from unstable markets: on the contrary, they often increase crop sales or engage in more off-farm employment in order to increase their liquidity. However, crops and techniques of production chosen on the basis of their flexibility in the short run, do not necessarily serve to enhance the sustainability of agricultural production in the long run. Under unstable economic and political conditions, farmers are reluctant to tie up land, labor, and capital in long-term projects, such as soil conservation, water control, or fixed capital formation, which may sustain soil fertility or augment available land and labor. Also, increases in time spent on off-farm employment or out-migration reinforce trends toward smaller farming units and investment in more liquid assets.

The implications of these patterns for agricultural performance and policy design are not obvious. If demand for commodities and labor is fixed in the aggregate, farmers' efforts to sell a larger share of their output and/or spend more time in off-farm employment will tend to drive down crop prices and wages, so that farmers gain liquidity and flexibility at the expense of income. In recent years of declining per capita incomes, African farmers' efforts to protect themselves against instability may therefore have intensified the impoverishment of their families and small-scale farming as a whole.

However, this argument rests on the implicit assumption that there is a relatively constant ratio between the level of real income in an economy and the volume of transactions in both commodity and labor markets—an assumption that may not hold in African rural economies. For many African farmers, selling a higher proportion of their output means that they also buy more of what they consume—a pattern that will be reinforced if time spent in off-farm employment undermines their ability to time their own farming tasks well and thus reduces their yields.[82] Also, African employers are often themselves farmers, traders, or artisans with political and social ties to the communities in which they live and work. Rather than take advantage of increasing labor supply to force down wages, they may prefer to absorb additional workers and/or dependents, thus enhancing their own status and influence within the community and, where supralocal politicians or administrators seek to work through local notables, beyond it. In such cases, farmers' efforts to increase their participation in trade, crop sales and/or off-farm employment may serve to increase the number of transactions in goods and productive services, rather than to raise or lower levels of real output. The result is a kind of inflationary process, whose effects on economic growth and distribution may well operate through changing expectations and strategies of investment, rather than through short-run shifts in prices and quantities.

Recent instability has also reinforced long-term trends toward the proliferation of social networks and people's memberships in them. Fluid, noncorporate networks have permitted such diversification, but clearly people cannot sustain regular, active participation in an indefinite number of networks. Accordingly, as social memberships proliferate, people tend to shift their attention and energy from one group or institution to another, depending on immediate needs. The result is a high degree of mobility of people and resources, but little tendency for institutions to develop into stable frameworks for collective action, resource management or the consolidation of capital and knowledge.

Thus, African farmers' struggles to cope with turbulent, unstable economic and political conditions in recent years have contributed to resource mobility and flexible patterns of production and social organization, but not necessarily to creating conditions for sustained agricultural growth, for becoming less "hemmed in." Structural adjustment policies, and other development programs predicated on the notion that markets with low barriers to entry and a high degree of resource mobility promote productive patterns of resource use may not be appropriate for African social realities.

Notes

1. Described in the Ravenhill, Green, and Gordon chapters of this volume. See also Kevin Cleaver, *Impact of Price and Exchange Rate Policies in Sub-Saharan Africa,* World Bank Staff Working Paper No. 728 (Washington, D.C.: World Bank, 1985); Carol Lancaster and John Williamson, eds., *African Debt and Financing* (Washington: D.C.: Institute for International Economics, 1986); and Tore Rose, ed., *Crisis and Recovery in Sub-Saharan Africa* (Paris: OECD, 1985).

2. See especially Gerald Helleiner, "Outward Orientation, Import Instability and African Economic Growth: An Empirical Investigation," in S. Lall and

F. Stewart, eds., *Theory and Reality in Development: Essays in Honor of Paul Streeten* (New York: St. Martins, 1986); "Balance of Payments Experiences and Growth Prospects of Developing Countries: A Synthesis, *World Development* 14, 8 (1986): 877–908; and "The Question of Conditionality," in Lancaster and Williamson, eds., *African Debt*; David Wheeler, "Sources of Stagnation in Sub-Saharan Africa," *World Development* 12, 1 (1984): 1–23.

3. World Bank, *Financing Adjustment with Growth in Sub-Saharan Africa* (Washington, D.C.: World Bank, 1986), p. 11; also see the Ravenhill, Green, and Gordon chapters in this volume.

4. Alfred Maizels, ed., *Primary Commodities in the World Economy: Problems and Policies,* a special issue of *World Development* 15, 5 (1987).

5. Patrick Guillaumont, "From Export Instability Effects to International Stabilization Policies," *World Development* 15, 5 (1987): 633–642.

6. Helleiner, "Balance of Payments." For a subgroup of seventeen African countries, plus six South Asian ones, no such relationship existed; see Helleiner, "Outward Orientation," pp. 146ff. It is impossible to tell from these aggregate calculations whether the difference between the sample of 24 low-income economies—17 of them in Sub-Saharan Africa—and the sample of 23 African economies was because the former sample included six Asian countries, or because it excluded Senegal, Zambia, Ghana, Liberia, Mauritania, Angola, and Kenya, most of which have experienced severe fluctuations in imports and/or exceptionally low rates of agricultural growth.

7. Also see Wheeler, "Sources of Stagnation;" Reginald Green and Stephanie Griffith-Jones, "Africa's External Debt" in Rose, ed., *Crisis and Recovery.*

8. Uma Lele and Wilfred Candler, "Food Security: Some East African Considerations," in A. Valdes, ed., *Food Security for Developing Countries* (Boulder: Westview, 1981); Frank Ellis, "Agricultural Price Policy in Tanzania," *World Development* 10, 4 (1982): 263–283.

9. See Michael Bratton, *The Local Politics of Rural Development* (Hanover, NH: University Press of New England, 1980); Johan Pottier, *Migrants No More: Settlement and Survival in Mambwe Villages, Zambia* (Bloomington: Indiana University Press, 1988).

10. World Bank, *Financing Development.*

11. See Kenneth Good, "Systematic Agricultural Mismanagement: The 1985 'Bumper' Harvest in Zambia," *Journal of Modern African Studies* 24, 1 (1986): 257–284, on Zambia's disastrous experience with a bumper maize crop in 1985, a third or more of which rotted or went unconsumed because of chaos in the marketing system.

12. See, for example, Nigeria's program of austerity, which began in 1986 with World Bank but no IMF funds; consult Thomas M. Callaghy, "Lost Between State and Market: The Politics of Economic Adjustment in Ghana, Zambia, and Nigeria" in Joan Nelson, ed., *Economic Crisis and Policy Choice: The Politics of Economic Adjustment in the Third World* (Princeton: Princeton University Press, 1990), pp. 257–319. Tanzania also adopted many of the policies advocated by the IMF in the early 1980s, while at the same time fail-

ing to reach an agreement with the Fund and therefore receiving no credits; see Reginald Green, "Political-Economic Adjustment and Conditionality: Tanzania, 1974–81," in John Williamson, ed., *IMF Conditionality* (Washington, D.C.: Institute for International Economics, 1983). Tanzania subsequently signed agreements with both the Fund and the Bank; see the Lofchie chapter in this volume.

13. World Bank, *Financing Adjustment*, p. 19.

14. Resource poor farmers face uncertainty on many fronts. In addition to variations in weather, pest attacks, or market conditions, illness or other family troubles can also cause significant, unexpected changes in farm production. In a study of farming households in Embu, Kenya, for example, Haugerud found that, in the wake of a domestic dispute, angry wives or adult sons would typically leave the household, sometimes for weeks at a time. Since most small farms depended almost entirely on household labor, domestic discord was a major source of poor yields due to disruption of labor supplies; see Angelique Haugerud, "Economic Differentiation among Peasant Households: A Comparison of Embu Coffee and Cotton Zones," IDS Working Paper No. 383, Institute for Development Studies, Nairobi, 1981; and "Household Dynamics and Rural Political Economy among Embu Farmers in the Kenya Highlands," Ph.D. dissertation, Northwestern University, 1984.

15. See, for example, Thomas Reardon, P. Matlon and C. Delgado, "Coping with Household-Level Food Insecurity in Drought-Affected Areas of Burkina Faso," *World Development* 16, 4 (1988): 1065–1074.

16. Good, "Systematic Agricultural Mismanagement," p. 268.

17. Andrew Shepard, "Agrarian Change in Northern Ghana: Public Investment, Capitalist Farming, and Famine" in J. Heyer, et. al., *Rural Development in Tropical Africa* (New York: St. Martins, 1981).

18. Professor Jane Guyer, personal communication.

19. For an example of fluctuations in government employment, see John Ayoade, "States Without Citizens: An Emerging African Phenomenon," in Naomi Chazan and Donald Rothchild, eds., *Precarious Balance: State and Society in Africa* (Boulder: Westview, 1988).

20. John Bruce, "A Perspective on Indigenous Land Tenure Systems and Land Concentration" in R. Downs and S. Reyna, eds., *Land and Society in Contemporary Africa* (Durham, NH: University Press of New England, 1988); Paul Bohannon, "Land, 'Tenure' and Land Tenure," in D. Biebuyck, ed., *African Agrarian Systems* (Oxford: Oxford University Press, 1963); John Cohen, "Land Tenure and Rural Development in Africa" in Robert Bates and Michael Lofchie, eds., *Agricultural Development in Africa* (New York: Praeger, 1980); Gershon Feder and Raymond Noronha, "Land Rights Systems and Agricultural Development in Sub-Saharan Africa," *World Bank Research Observer* 2, 1 (1987): 143–170.

21. A. G. Hopkins, *An Economic History of West Africa* (London: Longmans, 1973).

22. Paul Collier goes so far as to suggest that interlinked transactions in land, labor and/or credit, so common in rural Asia, do not exist in Kenya;

"Malfunctioning of African Rural Factor Markets: Theory and a Kenyan Case," *Oxford Bulletin of Economics and Statistics* 45, 2 (1983): 141–171.

23. Ibid.; Feder and Noronha, "Land Rights Systems."

24. Recommended reforms range from full privatization of land ownership, agricultural production, and rural trade to state ownership and collective production, depending on the author's political preferences.

25. Sara Berry, "Social Institutions and Access to Resources in African Agriculture," *Africa* 59, 1 (1989).

26. Paul Lovejoy, "Plantations in the Economy of the Sokoto Caliphate," *Journal of African History* 19, 3 (1978): 341–368.

27. Matt Schaffer, *Mandinko: The Ethnography of a West African Holy Land* (New York: Holt, Rinehart and Winston, 1980).

28. Norman Klein, "The Two Asantes: Competing Interpretations of Slavery' in Akan-Asante Culture" in Paul Lovejoy, ed., *The Ideology of Slavery* (Beverly Hills: Sage, 1981).

29. Charles Ambler, *Kenyan Communities in the Age of Imperialism* (New Haven: Yale University Press, 1987).

30. John Comaroff, "Bridewealth and the Control of Ambiguity in a Tswana Chiefdom" in J. Comaroff, ed., *The Meaning of Marriage Payments* (London: Academic Press, 1980); Colin Murray, *Families Divided* (Cambridge: Cambridge University Press, 1981); Francis Snyder, *Capitalism and Legal Change: An African Transformation* (New York: Academic Press, 1981).

31. Colonial administrators' relations with European enterprises in Africa were, accordingly, somewhat contradictory. Administrators depended on European firms and settlers to generate taxable revenue, but they were also potentially in competition with private firms for labor and essential supplies. See Jane Guyer, "The Food Economy and French Colonial Rule in Central Cameroon," *Journal of African History* 19, 4 (1978): 577–597.

32. I have developed this argument at length in an unpublished paper, "Hegemony On A Shoestring: Some Unintended Consequences of Colonial Rule for African Farmers' Access to Resources."

33. Michael Crowder, *West Africa Under Colonial Rule* (Evanston, IL: Northwestern University Press, 1986).

34. Also, officials' search for information about traditional cultures invited multiple, often conflicting testimonies from local informants, without establishing any clear guidelines for selecting among them. In dealing with European administrators, Africans defined "tradition" to advance their interests vis-à-vis the colonial structure. Colonial officials were often aware that tradition could be invented, as well as recalled, but were inclined to attribute the practice to African venality or incompetence—not to the possibility that stable, homogeneous precolonial African cultures may never have existed.

35. David Anderson, "Depression, Dust Bowl, Demography and Drought," *African Affairs* 83, 332 (1984): 321–344; William Bienart, "Soil Erosion, Conservatism and Ideas about Development: A Southern African Exploration," *Journal of Southern African Studies* 11, 1 (1984): 52–81.

36. John Lonsdale and D. A. Low, eds., *A History of East Africa*, vol. 3 (Oxford: Clarendon Press, 1976).

37. See, for example, Richard Crook, "Decolonization, the Colonial State and Chieftancy in the Gold Coast," *African Affairs* 85 (1986): 75–105.

38. Of course, the state sector grew after independence for political reasons, too; see Chazan and Rothchild, eds., *Precarious Balance.*

39. The view that the resulting structure of prices and domestic resource flows undercut agricultural development is a major part of the thinking underlying World Bank and IMF diagnoses of the African crisis and their recommendations for policy reform; see World Bank, *Towards Accelerated Development in Sub-Saharan Africa* (Washington, D.C.: World Bank, 1981); and *Financing Adjustment.*

40. Jan Kees Van Donge, "Understanding Rural Zambia Today: The Rhodes-Livingstone Institute Revisited," *Africa* 55, 1 (1985): 60–75. On land reform in Kenya, see H.W.O. Okoth-Ogendo, "African Land Tenure Reform" in J. Heyer, et. al., *Agricultural Development in Kenya* (Oxford: Oxford University Press, 1976); Jack Glazier, *Land and the Uses of Tradition Among the Mbeere of Kenya* (Lanham, MD: University Press of America, 1985); Angelique Haugerud, "The Consequences of Land Tenure Reform among Smallholders in the Kenya Highlands," *Rural Africana* 15/16 (1983): 65–90, and "Land Tenure and Agrarian Change in Kenya," *Africa* 59, 1 (1989). On rural consequences of the Nigerian Land Use Decree, see Paul Francis, "Power and Order: A Study of Litigation in a Yoruba Community," Ph.D. dissertation, University of Liverpool, 1981, and " `For the Use and Common Benefit of All Nigerians:' Consequences of the 1978 Land Nationalization," *Africa* 54, 3 (1984): 5–28. On IRDPs, see Michael Watts, *Silent Violence* (Berkeley: Universityof California Press, 1983); Judith Carney, "Struggles Over Crop Rights and Labour Within Contract Farming Households in a Gambian Irrigated Rice Project," *Journal of Peasant Studies* 15, 3 (1988): 334–349; Adrian Adams,"The Senegal River Valley" in Heyer, *Rural Development.*

41. Jacques Weber, "Types de surproduit et formes d'accumulation" in ORSTOM, *Essais sur la Reproduction de Formations Sociales Dominées* (Paris: ORSTOM, 1977).

42. For citations, see Sara Berry, "Property Rights and Rural Resource Management: The Case of Tree Crops in West Africa," *Cahiers des Sciences Humaines* 24, 1 (1988): 3–16, and "Social Institutions."

43. Terence Ranger and Eric Hobsbawn, *The Invention of Tradition* (Cambridge: Cambridge University Press, 1983).

44. Reardon, et. al., "Coping."

45. John Cleave, *African Farmers* (New York: Praeger, 1974); Kenneth Swindell, *Farm Labor* (Cambridge: Cambridge University Press, 1985).

46. Sara Berry, *Fathers Work for Their Sons* (Berkeley: University of California Press, 1985); Polly Hill, *Migrant Cocoa Farmers of Southern Ghana* (Cambridge: Cambridge University Press, 1963); Roger Southall, "Farmers, Traders and Brokers in the Gold Coast Economy," *Canadian Journal of African Studies* 12, 2 (1978): 185–211; Paul Clough, "Farmers and Traders in Hausaland," *Development and Change* 12 (1981): 273–292; Mahir Saul, "The Organization of a West African Grain Market," *American Anthropologist* 89 (1987): 74–95; Jannik Boesen and A. T. Mohele, *The "Success Story" of Peas-*

ant Tobacco Production in Tanzania (Uppsala: Scandinavian Institute of African Studies, 1979).

47. Brian Schwimmer, "The Organization of Migrant Farmer Communities in Southern Ghana," *Canadian Journal of African Studies* 14, 2 (1980): 221–238; Elizabeth Colson and Thayer Scudder, *For Prayer and Profit* (Stanford: Stanford University Press, 1988); Berry, *Fathers.*

48. William Watson, *Tribal Cohesion in a Money Economy* (Manchester: Manchester University Press, 1958).

49. Johan Pottier, "Defunct Labour Reserve? Mambwe Villages in the Post-Migration Economy," *Africa* 53, 2 (1983): 2–23, and *Migrants No More.*

50. Pottier, "Defunct Labour Reserve?" p. 2.

51. Returned migrants often avoided going back to their home villages, however, since they had few savings with which to reestablish themselves there, and knew what little they had would be immediately absorbed by relatives even poorer than they; see Pottier, "Defunct Labour Reserve?" and *Migrants No More.*

52. Pottier, "Defunct Labour Reserve?" p. 17.

53. See Shepard, "Agrarian Change;" Jean-Pierre Chauveau, Jacques Richard, and J.-P. Dozon, "Histoire de Riz, Histoire d'Igname," *Africa* 51, 2 (1981).

54. Opportunities for self-employment grew rapidly in other tertiary activities. To cite one example, the motor repair industry grew at a phenomenal rate during the 1970s, as oil revenues brought in a flood of imported vehicles, which wore down Nigeria's roads faster than the government could repair them or build new ones. This, in turn, created a booming market for the services of mechanics, panel beaters, vulcanizers, battery chargers, and a host of other specialities, whose buoyancy and low barriers to entry attracted many farmers' sons. See Berry, *Fathers,* chapter 6.

55. This is a complex issue, depending not only on differences in urban and rural investment opportunities, but also on struggles over control of labor and income within rural households and communities. See, for example, Murray, *Families Divided;* Andrew Spiegel, "Rural Differentiation and the Diffusion of Migrant Labour Remittances in Lesotho" in P. Mayer, ed., *Black Villagers in an Industrial Society* (Cape Town: Oxford University Press, 1980); Jean-Yves Weigel, *Migration et production domestique des Soninkes du Sénégal* (Paris: ORSTOM Travaux et Documents, 1982).

56. Megan Vaughan, *Story of an African Famine* (Cambridge: Cambridge University Press, 1987)

57. Angelique Haugerud, personal communication. The International Potato Center (CIP), headquartered in Lima, Peru, is part of the Consultative Group for International Agricultural Research, the international network of agricultural research institutes concerned with developing appropriate improved technologies for Third World farming systems.

58. Louise Fresco, *Cassava and Shifting Cultivation in Africa* (Amsterdam: Royal Tropical Institute, 1986); R. Weber, et. al. *Inter-Cropping with Cassava* (Ottawa: IDRC, 1979), and *Cassava Cultural Practices* (Ottawa: IDRC, 1980).

59. Michael Johnny, J. Karimu, and P. Richards, "Upland and Swamp Rice Farming Systems in Sierra Leone: the Social Context of Technological Change," *Africa* 51, 2 (1981): 531–579; Margaret Haswell, *The Changing Pattern of Economic Activity in a Gambian Village* (London: Her Majesty's Stationery Office, 1963); Olga Linares, "From Tidal Swamp to Inland Valley: On the Social Organization of Wet Rice Cultivation among the Diola of Senegal," *Africa* 51, 2 (1981): 557–595.

60. Paul Richards, *Coping with Hunger* (London: Allen and Unwin, 1986); J. P. Dozon, "Transformation et Reproduction d'une Société Rurale Africaine dans le Cadre de l'Economie de Plantation: Le Cas des Bete de la Région de Gagnoa" in ORSTOM, *Essai sur la Reproduction*; Olga Linares, "Farming Decisions and Household Composition: the Cultural Context of Production among the Jola of Senegal," paper prepared for a conference on African households and Farming Systems, Bellagio, Italy, 1984; and "From Tidal Swamp."

61. Johnny et. al., "Upland and Swamp Rice."

62. Chauveau et. al., "Histoire de Riz."; Dozon, "Transformation et Reproduction."

63. For a review of recent literature on cassava cultivation and its role in socioeconomic change in Africa, see Sara Berry, "Socio-Economic Aspects of Cassava Cultivation in Africa," paper prepared for the Rockefeller Foundation, 1986.

64. Christine Jones, "Intrahousehold Bargaining in Response to the Introduction of New Crops: A Case Study from North Cameroon" in J. L. Moock, ed., *Understanding Africa's Rural Households and Farming Systems* (Boulder: Westview, 1986); Carney, "Struggles Over Crop Rights."

65. Fresco, *Cassava*.

66. Richards, *Coping with Hunger*; Christine Okali and Sara Berry, "Alley Farming in West Africa in Comparative Perspective," Boston University African-American Issues Center Discussion Paper No. 1.

67. David Norman, "Rationalising Mixed Cropping under Indigenous Conditions," *Journal of Development Studies* 11, 1 (1974): 3–21.

68. George Abalu, "A Note on Crop Mixtures under Indigenous Conditions in Northern Nigeria," *Journal of Development Studies* 12, 3 (1976): 212–220; Deryke Belshaw, "Taking Indigenous Knowledge Seriously: The Case of Inter-Cropping in East Africa" in David Brokensha, et. al., *Indigenous Knowledge Systems and Development* (Washington, D.C.: University Press of America, 1986); Fresco, *Cassava*.

69. Fresco, *Cassava*, pp. 107–108.

70. Professor Jane Guyer, personal communication.

71. Others, such as livestock, form an important part of the capital stock in many African farming systems, but to do justice to the extensive literature on agro-pastoralism in Sub-Saharan Africa is beyond the scope of this chapter.

72. Pottier, "Defunct Labour Reserve?" and *Migrants No More*; Shepard,"Agrarian Change;" Berry, *Fathers*.

73. Weigel, *Migration et Production*; Richards, *Coping with Hunger*; Sally Falk Moore, *Social Facts and Fabrications* (Cambridge: Cambridge University

Press, 1986); Paul Ross, "Land as a Right to Membership: Land Tenure Dynamics in a Peripheral Zone" in Michael Watts ed., *State, Oil and Agriculture in Nigeria* (Berkeley: Institute of International Studies, 1986).

74. Berry, *Fathers*.

75. Glazier, *Land and the Uses of Tradition*, p. 183; Apollo Njonjo, "The Africanization of the 'White Highlands': A Study of Agrarian Class Struggle in Kenya, 1950–1974," Ph.D. dissertation, Princeton University, 1977; Fiona Mackenzie, "Land and Territory: The Interface between Two Systems of Land Tenure, Murang'a District, Kenya," *Africa* 59, 1 (1989).

76. For an extreme case, see John Sharp and Andrew Spiegel, "Vulnerability to Impoverishment in South African Rural Areas: The Erosion of Kinship and Neighborhood as Social Resources," *Africa* 46, 2 (1986): 133–152.

77. Carney, "Struggles Over Crop Rights;" Pauline Peters, "Struggles Over Water, Struggles Over Meaning: Cattle, Water and the State in Botswana," *Africa* 54, 3 (1984): 24–29.

78. Claude Raynaut, "Transformation du Système de Production et Inégalité Economique: Le Cas d'un Village Haoussa (Niger)," *Canadian Journal of African Studies* 10, 2 (1976): 279–306; Watts, *Silent Violence*; David Norman, M. Newman and I. Ouedraogo, *The Farmer in the Semi-Arid Tropics of West Africa* (Hyderabad: ICRISAT, 1981).

79. Ross, "Land as a Right."

80. Collier and Lal, *Labour and Poverty*.

81. Haswell, *Changing Pattern*; Richards, *Coping with Hunger*; Johnny et. al., "Upland and Swamp Rice;" Linares,"From Tidal Swamp;" Berry *Fathers*; Francis, *Power and Order*; Julian Clarke, "Peasantization and Landholding: A Nigerian Case Study" in M. Lofchie and S. Commins, eds., *Africa's Agrarian Crisis* (Boulder: Rienner, 1980); Christine Okali, *Cocoa and Kinship in Ghana: The Matrilineal Akan* (London: Kegan Paul, 1983); Chauveau, "Economie de Plantation."

82. Pottier, *Migrants No More*.

Chapter Eight

The Discovery of "Politics": Smallholder Reactions to the Cocoa Crisis of 1988–90 in Côte d'Ivoire

JENNIFER WIDNER

The February 5, 1989 edition of *Fraternité Matin* carried a picture of a rural scene and some children carrying a placard that read, "Oui Monsieur Le Président. Nous Vous Suivrons Pour La Lutte Contre Les Spéculateurs!"[1] The photo caption stated that the children came from Aboisso in southeastern Côte d'Ivoire, where cocoa farmers were suffering from "la chute"—the crisis in cocoa prices and purchasing. The banner supported President Félix Houphouët-Boigny's repeated statements that international speculators had forced the world price of cocoa to new lows to serve Western interests at the expense of Ivoirians.

To a social scientist, the photograph held special interest because it implied the existence of an agrarian "collective consciousness" or awareness of political interest that many Africa watchers have been hard-pressed to find on the continent. It is almost a truism in studies of contemporary Africa that agriculturalists have diverse economic and social interests, are weakly organized to participate in contemporary formal political institutions, and are incapable of influencing policy to their advantage or of lobbying for better government services because of their poverty, isolation, and large numbers.[2] With a few notable exceptions, cultivators have pressed their interests using what James Scott has called "small arms fire in the class war"—foot-dragging, retreat from official marketing channels, and participation in parallel markets.[3] The *Fraternité Matin* photograph conveyed a different view: that farmers might have a common understanding of political interest and the means of organizing collectively to advance their views.

The image coincided with three other events reported in the Ivoirian media that also suggested the beginnings of collective action by rural interests to influence public policy formation. The first of these was the hurried participation of the Minister of Defense, Jean Konan Banny, in a series of meetings with cocoa growers—meetings designed to denounce foreign speculators, cocoa buyers such as the French firm Sucres et Denrées and the American trading company Phillips Brothers, and to rally the farmers to the president's side. After several years of stagnating or declining revenues, the cocoa farmers had grown restless and demanded attention from senior officials. The second was the continual postponement of meetings between the president and a farmers' delegation during the spring of 1989, again a manifestation of increasing farmer dissatisfaction with the government and heightened official nervousness about the potential fallout from a public confrontation.[4] The third was the important place the treatment of cocoa farmers assumed in the mid-1989 "Days of Dialogue," during which the president met with representatives of a number of different social groups to discuss economic concerns. All three events suggested that Ivoirian farmers were beginning to mobilize for the first time since Independence.

The response departed from the farmers' reactions to earlier, similar crises. Those interviewed in this study recalled a period of comparable hardship during World War II, when the price of cocoa was also low. Farmers could afford to purchase neither adequate food nor other consumer goods. They remember eating cassava with a sauce made not of fish or meat but of green cocoa beans.[5] Absent money to buy clothes, they unraveled the fabric of old clothing and rewove it to make shirts. Their strategy for survival, they said, was to plant more cassava and hope that the price would go up again.

In the first phases of the current cocoa crisis, farmers in the cocoa zone pursued the same strategy: they planted cassava, trimmed their household budgets, and kept the cocoa bushes in the ground in the expectation that prices would again rise. Their attempts to protect their standards of living revealed barriers to many of the strategies that neoclassical economic theory and common sense had deemed potentially helpful. Some of the responses typical in other parts of Africa—diversification of crop choice and use of kin-based insurance systems—proved unavailable because of new shortages of land, which forced farmers to choose between cocoa and another crop, and the breakdown of extended households.

By 1989, however, farmer behavior had started to change. Gradually, frustration built over the lack of information available for making important investment decisions, over the inability to place trust in local firms and cooperatives, over the predominance of an "informal" guild system in many off-farm industries, and over the procedures the government used to control smallholder participation in the marketing of some crops. All of these loomed as obstacles to diversification, extension of credit, and other short-run and long-run adaptations to higher levels of market-related risk. None were subject to individual control; they required collective action on the part of communities and, in some cases, they required that the government involve itself as "umpire." Farmers turned their backs on the Parti Démocratique de Côte d'Ivoire (PDCI) and took matters into their own hands, sending small delegations to the headquarters of the Ministry of Agriculture and important parastatals in Abidjan and in some cases forming small unions to try to seek policy change.

The involvement of cocoa farming communities in new forms of political participation was not universal, however. Farmers in some parts of the Ivoirian cocoa zone were more likely than others to talk about government policies among themselves, protest to the *préfet*, travel to the capital to press their demands in the hearing of senior officials, or join regional or national meetings to express concern about their declining incomes. Even within the same region, the propensity to participate varied between villages. Although they faced similar climatic conditions, local income distributions, and economic environments, worked within the same formal systems of representation and administration, and shared demographic characteristics, some villages organized to improve the economic competitiveness of members and supported "militant" farmers while others did not.

To the social scientist, this pattern is especially interesting. We know that African farmers do sometimes organize to influence policy and participate in politics. We know little about how such collective action starts—about the process of interest formation and involvement, the "discovery of politics." Even though the Ivoirian cocoa farmers are just beginning to participate in formal party politics[6], the variation in "proto-political" militancy offers a rare chance to study the process by which political and economic identities or "cultures" change.

This research asked two questions. First, how is it possible to explain the pattern of response to the cocoa crisis? The study tried to identify the characteristics that distinguished "participant" from "nonparticipant" villages and make sense of them. Second, how, and under what conditions, does village-level activism begin to broaden and evolve into programmatic participation through formal channels, such as political parties and economic unions?

The study on which this analysis is based took place in the Aboisso region of southeastern Côte d'Ivoire during October and November 1989, and from June to September 1990, about two years after the cocoa crisis began. The 120 smallholders interviewed were randomly selected from several villages, each of which included growers of cocoa, coffee, and oil palms. The pattern of income distribution within each village was similar. Residents numbered farmers who had access only to small plots of land as well as a few farmers with 10 to 25 hectares, some of whom had won the government's annual prize for the smallholders with the highest yields. None of the villages included large land owners or members of the country's political elite.

The discussion has five main parts. The first introduces the existing literature on the "discovery of politics" among farmers in developing areas and outlines the argument. The second describes the dimensions of the crisis and explains the various ways in which the decline in the cocoa producer price affected smallholder standards of living. The third probes the economic adaptations farmers attempted to pursue as a first line of defense against the erosion of their incomes and the reasons for their frustration with these. The fourth explores the origin of variations in patterns of participation between villages. The final section summarizes the findings to date and discusses the process of political incorporation taking place today.

Patterns of Agrarian Response

The literature on patterns of agrarian political participation in Africa is part of a larger body of research and writing on farmer response to income instability induced by climatic variation, changes in tax policy, withdrawal of subsidies, or price fluctuation. This literature has identified three major farmer orientations toward economic "crises" including, first, changes in land tenure arrangements, with a shift away from pure rental or wage relationships toward share contracts instead; second, retreat from farming and reinvigoration of kinship ties as vehicles for movement into other sectors of the economy; and third, adoption of new forms of political participation designed to affect policy or implementation of policy directly. Existing research has little to say about two important questions, however: under what conditions do farmers choose one kind of response over the others? and how does collective action get started in the first place?

Redistributing Risk Between Households and Hired Labor

The economics literature has focused on diversification of income sources and the institution of share contracting as the predominant form of farmer response. A first line of attack for farmers is to diversify their choice of crops, but its utility as a survival strategy is constrained by the type of crops they choose (farmers are less likely to destroy perennial crops than annual crops to adjust to a short-term decline in returns), as well as the availability of land, and ecological conditions.

Share contracts are production relationships in which two or more parties agree to combine their privately held resources in a farming venture and share the output in prearranged proportions.[7] They become "rational" ways of organizing economic activities when there are multiple sources of risk associated with cultivation and/or information is costly. The starting point of this set of explanations is the recognition that if the only kind of risk farmers experience is production risk, then most of those without land will seek to become wage laborers instead of pursuing ownership, tenancy, or rental arrangements.[8] By choosing to work for a wage, the cultivator shifts the burden of risk to the owner of the land, who must pay the wage he or she has offered, regardless of the level of return—at least in the short run. At the other end of the spectrum, a rental contract shifts the burden of risk entirely to the "worker" or tenant.

In African settings there are usually multiple sources of risk in the farmer's environment, of course. Newbery and Stiglitz[9] have pointed out that where most people rely on agriculture for income, ups and downs in producer prices or the costs of critical inputs are likely to affect the labor market as well as the returns received by the landlord. Landlords are likely to reduce the wages they pay, lay off employees, or offer late payments, and potential workers are likely to sell their labor in the informal sector instead. If tenants are unable to reduce risk by diversifying into crops that each respond differently to drought, floods, or price changes—or that require different patterns of labor use or other inputs—share contracting becomes attractive.

The process of share contracting assumes two distinct parties: a landlord who brings land to the transaction and a landless worker, who brings his or her labor. In the models proposed, these are clear-cut roles. In Africa, however, individuals rarely occupy such distinct positions. More often a single person holds multiple roles and behaves as landlord, tenant, and wage laborer at the same time. For example, a producer might allow another community member to farm an inherited plot close to the village, while participating as a tenant in a share contract in an outlying area recently reclaimed from fallow and while devoting a day or two each week to wage labor on government "works" projects. Moreover, relationships become complicated when landlords and tenants are related to one another and have obligations toward each other that are outside the share contract. In these cases, the limited interests and maximizing behavior assumed by economists do not obtain; family obligations modify contractual relations.

Second, the notion of share contracting assumes individual rights of access to land and labor and ability to transfer these freely between individuals. Yet many African farming systems constrain individual rights of access and transfer—and even management patterns. Systems of entitlements vary greatly across the continent and are difficult to categorize, but many prevent transfer of land except to heirs. Indeed, in only four regions of Africa do share contracts stand out as dominant agricultural systems: in the Ghanaian cocoa belt, the Senegambian groundnut region, the cultivation of foodgrains in Lesotho, and production of cotton in the Sudan.[10]

Third, even if it turns out to be possible to model these other agricultural systems as functional equivalents of share contracts, it is important to note that bargaining over terms is unlikely to be a "frictionless" enterprise. The terms of share contracts extend in most cases not only to division of labor and output but also to contribution of a variety of inputs ranging from fertilizer to specialized skills. Because of the limits on labor but not on land that have prevailed in much of Africa until very recently, renegotiation of terms has typically benefited the tenant. Only now is that changing. In either case, modifications of community norms regarding appropriate shares requires signaling of the greater bargaining power or need of one of the parties, argumentation to establish the legitimacy of the new claims, reconsideration of the terms of performance and structures for enforcement, and mutual adjustment of parties affected indirectly by the change in terms. In short, achieving a change in the terms of the contract requires collective action on the part of tenants or landlords or both. It requires a "politics" noted in the economic theories only as an unmeasurable "transaction cost."

"Portfolio" Diversification Through the Household

Share contracts are only one of several ways to limit the consumption effects of income instability or economic "shocks." A large proportion of the literature on African agriculture suggests that farmers draw predominantly on kinship-based economic networks.[11] For example, in her study of Yoruba cocoa farmers in western Nigeria, Sara Berry has probed efforts to obtain larger shares of cocoa revenues during and after the drop in yields that occurred in the 1970s. Cocoa prices increased during the 1970s, but labor shortages, deterioration of land quality, and inflation reduced yields and incomes on the one hand and purchasing power on the other.[12] According to Berry, the first casualties of the downward trend were the village cooperatives and associations that had sought to improve terms of trade by bringing pressure to bear on buyers.[13] Berry's interviews suggested that the drop in incomes made it difficult for farmers to support the transactions costs associated with these associations. The farmers found their collective bargaining power vis-à-vis middlemen substantially reduced as cocoa dwindled in economic importance compared to oil.

Berry writes that the response was to rechannel economic activities and to "turn away from the cocoa sector politically as well as economically."[14] Farmers turned to kinship networks and the revival of descent group activities in an effort to advance the education of a few family members who could, in turn, obtain civil service jobs and channel state resources to their home areas. Farmers formed descent group-based "agencies of progress" to establish investment priorities and to help younger members tap the resources of wealthy or influential relatives. Stratification developed not on the basis of access to labor or to land but on the basis of educational attainment, as both income earning opportunities and ability to direct investment fell to those with the ability to read. Less educated "fathers" increasingly found themselves under the power of their sons.[15]

In his study of Hausa farmers in northern Nigeria, Michael Watts similarly found few instances of collective action to reduce the effects of income instability. In the portion of his study that deals with the 1970s, Watts has addressed the impact of climatic variations on income.[16] He has found that accommodation strategies vary first by "class," or economic position of the farmer, and divides Hausa cultivators into three such groups. The first group includes the "big farmers" who are able to hire labor, use the time saved to participate in trade and informal sector activities, invest in cattle (and so diversify their risk to some degree), and accumulate in excess of subsistence requirements. Group two includes the farmers who meet their domestic food demands under normal circumstances and participate in dry-season trade or manufacture. Group three includes the "poor," or those who under normal conditions are barely self-sufficient and rarely have the capital required to enter informal sector activities or to acquire access to land in floodplains suited to dry-season cultivation.[17]

Watts suggests that differences in survival strategies employed by these groups generate a process of impoverishment among group three Hausa farmers. To begin with, the stronger bargaining power of the group one farmers constrains the rise of share contracts between group one and group three farmers and colors the terms of these relationships.

> [Poor families] . . . generally don't have the political, familial, or economic capital to lubricate the rental process. Second, from

> the perspective of the landlord, a poor householder is an unattractive tenurial proposition in relation to a middle peasant with a larger gandu labor supply and availability of capital. And third, participation in the market garden sector presupposes some start up for seed, manure, labor, capital equipment, . . . and perhaps tractor hire.[18]

Just as Berry sees "exit" or abandonment of agriculture as the dominant strategy of Yoruba farmers facing declining cocoa yields, Watts sees "exit" to wage labor or to the urban informal sector as the strategy of the poor Hausa farmers. Collective action to modify policies is too "costly" compared to uncertain benefits, especially when many of the group three farmers are quasi-clients of wealthier community members and when group one farmers have used their wealth to secure control of local offices.

Political Protest

Other researchers have noted that forms of "informal" political participation or protest on the part of farmers are more common than previously suggested. Naomi Chazan has made the case that social scientists have too often overlooked direct attempts to influence policy because these have not always taken place through official channels, such as political parties.[19] Robert Bates has documented numerous instances of protest accompanying the commercialization of agriculture across the continent.[20] In most of these case studies, the researchers identify a pattern of increasing stratification, perception of impending permanent reduction in welfare, and discovery of the inefficacy of other forms of response to change the terms of the relationship with those who are better off and who control official channels of participation.

For example, C. E. F. Beer has tried to analyze the reasons for a particular form of collective action, resort to political violence as a response to tax changes that reduced real incomes for farmers. Beer has focused on the Agbekoya riots of 1968–69 among cocoa farmers in western Nigeria.[21] Economic and social change during the 1950s and 1960s had produced new elites who sought to turn existing mutual aid societies and cooperatives to their own benefit. Although the national leadership of Nigeria spoke at the time of campaigns to benefit the rural poor, levels of investment in agriculture languished. Toward the end of the 1960s, farmer grievances began to take specific form. The cultivators first objected to tax rates. During this period, the practice was to assess each farmer a flat tax on an estimated income base of 50 Nigerian pounds per year. Many of those in the region fell below this earnings level but local authorities expected all, including those retired from heavy farm work, to pay. The farmers' second concern was corruption among tax collectors, who often demanded bribes, and local councils, which were known to impose extra taxes for special services that rarely materialized.[22]

In 1968–69, tensions ran high. During the state governor's visit to one area, poorer farmers marched in protest against tax policies. The response of the governing elites was to call for a crackdown, a tax raid by council clerks before the main harvest, during a season when the farmers had insufficient cash even to bribe the officials. As in the Ghanaian case, the actions highlighted discrepancies in wealth and power and revealed the difficulty of working through official systems of representation. The cultivators organized in revolt, calling for a reduction of the flat tax, abolition of the district councils, and release of all detainees held after the earlier marches.[23] A series of dispersed but organized riots ensued until the tax collectors and an escort of riot police again entered the area and invited the farmers to take their grievances to the government in Ibadan. During the effort to articulate their demands, farmers and police clashed, and 300 people were killed.

Among the elements of a theory to explain the incidence of different types of response one must include, first, a recognition that cultivators usually pursue a series of strategies entirely under their control before leaving agricultural production or seeking changes in policies or institutions. Watts has usefully suggested that cultivators proceed through a series of adjustment strategies, preferring those over which they have complete control and that are consequently associated with relatively low transaction costs to those that require negotiation. If the farmer has anticipated instability it is likely that he will have attempted to limit the effects of price downturns or higher input prices by diversifying crop choice. In most cases, diversification is a measure to protect against weather- and pest-related risks, but it can be used to limit the effects of other forms of risk as well. Its use is far more constrained than social scientists often assume, however, as soil types and ecological conditions often limit severely the kinds of crops that will grow on a plot.

Second, the farmer can seek to reduce expenditures by exploiting family labor to a higher degree instead of hiring a contract worker or labor team, by skimping on labor-consuming soil- and moisture-conservation practices such as ridging of fields and frequent weeding, by cutting down on use of other inputs, or by withdrawing children from school. Third, the farmer can seek sources of supplementary income, either through work on casual labor contracts or by participating in informal sector enterprises such as automobile mechanics. Fourth, the farmer can try to induce other family members to seek additional income by engaging in some form of rural enterprise, such as basket weaving, pottery making, or animal husbandry. Fifth, the farmer can distance himself from obligations to supply food or assistance to members of the extended family, teenagers, or community members. And sixth, the farmer can seek to borrow funds.[24]

What, then, precipitates the rise of new forms of participation designed to influence government behavior and policy? Although methods by which farmers confront problems of collective action run through the literature, the actual attention devoted to conceptualizing efforts to build bargaining leverage and supply "solutions" or institutions (and thus the incidence of different types of responses) is limited, as is the effort to consider seriously the influence of formal systems of representation, which appear in most of these accounts as a kind of residual category.[25]

This study takes a step toward filling this gap in our understanding. It suggests that new forms of political participation emerge partly in response to changes in formal systems of representation that alter the costs of acquiring information, asking questions, speaking at meetings, sending delegations to speak with officials, and organizing economic interests. In themselves, these changes are not enough to produce collective action among households and villages, however. In many cases, a fundamental change in the understanding of appropriate forms of interaction and of authority relationships—or "political culture" more broadly—is essential. To adopt new forms of political participation requires that an individual have the skills and know-how to use new sources of information, the latitude to fail and try again, and special incentive for making the effort.

In the Ivoirian case, the commercialization of agriculture had reordered the social structures of villages in the cocoa zone and, in some cases, created local "space" for experimentation by destabilizing existing authority systems. It had also brought wealth, and with it, higher levels of formal schooling and greater access to media. It also brought new sources of risk. The commodity price "crisis" of the late 1980s accelerated a process of change in patterns of behavior already underway. It clarified perception of a "class-wide" economic interest and, by creating an economic recession in urban areas, it precipitated the return of highly educated and well-traveled young people to the countryside, bringing new skills to the villages. Finally, and most important, it encouraged those who remained in the cities to try to increase the impact of the increasingly limited funds they could remit to rural relatives, by joining together in associations, prioritizing village needs, providing funds to communities instead of households, and offering special incentives to farmers to submerge intra-household conflicts to broader economic interests.

The Cocoa Crisis of 1987–90

The trigger to the evolution of new patterns of political participation in Aboisso region was the crisis in cocoa production and its conjunction with decreasing returns to coffee and oil palm cultivation. Côte d'Ivoire's "economic miracle" had created problems for farmers unlike those in most African countries, where producer prices for agricultural commodities have typically been too low to make production profitable. In the Ivoirian case, the government maintained relatively high producer prices for its main agricultural exports and sheltered farmers from fluctuations in the world market by setting aside revenues when world prices greatly exceeded the producer price, paying out a subsidy from these revenues when world prices dropped. It established a special stabilization fund, the Caistab, to handle cocoa and coffee marketing and to manage revenues. Under these conditions, production of export crops, especially cocoa, expanded dramatically. Côte d'Ivoire became the world's largest producer and exporter of cocoa and, next to Ghana, the producer of the highest quality cocoa. Beginning in the 1980s, the growth of production began to depress the world market price, however, and by the second half of the decade the government found itself steadily subsidizing production and depleting government revenues in the process. The World

Bank and IMF eventually intervened, urging a reduction in the producer price.

A quick look at the relationship between producer prices and the world market price gives the false impression that the Ivoirian government was giving its farmers only a very small percentage of the revenues their commodity commanded on the international market. Because the government was bearing most of the collection, marketing, and transport costs, and because these costs are reflected in the world price, the actual differential between the producer price and the world market price was much smaller than the raw data suggest. By 1988, when farmers were earning 400 FCFA/kilogram, the world market price was only 450 FCFA/kilogram. Because transport and handling charges added about 300 FCFA/kilogram, the total cost of production exceeded the market price, and the government was losing about $1 on each kilogram sold.[26] The government's revenue base disappeared, and Caistab moved to borrow funds abroad, principally from French commercial banks.

The crisis affected urban areas first. Houphouët-Boigny imposed restrictions on government hiring, dismantled some of the parastatal organizations, and finally began to remove people from the government payroll. Publicly financed construction came almost to a halt. Differences in income levels between the countryside and the rural areas decreased. According to World Bank estimates, although in 1980 the average per capita income in urban areas was three times the level of rural areas, by 1985 it was only twice as great, and by 1988 it had fallen still farther.[27]

The cash crisis also struck the middlemen and shippers who handle Ivoirian cocoa. In an effort to improve efficiency in the cocoa marketing system, Côte d'Ivoire had long used private traders, or *traitants*, to carry out the actual transactions with farmers and to bring the fermented cocoa beans to port facilities, where it is turned over to licensed shippers or exporters, of whom there are about 40. The shippers pay the traitants. Both traders and shippers are allowed a certain profit margin on the cocoa they handle and are reimbursed for acceptable costs at the end of the cocoa season. In the interim, they finance the marketing and handling of the cocoa out of funds they borrow from commercial banks. When Caistab went into deficit in 1987, however, it was unable to make timely payments to the intermediaries, who, in turn, either failed to pay producers or failed to pay their bank loans (which triggered a liquidity crisis in the banking system). Further, it cut acceptable profit margins for traders, some of whom simply folded their operations.

The farmers themselves constituted the third group affected by the cocoa crisis. They felt the impact initially not through a reduction in the official producer price, which the government maintained until quite late in the crisis, but rather through the increasing unwillingness of the traitants either to offer the official price or to make payment for loads transported. During 1988, there was widespread evidence that traitants were paying as little as 200 FCFA/kilogram—or half the official price.[28] The government warned it would revoke traders' licenses and issue stiff fines for such behavior. Later, it urged that cooperatives (*Groupements de Vocation Coopérative,* or GVCs) take over responsibility for conveying cocoa to the exporters, although this practice did not spread quickly. Absent funds advanced from shippers, and given the risk of government censure, many traders either resorted to use of promissory notes or declared bankruptcy. Stocks of fermented cocoa began to accumulate in the country's interior.

The government's policy was initially to try to force the world price higher. In 1987, it held production off international markets, surrendering the tax receipts it would have earned from the sale. With the largest world surplus on record and the prospect of increasing production from Côte d'Ivoire in subsequent years, however, most of the cocoa failed to move. By the middle of 1987, the embargo on exports was lifted, and limited sales began again, the government seeking premiums for the high quality of its stock. It succeeded in obtaining limited sales to European confectioners at premium prices, but the effect of the two-tiered pricing system was to push returns to production of poorer grade cocoa still lower.

The lifting of the embargo did not improve the lot of the producers, however. Midway through the 1988–89 season, they still had not received payment for the previous year's crop. The traitants were either unable or unwilling to pay for what they had marketed; many waited for the government to drop the official price, which it seemed likely to do any day. Finally, on June 3, 1989, the government dropped the price for mid-season purchases to 250 FCFA/kilogram, although it suggested that the price for regular season purchases would go back up. In October, it dropped the price again, to 200 FCFA/kilogram, the price the World Bank had urged for several years.

In rural areas, the "Cocoa Crisis" also refers to a more generalized decline in the profitability of other key cash crops. Côte d'Ivoire is a coffee producer, and the Aboisso region has long produced significant quantities of robusta beans. During this same period, international coffee prices were also in decline, partly because of the new favor shown to arabica producers, and Côte d'Ivoire found both the price it received for coffee exports and its quota reduced. In the fourth quarter of 1989, it dropped the coffee producer price to 100 FCFA/kilogram from 200 FCFA/kilogram. Because farmers often produce both coffee and cocoa in combination, the price change reduced still further the incomes of farmers already affected by the cocoa crisis.

To make matters worse, the coffee growers of the region for the most part cultivated older bushes, near the end of their major bearing age. Just before the collapse in prices, the government had initiated a campaign to convince farmers that they would have to prune their bushes heavily, in order to rejuvenate them. Because this pruning (*récepage*) would prevent the bushes from bearing for some time, it too constituted a "shock" to farmers' incomes. Although the government eventually offered 60,000 FCFA per household to help cover the losses of the farmers who pruned their fields, it is not clear that any of the farmers in this study participated in the program. The program design created a conundrum by not stipulating exactly when payment was to take place—before the farmer cut the field, in which case the farmer might simply take the money and fail to do the work required, or after the process, in which case the government might forget to pay. Uncertainty hindered the expansion of the program and focused the farmers' attention on changes in price rather than pruning requirements.

Finally, the cocoa-growing areas are also oil palm production areas, and returns for this crop were also in decline, although the culprit was partly the change in producer price and partly the withdrawal of fertilizer and input subsidies under the new austerity regime. *Palmindustrie,* the palm oil parastatal, had responsibility for buying the fruit, and the government set the price. Although domestic demand for palm oil had increased, the world price had steadily fallen during the 1980s, and the nominal producer price had not increased since 1985, when it rose from 19 FCFA/kilogram to 21 FCFA/kilogram.[29] Coincident with the price increase, Palmindustrie had withdrawn most parts of its input subsidy package, limiting the effective price incentive for farmers to switch into oil palm cultivation.

It is not always the case that those who are victims of crisis perceive their situations as armchair analysts do. Subjective perceptions are a product not only of real circumstances but also of local systems of belief, which assign different significances and different priorities to important events. The multiple sources of risk African farmers routinely encounter have prompted one scholar to eschew studies of "risk and choice" for the theme, "coping with chaos." A farming household in Aboisso region encounters many types of risk to its annual income, including, most notably climatic variability, sickness of a household member, and market-related shocks (input shortages and withdrawal of subsidies, as well as price changes). The data collected suggest that during the period 1987–1990, however, smallholders in Aboisso were quite capable of distinguishing shocks of the third type from the others that plagued their lives, however. They were very much aware of the "cocoa crisis," although they preferred to extend the definition of *"la chute"* to the decline in profitability of coffee, coconut palms and oil palms as well. Of the cocoa producers, 24% identified the reason for diminished returns in the 1987–88 season, when traitants were issuing IOUs and bargaining to pay prices below official levels, as a change in the producer price. During the 1988–89 season, when the government announced the reduction in the official price, fully 96% attributed lost revenue to change in the government producer price policy.

Just before the crisis, farmers had been forced to cope with bad weather. Climatic variability is great in most parts of Africa, and Aboisso is no exception to the rule. In normal years, as part of the forest zone, Aboisso receives substantial precipitation in all months except November through February, when the Harmattan comes. Every so often—and in no predictable cycle or pattern—rainfall declines. If the regular dry season is drier than average or if the rains come a little late, the cocoa, coffee, and palm fruit crops may be unaffected. It is the pattern of rainfall and temperature during the most important part of the growing season that affects yields more than average levels of precipitation.

Although rainfall varied during the years leading up to the "cocoa crisis," causing persistent Western speculation that cocoa and coffee output would fall, only in 1983–84 and 1985–86 did drought constitute a serious problem. Some of the farmers in the region lost their cocoa holdings to brush fires in the 1983–84 season; yields dropped universally. In 1985–86, drought and heat struck both coffee and cocoa plantations during periods of heavy flowering, reducing the amount of fruit set, although rain arrived in time to limit the damage to the palm fruit crop. The perceptions of the farmers coincided with the evidence of rainfall patterns supplied by the local meteorological station. Sixteen percent of the cocoa growers identified the 1983–84 season as one in which returns were reduced by drought. The 1985–86 season proved difficult for "reasons of bad climate" in the view of 36% of the cocoa farmers and 30% of the coffee growers. By comparison, only a small handful of growers in all groups considered the 1987–88 and 1988–89 seasons difficult because of weather problems.

Shortages and other market-related, non-price sources of risk were identified as reasons for reduced returns during this period principally among the oil palm growers. The extension office for cocoa and coffee, SATMACI *(Société d'Assistance Technique pour la Modernisation Agricole de la Côte d'Ivoire)*, had withdrawn input subsidies many years before, when it was clear that to keep world prices high, the country would have to limit production. Only about 4% of the cocoa growers interviewed and 18% of the coffee growers reported regular use of fertilizer.[30] In consequence, few identified fertilizer prices or shortages as important reasons for reduced returns. Those who did use fertilizer (overwhelmingly those who believed producer prices would climb again), complained about the high cost, which, at 3 to 4 50 kilogram sacks per hectare, came to about 18,000–24,000 FCFA ($60 to $80).[31] The oil palm growers, who lost their fertilizer subsidy in the mid-1980s, were far more likely than members of the other groups to indicate rising fertilizer costs as a major component of the crisis, although the problem loomed largest as a source of lower returns in 1985–86 (when Palmindustrie removed the subsidy) and the two subsequent years. By the 1988–89 season, only 9% identified fertilizer costs as a major source of risk; all but 15% had stopped using fertilizer.

If the smallholders of Aboisso perceived the "crisis" as the concurrence of several sources of market-related risk, but especially of producer price variation, what expectations did they have about future changes in price? The overwhelming majority of cocoa, coffee, and oil palm growers believed the government's current price levels only temporary, but there was substantial debate among the farmers in each group about the direction of future changes. The cocoa farmers were evenly divided between those who thought the price would improve again and those who thought the price would drop further. The great majority of the other producers saw rising producer prices on the horizon.

To what did growers attribute price changes? Only a handful of the farmers interviewed understood the pricing system. Most knew only the official price—and the price traitants had asked them to accept during the 1987–88 season. They were unaware of the existence of a separate "world market price," although this information was available in two forms to local officials, *députés*, and larger planters. The *Chambre d'Agriculture*, a forum for discussion of agricultural issues, issued a monthly bulletin to subscribers, indicating cocoa and coffee prices on several different markets, as well as the volume of purchases by major international buyers. Although the smallholders did not participate in the Chambre d'Agriculture meetings, they had regular contact with some who did. This information was either not passed on or met with apathy. It was also possible to listen to crop reports and international prices on Ghanaian radio, which most could pick up in at least the eastern part of the region. Awareness of this information source appeared to be restricted to villages that were close to the border and that had members who were comparatively wealthy planters, as opposed to smallholders.

The reasons for the price changes were the source of much discussion in the villages. The government had promoted the view that foreign speculators, the European trading companies, had sought to reduce prices "artificially"—without relation to supply and demand. Most cocoa growers believed that oversupply had created their problem, however. Local economic science tended to downplay the role of non-Ivoirian producers (about whom they knew little) and pinpoint government mismanagement of its economic role as the real cause of oversupply. Farmers spoke of the need to invent uses for cocoa beans so that demand would increase, and turned silent when asked about the role of foreign speculators, indicating either extreme politeness to the interviewer, as a foreigner, or disagreement—more likely the latter. Most expressed concern about the government's ability to manage the economy. They commented that every time the government had urged them to plant a crop in the past, it had created plantations of its own, and the price had fallen. It had done so for copra—and, in the words of one farmer, "everybody knows that government officials own lots of coffee and cocoa, too."[32] Further, farmers were increasingly suspicious about the source of funds for the basilica at Yamoussoukro and spoke more frequently, as the crisis progressed, of the diversion of cocoa revenues to purchase the cathedral and of alleged sales of beans from the president's own plantations while the government allowed their own production to rot in the fields or in warehouses.[33]

Economic Adaptations

The first place the crisis made itself felt in farmers' lives was in the standard of living available to households. Retreat to subsistence agriculture was not a possibility in anyone's mind. Cash was essential for the education of children, and despite grumbling that girls made poor field assistants once spoiled by schooling, education was universally prized. At a minimum, the family had to supply 6,000 FCFA per child for books and 3,000 FCFA per child for a uniform. In most cases, schools required some tuition payments as well, but the boarding costs for older children who could not attend school nearby were the most prohibitive charges, and many despaired of the need to pay lodging expenses. Most farmers worked hard to continue payment of these fees, and the women interviewed in the study cooperated in trying to keep children in school by contributing the money from the trade in foodstuffs they would ordinarily have spent on soap, cloth, or jewelry.[34] Depressed incomes also meant more restricted diets, heavy in cassava and low in protein; even rice and yams had become too expensive to use as staples. Indeed, truck drivers complained that the roadside kiosks no longer made foutou with the yams that had been the mainstay only a year or two before.[35] There were fewer purchases of medicines and clothing, and households cut back their use of hired labor by as much as 50% in the early stages of the crisis, later moving entirely to family labor.[36] Family labor was diverted to cash-crop plots, where, in most cases, it was typical to employ workers for wages.[37] Women extended their workdays so that they could spend time tending the cocoa and coffee bushes, in addition to foodcrops. Household tasks suffered, in consequence. Both because of increased workloads and the growing inability of young men to make continuing payments of the brideprice, divorce rates increased, according to some.[38] Scrimping was a stopgap measure with definite limits, however, and most people looked for longer-term solutions to their predicament.

There were a number of possible economic adaptations to income instability. A farmer might borrow on local credit markets or from distant kin to ease the family through bad periods, draw on formal or informal sources of "crop insurance," diversify into production of other sorts of agricultural commodities or into "off-farm enterprises," or participate in share contracts with workers so that workers would bear some of the risks associated with production. Most farmers tried some combination of one or two of these. Because of the characteristics of kinship structure in these villages and imperfections in factor and producers' markets, however, most of these strategies proved difficult to pursue. To work, they required social and political institutions that did not then exist.

Borrowing and Insurance

There were technically four ways a farmer might borrow to support consumption expenditures, as opposed to agricultural investment, during this period. One was to take out a bank loan on the formal credit market, but that was extremely difficult for most farmers. Neither commercial nor development banks were inclined to loan money for consumption, few farmers had the kind of collateral the banks demanded, and the liquidity crisis meant that many banks would dole out cash in extremely limited quantities, at best (by 1990, even in Abidjan it was difficult to cash a check for more than the equivalent of $1000). Even the *Caisses Rurales d'Epargnes et de Prêts* (CREPs), of which there were three in the Aboisso area, were hard-pressed to provide funds, although two of the farmers, out of 120 interviewed, had borrowed from them.

More readily available, in theory, were three other types of credit transactions: receipt of loans through informal, village- or commune-based credit markets; diversion of funds from investment loans; and borrowing from relatives in urban areas or in other parts of the country, outside the cocoa zone. The statistics suggest that few people borrowed money at all, however. More than three-quarters of the cocoa producers said they had never borrowed during any period of reduced returns during the previous six years. Comparable proportions of other groups said the same. Overwhelmingly, they pointed to two reasons—inability to pay back the money, and since all farmers in the region were suffering reductions of income at the same time, no one really had money to lend.[39] Commented one farmer, "I try never to borrow money because everyone has problems right now."[40]

Several respondents spoke specifically about the difficulty of participating in local or regional credit markets—that is, of borrowing from other planters or from merchants. Credit was difficult to obtain because few had funds to lend, and the risk of default was great. Some commented that credit was so scarce on the informal market that they "would not know who to see about a loan."[41] Interest rates were exceptionally high, in consequence. In one village, the going rate of interest was 100 percent. "That's to say, a 5,000 FCFA loan would require reimbursement, within the year, of 10,000 FCFA," reported one village member. Only very rarely did farmers in this region obtain credit from the merchants who bought and sold their crops. On occasion, cassava dealers from Abidjan offered loans, which they would deduct, with interest, from the sales of the farmer's crop. This practice does not appear to have been widespread or to have lasted long because of the high implicit rates of interest charged (as estimated from the low prices offered), if the trader returned to make payment on the crop at all. In the few cases in which a farmer did secure a loan, the collateral used was almost always land, a commodity of increasing value in the Aboisso region. Although it is not clear from the available evidence it appears that in most cases the value of the land far exceeded the amount of money owed. The practice of "pledging" cocoa land was one with historical roots; cocoa farmers in Ghana and in Côte d'Ivoire had often used land as collateral during the price fluctuations of the colonial period. In Ghana, the practice had led to increasing concentration of ownership, but in the year after the Ivoirian cocoa crisis started, increasing concentration of ownership was not yet apparent, or even rumored in the Aboisso region.

An alternative possibility was to borrow investment funds from the traders or parastatal responsible for marketing the cash crop, whether cocoa, coffee, or oil palm fruit, and to divert the loan to consumption. In an earlier era, of course, a farmer would have received credit for purchase of fertilizer, insecticides, herbicides, and tools from the government marketing board, which would then have deducted the loan from the farmer's receipts at harvest time. In a bid to improve the efficiency of its cocoa and coffee marketing system, however, Côte d'Ivoire had placed crop purchases in the hands of private middlemen, or traitants, and the system of credit for agricultural investment had collapsed, as farmers accepted loans, then sold their crops to other middlemen, who would offer a price from which debt repayments were not deducted. Only Palmindustrie, the parastatal responsible for oil palm production, still maintained a system for extending credit, and it offered loans to support school fees in addition to investment funds. Most of the farmers in the sample who said they received credit had accepted loans through Palmindustrie, and Palmindustrie officials at the local factories[42] corroborated the information provided by the farmers. Several smallholders expressed interest in planting oil palms simply so that they might participate in the program, but the parastatal had shrewdly decided that it would not authorize planting of additional plots until 1990.

A third possibility often invoked by cultivators in studies of other parts of Africa was to borrow from members of the extended household living in urban areas or in other regions of the country. This system was less a kind of credit market than a family-based insurance system, to which people paid "premiums" throughout their lives in the expectation that they might call upon resources in time of need. Among the Aboisso cocoa growers, however, this strategy appeared to have little importance, at least in the first year after the effective drop in prices. Although a few farmers borrowed from neighbors, merchants, or, most especially, Palmindustrie, none reported loans from household members.

The key to understanding this choice appears to lie in the low social salience of kinship ties among the region's inhabitants. Where, at the turn of the century, the farmers of Aboisso came principally from two Akan groups, the Agni and the Attié, now they hail from many different regions within Côte d'Ivoire and from far-flung locations in Nigeria, Mali, Guinea, Burkina Faso, Togo, and

Ghana. Gone are the days when a single set of descent-based rights and privileges governed access to land, labor, and other critical resources in a village. In their stead are negotiated arrangements, supervised by chiefs and notables often from non-Agni or Attié backgrounds. Gone too are the extensive kinship networks that used to tie immigrants to relatives in the areas left behind. In most cases, immigrants appear to have limited the kin-based claims that could be placed on their resources by cutting themselves off from distant relatives.[43] In times of crisis, of course, the severing of kin ties meant that the cocoa farmers could not draw on the reserves of cousins in other regions, either. Even when sons, daughters, and cousins worked in nearby towns or in Abidjan, they were of relatively little assistance to their rural relatives. The cocoa crisis had affected urban incomes as well, and many were beginning to find that returns to labor on the land were increasingly comparable to returns to labor in the urban informal sector.

In the area covered by the study, there was only one "cluster" of instances in which commercial crop insurance was considered. A traveling insurance salesman had visited one of the villages, and several village members, including the chief, had thought the idea a good one. They paid their initial premiums, but they never heard from the salesman again. Absent government or quasi-public "umpiring" of the market, commercial insurance did not go forward, and in the presence of price-setting by government institutions, futures markets, which would potentially smooth producer price fluctuations and perform much the same function as insurance, failed to evolve.

Diversification of Crop Choice

In response to fluctuating cocoa prices, the farmer could attempt to diversify crop choice or to diversify into nonagricultural enterprises—informal sector businesses. By diversifying, the farmer could ensure that not all elements of his "income portfolio" varied in the same direction at the same time and could thus be relatively certain of receiving a basic level of return. Although this strategy could not and did not protect smallholder incomes when the government suspended cocoa sales and traders failed to pay farmers, most farmers had some inkling that cocoa and coffee prices would fall, in advance of the actual government decision to drop the price to 200 FCFA/kilogram. In the months before the decision the government had "protested too much" that it had no intention of reducing prices, and most farmers in the sample said they anticipated the drop.

Not all farmers pursued diversification. About a third of all coffee growers, a half of all cocoa farmers, and three-quarters of all oil palm growers reported increasing the number of crops cultivated in the wake of reduced returns. Cooperative members were less likely than others to add new crops to their programs. In almost all of these cases, the crops added were food crops, especially cassava. In fewer than 8% of the 120 cases studied did farmers attempt to earn money in nonagricultural enterprises or by participating in wage contracts on nearby plantations.

There were four principal forms of "crop diversification" during the cocoa crisis. The first and most important was increased production of cassava, which could be sold in the towns and in Abidjan. Typically production of cassava and other food crops was the preserve of women, who could use the proceeds from their sales to help finance children's education and to buy things they needed for themselves. With the advent of the economic crisis, men moved into cassava production, working land formerly cultivated by women and opening up new fields along rights of way. As people rapidly discovered, however, the problem was that as more and more farmers grew cassava and other food crops, prices for these commodities fell precipitously, lessening the stabilizing effects of the strategy on standards of living.[44]

The second major form of agricultural diversification was to expand fishing in the lagoons, rivers, and swamps of the department. Fish had long been an important part of the local diet. During the early 1980s when drought and bush fires reduced cocoa and coffee harvests, farmers discovered that they could market fish to passersby on the road between Ghana and Abidjan. Truck, taxi, and bus drivers would stop, purchase fish or crabs, and take the produce to the capital or to nearby towns for resale. Demand grew during the mid-1980s, then took off in the first year and a half of the cocoa crisis. Gradually, farmers began to notice that it was harder and harder to catch fish in the most accessible spots, and the price climbed higher. The city dwellers were willing to pay a high price for the fewer and fewer fish available, and, increasingly, Aboisso households began to forego fish in their own diets. They were too expensive to consume. By the end of 1989, women began to report that they had eliminated fish from family meals, except on important occasions or as a splurge once in a while, and when they did include it, it was often tinned fish from the town instead of fresh lagoon fish.

Harvesting of wild kola was another possibility pursued by many cocoa and coffee growers. Kola grew in the forest and could be found interspersed with coffee and cocoa bushes in many fields. Highly valued as a stimulant by Muslims and non-Muslims alike, kola nuts have long had a market in northern areas, and the Sénoufo and Dioula immigrants in the Aboisso region demonstrated particular skill in brokering a new kola trade during the first year and a half of the cocoa crisis. Several farmers interviewed in the study reported that the price for a kilogram of kola had exceeded the price for the equivalent weight of cocoa or coffee in the early months of the crisis and that it was now far more profitable than either beverage crop. Nonetheless, a highly perishable commodity with a limited market, kola was unlikely to support an entire region for long.

A fourth possibility debated hotly among village members was cultivation of rubber. Beginning in the early 1980s, the World Bank and the EEC had put pressure on the Ivoirian government to promote rubber production as a way of buffering farmer incomes from the ups and downs of the highly volatile cocoa market. A second campaign to promote smallholder cultivation of rubber began in 1983, with Bank support. Farmers who could produce deeds or some other evidence of land title, certify that their plots bordered passable dirt access roads, or *pistes*, farmed plots within 25 kilometers of the processing plant, and demonstrated that they or cosigners were at least 43 years old would receive authorization to plant rubber and to receive loans for fertilizer and other inputs. They would also be reimbursed for their labor in clearing and planting the plots of land.[45] The input packages ended after the initial phase of the program was over, and the farmers of Aboisso deliberated long and hard among themselves about the advisability of planting rubber. Oblivious to the use of synthetic substitutes, some argued that there would always be a demand for tires and that therefore they could not lose if they went ahead. Others commented that every time the government had urged them to plant a crop in the past, it had created plantations of its own, and the price had fallen. They believed that rubber was not going to be a solution to their problems.[46] By the end of 1989, however, only a handful of the farmers in the area had opted to plant rubber trees.

In their debates about rubber the farmers also noted a problem that was an important barrier to most kinds of agricultural diversification: increasing land scarcity. Of the barriers to agricultural diversification where perennial, or tree crops predominate, the new experience of land shortage was probably the greatest. As long as cocoa, coffee, or palm prices might go back up and the farmer believes he or she can earn an *average* return that exceeds the possible return from other crops, it makes sense to keep the bushes or trees in the ground. Except for kola, it is not possible to maintain other crops on the land while cocoa or coffee are in place; intercropping is not a real possibility. To diversify into other crops, the farmer either has to get rid of his trees or he has to gain access to more land.

Unlike most parts of Côte d'Ivoire, however, the Aboisso region now had a population density that puts pressure on land supply. Immigrants began to arrive in significant numbers during the colonial period, and they now outnumber the Agni and Attié in most villages. Most settled in the area during the mid-1900s, when land was abundant and participation in the cocoa and coffee trades appeared highly attractive. In some instances, young entrepreneurs first worked for Agni farmers and after a period of six years, or so, were given permission to cultivate plots of land on their own. They came in "waves," and most of the elders interviewed indicated a succession of migrations, which often started with an influx of Baule or Abouré from central Côte d'Ivoire, then Dioula and Sénoufo from the north, then people from other countries. The most recent settlers are the Togolese and Ghanaians, and older residents are fond of pointing out, half-jokingly, that in the latter case, Ghanaian women arrived first. As migrant workers became increasingly important in cocoa production, they obtained greater bargaining power vis-à-vis Akan groups and negotiated access to land and later to wives, loosening the hold of the original inhabitants over control of critical resources and weakening their political bases. In a few cases, the colonial government accelerated the cultural diversification of the region by rewarding young men for their military service or their work in road construction with gifts of cocoa land.

With the weakening of Agni power, lineage authority over land came into question. Although the form of the *Assassi Tuhô*, the

Agni system of land-transfer, is retained as an informal ceremony in some parts of the region today, it is no longer even an informal requisite.[47] The system eroded substantially during the middle part of the century and was dealt a final blow in 1971 by the passage of laws abolishing "traditional land tenure," or group rights of access. A land market did not immediately arise, however, and the buying and selling of land is still shrouded in secrecy, although both notables and farmers in all of the villages studied eventually "confessed" to participation in exchanges of land for money. It is possible to purchase land in areas of "classified forest" by approaching the administration of "Eaux et Forêts." These plots currently sell for about 80,000 FCFA (about $265) per hectare. It is also possible to purchase or rent land from other farmers, although officials often deny knowledge of some of these exchanges. The farmers surveyed in this study did participate in land deals and commented that the going rate for purchase of a hectare of land was about 70,000 FCFA at the time they purchased their land, about 15 years ago.[48] More recently, as land has become increasingly valuable, those with land appear to favor rental arrangements. Rental of a hectare for two years generally comes to 40,000 FCFA per hectare. The distinction between renting and buying is often obscure, and many of those interviewed said that the number of cases of land litigation had increased recently as people tried to ascertain the nature of their claims.

Without easy access to land, however, it becomes extremely difficult for the smallholders to diversify their crop choice. This situation places great pressure on the farmer's assessment of future price trends. If, in fact, a commodity is in long-term surplus worldwide, then the farmer is going to face not volatile prices and positive average returns but declining prices and declining returns—and he should cut down his bushes. None of the smallholders interviewed had adequate market information to make that judgment, however, and they emphasized their dependence on government policymakers in making critical assessments.

Diversification into Off-Farm Enterprises

Under these circumstances, one might expect households to seek nonagricultural sources of income—to manufacture stoves or shoes for sale along main roads or in towns, for example, or to sign up with the local labor bureau for work on industrial plantations or road contracts. The study results suggest, however, that in the early phases of the cocoa crisis, 1987–89, only a very few farmers pursued this option. Only 8% of those interviewed indicated participation in informal sector enterprises or wage contracts. This figure corresponds with a World Bank study which found that only 8% or fewer or rural household members in each of several age categories participated in petty trade or manufacturing, regardless of the part of the country.[49] In this instance, again, the structure of existing economic institutions made it difficult for most to modify their income portfolios, in the short run, in a way that would significantly protect their standards of living.

The only significant participation in "the informal sector," outside of agricultural trade, was illegal alcohol production—the tried and true backyard still. Because many of the palms in the area were reaching the end of their productive lives, enterprising young men negotiated with palm owners to get permission to tap the palms for their sap in exchange for cutting down the trees. A farmer who could produce 200 liters of palm wine a day for trade along main roads (with the complicity of the regular police, the customs police, the forest police, and the army, which all staffed roadblocks nearby) would net as much as 1,000,000 FCFA per year, after costs, or a little over $3,000. Of course, one had to be able to secure one's operations from interruption by the authorities or by competitors who might leak information about the still to local officials, and that could cost money. It is probably no accident that the most voluble palm wine producers had secure positions in the village leadership or strong ties with the local administration.

For most farmers, entry into the informal sector was blocked by lack of money, knowhow, and a severe labor constraint. Those interviewed said that to go into business required an apprenticeship. An informal guild system operated in local towns, and it was almost impossible to learn a trade or gain access to critical raw materials unless one worked with a member of the guild first. Apprenticeships cost money, of course, and few farmers had sufficient savings left to pay the fees required. Only one farmer in the study reported working as a mechanic, and he made it quite clear that he could do so because his grandfather, who had also been one, had taught him basic skills.[50] Most viewed entry into petty production and trade as nearly impossible for these reasons.

Participation in wage contracts or the informal sector was also limited by severe labor constraints. Although it is possible to neglect cocoa and coffee bushes for short periods of time without severe deterioration in the field quality, it is still necessary to invest enough labor to prevent catastrophic disease of plants and to produce food for household consumption. In most cases, the farmers interviewed indicated that, with children in school for part of the day, there were simply not enough hands to do the labor required. The loss of an able-bodied worker to another pursuit was not acceptable to them, in large part because they placed no faith in promises of high wage rates or high levels of return. Growing seasons are not divisible goods. Unless the farmer, or a relative, could guarantee high levels of earnings for an agricultural season and could convince the household that these earnings could be used to purchase food equivalent to what his or her labor would have produced on the land for the whole season, off-farm labor seemed a poor gamble indeed. Most respondents replied to continued probing of this issue with a curmudgeonly grumble that, "agriculture was still more remunerative anyway" and comments about the nobility of working the land.[51]

Share Contracts

Neoclassical economic theory suggests that another alternative for coping with increased risk, especially with multiple sources of risk, is for the farmer to abandon payment of wages to day laborers, which forces the employer to bear the burden of price variability, for a system in which those who cultivate the land assume some of the risk themselves by receiving a share of the output as payment for their work. This system also limits the need for close supervision of field labor, because the worker's earnings are tied directly to his or her productivity. Such share tenancies have had a long history among the Akan cocoa growers of Ghana and Côte d'Ivoire. The *abusa* system of the colonial period provided for the division of the output into thirds, and the return of a third to the person who had tended the land in the "owner's" absence. This arrangement operated alongside payment of wages to migrant workers. Sometimes it supplanted wages; at other times it existed in tandem.

With increased market-related risk, one might expect to see an increased incidence of share tenancies in the cocoa- and coffee-growing areas, but such does not appear to be the case—at least not yet. In late 1989, only 8% of cocoa growers reported giving part of their harvests to those who "owned" the land, and only 4% reported receiving part of another's harvest.[52] Those who believed that producer prices for their main crops would continue to drop were slightly more likely than others to participate in these contracts, a finding consistent with the theory. These findings appear to be in line with popular perceptions that abusa—and anything like it—had disappeared by the early 1960s, except in the management of land used for cassava production. Respondents showed little interest or enthusiasm for the system.

Why were share contracts unpopular ways of rewarding labor and allocating risk in the cultivation of perennial cash crops but practiced more widely in the food crop sector during the early stages of the cocoa crisis? The answer probably lies partly in the substantial bargaining power of labor, partly in the increasing shortage of land, and partly in the discovery of new ways of managing a labor force.

At the time of the crisis, affordable labor was still a scarce commodity even in this region of the country. The going wage on nearby pineapple plantations, the most direct competitor for the resource, was between 850 and 1000 FCFA per five-hour day (about $3.00). Few smallholders could afford to pay that much, although they generally agreed that they paid about 600 FCFA per day when they had to hire itinerant laborers. The high value placed on labor meant that workers were in a strong bargaining position vis-à-vis the household heads. They did not have to share the increased risk associated with cocoa, coffee, or oil-palm production. If asked to do so, they could simply turn around and go elsewhere, where their services were equally in demand but where the reward was higher.

For the farmers themselves, share tenancies held out not only the possibility of sharing the risk but also a way to avoid paying wages out of limited and stretched cash reserves. But increasingly the farmers of Aboisso lacked the one resource that could compel participation of workers in these arrangements: land. Under the abusa system, as practiced in this part of Côte d'Ivoire, the tenants who cultivated the land usually received their own plots on the periphery of village fields after about six years. Population density, increased settlement, and classification of some areas as protected forest had produced a land shortage in Aboisso by the time of the cocoa crisis, however. To make matters worse, many farmers had received subsidized input packages (fertilizer, pesticides, plants, for example) for oil palms, for which in return they had only to register the land and present a title to the parastatal. Titles had not been issued to those who admitted to participation in share contracts. Most smallholders had thus lost their ability to make share contracts attractive alternatives to higher wages.

Finally, all of the villages in the area had originated new forms of labor organization during the "mini-crisis" of the early 1980s that reduced the need of farmers to resort to share contracts as means of supervising labor. Several farmers in the study commented that individual workers could prove highly unreliable and required much supervision, which few had time to provide. Beginning in the early part of the decade, most villages had evolved competing "labor teams" of young men and women, who would clear, hoe, seed, weed, and harvest land for a fee, which the members would divide among themselves or, more often, invest in projects or ceremonies. Fees varied according to the size of the group, running from about 16,000 FCFA for a day's work by a team of eighteen to 25,000 FCFA for a day's work by a team of thirty-two.[53] The labor teams were more efficient, in the view of most farmers, because they created peer pressure for hard work and because one always knew to whom to go to complain about a lazy performance. In some villages labor participation was strictly voluntary. In others, a young man or woman who claimed exemption more than three times, whatever the reason, would be fined 1,000 FCFA. Although share contracts remained a way of spreading risk, the labor teams solved the problem of supervision, which loomed more important than distributing the burdens of a temporary downturn in price or increase in costs, in the eyes of many.

Share contracts did come into vogue between older farmers with few children and younger farmers who needed to grow food for sale to pay school fees. These differed from earlier arrangements, however, in that the parties were neighbors from the same village, both with access to land, and the contract involved no agreement to turn over rights of access to the plots.

The Insufficiency of Individual Responses

None of the major forms of economic adaptation could preserve household standards of living during the early phases of the crisis. Even in combination, the strategies barely kept people from despair. For the smallholders of Aboisso, who based their cash incomes on sale of perennial crops, there were four major problems in getting any standard economic strategy to work. One had to do with the emergence of a land shortage at precisely the time when urban job opportunities were few and the government had launched a "return to the country" campaign. Two were rooted in the absence of public- or quasi-public institutions for ensuring the integrity of market transactions. And the fourth was a consequence of the changed kinship structure in the region.

For growers of mature, perennial crops, diversification of crop choice in order to protect against market-related risk requires access to additional plots of land. It is difficult to cultivate alternative crops, especially food crops, on plots heavily shaded by cocoa or coffee bushes or oil palms, especially where roots compete for space. Farmers can cultivate land devoted to annual food crops more intensively, by extending intercropping and succession planting, but there are strict limits on the impact diversification carried out on these plots can have on cash incomes—especially if neighbors have the same idea at the same time. Few smallholders had the cash to buy more land. Some started to cultivate the rights of way between large estates and the main roads or access routes, as estate-owners rarely used this land fully. Most simply found agricultural diversification unworkable.

Those who did try to market surplus food as a short-run strategy encountered a second problem; they found that they could not always trust the traders who came from the city to buy their crops. When the farmers sold on credit, expecting the traders to return with their money after the sale in Abidjan, they rarely saw the proceeds. When they accepted credit from the merchants and agreed to deduct repayment from the revenues the sale generated, they ended up paying usurious interest rates. And they worried about the prices offered, too. Absent an umpire to guard against collusion among merchants, the farmers had no way to trust that the prices offered were fair market prices, and resentment over real or imagined "cheating" boiled right below the surface.

Theoretically, smallholders could take up opportunities in the "informal sector" or establish credit and insurance systems. But these routes, too, were at least partly blocked as a result of efforts by a few to segment and manipulate markets to their own advantage. As in the marketing of food crops, the absence of institutions to enforce contracts and to broadcast market information hampered the creation of insurance programs or credit systems that could have helped farmers through the crisis. As most African governments, the Ivoirian government has concentrated on the management role of the developmental state at the expense of its role as market "umpire." There are few procedures for resolving disputes between traders and farmers—or between farmers—and even fewer organizational vehicles for supporting these. If a dispute arises, the sous-préfet or préfet may choose to step in. These are busy officials, however, with many responsibilities, and few have the time to handle more than an occasional land dispute. Complaints about traders or insurance salesmen are nearly impossible to address, because there are few ways to track itinerant merchants with the resources the departments have available.

Second, the farmers viewed the "informal sector," quite rightly, as anything but the "free market," with low barriers to entry, low capital requirements, and high levels of competition, that Western analysts believed it was. At least in the rural areas, becoming a mechanic in an open-air garage, shoemaking, marketing cloth and other items villagers needed, smithing, and other "professions" required that one find the money to acquire an apprenticeship. Even then, some trades were open only to the sons of those who had practiced these before. And, of course, the returns from taking up one of these vocations would have to equal or exceed the average returns from agriculture, minus the extra wage costs required to replace the field labor lost. Few farmers thought such levels of return likely. The carpenters and vendors evident in the villages were strangers who had temporarily settled in the area from homes far away.

Finally, the smallholders of Aboisso were apparently unable to tap into kinship-based "insurance networks," because they had earlier cut themselves off from relatives in distant regions, in order to limit demands on their own resources. Unlike many parts of Africa, Aboisso is home to people from a wide variety of cultural backgrounds. Many had migrated to the region to take advantage of entrepreneurial opportunities and had severed ties with less enterprising cousins back home in order to preserve their capital from the constant demand to support funerals or weddings. They had done well, compared to more northerly neighbors or compared to relatives in neighboring West African countries, but few had succeeded so greatly that they had paid for a university education of a son or daughter and therefore few had salaried relatives. Even if household members had worked their way into the urban elite, the government's decision to impose a 15 to 40% tax on public and private salaries would have eliminated any savings well-to-do relatives might have provided.

The Rise of a "Proto-politics"

The futility of individual efforts to protect standards of living prompted some of the farmers to join together to communicate their concerns to the administration and to create a larger role for themselves in decision-making about agricultural policy. In the first phase of the crisis, their efforts were clear but limited. The farmers began to try out new forms of participation, to discard those they found wanting, and to sharpen their own understanding of their political interests. They stopped short of organizing the kind of farmers' interest lobby that an unidentified smallholder from the western region suggested necessary in a much-publicized interview with Radio France Internationale.[54] But many took issue, at least implicitly, with the farmer's comment, "We are not happy, but there is nothing we can do against the government." They reorganized the cooperatives that the extension service had constituted in each village and began to turn these to their own ends. They began to send delegations to the préfet and then to Abidjan, where they tried to meet with senior officials of the parastatals and the Ministry of Agriculture. Some began to join farmers from neighboring villages and towns to discuss marketing strategies, either through cooperatives, in the case of cocoa, or between individuals and international buyers, in the case of those who had planted pineapple next to their other crops.

Some farmers did decide to wait out the crisis, however, and for the political scientist, the interesting question is why some began to explore new forms of political participation while others did not. In particular, why did responses tend to vary by village, in the early phases of the crisis? By trying to explain the difference between "active" villages and "inactive" villages, it may be possible to illuminate the foundations of collective action.

"Participant" versus "Nonparticipant" Villages

The typical active village had several characteristics that distinguished it from those whose residents had chosen to cope with the crisis only through reorganization of household consumption and production patterns. These villages were "participant" in three different respects.

First, villagers had joined together to form decision-making groups that operated parallel to older systems of authority or to structures put in place by the state. Sometimes these informal groups used existing organizations to their own ends, and at other times they operated as ad hoc advisory committees. In either case, they made their influence felt by moving to solve disputes that had barred provision of community services—water towers and classrooms, for example—in neighboring communities. To do so, they had to overcome a problem common to most of the villages in the region.

Generally, villages in Aboisso included a small number of Agni or Attié families, descendants of the original inhabitants of the area, and a larger number of households from diverse cultural heritages. The latter had acquired access to land in the area in one of two ways. Earlier in the century, some had come to the region in search of work and had participated in share contracts, agreeing to care for the cocoa and coffee crops of resident farmers in return for part of the harvest and the promise of land several years hence. After they acquired their own plots, other members of their households joined them. Alternatively, some farmers had received grants of land from the colonial government as reward for military service or for work in the colonial administration.

The Ivoirian government installed two structures of authority within these villages. The first was a PDCI cell or *comité* that included a president, appointed by the chief or notables, and representatives of different quarters of the village. The purpose of this committee was to represent the village at regional party meetings, transmit messages from party headquarters and from the president of the country, and collect annual fees for identity cards.

The second authority structure was a cooperative organization with the power to choose cocoa and coffee buyers, collect and distribute crop payments, manage the local distribution of fertilizer in some cases, and collect revenues from each member to be used for provision of community services. Although the government had initially tried to promote cooperatives or Groupements de Vocation Coopérative (GVCs) and had been instrumental in their financing and organization in the early years, most of the GVCs of Aboisso had lost their strong ties to the administration or to parastatals and, by the time of the crisis, lived or died on the initiative of village farmers. Where they existed, GVCs provided a forum where farmers could argue about the sources of the crisis, about ways of improving their incomes, and about how they might try to influence the policies the government pursued. At this time, slightly more than half of the cocoa and coffee growers participated in annual cooperative meetings and elections. In many cases, however, the cooperatives had collapsed. In a few, they persisted but lost membership as residents disputed the choice of crop buyers and the use of funds collected and as the parastatal that had helped expand coffee and cocoa production, SATMACI, stopped subsidizing inputs.

Initially, some of the farmers thought about using the cooperatives both to make their views heard (it was easier for a cooperative president to get an appointment with the préfet than for an ordinary farmer to do so) and to appropriate some of the functions that "untrustworthy" intermediaries had previously monopolized. As one might expect, a higher proportion of those who envisioned future declines in producer prices, especially for lower grade coffees, participated than did those who believed that prices would remain stable, at their lower levels, or than those who believed prices might increase. Some of these groups contemplated marketing crops directly to exporters in Abidjan in the next growing season, to avoid problems with middlemen, whom they had grown to distrust, and to capture the traitants' margins for themselves.[55]

In most villages of the region, however, demographics and political structures, especially cooperative organization, conspired to produce conflict and disrupt the functioning of these groups. Cooperatives funded provision of public services or public goods by taking a fixed proportion of the revenues each farming household received in a given year and using that money to improve community amenities. Cooperative officers were able to monitor revenues of all farmers who sold their produce through the cooperative organization—and those of any additional farmers who received assistance from SATMACI's extension services. Revenues depended on yields, and typically newer residents generated higher returns on their land than did the Agni or Attié inhabitants, whether because of greater attentiveness to good farming practices, a higher proportion of household members of working age, or settlement on richer soils. The newer residents protested that their hard work meant that they supported a much higher proportion of the costs of community services and public goods than did the original inhabitants. The *autochtones* replied that as the original inhabitants, whose beneficence had allowed the newcomers to settle in the region in the first place, they were entitled to pay a lower proportion of the costs of community benefits.[56]

The first respect in which "participant" villages differed from "nonparticipant" villages was in the degree to which they had resolved or submerged this conflict either by creating parallel authority structures or by modifying the rules of operation of the existing cooperatives. In the "participant" villages, farmers had found some way to agree on an appropriate level of contribution from each member household and until the cocoa crisis depressed revenues greatly these villages had continued to improve water systems and classrooms and convince the government to help grade roads.

These farmers were also quick to defend their achievements. The general collapse of the cooperatives and the proliferation of new, small, uneconomic organizations in their stead attracted the notice of the Ministry of Agriculture, which tried to intervene to create larger, more viable units. The Ministry communicated its plans to extension agents in the Aboisso region through its newspaper, *Terre et Progrés*, where it argued that the management problems of the cooperatives had four components: the failure of the GVCs to repay loans extended by the BNDA and the consequent unwillingness of the BNDA and other credit sources to finance investment or trade by cooperatives, the tendency of private haulers and government security agents to impose high official and unofficial transport costs on the GVCs, eliminating profit margins in consequence, the inability of the factories to receive, process, and store the crops as they arrived, forcing return of truckloads to village storehouses, and "laziness, nepotism, and indiscretions" on the part of GVC officials.[57] Its analysis overlooked the relationship between farmer revenues and provision of public benefits and missed one of the major reasons for cooperative collapse. Its solution in many cases violated the arrangements the "participant" villages had forged. Farmers in these villages were predictably angry and made their displeasure known through delegates they sent to meetings with government officials.[58]

The second characteristic common to the "participant" villages but not shared by the others was the creation of "delegations" to represent grower interests locally and in Abidjan. By the end of the first year of the crisis, a new kind of participation had emerged. Dispensing with party representatives, farmers in several villages constituted delegations to take their complaints to the appropriate ministries or traveled to Abidjan on their own behalf. This step was no small accomplishment. It meant breaking with established systems of authority relations mentally, first. In other regions of the country, acceptable behavior toward people in power required that farmers with grievances take their complaints to the sous-préfet or to the préfet. To go above that level, unless invited, was unheard of. Second, it meant debating with others to define the main issues and frame a list of demands. Third, it meant spending money to travel by bus to Abidjan. Fourth, it meant negotiating bureaucratic red tape that would daunt the most clever of academics.[59]

An older farmer from one of these villages who had lived through the crisis of the 1940s commented on the village's experience in constituting a delegation to go to Abidjan. He said that in February 1990, when the transporters and other groups went on strike in the capital, some of the farmers in the region thought they should strike too. One person assembled some other farmers from neighboring villages, but when the men met they decided it would be difficult to carry out a successful strike. They decided to go to Abidjan instead. In May, they went to the headquarters of Palmindustrie and to the Caisse (Caistab). They were well received, he said. They urged the officials to raise producer prices and to offer "*primes d'encouragement,*" or monetary incentives for maintaining their plantings during hard times. The officials made lots of promises but did not act on them. The farmers of this village would consider sending another delegation to act on their behalf, he said.[60]

The interviews with farmers in "participant" and "nonparticipant" villages revealed that the former were far more likely to travel to meetings and seats of government to express their concerns than the latter, even though all of these villages had relatively easy access to road transportation. Senior parastatal employees in the region and in Abidjan confirmed reports that farmers often showed up in their offices, sometimes with advance warning and sometimes not, to seek action on individual complaints and convey information about problems experienced by the village. In some cases, parastatal officials had memorized the names and case histories of individual farming households, so often did the *chef d'exploitation* pay a visit to the headquarters.

The third difference between patterns of participation in these communities lay in media use. Residents of the "active" villages followed local and national news to a greater degree than did farmers in neighboring, "nonparticipant" communities. Asked about recent local meetings among *grands planteurs* to discuss marketing strategies and about meetings of the regional Chambre d'Agriculture, farmers in "participant" villages were far more likely to correctly identify the forum and the topics discussed than farmers in "nonparticipant" villages. None of the farmers in any of the villages surveyed had participated directly in those gatherings, which were generally the preserve of farmers with larger holdings or of growers of different kinds of crops. All had relatives of friends who traveled throughout the region during the week and could potentially return with news, however. Only those in the "participant" villages recalled the events or knew, in some cases, that the organizers of some of these meetings had urged creation of new systems of representation that would allow smallholders in the villages to send a delegate to future gatherings.

Further, the "militant" villages all had bamboo cinemas—VCRs and television sets attached to small generators or car batteries hooked up in series. The films obtained for show in these bamboo theaters rarely had anything at all to do with agriculture. Indeed, the favorites were the kinds of films that cause scholars to invoke the specter of "cultural imperialism" out of despair at the images displayed.[61] With a television set, however, it was also possible to catch the national news, in its local language edition, and the Wednesday evening agricultural special. Although government-controlled, this medium nonetheless allowed viewers some knowledge of the concerns of farmers in other parts of the country.

It offered exposure to the outside world less available to the residents of the other villages.

"Exposure to media" was an endogeneous variable too. The images the news conveyed may also have proven instrumental in the choice of the "delegation" as a form of political participation, instead of demonstrations or boycotts. Television watchers would have been familiar with the president's tactic of calling "days of dialogue" during times of crisis and of inviting representative groups to Abidjan to air their views in front of him. Just weeks before the farmers led their community delegations to the Ministry of Agriculture, the president had met with other, larger groups, whose members had not minced their words in voicing their complaints. It is likely that the form of participation the farmers chose was selected precisely because they had seen others use it and witnessed the president's acceptance of it. Although an exceptional form of participation, the delegation was sanctioned where other kinds of activities were not.

Non-economic Incentives for Collective Action

In his study of patterns of collective action among villages in south India, Robert Wade found that ecological and economic variables explained the emergence of "village republics" in some cases and not in others.[62] For example, communities at the remote ends of irrigation systems had greater economic incentive to organize than did those closer to the source of water and were more likely to fit the "active" pattern than the "inactive." The villages studied in the Aboisso region did not fit that model, however. All were similarly situated with regard to water, climate, soil fertility, transport, and availability of land. For the sources of the pattern observed, it is necessary to look to noneconomic variables.

The villages in which farmers organized and went to Abidjan to deposit themselves on the doorstep of the Minister of Agriculture were distinctive from others in three main respects. First, their chiefs did not appear to exercise strong control over the notables. In one case, the chief was extremely sick and unable to participate in village affairs. In another, the chief had no evident interest in governing, or at least seemed in practice to advocate an extremely laissez-faire approach to the job to which his neighbors had elected him. It is likely that the absence of the usual lines of authority in these two villages forced residents to solve problems among themselves, without the invocation of hierarchical authority, and that this experience encouraged them to think more flexibly about authority relations generally.

It is important to note that the legitimacy of the second center of political authority in the village, the PDCI, had also faded. Rates of participation in PDCI meetings remained high. As a way of hearing the latest from Abidjan and as social events, the gatherings are still attractive. The "discussion" was usually unidirectional, in the view of the participants, however. The role of the representative was to transmit the views of the party leadership and the president's words of wisdom, which some of the local representatives viewed as a sacred trust. Farmers may have voiced grievances about government policy, but the party had no clear mechanism for transmitting these, according to villagers.

More irksome, in the farmers' view, was that the party collected money but gave nothing in return. In displays of indignation that rarely occur in front of a visitor, village notables consistently chastised the PDCI representatives for trying to convey the impression that the farmers saw a return on the money spent on the identity cards. In more northerly regions, it was fairly common for villagers to assume that World Bank projects and aid-supported wells or infrastructure were PDCI contributions. The farmers of Aboisso labored under no such illusions, and they took their representatives to task for what they perceived as the party's failure to represent their interests in these times of crisis.

Just two months before the 1989 interviews, the party had also taken a step that was highly unpopular with many rural residents. A wave of violent crime had swept the capital in June, July, and August 1989. Growing fear of urban bandits, and, behind the scenes, the president's concern about the possibility of factional fighting between members of the growing Lebanese population, led the government to order the army out of the barracks and onto the streets of the capital to help police the city. It also installed the army along major rural roads, to supplement the customs police, gendarmerie, forest rangers, and other officials already on patrol. It lacked the money for stepped up security, however, and so, with great fanfare, the PDCI contributed substantial funds toward the cause—funds drawn from rural residents' already stretched pocketbooks. Because transport costs were already high as a result of the *"indélicatesses de certains agents de contrôle sur les routes,"*[63] to use the Ministry of Agriculture's phrasing, the farmers were none too pleased by the PDCI's proposal.

The second source of variation in patterns of participation was demographic. In the "participant" villages the "notables" were younger and more diverse in their cultural backgrounds than in the other villages. In most cases, how they became "notables" was not at all clear, except that they took an active interest in local affairs. Most were farmers who had participated in cooperatives and watched them fall apart or who had signed on to one or another of the government campaigns to diversify crops, only to have subsidy packages removed after they joined. It is likely that their experiences in these programs had given them a keener sense than their neighbors of which policies were inappropriate or poorly framed. To the extent that smallholders learned what their interests were by experimenting and trying to make their farms work, these people were among the most "educated," even if few had any formal schooling at all. Because of the loose authority structures in these villages, these younger and especially committed farmers were able to gain some control over their affairs within the village and build confidence in their views.

Some of these farmers had higher levels of education or experience than was the norm for the region, as well. In the mid-1980s, the government had initiated a campaign to return youth from the cities and towns to the land, on the grounds that the rural labor force was aging and needed the ideas and muscle-power of the young men and women who had left home. During the crisis, youth began to return to the countryside in increasing numbers, bringing both skills and problems. In contrast to most of the farmers surveyed, these return migrants could read and write—and speak French. One very successful farmer from an area adjacent to the study site commented that in his village, the labor invested in organizing the community and in maintaining the cooperative generated sufficient returns only if the farmers were literate.[64] Illiterate farmers, who could not read the accounting books of the cooperative, only caused trouble, in his view. The *"relève paysanne"* slowly began to increase the number of farmers with the skills necessary to monitor use of funds within the community.

The influx of young people also created new pressure to increase the returns to labor on the land. A prizewinning farmer on the outskirts of one of the less active communities noted that the dynamics of the household and community were beginning to change, with the need to accommodate the ambitions of the young men who chose to come home.[65] Two of his own sons had returned earlier in the year and already one had joined a delegation to go to Abidjan to protest low prices for oil palm fruit. He noted that there would be "real problems" if yields and prices did not increase and that his sons would probably become more involved in trying to influence government policy.

Third, these villages also differed from the less active or "nonparticipant" communities in that those who had left, students and urban workers, remitted part of their earnings to the community, not just to individual households, and took an active role in determining how that money should be spent. Urban-based village associations are common to both "participant" and "nonparticipant" communities. What varied was the kind of relationship the urban association maintained with the home area. As urban dwellers found themselves facing tougher economic straits, association members often decided to give to the home community as a group and to exert greater control over the use and management of the funds than they had previously. They constituted a new center of authority which further altered the role of the chief and notables but also made the managers of the cooperative or of the informal development association far more accountable for their actions than had been the case. The control over money combined with ability to exert pressure on household members provided instruments for reducing the costs of collective action within the village. Further, these groups reported important information that shaped the diagnosis of economic problems and interests and the selection of appropriate responses.

By way of illustration, the *ressortissants* of one village had decided that it had to take a stronger role in resolving the conflicts that perpetually afflicted the cooperative and undermined its effectiveness. In the very early years of the crisis, when price trends were still unclear, the members decided to open a headquarters in the village instead of in Abidjan, so that they would all have incentive to return home and monitor the problems farmers faced. They helped the new, young president of the GVC call residents together to meet as a group and then called the notables to witness the general support proposals for management change had among the villagers. Members returned regularly for GVC meetings and intervened when necessary to help resolve conflicts and ensure the wise use of funds contributed.[66]

In conclusion, therefore, the greater willingness of farmers in some villages to organize associations to bolster crop sales, lower costs, and provide basic amenities; constitute delegations to advance farmers' interests in negotiations with officials; and monitor local and national news about farming problems had its roots in three conditions. First, the authority for resolving conflicts and managing resources was already decentralized in these villages, partly because the cultural diversity of residents had already attenuated existing forms of central control and motivated farmers to think about their relationships with others in somewhat malleable, "contractual" terms and partly because illness or personality had weakened the influence of central figures, such as the chief. Second, in the "participant" villages, younger men and women, often literate and often with experience of travel through other parts of the country, had returned to play important roles in decision-making, either indirectly, by demanding the chance to realize new kinds of ambitions, or directly, by moving to fill power vacuums. Third, the "participant" villages received help and ideas in organizing their affairs from urban associations which, in economic hard times, increasingly pushed for a role in improving the economic lives of those who demanded resources from them and who controlled an important form of social security—agricultural land. Although the commercialization of agriculture and the process of industrialization and urbanization would probably have gradually yielded these conditions under any circumstances, the cocoa crisis accelerated this process.

The "Discovery of Politics": An Epilogue

By way of conclusion are some reflections on what happened after the period of this research and on the degree to which Côte d'Ivoire's agricultural development was "hemmed in" by the country's position in the international economy.

The Formation of a Farmers' Union

Delegations and strikes do not programmatic politics make. The farmers' early experiments with new forms of political participation stopped short of the formation of a political party or even a broadly based union. In May 1990, the government announced a move to multiparty democracy, which, however, failed to capture the imaginations of most farmers. And, indeed, the major parties made little effort (or could afford little) to influence rural voters. By the end of July 1990, none of the parties' representatives had stopped at these villages, accessible though they were to a main road. Party competition took place in urban centers and seemed a world apart even to farmers who were members of the delegations that had traveled to Abidjan earlier in the year.

That changed in July 1991. A little less than a year after the country's first multiparty elections, the farmers' growing predisposition to participate blossomed into the formation of a union, the *Syndicat des Agriculteurs de Côte d'Ivoire* (SYNAGCI). The first congress, a meeting of more than 1,000 delegates and hangers-on, took place at Boudépé, a village about 55 miles from the country's capital, Abidjan. A newly-organized opposition political party, the *Front Populaire Ivoirien* (FPI), had taken a hand in launching this first union congress—a fact state television took pains to point out. Since the legalization of multiparty competition in Côte d'Ivoire at the end of April 1990, FPI leader Laurent Gbagbo had criticized the government of President Félix Houphouët-Boigny and the *Parti Démocratique de Côte d'Ivoire* (PDCI) for transferring funds away from the *Caisse de stabilisation,* the commodity board charged with stabilizing producer prices and managing the marketing of key export crops. He argued that the government had used revenues from international sales to finance unproductive urban schemes and the Basilica Notre Dame de la Paix, a Florentine cathedral at the president's birthplace, Yamoussoukro. Although Gbagbo helped inaugurate the first congress, he announced to his listeners that the FPI would remove itself from union affairs after the initial meeting. In his view, SYNAGCI should operate independently of all political parties. "There is no such thing as PDCI cotton or FPI cotton," he remarked to his audience. "There is just cotton."[67]

A model of participation for SYNAGCI may lie in the unions that have formed in those parts of the agricultural sector where the government has already retreated as a major player and chosen to liberalize markets. The best example is the pineapple growers' union that has flourished in Bonoua, on the edge of the Aboisso region. In the pineapple sector, the presence of many small producers and the absence of a market umpire initially led to overproduction of poor-quality pineapples that depressed prices for Ivoirien produce on the European market and reduced farmer incomes. First larger growers, then smallholders organized to create cooperatives that would coordinate sales and provide some quality control. The cooperatives advanced the farmers a portion of the anticipated proceeds of the sale and paid the rest after transactions were complete. In many cases, however, the farmers ended up with negative net returns, so high were the marketing costs of these organizations. The union moved to work out agreements that would regulate quality but allow individual farmers or small groups of farmers to sign contracts directly with buyers, rather than work through a central company. Although only a few years old, it also started to act as an advocate for farmers' broader economic interests. Already well organized, this group provides a model of participation already closely watched by farmers in the more active villages.

The speed with which union involvement and party-centered political participation spreads in rural areas is likely to depend on the amount of contact between villagers and university students or younger urban relatives who currently constitute the major support and source of energy for all of the new political groups. The *année blanche*, or year without school, the president declared in the wake of street demonstrations, in March 1990, sent many youth back to their rural families. Although these students are without great exposure to the platforms of the new parties or the speeches of their leaders, they do constitute a link between these movements and the rural areas, or, at the very least, an attentive audience. Their own views are likely to shape those of their age cohort who have chosen to return to the land and to farming and who are the main experimenters in the "participant" villages.

Agricultural Development and Côte d'Ivoire in the World Economy

At their first congress, in July 1991, farmers throughout the country spoke of the need to make government more accountable in its use of resources. They recalled the support they had given Houphouët-Boigny in the country's first elections and suggested that the president had forgotten to whom he owed his political success. In their view, political elites had misspent revenues the farmers had generated over the previous years. Instead of paying attention to mechanization of agriculture, crop research, and training "les jeunes" to work the land, civil servants had sought to enrich themselves. If they had formed a union earlier, some said, they would not have suffered so.

In many respects, the farmers were quite correct; their incomes need not have declined so if government had invested funds from cocoa, coffee, and cotton sales more wisely. Like many other countries, Côte d'Ivoire had to accommodate to a world in which new producers of cocoa and coffee had appeared, increasing supply of these crops and lowering the prices countries received from their sale. The international terms of trade for these commodities deteriorated in the period after the "boom" of 1976–77. Yet farmers in southeast Asian countries, such as Malaysia and Indonesia, also poor and also growers of these crops, fared much better than Ivoiriens. Policy choices mattered. It is possible for incomes to remain stable when prices decline, as long as yields improve constantly, as they did in Malaysia and Indonesia, where output grew eightfold in the 1980s. That requires information, research, and improved extension, however.

One of the reasons southeast Asian farmers experienced less deterioration in standards of living (indeed, many saw their welfare improve) was that government had chosen to invest in agricultural research and infrastructure to a greater degree than did Côte d'Ivoire. Beginning in the late 1960s and accelerating throughout the 1970s, Houphouët-Boigny's appointees borrowed funds from the *Caisse* (or against its revenues) to build new public enterprises, which they subsequently managed with the aim of enhancing their own cash-flow. Monies invested in sugar development in the northern areas, in the mid-1970s, disappeared into untraceable construction invoices. The projects were guaranteed to yield negative returns from the outset; European markets were highly protected and the North American industrial countries already faced an oversupply. The main rationale for going ahead with the *sucriers* was partly to distribute patronage to restless northern regions but also, and more centrally, to let new generations of politicians accumulate resources and reduce the pressure they brought to bear on the elders who had fought for Ivoiriens to share the advantages of the French settlers. Similarly, state funds disappeared at this time into a large program to house civil servants, an operation whose directors managed to benefit political elites and French advisers who had properties to rent or sell above market prices. Both of these types of expenditure reached such scandalous and public proportions that the president eventually stepped in either to dismiss the ministers involved, in the first case, or to prosecute the civil servants in the courts, as in the second instance (the famous LOGEMAD scandal).

In short, the farmers who met at Boudépé had a good grasp of the source of their problem. The state was unresponsive to their long-term interests, its officers seeking short-term individual benefit at the expense of the "goose that laid the golden egg." It wasn't that the country did not invest. The problem was that it invested earnings in the wrong way. One way to try to avoid becoming "hemmed in" in the international economy was to organize to make the governors more accountable for their choice of investment targets. That was precisely what Côte d'Ivoire's farming population decided to do. In the long run, of course, export agriculture could not keep the government's accounts balanced and the standards of living of its citizens on the rise. That would require not only a healthy export agriculture but also a shift out of import-substitution industries into processing of agricultural exports and manufactures. Nonetheless, limiting the drain on rural resources was and remains an important component of that transformation, if the experiences of Malaysia, Indonesia, and the East Asian countries, most of them resource-poor, are any lesson.

NOTES

1. "Yes, Mr. President. We will follow you in the battle against the speculators." *Fraternité Matin*, Abidjan, February 5, 1989. The research for this chapter, which is part of a larger project, was carried out in Côte d'Ivoire between September 1989 and September 1990. The author wishes to thank Atta Brou Noël, Thomas Eponou, and Kouadio Yao of the Centre Ivoirien des Recherches Economiques et Sociales (CIRES) for their guidance and kind assistance and the World Bank McNamara Fellowship Program for financial support. The author has also benefited greatly from comments provided by the Harvard University Department of Government Political Development Study Group.

2. For example, see the discussion in Henry Bienen, "The Politics of Trade Liberalization in Africa," *Economic Development and Cultural Change*, 38, 4

(July 1990): 718. Although recognizing that farmers have employed various means of resistance to state policies over the past several decades, several researchers have documented farmers' efforts to influence policy. This work includes the essays of Robert Bates in *Essays on the Political Economy of Rural Africa* (Berkeley: University of California Press, 1983) and *Beyond the Miracle of the Market* (Cambridge: Cambridge University Press, 1989), as well as case studies that include Stephen Bunker, *Peasants Against the State: The Politics of Market Control in Bugisu, Uganda 1900–1983*, (Chicago: University of Illinois Press, 1987) and Jeffrey Herbst, *State Politics in Zimbabwe* (Berkeley: University of California Press, 1990).

3. James C. Scott, *Weapons of the Weak: Everyday Forms of Peasant Resistance* (New Haven: Yale University Press, 1985).

4. Economist Intelligence Unit, *Quarterly Economic Review of Côte d'Ivoire*, Third Quarter, 1989, p. 6.

5. See the interviews of July 13 and July 14, 1990 in Aboisso region.

6. President Félix Houphouët-Boigny announced in the spring of 1990 that Côte d'Ivoire would move toward a multiparty political system. At the time of this writing there are 23 political parties in addition to the Parti Démocratique de Côte d'Ivoire (PDCI).

7. Definition of share contracting drawn from the work of A. F. Robertson, *The Dynamics of Productive Relationships: African Share Contracts in Comparative Perspective* (Cambridge: Cambridge University Press, 1987).

8. David Newbery and Joseph Stiglitz, "Sharecropping, Risk Sharing, and The Importance of Imperfect Information," in James Roumasset, *Risk, Uncertainty and Agricultural Development* (New York: Southeast Asian Regional Center for Graduate Study, 1979) p. 315.

9. Ibid.

10. A. F. Robertson, *The Dynamics of Productive Relationships: African Share Contracts in Comparative Perspective* (Cambridge: Cambridge University Press, 1987) p. 26.

11. There is an extensive literature on this pattern of response. Among the political scientists who have written on this subject, Göran Hyden is perhaps the best known. See Göran Hyden, *Beyond Ujamaa in Tanzania* (Berkeley: University of California Press, 1981).

12. Although not a case of response to fluctuation around a secular trend per se, the drop in yields was corrigible and did not represent a change in a secular trend itself.

13. Sara Berry, *Fathers Work for Their Sons* (Berkeley: University of California Press, 1985) p. 98.

14. Ibid., p. 105.

15. Ibid., p. 107.

16. Michael Watts. *Silent Violence: Food, Famine, and Peasantry in Northern Nigeria* (Berkeley: University of California Press), 1983.

17. Ibid., pp. 411–412.

18. Ibid., pp. 437–438.

19. Naomi Chazan, "The New Politics of Participation in Tropical Africa," *Comparative Politics* (January 1982): 169.

20. Robert Bates, "The Commercialization of Agriculture and the Rise of

Rural Political Protest," in Bates, ed., *Essays on the Political Economy of Rural Africa* (Berkeley: University of California Press, 1983).

21. C. E. F. Beer, *The Politics of Peasant Groups in Western Nigeria* (Ibadan: Ibadan University Press, 1976).

22. Ibid., p. 164.

23. Ibid., p. 184.

24. The sequence draws on Watts's characterization but is not identical with his.

25. Robert Bates, "Contra Contractarianism: Some Reflections in the New Institutionalism," *Politics and Society* 16, 2/3 (1988): 387–401. Robert Bates has pointed out that the collective choice literature can offer an explanation of the demand for institutions such as share contracts but it offers no account of the supply. It affords no adequate explanation of the behavior of the political entrepreneurs who negotiate contract terms that approximate Pareto optimal or efficient solutions. The standard response that, given a special or selective incentive, a member of a community will sustain the costs of supplying an institution that is socially optimal or "efficient," or support the transaction costs associated with negotiation of the share contract, does not hold up under scrutiny. Offered a disproportionate share in the outcome, the entrepreneur is indeed likely to establish new contract forms, but these are likely to favor the entrepreneur's interests and result in socially suboptimal outcomes. Bates suggests that only when individuals are uncertain of one another's interests, intentions, and capabilities are they likely to choose terms that move the community toward the "efficient" set of relationships the economics approach envisions.

26. Economist Intelligence Unit, *Quarterly Economic Review of Côte d'Ivoire*. Second Quarter, 1988, p. 11.

27. Ibid., p. 8.

28. Ibid., Third Quarter, 1988, p. 10.

29. United States Department of Agriculture, IV0003, February 1, 1990.

30. This finding is in line with data collected by the World Bank Living Standards Measurement Study. See Angus Deaton and Dwayne Benjamin, "The Living Standards Survey and Price Policy Reform: A Study of Cocoa and Coffee Production in Côte d'Ivoire," LSMS Working Paper Number 44, Washington, D.C.: World Bank, 1988.

31. Provisional figure.

32. Although the economic logic in these statements seems incorrect upon first examination because Côte d'Ivoire is a price taker in every commodity market except cocoa, the farmers had accurately noted a correlation between government promotion and investment in certain crops and declines in the value of those crops. The example most often noted by the farmers was copra production, or cultivation of coconut palms, which the government had encouraged and in which it had invested extensively. Producer prices had subsequently collapsed, making it unprofitable to bother harvesting the trees. Many farmers were moved to chop down their palms and replace them with pineapples (for which prices have also started to diminish) or other crops. The farmers may be wrong in the way they phrase the problem, but their assess-

ment of the government's ability to pick winners and losers and their general understanding of the relationship between supply and demand are valid.

33. The sales of the president's cocoa during the period when smallholder cocoa was being held off the market to force the world price to increase is documented in Jean-Louis Gombeaud, Corinne Moutout, and Stephen Smith, *La Guerre du Cacao* (Paris: Calman-Lévy, 1990).

34. The Aboisso region is part of the Akan "goldbelt." Alluvial gold is common, and among the Akan peoples gold jewelry has special significance and remains a tie to the past.

35. *Foutou* is a staple of the diet in the southern and central parts of the country. It comes in the form of a small, hot loaf made variously of pounded yams, cassava, or plantain—or some combination of these ingedients—and is used to scoop up bits of *sauce*, or stew.

36. The survey results indicate a sharp drop in the use of hired labor between November of 1989 and July–August, 1990. In this region, farmers typically hired labor on annual contracts, paying food, housing, and medical expenses as well as a flat salary. By purchasing labor in this way instead of relying on family labor, sending children to school and young men and women to the towns, the household could improve its long-term earnings and hedge against the risk that a family member might become ill during a critical work period, forcing abandonment of part of a crop. By 1990, returns and household monetary reserves were so low that farmers were unable to engage workers, typically Burkinabé migrants. Unable to locate sufficient work at remunerative wage levels, the migrant workers left the region. The households still able to hire labor complained that workers were nowhere to be found.

37. For example, see Respondent #61, Group 4, Village 3 and Respondent #93, Village 4, both October 1989.

38. See, for example, the remarks of Respondent #103, Group 6, Village 1, October 1989.

39. Hans Binswanger and John McIntire, "Behavioral and Material Determinants of Production Relations in Land Abundant Tropical Agriculture," Operational Policy Staff Discussion Paper, #17, June 1984.

40. Respondent, Group 1, Village 1, October 1989.

41. For example, see Respondent #99, Village 4, October 1989.

42. There are two factories and industrial plantations in the region, one at Toumanguié, and the other at Ehania.

43. It is difficult to estimate how extensive this practice was and is in this region. When asked to describe the "household," including relatives living in town and in other areas who had provided assistance in cash or in kind, almost all of those surveyed described relatively small family units only rarely dispersed outside of the cocoa zone or towns within that zone.

44. It is important to note that the short-run effect of the collapse of the cocoa and coffee markets was to flood the cities with cheap food, keeping food prices low at precisely the time the government imposed an austerity plan on urban dwellers.

45. See *Terre et Progrés*, Ministère d'Agriculture, no. 69 (January 1987) and no. 64 (July 1985). Producer prices for rubber were to be indexed to an interna-

tional reference price, so that the farmer would get a floor price per kilogram, and an additional, variable premium.

46. See note 32.

47. Ministère de la Recherche Scientifique, "Le dynamisme foncier et l'économie de plantation," Abidjan: Publication Inter-Instituts de CIRES, IGT, Gerdat, ORSTOM, octobre 1978, p. 2.

48. This information corresponds exactly with data obtained by Jean-Philippe Colin in his study of the village of Djiminikoffikro in the 1980s. Colin reports a steady increase in land values, as follows:

PERIOD	VALUE/HECTARE	NUMBER OF TRANSACTIONS (FCFA)
1945–50	1,284	1
1950–55	5,236	3
1955–60	8,093	5
1960–65	22,572	2
1965–70	24,860	14
1970–75	41,374	12
1975–80	70,000	4

See Jean-Philippe Colin, "La Mutation d'une Economie de Plantation: Contribution à l'analyse de la dynamique des systèmes productifs agricoles villageois en basse Côte d'Ivoire." Montpellier: ORSTOM, 1987, p. 84.

49. Wim Vijverberg. "Nonagricultural Family Enterprises in Côte d'Ivoire." LSMS Working Paper No. 46, World Bank, 1988.

50. Respondent #59, Group 3, Village 2, October 1989.

51. The government had tried for several years to convince Ivoirians of just that. As part of its "back to the country" campaign, it produced a large quantity of buttons that read, "Je Suis Fier D'être Cultivateur!"

52. A puzzling anomaly appeared in the initial analysis of the survey data. A significant 24% of oil palm growers indicated that they received part of another's harvest in return for granting access to land, which, at face value, suggests that share contracts are practiced far more frequently than open-ended interviews suggested. This finding also flew in the face of oral histories offered by village elders about changing land tenure patterns. The leaders suggested that the abusa system had been replaced temporarily by a fifty-fifty split of the crop between the tender and the "owner" and then died out completely, with the introduction of oil palm cultivation. It is likely that the statistics reflect arrangements with palm-wine producers, who cut aging trees and give a portion of their liquor to the owner (if only to keep the owner quiet).

53. Interview with the notables of village #2, November 17, 1989 and interview with the notables of village #4, November 18, 1989.

54. Economist Intelligence Unit, *Quarterly Economic Report*, Third Quarter, 1989, p. 14. The RFI report was denounced by then Minister of Agriculture Denis Bra Kanon.

55. The government has tentatively authorized such arrangements after the collapse of parts of the cocoa marketing system. Because the traitants' gov-

ernment-determined allowances for marketing costs are widely believed to be below actual costs and because most of the cooperatives have loaned money to the members and cannot finance the trade, it is unlikely that this arrangement will work. Indeed, it may prove a further aggravation.

56. This description draws on interviews with village residents and with the "chef de zone" of SATMACI, who initially identified the problem as the major reason for the collapse of cooperative performance in some parts of his district.

57. *Terre et Progrés*, no. 69 (January 1987).

58. The farmers from the region maintain that they steadfastly objected to measures supported by representatives of the government and the International Labor Organization, which sent a consultant to help organize the unions. The officials offer a different account of the same events.

59. It is important to note, however, that unlike many Sub-Saharan governments, Houphouët-Boigny's government does not position armed soldiers at the doors to all ministries, and access is remarkably open.

60. See interview July 14, 1990, number 2.

61. The top three were, in order of preference: *Rambo* (the entire series), Bruce Lee's Kung-fu movies, and *Dallas*. The connection between the films' content and political behavior was remote, especially because the films were shown in their dubbed French versions while most of the viewers, save the school children, generally conversed in any one of a number of local languages.

62. See Robert Wade, *Village Republics: Economic Conditions for Collective Action in South India* (Cambridge: Cambridge University Press, 1988).

63. *Terre et Progrés*, no. 69 (January 1987).

64. See interview of July 14, 1990, number 1.

65. Ibid., number 3.

66. Ibid.,, number 1.

67. "Big Turnout For New Farmers' Union in Ivory Coast," Reuters News Service, July 29, 1991.

Chapter Nine

The Politics of Sustained Agricultural Reform in Africa

JEFFREY HERBST

Economic reform was at the top of the policy agenda for most African countries in the 1980s and, along with political reform, will remain the primary issue in the 1990s. On a continent where 70% of the labor force is involved in farming, it is only natural that reform of agriculture is one of the most important aspects of the effort to adjust economic institutions and policies to accelerate growth. Agricultural reform also exemplifies the complexity of the adjustment process in Africa. There is now widespread agreement that "getting prices right" is important if farmers are to have any incentive to produce. However, production will not increase markedly unless other aspects of the agrarian system function correctly: roads must be passable so that transport costs are kept low; inputs (e.g., seed and fertilizer) must be available if production is to be optimal; and extension agencies must function in order to keep farmers informed of research. Given the disintegration of African political systems and economies, the transportation, marketing, and extension infrastructure must all undergo significant renovation if increased prices are to be consequential. Thus, prices and several sets of economic institutions must be reformed if agriculture is going to undergo a resurgence.

For price and institutional reforms to be carried out in the agricultural sector, there must be a political system that rewards politicians for implementing changes beneficial to farmers. For instance, Delgado and Mellor elegantly call for "rural political processes to keep agricultural policy in the forefront of debate, to help mobilize and allocate national and local resources for agricultural development, and to provide legitimacy to decisions made."[1] Similarly, the World Bank, in its recent long-term study of Africa, cited the need for societal actors, including farmers, to hold "countervailing power" in order to affect the preferences of state officials.[2]

However, the means by which viable agrarian constituencies are to be created and the conduits through which they are supposed to exercise their countervailing power have not been analyzed. As Paul Streeten noted,

> Compared with the large and growing literature on rent-seeking and directly unproductive profit-seeking activities, relatively little research has been done by political scientists into the question of how to build constituencies for reform, how to shape reformist coalitions or alliances between groups whose interests can be harnessed to the cause of reform.[3]

Indeed, much of the structural adjustment literature implicitly assumes that if there is economic progress, new groups will coalesce and support the reform effort once they see that they are benefiting. However, as E. E. Schattschneider noted in his classic study of American tariff legislation, "spontaneous political response to economic interest is far less general than is commonly supposed."[4] There may be very high transaction costs (e.g., to peasants in the rural areas) that prevent certain constituencies from mobilizing to support a government that has embarked on significant reforms to help agriculture. Or, political systems may be structured in such a way as to prevent agrarian constituencies from being able to influence policy decisions.

The failure to describe political systems that might support agriculture is especially important because several different types of reform will have to be implemented if African agriculture is to flourish. Price reform is highly visible and can be done quickly and with relatively little administrative ability. However, raising producer prices for food crops can harm the interest of a very powerful constituency in most African countries: the urban population who are dependent on supplies of inexpensive food. Correspondingly, increasing the producer prices of export crops may put severe strains on government revenue, which may result in the curtailment of important government services. In contrast, reform of the infrastructure that supports agricultural production does not yield significant immediate benefits, requires a significant commitment over time, but does not automatically harm another constituency. Thus, the construction of a political system that will successfully support all aspects of agricultural reform in African countries poses especially difficult challenges.

After first briefly reviewing the nature of the agrarian crisis in Africa, I will survey the results of a decade of agrarian reform, after which I will analyze how the political systems in Kenya, Zimbabwe, and Ghana generate support for agriculture. I will pay particular attention to the ability of African political systems to create incentives for leaders to post higher prices and improve the underlying infrastructure. Finally, I will examine how the World Bank may be able to enhance constituencies favoring long-term improvements in the agrarian infrastructure.

The Agricultural Crisis in Africa

The extent of Africa's agrarian crisis is by now well-known. While food production in the 1960s roughly matched population growth, by the 1970s per capita agrarian production was decreasing. In addition, during the 1970s, Africa's share of the world market for many agrarian commodities decreased while food imports grew at three times the rate of population increase.[5]

Agricultural production did increase between 1980 and 1989 at a faster rate than in the 1970s (2.1% versus -0.3%), but this gain was still below the rate of population increase, estimated by the World Bank to be 3.1% across the continent.[6] As a result, the Food and Agriculture Organization (FAO) estimates that, by 1989, Africa's per capita food and agricultural production was actually 7% below the average for 1979 to 1981.

As table 9.1 suggests, a large number of countries actually experienced a significant decrease in per capita agricultural production during the 1980s. Just as important is the paucity of countries that have experienced significant production growth.

In comparison, during the same period, across the entire developing world, food and agriculture production in per capita terms increased by 9%.[7]

The crisis in agricultural production has many ramifications for African countries. At the most basic level, the stagnation and decline in the major sector of employment for most African countries obviously has an enormous effect on the life chances of the majority of people on the continent. For instance, daily calorie supply per capita, the most basic measure of consumption, actually declined in Africa by 3% between 1980 and 1987 and is now 12% below the average level for all low-income countries. By the late 1980s, caloric consumption in Africa was roughly equivalent to what it was in 1965; in comparison, Third World countries generally have increased their average consumption by 20% during the last 25 years.[8] Insecurity about food is most evident in the Sahel, Ethiopia, and Mozambique where long-term declines in the agrarian system have combined with natural or human-made disaster (especially war) to cause famine. More generally, this insecurity

TABLE 9.1

Percentage Change in Agricultural Production Per Capita Between 1979–1981 and 1989

10%<	10%> <0%	0> <-10%	-10%>
Benin	Kenya	Cameroon	Algeria
Burkina	Mauritius	Chad	Angola
Ghana		Congo	Botswana
Guinea Bissau		Gambia	Burundi
Senegal		Côte d'Ivoire	CAR
		Madagascar	Ethiopia
		Mali	Gabon
		Nigeria	Guinea
		Somalia	Lesotho
		Swaziland	Liberia
		Togo	Malawi
		Zaire	Mauritania
		Zambia	Mozambique
		Zimbabwe	Niger
			Rwanda
			S. Leone
			Sudan
			Tanzania
			Uganda

SOURCE: FAO, *Quarterly Bulletin of Statistics* vol. 2, no. 4 (1989), p.7.

causes malnutrition and engenders tremendous efforts whereby all other goals are sacrificed simply to get enough to eat. The World Bank estimates that to remedy the situation African agriculture will have to grow at 4% a year, a goal that only a handful of countries met during the 1980s.[9]

Second, declines in the production of export crops (e.g., cotton, tea, cocoa, coffee) aggravate shortages of foreign exchange because many African countries rely heavily on one or two export crops for most of their foreign exchange. When production of these crops decreases, there often is no other source of foreign exchange to replace them and the already weak economy declines further. Shortages of hard currency have an especially pernicious impact on African countries by making it much more difficult to secure imported inputs for manufacturing or to replace capital equipment. Perhaps the most spectacular example of agriculture-led decline was cocoa in Ghana during the 1970s. Because of poor prices and a deteriorating economic climate, the country's share of the world cocoa market decreased from 33% in 1970 to 17% in 1980,[10] a massive decline that propelled the economy into a steep depression. While other countries did not show so precipitous a decline, the travails of the first independent country in modern Africa are emblematic of what happened across the continent.

Finally, on a more general level, the vast majority of Africa's population remains in low-productivity agriculture so that there is essentially no chance of economic development. Indeed, the FAO estimates that 68.2% of Africa's total population is in agriculture compared to 56.5% for all developing countries, and that by the year 2000 this percentage will only have dropped to 62.6% (compared to 50.6% for all developing countries).[11] Sir W. Arthur Lewis noted the impact of such a large percentage of the labor force in low productivity agriculture several decades ago: "Industrialisation for a home market can make little progress unless agriculture is progressing vigorously at the same time, to provide both the market for industry, and industry's labour supply. If agriculture is stagnant, industry cannot grow."[12]

Lewis therefore recommended that Third World countries, while industrializing, keep increasing agricultural productivity. Unfortunately, most African countries neglected agriculture while attempting to industrialize and are therefore now faced with the problem of rebuilding agrarian systems before increases in industry can take place. Indeed, in good part, the current emphasis on agrarian reform in many countries is an effort to restore the agricultural sector to where it was at independence in order to begin the growth through agriculture that should have occurred during the early 1960s.

The Politics of Dysfunctional Agricultural Policies

During the early 1980s, a powerful critique developed of existing agricultural policies in Africa. The initial salvo was fired by the World Bank in its important 1981 report, *Accelerated Development in Sub-Saharan Africa.* The report argued that "agricultural output is the single most important determinant of overall economic growth" and "the principal factor underlying the poor economic performance of the countries of this region."[13] Where the report broke new ground was on focusing specifically on the issues of low prices paid to farmers as an especially important constraint to future agricultural production.

However, the focus on prices was criticized heavily during the 1980s, as many scholars cited the deficiencies of African markets and their inability, at times, to transmit price signals.[14] For instance, bottlenecks in transportation systems and poor delivery systems for basic inputs such as seed and fertilizer often present daunting obstacles to agrarian production even when prices are "right." In fact, African countries experience large regional variations in the prices of foodgrains because poor infrastructure prevents the integration of markets. Asian countries, with better infrastructure, do not experience nearly as significant intracountry price differentials.[15] Other factors, including the degree of monetarization in the economy, the relative self-sufficiency of households, and limited markets for such factors as land also restrict the power of prices alone to influence production.[16] Finally, limited supplies of consumer goods may also have a profound effect on farmer responses to an increase in producer prices.[17] Thus, correct prices are a necessary, but not sufficient condition, for promoting economic activity.

In the scholarly literature, Robert Bates' 1981 book *Markets and States in Tropical Africa* provided a theoretical grounding for much of the Bank's criticism of agrarian price policy. Bates was particularly interested in why most governments in Africa choose to tax producers of food and export crops. He focused his explanations on the need of African governments to placate the politically important urban population by keeping the price of food low and the revenue imperatives of government which caused them to take a substantial cut of the earnings of exporters.

What was particularly interesting about Bates' book was his explanation of the political weaknesses of agrarian producers. Bates assigned much of the blame for small farmers' political weakness to their atomistic nature, given that they are spread across large amounts of land with little communication. However, he also noted that African governments had consistently repressed any attempts to organize the rural majority. Finally, he suggested that governments had used various "sidepayments" including subsidized inputs, large agricultural projects, and other forms of government largesse to placate those who might lead farmer protests.[18] In fact, in accord with Bates' analysis, the proportion of the world price paid to farmers for export crops did decrease in the 1970s.[19]

Bates devoted far less attention to my primary question here: how to change political systems so that there are incentives to promote high producer prices and investment of significant resources in the agricultural infrastructure. Bates implied that simply increasing consumer prices would be too difficult for many African nations because of the fear of urban riots. Instead, he suggested that it would be necessary to alter domestic coalitions within African countries if farmers were going to garner enough political power to influence agricultural policy. For instance, he argued that if farmers could combine with a major urban extractive industry, they might have enough political clout to demand better government policies for agriculture. Similarly, he suggested that if non-food agrarian producers were brought into the dominant political coalition, government policy would be more favorable to exporters.[20]

However, he did not suggest why African governments, which he had portrayed as being opposed to any attempts by rural producers to organize and thereby increase their power, would suddenly allow farmers to form a powerful coalition with another set of important actors in Africa. The only other suggestion he made was that agrarian policies might change if leaders realized just how much the practices they pursued were causing long-term damage to their countries.[21] Clearly, given the dynamics that Bates outlined favoring low producer prices for farmers, a change in leadership preferences alone would constitute only weak support for agriculture.

The Results of a Decade of Reform

Given the magnitude of the agrarian crisis and the political weight of the World Bank, it was only natural that most countries said that they placed agricultural reform at the top of their agenda in the 1980s. In fact, 90% of all African countries now make agriculture the highest priority in their development plans.[22] However, these statements of priorities mean very little. Indeed, the World Bank noted that during the 1970s, African governments had devoted resources to agriculture at an unprecedented rate but there was still agrarian decline.[23]

It is therefore important to examine in a more concrete manner the extent of agricultural reform in African countries and the political reasons why these reforms did or did not take place. Given the importance of price signals in African countries, this section will first examine how successful governments were in improving incentives for farmers in the 1980s. It will then analyze efforts to improve other aspects of the agricultural system which will also have to be reformed if improved price signals are to be strong enough to affect farmers' decisions.

Price Reform

Evidence for price reform is unfortunately difficult to collect given the weaknesses of African statistical systems, especially in the rural areas. However, data collected by the World Bank on agricultural producer prices tentatively indicates that there has been some increase in the percentage of the world price paid to farmers for export crops. In 19 of the 25 countries for which data are available, the farmgate price as a percentage of the world price has increased.[24] Once again, it is worth noting that the data are so imprecise that they cannot support anything but rough analysis. However, the overall trend of the data suggests that governments have been able to increase the share of the world price that farmers receive. Other studies also report that there have been some improvements in the pricing practices of African countries. For instance, Jaeger and Humphreys estimate that while real prices for export crops fell 25% between 1977 and 1980, there was a recovery between 1983 and 1986, although a decline in prices in 1987.[25] Prices for food crops probably have also increased but empirical indicators are lacking to evaluate how governments have treated nonexport crops.

Prices were able to increase for several reasons. First, in part because of analysis like Bates' 1981 book and the World Bank's own 1981 report, the Bank, the IMF, and bilateral donors became major actors in the domestic struggle over agricultural producer prices. The conditionalities on aid that the Bank and bilateral donors constructed, especially demanding that governments raise producer prices, changed the political equations in agriculture. For instance, agricultural producer pricing has been a major component in more than 80% of all Structural Adjustment Loans for Africa that affected agriculture.[26] Also, the pressure that the Bank and the Fund placed on African governments to devalue aided exporters of agricultural products.

African farmers in many countries during the 1980s were therefore able to count on powerful international actors to present their case. These actors could offer consequential rewards to governments that changed agricultural pricing policies to favor farmers, and their sanctions to recalcitrant regimes were also quite persuasive. Indeed, when African governments set producer prices they are especially susceptible to pressure from multilateral and bilateral donors. Governments usually formally announce what price they are going to pay farmers, and it is relatively easy to calculate how farmers are doing since the world price of the good (at least for export crops) is readily available. Even for food crops, simple models that estimate farmers' costs can be constructed quickly to see if real prices are increasing.

The political barriers to price reform that the World Bank and other donors were demanding also now appear much less substantial because many governments in Africa and elsewhere in the world were able to raise prices substantially without causing urban riots. In a broad survey of "IMF riots" Henry Bienen and Mark Gersovitz found that many governments had actually overestimated the political difficulty of raising prices.[27] One reason urban unrest appears to have been less significant than predicted is that many consumers are forced to pay higher prices on the black market because of the deleterious effects of price controls. Thus, the urban population may be paying shadow prices long before a government announces the end of price controls on food. In such a case, only those who might have had privileged access to food at controlled prices will be hurt by an increase in the official price. Ironically, the greater a country's decline, the easier it may be to raise official prices because it is more likely that most of the urban population are paying prices which may even be above the market-clearing level.[28]

Also, several countries have changed their institutional structures so that it became much harder for the urban population to bring pressure to bear on pricing decisions. The most radical reform of this kind was Nigeria's, which in 1986, abolished six of its marketing boards. Similarly, the Central African Republic, Guinea, Madagascar, Mali, Niger, and Uganda have decontrolled pricing for some or all staple food crops.[29] By devolving pricing decisions to the market, these reforms emasculated the urban population because they could no longer use their old tactics, especially riots directed at the government, to influence the price of food.

While the urban population could demand that government recontrol the price of food, such a reversal of reforms would be difficult for a government to do given the pressure from the donors. At the very least, the urban population will have to bring significantly more pressure on a government to recontrol food prices (a drastic institutional reform) than in the past when it was trying to influence the prices that were already being set by the government. There have been no instances yet where a government has recontrolled prices after devolving pricing decisions to the market.

Therefore, there is reason to believe that governments are able to increase prices and some evidence to suggest that many farmers in Africa did, in fact, benefit from higher prices in the 1980s. While Bates had presented a very good analysis of why prices for many farmers had decreased in the 1960s and 1970s, his model did not anticipate the international pressures that developed in the 1980s to raise producer prices and probably overestimated the political problems governments face when they increase the cost of food. This is not to suggest that all countries in Africa have improved prices for all their farmers; clearly many have not. Rather, there is very good reason to believe that, especially since 1981, multilateral organizations have provided incentives for governments to post high prices and that it is easier than was originally thought for governments to increase consumer prices.

Reform of the Agrarian Infrastructure

However, as noted above, the reform of prices is only the first step in the effort to reform overall agriculture systems. A host of other institutions and systems must be overhauled to allow prices to have a powerful effect. Roads have to be built and (especially difficult in Africa) maintained. Systems to deliver fertilizer, seed, and extension services have to be established. Credit systems in rural areas must be expanded. Marketing systems should be extended to the rural areas so farmers can actually sell their produce. These types of reforms are very different from increasing prices for producers. Rather than a few well-publicized announcements, constructing, reconstructing, and maintaining agricultural infrastructure takes a large amount of administrative effort over a long period of time.

One potential measure of how countries are reforming their agrarian sectors is to examine the trajectory of crop yields. High yields, as Lele argues for Kenya, are, at least in part, a reflection of small farmers' relatively good access to research, extension, credit inputs, and markets.[30] Overall improvements in yield are particularly important to study because, while high prices may have the effect of increasing production of one crop, aggregate supply responses will continue to be sluggish unless there are improvements in the infrastructure.[31] Finally, now that the land frontier in most African countries has closed, higher yields will be the only way in which to increase total production.[32]

Table 9.2 presents basic yield data for 28 countries. The table shows the percentage of the main crops whose yield increased by at least 37% between the beginning of the decade and 1988. The 37% level is an important cutoff point: that is how much yields would have increased by if they had risen by 4% a year (the World Bank's growth target for African agriculture) for the first eight years of the 1980s. Of course, yield data are often of poor quality in Africa and data for many crops are unavailable. However, most of the countries listed in table 9.1 as having high overall production growth rates also appear to have high yield growth rates across their agrarian sectors.

The table does indicate that very few countries have experienced significant growth rates in yields across a wide variety of

TABLE 9.2
Percentage of Major Crops whose Yields Increased by more than 37%, 1979–1981 to 1988

Country	Percentage of Major Crops whose Yield Increased by more than 37% between 1979–1981 to 1988
Benin	20 (1/5) *
Burkina	40 (3/5)
Burundi	0 (0/6)
Cameroon	14 (1/7)
CAR	43 (3/7)
Congo	0 (0/4)
Côte d'Ivoire	0 (0/5)
Ethiopia	0 (0/4)
Gambia	0 (0/5)
Ghana	0 (0/4)
Guinea	0 (0/5)
Guinea-Bissau	50 (2/4)
Kenya	20 (1/5)
Liberia	0 (0/4)
Malawi	17 (1/6)
Mali	60 (3/5)
Mozambique	20 (1/5)
Nigeria	17 (1/6)
Rwanda	0 (0/5)
Senegal	40 (2/5)
Sierra Leone	0 (0/4)
Sudan	0 (0/4)
Tanzania	29 (2/7)
Togo	17 (1/6)
Uganda	40 (2/5)
Zaire	0 (0/4)
Zambia	33 (2/6)
Zimbabwe	0 (0/5)

*Figures in parentheses are the actual number of crops that had yield increases of more than 37% and the total number of crops.

NOTE: A country was not included in the chart unless data was available for at least four of its major crops. Marjor crops are identified by World Bank, *African Economic and Financial Data* (Washington, DC: The World Bank, 1989), pp. 135–145.

SOURCE: FAO, *FAO Production Year book 1988* (Rome: FAO, 1989); and FAO, *FAO Quarterly Bulletin of Statistics* vol. 2, no. 3 (1989).

crops. Almost all of the countries had one or two crops with very high increases in yields because of higher prices for that crop or specific efforts to boast production in one area. However, there have not been broad increases in yields, which suggests that there was very little improvement in the basic infrastructure that supports African agriculture in the 1980s.

Why did improvements in the agrarian infrastructure lag behind increases in agricultural producer prices in the 1980s? Obviously, infrastructural improvements are more difficult administrative tasks that will take years to complete while prices can be raised almost instantly. Thus, agrarian reform programs may lose momentum as poorly staffed African governments simply lack the institutional ability to accomplish complex tasks over a long period of time. Also, the political conflicts over the agrarian infrastructure may be much more difficult to resolve in favor of farmers. During the process of reform, interest groups that compete for resources with farmers may wage long political battles that cannot be decided in favor of agriculture with the precision and definitiveness that price increases bring. Thus, even a government committed to improving the agrarian infrastructure may be worn down by the competing demands of many other groups that also desperately need resources.

Unfortunately for the agricultural sector, the ability of the multilateral institutions to intervene is considerably less in the area of infrastructural development than in pricing policy. The multilaterals are best at imposing conditionality on a few government policies, especially prices, which they can easily monitor given their limited number of staff in most African countries. They are much less adept at monitoring long-term government policies because they have neither the personnel on the ground or the institutional memory to follow issues that are not as easily observable as prices. The IMF itself, in a review of structural adjustment policies, admitted that prices are much easier to change than other structural policies.[33] Thus, even if a government is encouraged by the multilateral organizations to post high agricultural prices, the same regime may face less effective political pressure to increase long-term investment in the agricultural sector.

Since the multilateral organizations cannot be particularly powerful proponents of long-term changes in agricultural systems, a fundamental question arises: what type of political system would guarantee continued political support for investment in agriculture? The question is important as it is conceivable that African countries could post relatively high prices to appease international donors but not proceed with the extremely difficult work of constructing agricultural support systems.

Three Examples of Political Support for Agriculture

Several African countries have been able to mobilize political support for agriculture. This section will examine Kenya, Zimbabwe, and Ghana to explore the different ways their political systems help to sustain the changes the different regimes implemented. These three cases do not represent all possible ways in which political systems have supported the agricultural sector but they are probably among the most important. They are interesting because there is a significant amount of variance among the three examples in terms of how important elections are, the relative significance of national political organizations, and the extent to which government structures have to become more open in order to promote agriculture.

Kenya represents perhaps the best known example in Africa of how a political system has been able to incorporate agrarian interests. In Kenya, much of the top leadership has strong personal ties in agriculture and these interests make politicians attentive to the fate of agriculture.[34] However, many African countries have ignored the overall agriculture sector even though the leaders own farms. Other aspects of the political systems are also be important in institutionalizing the interests of the agricultural sector. For instance, because Kenya holds elections frequently, parliamentarians have developed substantial patron-client ties with significant segments of the rural farmer population.[35] Indeed, because the elections are held within a one-party state, grand ideological issues are off the agenda. Rather, politicians are judged on how much they are able to do in terms of delivering goods to the local area they represent.[36] The harambee system of local self-help projects further emphasizes the importance of politicians contributing to visible projects in their constituency. Politicians are, in fact, often judged on the basis of who has done the most for self-help projects.[37] This is not to suggest that every peasant has benefited from Kenya's political system, just that the political ties between the state and a significant portion of the rural community are much stronger than in other countries.[38] As a result, Kenya has been a noticeable exception to the agrarian decline that has affected Africa for the last 15 years.[39] Indeed, not only have there been a plethora of individual projects sponsored by the government, but also the overall level of spending on agriculture and transport as compared to other sectors is more impressive than in some other African countries.[40] As a result, Kenyan farmers have much better access to infrastructure and byproducts of research. For instance, Lele found that more than 60% of Kenya's farmers grow hybrid or improved maize, compared to less than 10% in the other countries she studies.[41]

Two crucial lessons emanate from the Kenyan experience. First, elections per se are not the issue. Unless the elections force politicians by threat of losing office to deliver goods to their region, they will not matter. As Barkan notes, "Elections which are tightly constrained and/or orchestrated from the center as in Tanzania. . .may be worse than no elections at all if the ultimate goal is to make the state more accountable to the peasantry."[42] Indeed, civilian regimes based on elections in other countries, notably Ghana and Nigeria, failed to enhance the influence of the entire farming community.[43] Elections in these countries did not increase the power of the agricultural sector because the civilian regimes did not last long enough for a tradition of accountability through elections to develop. Second, the Kenyan experience demonstrates that institutional structures have to be developed if small farmers are to have strong ties with the ruling political coalition. Small farmers cannot simply be brought into the ruling group. Rather, there must be real institutional conduits that connect the state and the vast majority in the countryside. In the case of Kenya, these conduits consisted largely of frequent local elections whereby agricultural interests were, to some extent, institutionalized.

Thus, the central question is whether structures similar to those in Kenya could develop in other countries. Certainly, the system is under stress even within Kenya. As Barkan notes, the system worked best when Jomo Kenyatta was ruling. Kenyatta, the acknowledged father of the country, was politically secure and could afford to let local elections take their own course. In contrast, Daniel arap Moi, Kenyatta's successor, is in a much less secure position and has begun to interfere with local elections. As a result, the ties between the electorate and the politicians are weakening.[44] The present difficulties in Kenya, where the government is attempting to increase sharply its control over elements of the polity, indicates that an insecure government is probably incompatible in the long term with the type of electoral system that prospered under Kenyatta.

Also, electoral systems of the Kenyan type take an extremely long time to establish. Traditions must develop whereby incumbents know that they can lose and whereby farmers are assured that politicians can actually deliver a significant amount of resources in exchange for votes. At least in Kenya, the system began to evolve right after independence so the elections could be institutionalized relatively quickly. In other countries, where there is a long tradition of authoritarian rule and militaries overturning elected civilian regimes, the idea that even small farmers can hold politicians accountable may take much longer to develop.

The type of representation of agricultural interests practiced in Kenya probably is the most durable system for promoting farmer interests. Correspondingly, it is also the most difficult one to construct. Given the political trauma that adoption of the Kenyan model implies, it is not a short-run alternative for most countries.

Another example of institutionalizing political support for agriculture is Zimbabwe, where parliamentarians are not particularly important to the political system, elections are held only once every five years, and there is no direct link between electoral success and delivering political goods to a constituency.[45] However, black farmers directly influence producer prices because they, along with white farmers, engage in a highly structured bargaining process over how much they will receive for their goods from government each year. The Mugabe government aided the establishment of a nationwide peasant organization after independence in part so that black farmers would also have a voice in the price negotiations. In the price-setting process, all farmers are invited to negotiate with the agriculture bureaucracy over what producers should receive for their goods. Farmers are allowed to make detailed presentations and their concerns are taken seriously. In addition, they are able to lobby the senior national leadership while the final decisions on prices are being made.

Black farmers do not have a similarly institutionalized voice in Zimbabwe's infrastructure decisions. Unlike prices, which are set once a year in a structured process where farmers can easily be invited to participate, there is not an open, easily discernible process whereby infrastructural decisions are made. However, the competence of the bureaucracy and the commitment of the nation's top leaders to agriculture, forged in part by the long guerrilla war, has meant that significant resources have been invested in supporting the entire agrarian system. As a result, black farmers have increased the amount of food they grow remarkably. In 1980, Zimbabwe's black farmers produced roughly 10% of the nation's maize sold to the national marketing authority and approximately 20% of its cotton. Now, in years with good rainfall, they produce more than 50% of the maize marketed and a significant portion of the cotton.[46] This reflects large increases in actual production by small farmers rather than whites simply moving to other crops. For instance, in 1979, black farmers produced approximately 420,000 tons of maize while in 1985 they produced 1.5 million tons.[47]

Parts of Zimbabwe's experience clearly are not applicable to other African countries. In particular, the leadership's ability to help small farmer agriculture by expanding an already highly developed settler agricultural sector is clearly not an option open to most countries. However, there are other aspects of the Zimbabwe experience that may be relevant to African countries. In particular, the close consultation between the bureaucracy and major farmer groups (large-scale white commercial farmers and black farmers are represented by different organizations) over the setting of prices (and conceivably other aspects of the agricultural systems) could be replicated in many countries without the institutional trauma inherent in moving to systems where elections are central to the political system.

However, even the consultative aspect of Zimbabwe's system may not be able to be easily imported by other African countries. First, many other governments may not be willing to aid the establishment of a peasant organization as Zimbabwe did. Also, the Zimbabwe peasant organization, the National Farmers Association of Zimbabwe (NFAZ), is weak at both the bottom and top: it has only tenuous ties with many of its own constituents in the countryside and it has only the most limited ability to conduct competent economic analysis that might impress the government bureaucracy. The NFAZ therefore suffers from many of the same organizational problems that other farmer groups do across Africa.

However, the Zimbabwe black farmer group has a tremendous advantage in that it is able to piggyback on the white farmer group organization, which is also invited to the consultations with the government. In particular, the NFAZ is able to use the sophisticated analysis developed by the white farmers' group to buttress their claims on the government.[48] Thus, the black farmer organization in Zimbabwe has the best of both worlds: it has the political legitimacy of representing millions of black farmers but the analytical resources of a rich and highly organized lobbying group.

The third example of how agriculture could be promoted by a political system is Ghana,whose government, as part of the most comprehensive program of structural adjustment on the continent, has reinvigorated agriculture. The government has chosen to emphasize agriculture because of great pressure from donors and because government officials appear to have become convinced that previous regimes' neglect of food crops and cocoa was a prime cause of the country's decline. Between 1984 and 1988, the nominal price of cocoa increased fivefold. While cocoa farmers were still receiving less than 30% of the international price in the mid-1980s, the Structural Adjustment Credit with the World Bank called upon the government to provide cocoa farmers with 55% of the international price by 1988–1989.[49] Cocoa production, which bottomed out at 168,000 tons in 1983, is projected to increase to 300,000 tons in the early 1990s. For the period 1900–1995, the government has begun implementing the Medium Term Agricultural Development Program in order to increase food crop output and to have a more balanced agricultural sector. Overall, agriculture is projected to grow at a rate of 4.7% a year.[50]

However, agriculture has been promoted in Ghana without farmers gaining any institutional entree into the policy-making process. The PNDC, which took power in a coup in 1981, did not allow any elections to be held until 1988 and those were for District Assemblies with no immediate policy responsibilities. Nor has the government taken other measures that might institutionalize the voices of farmers. For instance, it has not aided the establishment of a nationwide farmer organization that would provide smallholders with a visible political presence in the capital through which they could influence policy. The PNDC's deliberations are also not open to this kind of participation from societal groups. Indeed, the government does not feel that it is necessary for farmers to have a formal voice in the policy-making process. As one Ministry of Agriculture official told me,

> Farmers have no comparative advantage in formulating policies. They have a comparative advantage in production. There is not a one-to-one relationship between farmer participation and their improved productivity. Improved extension and ensuring adequate supply of inputs at the doorstep is more important for productivity.[51]

Instead, farmers benefit because governments believe that agriculture should be reinvigorated and because the multilateral and the bilateral donors continually press for improvements in agriculture.

The Ghanaian method for improving agriculture is obviously the one most attractive to African governments. It does not require the dramatic changes needed to move to an electoral system or the significant alterations in the bureaucracy that institutionalized consultation would entail. However, a much greater danger in this type of system is that agriculture will be slighted during the long period of infrastructural reform because the only real impetus for resources being directed to agriculture is the leaders' own beliefs and pressure from the donors. For instance, although the Economic Recovery Programme (ERP) began in 1983, it was not until the PNDC reviewed the country's progress in the run-up to the second phase of the ERP in 1986 that a focus on food agriculture emerged. The country was fortunate that in 1984 there had been good rains so there had been an increase in agricultural production; but it was obvious that the ad hoc measures taken up to that point could not guarantee an adequate food supply.

A not particularly surprising tradeoff exists between the degree of political transformation required and the long-term political strength that farmers acquire. Elections in the form that Kenya had until recently undoubtedly would require vast changes in the operations of most African countries. Consultations, as in Zimbabwe, require far fewer changes in the governmental system but give less political power to farmers. Finally, the promotion of agriculture by preference of the leadership and pressure from donors, as in Ghana, is easy to do but does not guarantee that the political terms of trade will favor farmers.

Thus, the available evidence suggests that, while African political systems may indeed be able to raise prices for many of their farmers, they may be incapable of generating the commitment necessary for the difficult task of improving the underlying agarian infrastructure. As a result, production of individual crops may increase, but there probably will not be dramatic improvements in overall yield levels. Unfortunately, such an outcome will do little to redress the long-term problems afflicting most African countries. Indeed, price reforms without institutional and infrastructural improvements will guarantee that most African countries will not significantly alter the trajectory of either their agricultural sector or the economy in general.

The Multilaterals and the Empowerment of Farmers

Given these rather pessimistic conclusions concerning the ability of African countries to sustain agrarian reform, the World Bank's efforts to promote agriculture will be particularly important. As noted above, the presence of the World Bank and the IMF, while probably increasing the political power of those pressuring for short-term higher agricultural producer prices does not create an organized constituency with political clout favoring long-term investments in agriculture. However, since it is unlikely that the political structures most likely to evolve in African countries will result in an unambiguous increase in the political power of farmers, the multilaterals may eventually have to become more involved in empowering farmers.

The fundamental reason why the World Bank and the IMF cannot provide more assistance to farmers now is that they are still configured, at least politically, as if they were assisting in European reconstruction after World War II. In countries that had skilled labor and long industrial traditions, it made sense for the Bank in particular to have a small presence on the ground and then use visiting teams of experts to observe infrastructure projects that were being funded. However, the Bank is clearly involved now in very different types of lending in Africa. Today, a large percentage of the money that the Bank loans is related to policy changes rather than the funding of electrical power stations or infrastructure. The Bank's habit of using a large number of short-term consultants is particularly inappropriate for this type of lending because the organization does not gain the local knowledge or analytical ability to implement conditionality policy in a rational manner and promote the development of the agrarian infrastructure. Until the Bank realizes that it cannot be politically astute as a policy lender until it has a much bigger staff on the ground and acts in a more politically self-conscious manner, it will be unable to offer more support to farmers.

A World Bank that offered more support to agriculture would need, first, to have a significantly larger presence in many African countries. This expanded staff would be necessary if it were actually able to support improvements in agriculture beyond the raising of producer prices. Only a larger staff would be able to develop the ties with society, review mechanisms, and institutional memory so that the Bank could observe long-term improvements in the agrarian support system as well as follow prices. Indeed, it seems strange that the World Bank, which often provides loans many times the amount of money donated by the U.S. government, usually has a staff that is only a small fraction of the Agency for International Development's mission and the political section of the American Embassy. A larger, more politically conscious Bank mission would also be able to coordinate better with USAID and local nongovernmental organizations that have expert political knowledge.

Further, by having a larger physical presence on the ground, the World Bank would actually be able to reach out to the people it says should develop "countervailing power." At the very least, the Bank would be able to supply farmer groups with the same kind of analysis supporting reforms that it provides to governments. This would not be a radically new position for the Bank. After all, it already helps governments attract foreign investment and promotes policies that allow foreign investors to feel more comfortable with African governments. It is even possible that the Bank might at some future date provide some aid to farmers' organizations so that they become more of a political presence. Thus, provided governments are receptive to input from farmers, the Bank might be helpful to farmer groups trying to move from support for leadership commitment, as in Ghana, to something approaching the level of consultation, in Zimbabwe. If these changes were made, the Bank would be able to become as politically important an actor in the long-term policy debates over the agrarian infrastructure as it is during discussions over producer prices. These structural reforms would allow the World Bank to come to terms with its demands that institutions and "governance" be improved in Africa. If these reforms are not adopted, the Bank faces serious risks because it will not be able to participate in the very type of institutional reforms that it is increasingly suggesting are necessary if African countries are to grow again.

Of course, the Bank's bylaws explicitly prohibit it from becoming involved in politics. However, this is a fiction that is seldom adhered to even in theory. Given that the Bank has become heavily involved in programs that cause significant shifts of income, it is perceived by almost all actors in the developing and the developed world as a profoundly political organization. Adjusting to its political role and specifically supporting those it wants structural adjustment to benefit would only be logical. Indeed, it is ironic that the Bank's current position of not fundamentally recognizing its own political nature simply prevents it from helping those it is naturally allied with in the campaign to increase the long-term resources going to agriculture.

Conclusion

This is a crucial time for African agriculture. The economic crisis that almost all African countries are mired in demands that action be taken quickly. In addition, African states are also now under pressure from both their citizens and foreign governments to change basic political structures in order to promote agriculture, which has given farmer communities in Africa a window of opportunity in which to insert themselves into the policy-making process. It would be a shame if the new political structures that at least some African countries may experiment with in the years to come do not empower the largest single group in African countries. Indeed, it behooves foreigners, especially the multilateral organizations, now to think creatively how they can help African farmer communities.

Notes

1. Christopher L. Delgado and John W. Mellor, "A Structural View of Policy Issues in African Agricultural Development: A Reply," *American Journal of Agricultural Economics* 69 (May 1987): 391; also see the Widner chapter in

this volume. I am grateful to Tom Callaghy, John Ravenhill, and John Waterbury for helpful comments.

2. World Bank, *Sub-Saharan Africa: From Crisis to Sustainable Growth* (Washington, D.C.: World Bank, 1989), pp. 60–61.

3. Paul Streeten, *What Price Food?: Agricultural Price Policies in Developing Countries* (Ithaca: Cornell University Press, 1987), p. 80.

4. E. E. Schattschneider, *Politics, Pressures and the Tariff* (New York: Prentice-Hall, 1935), p. 286.

5. World Bank, *Accelerated Development in Sub-Saharan Africa* (Washington, D.C.: World Bank, 1981), p. 45.

6. World Bank, 1989, p. 222 and World Bank, *World Development Report 1992* (Washington, D.C.: 1992), p. 221.

7. FAO, *Quarterly Bulletin of Statistics* 2, 4 (1989): 7–8.

8. World Bank, *Sub-Saharan Africa*, p. 276.

9. Ibid., p. 89

10. World Bank, *Ghana: Policies and Program for Adjustment* (Washington, D.C.: World Bank, 1984), p. 10.

11. FAO, *FAO Quarterly Bulletin of Statistics* 2, 3 (1989): 21–25.

12. W. A. Lewis, *Report on Industrialisation and the Gold Coast* (Accra: Government Printer, 1953), p. 2.

13. World Bank, *Accelerated Development*, p. 45.

14. The debate between "pricists" and "structuralists" is now well known. Representative views include: Christopher L. Delgado and John W. Mellor, "A Structural View of Policy Issues in African Agricultural Development," *American Journal of Agricultural Economics* 66 (1984): 665–670; Michael Lipton, "Limits of Price Policy for Agriculture: Which Way for the World Bank," *Development Policy Review* 5, 2 (June 1987): 197-215; Robert Bates, "The Reality of Structural Adjustment: A Sceptical Appraisal," in Simon Commander, ed., *Structural Adjustment and Agriculture: Theory and Practice in Africa and Latin America* (London: Overseas Development Institute, 1989), pp. 221–227; World Bank, *World Development Report 1986* (Washington, D.C.: World Bank, 1986), chs 4–5.

15. Raisuddin Ahmed and Narendra Rustagi, "Marketing and Price Incentives in African and Asian Countries: A Comparison," in Dieter Elz, ed., *Agricultural Marketing Strategy and Pricing Policy* (Washington, D.C.: World Bank, 1987), p. 109.

16. Dharam Ghai and Lawrence D. Smith, *Agricultural Prices, Policy, and Equity in Sub-Saharan Africa* (Boulder: Lynne Rienner, 1987), p. 60.

17. See the fascinating study by David Bevan et. al., *East African Lessons on Economic Liberalization* Thames Essay no. 48 (London: Gower, 1987), ch. 3.

18. Robert H. Bates, *Markets and States in Tropical Africa* (Berkeley: University of California Press, 1981), pp. 106–119.

19. Paul Hesp, *Producer Prices in Tropical Africa*, Research Report no. 23 (Leiden: African Studies Center, 1985), p. 20.

20. Bates, *Markets and States*, pp. 130–131.

21. Ibid., p. 132.

22. See, The Secretary-General, *Mid-Term Review of the Implementation*

of the United Nations Programme of African Economic Recovery and Development 1986–1990, U.N. General Assembly Document A/43/500, 10 August 1988, p.17.

23. World Bank, *Accelerated Development,* p. 47.

24. Calculated from World Bank, *African Economic and Financial Data* (Washington, D.C.: World Bank, 1989), pp. 146–150.

25. William Jaeger and Charles Humphreys, "The Effect of Policy Reforms on Agricultural Incentives in Sub-Saharan Africa," *American Journal of Agricultural Economics* 70, 5 (December 1988): 1040. See also, Lionel Demery and Tony Addison, "Food Insecurity and Adjustment Policies in Sub-Saharan Africa: A Review of the Evidence," *Development Policy Review* 5, 2 (June 1987): 181.

26. Simon Commander, "Prices, Markets and Rigidities," in Commander ed., *Structural Adjustment and Agriculture,* p. 229.

27. Henry S. Bienen and Mark Gersovitz, "Consumer Subsidy Cuts, Violence, and Political Stability," *Comparative Politics* 19, 1 (1986).

28. The black market price may be above the market-clearing price because of rents that black marketeers can extract. I investigate this issue in Jeffrey Herbst, "Labor and City-Dwellers in Ghana under Structural Adjustment: The Politics of Acquiescence," in Donald Rothchild ed., *Ghana: The Political Economy of Reform* (Boulder: Lynne Rienner, 1991).

29. Country Economics Division, *Adjustment Lending: An Evaluation of Ten Years of Experience,* Policy Research Series no. 1 (Washington, D.C.: World Bank, 1988), p. 52.

30. Uma Lele, "Agricultural Growth, Domestic Policies, the External Environment and Assistance to Africa: Lessons of a Quarter Century," in Colleen Roberts ed., *Trade, Aid and Policy Reform: Proceedings of the Eighth Agriculture Sector Symposium* (Washington, D.C.: World Bank, 1988), p. 174.

31. J. G. Beynon, "Pricism v. Structuralism in African Agriculture," *Journal of Agricultural Economics,* 40, 3 (September 1989): 326.

32. David K. Leonard, "Putting the Farmer in Control: Building Agricultural Institutions," in Robert J. Berg and Jennifer Seymour Whitaker eds., *Strategies for African Development* (Berkeley: University of California Press, 1986), p. 184.

33. IMF, "Structural Reform in Fund-Supported Programs," in Development Committee, *Problems and Issues in Structural Adjustment* (Washington, D.C.: Development Committee, 1991), p. 6.

34. On Kenya, see Michael Lofchie, *The Policy Factor: Agricultural Performance in Kenya and Tanzania* (Boulder: Lynne Rienner, 1989), ch. 7; also see the Lofchie chapter in this volume.

35. The elections mattered even though the contestants were usually members of the ruling party. Joel D. Barkan, "The Electoral Process and Peasant-State Relations in Kenya," in Fred M. Hayward ed., *Elections in Independent Africa* (Boulder: Westview, 1987), p. 213.

36. Robert H. Bates, *Beyond the Miracle of the Market: The Political Economy of Agrarian Development in Kenya* (Cambridge: Cambridge University Press, 1989), p. 92. See Lofchie chapter on recent changes in Kenya.

37. See the very good review by Frank Holmquist, "Class Structure, Peasant Participation, and Rural Self-Help," in Joel D. Barkan ed., *Politics and Public Policy in Kenya and Tanzania*, revised edition (New York: Praeger, 1984), p. 185.

38. On the biases in the Kenyan system see, Stephen Peterson, "Neglecting the Poor: State Policy toward the Smallholder in Kenya," in Stephen K. Commins, Michael F. Lofchie, and Rhys Payne eds., *Africa's Agrarian Crisis* (Boulder: Lynne Rienner, 1986), pp. 59–83.

39. World Bank, *Sub-Saharan Africa*, p. 222.

40. Uma Lele, *Agricultural Growth, Domestic Policies, the External Environment and Assistance to Africa: Lessons of a Quarter Century*, MADIA Discussion Paper no. 1 (Washington, D.C.: The World Bank, 1989), p. 31.

41. Uma Lele, "Empowering Africa's Rural Poor: Problems and Prospects in Agricultural Development," in John P. Lewis ed., *Strengthening the Poor: What Have We Learned?* (New Brunswick: Transaction Books, 1988), p. 81.

42. Barkan, p. 234.

43. See, for instance, Naomi Chazan, "Ghana: Problems of "Governance and the Emergence of Civil Society," in Larry Diamond, Juan J. Linz and Seymour Martin Lipset eds., *Democracy in Developing Countries: Africa* (Boulder: Lynne Rienner, 1988), p. 120.

44. Barkan, "Electoral Process," p. 235.

45. I have described the workings of Parliament and of the ruling party in *State Politics in Zimbabwe* (Berkeley: University of California Press, 1990).

46. Agricultural Marketing Authority, *Economic Review of the Agricultural Industry of Zimbabwe* (Harare: The Authority, 1984 and 1987).

47. Central Statistical Office, *Statistical Yearbook 1987* (Harare: Central Statistical Office, 1987), p. 146.

48. See Herbst, *State Politics* 1988.

49. Simon Commander, John Howell and Wayone Seini, "Ghana: 1983–1987," in Commander ed., *Structural Adjustment and Agriculture*, p. 112.

50. Ministry of Agriculture, *Medium Term Agricultural Development Program* (Accra: Government Printers, 1990), p. 80.

51. Interview, Accra, August 10, 1989. See Martin and Callaghy chapters for recent changes in Ghana.

Chapter Ten

The Politics of Nonreform in Cameroon

NICOLAS VAN DE WALLE

Introduction: The Illusion of a Difference

As late as 1985, many Western observers were lauding Cameroon as a country that had avoided the economic policy mistakes of its African neighbors and might avoid the need for the bitter medicines of the World Bank and the International Monetary Fund (IMF).[1] Its agricultural policies were hailed as sensible, its finances sound and its leadership self assured, pragmatic, and competent. President Paul Biya's pledge to bring about the progressive democratization of the regime seemed to win him considerable domestic legitimacy and good will in the West. Today, this rosy assessment has been replaced by considerable pessimism. A severe balance of payments crisis emerged in 1986, causing a serious recession out of which the economy has not yet emerged. Cocoa and coffee farmers have not been fully paid for their efforts in recent years by the state marketing agency because state coffers are empty, while the banking system is in tatters and the parastatal sector is crippled with debts of over a hundred billion CFA francs.[2] Capital flight has increased dramatically despite repeated promises to clamp down.

As elsewhere in Sub-Saharan Africa, the international donors were brought in to help the government address the burgeoning crisis. After a stabilization package was signed with the IMF in September 1988, the country was able to get significant financial assistance from all the major donors in order to undertake the major economic reforms now judged to be essential to put the economy back on track again. In March 1989, the government rescheduled its public debt with the Paris Club for the first time, initiating its version of "the ritual dances of debt," to use Callaghy's appropriate expression.[3] Nonetheless, the slow economic slide has continued unabated. Promises of macroeconomic reform have remained mostly unfulfilled: parastatal reform, deregulation, and trade liberalization have proceeded slowly and fitfully if at all, while cuts in public expenditures have been insufficient to absorb the budget deficit. By early 1992, after six years of negative economic growth, nominal GDP stood at 75% of its level in 1985 and external public debt had risen to roughly half of GDP. On the political front, Biya's regime was increasingly contested by a pro-democracy movement, ethnic tensions were clearly on the rise, and Yaoundé was periodically being shaken by rumors of an impending coup.

What had happened? In retrospect, the earlier view of Cameroon was excessively optimistic, and the perception that it was different from other regimes in the area ill-founded. Cameroon's seemingly impressive growth rate until 1986 was inflated by the discovery of oil in 1978; it disguised a large and increasingly parasitic state sector, little or no productivity growth in the agricultural sector, and daunting infrastructural problems. Much of the oil windfall was invested in poorly conceived public sector schemes that lost money and imposed unsustainable recurrent expenditure demands on the state.

This chapter will provide a political explanation of Cameroon's economic crisis and its inability to bring about economic reforms today. It is sometimes argued that African state elites may not oppose reform but fear that imposing hardships on the population during the reform process will bring about unrest and political instability. I do not disagree with this view: urban unrest has been associated with reform programs in a number of countries and has resulted in regime changes in several. However, I do not believe that this fear poses the major obstacle to reform. Indeed, in Cameroon, the regime has been willing to hurt urban groups in the wallet. This chapter will argue that structural adjustment in Sub-Saharan Africa (SSA) is stagnating because it is opposed by the very state elites who are supposed to carry it out. This is the key to understanding the recent events in Cameroon. Using Bayart's Gramscian notion of a "hegemonic alliance," I will argue that Ahmadu Ahidjo, President of Cameroon from independence to 1982, cemented a complex intra elite accommodation process with access to state resources and rent seeking activities to ensure the regime's stability. Reform and economic austerity can be imposed on the general population; it is the state elite that will not tolerate the end of a system of prerogatives and privilege that is the glue that keeps it together.

Ahidjo combined the indigenous business and political elites that had emerged by the end of the colonial era with more traditional elites to create a ruling alliance. The expansion of the state, particularly into the economic arena, was promoted to manipulate and sustain the alliance, while Ahidjo's personal power and political skills allowed him to control the flow of resources. Fortuitous exogenous factors, in particular the discovery of oil in 1978, gave the regime a second breath that other similar regimes in SSA did not get, and gave the outside world the impression that somehow Cameroon was different.

However, his resignation in 1982 and Paul Biya's consolidation of his own power raised the costs of intra elite accommodation. In a process with parallels to the Senghor/Diouf and Kenyatta/Moi transitions in Senegal and Kenya respectively, new groups emerged in Biya's wake and jockeyed for added privileges while groups favored by Ahidjo were pushed aside or coopted. Biya's own ability to dominate the political game proved to be more limited than Ahidjo's, and when this political conjuncture was combined with a severe exogenous economic shock, the system fell apart. The regime has attempted to cut off some fat, to excise some of its patrimonial tendencies while maintaining its core logic. However, it has been unable to effectuate fundamental changes in governance, because this would mean the end of the hegemonic alliance on which the regime is based.

The Biya regime became even less likely to carry out substantial economic reform once a pro-democracy opposition movement emerged in 1990. At the time of writing (early 1993), domestic and international pressures had led the regime to concede some reforms of political liberalization, but Biya remained firmly in command and was proving quite capable of manipulating the internal divisions and rivalries within the opposition to his advantage.

Nonetheless, whatever momentum might have existed for economic reform was now eroded by the presence of the opposition. On the one hand, it made the government more sensitive to the popular discontent created by austerity policies and the worsening economy, since the regime could no longer prevent the emergence of organizational structures to channel this discontent. On the other hand, Biya's authority was being further diminished by defections from the single party, and the costs of maintaining his political coalition and the stability of his regime were being raised.

I begin with the background of the current crisis and the early signs of impending trouble, notably the rapid expansion of a parasitic state. I then briefly review the political dynamics of economic adjustment as theorized by a number of scholars. A third section argues that to understand the current developments it is necessary to analyze the sociological foundations of the Cameroonian state itself, particularly the loose alliance of elites that has benefited from past policies. A fourth section describes the onset of economic crisis and a fifth one evaluates the early implementation record of this reform program, in the context of the state's ambiguous interests in reform. I show that the state has been inconsistent and halfhearted, and that abuses have continued even within its own administration. In a sixth section, I assess the implications of the emergence of the pro-democracy movement in 1990 for economic reform. Finally, I argue that the present situation of stagnation, decreasing state efficiency and crisis is not necessarily unsustainable, even if it may well be self-perpetuating. Several lessons are then drawn from this case study for the process of economic reform in Sub-Saharan Africa.

A Cameroonian Economic Miracle?

Cameroon, with its land mass of 475,440 square kilometers and 10.9 million people, has one of the more diversified economies in SSA. With an estimated per capita GNP of $970 in 1987,[4] it is the world's fifth largest exporter of cocoa, as well as a major exporter of coffee, cotton, bananas, palm oil, rubber, and timber. Since 1979 it has exported oil, totaling some 7.7 million tons in 1985. Currently known reserves are to dry up sometime before the end of the century at the current exploitation rate. Other mineral reserves include bauxite, iron ore, and natural gas, and there is considerable hydropower potential as well.

With an annual growth rate of some 8% from 1970 to 1985, the Cameroonian economy was long considered one of the success stories in SSA. Its liberal investment code under Ahidjo's proclaimed economic philosophy of "planned liberalism" appealed to the Western donors and business milieux, as did the regime's lack of ideological posturing, and its apparent political stability.[5] Douala's importance as a business and commercial center was in constant progression, and the city was said to harbor one of the few strong business classes of the continent.

While not without foundation, this view of the country's economy was excessively optimistic and failed to take note of several disturbing trends by the end of Ahidjo's tenure. Much of the country's success was based on its rich resource base, yet the agricultural sector was stagnating: the growth registered was due mostly to increased acreage under cultivation, brought about by expensive government and donor programs, and it disguised the absence of sustained productivity growth. The bulk of government and donor investment had been devoted to capital intensive state farms and plantations, most of which lost money and required repeated infusions of capital.[6] Membership in the Franc Zone had the advantage of promoting economic stability and allowing an open trade regime, but it had established a tendency toward overvaluation of the currency and encouraged the development of imported consumer tastes.[7] The country's wealth obscured growing disparities and pockets of extreme poverty, particularly in the northern hinterlands. Moreover, the high levels of illiteracy, morbidity, and malnutrition were those of a much poorer country, and bespoke inadequate attention to these problems.[8]

Finally, the most disturbing trend was the rapid growth of a costly and ineffectual public sector. The point here is not to embark on a normative debate regarding the appropriate size of the public sector in African economies. Most of the institutions created in this period had valuable initial development functions and would have fostered more rapid development had they functioned correctly. They never came close to doing so, however, and soon became little more than vehicles for patronage and corruption. The agricultural sector is typical: more than 20 parastatal institutions were created during the 1970s, for example, at enormous cost to the state, yet cotton was the only crop that enjoyed significant productivity growth during this period.[9] One observer's severe critique of the effectiveness of a set of state-run cooperative structures could apply to most of the public institutions in the agricultural sector: despite a staff of more than a hundred employees and a budget of 122 million CFA, he argued, "the SOCOOPED are useless, perhaps even negative in their impact. They accomplish nothing for their members, they do not meet any of their needs. We recommend they be disbanded."[10] Ironically, traditional food crops, which were completely neglected by the authorities, fared significantly better than the rest of the sector.[11]

Overall, central government employment grew from some 20,000 employees in the early sixties to some 180,000 in 1988; in recent years, it was growing by 9% a year. Employment growth in parastatals and public enterprises, mostly after 1971, was even faster. By 1984, some 150 billion CFA a year were needed to cover parastatal sector deficits, even though most of them had been designed to be self-sufficient and possessed their own revenues.[12] Though much of the oil revenues after 1978 were initially kept in secret bank accounts abroad, their primary function soon became to cover parastatal deficits.

In the long run parastatal deficits proved unsustainable. It is not clear whether or not Ahidjo could have tempered spending demands had he remained in power, or whether he benefited from lucky timing. Certainly, the system began to fall apart after Biya's accession to the presidency in 1982 and particularly after his break with Ahidjo two years later—punctuated by the failed coup attempt of April 1984. The sharp deterioration in the country's terms of trade after 1985 did the rest.

The Politics of Adjustment

The fundamental political consequence of structural adjustment or of wholesale economic restructuring is that it redistributes resources within the economy.[13] It produces winners and losers, both in relative and in absolute terms, and the losers can be expected to oppose the reforms out of self-interest. Economists distinguish expenditure-switching reform policies from expenditure-reduction policies: the former result in absolute winners and losers, because resources are simply shifted across economic sectors, with no reduction in overall economic activity; the latter produce only losers since absorption is reduced equally across the economy. The way switching and reduction policies are combined in a stabilization package will determine whether or not the benefits and losses of the reform are absolute or relative.

It is easy enough to broadly identify the groups that have most benefited from Cameroon's political economy in the last decade and who is likely to suffer from reform, even if one takes into account the lamentable state of the country's economic statistics: public and parastatal employees are one group that has benefited. Exporters on the other hand have lost purchasing power because the CFA franc has had a tendency toward overvaluation, particularly in recent years (this is in real effective purchasing power terms, of course, since in nominal terms the exchange rate is fixed). The most obvious victims of overvaluation are export cash crop producers, whose real income has decreased since independence, despite belated increases between 1982 and 1986. The reverse is true as well: groups that are net consumers of imported goods have been net winners, everything being equal. They include urban dwellers, who consume the lion's share of nontraditional cereals, Western luxury goods, and electronic goods.

Relative and absolute losers will obviously oppose reform. Their ability to prevent it is much harder to predict, however. First, expenditure-switching reforms will presumably create new constituencies and state leaders may be able to garner political support for reform by skillful manipulation of the policy process.[14] Opposition to economy-wide austerity may be muted by the competing interests that exist even within single households. Urban civil servants who have invested in small cocoa or coffee plantations in their village of origin are an obvious example. Secondly, economic agents often choose their economic activities according to the policy mix and at least some can change their activities to gain from a new one. More generally, perceptions regarding the likelihood of success and of the long-term gains for the economy and for a given individual may condition the degree of tolerance for short-term duress. Groups who suffer from reform may grudgingly accept reform, or at least not mobilize against it, if they believe things will soon improve. Such perceptions are complex and bound to be affected by a number of intervening factors. They may not be predictable. Finally, the degree of the regime's legitimacy may well be instrumental in determining support for reform or at least the lack of opposition from groups that suffer; this too will depend on a number of factors that make prediction forbidding.

It has nonetheless been argued that the state's ability to undertake structural adjustment will be determined by its ability to impose hardships on the groups most favored by the current distribution of resources. Put differently, several authors have argued that the state elite's dilemma in periods of economic reform is to switch its base of support, to identify and assemble a new social coalition on behalf of the post reform policy mix.[15] These scholars suggest that successful reform is likely only to the extent that the state can assemble a viable coalition on behalf of an alternative policy mix. Other scholars have been more pessimistic about the state's ability to impose hardship on the population, or to switch its social base of support. Robert Bates has argued that there are important asymmetries in the political power of different groups.[16] Others assert that African states often lack the political legitimacy or toughness to impose hardships on their citizens. That the African state is unable or unwilling to impose austerity on the population has become a common explanation for the current failure of reform programs in a wide variety of African nations.[17] Yet, since the first oil shock in 1973, stabilization plans have brought about draconian compressions of national income in a number of African countries without noticeable increases in regime changes or political instability.

Elsewhere, I have argued that the obstacles to economic reform in SSA lie less in the opposition of those social groups that will be net losers—though it may be substantial and have an important impact on decisionmakers—than it does in the commitment of the state to reform and its limited capability to implement it.[18] Reform is undermined by the negative synergy that exists between implementation capability and the commitment to undertake a given reform. Here I would like to go further and argue that economic reform along the lines advocated by the IMF and World Bank is often unlikely to succeed because it would undermine the very sociological foundations of the state.

The Sociological Foundations of the Cameroonian State

In his seminal book on Cameroonian politics, Jean-François Bayart contends that post-independence politics has been marked by the successful efforts of the dominant social groups to establish their hegemony over society by taking over the political and economic institutions bequeathed by the colonial state.[19] This "hegemonic search" involved not only traditional rural elites, but also the emerging political class and the individuals who had profited most from the colonial economy. Ahmadu Ahidjo was instrumental in shaping a "post colonial historical alliance" out of these groups which have dominated the state apparatus ever since and used it to appropriate a disproportionate share of the nation's resources. He manipulated these elites to consolidate and then maintain his own power. This dynamic process is of course not unique to Cameroon[20] although it has acquired its own historical specificity. In most African countries, independence resulted in a power vacuum, just as the disparate social groups that had been privileged by the colonial political economy began to come of age and assert themselves.

Can this state elite be identified? In a fascinating analysis conducted in 1983 but still highly relevant, Ngayap answers the question "who governs Cameroon" by identifying roughly a thousand people.[21] Starting from the president himself, he identifies the people who hold the top positions in the government, administration, legislature, party, judiciary, army, and business world. This definition of the governing elite corresponds well with the members of Bayart's hegemonic alliance, although the latter also incorporates the leading traditional chiefs, who are born into positions of power. One may quibble with the exact delineations of this elite, but Ngayap's work does provide striking evidence regarding the personalized nature of power in African nations like Cameroon. In the poorly institutionalized, patrimonial political systems of SSA, small circumscribed elites can bolster their power through the personal networks that pervade the official structures of the state. It also may help explain how power can be so concentrated in the hands of one executive leader.[22]

As Gramsci theorized would happen when a class has secured social hegemony, the values of the ruling alliance and of its *modus vivendi* have seeped through Cameroonian society, shoring up its power.[23] In particular the acquisitive nature of state agents is something that is culturally accepted, even as it is resented and criticized. Common wisdom in Yaoundé has it that "*la chevre broute là ou elle est attachée,*" that in other words it can only be second nature for state officials to take advantage of their position.[24] The legitimacy of this system has been buttressed in part by the important social mobility that characterized Cameroon for a long time, and has given people the impression they too might benefit from state favors. Given the right studies and diplomas, positions of power and wealth could be attained at a young age, even by rural people.[25]

It is control of the state and its resources that has sustained this alliance, however. Its members have fought for the influence, wealth, and power that association with state institutions procures. Sklar's point is that in SSA political power preceded economic power; this has some truth, but in a country like Cameroon, the two have long been mutually reinforcing.[26] High-level positions in the government or administration grant their holders patronage possibilities and a mechanism for enrichment, through the selling of influence and rents. On the other hand, local and foreign businesspeople have accrued large fortunes by buying import licenses and monopolies over lucrative markets. The overlap of private wealth and state power is extensive, often realized within the same family if not the same individual.

As a consequence, the alleged presence of an autonomous business class in Douala is at least part mirage. Soppo Priso provides a fairly unusual example of a business empire being developed without the explicit complicity of the post-colonial state.[27] A Douala businessman, he made his fortune trading with the colonial state before independence and stayed at arm's length from politics after his failure to become prime minister in the early 1960s. Soppo Priso nonetheless continued to exert political influence through his contacts and family ties, which his rank as one of the richest men in the country abetted.

The career of Pierre Tchanque seems much more representative of the business elite that has emerged, particularly in recent years.[28] Of modest origins, this technocrat from the Bamiléké region of Western Province rose to the pinnacles of the state administration before starting his own business. After having been Secretary General in the Ministry of Finance from 1966–1969, Assistant Director General of the state investment company, the *Société Nationale des Investissements* (SNI) from 1969 to 1970, and Secretary General of the *Union Douanière des Etats de l'Afrique Centrale* (UDEAC) from 1971 to 1977, he left the public sector. In 1979, he launched a major brewery, NOBRA, with the help of capital from the SNI and important tax and tariff breaks. To reflect his new status, Tchanque was named to the Central Committee of the nation's single party, the *Rassemblement Démocratique du Peuple Camerounais* (RPDC).[29]

The private-public divide is often more illusory than real in a country like Cameroon. Private business strategies can be limited to exploiting rent situations granted by the state, but even legitimate businesses cannot be successful very long without accomodating the state. The unavailability of credit, building permits, or import licenses, as well as petty police exactions, harassment by the tax agents or by the water and electric company are all likely to result without the protection of well-placed friends: reaching an accommodation with the state is usually a precondition for staying in business, let alone thriving. That is why the current predilection for privatization in the donor community is likely to disappoint its proponents: privatization alone is unlikely to change the opportunities for rent seeking and state predation.[30]

The elite's drive for hegemony implied and directed state expansion. It would be wrong to argue that rent seeking and patronage were the only reasons the state promoted expansion after independence. Extensive public ownership conformed to prevailing development doctrines, was warmly supported by the donors, and responded to real development needs. Still, the scope state ownership was to achieve was helped by the fact that it afforded leaders like Ahidjo positions of prestige and power to distribute. Similarly with state intervention in the economy: tariffs, licenses, permits, and taxes had all sorts of purposes and justification—including the collection of revenue to finance state activities—but in many cases they were maintained because they created profitable rents to be rationed out.

Just as important, Ahidjo's attempts to dominate and manage his governing alliance shaped the nature of economic strategy. He sponsored the proliferation of ministries and parastatal institutions to increase the positions of power at his disposal. Economic development was inhibited when it appeared to favor certain groups unduly. Thus, in order to temper the development of Bamiléké and more generally southern economic power, Ahidjo always refused to pave the road between Yaoundé and Douala, the two biggest cities in the country, or the one between Yaoundé and

Bafoussam in the heart of the Bamiléké region of the Western Highlands.[31]

Similarly, the need to regulate the governing elite and to prevent any individual or group from developing undue power resulted in rapid turnover of high-level political and administrative personnel. Tenure in any position was kept short to prevent the holder from developing an autonomous power base, and to allow others to benefit from the position's advantages. Thus, both Ahidjo and now Biya have shuffled or changed ministerial cabinets at least once a year, keeping only a few close associates in key positions longer.[32]

Social mobility has declined in recent years. Income inequalities and social differentiation have increased as state elites have consolidated their positions and now are more intent on protecting their privileges. It is not only that the average bureaucrat's annual income is more than 50 times that of the average farmer's, as Hugon had already noted in 1967[33] or that egregious "urban bias" has been routinely identified in the developing world. It is also that the consolidation of the hegemonic alliance has resulted in increasingly little "trickle down" of this wealth throughout the economy. While the civil service as a whole is privileged, its internal inequalities have sharply increased. The administration spends roughly 30 billion CFA a year on housing construction and allowances for state employees, for example, yet these probably benefit 5% of all civil servants. Urban income data indicate a highly skewed distribution,[34] while the 1984 agricultural Census painted a picture of sharp rural differentiation, with some 28,000 farms (2.4% of all farms) enjoying gross incomes of one million CFA or more a year, while 60% of all farms make less than 100,000 CFA.[35] Access to education, modern medicine, and other social services have increasingly been rationed to rich urban populations.[36]

Clientelism has not disappeared, far from it. Sectional ties cut across and mediate class cleavages in the patron-client networks that permeate the state structures, much like those that Joseph has so well explored for Nigeria.[37] The most menial job in the administration attracts the minister's attention and mobilizes village and ethnic loyalties. But clientelism does not have the political role that it has in countries with vibrant machine politics. Individuals in the state elite do not cultivate an autonomous power base by promoting a given region or ethnic group, or even a functional category like trade unionists or teachers. It may be important for the Ewondo people (or any other group) that there is an Ewondo minister in Biya's cabinet—and certainly informal interviewing suggests it does—but it does not appear that the Ewondo minister feels obliged to do anything substantial for that ethnic group. That as Minister of Education he may promote the building of a school in his home village responds to a slightly different dynamic, not only because it involves relatively trivial resources but also, more important, it is the personal favor of the "local boy who made good," than it is the cultivation of a political base with ulterior motives.

The amount of income redistribution effectuated by state elites is insignificant. An interesting illustration is provided by the apportionment of arabica coffee revenues in the Bamiléké region of the Western Highlands.[38] Much is made of Bamiléké solidarity: rumors abound of a Bamiléké Mafia within the state bureaucracy, or of shady parallel financial networks that have helped Bamiléké businessmen.[39] In part, this reflects envy toward an ethnic group that has been more achievement oriented than others and has propelled more of its own up the social ladder. The Bamiléké's resulting prominence within the state apparatus, as well as its early support of the UPC Rebellion,[40] has spurred accusations from other ethnic groups of a Bamiléké ambition to dominate the country.

Almost all of the country's high-value arabica coffee is grown by Bamiléké farmers. Since the late fifties, the farmers have been organized in the production cooperatives run by rural elites, often traditional chiefs. The six largest cooperatives formed the *Union Centrale des Cooperatives Agricoles de l'Ouest* (UCCAO) in 1958 to help them commercialize their crops. About 100,000 small farms are obliged to market their coffee crop (some 20,000 tons) through the cooperative. UCCAO has always been allowed to export its arabica coffee directly, while other cooperatives and parastatals have had to pass through the ONCPB, the national marketing organization.

This unique decentralization of economic decision-making has given Bamiléké elites in the Western Province a unique opportunity to engage in "trickle down" to the benefit of their region. First, one might expect that the UCCAO's peasants receive a larger share of the world coffee price than other farmers receive for their crop. However, from 1971 to 1987 arabica producers received an average of 45% of the FOB price while robusta producers received 43% and cocoa producers received 45%.[41] Given the various difficulties with the data, this indicates no more than that a similar proportion of the crop's international value accrues to the producers of each of the three crops.[42] Strictly speaking, these numbers do not reflect the level at which producers are taxed, since they do not take into account the costs of marketing. As table 10.1 shows, however, the state has taxed all three crops at roughly the same level. The difference is that whereas the other two crops are providing ONCPB with handsome revenues, even after reasonable marketing costs are taken into account, the UCCAO cooperative kept the bulk of export revenues for itself, having to pay only a rather modest levy to ONCPB.[43]

Remarkably little of this considerable revenue has benefited the cooperatives' members, who are increasingly turning to food crop cultivation and losing their interest in arabica coffee. Arguments about UCCAO's technical assistance role in helping modernize local farming systems are belied by the fact that both yields and output are lower today than at independence, despite UCCAO's plethoric staff. Revenues have financed the growth of the UCCAO cooperatives, which now employ several thousand people. It has also encouraged much fraud, some prestige expenditures such as

TABLE 10.1
Breakdown of Marketing Revenues: Robusta, Arabica and Cocoa, 1986/87
(in CFAF/kg)

	Robusta	Arabica	Cocoa
F.O.B. Price	1028.0	1367.0	946.4
Marketing Costs	141.4	727.5	86.7
of which:			
- ONCPB Commission	3.0	0.0	1.0
- Exporters/Buyers	73.8	0.0	49.6
- Banks	39.2	0.0	20.7
- Others	3.7	28.7	5.0
- Cooperatives	21.7	698.8	10.4
Government Export Tax	71.2	83.5	59.7
ONCPB Levy	375.4	41.0	380.0
Producer Price	440.0	515.0	420.0

SOURCE: Adapted from J. Schwettmann, (1987). *Etude Préparatoire Pour le Séminaire national sur le Mouvement Coopératif au Camroun: Etude no. 3, Analyse Mesoéconomique.* Yaoundé: Deutsche Gesellschaft Fur Technische Zusmmenarbeit (GTZ). (August 1987).

the financing of football clubs in Western Province, and the local activities of the country's single party.[44] The shabby appearance of towns in the Western Province and the absence of industrial investments there provides subjective evidence that the bulk of UCCAO capital has made its way to the bigger cities south, and has not been recycled in the Western Province.[45]

We have described the UCCAO at length because it is a paradigmatic example of intra-elite accommodation processes in Cameroon. Ahidjo early on bought Bamiléké elite support by granting them complete discretion over vast coffee revenues. The success of this strategy was crucial during the UPC Rebellion and it has been maintained ever since to preserve the region's support. UCCAO revenues have nurtured the emergence of a provincial bourgeoisie, often linked to conservative traditional elites, that has tied its fortunes to the regime. UCCAO did not foster an autonomous Bamiléké political project, not only because Ahidjo would never have allowed it, but also because Bamiléké elites internalized the regime's values of material appropriation. While no doubt salient, ethnicity based solidarities have become secondary to strategies of individual enrichment.

The Onset of Economic Crisis

The regime we have just described was not necessarily unstable, even if it was unlikely to promote capitalist accumulation and economic growth. Two factors were to precipitate economic crisis: Biya's accession to the presidency and subsequent falling out with Ahidjo, and the deterioration of Cameroon's terms of trade with the outside world. Much has already been written about the struggle between the two men and its effects on Cameroon's political system after 1983.[46] Suffice it to say that the difficulties Biya encountered consolidating his own power raised the costs of maintaining the loose ruling alliance. Biya could not afford to exert as tight a control over state resources as Ahidjo, given that his hold on power was more precarious. He needed to please the state apparatus, notably those parts of the army which supported him during the 1984 coup attempt, and he wanted to mollify the north (Ahidjo's base of support) as well as meet the heightened expectations of his fellow southerners. A direct consequence was the acceleration of budgetary and state employment growth. He acceded to the donors' long-standing insistence that producer prices for the main cash crops be increased to improve farmer incentives. Increases were particularly generous for cotton producers in the north. By 1985, Cameroon farmers had the highest producer prices in all of Francophone Africa for coffee and cocoa, and cotton prices were a full 50% higher than in the other country of the Franc Zone.[47] Moreover, the new regime's barons to which Biya was beholden were much bolder in staking out claims on the state's resources than Ahidjo's supporters had been. Corruption and rent seeking had always been fundamental characteristics of the regime;[48] after 1984, they began to escape central control and became dysfunctional. In addition, the overvaluation of the CFA franc fueled rent seeking. Fraudulent trade with Nigeria reached dizzying heights after the naira's 1986 devaluation, for example. It is all but impossible to prevent, given the long history of occult trade between the two nations and the active complicity of state agents on both sides of the border.

The need to placate these diverse constituencies proved disastrous when the international environment turned against Biya. A sharp downfall in commodity prices and the rapid depreciation of the dollar after 1985 resulted in a 45% deterioration in the country's terms of trade.[49] The state soon ran deficits for all of the major export crops and could not even cover variable costs on its palm oil and rubber plantations. Most important, the world price of oil plunged and the state's oil revenues decreased from $350 million in fiscal year 1985 to an estimated $207 million in 1988.

The first consequence of the economic crisis was the collapse of the commercial banking sector. A number of bad loans—many of which had been contracted by northerners close to Ahidjo, now out of favor—were defaulted upon, causing a liquidity crisis. By 1987, most of the commercial banks in the country were insolvent, with effects that reverberated throughout the economy. The easy credit and state subsidies that had kept the economy going now suddenly dried up. The marketing process for the major cash crops was seriously disrupted, with not enough liquidity to provide seasonal credit. In addition, the ONCPB had illegally invested much of its accumulated reserves in the commercial banking system (65 billion CFA by some estimates), as well as in a number of private and semi-public corporations now verging on bankruptcy.

Farmers were as a consequence not paid more than a third to a half of the official price for their crop, usually with considerable delays. Between 1986 and 1989, GDP decreased by an estimated 11% in real terms.[50]

The IMF and the World Bank had been negotiating with the government on and off since mid-1986, without reaching agreement. At this time, Biya staked the national prestige by refusing the tough austerity programs of those two institutions. Throughout 1986 and 1987, he insisted that Cameroon would undertake an adjustment on its own, and seek only nonconditional capital from bilateral donors and the private banks.[51] The 1987 fiscal year budget was to be cut by several hundred billion CFA, the first of several hiring freezes was announced, along with new taxes on luxury goods, and in late 1987, Biya announced the creation of a new "anti-crisis" ministry, the Ministry for the Stabilization of Public Finances.[52]

In fact, deeds failed to follow Biya's tough rhetoric and the crisis continued to worsen, with expenditure overruns of 429 billion in 1986–87 (above the projected budget of 800 billion CFA), some 11.5% of GNP. Recourse to the international institutions became inevitable. Agreement was reached with the IMF on a stabilization plan in September 1988 and with the World Bank on a Structural Adjustment Loan in May 1989. The donors' adjustment strategies have contained the conventional prescriptions of important cuts in public expenditures, increased state revenues, and the compression of consumption, coupled with the promotion of selective investments to foster long-term growth. They have called for the privatization, rehabilitation, or elimination of almost all of the nation's parastatals, as well as thoroughgoing liberalization.

The Process of Reform Implementation

Given its sociological makeup, how can the regime come to grips with the economic crisis and the severe compression on its resources that it has brought about? Given that its power and legitimacy is based on the control and manipulation of state resources, can it survive liberalization? A kind of strategy can be gleaned from the desultory and half hearted implementation of adjustment policies since 1987. Some progress has been made cutting government expenditures; there is little choice anyway since state coffers are empty. The donors have been courted more assiduously than in the past to increase public external finance and to get the imprimatur needed to attract private capital back into the country, albeit with little success to date. Some donor-inspired reforms have been launched, usually laboriously although real progress has been achieved in some areas. At the same time, Biya's regime has not wanted—or known it would not be able—to turn systematically against its own barons in the administration and business world, or to change the "rules of the game" regarding the use of positions for personal enrichment. In addition, the state is too unwieldy and inefficient to execute economic policy consistently, and Biya is not confident that he can get his commands implemented by an increasingly undisciplined state bureaucracy. These inconsistent motivations largely explain the erratic and "stop-go" implementation of the specific reforms, which we now focus briefly on.

Cutting Expenditures

Government expenditures have been reduced from a high of 1,229 billion CFA in 1986–87 to 673 billion CFA in 1988–89, and a projected 572 billion for 1991–92. This achievement should be put into context. First, a concurrent fall in public revenues during the same period has meant that the budget deficit—some 207 billion CFA in 1990–91, or 7% of GDP—has remained much too high. Second, the spending cuts have been quite haphazard. Personnel expenditures have been little affected by the cuts, as the number of civil servants actually increased between 1987 and 1991.[53] The cuts have come from the rest of the budget: the investment budget has been cut by two thirds, while nonpersonnel related recurrent expenditures have been reduced to negligible amounts. To take one example, only 5% of the Ministry of Agriculture's total budget of 39 billion CFA was set aside in the 1988–89 budget for nonpersonnel related expenditures.[54] One consequence has been a near total breakdown of efficiency in the ministries, which are becoming increasingly short of working photocopy machines, typewriters, and even light bulbs. Maintenance, never adequately budgeted for, has now all but disappeared. The absurdity of this approach from a developmental point of view is well compensated by the political logic of placating the administration. This was the path of least resistance for the regime. If and when personnel expenditure cuts become necessary, the burden will fall disproportionately on the lower end of the hierarchy for the same reasons. Payroll arrears for new employees had already been allowed to slip to more than 20 billion CFA by early 1989.

The decision to impose new luxury taxes, to freeze new hiring in the administration, and to clamp down on fictitious employees won the government breathing space with the IMF and World Bank, but these changes were discreetly breached as political needs arose. Until the 1990 season the government noisily refused IMF advice to lower official producer prices for cotton, coffee, and cocoa, thus providing evidence of an admirable solidarity with the rural world. Meanwhile, it was increasingly unable to provide the marketing agencies with enough cash to pay peasants more than between 25% and 75% of the full producer price. In September 1989, under pressure from the donors, official producer prices for coffee and cocoa were cut by some 30%. Even the lower prices caused problems for the bankrupt state. State debts to cocoa and coffee farmers accumulated between 1988 and 1991 amidst much confusion, peaking at some 80 billion CFA before French and EEC grants provided the government with the necessary cash to begin honoring the IOUs farmers had accumulated.[55]

The decision to save money by selling off government vehicles provides an interesting micro case study of the reform process. The use and abuse of government vehicles have long been a highly charged symbol of state prerogatives in Cameroon. In July 1987, Biya proclaimed that the state had an excessive number of vehicles and that their misuses had reached an unacceptable level. He ordered that all state vehicles be impounded by the police and then either auctioned off publicly or reassigned according to clearly defined professional needs. The measure was initially popular, even though the likely savings would be minor, as it seemed to indicate a new get-tough policy on Biya's part. This enthusiasm made way for cynicism when his announcement set off an unseemly free-for-all that was to last several weeks.[56] Auctions were not publicized and local state elites were allowed to purchase personal cars at bargain prices. Car reassignments were either arbitrary, or the results of intense jockeying and haggling between local state agents, in a process that favored the politically powerful. Governors and prefects tended to be favored by the reassignments over developmental ministries like agriculture or health. The government never reported the savings made from the reform, but they came at the cost of reduced state efficiency and a further eroding of Biya's reputation.

Toughening up the Regime

Biya also toughened up his regime in more substantial ways. Perhaps fearful that his authority was eroding, in early 1989 he brought out of semi-retirement Jean Fochive to head the secret police, the *Centre National de la Documentation et de la Recherche* (CENER), and Andze Tchoungui to be Secretary of State for Internal Security.[57] Both men had been eminent members of Ahidjo's security apparatus and were closely associated in the public mind with the violent repression of the UPC rebellion in the late sixties and early seventies, as well as that regime's excesses. Indeed, they had dropped from view during the regime's period of democratization in 1983–1985. Their reappearance suggested that Biya wanted to intimidate would-be critics and opponents. A campaign against corruption and fraud was declared and crackdowns were prominently advertised in the state media.[58] The aim was to satisfy the donors, show the general population the regime's impartiality, and moderate the elite's acquisitive fervor. By strengthening his security apparatus, Biya hoped to shore up his own diluted authority and defend himself against potential coups.

Biya employed other methods to increase his own room to maneuver in the initial period of reform. Thus, he called for surprise presidential and legislative elections in April 1988, which were to see the defeat of several old barons of the regime and the election of Biya proteges. The elections were designed to provide Biya with a mandate. Given the degree of presidential meddling in both the constitution of the single party's electoral lists, and probably in the results themselves, it seems certain that Biya was promoting allies and undermining opposition to consolidate his position in preparation for the hard days ahead.[59]

Cutting Down on Corruption

Despite his exhortations against corruption, Biya continued Ahidjo's tactic of using the distribution of rents to regulate and dominate the different factions that constitute the country's elite. He sought less to eliminate rent seeking during this period of economic crisis than to better control and centralize it. The state's ability to moralize its own elite and cut down on corruption was limited in practice, moreover, as its capabilities for implementation were too limited to ensure the execution of policies, particularly when the state's commitment on their behalf is lukewarm. This negative synergy between lack of commitment and implementation capacity is exemplified by the stillborn Stabilization Fund (*Caisse de Péréquation*) for rice.[60]

Under considerable pressure from the donors, the government set up a stabilization fund that would tax rice imports enough to protect local rice production. The proceeds from this tax were to permit the rehabilitation of the SEMRY, the rice parastatal, which was under considerable financial pressure. In fact, the Stabilization Fund never functioned properly and did not accrue revenues. Until mid 1989, even the importers with official import licenses managed to avoid paying the stabilization tax, while the flow of illegal rice imports failed to abate; the evidence suggests widespread complicity in the Customs Office and in the Ministry of Industrial Development and Commerce, the ministry in charge of import licenses. Incompetence, confusion, and poor records in both institutions have abetted fraud. Biya spoke out on behalf of the Stabilization Fund but was not able or willing to clamp down on the corruption that destroyed it. His motives were ambiguous; it was alleged that the worst offenders were businessmen from the south who were encouraged by Biya and Nomo Ongolo, the Minister of Industrial Development and Commerce until December 1987, to compete with the traditional Bamiléké and northern importers.[61]

Parastatal Reform

Institutional reform in the public and parastatal sectors is another area where there was more rhetoric than action.[62] The World Bank made parastatal reform a cornerstone of its adjustment program and their excessive cost and inefficiencies had long been criticized by technocrats in the government itself. In May 1987, Biya appeared to side with the reformers when he appointed a national commission to review the performance of the parastatal sector. A group of five Cameroonian technocrats spent a year auditing more than 150 parastatals, with the assistance of foreign experts financed by the World Bank and the United Nations. They reported to the president in May 1988. Biya then procrastinated, expanding the Commission that summer and ordering it to examine the financial sector more thoroughly, before quietly shelving its report. Nonetheless, privatization has progressed, thanks to sustained donor pressures and budgetary exigencies. Initially, only several small parastatals were targeted for sale or liquidation,[63] but in mid 1991, the government published a list of firms to be privatized, including important public enterprises such as the Cameroon Sugar Company, although no deadlines or schedules were established. Outside of the banking sector, the most significant privatization has been the liquidation of the ONCPB.[64] Several thousand ONCPB employees were laid off and cocoa and coffee marketing channels were privatized. Significantly, considerable donor pressures could not prevent the process from taking several years, nor the government from establishing a new marketing organization, the *Office national du Café et du Cacao* (ONCC), to take over some of ONCPB's old functions.

There appears to be internal debate within the state elite regarding the steps to follow for the important parastatals. On the one hand, parastatal reform necessarily involves layoffs, management contracts, audits, and a tighter control of the purse, which it is loath to pursue; on the other hand, privatization has some appeal as a solution to the parastatals' problems, because discretion can be exercised over who the buyers are and the sale will provide revenues for the state. Perhaps as a result, the government has focused on parastatals that can be privatized rather than on those that have important noncommercial functions and where reform would focus on rehabilitation or liquidation. Privatization, however, involves daunting technical problems in a country with no stock market and a very sick banking sector.[65] Thus, again, reform seems to be slowed down by a mutually reinforcing combination of lack of commitment and lack of capability.

The Role of the Donors

The important donors have all offered capital to Cameroon to assist the process of adjustment; they are the IMF, the World Bank, and the European Development Fund (EDF) on the multilateral side; and France's *Caisse Centrale de Cooperation Economique* (CCCE), and USAID on the bilateral side. Donor finance provides the state with considerable discretionary resources and has become increasingly important as the state's own resources have decreased. As elsewhere in Africa, the conditionality of donor assistance has proven largely illusory: the donors disagree among themselves, promote difficult programs to monitor, and have strong incentives to avoid conflicts and showdowns with the national authorities.[66] The government has successfully played donors off each other: while still negotiating with the IMF it convinced France to extend 400 million francs for the rehabilitation of several parastatals, thus providing breathing space that lessened the need to accept the IMF's more draconian proposals. The parastatals France agreed to continue subsidizing included SEMRY and SODECOTON, two institutions originally slated for elimination by the World Bank. The IMF and World Bank opposed the construction of a new 88 billion CFA international airport at Yaoundé but the German government nonetheless provided subsidized loans for the airport.[67]

The state has manipulated donors in order to increase aid flows, with little attention to developmental concerns. It appreciates the discretionary, extra-budgetary nature of the aid, particularly in this time of austerity. Few parastatals exist that have not been financed in part by the donors and, today, continued donor support has been a sure way to safeguard institutional survival. When Biya cut down the number of ministries from 29 to 22 in 1988 to save money, it was alleged that the Ministry of Women's Affairs owed its survival largely to its ability to attract donor support.

Adjustment and Political Crisis, 1990–1992

As I argued above, the regime's political legitimacy was traditionally based at least in part on a high degree of upward social mobility, and the sense that the state's resources were being divided equally across region and ethnic group. As economic opportunity dried up in the late 1980s, popular resentment toward the regime was increasingly fueled by conspicuous disparities in wealth, high-level corruption, and the perception that specific ethnic groups were privileged by state policies. Yet, until 1990, the regime seemed safe from the kind of large-scale popular protest that might have led to systemic change. The regime's political elite seemed cohesive and the state had successfully eliminated or coopted all the organizations that might have given political expression to popular resentment. Occasional outbreaks, such as the taxi strike in late 1987 to protest police harassment, or the student demonstration at Yaoundé University in December 1988 to protest delays in student fellowships, embarrassed the state but were too ephemeral to undermine its stability. As the *Economist Intelligence Unit* put it in late 1989: "The man in the street is still taking the economic crisis and the rapid contraction of purchasing power with an astonishing degree of stoicism. It is the higher echelons of the army, government and civil service that are most likely to react to the erosion of their privileges."[68] The biggest threat thus seemed to be a palace coup against Biya, who had not shown great skill in managing the process of economic reform.

The emergence of a pro-democracy movement across Sub-Saharan Africa in late 1989 had a dramatic effect on Cameroon politics, however. Spurred in part by events in Eastern Europe and by the new international climate, as well as by domestic circumstances, major protests erupted in countries as varied as Benin, the Côte d'Ivoire, Gabon, and Zambia.[69] Initially, Cameroon appeared to be spared, but in February 1990, a prominent lawyer and ex-head of the national Bar, Yondo Black, was arrested for attempting to create an opposition political party. This led to a series of public demonstrations, notably by students at the University of Yaoundé, as well as the announcement of the creation of another new party in the Anglophone Northwest Province city of Bamenda. Antigovernment protests soon multiplied, growing in strength and reaching all parts of the country. They were reinforced by the adherence of prominent politicians from the Ahidjo era that Biya had pushed aside, as well as of several leading reformers of the single party who now defected. The absence of democratic freedoms, as well as governmental policy deficiencies and the lamentable state of the economy were the rallying cries of the protests.

Biya initially refused to compromise, arguing in April 1990 that the single party was needed to resolve the country's economic problems. Once it was clear that traditional repressive measures would not be adequate to silence the opposition, however, and under pressure from the Western donors, Biya responded with several reforms of political liberalization. Opposition parties were legalized, multiparty elections promised, and censorship relaxed in the second half of 1990. He also named a northerner as his prime minister, Sadou Hayatou, in April 1991, both to please the donors who had argued a prime ministry would increase governmental efficiency, and to attenuate growing accusations that his regime unduly favored the south. Hayatou's nomination did little to calm the north, however, and only exacerbated the unhappiness of the Bamiléké dominated western region.[70]

At the same time, Biya continued to try to intimidate the opposition with arrests, censorship, and the brutal repression of marches. He put the army in charge of administering seven of the country's ten provinces, further undermining the beleaguered local administration's credibility. Most important, Biya rejected the opposition's demand for a sovereign "national conference" along the lines of the ones held in a number of Francophone countries, and which had already led to governmental changes in Benin, Congo, and Togo.

Throughout 1990 and 1991, a deadlock prevailed between the opposition and the Biya regime, in an increasingly polarized and conflictual environment.[71] The opposition was constantly weakened by personal, regional, and ethnic rivalries, as well as legitimate differences over strategy. It attempted to overcome its internal divisions by forming the National Coordination of Opposition Parties and Associations (NCOPA), a coordinating committee to determine joint strategies and actions to follow. It agreed upon the *Opération Villes Mortes* campaign in May 1991. Under what amounted to a permanent general strike and civil disobedience campaign, people were encouraged to boycott their jobs, refuse to pay taxes of any kind, and withdraw their money from the formal banking sector. After a dramatic start, in which it more or less closed down the entire economy for a couple days, the *Villes Mortes* campaign appears to have been followed unevenly, with little effect on life in Yaoundé, a greater impact on Douala, and a strong and sustained impact in the western region. It nonetheless further undermined the state's extractive capabilities, and by the end of the year the state may have collected as little as 15% of the previous year's revenues.[72]

Nonetheless, thanks to the occasional infusions of donor capital, notably from France, the government managed to respect its most pressing budgetary obligations, and Biya stood firm in his refusal to agree to a national conference. Although Biya's credibility and legitimacy was further eroded,[73] his refusal to compromise with the opposition began to pay off, when the latter's unity weakened in the second half of 1991 and disagreements surfaced about whether or not to end the *Villes Mortes* campaign. The regime found it possible to manipulate the opposition's internal differences to its own benefit. Biya then caught the opposition off guard by announcing in a television address on October 11 his intention to hold legislative elections in February 1992, and his proposal that the prime minister meet with the leaders of the opposition to discuss the electoral code and access to the media during the election. The leaders of the NCOPA could not agree on the appropriate response to these proposals, amidst growing acrimony. Some opposition leaders favored some kind of negotiation with Biya to end the current stalemate, while other, more militant groups favored an extension of the economic boycott and refused to participate in an election they argued was sure to be rigged.

Eventually, much of the opposition agreed to forego the national conference and contest the elections, but Biya's political victory was tempered by the absence of several of the most prominent leaders of the opposition. These elections were held eventually on March 1, 1992, marred by procedural problems, violence, and some fraud. The CPDM, the ex-single party, won a narrow majority, and three other parties won seats in the new legislature. Although the election results indicated how little support the government retained outside of the Beti areas of the Center and South Province,[74] it did provide Biya with a much needed boost, demonstrating if nothing else his political survival skills. The presidential elections, scheduled for April 1993, were to be his next big test. Opposition leaders feared, however, that he would abruptly call the elections much sooner,[75] and this is precisely what he did. They were held hastily in October 1992, and Biya won by a narrow margin over five opponents, although serious allegations of fraud persisted.

The impact of these political events on the process of structural adjustment is complex. Obviously, the regime's political problems and the growing political instability had negative consequences for the economy and further eroded the government's willingness and ability to undertake reform. Within the administration, paralysis and indecision were probably heightened by a mixture of discontent, fear, and a wait and see attitude. Even more decisions were now referred up to the Presidency. The *Villes Mortes* campaign further weakened the state's extractive capabilities, as it provided a useful cover for widespread tax evasion, often quite unrelated to politics. Moreover, political instability fueled capital flight and deterred whatever little productive investment might have been forthcoming.

On the other hand, the deterioration of the political climate did not necessarily increase the unsustainability of the current situation and the need for economic reform. The donors appear to have decided to side with the regime against the opposition once Biya had agreed to the initial liberalization reforms in 1990. The fragmentation of the opposition and the absence of a clear alternative to Biya only comforted them in this choice.[76] The *Villes Mortes* campaign's impact on government revenues was so negative that there can be little doubt that the government was failing to respect the fiscal targets it had agreed to with its creditors.[77] Thus, the decision by France and the IMF to extend new capital to the country in December 1991, in the middle of the electoral campaign, signaled support for the regime in no uncertain terms, and provided it with a much needed boost. In other words, even though the economy was further undermined by the political events of 1990 and 1991, the situation was no less sustainable at the end of this period than it had been before.

The presence of an opposition, along with a media increasingly willing to test the limits of the regime's new tolerance, probably imposed a slightly higher level of accountability than in the past, moreover, and put pressure on the state to prevent the kind of abuses it had previously tolerated.[78] In addition, the opposition's policy views on structural adjustment were mixed, and did not much add to pressures on the government to change its policies. Beyond an agreement on the general proposition that excessive corruption was a major culprit for the crisis and must be eliminated, the diverse groups within the opposition offered sharply different views on the economy. Some leaders argued for a more rapid process of privatization and economic liberalization, to disengage the ineffectual state from the economy, albeit probably with various levels of sincerity.[79] Such views strengthened the reformers within the state itself and comforted the donors, even if they were often couched in terms of economic nationalism and were highly critical of donor conditionality. Other opposition groups criticized the government's implementation of past policies rather than the policies themselves, and seemed to imply that policy reform was essentially unnecessary as long as govenmental corruption was eliminated.[80]

Thus, the emergence of an opposition in the early 1990s did not on the whole constitute a strong force for or against adjustment policies. On the other hand, the period witnessed a further deterioration of the state's extractive and implementation capabilities, and only the relaxation of conditionality by the donors was keeping Cameroon from debt default. At the time of writing, the prospects for economic reform were worse than ever, while, having survived legislative and presidential elections, the Biya regime could look to the future with more confidence, and its long-term survival was by no means impossible. In the immediate run, thanks to oil and aid, the state retained enough discretionary resources to stave off opposition or buy support as needs arise. Opposition politicians could be placated with various material benefits and in time opposition parties could be convinced to rejoin the majority. Persistent rumors suggested that some oil revenues continue to be squirreled away in overseas bank accounts in anticipation of further political emergencies.[81]

Concluding Remarks: How Hemmed In Is Cameroon?

This brief description of the implementation of reforms so far suggests the prospects for structural reform are not good. Austerity will no doubt continue to impose budgetary cutbacks. In the absence of revenues, there will be haphazard expenditure cuts as the state peels off some its less important layers. The heralded opening up of the regime that Biya seemed to undertake in 1984–1986 was in some sense a process of enlargement of the ruling alliance. Oil money had made it possible and since 1987 austerity imposed the opposite process, with a retrenchment of the ruling alliance designed to save it. Biya's central challenge has not been to impose unpopular austerity measures on the population, although the regime's legitimacy may well collapse and the population express its unhappiness with increasing intensity. Certain constituencies will be treated more gingerly than others: the regime will be more hesitant to attack the purchasing power of civil servants than of peasants. But the regime has shown that it is not afraid to impose austerity if it is needed.

Biya's central challenge is rather to continue to manage this retrenchment of the state elite, in the context of diminishing resources. The inconsistent pace of reform, its recurring breakdowns and betrayals suggest Biya is maneuvering to placate the country's creditors while gingerly testing the political limits of the reform process. Ambiguity is an asset for Biya, as it keeps potential foyers of opposition off guard while cuts are made surreptitiously. Donor pressure and threats can be used to maintain pressure on recalcitrant allies. Still, Machiavellian machinations explain only a part of the reform's uneven progress. Some of the maneuvering may be little more than delaying tactics: time may after all solve some of the problems, while a rebound in world commodity prices could defer the crisis at least temporarily.

Moreover, it is not clear how much control Biya and the top echelons of the administration exert on events, or how much of what happens was designed. Can Biya raise the productivity of the administration, or get it to cut costs? Did he foresee what would happen when he ordered government cars sold? How much of government corruption occurs with his knowledge and at his discretion? The patrimonial logic on which the state is built subverts the capacity to implement change and lowers the internal discipline of the state apparatus; not only are managerial competence and technical expertise in short supply within the administration, but also they have never been the driving force behind the administration's work. Changing the social logic of the state apparatus would be a tremendous challenge for any would-be reformer.

The analysis of the preceding pages suggests that real structural adjustment—in the sense of a fundamental shift in the national allocation of resources—is unlikely without a change in regime. The current state elite is too dependent on the current pattern of allocation to begin dismantling it. Thus, even in areas in which implementation is not problematic, liberalization is unlikely if it undermines important rent seeking. Lip service will be paid to it, but specific reforms will be subverted or delayed.

At best, the egregious excesses of the boom years will be tempered. This supposes that Biya can muster enough personal prestige and power to persuade or coerce the ruling elite to behave with more discipline than it has since the beginning of the crisis. In the worst case scenario, Biya will not control the situation; reforms will then be systematically subverted by the regime's own barons and the state's ability and commitment to adjustment reduced to naught. Biya's power itself, after all, is based on the control of the state resources that are now melting away. He is the ultimate patron in the pyramid of prebendal networks that shapes political power: that is the source of his political legitimacy, such as it is. In this context, the prospects are not good. Before the pro-democracy protests, Biya had sought to gain a wider legitimacy with which to intimidate the state elite and increase his own autonomy. Albeit much too timidly, he had resorted to promises of liberalization, a populist discourse, and anticorruption campaigns, to gain new constituencies that might support or at least not oppose reform. Overtaken by the pro-democracy movement since 1990, Biya has increasingly become little more than the prisoner of his ruling alliance.

How stable is the current situation? Given African events of the last several years, predictions are doubtless foolhardy. Nonetheless, several comments can be safely made. First, events of the last two decades in Africa suggest that economic crisis and deterioration are not incompatible with political stability. In the absence of some unexpected exogenous event, the current patterns of economic stagnation are not necessarily unstable. The Côte d'Ivoire, with similar economic and political structures, has been in economic recession for almost a decade now. Houphouët-Boigny, like Biya, has proven unable or unwilling to push through radical reform, and has successfully concentrated his efforts on managing the retrenchment of the regime's traditional social base. The Côte d'Ivoire has not yet faced the succession crisis that destabilized Cameroon, as it has other regimes, but a decade of donor-managed economic austerity and the collapse of its agricultural sector have not yet shaken the regime.[82]

Nor is it unique. Several African countries have been rolling over debt and signing stabilization plans with the IMF since the first oil crisis almost twenty years ago. Cameroon's current predicaments would be the envy of many of these nations with their larger per capita debts and without Cameroon's diverse and rich resource base. The country's economic problems are not as severe—at least not yet—as those of say Ghana or Senegal, not to mention Sudan or Uganda. Between oil revenues and donor finance, there is no reason to think that the state's financial situation need deteriorate much beyond the current difficulties, even if complete recovery is also doubtful.

Over time, popular protest is less likely: the population begins to accept leaner times and expects less of the state; "urban exodus" may increase as it has in countries like Zaire or Nigeria and relieve some of the pressures in major cities. True, state effectiveness in fostering development will further deteriorate, but it was never that efficient anyway and the "exit" option is there for peasants to retreat back into subsistence agriculture. The point here is that countries much poorer than Cameroon have survived worse economic strains without a change in their regimes.

Several factors could undo this stabillity. First, of course, the political protests of 1990 and 1991 could revive with sufficient force to shake the regime. Sustained protests and street violence could lead the army to intervene on behalf of law and order. On the other hand, no organization appears capable of sustaining these protests or of unifying the opposition. The opposition leaders who emerged from the elections appear unlikely to promote a return to this kind of violence and appear for the most part willing to seek a *modus vivendi* with the regime. Strikes and student demonstrations may upset the government, but are unlikely to undermine the regime's stability.

Secondly, the possibility of large-scale ethnic violence has increased in recent years. Old quarrels have been reinvigorated both by economic hardships and by cynical politicians seeking short-term advantages. Biya himself has aroused considerable resentment by appearing willing to curry favor with his popular base in Beti country. Although still unlikely, widespread ethnic violence could conceivably destabilize the regime. In addition, resentment in the two Anglophone provinces has dramatically increased in the last couple of years and has given rise to secessionist sentiment. Legal, administrative, and even constitutional reforms could probably placate the Anglophone minority, but Francophone arrogance and the clumsiness of the regime on this issue could lead to an escalation of demands past a point of no return.

Thirdly, because the country can count on virtually no private capital, at least in the absence of Western public guarantees, the level of donor support essentially determines the government's budget constraint. It is clear that the end of the Cold War and budgetary difficulties are conspiring to reduce the West's interest in Africa. The consequence is a reduction in economic and military aid levels and a greater tolerance of instability and civil strife, if and when it occurs. The end of donor support for the regime could destabilize the current equilbrium. In particular, a more critical French attitude would impose on Biya the tough choices he has so far avoided. A tighter budget might impose cuts in the civil service salary mass, for example, arousing the wrath of the regime's leading constituency.

So much for factors that might subvert political stability. What factors are necessary to put the country on a virtuous economic path? To what extent, in other words, is Cameroon (and the rest of Africa) hemmed in? There is first and foremost, the governance dimension. In recent years, the link between the quality of governance and the economic crisis in Africa have increasingly become a subject of inquiry by scholars.[83] An emerging conclusion from this research is that state abuses have resulted from the lack of counterweights to state power in African civil society. There are fewer independent civic organizations in SSA than anywhere else in the developing world. Given state inefficiencies and low capabilities, associational life is vibrant and able to exert diffuse opposition to state policies, but it remains informal and too poorly organized to impose accountability on the state or to curb its excesses. Social forces have also been able to deflect and undo the impact of many policies, and often weigh on policy during its implementation phase. Few, however, have influenced the style of governance. Cameroon exemplifies these truths: every organized group to emerge from civil society has been coopted or destroyed by the state, from trade unions to farmer cooperatives. Until these groups are strengthened and develop an autonomous political project, pluralism and state accountability will remain unlikely. This process may have begun with the emergence of the pro-democracy movement in 1990. As I argued above, there are already signs that the opposition press has moderated government corruption.

It would be naive and historically incorrect to suggest that greater pluralism is a sufficient condition for sustained economic growth. On the other hand it is probably a necessary condition, at least in the African context. Clearly, authoritarian state structures have above all served to protect high-level incompetence and malfeasance. One may speculate that democratization alone can lead to the structures of state accountability and transparency that are needed for a vibrant private sector and effective governance in countries like Cameroon. Thus, Sklar has spoken of the need for "developmental democracy" in SSA, democratic regimes that promote economic growth.[84] One might further speculate that democracy would help promote a class-based politics in which numerically important groups in the population formed political alliances on behalf of economic growth. Democracy would then not eliminate patrimonial corruption, but it would limit its negative impact and potentially empower the groups that have the most to gain from economic reform: smallholders in the countryside and the private-sector middle class. By promoting the emergence of economic based interest groups, a class-based politics would moreover lessen the salience of ethnic solidarities.

Stable property rights and more effective governance will help promote economic growth. Secondly, however, it is clear that economic policy reform poses difficult dilemmas for any type of regime in SSA. Success stories in other parts of the world seem to indicate that true structural adjustment takes well over a decade of sustained effort and requires access to substantial international private capital to spearhead investment. In Africa, two decades of donor-inspired adjustment programs have not prevented a net disinvestment by private capital over the same period. Perhaps as a result, in countries as varied as Senegal, the Côte d'Ivoire, or Kenya, these programs have failed to deliver their promise of a "supply response" and healthy sustained development.[85] It is difficult to dispute the contention that this reflects the failure of state elites to implement these programs fully. Nonetheless, even committed reform governments, like the Rawlings regime in Ghana, have found it tough to sustain reform policies, as they provide few obvious dividends and as yet little extra private capital.[86] Where is the economic growth to come from? There are no obvious alternatives to the traditional commodity productions like cocoa and coffee whose value appear to be in ineluctable decline on world markets. A return to rapid growth in the world economy is probably necessary to stabilize commodity prices and stop the current trend toward increasing Western protectionism. Such a favorable international environment might then, along with improved governance structures, provide the conditions under which states like Cameroon could undertake sustained economic growth.

The current fiscal crisis of African states imposes cutbacks that undermine the little developmental capacity they had acquired, precisely when these are most needed to promote the infrastructural and social investments that will end economic stagnation. If it is true as I have suggested throughout this chapter that there is a negative synergy between state capacity and patrimonialism, then one of the ironies of adjustment is that it may end up strengthening the very features that brought about the present crisis, and cause a long-term period of stagnation. It will be difficult for Cameroon to devise new strategies to resolve these economic conundrums. Like many of its neighbors, it has so far preferred not to address them.

NOTES

1. An early draft of this paper was presented at the 1989 meeting of the African Studies Association, November 2–5, Atlanta, Georgia. It was revised thanks in part to a grant from the John D. and Catherine T. MacArthur Foundation. Helpful comments from Jean-François Bayart, Thomas Callaghy, and Juan Gaviria are gratefully acknowledged.

2. The CFA (*Coopération Financière en Afrique Centrale*) Franc is pegged to the French Franc, at a rate of fifty to one. One U.S. Dollar was worth some 409 in 1984, 400 Francs in 1986, 319 in 1989, and 272 in 1990.

3. Thomas M. Callaghy, "Africa's Debt Crisis," *Journal of International Affairs* 38 (Summer 1984): 61–79.

4. These statistics are from the World Bank, *Adjustment Lending: An Evaluation of Ten Years of Experience* (Washington, D.C.: World Bank, 1989). For a summary review of the Cameroonian Economy, see EDIAFRIC, *L'Economie Camerounaise* (Paris: EDIAFRIC, 1984); and "Cameroun, 1988," *Marchés Tropicaux et Méditerranéens* no. 2241 (October 21, 1988): 2793–2876. Early and somewhat dated reviews can be found in IMF, *Surveys of African Economies: vol. 1* (Washington, D.C.: IMF, 1968), chapter 6; and Philipp Hugon, *Analyse du Sous-Développement en Afrique Noire: l'Example de l'Economie du Cameroun* (Paris: Presses Universitaires de France 1968).

5. See the glowing assessment of the regime's policy orientation in "Cameroun: 1960–1980," *Marchés Tropicaux et Méditerranéens*, October 29, 1976, pp. 2812–2956. See also Salvatore Schiavo-Campo, et al., *The Tortoise Walk: Public Policy and Private Activity in the Economic Development of Cameroon*, Aid Evaluation Special Study No. 10, U.S. Agency for International Development, Washinton, D.C., 1983. A much less flattering view is provided by David Kom, *Le Cameroun: Essai d'Analyse Economique et Politique*

(Paris: Editions Sociales, 1971), and Richard A. Joseph, ed., *Gaullist Africa: Cameroon Under Ahmadu Ahidjo* (Enugu: Fourth Dimension Publishers, 1978).

6. Piet Konings, "L'Etat, l'Agro-industrie et la Paysannerie au Cameroun," *Politique Africaine* 22 (June 1986): 120–137; Jean Claude Willame, "The Practices of a Liberal Political Economy: Import and Export Substitution in Cameroon (1975–81)," in Michael G. Schatzberg and I. William Zartman, eds., *The Political Economy of Cameroon* (New York: Praeger, 1986); P. Baris, C. Freud, and J. Zaslavsky, "La Politique Agricole du Cameroun de l'Indépendence à nos Jours," mimeo, Paris, March 1987.

7. See Olivier Vallée, *Le Prix de l'Argent CFA: Heurs et Malheurs de la Zone Franc* (Paris: Karthala 1989), pp. 46–63.

8. Mokpokpo Muki Dravi, *The Alleviation of Rural Poverty in Cameroon*, FAO In Depth Studies Series no. 11, Rome, 1984; Bureau International du Travail, "Disparités de Revenues entre les Villes et les Campagnes au Cameroun," Report Submitted to the Government of Cameroon, Addis Ababa: International Labor Organization, 1982.

9. Mark Delancey, "Cameroon National Food Policies and Organizations: The Green Revolution and Structural Proliferation," *Journal of Modern African Studies* 7, 2 (Summer 1980): 121–128.

10. J. Schwettmann, *Etude Préparatoire Pour le Séminaire National sur le Mouvement Coopératif au Cameroun: Etude no. 3, Analyse Mesoéconomique*, GTZ: Yaoundé, August 1987; author's translation.

11. B. Essama Nssah, "Impact of Pricing and Related Policies on Agricultural Production in Cameroon," Yaoundé: U.S. Agency for International Development, mimeo, June 1984.

12. *Marchés Tropicaux et Méditerranéens*, "Cameroun, 1988," p. 2825. See also "Biya va Privatiser," *Africa International*, May 1988, pp. 88–90.

13. Deepak Lal, "The Political Economy of Economic Liberalization," *World Bank Economic Review* 1, 2 (January 1987): 273–300.

14. John Waterbury, "The Political Management of Economic Adjustment and Reform" in Joan Nelson, ed., *Fragile Coalitions: The Politics of Economic Adjustment* (Washington, D.C.: Overseas Development Council, 1989), pp. 39–56.

15. Henry S. Bienen and Mark Gersovitz, "Economic Stabilization, Conditionality and Political Stability," *International Organization* 39, 4 (1985): 729–754; Joan Nelson, "The Political Economy of Stabilization: Commitment, Capacity, and Public Response," *World Development* 12, 10 (1984): 983–1006; Stephan Haggard, "The Politics of Adjustment: Lessons from the IMF's Extended Fund Facility," *International Organization* 39, 3 (1985): 505–534.

16. Robert Bates, *Markets and States in Tropical Africa: The Political Basis of Agricultural Policies* (Berkeley: University of California Press, 1981), and *Essays on the Political Economy of Rural Africa* (Cambridge: Cambridge University Press, 1983).

17. John Ravenhill, "Adjustment with Growth: A Fragile Consensus," *Journal of Modern African Studies* 26, 2 (1988): 179–210; G. K. Helleiner, ed. *Africa*

and the International Monetary Fund (Washington, D.C.: International Monetary Fund, 1986).

18. Nicolas van de Walle, "Rice Politics in Cameroon: State Commitment, Capability and Urban Bias," *Journal of Modern African Studies* 27, 4 (December 1989): 579–600.

19. Jean-François Bayart, *L'Etat au Cameroun* (Paris: Presses de la Fondation Nationale de Sciences Politique, 1985).

20. Bayart's more recent work has extended this approach to the rest of the continent; see *L'Etat en Afrique* (Paris: Fayard, 1989). Similar approaches are to be found in Michael G. Schatzberg, *Politics and Class in Zaire: Bureaucracy, Business and Beer in Lisaala* (New York: Africana, 1980); Thomas M. Callaghy, *The State-Society Struggle: Zaire in Comparative Perspective* (New York: Columbia University Press, 1984); and Richard A. Joseph, *Democracy and Prebendal Politics in Nigeria: The Rise and Fall of the Second Republic* (Cambridge: Cambridge University Press, 1987).

21. Pierre Flambeau Ngayap, *Cameroun: Qui Gouverne? De Ahidjo à Biya, l'Héritage et l'Enjeu* (Paris: Editions l'Harmattan, 1983).

22. Robert H. Jackson and Carl G. Rosberg, *Personal Rule in Black Africa* (Berkeley: University of California Press, 1982).

23. See Antonio Gramsci, *Selections from the Prison Notebooks* (New York: International Publishers, 1971). Bayart provides a wide-ranging discussion of the nature of ruling class hegemony in *L'Etat en Afrique*, pp. 157–241; for a broader discussion of Gramsci's political theory, see Martin Carnoy, *The State and Political Theory* (Princeton: Princeton University Press, 1984), pp. 65–88.

24. This is translated literally as "the goat grazes where she is attached." See "Cameroun: Biya resserre les Boulons," *Jeune Afrique* no. 1481, May 24, 1989 p. 18. See also Bayart, *l'Etat en Afrique*.

25. Ngayap, *Cameroun: Qui Gouverne?*, describes at length the social and educational backgrounds of the governing elite.

26. Richard Sklar, "The Nature of Class Domination in Africa," *Journal of Modern African Studies* 17, 4 (1979): 273–293.

27. An amusing debate in the pages of *Africa International* as to which businessmen profited most from the state is instructive in this regard. See "Les Milliardaires Camerounais," no. 202, February 1988, pp. 67–68; and "Les Milliardaires Camerounais de l'Intox," no. 204 (April 1988): 51–53. Priso's political career is described in Bayart, *l'Etat au Cameroun*.

28. See "NOBRA: Les Lecons d'un Naufrage," *Africa International* 205 (May 1988): 22–24, and "Chronique d'un Pillage Annoncé," *Jeune Afrique Economie* 151 (January 1992): 177–178.

29. NOBRA would have a meteoric rise, producing 327,000 hectoliters of beer in 1983–84, but would soon fall apart amidst widespread allegations of fraud and mismanagement. A rehabilitation plan orchestrated by the SNI involving capital from a Danish government investment development fund in 1986 could not prevent final bankruptcy two years later.

30. Henry Bienen and John Waterbury, "The Political Economy of Privatization in Developing Countries," *World Development* 17, 5 (May 1989):

617–632; Nicolas van de Walle, "Privatization in Developing Counties: A Review of the Issues," *World Development* 17, 5 (May 1989): 601–616.

31. This is difficult to confirm, of course, but is widely believed in Cameroon. There is surely no good economic explanation for the lack of a decent road between these major economic and demographic centers. Indeed, when it was built in 1985, the Yaoundé-Bafoussam road resulted in an estimated 10–15% decrease in food prices in Yaoundé. See R. C. Kite, "Food Price Patterns in Cameroon: A Comparison of Yaoundé Retail Prices and West Province Market Prices," Yaoundé: USAID Agriculture Management and Planning Project, Ministry of Agriculture, mimeo, March 1988 .

32. See Ngayap, *Cameroun: Qui Gouverne?*, pp. 35–48. He notes that "in twenty four years, the Ahidjo regime had 7 different education ministers, 7 health ministers, 8 ministers of finance, 8 ministers of public administration, 9 ministers of justice, 9 ministers foreign affairs, 11 ministers of agriculture, 12 ministers of information and 12 ministers of the economy." (p. 45, my own translation). On the other hand, Ahidjo's fellow northerner and confidant, Sadou Daoudou, was in charge of the army for twenty years.

33. Hugon, *Analyse du Sous-Développement*, pp. 230–231.

34. Existing data is very spotty. The government's 1983/84 Household Expenditure Survey suggests that the top richest ten percent of the households in Yaoundé and Douala spent roughly 30 percent of those cities' total household expenditures. This understates inequalities at the national level, since the income of the average urban dweller is roughly 8 times that of the average rural dweller. See Ministry of Planning, Republic of Cameroon, *Enquete Budget-Consommation Auprés des Ménages: Septembre 1983–Septembre 1984*, September 1987; Dravi, *The Alleviation of Rural Poverty*.

35. Ministry of Agriculture, Republic of Cameroon, *1984 Agricultural Census*, Yaoundé, 1984.

36. Regarding the educational sector, see Philippe Lippens and R. A. Joseph, "The Power and the People" in Joseph, ed., *Gaullist Africa*, pp. 122–125.

37. See Joseph, *Democracy and Prebendal Politics*.

38. The Bamiléké are a loose knit set of distinct tribal groups in the densely populated Western Province. Though this region has extremely rich soils, overpopulation has contributed to extensive emigration to the rest of the country, including large groups to Yaoundé and Douala. Overall, as much as a fifth of Cameroon's population may be of Bamiléké origin, depending on how narrowly one defines the ethnic group and the region it occupies. See Hazel Mcferson, *Ethnicity, Individual Initiative and Economic Growth in an African Rural Society: The Bamiléké of Cameroon*, A.I.D. Evaluation Special Study No. 15, U.S. Agency for International Development, Washington, D.C., 1983; and Jean Louis Dongmo, *Le Dynamisme Bamiléké* (Yaoundé: Université de Yaoundé, 1981).

39. Mcferson, *Ethnicity, Individual Initiative*; interviews. See also E. Kengne Pokam, *La Problematique de l'Unité Nationale au Cameroun*. (Paris: Editions l'Harmattan, 1986).

40. There is now a long historiography of the UPC rebellion. See among others Joseph, *Radical Nationalism*, and J.-A. Mbembe, *Ruben Um Nyobe: Le Problème National Kamerunais* (Paris: Editions l'Harmattan, 1984).

41. Interestingly, the same percentages are 72, 67 and 57 for the 1961–1971 period.

42. These calculations have to be treated with circumspection for several reasons. First, the FOB values are nothing more than approximations and there are wide differences between the trade figures reported by the Cameroonian authorities, the ONCPB, and the FAO. Secondly, producers rarely get the official prices: there is systematic underweighing of their production during the marketing phase. The calculations used the price for the highest quality, and not the lower quality that the parastatal often arbitrarily assigns to a given farmer's crop. In this area too, there appears to be a good deal of corruption beyond the producer's control. These three factors suggest there may be large and unsystematic differences between the official producer price and the effective price paid to the farmers.

43. ONCPB's official function is to serve as a stabilization fund; the levy was designed to allow ONCPB to accumulate savings in order to maintain producer prices stable when world commodity prices decreased. In fact, the producer price has always been below the world price, and the levy has in effect been a permanent tax on cocoa and coffee producers. Besides financing its own not inconsiderable growth and shoring up the now bankrupt banking system, the ONCPB used this revenue to provide extra budgetary support to a number of loss-making parastatals. It has provided some assistance to farmers—including those of UCCAO—notably subsidized fertilizers, credit, pesticides, and free marketing bags. See among other sources, Schwettman, *Etude Préparatoire.*

44. Jacques Champaud, *Villes et Campagnes du Cameroun de l'Ouest* (Paris: ORSTOM, 1983), pp. 246–247.

45. See G. Courade, P. Eloundou-Enyegue, and I. Grangeret, "L'Union Centrale des Cooperatives Agricoles de l'Ouest de Cameroun (UCCAO): de l'Entreprise Commerciale à l'Organisation Paysanne," *Tiers Monde* 32, 128 (October/December 1991): 887–899 for a similar if somewhat more positive assessment of UCCAO's regional economic role.

46. Jean-François Bayart, "La Société Politique Camerounaise, 1982–1986," *Politique Africaine* 22 (June 1986): 5–36, Gilbert Moutard, "1983–1984: Deux Ans de Vie Tourmenté au Cameroun," *Afrique Contemporaine* 135 (1985): 38–45, and "Quelles Chances pour la Politique du Président Biya?" *Afrique Contemporaine* 139 (1986): 20–35.

47. Uma Lele, Nicolas van de Walle and Mathurin Gbetibouo, "Cotton in Africa: an Analysis of Differences in Performance." *Managing Agricultural Development in Africa Discussion Paper No.7.* Washington: World Bank, 1989.

48. Joseph, *Gaullist Africa*; J. F. Médard, "L'Etat Sous-Dévelopé au Cameroun," *L'Année Africaine* (Paris: Pedone, 1977).

49. République du Cameroun, *Déclaration de Strategie et de Relance Economique*, Yaoundé, May 1989.

50. Ibid.

51. This example of economic nationalism was applauded at home and by the Pan-African media. See "Cameroun: la Côte d'Alerte est Atteinte," and

"Scenario Classique," *Jeune Afrique Economique* 96 (April 1987): 22–24 and 118; (April 1989): 40–42 respectively; and "Peut on se Passer du FMI?" *Africa International* 203 (March 1988): 69–72; "Making Ends Meet," *West Africa*, December 27, 1987, pp. 2534.

52. *Africa International*, "Peut on se Passer du FMI?"

53. *Marchés Tropicaux et Méditerranéen*, April 3, 1992, reported that the total salary mass had gone from 280 billion CFA in 1986–87 to 264 billion in 1990–91. During that time, the civil service had increased from 168,000 to 182,000, despite a job freeze.

54. Charles Steedman, *Rural Development Planning and Budgeting in Cameroun* (Washington: Development Alternatives, April 1988).

55. G. Courade, I. Grangeret, and P. Janin, "La Liquidation des Joyaux du Prince: Les Enjeux de la Libéralization des Filières Café-Cacao au Cameroun, *Politique Africaine* 44 (1991): 121–128.

56. See "Country Report: Cameroon," *Economist Intelligence Unit*, No. 4, 1988; personal interviews in Cameroon in the spring of 1989 confirm these views.

57. See *Jeune Afrique*, "Biya resserre les Boulons," as well as "Country Report: Cameroon," *Economist Intelligence Unit*, No. 3, 1989, p. 11.

58. Thus 15,000 liters of illegally imported Nigerian gasoline was burned by the Customs Office in front of a big crowd in Maroua, northern Cameroon, in May, 1988. The government suffered some embarrassment when it was pointed out that the market value of the gasoline was more than 3 million CFA. See *Le Combattant* (Yaoundé), June 1, 1988. In a much commented speech to the party in December 1988, Biya loudly warned that corruption in high places would no longer be tolerated. See "La Colère de Biya," *Africa International.* 212 (January 1989): 31–32.

59. Most observers felt that the election was only a partial success for Biya, given a high absentee rate, and the suspiciously long time some precincts took to report on voting. See "Après la réelection de M. Biya: Le Cameroun se prépare à un Accord avec le FMI," *Marchés Tropicaux et Méditerranéens*, May 27, 1988, pp. 1357–1361; and "Cameroun: Et Maintenant?" *Africa International* 206 (June 1988): 21–23.

60. The following account of the stabilization fund is taken from van de Walle, "Rice Politics." Stabilization funds for sugar and vegetable oil were established at the same time and also did not function properly.

61. Interviews; Bayart, "La Société Politique Camerounaise."

62. See Paul John Marc Tedga, *Entreprises Publiques, Etat et Crise au Cameroun* (Paris: l'Harmattan, 1991) for a more comprehensive treatment. Also see *Marché Tropicaux et Méditerranéens*, "Cameroun, 1988," pp. 2825–2827; "Biya Spells in out," *Africa Confidential*, September 23, 1987, pp. 5–6; "The Privatization Stakes," *Africa Confidential* July 1, 1988, pp. 6–7; *Africa International*, "Biya va Privatiser."

63. See "Cameroun: Les Premiers Déchets de l'Ajustement," *Africa International* 219 (September 1989): 26–28.

64. Courade et al., "La Liquidation."

65. van de Walle, "Privatization."

66. Elliot Berg and Alan Batchelder, "Structural Adjustment Lending: A Critical View," CPD Discussion Paper No. 1985–21, World Bank, Washington, D.C., 1985; also see David Gordon, "Debt, Conditionality, and Reform," this volume.

67. "Country Report: Cameroon," *Economist Intelligence Unit*, 2 (1989): 15–16.

68. Ibid., p. 6.

69. This phenomenon is analyzed at length in Michael Bratton and Nicolas van de Walle, "Popular Protest and Political Reform in Africa," *Comparative Politics* 24, 4, (July 1992): 419–442.

70. See "Cameroon: An Unconvincing Premier," *Africa Confidential*, May 3, 1991.

71. Jacques Champaud, "Cameroun: Au Bord de l'Affrontement," *Politique Africaine* 44 (1991): 115–120.

72. See "Strike Aims to Bleed Cameroon's Economy to Force President's Fall," *The New York Times*, August 5, 1991; and "Cameroon: Crisis or Compromise?" *Africa Confidential*, October 25, 1991.

73. See "Cameroon: Biya Besieged," *Africa Confidential*, July 26, 1991.

74. See "Demi-Victoire Electorale en Forme de Désaveu," *Jeune Afrique Economie*, April 1992; and "Cameroun: Le Temps des Embrouilles," *Jeune Afrique Economie*, May 1992.

75. In early 1992, for example, there were rumors that Biya would surprise the opposition by resigning well before 1993 and conduct the elections quickly, not allowing his opponents to organize themselves. See "Cameroun: Cap sur l'élection Présidentielle," *Jeune Afrique*, March 25, 1992.

76. The U.S. position was more nuanced than France's generally uncritical support. On the one hand, the American embassy in Yaoundé has been critical of human rights abuses and has been openly sympathetic to the opposition; on the other hand, Washington forgave $73.4 million of Cameroonian debt in 1990 and welcomed Biya in his visit of the United States.

77. See "Avec un Nouvel Accord du FMI, le Cameroun Amorce un Tournant Décisif," *Marchés Tropicaux et Méditerranéens*, January 3, 1992.

78. *Jeune Afrique Economie* published two articles in 1992 on governmental corruption in the country that were widely distributed and of great embarrassement to the government. The first ("Chronique d'Un Pillage Annoncé," January 1992, pp. 175–183) identified some fifteen officials as most responsible for the country's economic ruin through their corruption and mismanagement. The second ("Ainsi a été Pillé la SCB," May 1992, pp. 106–130) provided detailed evidence that corruption by Biya and his wife had contributed to the bankruptcy of the leading commercial bank in the country, the Société Camerounaise de Banque.

79. Thus, for example, Bello Bouba Maigari, whose UNDP party (*Union Nationale pour la Démocratie et le Progrès*) would emerge from the March 1992 legislative elections as the leading opposition party with 68 seats, argued in an interview that his party's top economic priority was the "restoration of confidence and the flowering of economic freedoms." He went on to argue for tax cuts and more advantages to small businesses. See *Jeune Afrique*, May 27,

1992. On the other hand, this streak of economic liberalism had not been evident in the governmental posts he occupied in the seventies under Ahidjo, or as Biya's first prime minister in 1982.

80. See for example the different contributions in *Changer le Cameroun. Pourquoi Pas?* (Yaoundé, 1990), a collection of essays on policy issues produced by a group of anonymous Camerounian intellectuals close to the opposition.

81. Such a fund is a direct violation of agreements with the IMF and Franc Zone regulations. See *Nord Sud Export* 186, March 19, 1990.

82. République Française, Ministère de la Coopération, *Désquilibres Structurels et Programmes d'Ajustement en Côte d'Ivoire* (Paris, 1986); Y. A. Faure and J. F. Médard, *Etat et Bourgeoisie en Côte d'Ivoire* (Paris: Karthala, 1982); for similar processes in Kenya, see Michael Lofchie, "Trading Places," this volume.

83. Michael Bratton, "Beyond the State: Civil Society and Associational Life in Afica," *World Politics* 41, 3 (1989); The Carter Center of Emory University, *Beyond Autocracy in Africa: Working Papers from the Inaugural Seminar of the Governance in Africa Program*, Atlanta, 1989; Larry Diamond, Juan J. Linz, and Seymour Martin Lipset, *Democracy in Developing Countries: Africa* (Boulder: Lynne Rienner, 1988); Patrick Chabal, ed., *Political Domination in Africa: Reflections on the Limits of Power* (Cambridge: Cambridge University Press, 1986).

84. Richard Sklar, "Democracy in Africa," in Chabal, ed., *Political Domination*, pp. 17–29.

85. The World Bank, *Adjustment Lending: an Evaluation of Ten Years of Experience*, Country Economics Department, Policy, Planning, and Research (Washington D.C.: The World Bank, 1988); Carol Lancaster and John Williamson, eds., *African Debt and Financing* (Washington, D.C.: Institute for International Economics, 1986).

86. Thomas M. Callaghy, "Lost Between State and Market: The Politics of Economic Adjustment in Ghana, Zambia, and Nigeria" in Joan Nelson, ed., *Economic Crisis and Policy Choice: The Politics of Economic Adjustment in the Third World* (Princeton: Princeton University Press, 1990). pp. 257–319.

Chapter Eleven

Trading Places: Economic Policy in Kenya and Tanzania

MICHAEL F. LOFCHIE

For more than a decade, scholars of African development have grappled with the elusive and complex relationship between what Thomas Callaghy has elsewhere identified as *economic logic*—"the policies needed to pursue economic efficiency"—and *political logic*—"the policies needed to assure domestic stability."[1] The earliest scholarship on this topic emphasized the contradictory relationship between the two and the tendency for overriding political imperatives to yield poor economic policy.[2] The key arguments in this literature can be quickly summarized.[3] After independence, the need to create political support among urban pressure groups compelled political leaders to adopt policy frameworks marked by a sharp bias against agriculture. The purpose of these policies was to extract economic resources from the agricultural sector and shift them toward urban industries and clienteles that could provide stability for fragile regimes. Even though these policies have, almost everywhere, produced disastrous economic results, they have proven painfully resistant to change, for the constellation of interest group pressures and clientele demands that first led to their adoption has been sufficiently resilient to block major reforms.

The economic theme that dominates this literature is the notion of an ongoing, continent-wide policy bias against agriculture. Like any highly generalized social theory, this conception suffers from a number of striking shortcomings.[4] Two of these are especially important. The first is the theory's inability to explain the great diversity of policy choices that were made following independence and the wide differences in agricultural performance that followed. In the midst of apparently universal agricultural decline, some countries have done far better than others and a few have even done sufficiently well to attract a designation as "success stories." The second shortcoming in the theory is its inability to explain policy change. Interest group approaches, such as that utilized by Bates in 1981, tend to suffer endemically from this weakness. They provide powerful explanations of the tendency toward the persistence of policy, but offer little guidance for an understanding of why some governments implement far-reaching policy changes, often within a short period of time.[5]

The theoretical point of departure for the first part of this chapter is the first of these weaknesses. It is taken up with an examination of the wide differences in the agricultural policies of Kenya and Tanzania throughout most of the post-independence period. The Ravenhill article cited above refers to the "West African wager" between the market oriented approach of Houphouët-Boigny's Côte d'Ivoire and the statism of Nkrumah's Ghana.[6] East Africa also provides a variant of that wager in the contrast between the capitalist strategy of Jomo Kenyatta's Kenya and the socialist approach to development of Julius Nyerere's Tanzania.

The second part of this chapter takes as its point of departure the second weakness in the interest group approach, the inability to explain rapid changes in economic policy. It seeks to illuminate the reasons why Kenya and Tanzania have altered their approaches to the agricultural sector in recent years. For, during the 1980s, the two parties to the East African wager traded positions. Under President Daniel arap Moi, who succeeded to the presidency in late 1978, Kenya moved a considerable distance toward replacing policies of economic growth with those of redistribution. Under President Ali Hassan Mwinyi, who succeeded in the fall of 1985, Tanzania moved a considerable distance in the opposite direction, replacing policies of redistribution with policies of economic growth.

Comparing Agricultural Policy

The major economic differences between these two countries have probably been long familiar to most readers of this volume. They are quickly summarized in table 11.1.

Between 1965 and 1989, Kenya was able to attain an average rate of per capita increase in GDP of nearly 2%, compared with an average annual decrease for Tanzania of about 0.2%. Even this figure tends to understate the extent of Tanzania's economic decline. According to the World Bank, Tanzania had become the world's second poorest country, ranking only slightly above Mozambique. If Tanzania's GDP change were measured between 1965 and 1987, so as to rule out the economic gains caused by recent reforms, the average annual rate of economic decline was about 0.4%. Though both countries remained classified among the world's poorest nations, Kenya's GDP per capita at the end of the 1980s was more than triple Tanzania's.

Reduced to an elemental simplicity, the economic difference between Kenya and Tanzania was that between a country that enjoyed 25 years of agricultural growth sufficiently robust to afford important spillover benefits to other economic sectors, and a country that did not. The key to Kenya's positive performance in industry and manufacturing has been the productivity of its agricultural sector and especially the fact that agricultural exports generated sufficient foreign exchange earnings to permit the acquisition of the capital goods and other inputs that enabled these sectors to

TABLE 11.1
Kenya and Tanzania Economic Performance Compared

	1990 GDP in $	Per Capita Annual Growth in % 1965–90	Agricultural Growth	
			1965–80	1980-1990
Kenya	370.00	1.9	5.0	3.3
Tanzania	110.00	-0.2	1.6	4.1

	Industrial Growth		Manufacturing Growth	
	1965–80	1980–90	1965–80	1980–90
Kenya	9.7	3.9	10.5	4.9
Tanzania	4.2	0.0	5.6	-0.4

These figures are taken from World Bank, *World Development Report 1992* (Washington, D.C.: World Bank, 1992), Tables 1 & 2.

operate successfully. The key to Tanzania's inability to sustain positive growth rates in industry and manufacturing was the weak performance of its agricultural sector; the comparatively limited foreign exchange earnings it derived from agricultural exports meant a chronic and acute scarcity of capital and raw materials inputs for other sectors of the economy.

Kenya

Kenya must be reckoned among the most difficult countries in Africa to judge. By comparison with the economic performance of the vast majority of countries in independent Africa, it stands out as a rare example of successful economic development and constitutional stability. The distinctive feature of Kenya's economic record is its adoption, as early as 1965, of an economic strategy that anticipated many of the key ingredients in contemporary adjustment programs, including private ownership of the country's most productive economic assets, especially productive enterprises, a belief in individual incentives as stimulus for economic productivity, and a presupposition that the most important role for government was to provide a sound environment that would assure appropriate rewards for individual and corporate investors.[7] Kenya's leaders worked assiduously to create a political climate in which entrepreneurship was regarded as socially beneficial and profit-seeking was considered an indispensable source of economic growth.[8]

Although Kenya's economic system offered great latitude for private entrepreneurship, it would be incorrect to conclude that the basis of its economic success was a laissez-faire approach. For alongside its deep commitment to the importance of private economic activity as an engine of growth was a heavy state involvement in economic management. This involvement could be observed at virtually all levels. The government set and rigidly controlled the country's exchange rate and other vital aspects of monetary policy including interest rates. It was heavily involved in the protection of domestic industrial enterprise through the management of international trade and accomplished this through a highly complex system of tariffs and other trade restrictions, all of which were implemented through a cumbersome system of trade licensing. Through various co-investment schemes, the government became an active partner and co-owner in many of the country's largest business firms, including banks. It fixed and regulated the prices of agricultural commodities at the producer, processor, and retail levels. And it monopolized the procurement and marketing of the country's major agricultural commodities through a system of parastatal corporations.[9]

The underpinning of government involvement in the economy, however, was a concern that its policies be sensitive to the importance of market considerations and a belief that government-controlled prices be as close as possible to those that might prevail under equilibrium conditions. This concern was especially clear in the case of Kenya's agricultural policy, which was fundamentally driven by the classic economic notion of comparative advantage. Kenya's political leaders believed that maximum economic growth and improvements in human welfare could best be attained by pricing policies intended to increase the production of the highest value exportable crops, coffee and tea.

This approach to development afforded Kenya such a strong record of economic accomplishment that it has sometimes been judged by different and more difficult criteria than are commonly applied to other African countries. Economists in the World Bank and the U.S. Agency for International Development (USAID), for example, have taken the view that, although Kenya's performance has been impressive by African standards, its growth trajectory does not begin to compare with those of the more rapidly developing countries in Asia. These economists argue that Kenya does not compete for foreign investment with Uganda or Tanzania but, rather, with Singapore, Thailand, and Taiwan.

Agriculture has been the cornerstone of Kenya's economic growth. The figures in table 11.2 help provide a more detailed portrait of the performance of this sector since independence.

This table reveals the results of Kenya's high priority on increasing the production of export crops. Between the late 1960s and the late 1980s, coffee production more than doubled and tea production increased almost fivefold. The importance of high-value agricultural commodities as the country's principal source of foreign exchange has become even greater in recent years because of rapid increases in the production of horticultural products for export.[10] As Kenya's most lucrative exports, coffee and tea have been vital in providing the financial basis for infrastructural development in the agricultural sector as well as the wherewithal for high growth rates in industry and manufacturing. Kenya's average annual earnings from agricultural exports have recently climbed to about $600 million per year, a figure that has gone far toward ensuring that the country does not suffer from the acute scarcity of hard currency that has so constrained economic development elsewhere on the continent.

As the figures in table 11.1 also indicate, however, Kenya attained its greatest agricultural growth and highest rates of industrial growth during the decade immediately following independence. Not only did its agricultural growth rate decline during the 1970s and 1980s, but it is also now less than the rate of population increase, presently estimated at just under 4% per year. As agricultural growth has fallen, it has exerted a commensurate drag effect on the country's manufacturing and industrial sectors.

This decline can only be interpreted as a reflection of the Kenya government's reduced commitment to the policies that encouraged the maximum productivity of the agricultural sector. Under Moi, Kenya's commitment to the principle of comparative advantage has been diluted in at least two ways. First, there has been a tendency to treat export crop policy as a vehicle for economic redistribution. The present government has given greatly increased emphasis to encouraging the production of coffee and tea in nontraditional regions such as Rift Valley and Nyanza

TABLE 11.2
Kenya: Commodity Volume Increases

Commodity	Avg. Production 1967–69, in 1,000 metric tons	Avg. Production 1986–88, in 1,000 metric tons	Percent increase 1967–69/1986-88
Cash Crops			
Coffee	47.6	117.5	146.8
Tea	26.0	154.4	493.8
Cotton	14.0	27.6	97.1
Food Crops			
Corn	1544.3	2708.3	75.4
Wheat	206.7	236.7	14.5
Rice	19.3	23.0	19.2

NOTE: Figures for this table were supplied by the U.S. Department of Agriculture, Economic Research Service.

Provinces. Since these areas are less suitable for export crops and since the farmers there are less experienced in the cultivation of these crops, the result has been production of poorer quality commodities that do not realize high prices on world markets. The second change has been a tendency to place much greater emphasis on self-sufficiency in the production of food grains, especially wheat. Since grain production results in far less output value per unit of input, the emphasis on self-sufficiency in food has also resulted in a lowering of the agricultural growth rate.

The Moi government's emphasis on self-sufficiency in grain has been partly occasioned by the less impressive performance of Kenya's agricultural sector so far as food crops were concerned, as table 11.2 demonstrates. Although the production of corn, wheat and rice increased during the two decades from 1967–69 to 1986–88, these increases did not nearly keep pace with the growth of the country's population, which more than doubled during this period, from about 10 million to about 22 million. Indeed, only corn production came even remotely close to matching this population increase. As a result, grain imports, especially of wheat, began to escalate rapidly. These imports were relatively manageable because of a combination of factors, including the country's substantial hard currency earnings from the export crops and tourism and the willingness of the donor community to provide food aid. But, in recent years, Kenya has nevertheless been forced to allocate almost 12% of its total foreign exchange earnings, about $120 million/yr., for food imports.

The problem of greater and greater volumes of food imports had given rise to a debate within the Ministry of Agriculture as early as the late 1970s. Some agricultural planners continued to take a comparative advantage viewpoint and argued that Kenya should not alter its standing emphasis on agricultural exports since these continued to yield the greatest amount of economic output and foreign exchange per unit of resources expended. In their perspective, it would be economically unwise to shift scarce resources toward the production of grains. Not only is Kenya a relatively inefficient producer of corn, wheat and rice but, because of the glutted world grain market and the availability of heavily subsidized supplies through food aid programs, these crops are available from foreign suppliers at prices that are sometimes considerably lower than Kenya's cost of production.[11] The position of this group was officially adopted in the Kenya government's public statement on food policy, published in 1981.[12]

The idea of comparative advantage has been increasingly challenged during the Moi administration by those who advocate a greater degree of food self-sufficiency. The proponents of this policy acknowledge that programs to increase domestic grain production would be economically costly. Since grain crops are import-intensive, increased food production would inevitably involve considerable costs in foreign exchange, as in the importation of energy, equipment, and chemical inputs. Proponents of food self-sufficiency, however, believe strongly that the net effect of increased grain production would be a considerable savings in foreign exchange through a higher and higher annual savings on expenditures for grain imports. By increasing grain production, they argue, Kenya would free many millions of dollars per year in hard currency for further agricultural and industrial investment and to finance badly needed educational and medical imports. Although the government's 1981 Sessional Paper has never been officially repudiated, the views of the self-sufficiency group have been increasingly decisive since the early 1980s.

The debate over comparative advantage versus greater self-sufficiency is politically important because it is part of a greater conflict over which Kenyans will benefit most from the government's agricultural policies, the traditional export crop producers of the Central Highlands, who are predominantly Kikuyu, or the grain farmers of the Rift Valley, who are predominantly Kalenjin. From an economic standpoint, however, the important aspect of this debate is the fact that it concerns which agricultural subsector merits highest priority, not whether to shift the country's national priorities away from agriculture. Even as Kenya has sought to use agricultural policy as a means of attaining greater regional equality in the distribution of the gains from agricultural growth, its overall goal has continued to be the well-being of the agricultural sector. This emphasis is vividly reflected in its exchange rate and producer pricing policies.

Exchange Rate Policy

Among proponents of structural adjustment, it has become axiomatic that a country's exchange rate policy provides the clearest litmus test of its policy toward the agricultural sector.

An overvalued exchange rate imposes an implicit tax on the producers of export crops because it lowers the local price they receive for their commodity; it also imposes a tax on the producers of food staples by forcing them to compete with artificially cheapened imports. The tax on export production is of special importance to governments concerned with urban well-being. Since a large portion of this tax takes the form of a country's foreign exchange earnings, it can be used to finance the importation of capital goods, parts and raw materials for urban industries. Since these imports are artificially cheapened, overvaluation is a form of subsidy to both industrial entrepreneurs and industrial workers. Overvaluation also facilitates the acquisition and subsidization of consumer goods that today form a critical component of the urban lifestyle, further contributing to urban welfare at the expense of the countryside. It is not surprising that overvaluation is widely regarded as the first and most unmistakable symptom of urban bias.

There are two distinctly different viewpoints about overvaluation, however. According to economists who employ the concept of "public choice," a certain amount of overvaluation may be efficient at the early stages of a country's development. They argue that developing countries often lack the administrative capacity to collect more complex forms of taxation such as a sales tax or value added tax which would, in any case, involve considerable bureaucratic costs as well as a certain amount of corruption.[13] Moreover, peasant producers are the most difficult segment of society to tax since they have low cash incomes and are widely scattered. Economists who take this position also argue that, since the wage sector of these economies is relatively small, it might not be possible to collect more complex taxes, such as income tax or value added tax, in sufficient amounts to finance necessary levels of governmental activity.[14] In this perspective, a modest overvaluation may provide an efficient and necessary means of imposing a tax on a large, otherwise untaxable, segment of society.

Economists within the Bank, however, take the position that any amount of overvaluation inevitably introduces harmful distortions into an economic system since it lowers the production of tradable goods, discourages foreign investment and leads to a misallocation of scarce resources. They believe that the only appropriate exchange rate is one based on a policy of economic equilibrium; that is, a situation in which government controls are no longer required because the ratio between a local currency and the U.S. dollar is set strictly by market forces. For members of this group, the Bank's energies should be directed toward moving a country's official exchange rate *upward* until there is no longer any discrepancy between this rate and the informal currency market.[15]

Table 11.3 provides a comparison of official and unofficial exchange rates for the Kenya and Tanzania shillings from 1967, when they were created, through 1989. Kenya's exchange rate policy could be viewed in two ways. Compared with Tanzania, Kenya's exchange rate policy has been remarkably conservative.

TABLE 11.3

Official and Parallel Market Exchange Rates, Kenya and Tanzania

	Kenya			Tanzania		
Year	Official Rate	Parallel Rate	Ratio: Official to Parallel	Official Rate	Parallel Rate	Ratio: Parallel to Official
1967	7.14	8.68	1.22	7.14	8.68	1.22
1968	7.14	8.25	1.16	7.14	8.25	1.16
1969	7.14	9.10	1.27	7.14	9.10	1.27
1970	7.14	9.75	1.37	7.14	10.45	1.46
1971	7.14	9.10	1.27	7.14	15.00	2.10
1972	7.14	10.35	1.45	7.14	15.40	2.16
1973	6.90	9.75	1.41	6.90	13.45	1.95
1974	7.14	8.60	1.20	7.14	14.00	1.96
1975	8.26	8.95	1.08	8.26	25.00	3.03
1976	8.31	9.25	1.11	8.32	20.40	2.45
1977	7.95	8.15	1.03	7.96	15.15	1.90
1978	7.40	8.10	1.09	7.41	11.75	1.59
1979	7.33	8.30	1.13	8.22	13.50	1.64
1980	7.57	8.30	1.10	8.18	26.50	3.24
1981	10.29	12.50	1.21	8.32	24.35	2.93
1982	12.75	16.50	1.29	9.57	29.15	3.05
1983	13.70	16.20	1.18	12.35	50.00	4.05
1984	15.78	19.00	1.20	17.80	180.00	10.11
1985	16.28	19.50	1.20	17.80	180.00	10.11
1986	16.22	19.50	1.20	40.34	160.00	3.97
1987	16.45	22.00	1.34	63.48	180.00	2.84
1988	17.18	22.00	1.28	95.40	200.00	2.10
1989*	19.25	25.00	1.30	135.00	225.00	1.67

*1989 observations are for May.

SOURCES: Official and parallel exchange rates 1965–1984: Philip P. Cowitt (ed.), *World Currency Yearbook* (International Currency Analysis, Brooklyn, N.Y., 1985). p. 738; Franz Pick, *Pick's Currency Yearbook 1976–1977* (Pick's Publishing Corp, New York, 1978) p. 571; and *Pick's Currency Yearbook, 1970*, p. 485. Official exchange rates 1985–1989 supplied by World Bank. Unofficial rates 1985–1989 by interview in Nairobi and Dar es Salaam.

For most of the 23 year period covered by the table, overvaluation has generally been in the range of 20–30%, exceeding this amount only briefly during the early 1970s. Although this has imposed a price penalty on agricultural producers, those who view overvaluation as an efficient mechanism of taxation might not consider that this amount of overvaluation has been harmful to Kenya's development. It may also have been politically essential as a means of helping to enlist urban political support. This is a deeply controversial matter that is best treated as an open question: can Kenya's exchange rate policy be defended as a means of taxing the country's peasant population to generate resources for urban industries and services? Officials in Kenya hold this viewpoint and also point out that since exports of coffee, tea, and horticultural goods have generally increased during the 1980s, overvaluation cannot be criticized as a production disincentive. A recent study sponsored by the World Bank has supported that view affirming that Kenya had not greatly overvalued its exchange rate.[16]

Judged by the criterion of those who advocate an equilibrium exchange rate policy, however, Kenya's tendency toward overvaluation has always imposed a growth penalty on Kenya but only in recent years has this penalty begun to reach alarming proportions. For this group, the costs of overvaluation can now be readily discerned in the lowered growth rates of the 1980s. Those who hold this view also believe that Kenya's tendency toward overvaluation may also be important because it symbolizes a deeper economic malaise; namely, a decline in the quality of economic management.

Producer Pricing

The most useful point of departure for understanding agricultural producer pricing in Kenya is to recollect that the structural adjustment approach is deeply critical of the pricing policies of most African governments, holding that African countries have generally reduced production incentives by suppressing producer incomes. Kenya's status as independent Africa's clearest exception to this generalization has been documented by Cathy L. Jabbara, an economist with the U.S. Department of Agriculture. Summarizing the results of a study that surveyed Kenya's producer prices from 1972 to 1983, Jabbara drew the following conclusion: "Within the period covered by this analysis, Kenya has used agricultural pricing to create incentives for increased agricultural production and to meet its development goals of promoting smallholder production. This finding runs counter to the widely held notion that producer pricing in Africa is uniformly inimical to producer interests."[17] Jabbara concludes that the welfare of producers, not that of urban consumers, was consistently the paramount consideration in the determination of prices for Kenya's principal agricultural commodities.

One of the most commonly accepted economic concepts for evaluating agricultural producer prices is the nominal protection coefficient (NPC), a standard that compares the domestic price of a given commodity to its world market price. The purpose of the NPC is to determine the share of a crop's value retained by producers. The World Bank has explained the NPC in the following terms: "The NPC measures production incentives in a relative sense, comparing producer prices with the maximum price . . . that could be offered to producers without subsidies. A low NPC means high taxation; an NPC of about one implies no taxation; an NPC greater than one indicates subsidies to farmers."[18]

This method of evaluating a country's producer pricing policies has certain imperfections.[19] Since the world market price for agricultural commodities tends to fluctuate greatly from one year to the next, there are inevitably corresponding fluctuations in a country's NPCs without changes in domestic prices. And, in addition, NPCs do not reflect the various subsidies that agricultural producers sometimes receive. But its advantages far outweigh its shortcomings. NPCs not only provide an effective method for measuring changes in real producer prices over time but also are possibly the best means of comparing producer prices across countries that use nonconvertible currencies.

Export Crops

Kenya's pricing policy for its principal export crops, coffee and tea, differed from that of the vast majority of African countries in that the government did not set fixed producer prices for these commodities. Instead, it adopted a pricing policy commonly referred to as a "throughput" system; that is, the world market price of these commodities was passed on directly to the producers after a certain percentage had been deducted to cover the operating costs of the statutory boards that handle the procurement, processing, and transportation of these goods as well as applicable export and local taxes.

The critical question is whether these deductions have been so great as to constitute an onerous burden on the producer. The NPCs for coffee and tea from 1967 to1985 are presented in table 11.4, which reveals that Kenya's marketing and pricing system for coffee and tea has consistently passed a large proportion of the world market price for these products on to the producer. The producers' share of coffee and tea sales has averaged 70%. This helps to account for Kenya's success, as demonstrated in table 11.2, in boosting exports of these commodities. Between the late 1960s and the late 1980s, Kenya increased its coffee export volume by about

TABLE 11.4
Kenya Nominal Protection Coefficients, Export Crops: 1967–1985

Year	Coffee	Tea
1967	0.73	0.67
1968	0.83	0.64
1969	0.70	0.62
1970	0.62	0.61
1971	0.64	0.64
1972	0.60	0.51
1973	0.59	0.54
1974	0.67	0.58
1975	0.67	0.63
1976	0.78	0.76
1977	0.92	0.95
1978	0.85	0.88
1979	0.84	0.74
1980	0.81	0.89
1981	0.56	0.69
1982	0.51	0.62
1983	0.70	0.57
1984	0.62	0.81
1985	0.59	1.01
19 Year Average	0.70	0.70

Producer prices for coffee and tea were provided by U.S. Department of Agriculture, Economic Research Service. World market prices were taken from the World Bank, *Commodity Trade and Price Trends*, 1987–1988 Edition (Washington, D.C.: Johns Hopkins University Press, 1988), p. 50–51.

two and a half times and its tea exports nearly five-fold. The high producer shares for these crops are all the more remarkable in light of the fact that the dollar prices for these products have been calculated on the basis of parallel market exchange rates, a factor that, by itself, accounts for a reduction of between 10% and 30% in the throughput to the producer in any given year.

Food Grains

Kenya's record in increasing grain production has not matched its performance with respect to the export crops. As the figures in table 11.5 reveal, however, the relationship between agricultural performance and pricing policy is less clear for these commodities than in the case of coffee and tea.

For the period from 1971 to 1986, the average NPCs for maize, rice and wheat have been 61%, 45%, and 95% respectively. The surprising element in this picture is the lack of any readily dis-

TABLE 11.5
Kenya Nominal Protection Coefficients, Grains, 1971–1986

Year	Maize	Rice	Wheat
1971	0.55	0.43	0.80
1972	0.53	0.32	0.71
1973	0.34	0.15	0.38
1974	0.34	0.11	0.37
1975	0.51	0.18	0.65
1976	0.60	0.44	0.92
1977	0.95	0.62	1.55
1978	0.83	0.46	1.32
1979	0.60	0.52	1.11
1980	0.57	0.42	1.17
1981	0.47	0.25	0.86
1982	0.64	0.35	0.86
1983	0.61	0.60	1.00
1984	0.55	0.68	1.01
1985	0.74	0.81	1.08
1986	0.95	0.91	1.38
16 Year Average	0.61	0.45	0.95

Producer prices for maize, wheat and rice were supplied by U.S. Department of Agriculture, Economic Research Service. World market prices were taken from the World Bank, *Commodity Trade and Price Trends*, 1987–88 Edition, pp. 52–54.

cernible correlation between the NPCs for grains and production trends. Maize, which had the lowest NPC had the greatest production increase whereas wheat, which had the highest NPC, registered the smallest. (See table 11.2.) These results undoubtedly reflect the extent to which the production of any agricultural commodity is heavily dependent upon a wide variety of nonprice factors including infrastructure, capital investment, the availability of extension and marketing services, and the suitability of the physical environment.

The important conclusions sustained by the figures in tables 11.4 and 11.5 have to do with the extent and timing of the Kenya government's changeover from its emphasis on export crops toward a priority on grain production. The NPCs for food crops show that the increased emphasis on food production began in the late 1970s for wheat and in the mid-1980s for maize and rice. The striking feature of the NPCs for grains is the extent to which they have all increased markedly since 1983. As a result, the NPCs for rice, wheat, and maize now compare more than favorably with those for coffee and tea. Comparing the periods 1971–74 and 1983–86, the NPC for rice tripled; that for wheat nearly doubled and that for maize increased approximately 61%.

There could be an exogenous factor behind this trend. All three of these grains are in such acute oversupply in world markets that their international prices have dropped precipitously during this period. Even if the domestic prices set by the Kenya government had remained stable, falling world market prices would have resulted in increases in the nominal protection coefficients for affected commodities; (i.e., the local producer price would increase as a percentage of the falling world price). The magnitude of relative price shifts between exports and grains would be reinforced by the sharp drop in world prices of exportable commodities. This drop has been especially harmful to exporters of the beverage crops since the mid 1980s. Since Kenya's pricing system for coffee and tea passes on the shocks as well as the benefits of international price shifts for these commodities to the producers, it is to be expected that coffee and tea farmers would have suffered a loss in income relative to grain farmers in recent years.

The basic explanation, however, is that the administration of President Daniel arap Moi has made concerted efforts to increase the producer prices of grains. During the period from 1982 to 1986, the domestic producer price of wheat was increased 69%; that of rice, 121%, and maize, 45%.[20] These percentages alone demonstrate the extent to which the government of Kenya has sought to balance Kenya's previous priority on export crops, with a new emphasis on providing high prices for grain producers. This policy shift has undoubtedly had much to do with the very high levels of grain imports and the foreign exchange burden of sustaining them. By the early 1980s, Kenya's grain imports had begun to average well over 400,000 metric tons per year. Another factor in the policy shift is that the political support base of the Moi administration consists overwhelmingly of the Kalenjin grain farmers of the Rift Valley.

Kenya and the International Lending Institutions (ILIs)

The broadest conclusion sustained by these tables has to do with the timing of Kenya's willingness to undertake structural adjustment. By the time Kenya began to negotiate policy reform with the World Bank in the mid-1970s, the essential lineaments of a growth orientation toward the agricultural sector were already in place. As a result, the dialogue between Kenya and the Bank that took place in the intervening period was, for the most part, one between two parties basically aligned on the purposes of economic policy. Although Kenya's relationship with the World Bank and International Monetary Fund has been subject to occasional moments of strain, these do not begin to approach the levels of the lack of consensus characteristic of the dialogue between the Bank and nonadjusting or late-adjusting countries such as Tanzania.

Kenya's formal dialogue with the international lending institutions can be dated from mid-1975, when it received its first policy-based loans from the IMF. Characteristically, the Kenya government had taken the initiative to set the stage for these loans by developing its own set of policy responses to the balance-of-payments crisis created by the oil price increase of fall 1973. In 1974, for example, Kenya began a program to boost its export earnings by providing a 10% subsidy on manufactured exports.[21] This effort did not prove to be successful inasmuch as the cost of the export subsidies was well beyond the government's budgetary resources and because implementation was severely hampered by bureaucratic delays.

From the donor standpoint, however, the important feature of the attempt to boost exports was that it provided tangible evidence of Kenya's impulse toward economic reform. This impulse became even more apparent in mid-1975 in the government's official adoption of a comprehensive policy reform program designed to address the balance-of-payments problem in a manner that would ensure continued long-term economic growth. The basic strategy for accomplishing this objective was set forth in an important government sessional paper on economic policy published in early 1975. This document, which set forth a program of price, wage, and import restraints, had great importance as a direct signal to the ILIs of the government's willingness to take politically difficult steps, if these were necessary, to achieve a stable balance of payments.[22] Sessional Paper No. 4 of 1975 sounds a theme deeply familiar to both proponents and detractors of structural adjustment in Africa; namely, the need to impose domestic austerity as the precondition for Bank assistance and long-term economic health.

During the next 12 years, the Kenya government successfully negotiated at least 10 policy-based loans from the IMF. The conditions attached to these loans are well known to observers of the structural adjustment process. The Fund required the government of Kenya to accept sharp limitations on its budget deficits so as to help reduce inflation; to continue to impose wage restraint on public sector employees; to limit the growth of public sector employment; to reduce public borrowing from the banking system so as to facilitate a heightened level of lending to the private sector; to increase interest rates so as to encourage a higher rate of savings and discourage consumption; and to take concrete steps to move away from import-substitution toward an export-oriented industrial sector.

In the early 1980s, the World Bank, which was then initiating policy-based lending programs in Sub-Saharan Africa, began to press actively for trade liberalization. It required the government to curtail its policy of controlling certain imports through quantitative restrictions and to substitute tariffs wherever possible so as to make its controls more transparent. In addition, the Bank's conditionalities were an important impetus toward increased producer prices for grains and toward reforms in the management of the agricultural parastatal corporations.

Bank officials readily acknowledge that Kenya has done much to comply with these conditions.[23] Indeed, among some there is concern that precisely because of its deep commitment to structural adjustment, Kenya may have been subjected to conditionality stresses that overloaded its administrative capability. Kenya's record as regards exchange rate policy and agricultural producer pricing, for example, has already been shown to be exceptional. During the past decade, Kenya has also taken a number of steps to move away from a highly protected industrial sector based on import-substitution toward the production of manufactured goods intended for export. The Kenya government has complied with a number of the Bank's lending requirements: that bans on imports for protective reasons be abolished; that quantitative controls on imports be gradually replaced by tariffs; and that the tariff system be rationalized on the basis of an export orientation. To further reinforce the emergence of export oriented industries, the program for subsidizing exports of manufactured goods was improved and the subsidy level increased from 10% to 20%.

Kenya's principal failure has been its utter inability, under the Moi government, to maintain the prudent fiscal and monetary policies of the Kenyatta era. During the early 1990s, for example, the government's budget deficit grew to more than 5% of gross domestic product. To finance deficits of this magnitude, the government has resorted to increasing the money supply. But this has given rise to a high inflation rate, recently averaging about 20%, and seriously undermined efforts to move from negative to positive interest rates.[24] Although the government has indicated its intention to reduce the budget deficit by controlling spending, there are serious doubts that it will be able to do so. For there are severe political pressures to use government employment as means of coping with the country's growing unemployment problem.

Kenya has also failed to make any appreciable progress in the divestiture of state-owned enterprises whose losses account for about one-fifth of the total budget deficit. In the spring of 1991, the government announced plans to divest approximately 140 state concerns. But implementation of this goal was painstakingly slow. Although there are a variety of perfectly valid economic reasons that can help explain this, among them that even in Kenya capital markets are not sufficiently strong to finance large-scale corporate acquisitions, the principal factors are undoubtedly political. The parastatal corporations have proven to be politically indispensable in the government's efforts to maintain a support base. The possibility that large numbers of parastatal employees could become unemployed if privatization were to occur poses huge political risks.

Thus, despite Kenya's generally favorable record of economic growth, it would be misleading to suggest that all is or has been well in the relationship between Kenya and the World Bank and IMF. Tony Killick has shown that Kenya's structural adjustment agreements have not always worked out successfully and that, on several occasions, these agreements have provoked severe tension.[25] Structural adjustment credits were sometimes jeopardized because of disagreements over such matters as the extent or timing of currency devaluations, and on several occasions canceled because the Kenya government failed to comply with targeted ceilings for its borrowing from the banking system. In recent years, both the IMF and the Bank have become increasingly critical of certain aspects of Kenya's economic management. World Bank officials have been especially vocal in their criticism of Kenya's continued commitment to a parastatal system of grain procurement and distribution.

There is also sharp criticism of Kenya's rigid refusal to reform its bureaucratically cumbersome system of trade restrictions that classifies imports into various categories and imposes restrictions on various imports according to their classification. Bank officials also feel that although Kenya has made considerable progress in shifting trade policy toward a greater emphasis on exports, its reforms have proven insufficient to prevent an unacceptably high growth in the balance-of-payments deficits on trade. Kenya's international lenders are convinced that Kenya's system of trade management continues to give far too much control to state institutions such as the Ministry of Commerce and the Central Bank. In their view, Kenya's continued insistence on a bureaucratically managed system of trade is not only a serious constraint on industrial growth, but also an open invitation to bureaucratic and political corruption.

Tanzania

If the relationship between Kenya and the international lending institutions can at present be characterized as one of increasing strain between friends who once shared a common underlying commitment to growth-oriented economic policies, that between Tanzania and the lenders is its exact opposite. Between the late 1960s and the mid-1980s, a period when Kenya was able to negotiate and implement a series of policy-based loan agreements with the World Bank and IMF, the relationship between Tanzania and its international creditors was one of complete mistrust and fundamental dissensus over the goals of development policy. While Kenya's relationship with the ILIs ranged from cordial to mildly difficult, the pattern of Tanzania's relations with these institutions was a tortured one, with negotiations begun and broken off, agreements completed but never implemented, ceaseless bickering over technical matters such as the timing of Bank payments or the extent to which Tanzania was meeting its adjustment targets—all of this conducted in an atmosphere that was politically charged and often ideologically accusatory.[26]

The reasons for this strain are readily apparent. Between the mid-1960s and the mid-1980s, Tanzania identified and perceived itself as a socialist country whose principal developmental goals had to do with the creation of an egalitarian society and the elimination of class antagonisms. Because of the influential writings of President Julius Nyerere, Tanzania became a global exemplar of a development strategy whose primary objective was to build a communal society in which inequalities of wealth and power would be minimized. From Tanzania's standpoint, the World Bank and IMF were adversarial institutions. Their commitment to the implementation of growth-oriented strategies based on the operation of economic incentives and free market forces ran directly counter to Nyerere's belief in state-managed socialist equality.

From the standpoint of the Bank and the Fund, Tanzania offered an excellent example of why an internationally supervised program of structural adjustment was necessary. Tanzania's post-independence economic performance provided a perfect illustration of the Berg Report's contention that inappropriate economic policies produce ruinous effects. Bank officials believed that Tanzania should be judged not by the lofty idealistic goals of its philosophical president, but by its concrete economic performance and, by this criterion, everything had gone wrong that could possibly go wrong. Gross domestic product and per capita income had declined disastrously; production of exportable agricultural commodities had fallen sharply causing a major deficit in the country's balance of payments; excessive expansion of public services in the face of severe revenue contraction had led to excessive budget deficits and these, in turn, had contributed directly to spiralling inflation, declining per capita food production and corruption in the public sector.

Tanzania's relationship with the international lenders has been improving dramatically just as Kenya's has become more strained. The turnabout can be dated roughly to the presidential succession in the fall of 1985, when President Ali Hassan Mwinyi replaced Julius Nyerere, a change that signalled Tanzania's intention to initiate a major program of economic reform. The presidential succession was quickly followed, in the summer of 1986, by a structural adjustment agreement with the IMF. More important, it has brought about a gradual but extremely comprehensive process of economic reform. The difficulty Tanzania currently faces is that the economic crisis preceding its present reform efforts was so deep that restoration of a healthy, diversified, and growing economy continues to prove an elusive target.

Tanzania's Economic Crisis

The precise extent of Tanzania's economic decline is difficult to measure because of the extreme unreliability of statistical materials. For any number of reasons, it is especially important to treat statistics about Tanzania with great caution. There can be little doubt, however, that the Bank's basic image of Tanzania as having one of independent Africa's worst performing economies is substantially correct. The figures in table 11.1 of the Bank's 1992 *World Development Report* indicate that Tanzania's GNP/Capita in 1990 was the second lowest in the world, exceeding only that of Mozambique, which had been devastated by more than two decades of civil war.[27]

The aspect of Tanzania's economic decline that gave international lenders their greatest leverage was its acute balance-of-payments crisis, a factor that resulted in a growing debt crisis and extreme scarcities of foreign exchange. Tanzania's balance-of-payments deficits first began to escalate sharply in the early 1970s, at which time, however, they were of relatively manageable proportions averaging only about $120 million per year for the period 1970–74. During this time its debt service ratio (debt payments as a percentage of export earnings) averaged about 29%. By the early 1980s, however, the country's balance-of-payments deficits had skyrocketed out of all proportion to its capacity to service its debts, averaging more than $340 million/yr for the period 1980–84. The IMF estimates that Tanzania's debt service ratio in the mid-1980s had climbed to a staggering 66%. As a result of balance-of-payments deficits, Tanzania had begun to suffer acute scarcities of every commodity that had to be purchased abroad, ranging from vital necessities to everyday consumer items.

The major cause of Tanzania's balance-of-payments deficits was not declining terms of trade or falling world prices for its exports, but rather the problem of stagnation or decline in the country's production of exportable goods.[28] Table 11.6 demonstrates the poor quality of Tanzania's agricultural performance with respect to its key exports. Of Tanzania's five most critical agricultural exports, only one, coffee, registered a slight production increase between the mid-1960s and the mid-1980s. This increase could be attributed largely to the vast inpouring of donor assistance to improve coffee production. Tanzania's other four key exports suffered decreases ranging from moderate to disastrous. By the early 1980s, cotton production, for example, had fallen to just below two-thirds of its 1970–72 peak; sisal production, Tanzania's key export in the 1960s, to only 28% of its 1964–66 peak; and cashew production, Tanzania's key export in the early 1970s, to only about 30% of its former level. Tea production had fallen slightly to about 95% of its late 1970s peak.

The contrast with Kenya could not be greater. By the mid-1970s,

TABLE 11.6

Tanzanian Export Crop Production and Ratio of 1980–1984 Production Average to Peak Period Production

Crop	1980–1984 Avg (in 1,000 metric tons)	Peak Period	Peak Avg.	Ratio of 1980–1984 Average to Peak Period Average
Cotton	47.00	1970–72	72.67	0.65
Tea	16.40	1977–79	17.33	0.95
Coffee	58.60	1966–68	53.67	1.09
Sisal	62.60	1964–66	225.67	0.28
Cashews	39.00	1972–74	131.00	0.30

Figures were provided by U.S. Department of Agriculture, Economic Research Service.

if not earlier, both countries had become primarily dependent upon coffee and tea exports as their principal source of foreign exchange earnings. Between the early 1970s and early 1980s, a period when Tanzanian tea and coffee export levels were flat, Kenya increased its exports of these crops by 300% and 200% respectively. Its tea exports during this period increased from about 43,000 metric tons per year to about 128,000, and its coffee exports from about 60,000 metric tons per year to about 120,000.

The ripple effects of declines of key exports touched virtually every sector of Tanzanian society. Industrial production, for example, plummeted because of acute scarcities of funds for the importation of capital goods, spare parts, and raw materials. According to the 1986 budget address by the Minister of Finance, the majority of Tanzanian industries were operating at 30% or less of installed capacity.[29] Acute shortages of equipment and supplies also had profoundly negative effects on the country's infrastructure. By the early 1980s Tanzania's system of roads and railroads had deteriorated to the point where transportation bottlenecks alone constituted a major constraint on economic recovery. Indeed, labor and input shortages in both agriculture and industry could be accounted for by the sheer difficulty of transporting workers and vital inputs to different regions of the country.

Foreign exchange shortages also made a mockery of Tanzania's claim to have sustained a high physical quality of life index (PQLI) during this period.[30] Throughout the 1970s, the notion that basic needs had to be provided for had constituted a major line of defense for proponents and supporters of Tanzania's sociopolitical system. But the country's unremitting balance-of-payments deficits badly undermined this argument. The scarcity of hard currency had drastically reduced the country's ability to import medical and educational supplies, which had a profoundly negative effect on the quality of services in its hospitals and schools. For all practical purposes, vast portions of Tanzania's medical and educational systems had ceased to function in all but name. Doctors at Tanzania's principal national hospital in Dar es Salaam were regularly reporting that even the most basic supplies were unavailable. Librarians at the university of Dar es Salaam reported comparable shortages in the acquisition of critically important journals and monographs. By the late 1970s, the day-to-day operation of clinics and schools in the countryside was even more severely curtailed and services had to be provided without even the most rudimentary of medical or educational materials.

To help resolve its balance-of-payments problems, Tanzania adopted self-sufficiency in food as an official policy. This policy was partly occasioned by the severe drought in 1974–75, which had resulted in the need to import huge volumes of food at considerable cost. In addition, there was a heightened concern that the only alternative to commercial food imports, food aid, would involve a heavy and unwanted political dependency on the principal food donors. Since the World Bank and IMF were already beginning to express reservations about Tanzania's approach to socioeconomic development, food self-sufficiency appeared to represent one way to avoid their early strictures about the need for policy reforms.

Since numerous other African countries have committed themselves to the same goal for approximately the same reasons, Tanzania's experience with this strategy has broad significance for the continent. There can be little doubt that the strategy significantly worsened the country's economic crisis by exacerbating its balance-of-payments difficulties. The reasons for this have to do partly with a widespread misconception about the nature of food production in modern Africa; namely, that food production requires relatively few imported inputs. While this may have been the case in traditional, subsistence-oriented village communities, the food systems of contemporary African nations are heavily import-intensive. Not only does the process of production itself increasingly rely upon such imported inputs as fertilizers and pesticides, but the supplemental processes of milling, packaging and distribution are also heavily dependent upon imports of equipment, energy, and materials.[31] Self-sufficiency is thus, paradoxically, utterly dependent upon success in the export sector. And it was here, of course, that Tanzania had its worst failure.

Tanzania seemed, as a result, to suffer the worst of all worlds. Not only did its policy fail to halt the increase in food imports, but also the cost of food imports as a percentage of total imports climbed steadily. Table 11.7, which compares Tanzania's grain imports with Kenya's, demonstrates this problem.

This table makes it clear that although Kenya was paying a heavy and increasing price in grain imports for its emphasis upon an export oriented agricultural system, the burden of these imports on its national economy was less than Tanzania's. Tanzania's program of food self-sufficiency succeeded in lowering the volume of grain imports to a level substantially below that of Kenya, but the cost of food imports as a percent of total imports remained measurably higher. Despite efforts to achieve self-sufficiency, Tanzania's food imports as a percentage of total imports increased considerably between the two periods.[32]

There was, however, one critical difference: food imports had far greater political consequences for Tanzania than for Kenya. For Tanzania's dependency upon food aid gave the international donor community considerable leverage to influence its domestic policy orientation. And, by 1985, the vast majority of Tanzania's donors had made it clear that food assistance, like development aid generally, would not be easily forthcoming in the absence of a structural adjustment agreement. Although the financial leverage of the World Bank and IMF does not by itself constitute an adequate explanation for Tanzania's recent policy changes, it was an important element in empowering those Tanzanians who sought economic reforms.

Tanzania's economic crisis was so all-pervasive that it imperiled the country's major social objective, the creation of an egalitarian society. One of the most conspicuous symptoms of the country's economic decline was the emergence of an informal economy in which goods and services that could not be obtained

TABLE 11.7

Total Grain Imports, 1976–1985 (in metric tons) and Food Imports as % of Total Imports by Value

	Kenya	Tanzania
1976–1980	649,000	906,100
5 Yr. Avg.	129,700	181,200
Food Imports as % of Total	5.9	10.1
1981–1985	2,081,200	1,466,700
5 Yr. Avg.	416,400	293,300
Food Imports as % of Total (by value)	9.9	13.5

SOURCE: U.S. Department of Agriculture, Economic Research Service.

in the official marketplace were openly traded. The most significant feature of the informal economy was that incomes earned there were neither regulated by the government's wage policy nor subject to the country's steeply progressive system of income taxation. Indeed, but for a few attempts by government agencies to compare the prices of goods in the formal and informal economies, the existence of an informal economy was barely acknowledged by the Tanzanian state. Hence, the traders, transporters, and independent producers whose incomes were derived from informal economic activity came increasingly to represent an economic class whose wealth was entirely exempt from the government's efforts to maintain social leveling.

It is impossible to determine with accuracy the absolute extent of Tanzania's informal economy, much less the level of wealth of the successful traders who operated within it, because the transactions that occur there are not recorded in official statistics.[33] But there is little doubt that in certain major spheres of economic activity, the informal economy was of far greater dimensions than the legitimate or official economy. It became commonplace, for example, to speak of Tanzania as having two food delivery systems, only one of which was official. The official system operated principally through the National Milling Corporation (NMC), Tanzania's parastatal corporation for the procurement, processing, and marketing of grains, and provided food for the country's major institutional consumers. The informal system consisted of innumerable private traders and transporters who illicitly sold food staples such as maize meal to the overwhelming majority of Tanzanians who could not obtain them through official outlets.

Many of the transactions that Tanzanians had to undertake with the public sector were also illicit and involved that classic and irremediable source of informal sector wealth, corruption. By the late 1970s, Tanzanian informants often complained that virtually every interaction with a public sector official involved some sort of bribery: bribes were required to acquire passports, to purchase tickets on Tanzania Airways, to obtain school transcripts or other vital documents, and to have repairs undertaken at their state-owned apartments.[34] Bribery was also a major factor in the process of obtaining government jobs, promotions, and special allowances. One of the great ironies, if not hypocrisies, of Tanzanian socialism was that some of the highest informal incomes in the country accrued to persons entrusted to administer the country's system of social equality.

The Policy Roots of Crisis

Tanzania's economic collapse followed directly from precisely the sort of inappropriate economic policies economic adjustment is intended to correct. Throughout the period of economic decline, Tanzania was a textbook example of such policy mistakes as currency overvaluation, a pattern of commodity pricing that suppressed incentives to agricultural producers, and a politically derived tolerance for poor management in its agricultural parastatal corporations.

Currency Overvaluation

Table 11.3 showed the extent of overvaluation of the Tanzanian shilling from the time of its creation in 1967, through May 1989. Throughout most of the 1970s, Tanzania's currency was overvalued by between 200% to 300%. In the early 1980s, however, the extent of overvaluation increased, and by 1984 the gap between the official and unofficial exchange rates was greater than 10 to 1.

The effect of overvaluation on Tanzania's economic development cannot easily be exaggerated. It was manifestly a factor in lowering the production of exportable agricultural commodities, while acting as a disincentive to local food production by cheapening the cost of imported foods. This helps explain the continuing high levels of grain imports even during a period when the government's official goal was food self-sufficiency. Overvaluation also contributed to the problem of balance-of-payments deficits since it reduced the cost of imported consumer goods, thus stimulating both demand and consumption. Overvaluation can also be held partly responsible for the constant hemorrhage of hard currency to external bank accounts in European countries and North America and hence for the country's chronic scarcity of foreign exchange. Overvaluation may also have retarded Tanzania's industrial growth by raising the real cost of wages, thus discouraging foreign investment in any enterprise that required a substantial labor force.

Price Suppression

Overvaluation of the exchange rate also contributed to the country's balance-of-payments problems by suppressing the real value of official producer prices for the country's key export crops. Table 11.8 compares the Tanzanian NPCs for coffee and tea with those of Kenya and also presents the ratio of Tanzania's producer prices to those of Kenya.

The figures in this table alone provide an adequate explanation for Tanzania's economic crisis. During the 1970s, the producer prices for the country's key export crops collapsed. By 1980, the local price being paid to Tanzanian coffee producers was only about one-eighth of the world market price for their crop and only about one-sixth that being offered to coffee growers in Kenya. Tanzanian tea growers did not fare significantly better, receiving less than one-sixth of the world market price and about 17% of the Kenya price. In the light of these figures, it is no mystery why Tanzania's export levels plummeted and the country experienced an ever worsening deficit in its balance of payments.

Parastatal Mismanagement

Until the initial implementation of its structural adjustment agreement in fall 1986, Tanzania was structurally identical to Kenya in administering its agricultural sector through a parastatal

TABLE 11.8
*Tanzania Export Crop NPCs and Ratio of Prices to Kenya; 1967–1980**

	Coffee		Tea	
Year	NPC	Price Ratio to Kenya	NPC	Price Ratio to Kenya
1967	0.53	0.72	0.61	0.91
1968	0.57	0.69	0.74	1.15
1969	0.41	0.58	0.64	1.03
1970	0.48	0.77	0.51	0.83
1971	0.40	0.62	0.30	0.47
1972	0.40	0.67	0.24	0.48
1973	0.44	0.75	0.29	0.54
1974	0.30	0.45	0.34	0.58
1975	0.39	0.58	0.20	0.32
1976	0.24	0.31	0.28	0.37
1977	0.22	0.23	0.29	0.30
1978	0.24	0.29	0.31	0.35
1979	0.23	0.28	0.30	0.40
1980	0.12	0.15	0.15	0.17

*The basic data for this table was provided by the U.S. Department of Agriculture, Economic Research Service.

corporation that had a legal monopoly in the procurement, processing, and marketing of the country's principal commodities. Here, however, any similarity ceased. Whereas Kenya's agricultural parastatals generally performed well in passing on a relatively high proportion of the market price to their producer-clienteles, in expanding their capital base of transportation and storage facilities, and in providing a range of additional services such as the provision of inputs, Tanzania's did not.[35] Indeed, the quality of management in Tanzania's agricultural parastatals was sufficiently poor to be ranked alongside currency overvaluation and price suppression as one of the principal causes of the country's agroeconomic decline.

The inadequacies in the performance of Tanzania's agrarian parastatals substantially corroborate the critique of these institutions articulated in the Berg Report. Official studies by the Tanzanian government demonstrated that the operating costs of these corporations tended to absorb a higher and higher proportion of their sales revenues. As a result, there were often no funds remaining to pay the farmers or else the payments were badly delayed or consisted of only a small fraction of the amount actually owed.[36] The performance of Tanzania's agricultural parastatals was so consistently poor that one scholar has posited a "law" of rising parastatal marketing costs. According to Frank Ellis, the problem of nonpayment or late payment was so severe that Tanzanian farmers sought by any means available, including the informal market, to avoid the official marketing system. The result was that the parastatal corporations processed smaller and smaller volumes of the commodities for which they were legally responsible relative to their costs of operation which tended to remain stable or even to increase. The result was that the per unit costs of parastatal operations often rose precipitously, further aggravating the problem of nonpayments to farmers.[37]

Poor parastatal performance contributed to Tanzania's economic crisis in other ways as well, most notably through its impact on the government's budget deficits and, hence, on inflation. This occurs because the parastatals are governmental corporations and as such are entitled to call on the government to make up their annual deficits through budgetary appropriations. Since the Tanzanian government financed its deficits through a rapid expansion of the money supply as well as through heavy borrowing from its banking system, fiscal policy significantly intensified the country's steep rate of inflation.

World Bank personnel in Dar es Salaam generally considered the budgetary position of the parastatal corporations to be financially intolerable. The parastatal authorities were able to act as autonomous corporations with independent jurisdiction over their cost of operations.Therefore they had the latitude to raise their cost-base without any exercise of control by the central government. But, at the same time, they were able to take advantage of their official status as governmental agencies when it came to the funding of their perennial cost overruns. Before the signing of the IMF agreement, the parastatals' deficits became so huge that they accounted for a large proportion of the government's budget deficits.

The World Bank has sometimes used the metaphor of medical treatment to describe its relationship with ailing countries such as Tanzania: the Bank as doctor formulates a specific remedy to cure the illness of its country-patient. In this metaphor, there are clear and readily observed differences between the viruses that cause an illness and the symptoms that are its result. The daunting feature of Tanzania's economic crisis, however, was that each of its different facets was so closely interwoven with others that cause and effect could not always be clearly identified. Poor export performance, for example, contributed to the country's balance-of-payments difficulties but these, in turn, affected the production of exportable commodities by reducing the flow of imported inputs. Similarly, the balance-of-payments problems resulted in failing industrial performance that reduced the availability of capital goods and raw materials while also contributing causally to these deficits by increasing demand for imported goods.

This quality of interrelatedness makes the process of structural adjustment a difficult and prolonged one in Tanzania and other countries that have experienced severe economic decline. For it means that there is no single feature of the country's policy framework that a structural adjustment agreement can isolate as having special potential to cure the economic malaise. In this respect, structural adjustment does not lend itself to the medical metaphor. It not only involves a simultaneous assault on both the causes and the symptoms of a country's economic malaise, but also often proceeds without any certainty as to which is which.

Adjustment in Tanzania

Both the impetus toward structural adjustment and the implementation of a process of policy reform preceded Tanzania's August 1986 agreement with the IMF. An internal momentum favorable to liberalization of the country's economic policies had been discernible since the early 1980s and was a visible part of the Tanzanian political scene as early as 1982 when the Ministry of Planning and Economic Affairs published a document that committed it to an economic reform agenda.[38] The first major steps toward structural adjustment took place as early as the summer of 1984, two years before the IMF agreement and about 18 months before President Julius Nyerere left office. Thus, it would be an oversimplification to suggest that the 1986 agreement was thrust upon an unwilling Tanzanian government as a condition of its grudging compliance in a process of policy change or that the process of structural adjustment had to await a presidential succession. Since the very beginnings of the country's socialist experiment, there have been a variety of political forces at work in Tanzania, some favorable toward and some bitterly opposed to a more liberal politicoeconomic orientation.

The difference in the mid-1980s was simply that leaders favorable to policy changes began to have a decisive influence over the policy process. This is by no means to suggest that the process of policy reform even now is smooth and systematic. Structural adjustment in Tanzania has had something of a lurching quality, moving ahead often abruptly in some areas while little progress is made in others. This is perhaps to be expected in a country in which the balance of political forces is shifting only gradually and in which powerful factions unfavorable to policy change continued through the early 1990s to hold important positions within the government.

The Tanzanian experience illustrates the most important and difficult aspect of structural adjustment; namely, that it is, in the final analysis, a supremely political process, one that requires the methodical building of a reform-oriented governing coalition. Because the economic benefits from policy reform sometimes require a considerable period of time to become apparent, this is often painfully difficult.

If a single date were to be chosen as the unofficial starting point of Tanzania's present program of structural adjustment, it would undoubtedly be the June 1984 budget address. That address announced a series of economic reforms intended to affect virtually every important facet of the country's economic life. Among the most significant policy reforms were a major devaluation of the Tanzanian currency, substantial real increases in the producer prices of agricultural commodities (particularly export crops), the phased elimination of agricultural subsidies both on food prices and for production inputs, the complete restructuring of the country's system of agricultural marketing through the reintroduction of producer cooperatives and a series of sweeping steps to liberalize international trade. Tanzania's policy changes have been so extensive that in some major areas such as grain marketing, foreign exchange management, and international trade, its policies are now substantially more liberal than those in Kenya. Although it is too early to determine the full effects of these policy changes on the country's economic performance, there can be little doubt that Tanzania has taken fundamental steps to set aside the statist system of economic governance it employed throughout most of the post-independence period in favor of a more market based economic approach.

The breadth of policy change in contemporary Tanzania is so great that it would be impossible to inventory all the changes that have taken place. It is more feasible to illustrate the pace and magnitude of changes taking place by focusing on selected policy reforms. Four areas of structural adjustment stand out as having special political and economic importance: exchange rate reform, budgetary reform, trade liberalization, and reform of the grain marketing system.

Exchange Rate Reform

Currency devaluation has been by far the most dramatic aspect of economic reform in Tanzania. The June 14, 1984 budget address announced a substantial devaluation of the Tanzanian shilling to take effect as of the following day. The devaluation was from TS 12.35 = 1$U.S. to TS 17.80 per 1$U.S., a drop of 44%. Although the Shilling was then frozen in value for 1985, the year of the presidential succession, it has since been devalued further. As the figures in table 11.8 reveal, Tanzania's exchange rate in April, 1989, was TS 135 per $1, less than one-tenth its 1984 value. In June of 1991, following a new IMF agreement, the exchange rate for the Tanzania shilling was further lowered to TS 230 per $1. While this meant a devaluation of nearly 2000% in only eight years, the gap between the official and unofficial exchange rates remained persistently large. With the dollar worth TS 365 in informal markets, Tanzania's currency remained about 60% overvalued throughout 1991.

To remedy this gap, the Tanzania government decided to alter fundamentally the mechanism for determining exchange rates. In June 1992, Tanzania followed the Ghanaian example and allowed the creation of private exchange bureaus that could buy and sell international currencies openly. This reform has had dramatic short-term effects and can be expected to have even more fundamental long-term consequences. Its immediate effect was to lower the Tanzanian exchange rate even further, to about TS 400 = $1. The long-term result may be even more consequential. The bureau system provides greatly increased insurance that exchange rates reform will be institutionally irreversible. For it not only takes exchange rate policy out of the hands of the Ministry of Finance and the Central Bank, but also creates an influential lobby of the owners, managers, and clients of the bureaus. This adds greatly to the long-term political credibility of the of the reform effort and can be expected, as a result, to stimulate entrepreneurial activity.[39]

Budget Reforms

Budgetary reform is a matter of vital political importance. For fiscal discipline gives a powerful signal of the government's willingness to sustain the politically unpopular austerity measures that are part of the adjustment effort. The Tanzanian government has performed less well in this regard than in devaluing the currency. The broad outlines of the problem are as follows. On the eve of Tanzania's experiment with socialism in 1966–67, government expenditures constituted approximately 20% of GDP and revenues, about 15.5%, thus producing a deficit of only about 4.5% of GDP. Twenty years later, when economic reforms began, the Tanzanian budget was about 28% of GDP, and revenues about 17%. This left a deficit amounting to about 11% of GDP. The first three years of economic reform did almost nothing to correct this problem so that Tanzania's budget deficit at the end of the 1980s remained at 11% of GDP. The government's principal problem did not lie with revenue collection, which increased about 335% during this period, but rather with its failure to curb expenditures, which increased by almost the same amount.[40] As a result, inflation has remained high at approximately 20%.

Much of the government's budgetary difficulty was caused by its chronic inability to reduce subsidies to politically powerful parastatal corporations, especially the crop authorities. To underscore the depth of its commitment to structural adjustment, the Tanzanian government, in late 1991, announced plans for budgetary reform that if fully implemented would end the ability of the parastatal corporations to make seemingly limitless claims for governmental support. As of fiscal year 1992–93, expenditures for parastatal corporations must be approved as part of the government's annual expenditures estimates.[41] This is a highly risky political strategy. Since parastatal corporations whose losses exceed the limits approved by the National Assembly can no longer count upon the Treasury to fund the difference, there is, for the very first time, the very real possibility of parastatal employees and suppliers going unpaid.

Trade Liberalization

The Tanzanian government has made significant progress in liberalizing its policies governing international trade. In early 1984, it introduced a program of "own exchange" imports, which has done much to ease the shortage of consumer goods in Tanzania and, thereby, to diminish the unofficial flow of privately held hard currencies to overseas accounts. Basically the plan allowed Tanzanians who held foreign exchange accounts overseas to import certain categories of goods on a no-questions-asked basis. While it was originally limited to a fairly small range of economically utilitarian goods such as pickup trucks and automobile spare parts, it proved so popular and so successful that it was gradually expanded to allow virtually any kind of import. Goods that have been imported under the own exchange scheme can be resold without any restrictions. Estimates of the value of own exchange imports vary considerably but governmental officials believe that between $300 million and $500 million worth of goods are imported annually through this program.

The government has also sought to ease the flow of imports by introducing a foreign exchange retention scheme, which allows exporters to retain control of a certain percentage of their foreign exchange earnings. The hard currency thus retained can be used to purchase inputs vital to continue the exporting process. In this scheme, the amount of foreign exchange that a given exporter might retain varied considerably, depending upon whether the export was a traditionally exported commodity such as coffee or tea, or a new export. The idea behind foreign exchange retention has been to encourage the development of new export markets by allowing successful exporting companies a high degree of flexibility in the management of their hard currency earnings.

Perhaps most important, the government has made major strides in eliminating its cumbersome and corruption-riddled system of quantitative import restrictions. As early as 1988, the government established an Open General License (OGL) system that allowed Tanzanians to import large volumes of permissible goods relatively freely. In 1991, this system was extended further by changing the OGL system from a list of permitted goods to a "negative" list, one that identifies only those items that are specifically excluded. By the end of 1991, the most significant deterrent to free trade confronted by Tanzanians was the difficulty of obtaining a foreign exchange allocation through the banking system. With the establishment of private currency bureaus, even this constraint has been largely eliminated.

Grain Marketing and Pricing

Structural adjustment in Tanzania has had perhaps its greatest achievements in the field of grain marketing and pricing. The Tanzanian government has both announced and implemented a whole series of measures to liberalize the procurement and marketing of agricultural commodities and to increase the price incentives for producers. Most of the major changes had to do with ending the monopoly status of the parastatal corporations. As early as 1984, the government announced that parastatal bodies would no longer enjoy monopsony status as the sole legal purchasers of specific agricultural commodities but, instead, that regional cooperative societies would be established and given permission to purchase directly from farmers. The government is striving to move toward an arrangement in which crops will be purchased from farmers by primary cooperative societies which will then transfer the crops to regional cooperative unions. These will then transfer the crops to marketing boards whose role in national and international marketing will be supplemented by private companies and individuals.

Similar measures have now been taken to end the parastatal monopoly over the purchase and distribution of agricultural inputs. By 1987, these functions had been opened to cooperative unions and private importers. To facilitate the entry of private actors into the agricultural services sector, such organizations were also made eligible for foreign exchange allocations. An even further curtailment of the role of the parastatal corporations had to do with their role as monopolistic exporters of the country's key agricultural commodities. As early as 1985, privately held sisal and tea estates were given permission to market their products independently, both to internal processors and to foreign purchasers. This reform was slower in being made available to coffee producers, but by the end of the 1980s it had been extended to coffee growers as well. Since producers of these crops are able to take advantage of the foreign exchange retention scheme, production has begun to respond not only to more favorable prices but also to the greater availability of imported inputs.

In the field of grain marketing, the government has basically legalized the dualistic system of purchasing and distribution that had already become a de facto part of Tanzania's economic reality. The most important change has been the government's official acceptance of the role of private traders in purchasing and marketing the country's basic food staples. The National Milling Corporation (NMC), formerly the monopsony buyer at official prices, has now become a residual purchaser obligated to purchase only those supplies of grain that are not channeled through private markets and cooperatives. To facilitate the participation of cooperative societies and private traders in the procurement and marketing of grains, the government has dismantled the system of restrictions that formerly prevented the private transportation of grains between regions. Although there has been some debate about whether private traders should be legally allowed to purchase directly from peasant smallholders or limited to purchases from village and regional cooperative societies, the fact is that private traders operate in virtually unrestricted fashion throughout both the countryside and the urban centers.

Tanzania has also committed itself to a policy of increasing the real producer prices of all of the country's agricultural commodities, both export crops and food staples. Although this commitment is as great as the commitment to structural reform, progress in this area has been less dramatic, and for many of Tanzania's key crops, real prices remained relatively stagnant during the early years of structural adjustment. There are a number of reasons for this: the world prices of Tanzania's key agricultural exports have fallen greatly in recent years and these pose an outer limit on the government's efforts to improve price levels internally. More important, the country's high rate of inflation has substantially eroded the nominal price increases offered by government purchasing agencies.

Of greatest concern, however, is that market forces now have a much greater role in setting producer prices in Tanzania. The nation's experience demonstrates that liberalization can reverse the pre-adjustment pattern in which a parastatal corporation, by suppressing producer prices, would gradually alienate its farmer-clientele and create an opportunity for private traders in the informal market. The difficulty with informal markets was that so much of the profit was made by the middlemen, the transporters and traders who bore the risk of bypassing the state marketing system. Although informal markets did deliver the goods, they provided little to help farmers while resulting in considerable price increases for retail consumers.

Legalization of informal markets has helped both farmers and consumers. As supplies of most of the country's agricultural commodities, especially grains, have increased, retail price levels have generally tended to fall in response. But legalization of private markets has, paradoxically, enabled farmers to benefit from the price-setting capabilities of state corporations. When the free market producer price falls in response to added supply, it is occasionally lower than the official price. As a result, the NMC, formerly avoided by farmers who regarded it as an agent of governmental exploitation, has occasionally become a preferred purchaser, especially in the more distant regions of the country where private traders are reluctant to operate.

In sum, Tanzania's economic reforms have made it, in certain major respects, a more liberal society than Kenya. Its currency is now traded freely whereas Kenya's remains governmentally managed. Its export and food crop producers are much freer to bypass government purchasing agencies and market their crops privately or through cooperatives, whereas Kenya's are not. Its parastatal corporations have been put on strict notice that losses must be contained within limits and that staff reductions are inevitable for those that cannot do so whereas Kenya's parastatals, especially in agriculture, continue to depend heavily on government support. And its trade policies have become far more open than Kenya's.

Trading Places: Political Change in Kenya and Tanzania

We will now examine the process of policy change in contemporary Kenya and Tanzania. Our theoretical instruments for this purpose are regrettably weak. As Grindle has suggested, the advantages that first attracted development scholars to political economy—its ability to explain why inappropriate economic policies are first introduced and why they then persist for so long—are critical weaknesses when it comes to explaining why policies change.[42] No single theorem suffices. Policy change, like policy diversity, can at present best be understood as the product of a variety of factors.

One of these is contextual. The longstanding economic differences between these two countries have had a considerable bearing on the nature and course of economic changes during the 1980s as well as on the extent to which they have been prepared, in recent years, to undertake structural adjustment. As in so much of their political history, the two countries tend to mirror one another. The present government of Kenya has been profoundly aware of its international reputation as an African success story much favored by Western bilateral donors, international lenders, and multinational investors. The administration of President Daniel arap Moi has behaved as if this legacy could be taken for granted and has not been greatly preoccupied with improving upon the growth-oriented policies of the past. Instead, it has identified economic redistribution as its primary agenda. As a result, some of the more recent policy changes in Kenya have introduced a pronounced tendency toward economic stagnation.

The government of Tanzania, on the other hand, has been fundamentally motivated by the urgent need to improve upon the economic record of the past. The administration of Ali Hassan

Mwinyi, painfully aware that twenty years of socialism produced a dismal economic record that had become increasingly unacceptable to the majority of the Tanzanian people, therefore signed a structural agreement with the IMF in the summer of 1986. This government has identified as its highest political priority the introduction of a set of policy reforms that will produce economic growth. It has sought so assiduously for ways to eliminate political and institutional blockages to economic growth that the pace of policy change outstrips that in Kenya.

The figures in table 11.1 provide a partial economic reflection of the changes in the two countries' approaches to development policy during the 1980s. The recent economic story is clearest for Kenya whose growth rates for agriculture, industry and manufacturing for the period 1980–90 have all declined substantially from the early post-independence period. Kenya's rate of agricultural growth fell by 34%, industrial growth, by almost 60%, and manufacturing growth, by 53%. Although Kenya's growth rates remain higher than Tanzania's, their trajectory suggests that this may not long remain so. The analytic challenge posed by these figures is relatively simple: identify the policy changes that have induced economy wide tendencies toward economic decline.

The economic picture for Tanzania is more complex. Agricultural growth has recovered dramatically during the 1980s and now substantially exceeds Kenya's. Indeed, because agriculture accounts for such a large proportion of the Tanzanian economy, improved agricultural performance during the second half of the 1980s contributed to a positive overall per capita growth rate for the first time since the economic decline of the 1970s. Tanzania's industrial and manufacturing sectors, however, have continued to perform poorly, suggesting that Tanzania, like so many other societies that have recently embarked on structural adjustment, is plagued by the seemingly pandemic problem of a slow supply response. The intellectual challenge posed by Tanzania is to provide a political answer for why industrial recovery has lagged so far behind improved agricultural performance.

Kenya

One important lesson to be derived from a comparison of Kenya and Tanzania is that the benefits of a market-friendly approach to development have much to do with the timing of its introduction and the duration of a government's commitment to it. After independence, Kenya adopted economic policies that gave prominent importance to individual economic incentives and remained basically committed to those policies for twenty years. The sheer longevity of the government's commitment to prudent policies that created a favorable macroeconomic environment has been a vital factor in Kenya's ability to sustain a positive record of economic growth. For it has meant that sound economic policies were by and large predictable and dependable. Unlike Tanzania, Kenya did not have to turn to structural adjustment 25 years after independence as a desperate means of restoring health to an economy badly undermined by a set of egregiously inappropriate economic policies. Nor has Kenya had to deal with the task of building a completely new political climate, one that treats entrepreneurship as economically beneficial rather than socially exploitive.

Despite its long record of economic growth, Kenya's policy framework no longer satisfies the structural adjustment metric of the World Bank whose growth model features a minimalist state that allows maximum latitude for free market forces. Judged by that criterion, the statist side of Kenya's economic system has always left a great deal to be desired. But worsening economic performance has given the Bank and other donors a stronger basis for insisting upon changes in areas where free market approaches are likely to produce better economic results. The reason has to do with the economic downturn that has occurred during the Moi administration. As long as Kenya's special mixture of statism and market-based approaches to development was economically successful, a period that roughly coincided with the Kenyatta years, its system was relatively immune to the Bank's criticism. Indeed, Kenya's economic successes gave the Kenyans a good deal of independent leverage in their negotiations with the Bank and this leverage was consistently used to resist its demands for structural changes. Now that Kenya's system has begun to perform poorly, its interventionist approach to economic management is far more vulnerable to the Bank's insistence upon economic reforms that will drastically reduce the government's economic role.

Kenya's critics in the World Bank point reproachfully to a whole range of economic policies they would like to see structurally corrected. The exchange rate, for example, is still set by the government and private transactions are strictly proscribed; hard currency is allotted to licensed importers through a cumbersome, time consuming, and corrupt bureaucratic process; the procurement, processing, and marketing of all of the country's major agricultural commodities are still conducted almost entirely through a system of monopolistic parastatal corporations; the producer, processor, and retail prices of the country's basic food staples (maize, wheat, rice, and sugar) are also set by the government and, in general, strictly enforced; the country's import and export trade are also strictly regulated and trade licenses are still required for all imports. Kenya's industrial system also contravenes the Bank's strong commitment to free trade inasmuch as it has been based largely on the principle of import-substitution with domestic manufacturers given varying degrees of protection from foreign competition.

There is little doubt that the economic costs of these heavily statist systems of regulation and control have become more and more visible. Since the early 1980s, the quality of Kenya's economic management has deteriorated visibly. As a result, World Bank economists now place even greater emphasis on the urgent need for timely reforms of its highly bureaucratic system of economic controls. No small part of the Bank's urgent insistence on privatization in Kenya stems from a concern it shares with numerous foreign donors that an economic system that performed well for the first 20 years after independence is being increasingly subordinated to political expediency in ways that conflict with economically sound management. There is a growing consensus that, under President Moi, Kenya is squandering its precious legacy of economic credibility.

The conspicuous falloff in Kenya's recent growth rates is partly related to a dramatic reversal in its ability to attract foreign capital. Whereas Kenya was among Africa's most popular countries for external investment during the 1960s and 1970s, such investment has now all but disappeared and, according to recent reports, Kenya has recently begun to experience critically serious problems of capital flight.[43] That flight, however, is itself reflective of a deeper malaise.

To understand the contextual political roots of economic decline in contemporary Kenya, it is essential to begin with the fact that the benefits of the two decades of booming agricultural and economic growth following independence were not uniformly distributed throughout the country.[44] Take, for example, the cultivation of coffee and tea. Because of a combination of ecological factors that included suitability of soils and the geographical distribution of its annual rainfall, as well as historical considerations that included colonial policy and the regional preferences of colonial settlers, those crops are grown principally in the Central Province. The major African beneficiaries, as a result, were the Kikuyu people or, more specifically, the land-owning stratum of the Kikuyu people, who benefited not only agriculturally but also in such spheres as education, government service, and business.[45]

The Kenyatta government did little to ameliorate the country's ethnic inequality. Its political record suggests, instead, that it viewed its principal task as one of ethnic management and cooptation: maintain political domination by the Kikuyu elite while, at the same time, allotting sufficient opportunity for political and economic advance to individual members of other groups to avoid severely destabilizing ethnic confrontations. This is not to suggest that the Kenyatta administration was able to avoid political pressures for a more equitable distribution of the country's wealth. Such pressures were sometimes severe.[46] But it was able, through adroit manipulation of the rewards and punishments available to it, to contain these pressures within the broad political framework of a constitutional and relatively pluralistic single-party system.

Toward the end of the 1970s, however, the pressures for economic redistribution became especially intense. The principal cause of this intensification was an exogenous event—the beverages boom of 1975–77. Since Kenya's pricing policy for export crops was to pass on as much of the world price as possible to the growers, the benefits of booming world prices for coffee and tea during this period meant little to most of the country and became a huge economic windfall for export-oriented Kikuyu farmers.[47] As a result, the widespread resentment among other ethnic groups of Kikuyu wealth and power was abruptly intensified on the eve of Moi's succession. Chege, commenting on Moi's succession, notes that "he inherited a country seething with popular discontent produced by the political and economic domination of national affairs by the Kikuyu."[48]

The demands for economic redistribution Moi inherited from his predecessor fitted perfectly with his personal political agenda.

Recall that he had always been politically motivated by resentment of Kikuyu wealth and power. He had begun his political career in the early 1960s as national chairman of a political party called the Kenya African Democratic Union (KADU), an organization best understood as a loose alliance of Kenya's ethnic have-nots drawn together by fears of Kikuyu politico-economic domination. Moi joined KANU only after KADU's dissolution in 1964 and his long career within KANU is both a tribute to the Kenyatta government's powers of cooptation and to his own patient willingness to occupy the political sidelines.

Since Moi's personal resentment of Kikuyu preeminence was widely shared throughout the country, he could potentially have gathered a governing coalition that comprised an overwhelming majority of the population. The supporters of economic redistribution included not only the have-not regions of the country that had formerly supported KADU, including Coast, Rift Valley, and Western Provinces, but substantial elements of Kikuyu society itself, such as the large landless population in the rural areas, low-paid agricultural and industrial workers, and the massive Kikuyu urban underclass.

During its earliest years in office, the Moi government undertook a number of steps intended to create and solidify a broad multiethnic coalition for socioeconomic reform. Admission to the university, for example, was no longer to be strictly by merit—a system that had decidedly favored the Kikuyu graduates of the country's best high schools, which were overwhelmingly located in Nairobi and the Central Province—but by merit within regions, with each region entitled to a proportion of the entering class according to its population. High schools in the various provinces were also required to restrict admissions to children of indigenous residents, thereby debarring the children of more recent Kikuyu immigrants. Similar steps were taken to broaden the ethnic basis of recruitment to the civil service and promotion to the highest ranking government positions with each region given a proportional allocation. In addition, the government sought to locate new educational and medical facilities in historically disfavored regions.[49]

The Moi administration also took a number of steps to broaden ethnic participation in business enterprise. Through a variety of formal and informal means, including leverage over the country's banking system, the government has sought to deny important benefits such as credit, trade protection, and import licenses to Kikuyu-owned businesses in order to provide business opportunity to non-Kikuyu. A determination to reduce Kikuyu domination of the business sector has also been an important consideration in the government's unwillingness to divest state-owned enterprises. Members of the Moi government have been fearful that only Kikuyu entrepreneurs possess sufficient wealth to acquire these large assets from the government.

The government's interest in redistribution has also been extended to the agricultural sector where the Moi government has initiated programs to broaden the ethnic basis of cash crop cultivation. New projects for coffee and tea cultivation, for example, were initiated to disseminate the production of these crops to the Coast, Rift Valley, and Western Province. The Moi government also shifted its sectoral agricultural priorities away from the historic emphasis on exportable commodities toward an increase in grain production for domestic consumption. This, too, was a product of the redistributive political impulse. The principal beneficiaries of the pricing policies that currently favor wheat and rice are non-Kikuyu grain farmers, especially wheat farmers in the Rift Valley.

In implementing its shift toward grain production in non-Kikuyu areas, the government has treated the traditional export crop producers, especially Kikuyu coffee farmers, as its political and economic adversaries. It has intervened actively and destructively in the network of organizations that served the needs of the export sector, eliminating or undermining those that had been of vital importance to coffee farmers and creating new ones to represent non-Kikuyu grain growers. In 1985, for example, the government banned the Kenya Farmers Association (KFA), a hybrid organization that functioned as part interest group and part grain marketing cooperative for the predominantly Kikuyu mixed farmers of the Central Province. In its place, the government established a new organization, the Kenya Grain Growers Cooperative Union (KGGCU), which was dominated by the Kalenjin wheat farmers of Rift Valley Province. In 1989, the banning of the KFA was followed by the banning of the Kenya Coffee Growers Association (KGCA), another organization vital to the interests of coffee growers. The KGCA had functioned as a lobby for trade and tax policies favorable to coffee. Throughout this period, the government was also attempting to influence the selection of leaders of the Kenya Planters Cooperative Union (KPCU), an important producers cooperative. Its goal was to remove those who had long held the growers confidence and replace them with leaders more amenable to the new policies.

That these policies should have led directly to lower rates of agricultural growth and indirectly to lower rates of growth in industry and manufacturing requires little explanation.[50] It is axiomatic among many scholars of economic development that when governments intervene on the basis of Callaghy's *political logic* in the allocation of economic resources, those resources are often used in a less than optimal manner.[51] The political actions of the Moi administration caused economic decline because they alienated and demoralized some of the country's most skilled agriculturists and business leaders, disrupted organizations that had contributed greatly to the country's economic growth, and produced higher and higher levels of inefficiency in the government agencies whose function was to serve the economic needs of the society. From the standpoint of long-term economic growth, perhaps the most important casualty of the Moi policies was the atmosphere of economic trustworthiness and credibility that the Kenyatta government had nurtured as the cornerstone of its growth orientation.

The great puzzlement of the Moi administration, then, is not the wrenching downturn of economic growth caused by its redistributive policies, but the fact that its attempts to build a broad coalition of ethnic have-nots has also failed so miserably. Far from having created such a coalition, the government has become ethnically and politically isolated and forced to depend upon extreme levels of political repression to remain in power. Its basis of support has been reduced for all practical purposes to the members of one ethnic group, the Kalenjin.[52] As a result, the stability of this increasingly unstable regime rests not on the sort of broad political underpinning that, for so many years, helped buoy the Tanzanian administration of Julius Nyerere despite its economic woes—that is, the widespread popular support inspired by socially egalitarian policies—but, rather, on the government's apparent willingness to go to any lengths to terrorize and intimidate its political opponents.[53] Once a symbol of constitutional pluralism,

Kenya today is best known for having one of modern Africa's worst records in the area of human and political rights.

The reasons for this failure are by no means clear. Journalistic observers attribute it to personality factors, the combination of ineptitude and venality that characterizes Moi and his closest followers. There is an element of validity in this perception. It seems painfully clear that at some point in the early years of the Moi administration, its progressive social agenda—the goal of redistributing the wealth and privilege of the Kikuyu few to benefit the non-Kikuyu many—became transformed into something very different: an opportunity to use the power of government to confiscate and personally acquire the wealth of an older but now politically marginalized elite.

The concept of prebendalism, used by Richard Joseph to describe Nigeria, seems perfectly suited to describe the behavior of Kenya's new political elite.[54] According to this concept, a state is prebendal when its leaders employ political power to amass personal wealth. This is exactly what has been occurring in Kenya. The economic and social assets of the Kikuyu upper class have been diminished in value. But this diminution was not so much an aspect of social redistribution as it was a matter of treating the wealth of Kikuyu farmers and business entrepreneurs in ways that augmented the private assets of the new ethnic hegemon, the Kalenjin followers of President Moi. Joseph's concern for Nigeria applies to Kenya: once prebendalism has become institutionalized as a feature of elite behavior, successor governments, even those that are democratically elected, seem prone to engage in it.

Prebendal behavior on the part of the Moi administration accounts well for the extraordinary breadth of opposition it has aroused. The coalition against the present government is an extremely disparate one. It includes first and foremost, of course, the old Kikuyu establishment that surrounded the Kenyatta government. Their political agenda could be best described as a conservative one: a return to pure meritocracy in government, nondiscriminatory approaches to business opportunity, and a return to the principle of comparative advantage in agricultural pricing policy.

Moi's opposition further includes the lower strata of Kikuyu society, ethnically offended that the notion of redistribution has transparently become a mere excuse for engaging in economic warfare against the leading members of Kikuyu society. Their agenda is more radical, and includes the calls for redistribution of wealth that have been a part of Kenya's political system since colonial times. The Kenyan left has also taken the conspicuous personal enrichment of the new Kalenjin establishment as an occasion to reassert old demands for genuine redistribution of the agricultural land in the central highlands. The Kikuyu radicals are in an especially difficult position. They have been unable to align themselves with the Kikuyu conservatives because of ideological differences and unable to align themselves fully with radicals of other ethnic groups because of their strong Kikuyu identity.[55]

The anti-Moi coalition further includes a variety of important ethnic groups that should have benefited from the redistributive efforts of the Moi government but that feel they have not. Such groups as the Luo, for example, are deeply offended that such distribution as has occurred seems largely to have bypassed their communities.

Moi's opposition is by no means wholly ethnic in character; it also includes a considerable variety of other professional, religious, and ideological elements. Members of Kenya's legal profession, for example, have been outspoken critics of the government because of its willingness to violate the rule of law and the independence of the judiciary in its zeal to repress political opponents; members of the clergy have openly criticized the government for its transparent cynicism and amoral insensitivity to the needless suffering its policies have caused. Even members of Kenya's nascent environmental movement have become an active part of the opposition because of the government's willingness to disregard ecological considerations in the raw pursuit of personal enrichment.

Kenya's internal political opposition has been significantly reinforced by the pressure of Kenya's international donors who, now, with the end of the Cold War, find it politically easier to apply added pressure by threatening to withhold financial aid until major political reforms occur. Some formerly friendly governments such as Norway have broken openly with Kenya and others, including Britain and the United States, have been outspoken in their criticism of the government's human rights record. Indeed, donor pressure for political reform is now so great that it is widely credited with having forced the Kenya government to accept multipartyism in early 1992.

Kenya's principal opposition group, the Forum to Restore Democracy (FORD), reflected the pluralism of Moi's opposition. From the beginning, it was a fragile admixture of formerly powerful Kikuyu conservatives who felt excluded from the Moi administration, Luo populists who, in the immediate post-independence era, championed the interests of small farmers against the large estates, and political reformers from a variety of ethnic groups. It was divided not only by its ideological and ethnic diversity, but also by a generational split, raising the larger question of whether political power in any post-Moi era would be held by a new generation of Kenyans or by individuals who were active in the country's independence movement and the Kenyatta government that followed it. By the fall of 1992 FORD had split into two parties. The principal source of the fragile cooperation that existed among the highly disparate elements of the opposition was their determination to oust Moi personally from political power.

The power of Kenya's opposition groups brought the ultimate survival of the Moi government into question. Further political reform, including open elections to the National Assembly, seemed inevitable. In an abrupt move in early November 1992, Moi caught the opposition off guard by announcing elections for early the following month, but the opposition managed to get the High Court to provide more time to nominate candidates. Complaining of harassment and impending electoral fraud, the opposition considered boycotting the elections. The elections were held on December 29, accompanied by charges of serious fraud. The badly fragmented opposition split the anti-government vote, allowing Moi to retain the presidency and KANU to maintain control of the National Assembly, even if only marginally. The major opposition leaders charged that democracy had been hijacked. Nevertheless, the political openness Kenya enjoyed during the early Kenyatta years has been partially but ambiguously restored.

The more difficult question is whether Kenya will also be able to recapture the economic growth it enjoyed during the immediate post-independence period. The prospect of this happening is less favorable. Moi's spending on the elections seriously aggravated Kenya's already precarious economic condition, and his post-election cabinet failed to inspire confidence in his commitment to viable economic reform. After consultations with the Moi government in late February 1993, the IMF was unwilling to resume assistance to Kenya despite the government having effectively floated its currency and made other economic changes. Powerful older political logics still held sway. If it has done nothing else, the Moi government may have permanently discredited the notion of comparative advantage by associating it with the notion of wealth for a single privileged ethnic minority.

Tanzania

The process of structural adjustment in contemporary Tanzania raises questions of profound importance for students of economic reform. Among the most difficult of these is the very basic issue of why governments change policy. In the case of countries such as Ghana, where a puritanical military coup suddenly replaced decadent civilian leadership and swept aside an older generation of equally decadent senior officers, a superficial answer, at least, is available: reform takes place because a reform-minded group of leaders replaces one that is disinclined toward change. But in Tanzania, no such violent succession occurred and important reforms such as currency devaluation had, in fact, begun under the Nyerere regime, several years before the constitutional succession. Clearly, an intellectually persuasive explanation of policy change must rest on factors more intellectually persuasive than such idiosyncratic events as a change of regime.

Perhaps the best answer to the question of "why change?" is that there is no single answer. In countries such as Tanzania, which have made important change from statist economic systems to a greater reliance on the market mechanism, a variety of factors, both external and internal, have come into play and, at some moment, converged in their effects. Among the most powerful forces at work are the internal political consequences of acute economic decline, the preeminent intellectual influence of orthodox economics since the early 1980s, and the leverage enjoyed by international lending institutions.

Perhaps the most powerful source of policy change is the economic crisis that precedes it. As John Ravenhill has elsewhere suggested, "the greater the deterioration of an economy, the more ruptured the social fabric, then the greater tolerance that government and society will have for . . . adjustment programs."[56] Because of its overriding importance, the relationship between economic crisis and policy reform is one that cries out for theoretical precision. But there is great difficulty in becoming more precise about this relationship because governments seem to vary so greatly with respect to how deep an economic crisis must become before they become willing to change their policies. Perhaps the greatest challenge for the next generation of scholars of structural adjustment is to shed greater light on exactly how an economic crisis launches a new political dynamic.

One possible way to begin is through the conceptual prism of the rent-seeking model.[57] In this model, the tendency for inappropriate economic policies to persist long after they have inflicted great economic damage is explained on the basis of the material rewards these policies make available to politicians and bureaucrats. It suggests that political elites have no incentive to change policies that benefit them personally and that also provide them the resources to cement together powerful coalitions of clienteles. This model may help us develop a slightly better profile of the relationship between economic crisis and policy change. For it directs our attention toward an important political process: when an economy has declined to the point that it no longer generates an adequate supply of rents to bind together the component parts of the old policy coalition, change is imminent and likely.

Tanzania had reached that point by the end of the 1970s. High and growing levels of unemployment had forfeited the regime the support of industrial workers hitherto cushioned from economic pain by the country's rigid protectionism and the security of guaranteed employment in state-owned industries. Virtually all urban wage earners, ranging from middle class civil servants and parastatal officials to low paid service sector workers, had become profoundly disaffected because of the precipitous decline in the purchasing power of their salaries and the extreme unavailability of even the most basic goods. Even university graduates, the country's presumptive elite, had begun to question the economic system. Long accustomed to a government that had always acted as employer of last resort (and often as employer of first resort), they increasingly found that the government's impossibly bloated ministries had finally reached the point where they simply could no longer add additional staff.[58] When all these groups faced the collective prospect of long-term and growing economic hardship under the statist regime, the stage was set for policy reform.

A government that is perched on the edge of political transformation can also be decisively influenced by shocking events that so jar the existing economic system as to make its further continuation impossibly difficult. Between 1979 and 1981, Tanzania suffered three of these; two were exogenous and one was internal.[59] The first exogenous shock was the oil price increase of late 1979. This had a variety of effects beginning immediately with an inflationary impact on urban consumers and, because fuel purchases consumed a larger portion of foreign exchange earnings, an additional impact in constricting the country's ability to import the equipment and materials necessary to operate its industrial plants, transportation networks, and medical and educational supplies. The second external shock was the sharp decline in the international terms of trade suffered by primary agricultural exporters between 1979 and 1981. The decline drastically reduced Tanzania's foreign exchange earnings and, like the oil price increase, reduced the country's capacity to maintain an operating economic system. These events worsened the economic circumstances of urban Tanzanians and, by themselves, could well provide an adequate explanation of the policy changes that began to take place in the early 1980s.

The political effect of external shocks, however, is difficult to assess and has probably been exaggerated by most observers. Even the most restive social groups tend to be aware that they cannot hold a government accountable for events that are beyond its control. In addition, the explanatory usefulness of external shocks is weakened by their very universality: the same exogenous shock (e.g., an oil price increase) that launches an economic revolution in one struggling country may produce few tangible political effects in another. The shock events that are unique to a specific country, therefore, are of greater explanatory utility.

It is likely, therefore, that the shock event that contributed most to Tanzania's change of political course in the early 1980s was internal, the government's decision to conduct the enormously costly 1979 war that led to the overthrow of the Idi Amin regime in Uganda. Whatever meager resources of hard currency remained to Tanzania at the end of the 1970s seemed to be devoted almost entirely to the war effort and, as a result, virtually every civilian sector of Tanzanian society seemed to suffer visibly from the effects of the government's need to supply a massive and prolonged military operation more than a thousand miles from the capital city.[60] Many Tanzanians did not understand or accept the reasons for the government's decision to engage in a war with Uganda and, as a result, came to feel that the economic deprivations it occasioned could have been avoided.[61] For the very first time since independence, there was widespread and open criticism of Nyerere's leadership and a public outcry for an end to the economic system he had personally sponsored.[62]

The hardships suffered by Tanzanians during the late 1970s and early 1980s produced an all-pervasive belief that the old system had failed. While some political leaders remained vocally supportive of the country's socialist approach, their reasons for doing so were transparently self-interested. The vast majority of Tanzanians were not only deeply frustrated by the chronic shortages of goods, inadequacies of government services, and unfulfilled promises of better things to come, but also increasingly prepared to endure the uncertainties of a wholly new strategy of economic development.

Economic crisis, then, induces a willingness to change and a determination to support leaders who will bring it about. But it does not provide a satisfactory answer to the question of why policy reform has, virtually everywhere, become synonymous with economic liberalization. To deal with this question, it is essential to consider intellectual influences. For ideas inspire and empower political choice and, on a global basis, the most consequential and persuasive ideas of the past decade have been those that embraced and adumbrated the superiority of market-based economic systems.

Why these ideas should have attained such seemingly universal ascendancy at this time is a question far beyond the scope of this chapter. But part of the explanation undoubtedly lies in real-world economic trends. And the most conspicuous of these, in recent years, has been the glaring contrast between the dismal performance of statist economic systems that have disregarded the vitally important role of free markets and the superior performance of economies where governmental interventions have supplemented and reinforced the growth possibilities inherent in production for the international marketplace. By the end of the 1970s, innumerable Tanzanians, including countless students, scholars, journalists, bureaucrats and politicians, had been personally exposed to this contrast and would have drawn obvious conclusions about the policy changes necessary to rekindle a process of economic growth in their society.

Ideas also attain an impact on policy when they become the official doctrine of powerful financial institutions. The role played by the World Bank, IMF and bilateral donor agencies such as USAID has been widely referred to and, in many cases, is probably greatly exaggerated. Such organizations are undoubtedly important as the institutional transmission belts of orthodox economic analysis and they can apply great pressure for the adoption of orthodox economic reforms through their capacity to provide or withhold financial assistance. But it would be wholly incorrect and completely unfair to Tanzania and to a host of other African countries to explain policy change on the basis of the power of international lenders. Such explanations completely ignore the importance of internal political changes. The most accurate description of the role of the international lenders is that they become involved only when governments are themselves actively considering policy changes. Their role is then to lend support to groups and leaders favorable to change, thereby strengthening the internal political impulse toward economic adjustment.[63]

The search for causal factors, whether internal or external, misses a major part of the drama of political reform. Social science has yet to capture, even descriptively, a portrait of the way an existing policy coalition disassembles itself and gives way to a new one. Recent scholarship on Tanzania is especially weak on this subject and, as a result, little is yet known about the exact sequence of internal political changes that have fundamentally transformed the policy framework of the Tanzanian government.[64] All that can be said with utter certainty is that, by the early 1980s, a growing number of Tanzania's leading politicians had become supportive of policy reforms that would involve a major increase in the role of market forces.

The outward signs of this receptiveness were everywhere. The most important ministries, such as Agriculture and Finance, had come under the jurisdiction of ministers favorable to reform. And, within these ministries, officials who favored reform had risen to highly influential positions and were engaged in a visible effort to transform their country's most important economic policies. Tanzania's rapidly changing intellectual climate could also be discerned at the University of Dar es Salaam, where a growing number of members of the Economics faculty and economists associated with the university's highly influential Economics Research Bureau had begun to take public positions favoring reform. Indeed, from the very beginning, Tanzanian economists were among the most important actors pressing for political changes. Through the intellectual strength of their research, through the force of their presentations at professional conferences and seminars, through their influence as consultants to government ministries, and, perhaps most importantly, through personal friendships with some of the country's highest ranking politicians, they had a profound effect in bringing about a greater openness to economic change.

One of the most frustrating aspects of policy reform in societies such as Tanzania has to do with the tendency for economic recovery to lag behind policy change. There is an implicit assumption among many proponents of structural adjustment that, once significant reforms have been introduced, private sector actors that have been patiently waiting on the sidelines will become actively involved and buoy the process of economic recovery. But this has rarely occurred, producing frustration among economists who tend to view structural adjustment as principally a matter of getting the policies right. Important as that is, it overlooks the supremely political aspect of the connection between policy change and economic recovery, the factor of policy credibility.

The timing of official reform efforts may be something very different from the moment at which those efforts become sufficiently credible to energize the involvement of segments of the population whose participation is economically indispensable. The distinction between policy change and credibility is especially salient in formerly socialist countries, such as Tanzania, where private entrepreneurs have been subjected to decades of harassment and official political disparagement. Here, mere policy changes may not suffice to provide assurance that those who engage in business activity are no longer personally or economically at risk.

Political economy has also been regrettably weak in dealing with this issue. The disturbing fact of the matter is that very little attention has been directed toward the question of how long a reform effort must be in place before it becomes credible or whether some institutional arrangements for reform can inspire more confidence than others.[65] The factor of credibility is of overriding importance in areas of economic liberalization that require individuals and organizations to invest resources and skills in the reform process and in sectors of the economy where whole institutions must be reformed or created in order to generate an economic response. There are numerous examples of areas where credibility is absolutely vital to a reform effort, including divestiture of state enterprises, which requires that private investors risk capital to acquire ownership. Where the credibility of a reform effort is uncertain, it is to be expected that such sectors will exhibit an especially slow response to a reform program.

Perhaps the best example in Tanzania has to do with the restoration of cooperative unions which, the present government hopes, will replace parastatal corporations in the local procurement and marketing of agricultural commodities. The difficulty lies in the fact that cooperative unions are such enormously complicated organizations; they require highly sophisticated accounting skills to deal with complex financial matters and equally sophisticated managerial skills to handle such daunting tasks as the management of large inventories of physical equipment, crop storage facilities, and rolling stock. Cooperatives must also be able to administer such widely assorted activities as credit provision and delivery of farm inputs. Under the best of circumstances, then, the creation of an effective cooperative society requires years and sometimes generations of laborious and painstaking effort.

In contemporary Tanzania, those with the experience and skills required to perform these tasks are in desperately short supply. The most likely candidates for the rebuilding of cooperative societies are those with previous cooperative experience. But, among members of this group, the government's sudden and arbitrary decision, in 1976, to ban the producer cooperatives and assign their functions to governmental crop authorities remains a bitter memory. In such agriculturally vital regions as Kilimanjaro, West Lake, and Mwanza, the banning of cooperatives continues to evoke pervasive feelings of suspicion and mistrust. It thus provides an important component in an explanation of the slowness in the recovery of the cooperative movement.

The most visible source of Tanzania's on-going credibility constraint has been the political difference between the government, which is dedicated to economic liberalization, and the governing party, which officially remains a socialist organization. During the years immediately preceding the structural adjustment agreement of 1986, and throughout the period since, it has been an obvious, sharp division within Tanzania's political leadership between those in favor of policy reform, who generally identified themselves as "pragmatists," and those who remained committed to the old statist system of economic management, generally referred to as "socialists." In this respect, Tanzania manifested its own version of the classic "reds" versus "experts" confrontation. It would be an oversimplification to suggest that this division conformed entirely to the institutional division between the country's socialist governing party, the Chama Cha Mapinduzi (or Party of the Revolution [CCM]) on the one hand, and its state apparatus on the other; for pragmatists and socialists were to be found in both the government and within the CCM. But by and large, the CCM has been the most important source of resistance to the process of economic reform.

Not only did the party remain officially committed to a socialist vision of Tanzanian development, but, until early 1992, it also remained the supreme organ of government. For these reasons, there was a tendency for the country's leading socialist politicians to congregate within the CCM and use its policy-making authority in ways that frustrated the country's economic reformers. Not the least of Mwinyi's difficulties was the brooding presence of his predecessor, President Nyerere, who, while never explicitly denouncing the government's reform policies, took numerous occasions to remind Tanzanians, many of whom continued to revere him personally, of his own devotion to a socialist outlook and distaste for market-oriented approaches to development.

Nyerere's highly visible role as implicit critic of economic reform was an acute source of unease to reform-minded Tanzanians and a constant reminder of the potential fragility of the reform process. Since the ultimate triumph of the pragmatists could not, even until recently, be taken for granted, the prudent course for a rational economic actor would have been to refrain from making a potentially risky investment of personal skills and resources in the reform effort.

The first political challenge for Tanzania's economic pragmatists, therefore, was to dislodge the party's most prominent socialists from important ministerial positions without inducing a destabilizing rupture between the party and the state. The early years of the administration of President Ali Hassan Mwinyi were much taken up with this process and were characterized by the increasing political ascendancy of the pragmatist group, with socialist conservatives being gradually displaced from virtually all key governmental positions. But the process of pragmatic consolidation was a frustratingly slow one and the removal of conservatives was not basically completed until the end of 1991.[66] The process of reform proceeded, however, because the party's power was ultimately more symbolic than real: it could pass resolutions that implicitly criticized the process of liberalization, it could conspicuously embarrass the government by refusing to renounce its commitment to a socialist ideology, and it could continue to insist on some representation of the socialist position within the cabinet. But, by the early 1990s, the party's socialist stalwarts no longer controlled the key organs of government within which economic policies were formulated and implemented.

The party's ability to maintain a high political profile, even as major policy reforms were proceeding without its formal assent, was, however, a source of unease to those awaiting signals of credibility from the reform effort. For it meant that the process of economic reform was largely a matter of administrative changes in policy implementation rather than legal changes legislatively authorized by a majority of the National Assembly. So far as the credibility of the reform effort was concerned, the difficulty for contemporary Tanzania was that the power of the CCM created the bewildering anomaly of a reformist government coexisting in the same political space with a socialist party whose representatives continued to dominate the country's most important representative body.

The political changes that might begin to resolve this anomaly did not occur until the beginning of 1992, when the governing party approved a series of constitutional reforms that effectively removed two of the most important pillars of the old Tanzanian system. In the spring of 1992, the CCM officially accepted political pluralism and also agreed to end its status as the supreme organ of government. The CCM must now contend with a vast proliferation of more than a dozen opposition organizations seeking to position themselves for Tanzania's next general election, presently scheduled for late 1995. Since some of these parties seem certain to oppose economic reform, the credibility constraint posed by a reformist government coexisting uncomfortably with a socialist party may not be fully resolved until that time.

Multiparty Democracy and Structural Adjustment

It would be wholly premature to assess the long-term political sustainability of economic reform in Tanzania but the country's present political situation typifies the dilemma confronting a number of African nations undergoing far-reaching economic liberalization: is economic reform compatible with political democratization? To address this issue, it is useful to begin with the conventional wisdom on the topic: the view that structural adjustment cannot readily coexist with democratic politics. The reasoning generally offered for this position holds that because structural adjustment imposes painful and prolonged austerity on large numbers of people, it creates a ready-made opportunity for would-be political entrepreneurs to mobilize opposition sentiment. Under democratic conditions, the parties formed by these entrepreneurs could be expected to enjoy sufficient levels of electoral support to capture political power. The politically reformed government would then find itself electorally committed to repeal major components of the economic reform package. Therefore, it is argued, only authoritarian regimes capable of repressing or withstanding adverse public opinion can sustain reform efforts.

The weaknesses in this position are glaring. The first is its uncritical assumption that neither ordinary citizens nor political elites learn from experience. This would be completely untrue in the Tanzanian context. One of the most powerful political forces in Tanzania today is the memory of the severe day-to-day hardships experienced during the Nyerere regime. The shortages and deprivations of that period remain a living memory for vast numbers of Tanzanians who, as a result, would be deeply loathe to see a return of a socialist or statist approach to development. An additional memory of the socialist period has to do with the constant need to bribe government officials for even the most trivial services. The memory of pandemic official corruption continues to foster a vast amount of social rage toward politicians who enriched themselves while articulating the phraseology of socialist egalitarianism. Today, these memories constitute a formidable barrier to politicians who base their appeal on a return to the old system.

A second shortcoming of the conventional wisdom is its tendency to overlook the fact that large and potentially influential segments of society do well under adjustment even in the short run. The list of "winners" includes not only export-oriented farmers but also a wide variety of other important social groupings. Since currency devaluation, insofar as it increases the domestic price of imported goods, constitutes a natural form of protectionism, it can provide considerable stimulation for a host of import-competing industries. Food-producing farmers, for example, benefit as the prices of imported foods increase and as the increased incentives for agricultural exports provides a more generalized buoyancy for the agricultural sector.[67] Structural adjustment can also provide small-scale productive enterprises since these also benefit from the protective cocoon of devaluation. Examples include small-scale machining firms that remanufacture truck, bus, and automobile parts, tailoring and clothing shops that benefit as imported clothes increase in price, and furniture manufacturing firms that can provide local substitutes for imported goods. Indeed, one of the ironies of structural adjustment is that devaluation provides natural protection for some of the same industries that formerly received protection through quantitative restrictions.

A third shortcoming of the conventional wisdom lies in its repeated assertion that structural adjustment is merely a developmental version of "trickle down" economics and that, as a result, it provides few benefits for lower socioeconomic strata. The fact is that it provides substantial and immediate benefits for large segments of the working class. Workers in trade-related sectors such as plantation workers, mineworkers, and transportation and dock workers, for example, benefit quickly as increased international trade stimulates increased labor demand in these areas. And workers in the construction trades also tend to benefit because adjustment tends to stimulate immediate investment in the rehabilitation of infrastructure, especially road building and railroad reconstruction. Workers in building construction have also benefited with a boom in commercial real estate and housing. And as government revenues improve, civil service salaries may also be allowed to rise, easing the inflationary pressure on middle- and lower-level public servants. As the incomes of these groups improve, there are often ripple effects that include a heightened demand for labor-intensive services such as automobile and truck repair, dry cleaning, and food preparation.

Since there has been so much misunderstanding and so much misrepresentation of the socioeconomic effects of economic reform, it is vitally important to be as precise as possible about the question of which members of society are, indeed, the losers. There are only two groups that obviously fall into this category. The first and most obvious consists of those who were the most conspicuous winners under the old system; that is, the rent-seeking politicians and bureaucrats who were able to benefit from the governmentally induced scarcities that were integral features of an economic approach that justified trade restrictions as a means of attaining economic growth. About the declining fortunes of this group, little need be said except possibly that this group of economic losers should never have been winners in the first place.

The second group of losers is more elusive but consists generally of the workers, managers, and suppliers of formerly protected enterprises. The effect of adjustment on this group is complex and, because of severe information scarcity, difficult to assess. The little that is known with certainty can be quickly summarized. Both the size and the plight of this group have probably been considerably exaggerated. Since rates of capacity utilization in protected industries had already fallen to abysmally low levels well before structural adjustment began, unemployment and underemployment were already severe. Indeed, as production levels fell, many of the workers in these firms had already begun to drift away, to seek employment elsewhere in the system. Moreover, even before the period of severe economic decline, a certain proportion of the labor force in the protected industries had always consisted of "ghost workers," the relatives, friends, and political clients of politically influential persons, placed there purely for the purpose of patronage.

The relationship between structural adjustment and real industrial unemployment, then, is unclear. Undoubtedly, some proportion of the industrial workforce has suffered economic misfortune as a result of the withdrawal of protections and subsidies. But, given the extent and rapidity of recovery in import-competing industries, construction activity, and the extractive sectors, it is by no means clear that industrial workers as a whole are worse off under adjustment.

The fact of the matter, then, is that the relationship between democracy and adjustment may be exactly opposite to that stated in the conventional wisdom. It is wholly plausible to this observer that the number of those benefiting from economic reform substantially exceeds those who have suffered from it and that their improved fortunes, combined with even broader social memories of the inequities of the earlier rent-seeking society, would provide a solid electoral basis for further reform efforts.

NOTES

1. Thomas M. Callaghy, "Toward State Capability and Embedded Liberalism in the Third World: Lessons for Adjustment," in Joan M. Nelson, ed., *Fragile Coalitions: The Politics of Economic Adjustment* (New Brunswick, N.J.: Transaction Books, 1989), p. 115. The author wishes to thank Michael Kurtzig and Margaret Missiaen of the Economic Research Service of the U.S. Department of Agriculture for their willingness to make available the agricultural data used in this chapter.

2. The "classics" in this literature are widely familiar and include most notably The World Bank, *Accelerated Development in Sub-Saharan Africa: An Agenda for Action* (Washington, D.C.: World Bank, 1981), referred to hereafter as the "Berg Report" and Robert H. Bates, *Markets and States in Tropical Africa: The Political Basis of Agricultural Policies* (Berkeley and Los Angeles: University of California Press, 1981).

3. For a full discussion of this scholarly genre, see John Ravenhill, "Africa's Continuing Crises: The Elusiveness of Development," ch. 1 in Ravenhill, ed. *Africa in Economic Crisis* (New York: Columbia University Press, 1986).

4. One recent article that compiles an inventory of these shortcomings is Robert H. Bates, "Agricultural Policy & the Study of Politics in Post-Independence Africa" in Douglas Rimmer, ed. *Africa 30 Years On* (Portsmouth, N.H.: Heinemann, 1991), pp. 115–129.

5. For an excellent discussion of this issue, see Merilee S. Grindle, "The New Political Economy: Positive Economics and Negative Politics." (Cambridge, Harvard Institute for International Development, *Development Discussion Paper No. 311*, 1989).

6. Ravenhill, "Africa's Continuing Crises.," p. 3.

7. Republic of Kenya, Sessional Paper No. 10: "African Socialism and its Application to Planning in Kenya" (Nairobi: Government Printer, 1965).

8. Ibid.

9. The Kenya case provides strong support for Robert Wade's argument that neoliberalism does not provide an adequate explanation for economic growth in developing countries. See his article "East Asia's Economic Success," *World Politics* 44, 2 (January 1992): 270–320.

10. Between 1985 and 1990, horticultural exports increased 225% in volume and 375% in value. By the early 1990s, horticulture nearly equaled coffee

exports in total annual earnings. In 1990, tea exports earned approximately $257 million; coffee exports, $151 million; and horticultural exports, $148 million. Economist Intelligence Unit, *EIU Country Profile 1991–92, Kenya* (London: Economist Intelligence Unit, 1992), pp. 16–17.

11. In interview, one agricultural planner claimed that the foreign exchange component alone of wheat produced in Kenya was higher than the world market price of this commodity.

12. Republic of Kenya, Sessional Paper no. 4 of 1981: "National Food Policy" (Nairobi: Government Printer, 1981), esp. pp. 20–21.

13. The author is indebted to Professor Charles Hickson, School of Business, University of Belfast, for this observation.

14. For a theoretically generalized treatment of the political efficiencies of different tax systems, see Margaret Levi, *Of Rule and Revenue* (Berkeley and Los Angeles: University of California Press, 1988).

15. The terminology is sometimes confusing. *Overvaluation* of a currency consists of offering too *few* units of local currency per $ U.S. *Devaluation*, therefore, consists of *increasing* the number of units of local currency per $, an *upward* movement in the exchange rate.

16. Uma Lele and Richard Meyers, *Growth and Structural Change in East Africa: Domestic Policies, Agricultural Performance, and World Bank Assistance, 1963–1986* (Washington, D.C.: World Bank, 1987), p. 14.

17. Cathy L. Jabbara, "Agricultural Pricing Policy in Kenya," in *World Development* 13, 5 (May 1985): 624.

18. The World Bank and the UNDP, *Africa's Adjustment and Growth in the 1980s* (Washington, D.C.: World Bank, 1989), p. 22.

19. For an excellent discussion, see Michael Westlake, "Nominal Protection Coefficients and the Measurement of Agricultural Price Distortion in Developing Countries" (Cambridge: Harvard Institute for International Development, Discussion Paper, No. 214, January, 1986).

20. Since the World Bank calculates NPCs using official exchange rates, its figures show even higher increases for grain crops than table 11.5. Figures generously supplied by the Bank place the NPCs for maize, wheat and rice at 131, 115 and 113 respectively, indicating considerable "subsidies" for these crops.

21. This legislation was the Local Manufactures (Export Compensation) Act. A detailed discussion of this law and its effects can be found in Patrick Low, "Export Subsidies and Trade Policy: The Experience of Kenya," *World Development* 10, 4 (1982).

22. Republic of Kenya, Sessional paper No. 4 of 1975, "Economic Prospects and Policies" (Nairobi: Government Printer, 1974), p. 4.

23. See, for example, The World Bank, *Kenya: Growth and Structural Change*, pp. 97–99.

24. *Financial Times* (London), January 8, 1992.

25. Tony Killick, "Kenya, the IMF and the Unsuccessful Quest for Stabilization," in John Williamson, ed., *IMF Conditionality*, (Washington, D.C.: Institute for International Economics, 1983).

26. For a different view that considers Tanzania's negotiating position as substantially closer to the conditionality requirements of the IMF, see Regi-

nald Herbold Green, "Politico-Economic Adjustment and IMF Conditionality: Tanzania 1974–1981" in Williamson, *IMF Conditionality.*

27. World Bank, *World Development Report 1992* (New York: Oxford, 1992), p. 218.

28. John de Wilde has also suggested that part of Tanzania's foreign exchange crisis may have been caused by the declining quality of agricultural exports and the fact that, as a result, the prices it received were increasingly at the low end of the world market scale. See his *Agriculture, Marketing and Pricing in Sub-Saharan Africa* (Los Angeles: African Studies Center and Crossroads press, 1984), p. 35.

29. *Daily News* (Tanzania), June 20, 1986.

30. The physical quality of life index is a United Nations standard of measurement that is a statistical composite of such indices as infant mortality, adult literacy, life expectancy, and availability of food.

31. Jennifer Sharpley has shown that, as a percentage of market value, food crops in Tanzania are twice as import-intensive as export crops. See "External Versus Internal Factors in Tanzania's Macro-Economic Crisis" (unpublished manuscript), table 11.5, p. 16a.

32. If the drought year 1984 is dropped from the calculation, and grain imports are calculated on the basis of 1981–83, and 1985–86, Kenya's grain imports averaged 337,000 metric tons and its grain imports as a percentage of total imports were 9.0. Tanzania's grain imports averaged 263,000 metric tons and its food imports as a percentage of total imports were 12.9.

33. According to one estimate, the informal economy GDP ranged between 21% and 31% of the official economy GDP throughout most of the 1980s and did not begin to decline significantly until 1988. See M. S. D. Bagachwa, "The Nature and Magnitude of the Second Economy in Tanzania," *Tanzanian Economic Trends* 2, 3 (October 1989) and 2, 4 (January 1990): 32.

34. According to one informant, the bribe to be assigned a preferred place on the waiting list for a state-owned apartment was equal to 20 years rent.

35. For a detailed survey of Kenya's experience, see Barbara Grosh, "Agricultural Parastatals Since Independence: How Have They Performed?" (Nairobi, Institute of Development Studies, Working Paper No. 435, 1986).

36. See, for example, The United Republic of Tanzania, *Analysis of Accounts of Parastatal Enterprises* (Dar es Salaam, Bureau of Statistics, Ministry of Planning and Economic Affairs, 1983), and United Republic of Tanzania, Ministry of Agriculture, *Crop Authorities: Financial Position and Financial Performance 1977 to 1981/82* (Dar es Salaam: Project Preparation and Monitoring Bureau, 1983).

37. Frank Ellis, "Agricultural Pricing Policy in Tanzania 1970–1979: Implications for Agricultural Output, Rural Incomes and Crop Marketing Costs," (University of Dar es Salaam, Economic Research Bureau, 1980), p. 38.

38. The United Republic of Tanzania, *Structural Adjustment Programme for Tanzania* (Dar es Salaam: Ministry of Planning and Economic Affairs, 1982).

39. For an article on the vital importance of credibility in a reform effort, see Dani Rodrik, "Credibility of Trade Reform—A Policy Maker's Guide," *World Economy* 12, 1 (March 1989).

40. Economist Intelligence Unit, *EIU Country Report 1991–91, Tanzania* (London: Economist Intelligence Unit, 1992), pp. 19–20.

41. This reform is intended to replace the system that grants parastatal corporations guaranteed lines of credit with the nation's banking institutions. Initially intended to allow parastatals to conduct business on a month-to-month basis before crop sales produced an end-of-year surge in revenue, the line of credit system was an open invitation to abuse.

42. Grindle, "The New Political Economy," p. 45.

43. Roger Thurow, "Capital Flight Strains Kenyan Economy," *Wall Street Journal*, August 17, 1989.

44. The following observations are much indebted to Michael Chege and especially to his unpublished ms., "The Search For Optimal Sequence Between Production and Distribution: Kenya and Tanzania After Their Founding Presidents." This ms. is intended for publication in David E Apter and Carl G. Rosberg, eds., *Political Development and the New Realism in Sub-Saharan Africa* (Charlottesville: University of Virginia Press, forthcoming, 1993).

45. Income inequality in Kenya became the subject of extensive research by scholars and international organizations. The most well known and carefully documented study was International Labour Office, *Employment, Incomes and Equality: A Strategy for Increasing Productive Employment in Kenya* (Geneva: International Labour Office, 1972), see esp. ch. 5.

46. The assassinations of Pio Gama Pinto, Tom Mboya and J. M. Kariuki indicate that the Kenyatta government was fully prepared to deal severely with the most outspoken proponents of economic redistribution.

47. This 1970s beverages boom and the differences in the way Kenya and Tanzania responded to it are the subject of an excellent volume. See David Bevan, Paul Collier and Jan Willem Gunning, *Peasants and Governments: An Economic Analysis* (Oxford: Clarendon Press, 1989).

48. Chege, "The Search For Optimal Sequence," p. 10.

49. The best example is the creation of Moi University in western Kenya.

50. Not surprisingly, the effects on coffee production have been calamitous. Total production fell from an all time high of 129,000 metric tons in 1986–87 to 104,000 metric tons in 1989–90.

51. Mancur Olson has further suggested that distributional governments "slow down a society's capacity to adopt new technologies and to reallocate resources in response to changing conditions." See his *The Rise and Decline of Nations: Economic Growth, Stagflation, and Social Rigidities* (New Haven: Yale University Press, 1982), p. 65.

52. The designation Kalenjin does not refer, in fact, to a single ethnic group but to a language family that includes such diverse groups as Nandi, Kipsigis, Elgweyo, and Tugen. The president himself is a member of the Tugen subgroup of the Kalenjin people.

53. For an excellent analysis, see Joel D. Barkan, "The Rise and Fall of a Governance Realm in Kenya," in Goran Hyden and Michael Bratton, eds., *Governance and Politics in Africa*, (Boulder: Lynne Rienner, 1992).

54. See Richard A Joseph, *Democracy and Prebendal Politics in Nigeria: The Rise and Fall of the Second Republic* (New York: Cambridge University Press, 1987).

55. The most obvious example of this group is the famous Kenyan novelist, Ngugi wa Thiongo.

56. John Ravenhill, "Reversing Africa's Economic Decline: No Easy Answers," *World Policy Journal* 7, 4 (Fall 1990): 716.

57. The classic article by Anne O. Krueger, "The Political Economy of the Rent-Seeking Society," *American Economic Review* 64, 3 (1974).

58. Lele and Meyers estimate that public sector employment in Tanzania had grown at a rate of nearly 16% annually between the late 1960's and late 1970s, *Growth*, p. 21.

59. See R. H. Green, D. G. Rwegasira and B. Van Arkadie, *Economic Shocks and National Policy Making: Tanzania in the 1970s* (The Hague: Institute of Social Studies, 1980).

60. The country's transportation system, for example, suffered greatly as its railroads, trucks, and even busses from the Dar es Salaam municipal transport authority were devoted to transporting troops and equipment to the Uganda border.

61. One of the worst after-effects of the war was a sudden, sharp rise in violent crime as demobilized soldiers, many of whom had weapons that had been captured or not handed in, returned to a depressed economy that was unable to provide employment.

62. At the University of Dar es Salaam, some scholars spoke of "Tanzania's Viet Nam" pointing to opposition to certain forms of conscription, the social demoralization occasioned by battlefield casualties, the adjustment difficulties experienced by demobilized and unemployed soldiers, and the budgetary squeeze on social programs that had been the pride of Tanzanian socialism.

63. The author is indebted to Professor Anne O. Krueger of the Department of Economics, Duke University, for this observation.

64. See, for example, John Loxley, "The Devaluation Debate in Tanzania," ch. 1 in Bonnie K. Campbell and John Loxley, eds. *Structural Adjustment in Africa* (New York: St. Martin's Press, 1989). While comprehensive as an exposition of the arguments for and against devaluation, Loxley's argument says little about which groups of Tanzanians took either position and why, in the end, the pro-devaluation group won.

65. For example, an auction method of setting exchange rates is not credible because it can be canceled or suspended so easily by a central bank. An exchange bureau system is more credible because the bureaus and their clienteles become an institutional lobby.

66. In October 1991, one of the major socialists, Joseph Warioba, a former Prime Minister and relative of President Nyerere, was removed from his position as Minister for Regional Administration and Local Government. Another, Rashid Kawawa, retained a position as Minister without Portfolio, an assignment that reflected the party's continuing ability to influence cabinet-level appointments.

67. Before economic reforms began, overvaluation was sufficiently great that coffee production had become so unprofitable that a number of coffee farmers had abandoned this crop to engage in the cultivation of uncontrolled food crops. As real coffee prices rose with devaluation, these coffee farmers returned to the export crop, thereby creating an important niche for traditional food crop cultivators.

Chapter Twelve

Political Passions and Economic Interests: Economic Reform and Political Structure in Africa

THOMAS M. CALLAGHY

Introduction: Beyond Authoritarianism or Democracy?

This chapter is about the relationship between economic and political liberalization in Africa. Among many Western scholars and politicians the explicit or implicit assumption was long that major economic restructuring required authoritarian regimes. Now both Western scholars and politicians are arguing that such economic restructuring *requires* simultaneous democratic political liberalization. Neither position is fully correct; neither is fully wrong. A more nuanced view is required, and time frame, sequence, and political conditions are central to such a perspective.

The key argument is an institutionalist one about the conditions under which economic policy is formulated and implemented in regimes of all types. If certain institutional features are present, economic liberalization is greatly facilitated, but not assured. Such features can be present under authoritarian, semidemocratic, and democratic conditions, but they are more likely to last and be effective under the first two, at least in the medium run. Propitious structures and conditions can disappear under any type of regime, but, because of the political logics of democratic coalitional and electoral support and legitimacy, they are more likely to do so under fully democratic conditions. I argue that established Third World democratic regimes engage in economic stabilization as well as most authoritarian regimes and better that most new or transitional democratic regimes but do not do as well at structural adjustment. While cases of established democratic regimes will be used here, the focus will be on new or transitional democratic regimes, as that is the primary issue facing African countries in the 1990s. Our time frame will be the short and medium run.

The chapter will first look at the old debate on the relationship between regime type and economic change and examine recent Third World evidence on it. Then it will sketch Africa's current economic and political marginalization and dependence as well as the efforts at economic reform in the 1980s that flowed from them. It will present an argument about the requisites of successful economic restructuring under African and other Third World conditions—one that focuses heavily on the politics of delegation under a variety of regimes. Other factors that facilitate successful reform will then be discussed as will the reactions of external actors to the quite limited success of neoorthodox economic reform in Africa. From two originally separate paths, these reactions converged on the new phenomenon of political conditionality stressing "governance" and democratization. In order to assess the prospects for mutually reinforcing processes of economic and political liberalization in Africa the difficulties facing new or transitional democracies will be examined and then three country cases will be analyzed—Ghana, Nigeria, and Senegal. Finally, the conclusion will look at the prospects for economic and political liberalization in Africa, especially its version of the "cruel choice" and the tension between everyday politics and developmental visions.

Economic Change and Regime Type: The Old Debate and the Recent Record

As Laurence Whitehead has pointed out, in many Western "policy-making circles it is virtually an unexamined axiom that market economics and participatory politics are parallel processes that accompany each other. Capitalism and democracy are seen as two sides of the same coin, united by commitment to individual free choice in both economic and political matters."[1] This belief was greatly reinforced by events in Eastern Europe and is now assumed to hold for the Third World as well. There is, in fact, a long tradition of scholarship that readily admits "the historical and the logical connections between capitalism and democracy,"[2] certainly for much of Europe and frequently for other places in the world *over the long run*. This link has been seen to hold particularly for historically stable countries with high levels of economic development.[3] But the rise of bureaucratic-authoritarian states in Latin America in the 1960s and 1970s generated a more pessimistic mood. Discussions of East Asian newly industrializing countries (NICs) led to similarly pessimistic conclusions. For Africa it is even less clear that there is an historical or logical connection between the two, for at least the foreseeable future.

One analyst points to "the inconclusiveness of the debate" about "the impact of democracy on economic development."[4] While he does admit that "most cases of very high growth rates have involved authoritarian regimes, and authoritarianism may be a nearly necessary, though not a sufficient, condition for rapid economic growth," he asserts that "the economies of many democratic Third World countries have grown at satisfactory rates."[5] Most of his "satisfactory" cases are established democracies, however, such as India and Venezuela. He is more pessimistic about the prospects for transitional or newly established democracies facing the tasks of economic restructuring and points to the difficult political logics they confront:

> The capacity of democratic regimes to extricate themselves from social ties so as to restructure the economy is minimal. Generally, only incremental shifts are possible. Moreover, leaders in democracies concern themselves with what appears to be politically "rational"—namely, how to generate and enhance political support. Thus economic policies often are chosen because of the political benefits they may bring to the leaders. Policy incrementalism and the use of economic resources for sustaining political support generally tend to retard economic growth in democracies.[6]

A study comparing the performance of twenty-five Third World countries for 1978–86, a sample that included "continuous democracies, authoritarian regimes, and countries that have undergone a democratic transition," found that "established democracies have performed about as well as authoritarian regimes in implementing stable macroeconomic policies," but that "new democracies as a group did appear to have difficulties controlling fiscal and monetary policy during the period of transition." The study noted, however, that there were striking differences among the new democracies based on different structural and institutional characteristics.[7] Considerable variation also existed among authoritarian regimes, reemphasizing the point that authoritarian regimes do not guarantee good economic performance; Africa is replete with such examples. The key finding for Africa is that "democratic political transitions are associated with difficulties in managing macroeconomic policy."[8] The differences become even more striking, however, when looking at major structural adjustment efforts rather than stabilization measures.

In a study of East Asian and Latin American NICs, it is clear that "authoritarianism contributed to economic growth," that "crucial policy reforms in the NICs have historically been associated with authoritarian rule; any assessment of the NICs must weigh this high cost of `success.' "[9] In discussing the bottom line, the author notes that:

> One way to circumvent this problem is to go beyond regime type to other institutional factors that have affected the NICs' performance. . . . I have attempted to show how other institutional features of the state, including the organization of interest groups, the centralization of decision-making authority, and the instruments available to government officials, also affected ability to formulate and implement coherent policy. *Yet as the case studies have shown, many of these institutional characteristics were themselves a by-product of the consolidation of authoritarian political power.* Thus while there are good reasons to disaggregate the state, disaggregation does not reduce the analytic utility of beginning with the authoritarian-democratic distinction.[10]

He goes on, however, to express a common hope:

> Nevertheless, . . . there are no *theoretical* reasons to think that authoritarian regimes are *uniquely* capable of solving the collective-action problems associated with development. This absence [of theoretical reasons] provides hope that newly democratizing countries will develop institutions conducive to both political liberty and economic growth . . .

> Authoritarian rule may have facilitated reform in the past, but a variety of institutions may be functionally equivalent in their ability to induce restraint from competing social groups.[11]

Thus we appear to have a high historical correlation in the contemporary era between authoritarian rule and the ability to engage in major economic restructuring in the Third World, but not a necessary theoretical one. The search then becomes one for what might be called "effective and sustainable democratic functional equivalents." I will return later to the issue of the nature of these equivalents and how commonly they are likely to be found. If they are not found, current disturbing trends in Africa are likely to accelerate. It is to these that we now turn.

African Economic and Political Marginalization and Dependence

Referring to the precolonial era, a leading historian of Africa has pointed to "the paradox of Africa's simultaneous involvement and marginalization in the world economy," that "Africa was becoming less significant to the world economy at the same time as it involved itself more closely in international commercial relationships." This paradox "operates in the opposite direction" as well: the world's "increasing involvement in the African economy . . . is also at odds with the decreasing economic importance of Africa" for the world economy.[12] In the early 1990s, this paradox is still valid; in fact, it is probably more applicable now than it was earlier.

The increased marginalization of Africa is twofold—economic and politico-strategic, and both aspects are tightly linked in their consequences. The first is primarily economic: that Africa is no longer very important to the major actors in the world economy and its changing international division of labor—to multinational corporations, international banks, the economies of the major Western countries, or those of NICs such as Korea, Taiwan, Brazil, and Mexico. Africa produces a declining share of world output. The main commodities it produces are becoming less and less important or are being more effectively produced by other Third World countries. Trade is declining; nobody wants to lend; and few want to invest except in narrowly defined mineral enclave sectors.[13]

The second aspect of Africa's marginalization is politico-strategic, but with very negative economic consequences. Africa has become of much less interest to the major world powers with the dramatic changes in the international arena in the 1980s and early 1990s, especially the end of the Cold War with a disintegrating Soviet Union, a liberated Eastern Europe, the rise of Japan as a major world power with more influence in the IMF and the World Bank, the dynamism of East Asian NICs, and the preoccupations of the Latin American debt crisis, which, unlike the African one, posed a threat to international financial stability. As one senior African diplomat put it, "Eastern Europe is the most sexy beautiful girl, and we are an old tattered lady. People are tired of Africa. So many countries, so many wars."[14] Even the French are beginning to reassess their "special relationship" with Africa.

Debates about Africa used to pit "internationalists" concerned about big-power rivalry against "regionalists" concerned with African issues.[15] Ironically, the internationalists have now voluntarily ceded the field to the regionalists. The latter used to call for the major powers not to turn Africa into an international security battlefield of the Cold War, but rather to let Africans solve their own problems, to leave Africa alone. The regionalists still wanted Western powers to provide substantial development assistance, but, at the same time, to let these countries decide how to use it. Now that the internationalists have declared the game over, the regionalists are desperately searching for a rationale to keep external interest and resources focused on Africa, especially in areas of intense desperation such as the Horn. The dramatic changes of 1989, Africa's politico-strategic marginalization, and the search for a new foreign policy rationale by Western industrial democracies meant that economic conditionality was joined by forms of political conditionality, under the assumption that, as in Eastern Europe, economic and political liberalization must go hand-in-hand.

What to Do?: The Political Economy of Attempted Economic Reform

As in other areas of the Third World, a difficult external debt burden and the resulting desperate need for foreign exchange have made African countries very dependent on a variety of external actors, all of whom have used their leverage to "encourage" economic liberalization.[16] This process, which some have referred to as "the new neocolonialism," means intense dependence on the International Monetary Fund, the World Bank, and major Western countries for the design of economic reform packages and the resources needed to implement them. This leverage has been converted into economic policy conditionality: specific economic policy changes in return for borrowed resources.[17] The primary thrust of these economic reform efforts is to more fully integrate African economies into the world economy by resurrecting the primary-product export economies that existed at the time of independence and making them work right this time by creating a more "liberal" political economy.

By the early 1980s the key question was not whether Africa had a serious economic crisis, but rather what to do about it. Avoiding the problem and policy drift were common African reactions, despite external warnings and pressure. Much of the African response was to rail against the prescriptions of external actors. For those governments which did decide, out of conviction or desperation, to attack the problem, the dilemmas were enormous, the risks great, and the uncertainties pervasive. Throughout the 1980s economic reform did take place in Africa, in large and small ways. A fair number of countries went through the motions or at least appeared to do so, resulting in a series of "small reforms." Few cases of "large reform" appeared, however, that is, multisector and sustained over time. By 1992 Ghana was still the only clear-cut example, although Tanzania had also made important changes. Yet Ghana illustrates the enormous difficulties of such efforts. Dr. Kwesi Botchwey, Ghana's long-time finance minister, portrays them vividly:

> We were faced with two options, which we debated very fiercely before we finally chose this path. I know because I participated very actively in these debates. Two choices: We had to maneuver our way around the naiveties of leftism, which has a sort of disdain for any talk of financial discipline, which seeks refuge in some vague concept of structuralism in which everything doable is possible. . . . Moreover, [we had to find a way between] this naivete and the crudities and rigidities and dogma of monetarism, which behaves as if once you set the monetary incentives everybody will do the right thing and the market will be perfect.[18]

As the regime of Jerry Rawlings in Ghana discovered, neither position is fully correct: everything is not possible and policy incentives do not ensure that markets will work well. In addition, a revenue imperative exists whatever path is chosen. Resources have to come from somewhere. As we shall see, a quite rare conjuncture of factors allowed the economic reform efforts in Ghana to be sustained, and Ghana's success at "large reform," itself still fragile, is rare on the continent.

Reform and the Political Economy of Delegation: An Institutionalist Argument

How, then, do we explain the varied ability of African governments, caught as they are between strong and often contradictory internal and external pressures, to engage in sustained economic reform? The degree to which an African government can adjust appears to be determined by its ability to insulate itself from the political logics, social pressures, and characteristics of the rent-seeking statist syndrome that has dominated Africa since independence while adopting externally- and market-oriented policies, largely through the delegation of economic policy-making and implementation to a core of powerful and protected technocrats.[19]

The ability to insulate and delegate is affected primarily by the following variables: (1) how the economic crisis is perceived by African rulers—particularly whether it is caused by external or internal factors and is temporary or systemic; (2) the degree to which decision-making is influenced by technocratic and economic rather than political considerations such as patron-client politics and rent seeking; (3) the degree of autonomy of the government from powerful sociopolitical forces and groups, particularly relating to distributional demands; (4) the levels of *stateness* or administrative capabilities of the state apparatus and of *cosmopolitanism*, defined as the degree of sophisticated knowledge about how the international political economy actually works; and (5) the nature, dependence on, and extent of external influence, support, and resource flows, including the market forces of the world economy.

This argument maintains a balance between agency and structure, between voluntarist perspectives that stress "political will," so common to external actors, and pessimistic ones that stress structural constraints, so common to academic and African analyses. Proper policies and adequate levels of understanding, cosmopolitanism, commitment, and statecraft (plus luck—a variable we greatly underestimate) are necessary but not sufficient. Stateness, sociopolitical insulation, and adequate external resources are also necessary but not sufficient. Some combination of both sets of factors is required. Leaders need to rely on, insulate, and protect the technocratic staff while keeping it informed of the political and social effects of the reforms on both domestic and external actors. This places the technocratic team at the heart of complex two-level policy-making and implementation "games"—economic and political games played simultaneously at domestic and international levels for very high stakes. Given this argument, and the nature of African postcolonial political economies, it is not surprising that there have been few examples of sustained neoorthodox economic reform in Africa.

In many ways delegation is a statecraft strategy that attempts to create or reassert key Weberian bureaucratic attributes in a small but intense manner under conditions of stress, characteristics that have become greatly diluted by "politics as usual," and the rooted effects of older strategies and policies. Using insulated but informed delegation is an attempt to expand the arena of discretion and maneuver in order to diminish the constraints of the everyday "rules of the game"—legal, political, administrative, and social.

Given the effort to reassert these characteristics in a small but powerful "core" of officials and institutions, the strategy is, at least in the short run, an additive rather than a transformatory one in regard to overall state capabilities. As an additive statecraft variable, however, it exists and operates in a larger and much less variable and malleable historically defined political, administrative, social, and international context, which greatly affects the likelihood that such a strategy can become institutionalized and historically rooted. The larger contextual variables are not to be underestimated. By the early 1990s the IMF and the World Bank were increasingly, if grudgingly, giving them more analytic and policy weight.

The effective operation of a technocratic core is largely determined by its size, its level of technical and administrative capability, and the quality and availability of data. Also important are the technocratic staff's own depth, cohesiveness, continuity over time, and its degree of insulation and freedom to interact and bargain with external and internal actors. The technocratic staff's insulation and protection, political awareness, influence, and level of interaction with external and internal actors can vary over time given the statecraft of the leadership, political structure, and the economic and political impact of the attempted reforms. This is true of authoritarian as well as democratic regimes. The nature and use of an adjusting country's technocratic and bureaucratic capabilities are also directly affected by the behavior of external actors and the level of resources they provide.

Technocratic and bureaucratic capabilities vary considerably from country to country—as well as from region to region—reflecting different levels of overall development, political structure, and historical legacies. But, as we shall see, successful cases of delegation and economic reform cut across both regime type and level of economic and administrative development. In addition, they pose a significant challenge, at least in the medium run, to societalist views of social and economic change, which assert that successful economic reform requires the existence of sizeable supporting societal coalitions. Clearly, in some cases viable economic reform can come without major coalitional support in the short to medium run as part of a statecraft strategy that is heavily institutional in its thrust. How such a strategy can become institutionalized and relinked to society in the longer run is a larger and more complex question, one that now confronts Korea, Taiwan, Mexico, Chile, and Turkey in a very stark fashion.

A relatively common set of characteristics appears to make delegation possible. These characteristics are more commonly found in, but not restricted to authoritarian regimes (Korea, Chile under Augusto Pinochet, Ghana).[20] Under certain conditions, formally or partially democratic regimes can manifest functional variants which allow delegation to operate effectively, at least for awhile (Mexico, Turkey, Argentina). The bases for delegation can also exist in regimes of very different levels of socioeconomic development (Bolivia and Turkey, Ghana and Chile).

The most important of these characteristics is the ability to insulate the economic teams from pressure, opposition, and requests for particularistic exceptions from major social and political groups, from elements of the state bureaucracy, *and* from the top leadership itself. This insulation can be provided by the repressing or fragmenting opposition groups via direct coercion, states of emergency, internal or external exile of opponents (Chile, Ghana, Nigeria), corporatist control mechanisms in military or single-party regimes (Mexico), formal and informal political pacts (Bolivia), co-optation via selective and controlled patronage (Turkey, Bolivia), and the emasculation of legislative bodies (Jamaica, Bolivia). The formal structure of executive authority may also be important, such as the constitutional power to rule by decree or the strong executive power provided to a prime minister by a Westminster parliamentary system (Edward Seaga in Jamaica, Carlos Menem in Argentina).

Less tangible sources of executive authority may also be important—the personal popularity, at least initially, of a ruler (Rawlings in Ghana, Fernando Collor in Brazil, Menem), a positive international reputation for the ruler, increasing the probability of external support (Seaga, Raul Alfonsin in Argentina), an electoral mandate (Seaga, Turgut Ozal in Turkey, Collor), the chaos and decline left by previous governments (Ghana, Bolivia, Argentina), and even classic obfuscation efforts.

Just as executive authority and protection are key bases for delegation, they can also be its worst enemy. Often the major threat to the productive insulation of the technocratic team comes from the executive itself. Deviations from technocratic rationality can be productive or unproductive for the viability of economic reform. Political "buffering," via side payments, for example, that facilitates the continuation of a reform program without unduly undermining it, may well be very rational (Chile, Turkey); we will return to this point in the conclusion. Much executive meddling is driven by the clash of economic and political logics, related to the need to stay in power, especially in democracies (Ozal, Victor Paz in Bolivia). Such executive intervention can quite easily cross the fine line into the unproductive, however (Kenneth Kaunda in Zambia, José Sarney in Brazil). A good deal of meddling, however, is, often quite intentionally, of a much more predatory variety (Fernando Belaúnde in Peru, Ferdinand Marcos in the Philippines, Mobutu Sese Seko in Zaire).

Unity of views and continuity of personnel—both indicators of coherence—are central to the effective performance of insulated economic teams in the short to medium run (Korea, Mexico, Ghana, Turkey). Several other factors are important, however, to the longer run coherence and eventual institutionalization of these processes and forms of statecraft. Two of the most important of these "nonbureaucratic elements of bureaucracy" are: (1) intrabureaucratic and extrabureaucratic informal networks of cohesion, and (2) the development of a bureaucratic political culture/esprit de corps/ideology. Both of these have been very important in the development of the Japanese state's role in the political economy, for example. The former has two parts. The first is the development of informal recruitment and performance networks that are based on competence and role definition. It is not a question of competence versus connection, as in the distinction between bureaucratic and patrimonial administration, but rather the *fusion* of connection and competence in the service of bureaucratic coherence and effectiveness. The second set of informal networks is extrabureaucratic, linking the bureaucracy with social groups, mostly business, in a way that facilitates economic transformation rather than retards it: what Peter Evans calls "embedded autonomy."[21]

The difficult task is to institutionalize such a technocratic political culture while finding ways to relink it to society in a productive balance between insulation and social connectedness. These are challenges that remain of central importance to the ongoing development of Korea, for example. They can be affected both positively and negatively by political liberalization depending on how various forms of "democracy" are institutionalized. Both the development of informal networks and a bureaucratic political culture help to make possible the emergence of a distinctive outlook among state officials, one that focuses on the "general interest" rather than on particularistic interests. This is one of the key things that separates developmental from predatory states. Although the long-run institutionalization of delegation requires some form of "embedded autonomy," usually democratic or semidemocratic of one sort or another, it can be sustained most effectively after major economic change has taken place. But in the shorter run the line between productive relinking with society and succumbing to particularistic rent-seeking behavior by state and societal groups, especially business, is very fine indeed.

The search for this balance between economic and political logics generates delegation cycles, even in authoritarian regimes, as we shall see for Nigeria. Productive delegation is very difficult to sustain. It is a highly contingent statecraft variable, especially in democracies and plebiscitary authoritarian regimes. It is now clear that effective delegation is not necessarily restricted to more developed states, but it is more difficult to achieve and sustain in less developed states (Ghana, Nigeria, Zambia, Bolivia, Jamaica). As we shall see, Ghana demonstrates that countries with low levels of overall development and state capabilities can effectively use delegation as a statecraft strategy for economic reform, that small teams with enormous burdens can survive, learn, and win battles with powerful external actors.

African Economic Reform, an Implicit Bargain, and Learning

But is an intelligent delegation strategy sufficient? The answer is no. Africans and external actors alike have asked how serious attempts at economic reform can be prevented from collapsing, as one such program did in dramatic fashion in Zambia in 1987.[22] How can others that are limping along become more effective and sustainable? How can the enormous burdens of such efforts be softened, ameliorated? In a very real sense, these are classic issues of statecraft, at both the national and international levels.

Africans have long maintained that substantial resource flows and debt relief are required for sustained reform. One of the lessons of Ghana is that this is certainly a necessary but not sufficient condition. By the late 1980s external actors began to realize that increased resource flows and debt relief were going to be required. This realization began to sink in as the enormous obstacles to reform and the possibility of widespread failure became increasingly apparent. Whether adequate resource flows and debt relief will come is another matter. The special new lending facilities of the IMF and the World Bank are steps in that direction, but substantial support for them will be needed from all donor countries, probably much more.[23] Given the economic and political difficulties of major industrial democracies, it is not at all clear how likely this will be.

A larger problem exists, however, which is directly linked to Africa's increasing marginalization from the world economy. An "implicit bargain" has existed between the international financial institutions and the major Western countries on the one hand and the Africans on the other. It is that if African countries successfully reformed their economies in a neoorthodox direction with the help and direction of the IMF and the World Bank, then new international private bank lending and foreign direct foreign investment would be available to underpin and sustain the reform efforts.

This "implicit bargain" has not held for Africa. The failure is not the fault of the IMF and the World Bank alone, both of which have worked to increase voluntary lending and direct foreign investment, or of reforming African governments. It is a legacy of Africa's thirty-year history of dismal economic performance, a track record that banks and investors do not forget easily, and because of structural shifts in the world economy and state system that make other areas of the world more attractive. Proponents of neoorthodox reform in Africa have argued that the track record of poor performance can be overcome if Africa provides relatively predictable opportunities for profit. Even if the African end of the bargain were to be fulfilled (not likely in very many places, however), this would hold only if other areas of the world did not provide better opportunities. As some French scholars have noted, an "*afro-pessimisme gagne du terrain et tend a réduire le continent à la portion congrue dans l'esprit des investisseurs et de nombreux dirigeants politiques.*"[24]

But are delegation and sufficient resources enough? Once again the answer is no. By the middle of the 1980s some international officials began to realize that many efforts at economic reform in Africa would fail unless changes were made in how the programs were designed and implemented. This often quite palpable fear of failure became an impetus to international learning. This realization prompted some reassessment of the economic reform process, and by the end of the decade important learning was taking place, slowly and unevenly, by both external actors and some African officials.[25]

Although some policy lessons are being learned, Africa's problems are larger still. The task of confronting this decline is enormous, much more so than for any other region of the world. External actors have learned that Africa is a special case; it has not responded as neoclassical theory predicted it should. In 1989 the World Bank noted that:

> The supply response to adjustment lending in low-income countries, especially in SSA [Sub-Saharan Africa] has been slow

> because of the legacy of deep-seated structural problems. Inadequate infrastructure, poorly developed markets, rudimentary industrial sectors, and severe institutional and managerial weaknesses in the public and the private sectors have proved *unexpectedly* serious as constraints to better performance—especially in the poorer countries of SSA. Greater recognition thus needs to be given to the time and attention needed for structural changes, especially institutional reforms and their effects.[26]

Note the revealing use of "unexpectedly"; it indicates a changed perception—the lesson that Africa is a particularly difficult case.

It is not just a case of reordering policies, but rather one of constructing a whole new context,[27] what the World Bank is now calling an "enabling environment." At the end of the 1980s, a new tenet was added to neoorthodoxy—political liberalization.

Governance and Democracy: The New Political Conditionality

Ultimately, it is not just a question of finding the "precarious balance" between state and market or state and society, but rather searching for the precarious trialectic between state, market, and the international arena. Such a precarious trialectic can be very difficult to achieve, however, as domestic politics and the international arena have a habit of presenting new and unexpected challenges for African rulers. While the World Bank's 1989 long-term perspective study, *From Crisis to Sustainable Growth*, was initially well received by many Africans, it contained a quiet time bomb—"governance," which has brought considerable new tension and uncertainty to African-external actor relations.[28] The World Bank's emphasis on governance emerged out of its learning about the primary importance of creating a more facilitative sociopolitical context for structural adjustment in Africa.

In the long-term perspective study, the World Bank, and indirectly the IMF and the major donor countries, raised governance as a major issue for the first time:

> Efforts to create an enabling environment and to build capacities will be wasted if the political context is not favorable. . . . Ultimately, better governance requires political renewal. This means a concerted attack on corruption from the highest to low-

> est levels. This can be done by setting a good example, by strengthening accountability, by encouraging public debate, and by nurturing a free press. It also means . . . fostering grassroots and nongovernmental organizations (NGOs), such as farmers' associations, cooperatives, and women's groups.[29]

Better governance, according to the Bank, also means less unpredictability and uncertainty in policy and administration, more rule of law, maintenance of judicial independence, and transparency and accountability to representative bodies.

Because of the dramatic changes in the world after 1989, especially in Eastern Europe, and the search for a new foreign policy thrust to replace anti-communism that resulted from these changes, governance was transformed quite explicitly by the major Western industrial democracies into political conditionality focusing on the promotion of democracy.

The convergence of these two external policy thrusts—one largely technocratic, the other distinctly political—merged in dramatic fashion with a third domestic thrust to pose a real dilemma for African leaders. Domestic opposition to authoritarian African governments erupted in a large number of countries in the early 1990s. Many of these tensions had been building for well over a decade, and while not all of them were directly related to the socioeconomic crisis many of them were.[30] The crisis brought great suffering in itself; this was further compounded by the hardship effects of attempted economic reform programs undertaken under the supervision of the IMF and the World Bank. In short, attempted economic reform was itself an important contributing cause of domestic unrest. Most of this opposition was put in "democratic" terms, much of it genuinely so, some of it not. When linked with the two strands of external pressure for political liberalization, domestic unrest dramatically increased the pressure on African rulers, on both those resisting economic reform *and* on those, such as Rawlings, attempting serious economic reform. These combined external and internal pressures for political liberalization can make economic reform more rather than less difficult.

Warnings about governance and political liberalization have come from the highest levels of the international financial institutions and the most important Western industrial democracies. In April 1990, Barber Conable, then president of the World Bank, put the case in very blunt terms:

> The development of many Sub-Saharan African countries has been quite unnecessarily constrained by their political systems. Africans can and must tackle this issue. . . . Indisputably, three decades after independence too many African countries have failed to produce political and economic systems in which development can flourish. . . . People need freedom to realize individual and collective potential. . . . Open political participation has been restricted and even condemned, and those brave enough to speak their minds have too frequently taken grave political risks. I fear that many of Africa's leaders have been more concerned about retaining power than about the long-term development interests of their people. The cost to millions of Africans . . . has been unforgivably high.[31]

Douglas Hurd, the British Foreign Secretary, asserted that the distribution of aid should favor countries tending toward pluralism, public accountability and human rights, and market principles. While saying that France did not intend to impose models, President François Mitterrand made a similar declaration and noted, that for him, democracy would include free elections, multiparty systems, press freedom, and an independent judiciary. U.S. officials also treaded a similar path, pushed with considerable vigor by Congress. In July 1990, for example, a senior U.S. official declared: "We believe that democratization is vital for Africa's long-term future, and that economic liberalization goes hand in hand with political liberalization."[32]

Political conditionality promised to increase African dependence on external actors. African leaders feared its consequences, including some such as Rawlings who were committed to economic reform. A few leaders resisted energetically (Mobutu), others stalled or played charades with both internal and external critics (Paul Biya, Daniel arap Moi). But how viable is this vision of simultaneous democratization and economic reform?

Neoclassical Theory, Democratic Transitions, and African Reality

New or transitional democracies confront particularly serious difficulties in any attempt at economic stabilization and/or structural adjustment. They must deal with greatly increased political mobilization, which often feeds on long-repressed tensions, demands, and expectations. These usually relate to lingering conflicts over the character of political structure, control over the instruments of power, the distribution of resources, the legacy of the outgoing authoritarian regime, and the effects of socioeconomic crisis and any attempts to deal with it. For countries such as Ghana and Nigeria, whose authoritarian governments engaged vigorously in economic reform, many of the tensions released by political mobilization were themselves the direct result of the hardships of reform.

The advent of a new democratic regime usually generates very high expectations about positive change, especially strong distributional ones. New democratic leaders must worry about gaining and sustaining sufficient legitimacy and coalitional support to stay in power. Frequently, the short time horizon generated by such concerns is intensified by fears of the return of authoritarian domination. The predicament of the Hilla Limann government in Ghana in the late 1970s is a classic example. All of these pressures greatly constrain economic policy-making and implementation. Even when productive policies are announced, what actually transpires may be at great variance. As a result, "countries undergoing democratic transitions appear to pursue more expansionist policies than either established democracies or authoritarian governments," and the more difficult structural adjustment issues get delayed or set aside.[33]

The number of political parties, especially two-party versus multiparty systems, and the degree of political factionalism and fragmentation are central variables to any attempt to produce and sustain productive economic policies, particularly as they affect the ability of political elites to bargain and cooperate. In the search for legitimacy and coalitional support, the temptation to adopt populist rhetoric and political action is strong, as powerful symbols that can be used to mobilize major support for painful adjustment measures are hard to find. For countries whose authoritarian governments engaged in systematic reform before the transition, the continuity of economic policy-making is often broken as experienced people are replaced by new ones and pressure mounts to restructure policy institutions, particularly to make them more open to outside influences. This is a special problem for countries, such as African ones, which have a very thin layer of technocratic talent.

As indicated above, factors that facilitate economic policy-making and implementation can begin to overcome some of these problems in new democracies, at least for awhile. Widespread success is not to be expected, however. Factors that foster the creation or continuation of a delegation strategy are the most important ones. A strong legacy of repression, corruption, and economic mismanagement can provide a "honeymoon" period for a new democratic government to initiate economic reforms and legitimate them. Where previous authoritarian regimes were already engaging in serious economic restructuring, however, the costs of such efforts are often the legacy that comes under attack unless the benefits of the reforms are so clear cut and widespread that the incoming democratic administration is at least willing to admit to some economic learning (Chile under Patricio Aylwin, for example).

Mechanisms that control the degree and intensity of popular sector mobilization are particularly important. Where the popular sector includes distinct particularistic as well as class components, as in Africa, this is an especially difficult task. Compared to the rest of the world, in Africa the processes of state formation are still quite incipient. A number of analysts have pointed to the hope for forms of democratic corporatism to overcome these collective action dilemmas, as has existed in some West European countries.[34] Unfortunately for Africa, such structures emerge only very slowly and incrementally and are thus not likely to play a major role in the short to medium run required for current economic restructuring efforts. Whatever the difficulties, however, mechanisms for elite consultation remain a primary need. Many Latin American countries have experimented with social pacts, with quite uneven results, however.[35]

If these and other facilitating mechanisms remain weak, the need for strong and autonomous executive authority becomes even more important and calls for especially creative statecraft. All of these efforts are more difficult, but not impossible, at least for awhile, under conditions of low levels of overall development, highly personalized politics, pervasive corruption, permeable bureaucracies, and fragile democratic political cultures, as in Africa today.

Thus, a major contradiction between economic and political conditionality may indeed exist, one that the major Western governments and the international financial institutions either do not see or choose to ignore. The primary assumptions appear to be that economic structural adjustment and political liberalization are mutually reinforcing processes and that since authoritarian politics in large part caused the economic malaise, democratic politics can help change it. These may be incorrect assumptions, however. Evidence from the Third World over the last three decades, and now from the former Second World, does not support widespread optimism about the mutually reinforcing character of economic reform and political liberalization in a large number of cases.

The presumption of the mutually reinforcing character of political and economic reform in Africa and elsewhere relies on an extension of neoclassical economic logic, as follows: economic liberalization creates sustained growth, growth produces winners as well as losers, winners will organize to defend their new-found welfare and will create sociopolitical coalitions to support continued economic reform. This logic, however, does not appear to hold for Africa, even under authoritarian conditions, much less under democratic ones. As Herbst notes:

> African reality simply differs too radically from the assumptions of properly working governments or economies for the application of general precepts to be fruitful. Ironically, economic and public choice theories, which their proponents claim are completely opposed to the ideologically-driven rhetoric of socialists or free-marketeers, . . . cannot make a substantive contribution to the demarcation of the African state because these theories are . . . incapable of taking account of African realities. Only an eclectic mix of guidelines which are grounded in the realities of how the economy and the state actually work in Ghana and the rest of Africa will usefully suggest what the state should do for whom.[36]

Under these conditions, the consequences of simultaneous economic and political liberalization, based on faulty assumptions about cause and effect, could be very serious.

The evidence from Africa in the 1980s indicates that successful economic reform requires a quite rare conjuncture of factors, such as those that existed in Ghana after 1983. Ghana under Rawlings demonstrates that successful and sustained economic reform is possible without the presence of an existing societal support coalition. There have been economic "winners" in Ghana, especially cocoa farmers and resident expatriate business people, but the former are difficult to organize specifically to support the economic reforms and the latter cannot form a viable element in a new support coalition under democratic conditions. Besides, private sector actors, domestic or foreign, are not uniformly supportive of full economic or political liberalization; they can be just as interventionist and particularistic as state actors. It depends on whether such intervention and particularistic discretion benefits them or not.

The winners of economic reform in Africa are few, appear only slowly over time, and are difficult to organize politically. The neoclassical political logic of reform is too mechanistic for the African context; there are real "transaction costs" to organizing winners, and not just infrastructural ones. Direct linkages between economic interest and political outcome are rare, thus making reliable theoretically based predictions about the emergence of coalitional support extremely difficult. Farmers, for example, have other interests, political loyalties, and histories of organization that make direct political organization in support of a given set of economic policies difficult. Other organizational bases of political solidarity exist—ethnic, regional, religious, linguistic, and patron-client, which make mobilization around policy-specific economic interests difficult in much of Africa. Speaking of Ghana, for example, Herbst points out that:

> rural dwellers are the obvious constituency for the PNDC regime because so much of the structural adjustment program is devoted to promoting agriculture. However . . . the high proportion of Ewes in the national leadership has made it particularly difficult for the PNDC to establish support in the Ashanti Region, despite the fact that cocoa farmers there have clearly benefited from the regime's policies.[37]

Even where they might so organize, it would not likely be to support the full range of economic measures, thereby threatening the viability of reform.

Some have argued that Africa does not have a democratic tradition, but it does have one. It was just brief, vivid, and a failure, and the reasons for its demise have not disappeared.[38] The periodic reemergence of democratic regimes in Ghana and Nigeria over the last two decades indicates that old patterns of political organization reappear with quite amazing vigor under conditions of free political association.[39] As political transitions reached the final stage in both countries in 1992 this point was demonstrated yet again. For many countries, national unity, a factor analysts have asserted to be a basic prerequisite for viable democracy, is also still very tenuous.[40] Political liberalization is not likely to guarantee the appearance of new political alignments that favor sustained economic reform. Other issues may be more important, such as the definition of the state and nation or the shape of the political order. Besides, no strong evidence exists that African politics has shifted from distributional to productionist logics and forms of behavior.

Political openness without coalitions supporting a production-oriented rather than a distribution- or welfare-oriented political economy will simply make matters worse. It might end existing reform efforts and make new ones hard to initiate. Openness might simply empower old political and economic logics that have dominated African life since independence. More so than in any other region of the world, the political dilemma of structural adjustment in Africa is that no supporting societal coalition is even on the horizon. Neoorthodox economic reform in Africa is very unpopular because its political, social, and distributional effects are quite negative even in the medium run. Economic learning by political leaders and societal groups is possible, as Chile demonstrates, but it is usually a fragile creature, requiring special circumstances to survive, and can be easily upset. Renewed democratic politics on a diminished and still shrinking production base might be even more difficult to sustain than in the 1960s, making such learning very difficult indeed.

It is important to stress yet again that authoritarian regimes cannot guarantee economic reform or even produce it very often. Nor is this to say that economic reform under democratic conditions is impossible; it is just very difficult. There is evidence that economic reform can take place in existing democracies, such as Costa Rica and Jamaica, at least for awhile. In Costa Rica, however, there was much more economic stabilization than structural adjustment, and it is a long established democracy. In Jamaica under Edward Seaga very particular institutions and circumstances existed which reinforced executive autonomy and fragmented the opposition, but again progress was only temporary.[41] That military regimes already engaging in successful economic reform can become democratic is demonstrated by Turkey under Ozal and Chile under Aylwin, but again institutions and circumstances that reinforce executive autonomy, continuity in delegation, and controlled opposition appear essential. In Turkey, however, hard fought economic progress was once again being weakened in 1992 by democratic political logics.[42]

Political Structure, Sequence, and Economic Reform: Three Cases

In order to more fully explore these points, we will examine three cases—Ghana under Rawlings, Nigeria under Ibrahim Babangida, and Senegal under Abdou Diouf. These three cases range across a continuum from an authoritarian regime that made real economic progress before initiating political liberalization (Ghana) to an authoritarian regime that attempted economic reform while simultaneously carrying out a protracted, highly structured, and multistaged political liberalization process (Nigeria) to a regime that attempted economic reform after important democratization had been achieved (Senegal).

Ghana

In late 1981, Flight Lieutenant Jerry Rawlings, a young populist military officer, staged his second successful coup d'état in Ghana and promised to make dramatic changes.[43] He did so in the context of a low level of socioeconomic development, serious economic decline over a 20-year period—approaching collapse, in fact—and cycles of ineffective change between democratic and authoritarian regimes. After trying radical populist mobilization techniques with only modest results, he and his advisors realized that something different had to be attempted. When asked for major help, the Soviet Union suggested the Ghanaians turn to the IMF and the World Bank. Given their desperate need for foreign exchange, the new Ghanaian leaders felt they had little choice but to do so.

As a result, the IMF and the World Bank jointly played the major formulation role for Ghana's economic reform effort, but did so in conjunction with a small but capable and stable economic team which received strong and consistent support from Rawlings. He provided this support for IMF and World Bank-style economic liberalization while having almost no knowledge of economics of his own. After its initial diffuse legitimacy dissipated, the new regime, the Provisional National Defense Council (PNDC), found that it had almost no coalitional base in society for such a strategy. Thus a delegation strategy was based almost solely on the insulation provided by the military, which was itself not fully united as demonstrated by several countercoup attempts. By the early 1990s, however, the result was a remarkably sustained and successful economic recovery program, in fact, the only major African success story.

Despite the PNDC's political commitment to a delegation strategy of economic liberalization and its success, the Ghanaian case illustrates other tensions inherent in such an approach, even under authoritarian conditions. One of the strengths of the reform effort was the quite striking stability, quality, and unity of the senior officials involved in it. The small economic team was loosely but effectively organized, without being very institutionalized. But the pervasive administrative weakness of the Ghanaian state clearly limited the program. It affected policy formulation and, above all, implementation. Long-term government planning was almost nonexistent. Even basic data gathering and analysis capabilities and accounting skills were rudimentary. The most effective reform policies were those that did not involve direct administrative action on a continuous basis.

Despite these enormous constraints, the Ghanaian economic team learned quickly, and over time it was able to bargain effectively with the Fund and the Bank and obtain concessions. The Ghanaians often agreed with the principle, but bargained vigorously over scale, speed, and sequence, especially after major unrest in 1986. On a number of issues they formed a coalition with the Bank against the Fund and were able to carry the day, on the nature and workings of the foreign exchange auction, for example.

To compensate for the low level of stateness, the economic recovery program generated a real and quite visible resurgence of expatriate influence in Ghana—the near constant presence of IMF and World Bank personnel, visiting missions, hired consultants, and seconded bureaucrats and managers. The World Bank, for example, sent more than 40 missions to Ghana in 1987. The whole recovery effort was a high-conditionality process, and the Fund, the Bank, and the donor countries believed that expatriate personnel and their skills were necessary to ensure that external funds were used wisely. Without much of this expatriate work, the adjustment effort would not have progressed nearly so far, but a real political problem was created in the process. The often bitter resentment of the role of expatriates clearly identified the program with external actors, further intensifying opposition among key groups in Ghana.

These difficulties were also directly linked to Ghana's ability to absorb effectively newly increased amounts of external resources resulting from the sustained success of the reform program. The official side of the "implicit bargain" was fulfilled for Ghana, as bilateral and multilateral resource flows were relatively high. Given the needs in Eastern Europe, the former Soviet Union, and strategically more important parts of the Third World, it is not clear that such support can be provided to many African adjusters, however. On the other hand, the private half of the implicit bargain has been close to a complete failure, as direct foreign investment and voluntary international bank lending have been very weak in Ghana.

Given its rare conjuncture of factors, and despite the enormous difficulties linked to low levels of stateness and economic development, the Rawlings government managed to pursue successfully a delegation strategy of economic liberalization with an average annual growth rate of more than 5 percent after 1983. This is a remarkable achievement in the African context, especially given the extent of Ghana's decline. The predatory rent-seeking state of the first 25 years of independence was held at bay, at least for awhile. The military government successfully attacked many of the "easy" adjustment issues, but several particularly tough ones remain—effective privatization, parastatal reform, and a major restructuring of the financial and banking sector, for example—issues that restrict foreign investment and lending.

By the early 1990s, the primary dilemma was still that the impressive success had been achieved by the insulation provided by the military regime. The government continued to lack major coalitional support and the institutional bases to relink the delegation strategy to society in a way that might sustain the reform effort beyond the life of the military regime.

The continued fragility of this successful case was made apparent in 1990, one of the toughest years since the reform effort began in 1983. Growth dropped to about 3%, inflation increased from 25 to 37%, and the budget deficit ballooned due in part to a peacekeeping role in Liberia and the early fallout of the Gulf crisis. In addition, both cocoa production and revenue, the primary source of foreign exchange, were down. This was due in part to a 30% drop in cocoa consumption by the Soviet Union, which did not have the hard currency to pay for it. External support from donor countries and institutions continued at high levels, however.

At the same time, pressure for political liberalization grew substantially. As a result, after doggedly resisting such pressures for years, Rawlings announced political liberalization measures for 1992. A new constitution was approved overwhelmingly in April 1992, even though it protects the Rawlings regime from prosecution by future governments. The eleven-year-old ban on political parties was lifted the next month, and legislative and presidential elections were scheduled for late in the year. The opposition charged the government with stage managing the transition to protect the economic reforms and itself. In late September, Rawlings finally announced that he would run for president as the candidate of the National Democratic Congress. He won the early November presidential elections with about 60% of the vote over four challengers, although opposition parties contested the results. Much still rested, however, on the outcome of the early December parliamentary elections.

The primary fear was that even managed political liberalization would "hollow out" the hard-won economic changes, as it was far from clear that a social coalition supporting them existed yet. The uncertainty of the controlled political transition process bred some public caution by the new political parties in regard to the economic reforms. Nonetheless, resistance to the reforms still appeared to be strong, at least among urban groups. For example, Dr. Hilla Limann, the civilian president overthrown by Rawlings in 1981 and a presidential aspirant himself, attacked the reform program, especially devaluation, as a "terrible disaster" that the "dictatorship" of the IMF and the World Bank had imposed on Ghana in order to "stuff their own pockets." As one leading Ghanaian businessman noted in discussing the opposition parties, "Many of them seem unable to see the enormous changes that have taken place in the world. If they get it wrong again there will be no more chances for Ghana."[44] The makeup of the new parliament would be very important.

Rawlings and key members of his government remained hopeful, however. As Joseph Abbey, long a key member of the economic team, expressed it, "We are hoping that Ghanaians will have the political maturity to judge the programme not on their direct material benefits but on the solid foundations we have laid down for future economic take-off."[45] Rawlings himself believed that "the people have become a lot more defiant. You can't fool the people any more with sweet promises. Thank God for it. The politicians would be better talking about the reality of hardship ahead which faces us, instead of trying to con people."[46] But the new parties tended to reflect long-standing political attitudes and patterns in Ghana, many with roots in the 1960s, rather than new realities.

The opposition was stunned by Rawlings' victory in the November presidential elections. As a result, following intense debate, the anti-PNDC parties fatefully boycotted the December 29 parliamentary elections, allowing Rawlings's National Democratic Congress and two other small pro-government parties to control completely the new parliament.

After the elections, the opposition parties formed an Interparty Coordinating Committee and vowed to create an effective shadow cabinet. It will be difficult, however, for the opposition to contain the tensions between its conservative and Nkrumahist wings. Hence, the outcome of the presidential and parliamentary elections in Ghana was closer to a return to one-party rule than to multiparty democracy. The economic reform process was likely to continue, however. In this sense, Ghana may be following the Korea, Taiwan, and Chile[47] pattern of sequential vigorous economic reform followed by halting, incremental, but increasingly full political liberalization.[48] Such a propitious outcome appears far less likely in our next case, however.

Nigeria

The excesses of the Nigerian civilian democratic government of the Second Republic from 1979–83 had been spectacular, and the military government that replaced it made only minor progress on reform. In 1986 General Ibrahim Babangida's new military regime set in motion a neoorthodox delegation strategy for reforming the quite predatory and rent-seeking Nigerian political economy.[49] But because of intense domestic antipathy toward the IMF, the World Bank quietly played the central role in formulating the structural adjustment program. World Bank personnel worked directly with Nigerian officials in an interministerial committee established by the military regime. They also attempted to engage in extensive "policy dialogue" with influential members of the Nigerian elite. The resulting package was presented by General Babangida to his people as a "home-spun" indigenous solution. It was then quietly formalized as an IMF standby agreement, although Nigeria did not draw on the available funds. These were provided by the World Bank instead, again because of political sensitivities. Without its long-standing presence in Nigeria and the key background studies it had already conducted, the Bank would not have been able to play this extraordinary role.

Until the early 1990s this neoorthodox effort at economic reform was supported by a small, but capable and relatively stable economic team, increasingly centralized economic and repressive capabilities, strong political support and insulation by the military regime, and aggressive executive authority on the part of Babangida. Nigeria had greater levels of stateness and cosmopolitanism than the Rawlings military government in Ghana, but they were still weak by world standards.

The main dilemma of the Nigerian delegation strategy of economic adjustment was Babangida's promise to return Nigeria to two-party democracy, to a Third Republic, first by October 1992 then by January 1993. This difficulty arose precisely because, unlike Rawlings, he attempted from the beginning to carry a serious economic reform effort beyond his own regime by using political and institutional engineering during a simultaneous process of political liberalization. Well aware of the political logics that threaten efforts at economic reform, however, Babangida began to have second thoughts about how freely participatory these new democratic structures should be. He reneged, for example, on a promise to chose the two strongest political parties that emerged after the lifting of the ban on party activity as the two legal parties in the next regime. Instead he decided that the military government would create two parties which everybody would be "free" to join. His government chose the names and wrote the platforms of the two parties—the Social Democratic Party and the

National Republican Convention. Nonetheless, Babangida found it increasingly difficult to control fully the political liberalization process.

Despite decent early progress made by a skilled and dedicated economic team, the Nigerian reform effort became increasingly driven by the need for debt rescheduling rather than a commitment by the military to economic transformation. Well-rooted political logics proved very resistant to change, including those within the military itself. A vicious circle of reform became the dominant and debilitating pattern. Fiscal difficulties would increase the need for debt rescheduling; this could not take place without an IMF agreement, even if Nigeria did not draw funds from it; the Fund would demand specific policy changes; these would eventually produce unrest; in response the government would ease off the policy reforms; these policy "wobbles" of the vicious circle would led to the suspension of the IMF approval; new macroeconomic imbalances would be generated, which required new debt rescheduling and hence a new IMF agreement. . . . These policy wobbles became stronger and more frequent over the course of the late 1980s and early 1990s.

Nonetheless, beginning in late 1990, with the early steps of the political transition already well underway, the military government made yet another round of concessions and policy changes, leading to a new set of IMF, Paris Club, and London Club agreements by March 1991. With these new agreements, the Nigerians felt that they had slain the debt dragon, ending the vicious circle of adjustment and setting up the political transition with a manageable projected debt service ratio of under 25%. It was not to be. As with all things in Nigeria, the proof was in effective implementation—or rather the lack of it. The old political and rent-seeking political logics were far from dead. They surged back with renewed vigor, and the overall reform effort began to disintegrate. It also had become clear that no political or social coalition had emerged that was likely to support continued structural adjustment under democratic conditions.

Two primary examples of the unraveling process will be presented here: (1) the greatly expanded banking sector as the new functional equivalent of the old corrupt import licensing system, and (2) the political logics of the Gulf War foreign exchange windfall.[50]

Resurgent Logics I: the Banking Sector

Bank deregulation was one of the reform measures set in motion in 1986, but, as with changes in the exchange rate mechanism, the reform was only partial, allowing the powerful old political rent-seeking logics to surge back in the guise of positive change. The frantic search for foreign exchange simply moved from import licenses to bank licenses after the former were abolished. Bank licenses became as political and rent-seeking as import licenses had been. Bank deregulation and lax supervision (intentional and unintentional) allowed a wide variety of unproductive economic activities to flourish, including the subversion of the centerpiece of the reform effort—the foreign exchange auction as a market-based structure for determining the exchange rate and allocating foreign exchange.

In 1986 there were 41 licensed banks. By 1988 there were 66 banks; by 1990 107 banks existed. At the end of 1991 there were 120 banks "bidding" in the foreign exchange auction, and there were more than thirty pending applications when the licensing of new banks was finally suspended. The application and licensing processes were very political. Both the federal and state governments held substantial shares in many of these banks, and thus they had strong formal and informal ties to the government. Hence the structure and operation of these banks were also heavily politicized.

Under lax supervision, fraud, forgery, widespread corruption, political lending, and poor management, especially shoddy accounting, all flourished. The aim of the new banks was clearly quick profit, political deals, and access to foreign exchange. As one savvy external observer noted, "The banks continued to thrive against the background of rapid credit expansion and the wholly-artificial foreign exchange auction system in which all are winners." This multi-tiered mechanism, heavily managed and based on informal consultation, guaranteed access to foreign exchange for all banks. It allowed scores of them, large and small, to make major profits via arbitrage and "roundtripping" funds between the official auction and the more market-based rates of the parallel and, after September 1989, exchange bureau markets. The wider the gap between the rates the higher the profits, and the more managed the official rate, the higher the gap, usually further aggravated by poor fiscal and monetary policies. The World Bank estimated the effective rent for 1990 at about $500 million when the average spread was about 20%.

Under strong IMF pressure, the Nigerian government switched to the Dutch auction system in early 1991. But even this reform was perverted. After the middle of the year, because of informal discussion among the banks and with the government, all 120 "bidding" banks quoted the same buying rate. This assured that each bank met the "pod" price and thereby received foreign exchange based on a carefully negotiated distribution quota. By late 1991 the spread was more than 80%. Clearly the old political logics were resurgent in the face of reform.

Resurgent Logics II: Of Wobbles and Windfalls

In the first half of 1990, government spending was 33.7% above budget. Then came the Gulf crisis and an oil revenue windfall of about $5 billion from a 6% increase in production and an average 31% increase in price. An existing policy wobble was thus reinforced by a windfall. By early 1991 both spending and economic management were once again out of control. The normal vicious circle returned with an intensified vengeance: expansionary fiscal policy (both on and off budget), a surging budget deficit, substantial internal borrowing, an increase in the money supply, rising inflation, a growing exchange rate spread between the official and parallel/exchange bureau rates, and external concern and pressure. The government had projected a slight budget surplus for 1991. It was not to be.

In late June 1991, William Keeling, the resident *Financial Times* journalist in Lagos, reported that Western officials believed that about $3 billion of the windfall was unaccounted for and that much of it was being spent unwisely. The Nigerian government expelled him, charging "a deliberate attempt to mislead the public, including Nigeria's development partners."[51] The IMF, the World Bank, and Nigeria's other creditors were indeed worried. As a result, in November 1991, the World Bank produced a confidential internal report entitled "Nigeria: Public Expenditure Management." It reached very damaging conclusions about Nigerian economic management, which was described as lacking "transparency and accountability." It vividly indicated the degree to which old political logics were resurgent. The report asserted that:

> Public expenditures are used more to distribute oil riches and generate lucrative business and employment opportunities for

> selected groups than to ensure efficient delivery of goods and services to the public at large. . . .
>
> [Pressures of the transition to civilian rule] led to a breakdown in fiscal and monetary discipline during 1990 . . . not only characterised by additional spending and monetary expansion, but also by a major surge in expenditures bypassing budgetary mechanisms of expenditure authorization and control . . . [52]

The massive on- and off-budget expenditure surges had many causes, but they focused on debt service, massive corruption and unusual spending within the military, resurgent political logics among major societal groups, efforts to dampen opposition to the economic reforms, and the political business cycle of the democratic transition. The windfall greatly increased spending expectations of major social groups, and state and local government expenditures were difficult to control, especially with the creation of nine new states. By the time newly elected civilian governors took office in late 1991 as the multistage transition process unfolded, many of the state treasuries were nearly empty and heavily debt-ridden.

Defense and internal security spending were nearly double projected levels, partly because of the military peacekeeping operation in Liberia, but also because of the purchase of 150 new Vickers tanks from Britain, twelve Czech jet fighters, and 300 new Peugeot sedans for military officers ("toys for the boys" as one analyst put it). Spending linked to the looming political transition included funding for the two new parties, several sets of elections, a national census, placating payments to banned "old breed" politicians, and expenditures for the maintenance of old patron-client networks and the creation of new ones, both inside and outside the military. Other groups wanted to take what they could before the transition arrived.

As the return to democratic rule came closer, the economic reform effort continued to fray, especially macroeconomic policy. The IMF finally refused to certify that Nigeria was performing adequately under the terms of its January 1991 fifteen-month standby agreement. This put in jeopardy Nigeria's right to reschedule its Paris Club debt again in early 1992.

In March 1992, the IMF forced the Nigerian government to terminate its foreign exchange auction and to effectively float its currency, the naira. The exchange rate fell from 10 to nearly 20 naira to the dollar. Major riots broke out in May; they were linked to the renewed sting of the economic reform measures, but complicated by ethnic, religious, regional, and political tensions generated by the political liberalization process. The economic reforms were very unpopular, and, as in Ghana, the opposition charged that the military regime was manipulating the transition process in order to protect the reforms and itself.

At the same time, Babangida found the political liberalization process increasingly difficult to control. For example, presidential primary elections were invalidated in August and then postponed twice because of massive vote fraud and intimidation. By late September 1992 the government still did not have a new agreement with the IMF. Then in mid October Babangida nullified the results of the latest attempt to conduct presidential primaries, dissolved the leadership of the two parties, and ordered their reorganization. Babangida subsequently announced that the political transition would be delayed until August 27, 1993, the eighth anniversary of his coup d'état, and that the military was turning the day-to-day administration of the government over to a civilian Transitional Council as of January 1, 1993. Presidential elections would now be held in June 1993, and by late February there were more than 300 declared candidates ready to engage in a new, complex, and multistaged primary process. The Transitional Council was headed by a respected businessperson, Chief Ernest Shonekan, who surrounded himself with competent technocrats. Babangida made it clear that the primary aim of the Transitional Council was to relaunch the economic reform program, noting that it would be a rare feat to make a successful transition to democracy with a declining economy. Chief Shonekan faced strong opposition from both military and civilian groups, however, and was not likely to succeed. By early March 1993 Nigeria was still without a new agreememt with the IMF, and one would not come easily or quickly.

Despite these troubles, the Babangida government vowed to continue with the transition and return the country to civilian rule. Unlike Ghana, however, the economic reform effort in Nigeria was nearly dead *before* the actual transfer of power to a civilian democratic regime. Despite an auspicious beginning in 1986, the crippled economic reforms are likely to be "hollowed out" of real substance even more quickly in the Third Republic than under the Babangida military regime. Economic reform programs, whether imposed or voluntary, are rarely ever repudiated or terminated formally by governments because they are so dependent on external resources. Most programs die unobtrusively, eaten out quietly from within, and the IMF is eventually forced to suspend them. If the Babangida economic reforms continue to be "hollowed out" in the Third Republic, Nigeria will then have achieved political liberalization without economic liberalization, an outcome similar to that of our last case—Senegal.

Senegal

In the postcolonial period, Senegal became a patrimonial administrative state built around clientelist networks of single-party politicians from the *Parti Socialiste* (PS) and of *marabouts* from Islamic brotherhoods.[53] The material base of this political structure was a very fragile economy with a weak and inefficient manufacturing sector and a declining groundnut agricultural sector. In the late 1970s, President Léopold Senghor started a halting process of democratization as an economic crisis deepened under the weight of the old clientelist politics and the collapse of peanut and phosphate commodity booms. At the same time, Senghor's longtime prime minister, Abdou Diouf, began to assemble a group of fellow technocrats who would be able to attack the economic crisis.

When Senghor decided to retire from politics, Diouf became president in January 1981. As part of a political logic to ensure the survival of the regime, Diouf accelerated the process of democratization. The result was twelve political parties, only one of which posed a potential threat—the *Parti Démocratique Sénégalais* (PDS) of Abdoulaye Wade. The process of democratization also led to an explosion of associational life including the creation of new and autonomous unions and business and civic associations.

Diouf took power with the obvious intention of engaging in serious economic reform, something he made very clear through the use of slogans such as *"moins d'Etat, mieux d'Etat."* Over the course of the 1970s he had come to understand the serious nature of Senegal's economic problems. In conjunction with his deepening of the democratization process, this willingness to attack the economic problems increased Diouf's legitimacy, which was reinforced by his technocratic image. A *"débat sur la technicité"* further underscored the political credibility of the reform intention, at least for awhile.

President Diouf either benefited from or created many of the conditions discussed earlier in the chapter that can facilitate serious economic reform, even under democratic conditions. He assembled a very strong team of experienced technocrats and provided it with strong backing. The new economic team also had the confidence of the IMF, the World Bank, and the major donor countries. In order to further strengthen the technocrats, Diouf set out to weaken the old "barons" of the PS, a process he felt would be facilitated by democratization.

Diouf likewise moved to increase the powers of the presidency by eliminating the post of prime minister, restricting the powers of the National Assembly, and removing old barons from sensitive positions in the government and replacing them with people with more technocratic qualifications. The President launched administrative reforms aimed at enhancing data collection and analysis capabilities and policy coordination, including the creation of policy analysis cells in key ministries. With external help, several interministerial committees were created. Above all, the *Comité de Suivi du Programme d'Ajustement Structurel* (CPSA) was formed to provide overall coordination of the economic reform effort. It was to be insulated from countervailing pressures from the rest of the state administration and the party barons and was to work closely with the international financial institutions (IFIs).

In addition, Diouf's economic reform effort received substantial external support, with assistance growing at 18% a year over the 1980–87 period. This made Senegal the leading per capita recipient of aid in Africa. These external resource flows did increase the debt burden, but it was partially offset by repeated Paris Club reschedulings and some debt forgiveness.

Finally, Diouf benefited from an early political honeymoon, especially from urban groups, because of his acceleration of the democratization process. This was reinforced by a very strong mandate derived from the 1983 presidential elections. Thus, Diouf's effort seemed to start under very propitious conditions with a leader who understood the economic crisis and had both the legitimacy and the mandate to attack it, a fine and insulated team of technocrats, administrative reforms to enhance policy formulation and implementation, and external support and resources.

The reform effort had a rough start, however. The first plan for 1981–84 proved to be quite weak and was badly implemented. Above all the government was unable to control spending. Agreements with the IFIs were canceled and had to be renegotiated. The peak of the reform effort came in the 1985–87 period when it was led by Mamadou Toure who had worked for the IMF. It coincided with better rains and more favorable commodity prices and external demand. After 1987, however, the reform effort was quite systematically "hollowed out," such that by 1991 it could be characterized as having failed, leaving both the state and the economy weaker than they were in 1981.

The political weaknesses of the reform effort will be stressed here, but it is important to point out that it was also constrained by the inability to use devaluation because of Senegal's membership in the West African Franc Zone;[54] by policy design errors, especially in industrial policy and trade liberalization; by the country's extremely weak agricultural base; by the near collapse of the corrupt banking sector; and by a very weak overall supply response.

Agricultural policy was quite feeble and unevenly and incompletely implemented, particularly in response to pressure from the marabouts. Despite some new producer associations, farmers were never mobilized in support of the reform effort, underscoring the difficulty of organizing them. They usually found that their interests could be defended more effectively if they acquired particular policy exceptions and resources via their client ties to the marabouts. In short, dominant social and economic relations in the rural areas were essentially untouched.

The New Industrial Policy was also badly conceived and poorly implemented, especially a trade liberalization that was much too rapid. Compensating policies that were to mitigate the loss of protection were poorly formulated and only partially implemented, for reasons of politics and state capacity. A number of the old, mostly foreign, trading houses and light industrial firms simply went out of business; others survived only by obtaining protection and subsidies via old clientelist networks. The policy shift was compounded by the continuing overvaluation of the Communauté Financière Africaine (CFA) franc, which is pegged to the French franc. Deindustrialization loomed and as many as 20,000 jobs may have been lost. These changes had a devastating effect on state revenue levels, largely because of the emergence of new trader groups who flooded the country with cheaper foreign goods but were not forced to pay import taxes or other related fees on them.

In the 1970s, with the groundnut economy clearly declining, the marabouts of the Islamic brotherhoods, particularly the Mourides, sought to find a new economic base in order to reproduce their social order outside the rural agricultural economy. Moving into commercial trade and distribution was the most logical answer. It extended their reach into the urban areas while providing jobs for increasingly distressed rural followers. In order for it to succeed, however, it required at least de facto trade liberalization; with the complicity of the state and its agents, this began to happen in the 1970s. The process was accelerated by the formal trade liberalization of the 1980s and its devastating impact on the long-protected trading houses and light industry. The switch into trade was controlled largely by Mouride marabouts, who had long been a political pillar of the regime, and was first accomplished by smuggling via Gambia. With later changes, the Mourides, playing by old political rules, moved systematically into the urban areas. For example, the Sandaga market in Dakar, commonly referred to as the "Mouride market," became a quasi-"free trade area" or "tax haven" with increasing amounts of import fraud and nonpayment of import duties. Over time, this trade was increasingly run through the port of Dakar rather than Gambia.

This transformation amounted to what Catherine Boone has called a vast "informalization" of the import/distribution trade which benefits groups of state agents but greatly weakens the fiscal health of the state by depriving it of badly needed resources. The regime allowed it because of its political dependence on the marabouts, and this dependence was intensified by the democratization process. Permitting this process also helped the regime buffer the social costs of austerity by providing cheaper goods and jobs to the urban population while helping to integrate marginalized groups into a supportive social order. Thus, drawing on social and political changes already under way, trade liberalization had consequences hardly imagined by the IFIs. It certainly did not depoliticize trade, strengthen the fiscal basis of the state, or integrate the informal economy into a revitalized and expanding formal one. It did, on the other hand, help to solve major political problems by shoring up both the Mouride social order and the Diouf regime. The result was not economic reform, however; the old patrimonial administrative state and its politicized economy was only partly reconfigured, not transformed in a more productive direction.

As the 1988 elections approached, generalized opposition to the economic reforms intensified and diversified as their costs continued to mount. From the beginning very few members of the dominant political class in the state and the PS believed that the reforms would succeed. They certainly did not see any ready alternative to the declining groundnut economy or believe that Senegal could compete with manufacturing exports in the world economy. They did believe, however, that Senegal could muddle through with periodic commodity booms and donor assistance. Above all, they feared the high political costs of IFI-style economic reform. These views were reinforced by a long-standing distrust of the market that was so much a part of the decolonization process and by the overselling, by both Diouf and the IFIs, of the reforms, which created greatly unrealistic expectations. Given Diouf's strong support for such reform in the early 1980s, however, many of these people simply bided their time while quietly diverting the reforms from the most dangerous political shoals. As the costs mounted, however, they began to shift into more overt opposition.

Much of this same skepticism existed among major social groups as well, and opposition to the reforms was facilitated by the explosion of associational life that resulted from the democratization process. Reform of the labor code, for example, which was central to the compensating measures of the New Industrial Policy, was blunted by opposition from newly autonomous unions as well as the state corporatist labor federation—the *Confédération Nationale des Travailleurs Sénégalais* (CNTS) as it responded to pressures from the new unions. Strikes and demonstrations became commonplace and resulted in a largely successful effort to get the National Assembly to resist labor code reform creating a freer labor market. Student opposition also intensified greatly beginning in 1987. In the face of this opposition, the government eventually made very costly concessions, greatly aggravating the already serious fiscal health of the state. In April 1987, government concern was galvanized by a police strike. Although triggered by a professional dispute, it was aggravated by the general conditions of austerity and declining working conditions resulting from the reforms.

As the elections approached, Wade's PDS and other parties campaigned vigorously against the economic reforms, bringing preemptive government concessions such as lowering the price of rice. On the whole, however, the government did not see the opposition parties as a major threat because it continued to receive the support of the marabouts, support purchased via particularistic concessions in agricultural policy, and generalized support for the move into import trade and distribution. Diouf and the PS won the elections with more than 70% of the vote. They were followed by protests alleging vote fraud and challenging the economic reforms, leading to the declaration of a state of emergency.

A major blow to the government's confidence that it could control the effects of democratization came with a serious outbreak of social violence in April 1989. It emerged out of a complicated land dispute with Mauritania, but tapped long-standing tensions over the role of Mauritanians in the informal trading sector. The violence scared the government because it was fueled by marginalized groups beyond any of the normal control structures of the party, the unions, or the marabouts: discontent it feared could be organized by opposition political parties, and the new vigor of associational life. Unemployment became a major concern again, undercutting plans to cut the civil service, push privatization, pursue trade liberalization, and regulate informal trade. Some taxes were cut, wages raised, and the government began to harden its position to external demands. These events accelerated a move by the government to back off from the economic reforms; political logics were beginning to take precedence over economic ones.

In August 1989, for example, the government reintroduced some protective tariffs and retreated from other industrial reforms. This angered new traders who went on strike. These mostly Mouride interests were now represented by a new organization—the *Union Nationale des Commerçants et Industriels du Sénégal* (UNICOIS). The government attempted to engage in a delicate balancing act in the face of these contending forces. It pulled back from industrial reform and gave out particularistic concessions to individual businesses while it refused to control the new trading activities of the Mourides. Reconfiguration of older patterns, not economic transformation was the result, one that intensely frustrated the IFIs. As one World Bank official put it in 1991, "We are almost back to where we were in 1986."[55]

Diouf's new concern about controlling the political costs of democratization led him to view the PS in a new light; it was his only major instrument of social control beyond the alliance with the marabouts. An attempt to revitalize the party by a renewed attack on the barons failed, in large part because of the now very clear political and social costs of the economic reforms. With this route blocked, Diouf reversed course and sought to come to terms with the barons.

In addition, Diouf sought reconciliation with the opposition. In April 1991, he created a coalition government of national unity or *cohabitation* with Wade's PDS and another opposition party. He also recreated the position of prime minister and appointed Habid Thaim to fill it. Thaim had been prime minister from 1980 to 1983 and was known for his anti-reform views.

Even before the 1988 elections, Diouf had begun to diminish his support for the technocrats. The CSPA had made many enemies inside the state administration. Diouf allowed long-simmering bureaucratic tensions to undermine the technocrats and allowed disputes among them to go unresolved. In March 1988 Mamadou Toure and Chiek Hamidou Kane, the two key technocrats, left the government, and the next month the CSPA was moved into the presidency where it became far less insulated from countervailing meddling by the executive itself and by powerful political and social forces opposed to reform.

Thus, by the middle of 1991, as Ka and van de Walle put it, "economic reform had been dislodged from the top of President Diouf's agenda by the exigencies of Senegalese politics," the reforms had "succumbed to the changing political context." Diouf's "top priorities related to his own political needs rather than the needs of reform," and these needs were greatly magnified by the effects of democratization.[56] What had started out as a propitious attempt at economic reform under democratic conditions, one supported by committed leadership with a honeymoon period and an electoral mandate, capable and insulated technocrats, and external advice and resources, ended in failure, having been effectively "hollowed out" by the old political logics of the patrimonial administrative state. The process of democratization had been an early and quite temporary advantage for the economic reform effort. Ultimately, however, it became a major contributing factor to its failure.[57]

This conclusion has major implications for economic and political reform efforts now underway in the rest of the continent. This is particularly so for the one launched in late 1991 by Frederick Chiluba in Zambia after the electoral defeat of the authoritarian single-party regime of Kenneth Kaunda.[58] Even under the most propitious political and institutional conditions, serious and sustained economic reform under democratic conditions in Africa is not likely to take place in very many countries. In most places, limited reform for a limited period of time is the more probable outcome, before it is swamped by the host of political, social, attitudinal, capacity, and ecological constraints that are inherent in the continent's current conjuncture.

In Senegal, all the normal problems confronting economic reform in Africa—low overall level of development, thin state capabilities, weak supply response, flawed program design, and, above all, the persistence of old rent-seeking political logics—were further aggravated by the democratized political context that focused political calculations on the survival of the regime. This led to premature compromises with state and non-state groups alike. These compromises not only "hollowed out" the reform effort; they also seriously undermined the state itself, making it an even weaker vehicle for possible transformation. Senegal's unusually fragile ecological and agricultural base, with no ready primary product alternative, constituted an additional constraint.

Furthermore, this agricultural base was still controlled by a well-entrenched social formation desperately seeking a new way to reproduce itself. It picked the route of least resistance, a sort of crony commercial capitalism, one with negative consequences for the Senegalese state and the economic reforms, if not for the political elite.[59] Unlike Senegal, both Ghana and Nigeria have more viable resources bases and rural social formations that are less politically dominant in ways that rule out reform. As in Ghana and Nigeria, however, the Senegalese technocrats had no real coalitional support base in society from which to fight, and it is not at all clear that they could have created one even if they had tried assiduously. But unlike the Ghanaian economic team, the Senegalese one lost its one real domestic pillar of support—the chief executive. As we have seen, the Nigerian case is more mixed in this regard.

It would thus not be correct to say that democratization was the dominant or overriding reason for the failure of the economic reform effort in Senegal, but, given its effect when combined with all the other constraints, democratization was certainly a very important contributing reason. By accelerating the "hollowing out" process, it certainly intensified the degree to which Senegal is "hemmed in." This is a constraint Jerry Rawlings did not confront in Ghana until almost ten years into a quite, by African standards, effective reform effort; in fact, the reform efforts of the two countries covered roughly the same period of time, but had very different outcomes. In Nigeria, which started the democratization process during a less systematic economic reform effort, the negative effects came sooner than in Ghana, but later than in Senegal. In Senegal democracy survived, but economic reform died.[60] Ironically, although Diouf wanted "less state, better state," he got "less state, worse state," one much less capable of ever transforming the Senegalese political economy. In effect, major economic reform is likely to be out of the question for some time, although the ritual dances of the reform game with external actors will most likely continue because of Senegal's dependence on external resources and debt rescheduling.

Conclusion: Prospects for the Future

In a passionate discussion of "reactionary rhetoric," Albert Hirschman points to what he calls "the thesis of the perverse effect": the situation where "unwilling to argue directly against reform, opponents of progressive impulses in society have attempted to show instead that reformist measures will invariably have effects that are contrary to the ones intended."[61] Is the version of the "thesis of the perverse effect" presented here—that political liberalization might have a negative impact on the chances for desperately needed economic reform—likely to hold across the board for Africa? No, not necessarily. It is important to assess the cases in particular countries. Kenya, for example, might be a case where political liberalization could allow formerly powerful political actors who had to retreat into the private economy in order to survive under the Moi government to return to political influence without impeding continued economic reform, but it would have to be done carefully and without allowing the returning political forces again to dominate political and economic life so totally. It is also possible that the elite learning that has taken place in Tanzania might survive electoral scrutiny.[62]

It might be possible to facilitate economic reform under certain democratic conditions in two major ways: by careful and clever political "engineering" and "buffering." The first or "engineering" way is to shield key areas of policy from distributional and other political pressures by delegating them to autonomous institutions or processes, such as auctions for exchange rate fluctuations and central banks for certain types of macroeconomic policy. The second or "buffering" way is to attempt to link political and economic logics by selective, but balanced political amelioration of the costs of economic adjustment—what has been called "embedded liberalism" in the context of the Western industrial democracies.

In regard to the "engineering" method, Paul Collier identifies "agencies of restraint" as one type of democratic functional equivalent of insulation and delegation: "At the macroeconomic level the main function of agencies of restraint is to prevent public expenditure from out pacing public revenue . . . ; the typical business of such agencies is to say no to spending requests or to punish the politically well-connected for abuses of power." As he points out, "For such agencies to function effectively they must be protected from the pressures they are designed to hold in check. They must therefore be autonomous centers of power."[63] But there are attitudinal as well as institutional aspects to the creation and effective operation of agencies of restraint. For them to be most successful both aspects must be present.

The most common institutional example of an agency of restraint is the central bank. The most typical example is the German Bundesbank, although Chile was the first developing country to establish an effective one. As John Goodman observes:

> Creating an independent central bank can be seen as a way for governments to prevent themselves (and their successors) from pursuing overly expansionary policies. Central bank independence is thus considered a solution to what economists term the dynamic inconsistency of policy. Dynamic inconsistency refers to the inability of politicians to commit to and implement poli-

cies that may be best for the economy in the long run, but are politically harmful in the short run.[64]

This is the tension between political and economic logics discussed at the beginning of this chapter.

As part of the conditionality inherent in externally supported economic reform, the IMF and the World Bank can insist on the creation or strengthening of central banks. Such has been the case in a number of Third World countries: Nigeria and Zambia, for example.[65] In Zambia, the stautory authority of the Central Bank was greatly strengthened in 1992 and early 1993, and, as part of an effort to revise the Kaunda-era constitution, the Chiluba government was working on a constitutional formula to prevent overspending. In fact, however, we know very little about how to create viable institutions in contexts where other facilitating factors are absent. Most central banks in the Third World are weak because they lack autonomy and attitudinal support for generalized restraint.

Collier takes his argument one step further, however, by asserting that "both for fiscal rectitude and adherence to the law, democratic institutions can serve as powerful agencies of restraint because they can produce "informed domestic constituencies of restraint"[66] at the level of organized social groups and the mass electorate. Most of the evidence from Africa, the rest of the Third World, and now the former Second World does not support such an optimistic conclusion. In large part, this is because powerful populist and distributive political logics are at play and because much of the debate about the need for economic reform and what to do about it has been externalized, making the foreign actors, especially the IMF and the World Bank, the lightening rods of opposition to serious economic reform.

In most places, no serious domestic debate about restraint has taken place, and there are few organized social constituencies for such restraint. Indeed, the very political language and set of symbols through which such a debate could take place do not usually exist. Some learning about economic reform and the necessity of macroeconomic restraint has taken place, but the question becomes *who* has learned—technocrats, rulers, military officers, government officials, politicians, leaders of groups in "civil society," or the mass electorate?[67] So far the learning has mostly been at the technocratic level. Collier's "informed domestic constituencies of restraint" are not likely to emerge in very many places.

The second or "buffering" method of facilitating economic reform under democratic conditions is linked to the practice rather than the rhetoric of the Western industrial democracies. A striking thing about the Western vision of simultaneous economic and political liberalization is that it is not the accurate representation of Western economic and political realities that it is alleged to be. Western industrial democracies have been preaching the vision and doing something else all along, especially on the economic side. Contrary to popular assumption and official rhetoric, orthodox liberalism, especially its free-market core, has not been the dominant form of political economy in the industrial West since World War II. Instead, the dominant political economy has been a form of compromise called "embedded liberalism," which involves the use of quite extensive state power simultaneously in the interests of domestic political and social stability and well-being on the one hand and international economic adjustment on the other.[68]

At the international level, market forces have been permitted to move, if haltingly, toward comparative advantage and adjustment. Within industrial countries, state power has been employed to varying degrees to restructure the economy while minimizing and buffering the disruptive domestic political and social consequences of liberal economics at the international level as trade, finance, production, and technology have evolved. As a result, modified international economic liberalism and domestic political stability and prosperity via state intervention coexist in a strained and uneasy balance, mediated by the pressures of democratic politics. This is not the autonomous interplay of free markets and minimalist states.

The compromises of the postwar political economy are sometimes viewed as liberalism with lots of cheating. But the "cheating" (protectionism, for example) as a form of political buffering and economic adjustment is, in fact, an inherent and defining characteristic of the system. In other words, international economic liberalism is real, but "compromised" by being "embedded" in the political and economic realities of domestic state-society relations. International economic efficiency is not sacrificed to domestic political stability, nor vice versa; a modus vivendi is established through embedded liberalism by uniting the entanglements of domestic and international politics and economics.

Embedded liberalism is an inherently unstable equilibrium, based on a delicately balanced tension between state and market and between economic and political logics, which can easily tip into unbalanced and unproductive statism, a form of malign mercantilism, on the one hand or the instabilities of unbridled market forces on the other. Maintaining this balanced tension, and getting economic and political logics to reinforce rather than contradict each other, requires special state capabilities, sophisticated statecraft, and considerable resources.

The compromise of embedded liberalism has not been extended by the major powers to the Third World since the onslaught of the debt crisis in 1982 or now, with the collapse of communism, to the former Second World. It is likely that the need to extend it may be learned most easily for Eastern Europe and the former Soviet Union because central, and threatening, interests are at stake. Until now developed countries have attempted to force Third and Second World countries to adjust to full orthodox liberalism without embedding it in the realities of their domestic state-society relations. Embedded liberalism is not likely to be extended to the Third World, especially Africa, because of its combined economic and strategic marginalization and the lack of sufficient Western resources. This lack of resources results from the fact that in the 1980s the embedded liberal compromise started to come under increasing strain in the West itself, largely for fiscal reasons.

Without the effective implementation of these "engineering" and "buffering" processes, simultaneous economic and political liberalization is not likely to be successful. As recent Western experience indicates, this is difficult to achieve because the two methods are partially contradictory and therefore hard to balance. Thus, a probabilistic rather than a deterministic perverse effect is likely to operate in Africa. As Hirschman himself finally admits, "there is no denying, to be sure, that the perverse effect does show up here and there. . . . I have merely intended to raise some doubts about whether it occurs with the frequency that is claimed."[69] If not handled properly, political liberalization might well impede rather than facilitate the productive relinking of Africa to the world economy that the continent so desperately needs.

Given the enormous constraints discussed here, what are the prospects that African countries will engage successfully in economic reform and establish more effective linkages to the world economy? The answer appears to be that simultaneous marginalization and dependence are likely to continue, and probably increase, for most countries. A few, with hard work, propitious facilitating circumstances, and luck, may begin to lessen their marginalization and dependence. Differentiation among African states, already long evident, may well increase. A few will stay in the Third World and do relatively better economically, while many will continue to descend into the Fourth and Fifth Worlds—fulfilling the Economic Commission for Africa's own "nightmare scenario."[70]

In regard to the relationship between economic and political liberalization, one analyst concludes that: "any justification of non-democratic regimes that relies on their developmental capacities is, at best, weak."[71] Yes, effective authoritarian regimes are quite rare, but, in regard to the ability to carry out badly needed economic reform, especially in a region like Africa, the following holds even more so: any justification of democratic regimes that relies on their developmental capabilities is, at best, weak. This dilemma underscores just how "hemmed in" Africa really is. Assertions by external actors to the effect that economic liberalization requires political liberalization ring more than a little hollow.

As the evidence presented here suggests, it is possible in some cases that political and economic liberalization can positively coexist in transitional democracies, at least for awhile, but it requires a difficult, rare, and fragile conjuncture of factors. The probabilistic perverse effect holds—it is possible, but not probable in many cases or for very long. Are we thus to ignore the pessimism of the historical record of the last three decades in the Third World and put our faith in the theoretical vision of widespread democratic functional equivalents in a large number of cases? Ignore the historical pessimism and opt only for policy optimism? It all boils down to how much stock, or hope, we put in democratic functional equivalents of authoritarian delegation and where we place our normative bets. One could argue that African countries are so unlikely to become Koreas, Chiles, or Turkeys that why not ignore the analytic conclusions and go with our instincts? In fact, this seems to be what is happening. But if we place our bets on the side of democratization as a valued end in itself, we need to do so with our analytic eyes and pocketbooks wide open and our expectations well in check.

If Western actors are to go ahead and encourage political liberalization as an explicit policy, they should at least do it with some of the democratic functional equivalents of a delegation strategy firmly in mind, to specifically foster them. This would require a clear recognition of the constraints facing leaders of transitional democracies, a strong willingness to allow more gradual economic liberalization accompanied by increased policy experimentation drawing on the structural adjustment lessons of the 1980s, and an intention to commit substantially increased resources, including major debt relief.

Above all, external actors should avoid the "faults of analytic and policy hurry" and not create undue expectations about what can be achieved in Africa over the medium run. Given the enormous obstacles confronting African countries, overly optimistic expectations can be very dangerous. Slow, steady, consistent progress is far preferable; there are no shortcuts after all. Change is incremental, uneven, often contradictory, and dependent on the outcome of unpredictable socioeconomic and political struggles. Policy-makers, both international and African, can try to bring about important changes, but they need to retain a sense of the historical complexity involved. Today's policy fads can easily become tomorrow's failed initiatives. External actors need to work closely with Africans to find ways to implement effectively the lessons learned from the experience with structural adjustment in the 1980s, lessons apparent in the World Bank's long-term perspective study. If not, "adjustment with a human face," "capacity building," "governance," and "democratization" will just become the latest in international passing fancies. To rely solely on the hope that democratic functional equivalents might just magically appear is a quite sizeable leap of faith. Indeed, both Africans and external actors face difficult and cruel choices.

If simultaneous economic and political liberalization is not likely, is democracy possible in many countries in Africa without major reform and a solid economic base? Evidence from the rest of the world is not encouraging. Africans may well use democratic structures to choose not to engage in economic restructuring, but they will then have to live with the consequences of that choice until accelerated decline and sufficient learning turns policy around. By then, however, it might well be too late to recover economically, leaving the continent marginalized or hemmed in beyond salvation. A cruel choice indeed.

More than thirty years of independence have shown that there are no panaceas, authoritarian or democratic, conservative or revolutionary, but at the same time, that it does matter what rulers and their subjects do and how they do it. The experience of nineteenth-century Latin America indicates that the nature of patrimonial administrative states changes only very slowly and incrementally. Structural and contextual constraints to action are real and set serious limits to political action, but they do not unilaterally determine it. Expectations of swift and dramatic change are likely to be dashed; new cycles of authoritarian rule are likely. There is little prospect for what Richard Sklar has called "developmental democracy." The harsh realities of African politics over thirty years make his vision of "a democracy without tears" appear strikingly utopian.[72] What "Africa needs" may well not be what it is likely to get. Modest expectations about democracy are required. Like Tocqueville, it is important to bring to democracy neither the enthusiasm of those who expect from it a transfiguration of the human lot nor the hostility of those who see in it no less than the very decomposition of human society. Democracy is risky after all and often lacks brilliance and grandeur . . . [73] The day-to-day politics of African patrimonial administrative states makes the effective translation of political vision into reality very difficult, but not necessarily impossible.

Notes

1. Laurence Whitehead, "Economic Liberalization and the Consolidation of Democracy in Latin America: Mutually Reinforcing or Potentially Conflicting Processes?" paper prepared for the Inter-American Dialogue workshop on Political and Economic Liberalization, June 1990, p. 1.

2. Atul Kohli, "Democracy and Development" in John P. Lewis and Valeriana Kallab, eds., *Development Strategies Reconsidered* (New Brunswick, N.J.: Transaction Books, 1986), p. 164; as examples he cites Charles E. Lindblom, Samuel Huntington, Barrington Moore, Jr., Seymour Martin Lipset, and T. H. Marshall; also see Robert Dahl, *Polyarchy* (New Haven: Yale University Press, 1971).

3. See Kenneth A. Bollen and Robert W. Jackman, "Economic and Non-Economic Determinants of Political Democracy in the 1960s," *Research in Political Sociology*, vol 1 (Greenwich, CT: JAI Press, 1985); Dietrich Rueschemeyer, Evelyne Huber Stephens, and John D. Stephens, *Capitalist Development and Democracy* (Chicago: University of Chicago Press, 1992), pp. 12–39.

4. Kohli, "Democracy and Development," p. 156.

5. Ibid., pp. 159, 156.

6. Ibid., pp. 159–160.

7. Stephan Haggard and Robert R. Kaufman, "Economic Adjustment in New Democracies" in Joan M. Nelson et al., *Fragile Coalitions: The Politics of Economic Adjustment* (New Brunswick, N.J.: Transaction Books, 1989), p. 58.

8. Ibid., pp. 62, 64.

9. Stephan Haggard, *Pathways from the Periphery* (Ithaca: Cornell University Press, 1990), pp. 265, 256.

10. Ibid., p. 264, emphasis added.

11. Ibid., pp. 256, 267, emphases added.

12. Ralph Austen, *African Economic History* (London: James Currey, 1987), pp. 102, 109.

13. For data on marginalization, see Thomas M. Callaghy, "Africa and the World Economy: Caught Between a Rock and a Hard Place" in John W. Harbeson and Donald Rothchild, eds. *Africa in World Politics* (Boulder: Lynne Rienner, 1991), pp. 39–68; and the Ravenhill and Green articles (chapters 1 and 2) in this volume.

14. B. A. Kiplagat quoted in "Africa Fears Its Needs Will Become Secondary," *New York Times*, December 26, 1989.

15. See Gerald Bender, James S. Coleman, and Richard Sklar, eds., *African Crisis Areas and U.S. Foreign Policy* (Berkeley: University of California Press, 1985).

16. On Africa's debt problems, see Tony Killick and Matthew Martin, "African Debt: The Search for Solutions," United Nations Africa Recovery Programme Briefing Paper No. 1, New York, June 1989; Charles Humphreys and John Underwood, "The External Debt Difficulties of Low-Income Africa," in Ishrat Husain and Ishac Diwan, eds., *Dealing with the Debt Crisis* (Washington, D.C.: World Bank, 1989); Thomas M. Callaghy, "Debt and Structural Adjustment in Africa: Realities and Possibilities," *Issue*, 16, 2 (1988): 11–18; and Trevor W. Parfitt and Stephen P. Riley, eds., *The African Debt Crisis* (London: Routledge, 1989).

17. On conditionality, see the Gordon article (chapter 3) in this volume.

18. Quoted in "Ghana: High Stakes Gamble," *Africa News*, 31, 2 (January 23, 1989): 10.

19. On the African postcolonial syndrome, see Thomas M. Callaghy, "Lost Between State and Market: The Politics of Economic Adjustment in Ghana, Zambia, and Nigeria" in Joan M. Nelson, ed., *Economic Crisis and Policy Choice* (Princeton: Princeton University Press, 1990), pp. 257–262.

20. Much of the comparative evidence comes from the results of a multi-year, six-person research project in which I participated. It was entitled "The

Politics of Economic Stabilization and Structural Change in Developing Nations" and was funded jointly by the Ford and Rockefeller Foundations. The project produced three books: Nelson, *Economic Crisis and Policy Choice*; Nelson, *Fragile Coalitions*; and Stephan Haggard and Robert Kaufman, eds., *The Politics of Economic Adjustment* (Princeton: Princeton University Press, 1992). Also see Thomas M. Callaghy, "Vision and Politics in the Transformation of the Global Political Economy: Lessons from the Second and Third Worlds" in Robert O. Slater, Barry M. Schutz, and Steven R. Dorr, eds., *Global Transformation and the Third World* (Boulder: Lynne Rienner, 1993). On Bolivia, see James M. Malloy, "Democracy, Economic Crisis and the Problem of Governance: The Case of Bolivia," typed manuscript, August 1989, pp. 29–30, and Catherine M. Conaghan, James M. Malloy, and Luis A. Abugatta, "Business and the 'Boys': The Politics of Neoliberalism in the Central Andes," *Latin American Research Review* 25, 2 (1990): 3–30.

21. Peter B. Evans, "The State as Problem and Solution: Predation, Embedded Autonomy, and Structural Change" in Haggard and Kaufman, *Politics of Economic Adjustment*, pp. 139–181.

22. On Zambia, see Callaghy, "Lost Between State and Market," pp. 268–69, 286–303.

23. See the Gordon and Martin articles (chapters 3 and 4) in this volume.

24. Letter of invitation dated July 10, 1990 from the staff of *Politique Africaine* to an October 1990 conference in Bordeaux.

25. See the Green article (chapter 2) in this volume.

26. World Bank, *Adjustment Lending: An Evaluation of Ten Years of Experience* (Washington, D.C.: World Bank, 1988), p. 3, emphasis added.

27. See Thomas M. Callaghy, "The State and the Development of Capitalism in Africa" in Donald Rothchild and Naomi Chazan, eds., *Precarious Balance: State and Society in Africa* (Boulder: Westview Press, 1988), pp. 67–99.

28. World Bank, *Sub-Saharan Africa: From Crisis to Sustainable Growth* (Washington, D.C.: World Bank, 1989); also see Deborah Brautigam, "Governance and Economy: A Review," Working Paper, Policy and Review Department, World Bank, Washington, D.C., December 1991.

29. World Bank, *From Crisis to Sustainable Growth*, pp. 192, 6.

30. See the Chazan and Rothchild article (chapter 5) in this volume. Also see Goran Hyden and Michael Bratton, *Governance and Politics in Africa* (Boulder: Lynne Rienner, 1992); Larry Diamond, Juan J. Linz, and Seymour Martin Lipset, eds., *Democracy in Developing Countries: Africa* (Boulder: Lynne Rienner, 1988); Michael Bratton and Nicolas van de Walle, "Popular Protest and Political Reform in Africa," *Comparative Politics* 24, 4 (July 1992): 419–22, and "Regime Type and Political Transition in Africa," paper for the Annual Meeting of the American Political Science Assoication, Chicago, September 3–6, 1992; Peter M. Lewis, "Political Transition and the Dilemma of Civil Society in Africa," *Journal of International Affairs* 46, 1 (Summer 1992): 31–54; John Healey and Mark Robinson, *Democracy, Governance and Economic Policy: Sub-Saharan Africa in Comparative Perspective* (London: Overseas Development Institute, 1992).

31. Barber B. Conable, "Address As Prepared for Delivery to the Bretton

Woods Conference on Africa's Finance and Development Crisis," Washington, D.C., April 25, 1990, World Bank, typed manuscript, pp. 2–3.

32. Director of the U.S. Agency for International Development, "Realizing Africa's Dream," speech to a conference in the Netherlands, July 4, 1990, typescript, p. 2.

33. Haggard and Kaufman, "Economic Adjustment," p. 61.

34. Haggard, *Pathways*, p. 267; Joan M. Nelson, "The Politics of Adjustment in Small Democracies: Costa Rica, the Dominican Republic, and Jamaica" in Nelson, *Economic Crisis and Policy Choice*, pp. 211–213; see Peter J. Katzenstein, *Small States in World Markets: Industrial Policy in Europe* (Ithaca: Cornell University Press, 1985).

35. See, for example, Terry Lynn Karl, "Dilemmas of Democratization in Latin America," *Comparative Politics* 23, 1 (October 1990): 1–21.

36. Jeffrey Herbst, "The Economic Frontiers of the State in Africa," typed manuscript, 1990, p. 26.

37. Herbst, "Labor in Ghana," pp. 24–25.

38. For the classic assessment of this period, see Aristide R. Zolberg, "The Structure of Political Conflict in the New States of Tropical Africa," *American Political Science Review* 62, 1 (March 1968): 70–87.

39. See, for example, Naomi Chazan, *An Anatomy of Ghanaian Politics* (Boulder: Westview Press, 1983); Richard Joseph, "The Overthrow of Nigeria's Second Republic," *Current History* (March 1984); Larry Diamond, "Nigeria in Search of Democracy," *Foreign Affairs* 62, 4 (Spring 1984).

40. See Robert H. Jackson and Carl G. Rosberg, Jr., "Why Africa's Weak States Persist: The Empirical and the Juridical in Statehood," *Comparative Politics* 35, 1 (October 1982): 1–24; Robert H. Jackson, *Quasi-States: Sovereignty, International Relations and the Third World* (New York: Cambridge University Press, 1990).

41. See Nelson, "The Politics of Adjustment in Small Democracies."

42. On Turkey and Chile, see Callaghy, "Vision and Politics." On Chile, also see Barbara Stallings, "Politics and Economic Crisis: A Comparative Study of Chile, Peru, and Colombia" in Nelson, ed., *Economic Crisis and Political Choice*, pp. 113–67, and "The Political Economy of Democratic Transition: Chile in the 1980s" in Barbara Stallings and Robert Kaufman, eds., *Debt and Democracy in Latin America* (Boulder: Westview Press, 1989), pp. 181–99; Pamela Constable and Arturo Valenzuela, *A Nation of Enemies: Chile Under Pinochet* (New York: Norton, 1991); Carol Graham, "Democracy, Economic Reform, and Civil Society in Chile: The Merging of Democratic and Authoritarian Traditions," paper for the conference on "Economy, Society, and Democracy," Washington, D.C., May 1992. On Turkey, also see George Kopits, *Structural Reform, Stabilization, and Growth in Turkey* (Washington, D.C.: IMF, 1987); Ziya Onis, "Redemocratization and Economic Liberalization in Turkey: The Limits of State Autonomy," typed manuscript, n.d.; Ziya Onis and Steven B. Webb, "The Political Economy of Policy Reform in Turkey in the 1980s," paper for the conference on "The Political Economy of Structural Adjustment in New Democracies," Washington, D.C., May 1992; John Waterbury, "The Export-Led Growth and the Center-Right Coalition in Turkey,"

Comparative Politics 24, 2 (January 1992): 127–145; Ergun Ozbudan, "Turkey: Crises, Interruptions, and Reequilibrations" in Larry Diamond, Juan J. Linz, and Seymour Martin Lipset, eds., *Democracy in Developing Countries: Asia* (Boulder: Lynne Rienner, 1989), pp. 187–230.

43. Since the Ghanaian case is also discussed in the chapter by Matthew Martin, the treatment here will be relatively brief. Also see Callaghy, "Lost Between State and Market"; Donald Rothchild, ed., *Ghana: The Political Economy of Recovery* (Boulder: Lynne Rienner, 1991); Jeffrey Herbst, *The Politics of Economic Reform in Ghana* (Berkeley: University of California Press, 1993); and Matthew Martin, *The Crumbling Facade of African Debt Negotiations: No Winners* (London: Macmillan, 1991).

44. Both quotations are from Julian Ozanne, "Ghana's Tough Economic Reforms Face the Ballot Box Test," *Financial Times*, August 14, 1992.

45. Ibid.

46. Quoted in Julian Ozanne, "The Riddle of the Chairman," *Financial Times*, August 17, 1992.

47. See Callaghy, "Vision and Politics."

48. As Michael Lofchie notes in his chapter, the impressive economic changes in Tanzania have yet to be tested electorally.

49. On the Nigerian reform efforts, see Callaghy, "Lost Between State and Market," and "Democracy and the Political Economy of Restraint and Reform in Nigeria," paper for the conference on "Economy, Society and Democracy," Washington, D.C., May 1992; Adebayo Olukoshi, ed., *Crisis and Adjustment in the Nigerian Economy* (Lagos: JAB Publishers, 1991); and Jeffrey Herbst and Adebayo Olukoshi, "Nigeria," draft manuscript for the Project on the Political Economy of Structural Adjustment in New Democracies, 1992. On Nigeria's older political logics, see Richard A. Joseph, *Democracy and Prebendalism in Nigeria* (New York: Cambridge University Press, 1987); Larry Diamond, *Class, Ethnicity and Democracy in Nigeria* (Syracuse: Syracuse University Press, 1988); Thomas J. Biersteker, *Multinationals, the State, and Control of the Nigerian Economy* (Princeton: Princeton University Press, 1987); Sayre Schatz, *Nigerian Capitalism* (Berkeley: University of California Press, 1977), and "Pirate Capitalism and the Inert Economy of Nigeria," *Journal of Modern African Studies*, 22, 1 (March 1984): 45–58; Douglas Rimmer, "The Overvalued Exchange Currency and Over-Administered Economy of Nigeria," *African Affairs*, 84, 336 (July 1985): 435–446.

50. The next two sections are based on confidential interviews in Washington, D.C., August 1990, March 1992, and in Lagos, January 1991; discussions with a former student who became the head of a state bank; and press reports from *Financial Times, West Africa, African Business, Newswatch*, and *Africa Report* covering August 1990 to March 1992.

51. *Financial Times*, July 1, 1991.

52. These quotations from the report come from *Financial Times*, March 16, 1992, pp. 1, 18; and *Financial Times Survey*, "Nigeria," March 16, 1992, pp. i, xiv; the discussion here is based on these and *Financial Times*, June 27, 1991; July 1,4 and 10, 1991; August 14, 1991. William Keeling clearly based his reporting in June and July 1991 on work that went into this very damaging

report, and his findings are confirmed by confidential interviews I conducted in Lagos in January 1991while the data for the report was being collected.

53. This section draws on two particularly fine papers: Samba Ka and Nicolas van de Walle, "The Political Economy of Adjustment in Senegal, 1980–91," paper for the World Bank Project on the Political Economy of Structural Adjustment in New Democracies, directed by Stephan Haggard and Steven B. Webb, Washington, D.C., May 1992, and Catherine Boone, "Trade, Taxes, and Tribute: Market Liberalization and the New Importers in West Africa," a paper presented at the Annual Meeting of the American Political Science Association, Chicago, September 3–6, 1992. Also see: Catherine Boone, "State Power and Economic Crisis in Senegal," *Comparative Politics* 22, 3 (April 1990): 341–357; Victoria Ebin, "Mouride Traders vs. the State: Strategies for the Development of International Trade in a Time of Crisis," and Momar Coumba Diop and Mamadou Diouf, "Notes sur le réconversion des marabouts mourides dans l'économie urbaine," papers presented at the Colloque "Etat et Société au Sénégal: Crises et Dynamiques Sociales," Centre d'Etude d'Afrique Noire and Institut Fondamental d'Afrique Noire, Bordeaux, October 22–25, 1991; Gilles Duruflé, *L'Ajustement Structurel en Afrique: Sénégal, Côte d'Ivoire, Madagascar* (Paris: Karthala, 1988); Christopher L. Delgado and Sidi Jammeh, eds., *The Political Economy of Senegal under Structural Adjustment* (New York: Praeger, 1991); Catherine Boone, "Politics under the Specter of Deindustrialization: "Structural Adjustment" in Practice" in Delgado and Jammeh, eds., *Political Economy of Senegal*, pp. 127–149; John Waterbury and Mark Gersovitz, eds., *The Political Economy of Risk and Choice in Senegal* (London: Frank Cass, 1987); S. Commander, O. Ndoge, I. Ouedrago, "Senegal 1979–88" in Simon Commander, *Structural Adjustment and Agriculture* (Portsmouth, N.H.: Heineman, 1989), pp. 145–174; Crawford Young and Babacar Kante, "Governance, Democracy and the 1988 Senegalese Elections" in Hyden and Bratton,*Governance and Politics in Africa*, pp. 57–74; Christian Coulon, "Senegal: The Development and Fragility of Semidemocracy," in Larry Diamond, Juan J. Linz, and Seymour Martin Lipset, eds., *Politics in Developing Countries: Comparing Experiences with Democracy* (Boulder: Lynne Rienner, 1990), pp. 411–448; Robert Fatton, *The Making of a Liberal Democracy: Senegal's Passive Revolution, 1975–85* (Boulder: Lynne Rienner, 1987).

54. See Nicolas van de Walle, "The Decline of the Franc Zone: Monetary Politics in Francophone Africa," *African Affairs* 90 (July 1991): 383–405.

55. Cited in Boone, "Trade, Taxes and Tribute," p. 14, from an interview she conducted in Dakar, December 1990.

56. Ka and van de Walle, "The Political Economy of Adjustment," pp. 66, 65.

57. In "The Political Economy of Adjustment," Ka and van de Walle attempt to take a less pessimistic view of the impact of democratization on economic reform than the one presented here, but I do not believe that their own evidence supports a less pessimistic assessment. They do note that "social pressures were indeed in part to blame for the failure of reform" by pushing "the state to return to pre-adjustment policies of subsidies, regulation and trade protection" and that "regular and reasonably honest elections obvi-

ously did put some pressure on the government to lessen the bite of economic austerity" [p. 64]. They go on to conclude, however, that the "common wisdom on Senegal" which suggests that "its economic stagnation is linked to the fact that it has been one of the most democratic regimes in Africa" is flawed. For them, the fact that Diouf won the 1988 elections by nearly the same percentage as the 1983 ones points to "the limits of this kind of analysis" [p. 64]. They contend that "interest group pressures must be put into a larger context to properly understand the failure of reform" [p. 64], a context dominated by constraints such as the inability to use devaluation, weak supply response, personal rivalries within the economic team, little faith in the reforms etc. which become reasons for failure. Yes, such constraints have long weakened economic reform efforts by authoritarian regimes as well in Africa, but I would argue that these weaknesses were further aggravated by democratization in Senegal, making a successful outcome of the reforms even less likely. Lastly, speaking about Diouf, they argue that "democratization held relatively few risks for him, *particularly as long as he maintained the support of the marabouts*" [p. 65, italics added]. This caveat is the key; the point is precisely that maintaining such support was one of the chief reasons for the failure of the reforms, as their evidence and that provided by Boone and others demonstrates quite clearly. By placating the marabouts and other groups, the Diouf government won the 1988 elections by a comfortable margin but killed the economic reforms. This more pessimistic assessment is likely to hold for other African countries undergoing democratization as well, and shows just how "hemmed in" Africa is.

58. In chapter 4 in this volume, Matthew Martin indicates that, at minimum, Chiluba will need all of these propitious factors, plus much more sensitive program design and negotiating procedures.

59. For a discussion of a strikingly similar situation in another patrimonial administrative state, see Paul D. Hutchcroft, "The Political Foundations of Booty Capitalism in the Philippines," paper delivered at the Annual Meeting of the American Political Science Association, Chicago, September 3–6, 1992.

60. For Latin America, Karen Remmer argues, contrary to much of the literature on the region, that economic crisis does not necessarily lead to the end of democracy. I would argue for both Latin America and Africa, certainly for Senegal, that although, or rather because, democracy survives, at least in the short run, major economic reform is made more difficult and thus will not be very common. This clearly runs counter to the Western vision of the need for simultaneous economic and political liberalization; see Callaghy, "Vision and Politics." For Karen Remmer's argument, see "Democracy and Economic Crisis: The Latin American Experience," *World Politics* (April 1990), pp. 315–335, and "The Political Impact of Economic Crisis in Latin America in the 1980s," *American Political Science Review* 85, 3 (September 1991): 777–800; also see Stephan Haggard and Robert Kaufman, "Economic Adjustment and the Prospects for Democracy" in Haggard and Kaufaman, *The Politics of Economic Adjustment*, pp. 319–350.

61. Albert O. Hirschman, "Reactionary Rhetoric," *Atlantic Monthly* 263, 5 (May 1989): 63.

62. On the Tanzanian case, see Lofchie's article (chapter 11) in this volume.

63. Paul Collier, "Africa's External Economic Relations: 1960–90," *African Affairs* 90 (1991): 340, 339.

64. John B. Goodman, *Monetary Sovereignty: The Politics of Central Banking in Western Europe* (Ithaca: Cornell University Press, 1992), p. 6, note 12; also see Stanley Fischer, "Dynamic Inconsistency, Cooperation, and the Benevolent Dissembling Government," *Journal of Economic Dynamics and Control* 2 (1980): 93–107; William Nordhaus, "The Political Business Cycle," *Review of Economic Studies*, 42 (April 1975): 169–190.

65. See Callaghy, "Democracy and the Political Economy of Restraint and Reform in Nigeria."

66. Collier, "Africa's External Economic Relations," p. 134, and his talk of the same title, Center for International Affairs, Harvard University, March 6, 1992.

67. The notion of "civil society" has generated considerable discussion, and hope, by academics and political actors alike, in the context of efforts at political liberalization in Africa. At the same time it remains a contested concept. For a discussion of the concept and its applicability to Africa, see Naomi Chazan, John W. Harbeson, and Donald Rothchild, eds., *Civil Society and the State in Africa* (Boulder: Lynne Rienner, forthcoming 1993); for my skeptical views, see Thomas M. Callaghy, "Civil Society, Democracy, and Economic Change in Africa: A Dissenting Opinion" in *Civil Society and the State in Africa*. Also see Lewis, "Political Transition and the Dilemma of Civil Society in Africa."

68. The concept of "embedded liberalism" is John Gerard Ruggie's; see his "International Regimes, Transactions and Change: Embedded Liberalism in the Postwar Economic Order," *International Organization* 36, 2 (Spring 1982), especially pp. 398–399, 405, 413, and "Political Structure and Change in the International Economic Order: The North-South Dimension" in Ruggie, ed., *Antinomies of Interdependence* (New York: Columbia University Press, 1983), pp. 423–487. Robert Gilpin and Barry Buzan both prefer the term "benign mercantilism;" see Robert Gilpin, *The Political Economy of International Relations* (Princeton: Princeton University Press, 1987), pp. 404–5. I prefer "embedded liberalism" because it more accurately reflects the direction of policy change and the balancing point between state and market. On the Japanese version of it, see Kent E. Calder, *Crisis and Compensation: Public Policy and Political Stability in Japan* (Princeton: Princeton University Press, 1991).

69. Hirschman, "Reactionary Rhetoric," p. 70.

70. On the "nightmare scenario," see Economic Commission for Africa, "ECA and Africa's Development: 1983–2008," Addis Ababa, April 1983, and "Beyond Recovery: ECA—Revised Perspective of Africa's Development, 1988–2008," Addis Ababa, March 1988.

71. Kohli, "Democracy and Development," p. 178.

72. Sklar's discussion of "developmental democracy" in his "Democracy in Africa" in Patrick Chabal, ed., *Political Domination in Africa* (Cambridge: Cambridge University Press, 1986), pp. 1–29.

73. See Raymon Aron's discussion of Tocqueville's views on democracy in Raymond Aron, *Main Currents in Sociological Thought*, vol. 1 (New York:

Anchor Books, 1968). Adam Przeworski recently echoed Tocqueville's point in the context of Eastern Europe, as well as one of its inherent dangers: "The everyday life of democratic politics is not a spectacle that inspires awe: an endless squabble among petty ambitions, rhetoric designed to hide and mislead, shady connections between power and money, laws that make no pretense of justice, policies that reinforce privilege. This experience is particularly painful for people who had to idealize democracy in the struggle against authoritarian oppression, people for whom democracy was the paradise forbidden. When paradise turns into everyday life, disenchantment sets in. Hence the temptation to make everything transparent in one swoop, to stop the bickering, to replace politics with administration, anarchy with discipline, to do the rational—the authoritarian temptation" [*Democracy and the Market: Political and Economic Reforms in Eastern Europe and Latin America* (New York: Cambridge University Press, 1991), pp. 93–94]. This point and its inherent warning are particularly pertinent to Africa.

Chapter Thirteen

How Hemmed In? Lessons and Prospects of Africa's Responses to Decline

THOMAS M. CALLAGHY AND
JOHN RAVENHILL

Introduction: A New Leader's Challenge

On November 2, 1991, Frederick Chiluba was sworn in as Zambia's newly elected president. An eloquent labor leader who had passionately opposed an IMF/World Bank economic reform effort in 1985–87, Chiluba is truly a democratic leader. Yet he was one well aware of the challenges that face him and his country, for few African countries have declined as seriously as Zambia. As a result, his inauguration speech is worth quoting at some length:

> The stream of democracy—damned up for 27 years—is finally free to run its course as a mighty African river. Not because of arms, not because of bullets, not because of any other time, but the patience of Zambia with corruption, repression, and dictatorship had run out. The voice of the Zambian people, weak as it was at one stage, faint against the thunder of one party and one man, is once again strong, a roar asserting itself. But let us not forget that we cannot replace the tyranny of an elite with the tyranny of the many. The Zambia we inherit is destitute—ravaged by the excesses, ineptitude and straight corruption of a party and a people who have been in power for too long. When

our first President stood up to address you 27 years ago, he was addressing a country full of hope and glory. A country fresh with the power of youth, and a full and rich dowry. Now the coffers are empty. The people are poor. The misery endless.

The economic ills we suffer have come upon us over several decades. They will not go away in days, weeks or months. But we are determined that they will go away. They will go away because we as Zambians have the will to apply ourselves to do whatever needs to be done to rebuild this glorious country.

In this present crisis, government alone is not the solution to our problems. For too long, government was the problem. The crisis needs discipline, hard work, honesty, clean government and a determination to grit our teeth, to look our problems squarely in the face, and to tackle them head-on. . . . We have the right to dream heroic dreams. But more importantly, we have the obligation to make them come true. For we know what works—freedom works. We know what is right—democracy is right.

But what exactly is to be done? I believe we ought to concentrate on the basics. Our priorities must be the basic needs of the people of Zambia. One such priority is education. . . . Another is health care. . . . But most important of all is the need to create a sustained confidence in the socio-political stability of our country. . . . In our time of need, we will look to the world. Not for hand-outs, but for help to stand on our own feet again. To get well. . . . Zambia is not the center of the universe, but Zambia is the center of our universe. . . . Let's do whatever we can, every day to slowly pull ourselves through our sweat and toil, out of mud and to build a new Zambia where prosperity, decency, [and] Human rights are normal parts of life.[1]

Chiluba clearly has a vision. He believes that Zambia is not hemmed in, but knows that difficult tasks lie ahead. Is Zambia, or the rest of Africa, hemmed in?[2] If so, how and how much? Can it become less so? Can it pull itself out of the mud to become less hemmed in? And do it with democracy and outside help? After nearly thirty years of decline, can Zambia start over or will old logics, dilemmas, and tensions once again tear it to shreds? Can it, for example, switch from distributionist logics to productionist ones? What lessons have the chapters in this book elucidated as possible answers to these questions? The most obvious is that it will not be easy for Chiluba or other reform-minded leaders to break through the constraints they face.

Lessons: Can Africa Become Less Hemmed In?

Intractability and "Laundry Lists"

Few signs of economic recovery exist as Africa moves well into the 1990s. As several of the authors in this volume have stressed, the track record of attempts at economic stabilization and structural adjustment over the 1980s is very modest indeed. There were very few cases of successful "large reform," such as Ghana, and while there have been many cases of "small reform" the impact has been negligible on the overall economy. Is this the fault of the externally sponsored strategy? That depends on the expectations attached to it. The international financial institutions believed that altering the policy framework would bring relatively rapid improvement. They were wrong. As a result, they now talk quietly among themselves about Africa's "intractability," while cheerleading those seriously attempting economic reform in order to combat an increasingly prevalent "Afro-pessimism." Is there is a "better" counterfactual strategy, one more suited to African realities, out there somewhere just waiting to be discovered? Our answer, elaborated below, is a qualified no, itself a striking reflection of the degree to which Africa is "hemmed in" and of the fact that everybody's expectations have been unduly high given the complexity of African conditions.

As a result of this "intractability" in the face of policy change, the IMF and the World Bank have developed an increasingly long "laundry list" of relevant variables, ranging from defending the fragile ecology to protecting property rights via good "governance." In Africa, the Fund and the Bank have been learning by doing, and often experimenting without buffering much of the negative consequences of their often creative efforts. This laundry list is most evident in the World Bank's 1989 long-term perspective study, *Sub-Saharan Africa: From Crisis to Sustainable Growth.*[3] Most of these variables are not easily susceptible to the effects of policy change. External actors have discovered that many things are necessary but not sufficient—correct policies that "get the prices right," investment, aid, voluntary lending, debt relief, political will and stability, accountability, decent levels of state capacity, and institutional and attitudinal change, for example. In a sense, this expanding laundry list is a "wish list" not generically unlike the one contained in the OAU's Lagos Plan of Action, which the Fund and the Bank criticized so strongly.

Consequently, the projected time frame for reform has moved, first from three to ten years and now from ten to twenty years. But as Green points out, the international financial institutions do not really know how to operate in such a lengthened time frame. Learning lessons and being able to apply them are different things. The IMF and the World Bank, and all other major actors, have their own capacity problems; they lack the detailed knowledge and data, analytical frameworks, institutional structures, and resources to implement the new lessons, especially since the larger contextual variables are both diffuse and daunting. The inability of the international financial institutions (IFIs) to come up with a clear and operational definition of "governance" is but one vivid example.[4] In addition, the laundry list is now so long and broad that it is difficult to decide which items to work on first, how to go about doing so, and how to allocate scarce resources.

Thus, as Ravenhill points out in the opening chapter, there exist both a growing realization of complexity and a growing uncertainty about what to do. Creeping conditionality is but one indicator of this situation. The neoclassical economic strategy is elegant and parsimonious, a tight analytical framework; it is also off target in its expectations about what it calls "supply response." It is so because it has *assumed* the prior existence of a panoply of contextual factors that were linked to the rise of capitalism in Europe, and more recently in East Asia and selected parts of Latin America. These variables are the result of long-run historical processes that cannot be easily or quickly "built" through short-term policy manipulation. In short, neoclassical policy prescriptions have been extracted from the sociopolitical contexts in which they were historically embedded. Many Africans also see the task as daunting and the neoclassical prescription of linkage to the world economy as dangerous. They are quite understandably shaken by Africa's simultaneously accelerating marginalization and dependence. As a result, a "fear-flight" reaction sets in, which sends many of them running from the world economy in search of a less daunting and dangerous counterfactual strategy. Events around the world over the last several decades do not breed encouragement about the existence of a strikingly different counterfactual appropriate to African conditions. A modified, more statist one may exist, but whether African countries have the "laundry list" of factors that might make it work is another question. The track record of the 1980s and the early 1990s illustrates how little anybody, African or non-African, knows about how African political economies function, much less how to improve them. The basic data base is still quite thin and unreliable, although improving rapidly.

All of this is greatly complicated by high social costs, weak or nonexistent societal coalitions supporting reform, slow and shallow learning by political actors, a long time lag before major benefits appear, donor fatigue, and the failure of the implicit bargain, especially as new demands and opportunities emerged in Eastern Europe and the old Soviet empire, and now the pressures and dilemmas of political liberalization. It should not be surprising then that there is little consensus between African and external actors about how to proceed—what Green describes as "a dialogue of the mutually deaf" or "two prophets speaking at each other in tongues." As a result, the ritual dances of economic reform go round and round, leaving few grounds for optimism about major recovery. Adjustment, planned or unplanned, will come eventually, but unplanned adjustment may be far worse than economic reform now. As we shall see below, some African learning has taken place in a few cases; but it remains a question of who learns—technocrats, rulers, leaders of organized groups in a reemergent "civil society" or a newly reconstituted mass electorate—and with what consequences.

"Back to the Future"?

What then is this strategy or vision that Western actors have insisted that African countries follow? As it emerged and was modified over the course of the 1980s, it can be characterized as a "back to the future" strategy. It is an attempt to take African countries back to the 1960s, both economically and now politically, in order to start the development process over and do it right this time. On the economic side, it means rehabilitating primary product export economies and making them work properly, without the pernicious effects of countervailing political logics and weak capabilities. From this reestablished revenue platform, slow and careful moves can be made in the direction of expanding a manufacturing base via new investment, privatization, and parastatal reform. By creating a new "enabling environment" and policy framework, it is also hoped that the entrepreneurial talents of the now greatly expanded informal economy can be relinked to the domestic formal economy and through it to the world economy. In the process, the hope is to eliminate the "missing middle" problem that has plagued Africa since the 1960s, that is, the absence of a vital domestic private business sector in the formal economy between the parastatals and the multinationals on the one hand and the informal sector on the other. On the political side, the back to the future strategy means resurrecting democracy and making it survive this time and in the process turning predatory, rent-seeking governments into developmental ones. The Western vision asserts that the economic and political sides of this effort will mutually reinforce each other.

The critics of the economic part of the back to the future strategy assert that is not an optimum strategy appropriate to African conditions. True enough; but other than focusing on its very real social costs, they really do not have a viable counterfactual strategy. Even when correctly and powerfully describing the social costs of the back to the future strategy, critics do not explain where the resources might come from to ameliorate these costs. Nor have they articulated alternative policies that would avoid them. Given the fallacy of composition problem that haunts it, the back to the future strategy is clearly a weak option, with only limited potential, especially since Africa may already be closer to its production frontiers than anybody wants to admit. But nobody has been able to generate a more viable strategy for Africa, in large part because the state capabilities necessary for an alternative, heavily statist, strategy along East Asian lines, simply do not exist. So it appears that back to the future is the only viable alternative, albeit one about which there should be greatly lowered expectations. In this sense Africa really is "hemmed in," as it tries to navigate between weak states and weak markets and do so with more open political structures. But the hope is that by attempting to go back Africa will not go forward to the OAU's "nightmare scenario."[5] The viability of this minimalist strategy is one of the central questions of this book.

The Limits of External Actors

One of the key factors affecting the viability of the back to the future strategy is the limited ability of external actors to implement it in Africa, hence their sense of the intractability of African reality. As Gordon, Green, and Martin point out, two of the central limitations on external actors are the constraints of African debt and the weakness of conditionality. Gordon notes that the IFIs are caught in a trap of their own design because they are simultaneously creditors and reformers. Debt itself is a source of reform because it creates financial leverage for Western actors, while it acts as a serious constraint on reform given the scarcity of resources the continent faces. To insist that African countries meet their debt repayments weakens reform, but not to enforce arrangements weakens the IFIs as creditor agencies. Given these ambiguities, the new world context, and the political sensitivities of Western industrial publics, Gordon argues that major new debt relief for Africa is not likely. The absence of such relief might be mitigated somewhat by creative new mechanisms such as the "rights accumulation" procedure used to cope with Zambia's problems that he and Martin discuss.

Financial leverage permits conditionality, and it can be powerful in initiating reform efforts, especially, as Lofchie points out for Tanzania, when it is linked to economic learning. Over time, however, as conditionality proliferates in the face of intractability, financial leverage becomes more apparent than real. In large part, this is because, as creditors, the IFIs need both to lend and collect. In addition, the IFIs do not really have the capabilities to monitor proliferating conditionality; Herbst's proposal to greatly expand the field presence of the World Bank is probably not a practical idea from a political point of view nor is it likely to solve the Bank's own capacity problems. Conditions are fudged, and the "conditionality game" becomes just one major aspect of the ritual dances of reform, as van de Walle demonstrates for Cameroon. Thus, withholding resources systematically becomes increasingly difficult and conditionality harder to "enforce." Countries have incentives to start (and restart) reform because of the associated improved access to resources, but fewer incentives to sustain reform efforts. Gordon also notes that the model of pure conditionality has failed because it has not acted to "catalyze" private resource flows; hence the failure of what Callaghy calls the implicit bargain between African governments and Western sources of finance.

Despite these limitations, both Gordon and Lofchie argue that the IFIs and other Western actors do have intellectual influence, that they are the conduit of new ideas. While we agree that this is certainly one avenue of influence, we believe that it is still a relatively modest one in Africa. The question becomes influence with whom—technocrats, rulers, government officials, politicians, leaders of groups in civil society or the mass electorate under democratic conditions? This becomes an increasingly important question with the widespread political liberalization moves of the early 1990s. Callaghy's discussion of Senegal and Nigeria should give pause to those who see a simple linkage between the influence of international financial institutions and policy outcomes. Lofchie makes a case for the role of influence and learning in Tanzania, especially among technocrats and some government officials, but he also attests to their halting and uneven nature and potential fragility. This learning certainly has not yet been tested in democratic elections, and we do not share Lofchie's optimism about such an outcome. His view shares too many of the overly mechanistic linkages between *presumed* economic gain and actual political practice that are at the core of the neoclassical view of economic reform examined by Callaghy. Nevertheless, the argument made by Lofchie and Gordon that we need to focus on the interplay of financial, intellectual, and political influences is an important one.

Gordon underscores the fragility and limits of these processes of influence, pointing to a "new dependency syndrome" and to the fact that the donors "have 'hemmed in' Africa in a very peculiar way; not by imposing inappropriate strategies or policies, but by substituting external pressure and financial resources for domestic leadership and an indigenous process." Callaghy also observes that much of the public debate in Africa about economic reform has been externalized by blaming the IFIs for Africa's problems and that there are few mass agencies that can restrain traditional rent-seeking behavior in Africa's new democracies.

For some countries such as Nigeria effective mass learning may come only after several more rounds of democracy, failed economic reform, and accelerated economic decline. In such cases external actors might actually facilitate learning by staying out until democratized polities have learned these hard lessons, for ultimately, as Gordon remarks, "the main initiatives for African development must come from Africans themselves." This point is particularly true under conditions of political liberalization.

Many of the points made by Green and Gordon about negotiating with the IFIs, especially those about the nature and limitations of conditionality, are nicely illustrated by Martin's two cases studies of Ghana and Zambia. The international financial institutions are not, by nature, humble organizations, and Martin argues that the manner in which they have negotiated with African governments is another limitation affecting the viability of their strategy. In particular, he stresses the lack of flexibility and dialogue and the quite striking inattention early on to how their policy preferences would be implemented. He also notes how quite crude political assessments by IFI officials can limit the impact of their own efforts. Zambia is a clear case in this regard. Beginning in the middle of the 1980s, the Fund and the Bank did revamp some of their negotiating practices and did so in time to help Ghana but not Zambia (whose adjustment program was probably doomed in any event by the lack of domestic political commitment). Martin argues properly, however, that there is still considerable room for further improvement. One would hope that such additional improvement will come in time to help President Chiluba. Although Martin notes that "the past experience of both countries is that political liberalization has tended to undermine reform by increasing the demands on government for expansionary policies," he asserts that "at the moment, both countries are well-placed to sever this connection." We only hope that he is correct.

Reform in Agriculture and Manufacturing

One of the lessons of the 1980s is that under certain conditions farmers will respond to price incentives, but that there are clear limitations to this response in terms of aggregate supply, especially a quick one. The structural and behavioral constraints on a systematic and sustained response to price incentives are considerable. This reinforces the point that while the back to the future strategy may be the only viable one for now, it still has distinct limits as a means of economic transformation. This underscores just how "hemmed in" Africa is.

Taking a longer-range historical perspective, Berry shows how African smallholder producers have responded over time to economic change, instability, and volatility. By focusing on struggles to gain access to the means of agricultural production, she shows how African farmers use a wide array of social networks and different production strategies in seeking liquidity and flexibility. Over time claims on resources from such networks have multiplied and become increasingly complex. Without the full commercialization of the means of production, investing in a variety of social networks is a rational strategy for coping with confusion, but it also limits sustained, major, medium-term investment in agricultural production that might allow a major response to changes in price incentives. The instability of the late 1970s and 1980s reinforced these older patterns of response, negatively affecting the ability of the new price incentives that are central to reforms aimed at generating a significantly increased supply. As Berry, Herbst, and Widner all stress, many other factors constrain farmers' responses to price incentives; these include the limited availability of improved crop strains, pointing to the poor returns from post-independence investment in agricultural research, the scarcity of viable agricultural support and outreach infrastructure, and the deterioration of the transportation network. These are a direct product of weak state capabilities and the import strangulation that has accompanied structural adjustment. All of the indicators suggest that the overall price elasticity of supply in Africa is low; without research breakthroughs and substantially improved availability of key inputs to go beyond price reform, Africa may be closer to its production frontier than many observers believe.

In the manufacturing sector, Africa is really "hemmed in." As Riddell shows, IMF-World Bank reform programs have had very negative consequences for the manufacturing sector. If the back to the future strategy is fully implemented systematically across the continent, deindustrialization might be a real phenomenon from an already small base. The "harsh withdrawal" thrust to these reforms is considerable, as has been the IFI's opposition to any form of "benign interventionism." To their dismay, the Fund and the Bank have discovered that privatization is not likely to have a major impact in Africa, that parastatal reform is very difficult, and that major new investment, domestic or foreign, is not taking place. The result is that the "missing middle" is still missing despite a vibrant informal sector. While the negative consequences and limitations of the IFI's back to the future strategy for manufacturing are significant, the constraints for the strategy of "benign interventionism" that Riddell proposes are much more serious. Given the limited technical, policy, administrative, and infrastructure capabilities that plagued parastatal efforts in the first three decades of independence, where is the ability to implement such policies going to come from? His answer is that the help will have to come from external sources. Ultimately, he notes that "the environment of the 1990s provides little optimism that any policy to promote and accelerate the development of the manufacturing sector is going to be easy" and that "most countries . . . are going to continue to be `hemmed in' by a range of factors that will dampen demand, and thus limit the pace of industrial expansion and the scope for diversifying the manufacturing base." Can African countries do what Korea and other East Asian countries have managed to do?[6] As we will argue below, the answer for now is quite clearly no, once again reinforcing the fact that Africa is "hemmed in" between weak markets and weak states. We also argue, however, that Africa needs to work in that direction, albeit slowly and carefully this time.

Politics and the Limits to Reform

As Herbst argues, it will take a favorable political system to begin to lessen the structural constraints affecting agricultural production, including those discussed by Berry, Green, and Ravenhill. The key questions become what kind of political system and how is it achieved. Clearly it takes one with important administrative and technical capabilities and one that reflects agricultural interests. The discussion of Kenya by Herbst and Lofchie demonstrates the historical complexity of the factors needed for sustained and effective representation of agricultural interests—especially elite responsiveness, institutionalized linkages that can deliver resources and support infrastructure, and relatively stable participatory elections over time. Their discussion also indicates that even long-standing productive political economies can be amazingly fragile when confronted with counterproductive political logics. In Kenya, for example, it remains unclear whether the old consensus that supported policies favorable to agricultural growth can be re-created in a post-Moi democratic Kenya. Herbst stresses that elections by themselves are not likely to be sufficient, raising doubts about the positive effect of political liberalization for economic reform, at least in the short run. He observes that democratic political structures need to "last long enough for a tradition of accountability through elections to develop." Thus, even assuming that agricultural interests are well organized (a point we shall return to shortly), democratic political logics of electoral punishment for policy failure need to become well rooted; this takes time and basic political stability. As he points out, democratic regimes in Ghana and Nigeria "failed to enhance the influence of the entire farming community," the one social group that can potentially benefit the most from structural adjustment.

In his discussion of Zimbabwe, Herbst also underscores the historical roots of effective patterns of representation. Since elections are not sufficient, this requires the development of "real institutional conduits that connect the state and the vast majority in the countryside." Much of the current thinking about political liberalization in Africa implies that "institutional conduits" will develop via the emergence of stronger "civil societies." As a result, successful economic reform requires not only increased levels of state capacity but also higher levels of "civil society capacity," that is, the effective and sustained organization of social interests over time. Callaghy stresses the initial "transaction costs" of effective organization, but the difficuties of sustaining capacity are even higher as the history of failed agricultural cooperatives in Africa all too vividly illustrates. Herbst points to the National Farmers Association of Zimbabwe as a possible model, yet he notes that it is "weak at both the bottom and top" with "only tenuous ties with many of its own constituents in the countryside" and "only the most limited ability to conduct competent economic analysis that might impress the government bureaucracy."

Civil society capacity is therefore a major issue in assessing the effects of political liberalization on economic reform in Africa. As with state capacity, it cannot be assumed to exist. This again points to the limits of any mechanistic view of the link between presumed economic benefit and political outcome. Herbst concludes that ultimately "it is unlikely that the political structures most likely to evolve in African countries will result in an unambiguous increase in the political power of farmers." Thus, while his three country examples are analytically interesting, they are not likely to represent major trends in Africa in the foreseeable future. Given this situation, he proposes that the external actors, particularly the World Bank, play a more intrusive role in helping agricultural interests organize themselves. While this is an intriguing proposal, it is not likely to be adopted, and would be unlikely to succeed even if it were. Thus, the structural limitations to systematic and sustained responses to price incentives are likely to remain strong, again diminishing the viability of a back to the future strategy.

In her detailed case study of the agricultural "proto-politics" in Côte d'Ivoire generated by a very serious agricultural crisis, Widner illustrates points made by both Berry and Herbst. She demonstrates both that small farmers are able to organize politically to defend their interests and that these efforts can have quite distinct limitations. She notes that these "beginnings of collective action" in Côte d'Ivoire become possible precisely because many of the older coping strategies discussed by Berry did not work well in the villages she studied, particularly because of the closure of the land frontier. The propensity to "discover politics" varies, however, having to do with the structure of local politics, the presence of leadership and resources, available models, and changes in the structure of national-level politics. All of these factors affect the transaction costs of collective action. Sustained collective action, however, was both unusual and relatively ineffectual (garnering "lots of promises"), vividly illustrating the difficulties of generating highly organized collective action over time. In short, "delegations and strikes do not programmatic politics make." She also indicates that national electoral politics, in and of itself, is not likely to further small farmer interests, at least in the short run. She indicates that in the 1990 Côte d'Ivoire elections, "the major parties made little effort (or could afford little) to influence rural voters." The "could afford little" is particularly important as political parties and major civil society groups also require solid economic bases. Hence, as in the 1960s, political liberalization is still likely to be largely an urban phenomenon with weak backward linkages to rural areas.

In her epilogue, however, Widner ends on a more optimistic note by pointing to the creation in 1991 of the *Syndicat des*

Agriculteurs de Côte d'Ivoire (SYNAGCI) with help from the head of a newly created political party. It resulted from widespread discontent about the corrupt manner in which the *Caisse de Stabilisation* had functioned under President Houphouët-Boigny. She links this to the experience of southeast Asian countries such as Malaysia and Indonesia where it was clear that "policy choices mattered." These countries can cope with price fluctuations "as long as yields improve constantly," this "requires information, research, and improved extension, however." In short, "one way to try to avoid becoming 'hemmed in' in the international economy was to organize to make governors more accountable for the choice of investment targets." Hence, effective and sustained agricultural reform requires proper policy choices, state capacity for research and extension support, and civil society capacity for effective representation, as elections are clearly not enough. The degree to which SYNAGCI will be able to perform its representation functions effectively over time remains open to question. It may, as Herbst notes for NFAZ in Zimbabwe, "suffer from many of the same organization problems that other farmer groups do across Africa."

Policy choices in agriculture and other sectors thus do matter as the southeast Asian cases demonstrate, but, as these chapters indicate, any positive correlation between economic and political liberalization entails a number of crucial "ifs." It requires a fragile, long-linked chain of conditions and events. Farmers need to put pressure on governments to make proper policy choices and provide the extension support to make them effective; this presumes organization of farmer interests and the civil society's capacity to make such organization efficacious over time. The government must believe that it has to respond to farmer pressure; this presumes sufficiently rooted repetititive electoral cycles to ensure that pressure is credible. The government must then have both the resources and the state capability to make the right policy choices and provide the necessary support infrastructure consistently in the medium to long term to compete effectively in the world economy with countries that have already proved themselves capable of doing so. Similar long-linked chains exist for other major groups that are presumed to benefit from structural adjustment.

In short, the discussion in the chapters by Berry, Herbst, and Widner indicates the naiveté of those who see democratization as a panacea for Africa's economic problems. A far more nuanced understanding, rooted in careful empirical work at the village and town as well as national levels, illustrates powerful constraints on collective action and the improbability that democratization will work to the benefit of rural interests in many countries in any major way.

While Africa's economic decline and halting attempts at reform were going on in the 1970s and 1980s, other powerful socioeconomic and political processes were emerging underneath the formal facades of both the state and the economy. Of particular importance were the striking growth and spread of the informal economy as the formal one weakened. These were accompanied by an enriched associational life which emerged as effective central political control diminished despite efforts to prevent it, constituting what Kohli and Shue call "increasing centralization with powerlessness."[7] Yet, as Chazan and Rothchild argue, this expanded informal sphere, with its economic and political aspects and coping mechanisms, was highly fragmented. It "accentuated protest but did not usually point to any nonstatist models of power restructuring," although it certainly limited the impact of formal attempts to engage in neoclassical economic reform.

Chazan and Rothchild sketch an evolving relationship between the formal and informal sectors over the course of the 1980s and early 1990s. The first half of the 1980s was dominated by patterns of informal disengagement from both the state and the formal economy. The latter half of the decade witnessed a halting and uneven partial reengagement, leading to resurgent and more aggressive "civil societies." With continued economic decline and the very real costs of attempted economic reform, the 1990s opened with vigorous political struggles over political liberalization in a significant number of countries. Chazan and Rothchild note that economic decline and political ferment, often fueled by attempts at economic reform, helped to rearrange power concentrations in Africa.

Although they stress the "fragility of political reform," Chazan and Rothchild do assert that "if future African governments can implement political liberalization measures, they will greatly enhance the capacity of the state to establish the routines and institutions for sustained economic reform." While "more regularized responsiveness to the demands of civil society" is seen as the key, they do not rule out less sanguine outcomes. These range from "a kind of enforced self-reliance," characterized by "destructive internal conflict" and continued economic decline whereby countries "are involuntarily de-linked for all intents and purposes from the international community" to a more likely continuation of the clientelistic practices and "expansion of informal social and economic activities at the expense of the political center" that were characteristic of the 1980s. As Callaghy illustrates, this is precisely what happened in Senegal, the one case that clearly linked attempted economic reform with political liberalization.

As van de Walle illustrates with Cameroon, one of the major responses to economic decline in Africa, even in the late 1980s, was nonreform. Zaire, Zambia, and a host of other countries fit into this category—those that choreograph the ritual dances of reform play the conditionality game, and do so without any positive economic impact. As Zaire has demonstrated since the 1970s, the impact of nonreform is cumulative, and when political change finally comes, the effects can be devastating, both politically and economically.

Nonreform in Cameroon was the result of elite opposition because real reform threatened its "hegemonic alliance," leading to a synergy between weak, ambivalent commitment and very limited implementation capability. Like Moi in Kenya, President Biya found that consolidating his inherited political position was very costly especially in the middle of an economic downturn. Biya attempted to manage retrenchment and failed, seriously damaging the functioning of the state in the process and forcing a turn toward the more extensive use of coercion and the ritual dances of political liberalization. The latter permitted external actors to provide more resources for the government, which partly mitigated the effect of a weakening economy and a seriously declining revenue base. Any positive influence of external actors was very limited, however, and economic conditionally was largely illusory, illustrating points made by Gordon and others in this volume. Biya benefited from external acquiescence justified by the ritual dances of political liberalization. Under such conditions, it is possible for a regime to survive—a point also illustrated by Senegal where the continuation of older political logics seriously weakened the revenue base and administrative functioning of the state. A resurgent but fragmented civil society in Cameroon led to rampant *incivisme fiscale*, where opposition groups worked systematically to keep revenue out of the hands of the state.[8]

Much of the opposition in Cameroon remained quite ambivalent about the need for economic reform, however, a point echoed by Gordon for other countries. One position, for example, was that "policy reform was essentially unnecessary as long as governmental corruption was eliminated"! Nonetheless, van de Walle concludes that "it would be naive and historically incorrect to suggest that greater pluralism is a sufficient condition for sustained economic growth. On the other hand, it is probably a necessary condition, at least in the African context." If one links the ambivalence of the opposition about economic reform to his central point that there is a negative synergy between weak commitment to reform and weak implementation capacity, his necessary but not sufficient assertion about political liberalization rings less true. As Senegal demonstrates, political liberalization is likely to strengthen the patrimonial features of African states. Hence, this negative synergy is likely to be intensified by political liberalization. As van de Walle observes, "the patrimonial logic on which the state is built subverts implementation capacity and lowers the internal discipline of the state apparatus." In addition, despite all the rhetoric about accountability, efforts at structural adjustment have done little to control corruption; the same is also likely to hold true for political liberalization. This was certainly true for Nigeria's Second Republic and is likely to be so for its Third Republic as well, despite the early progress made by the Babangida military regime on economic reform, and there are already indications of this under Chiluba in Zambia.

As Lofchie indicates with Tanzania, while it is possible to shift ruling coalitions, the process is an extremely difficult, uncertain, and fragile one. Such a shift may be most feasible where there is a generational change in leadership, as occurred in Tanzania, or where the economy has deteriorated to such an extent that there is a widespread belief that something has to be done, as in Ghana. In such circumstances, leaders may enjoy a honeymoon period that gives them a certain amount of temporary autonomy, enabling them both to refashion the governing coalition and reorient economic policies. Whether new leaders who emerge through the democratization process will really benefit from such honeymoons in many cases in Africa remains to be seen. They will be under immense pressure for rapid improvement in living standards, yet leaders can expect significant opposition to meaningful reform from the "old guard," organized labor, and other groups. The logics of politics do not disappear just because economic reform is required—as President Chiluba is finding out in Zambia. So will any successors to Mobutu in Zaire, be they authoritarian or democratic.

Lofchie thus makes an interesting, important, and more hopeful argument about the African political roots of reform in two polar cases—Kenya, which had relatively good policy all along (despite being relatively statist), and Tanzania, which violated almost every neoclassical policy rule in the book. In some ways, his argument parallels that of Gordon about the importance of intellectual influence and learning. Reform can be imposed without a supporting societal coalition, as Ghana demonstrates, or it can result from the emergence of a relatively supportive coalition that develops over time. This "internal origins" thesis about the development of a productive political economy "as a product of domestic political forces" holds for both Kenya under Jomo Kenyatta and Tanzania after Julius Nyerere. Kenya demonstrates the rare benefits of a stable and workable, if not perfect, political economy over time. It also illustrates, however, that even such a consolidated one can be shredded by new negative political logics with amazing ease and speed. Increasingly over time, Moi's attempts to consolidate his political position weakened the basic supports of Kenya's prolonged progress, especially general macroeconomic management, culminating in a major domestic and international crisis in 1991-93. This crisis precipitated the first major use of simultaneous economic and political conditionality by external actors.

Tanzania, on the other hand, illustrates the ability of a government to respond to the terrible costs of prolonged economic decline and external pressure to quietly build a new coalition willing to support major economic reform. As Lofchie argues, this coalition appeared slowly, haltingly, and unevenly, with important consequences for the lurching quality of the implementation of new policies. And it did so despite the "profound mistrust, deep misunderstanding, and fundamental dissensus" of the "tortured," "politically charged," and "ideologically accusatory" relations between Tanzania and the IFIs. One of the factors facilitating this coalitional shift from the "socialists" to the "pragmatists" was the long-term stability of the government, a factor not yet tested by free electoral competition.

After making this more hopeful "internal origins" domestic coalition argument about the possibility of economic reform in Africa, Lofchie vigorously defends the current Western position which sees economic and political liberalization as positively reinforcing phenomena. As already indicated, we are skeptical of Lofchie's overly mechanistic view of the positive link between presumed economic benefit and political action in democratic contexts. It assumes the existence of a sizeable potential support coalition and makes unwarranted assumptions about the necessary connections between perceived economic interest, social learning, political organization, and policy outcome. This viewpoint also greatly underestimates the degree to which economic reform can be "hollowed out" by patrimonial political logics under democratic conditions.

Our skepticism is reinforced by a telling argument Lofchie himself makes about the relationship between political uncertainty, credibility, and economic reform. He calls "the factor of credibility the supremely political aspect of the connection between policy change and economic recovery." Thus, "the factor of credibility is of overriding importance in areas of economic liberalization that require individuals and organizations to invest resources and skills in the reform process in sectors of the economy where whole institutions must be reformed or created in order to generate an economic response." Lofchie observes correctly that the long-term struggle between Tanzania's "socialists" and "pragmatists" created a high level of uncertainty about the sustainability of the new and fragile reform orientation. In turn, this weakened the credibility of reform and dampened both domestic and external interest in the medium-term investment that is so necessary to a supply response strong enough to sustain the reform effort. He points out that the importance of credibility has long been underestimated by many proponents of structural adjustment who make an "implicit assumption . . . that once significant reforms have been introduced, private sector actors that have been patiently waiting on the sidelines will become actively involved and buoy the process of economic recovery." He indicates that this has rarely occurred and identifies uncertainty as the key: "Where credibility of a reform effort is uncertain, it is to be expected that such sectors will exhibit an especially slow response to a reform program."

The post-Nyerere Tanzanian government thus suffered from an "ongoing credibility constraint" which, Lofchie argues, might begin to be resolved by upcoming multiparty elections. He notes that in 1992 "a vast proliferation of more than a dozen opposition organizations" sought to position themselves for the elections, and he concludes that "since some of the parties seem certain to oppose economic reform, the credibility constraint posed by a reformist government coexisting uncomfortably with a socialist party may not be resolved until that time." Unfortunately, however, the elections might not end the problem, as uncertainty about policies is often pervasive in new democracies. This is a major problem in Eastern Europe now, for example, especially in Poland.[9]

The Tanzanian case has major implications for the tasks that confront President Chiluba in Zambia. Is such a shift possible there, especially given the advent of democracy in late 1991 and the need to consolidate power while engaging in major economic reform? As Callaghy points out, the experience of Senegal is not encouraging. The question raised earlier of who learns and how much they learn is central here. Another issue raised by the Tanzanian case with applicability to Zambia is how such "learning" processes and coalitional shifts get started and how they are sustained. One argument is that, as in Tanzania, change will not come until things become so bad that serious internal political economy debates and struggles are precipitated by the terrible nature of social conditions. A fear generated by this argument is that if one waits too long, the economic situation will be so devastating that altering it will be extremely difficult, if not virtually impossible. Zaire may be such a case. Lofchie does point to the negative consequences of the duration and tightly interrelated nature of Tanzania's policy errors, which makes altering them even more demanding. In addition, the decline of Tanzania's economy was so steep that repairing the damage raises the level of effort, and resources, required. These facts are seen in the halting and "mixed" nature of Tanzanian adjustment to date. Under such conditions, the maintenance of political stability is central, something not yet tested in Tanzania and to be sorely tried in Zambia.

Drawing on experience elsewhere in the Third World and that

of Ghana, Nigeria, and Senegal in Africa, Callaghy makes a probabilistic institutionalist argument that the reverse relationship holds: that increased participation in the formal political arena usually, but not always, makes systematic economic reform more difficult. In the process, he challenges the political half of the back to the future strategy and the current Western vision. Given the wave of political liberalization in Africa in the early 1990s, the limits on successful economic reform may be even greater in the last decade of the century than they were in the 1960s or the 1980s. In 1992, as Martin observes, "Zambia is if anything more `hemmed in,' because of a combination of intermittent reform and foreign exchange shortage," while "Ghana is much less `hemmed in,' because of its economic policy reforms, although these remained dependent on large volumes of aid and imports." Democratization is thus difficult under the best of circumstances; democratization with a diminished and still shrinking economic base is a haunting challenge.

In short, President Chiluba faces a Herculean task, given resurgent political logics and the very uneven learning curves of technocrats, officials, politicians, groups in civil society, and the mass electorate. Callaghy begins to explore institutional arrangements and agencies of restraint that might facilitate the maintenance of sound economic policy under democratic conditions. He stresses, however, that just because such structures are needed is no guarantee that they will be produced because institutions are the result of concrete political struggles the outcome of which are intrinsically unpredictable. Older political and economic logics may not be dead, and new learning patterns can be swamped easily.

While in Geneva in June 1992 in search of new investment, debt relief, and understanding to support Zambia's new attempt at IMF-sponsored economic reform, President Chiluba observed that, "The thrill of victory was soon replaced by an ominous realization that the country was not only run down and ravaged by mismanagement, but indeed also that the treasury was bare."[10] At the same time, he was confronted by a devastating regional drought, a serious AIDS crisis, political conflict with the former ruling party, and strikes from labor groups opposing 200 percent increases in staple food prices and plans for extensive privatization, both of which were demanded by external actors as the price of a new and innovative debt-relief plan. Chiluba noted that the strikes reflected "some excitement and some abuse, now that we are all free." He was also aware of a key obstacle: "But again I must admit that there has been a genuine feeling of disappointment, because generally when we started, an atmosphere was generated that created a crisis of expectations. Some people, in spite of what we told them, still felt that relief would come overnight, and when we said we have to show more responsibility, they thought we were running way from the promised way of life." Chiluba continued to believe, however, that "the people will learn that democracy is their own creation and that they don't have to destroy their own baby."[11] But will this learning come soon enough? Or will the IMF economic reform program once again "sow the seeds of unrest and undermine the spirit and unity of the nation" as former President Kenneth Kaunda put it in 1987,[12] and lead Zambia's new civil society to use its new found democracy to choose of its own free will to end the IMF program, as some of Chiluba's opponents hope?

External actors, as Martin notes, will share major responsibility because "it will be impossible to sustain this combination of economic and political liberalization without major changes in the way reform programs and external finance are negotiated." It is far from clear that such changes will be forthcoming, given the current international conjucture. Can Chiluba then take Zambia back to the future? The lessons of this book do not lead to optimism. As Green observes, most African governments "have few degrees of freedom left. They are 'hemmed in' by present resource levels, by poor external economic environment prospects and limited probability of large net resource inflow increases—as well as by the need to deliver perceived benefits to voters." In the process, Africa becomes even more disadvantaged relative to other regions of the world.

Current Conjuncture: African Performance in Comparative Perspective

As the World Bank correctly points out, "the 1980s saw a sharp divergence in economic performance across developing regions," and these "regional disparities in growth will continue."[13] A continuum, representing an enormous chasm, runs from East Asia, down through Latin America, Eastern Europe, the Middle East, and South Asia to Africa. The disparities between these regions preceded the 1980s, but they were seriously aggravated by "the lost decade." See tables 13.1 and 13.2 for data on the 1965–1989 period.

The average annual aggregate per capita real GNP for developing countries increased 2. 5% between 1965 and 1989, but in East Asia it grew 5.2% a year while in Africa it "increased" at only 0.4% a year. Thus, some regions have performed better than others, and some countries in each region have outperformed others in the same area.

Despite the diversity of these regions and countries, the key seems to be linkages to the world economy: "a recognition of the importance of international trade and finance for improving growth and per capita incomes. . . . Economies that chose to limit their links with the world economy have not fared as well." Countries that stressed linkages also "tended to do better during the turbulent 1980s than did others."[14] This held particularly for East Asia, including Korea, Taiwan, Thailand, and Malaysia, for several countries in Latin America, especially Mexico and Chile, and even for a couple of countries in Africa—Ghana and Botswana. As we shall see, however, outward orientation does not have to be of the "liberal," minimal state-variety recommended by the IMF and the World

TABLE 13.1

Growth of Real GDP Per Capita, 1965–2000

(average annual percentage change, unless noted)

Group	Population 1989 (millions)	1965–73	1973–80	1980–89	Production for 1990s[a]
Industrial Countries	773	3.7	2.3	2.3	1.8-2.5
Developing countries	4,053	3.9	2.5	1.6	2.2-2.9
Sub-Saharan Africa	480	2.1	0.4	-1.2	0.3-0.5
East Asia	1552	5.3	4.9	6.2	4.2-5.3
South Asia	1,131	1.2	1.7	3.0	2.1-2.6
Europe, Middle East, and North Africa	433	5.8	1.9	0.4	1.4-1.8
Latin America and the Caribbean	421	3.8	2.5	-0.4	1.3-2.0
Developing countries weighted by population[b]	4,053	3.0	2.4	2.9	2.7-3.2

[a]Projected on the basis of the two main scenarios (baseline and downside) discussed in Chapter 1 of *World Development Report 1991.*

[b]Using population shares as weights when aggregating GDP growth across countries.

SOURCE: World Bank, *World Development Report 1991* (New York: Oxford University Pres, 1991), p. 3.

Bank. In fact, explaining differentiation and its speed requires taking into account much more than externally oriented policies and the international economic environment. Stateness (administrative and technical capability), cosmopolitanism (the degree of sophisticated knowledge about how the international political economy works), regime type, politico-strategic linkages, overall level of development, and historical context all play a key role.

Recent developments are not encouraging, but need to be disaggregated by region and country. In 1989 the overall GDP growth rate for developing countries was 2.9%; it fell to 2.3 in 1990. In East Asia, however, it rose from 5.5% in 1989 to 6.7 in 1990; in Latin America, without Brazil, it rose from -0.2% to 2.0%; in the Middle East it increased from 2.6 to 3.2%. These increases were counterbalanced, however, by significant drops in Brazil, Eastern Europe, much of Africa, and, above all, what used to be the Soviet Union.

While the World Bank correctly expects these disparities to

TABLE 13.2
Growth in Developing Countries, by Region and Analytic Group, 1965–89 and the 1990s
(average annual percentage change)

			Scenarios for the 1990s			
Region or group	1965–89	1980–89	Low	Downside	Baseline	High
All developing countries	4.7	3.7	2.9	4.1	4.9	6.5
Geographic regions						
Sub-Saharan Africa	3.2	2.0	2.8	3.5	3.6	4.4
East Asia	7.2	7.9	3.9	5.6	6.7	8.8
South Asia	4.2	5.4	3.3	4.2	4.7	6.5
Europe, Middle East, and North Africa	4.2	2.5	2.5	3.2	3.6	4.7
Latin America	4.3	1.7	1.9	3.1	3.8	5.3
Analytical groups						
IDA-only adjusting Africa	2.3	2.5	3.2	4.0	4.5	5.6
Severely indebted middle-income countries	4.4	1.9	1.9	3.1	3.8	5.4
Exporters of fuels	3.2	1.8	3.5	4.5	4.1	3.5

SOURCE: World Bank, *Global Economic Prospects and the Developing Counties 1991* (Washington, D.C.: World Bank, 1991), p. 48.

grow, its assessments have often been overly optimistic. This has long been the case for the weakest of the regions—Africa. In 1991 the Bank for the first time candidly admitted in the *World Development Report* that many of its past projections, even the low-case ones, were overly optimistic. The Bank forthrightly declared that it had been "generally too hopeful about growth in the 1980s." Except for East Asia, the high cases were too favorable, with the low cases being "much closer to the mark." For Latin America, however, "even the low-case projections were too optimistic." For Africa, both the high and low cases "were revised downward" over time to a "fairly significant" degree as a result of "sharp economic deterioration." Why such undue optimism? Projections of world trade levels and inflows of capital were way too high, real interest rates did not come down as expected; and the "potential severity of the debt crisis" was underestimated, especially "the large negative transfer of resources from developing countries after the mid-1980s." Finally, and "perhaps most important," was the fact that "domestic policy weakness" was underestimated.[15]

The Bank is now carefully hedging its assessments for Africa. In 1991 it saw "the first tentative signs" of a "fragile" economic recovery, with many economies remaining in "precarious" conditions. But, for the countries that it saw as reforming, it was much more optimistic. They were "expected to grow relatively fast in the 1990s and to show significant improvement in performance over the 1980s." The "ifs" were quite substantial, however:

> Such sustained growth could be achieved if these countries maintain steady progress in implementing structural reforms, if their terms of trade do not deteriorate significantly, and if gross disbursements of official development assistance increase by about 4 percent a year in real terms. Much depends on the supply response induced by these conditions. So far, supply has responded hesitantly because of inadequate infrastructure and little confidence in the permanence of the reforms.[16]

The Bank's assessment for Africa's nonreformers is more likely to hold for the continent as a whole, precisely because reform is so very difficult: "these economies can expect significant deterioration in coming years. . . . They have become estranged from the world economy, and their isolation is expected to grow in the coming decade unless their domestic political and economic policy situations turn around significantly and international efforts to support growth in these economies are renewed." Unfortunately, "the composition of Africa's sources of external finance reinforces the composition of its production, exports, and debt in limiting Africa's opportunities in the medium term."[17]

The East Asia to Sub-Saharan Africa continuum thus constitutes an enormous chasm, especially as to the existence of effective linkages to the world economy, and this chasm is growing, not shrinking. This can be illustrated vividly by noting the response in the end point regions of the continuum to a one percentage point a year rise in OECD growth. For the developing countries as a whole it would bring a 0.7% increase in growth, but for Africa it would be only 0.5% while for East Asia it would be 1.0%. Can Africa do significantly better? Can it begin to perform like the East Asian "tigers," for example?

If Korea Can Do It, Why Not Africa? Or: Limited Current Relevance But Possible Future Model

In the late 1980s, a working group of senior African policy advisors examined the experience of the newly industrialized countries (NICs), particularly the Republic of Korea, "to see if there were any peculiar attributes in the social and political leadership that underlay these countries' success." The conclusion of this group was that "other than favorable economic conditions prevailing at the time most newly industrializing countries embarked on their development paths, nothing suggests that the social and political regimes existing were much different from other countries."[18]

As disappointment grows with Africa's economic record and with the lack of transformation brought about by structural adjustment programs, the East Asian NICs have come under increasing scrutiny in an attempt to derive lessons that might be applied in the African context. Politics cannot of course be abstracted from the historical and institutional context in which they were successful and be expected to work with similar effect elsewhere. Nevertheless, a study of the East Asian NICs is a useful exercise because lessons can indeed be learned—although their content may not be pleasing to many (including the African policy advisors quoted above who seem to interpret the East Asian experience so woefully) as they identify the crucial role of such factors as specific forms of political and socioeconomic structures and relationships that are missing from Africa.

South Korea is the obvious point of comparison. In 1950 it had a per capita income of $146 (in 1974 US dollars), less than that of Nigeria ($150) and only slightly more than those of Kenya ($129) and many other African countries.[19] Forty years later, Korea had become an impressive economic and industrial power—a transformation of quite startling speed and scope. Nigeria and Kenya, on the other hand, while among the better-performing African economies, had not achieved significant transformation despite, in the Nigerian case, considerable oil wealth. In 1989, the respective GNP per capita figures (in current dollars) and their average annual growth rates for 1965–89 were: Korea $4,400 and 7.0%; Nigeria $250 and 0.2%; and Kenya $360 and 2.0%. Comparable transformation has simply not taken place anywhere in Africa

Korea is almost the paradigmatic case of economic transformation in the Cold War era. It is also a case around which swirls a considerable debate, in large part because it does not match the neoclassical liberal prescriptions of the IMF and the World Bank.[20] These two institutions have finally begun to confront the implications of the Korean case, a point we shall return to in the conclusion.

In the years immediately after the Second World War, Korea was governed by a U.S. occupying administration which appeared to lack any clear sense of direction, and it subsequently fell victim to the personalized, corrupt administration of Syngman Rhee. In its rent-seeking and pursuit of patronage politics, and the subordination of economic rationality to short-term political gain, the Rhee regime was similar to many of the governments that have hastened Africa's economic decline in the last three decades. Under Rhee, Korea pursued import-substitution policies based on an overvalued exchange rate and political control of foreign exchange and imports (including the substantial volume of goods made available under the U.S. aid program). Access to foreign exchange and imports was an important source of rents which were employed to buy the loyalty of the army, the bureaucracy, and the emerging middle class.

Despite these problems, Korea's starting point on its path to economic development in the 1950s was not the same as that of Africa in the 1990s. The Japanese colonization of Korea in the years 1910–45 laid far stronger foundations for future economic growth than did the Western colonial powers in their much longer occupation of Africa. The Japanese administration introduced land reform and modernized agricultural production, built a strong centralized state apparatus around a well-educated colonial bureaucracy and a large police and military apparatus, and developed the country's transport and communications infrastructures. Although Korea was initially used primarily as an exporter of agricultural products, the Japanese also built a substantial industrial capacity, particularly after the invasion of Manchuria.

In the 1950s, the economy was saved from the worst depredations of a rent-seeking polity by massive inflows of foreign assistance. USAID contributed close to $6 billion to Korea which also benefitted from about $7 billion in U.S. military assistance; most of this was in grant form.[21] Foreign aid financed 70% of all of Korea's imports in the years 1953–62; the sum was equivalent to 75% of the country's total fixed capital formation.[22] Industry grew quite rapidly in the Rhee years (more than 11% annually) benefiting both from high tariff barriers and the effect of aid inflows in considerably reducing foreign exchange constraints.[23] But the overall rate of economic growth was modest (an annual average of 4.2% in 1953–62).[24] Rhee resisted the efforts of U.S. advisers to push for more rational economic policies—decreased government expenditures, higher taxes, and lower exchange rates—because they would have posed a threat to the government's patronage system. And despite his dependence on U.S. assistance, Rhee was able to do this successfully by playing on the country's geostrategic importance.

By the end of the 1950s Korea had failed to capitalize on the strong foundations for economic growth inherited from the Japanese. In a survey of 74 Third World countries conducted by Adelman and Morris, Korea displayed the biggest discrepancy between per capita income achieved and a composite indicator of sociopolitical development. Whereas Korea ranked 60th in 1961 in per capita income, it was ranked 14th on the composite indicator, which included "size of traditional sector, extend of dualism, character of basic social organization, size of the indigenous middle class, extent of social mobility, extent of mass communication, crude fertility rate, and the degree of modernization of outlook."[25]

However imperfect such quantitative indicators, Korea was clearly a country of significant unfulfilled potential.

A restructuring of the state and its relations with society was necessary; to unlock this potential the state and its relations with society had to be restructured. And this is where the African policy advisers quoted at the beginning of this section are so wrong. While the Korean state under Rhee may have been very similar to many contemporary African states; that which evolved after the military coup of 1961 was very different. The military leadership that seized power justified its move as necessary for ending corruption and for achieving real economic development. It set out to eradicate the old crony networks and the rentier predatory state. Pivotal to this effort was the centralization of political power, the gaining of autonomy from pressures from societal groups, and the institutionalization of centralized decision-making by technocrats who again enjoyed substantial autonomy from societal pressures.

The military moved quickly to curtail political pluralism and participation, temporarily banning more than 4,000 politicians. It also purged the bureaucracy and the military, using as its main instrument the powerful newly created Korean Central Intelligence Agency. All major social groups, especially peasants, students, and above all, labor, were kept at bay via coercion and institutional control structures. There was, however, important societal opposition, and it was quite consistent; but it was tightly contained by the government's coercive apparatus.

On seizing power, the military arrested most leading businessmen but exempted them from prosecution for their previous corrupt activities provided they agreed to establish new industrial firms and donate shares to the state. The military realized that its own legitimacy rested on success in fostering rapid economic growth, and that this was ultimately dependent on the performance of the private sector.[26] The government provided the large business groups, the *chaebol,* with credit, subsidies, information, logistical assistance, protection, and controlled labor. But although it recognized the necessity of creating an economy conducive to business success, the government was never captive to any particular business interest. By making its support to companies conditional on performance criteria, very often success in expanding exports, the government was able to force business out of rent-seeking into productive activities. Companies that failed to meet government expectations were allowed to go bankrupt and their assets taken over by better performers. There may have been a partnership between business and government in Korea but government was the dominant partner.[27]

To manage this new structure of benign mercantilism an institutional revolution of economic centralization was carried out that allowed a major role for insulated technocratic endeavor and external advice aimed at the very top of the presidential political structure. Of key importance in this new policy framework were the Economic Planning Board, staffed by technocrats many of whom were educated overseas, and extensive external economic advice, primarily from the U.S. and the World Bank. These changes built on the halting, but ineffective reform efforts that the Rhee government had undertaken in order to pacify the American government.[28] The new economic institutions used and reshaped the existing bureaucracy, thereby increasing its status and power, and eliminated any significant opposition within the administration to economic reform.

While corruption and rent-seeking were never fully eliminated and were often the substance of opposition charges, they were significantly reduced. And while government encouraged the accumulation of wealth, it acted to direct the uses to which private accumulation could be put. The state was no longer the predatory one of the Rhee era; it was becoming a developmental state, albeit a harsh one.[29] Both the overall rate of economic growth and the rate of growth of industry more than doubled after the military coup.

Of course the Korean success story was engineered within a specific historical context. Rapid growth of exports began in a period in which world trade was expanding rapidly and there were relatively few barriers to exports of manufactures. Korea continued to benefit from significant amounts of U.S. assistance; the country's geostrategic importance caused the U.S. to turn a blind eye to its predatory, mercantilist trading policies. Based on substantial societal and cultural integration, relatively high levels of educational achievement, and low dependence on foreign direct investment, the Koreans managed to achieve higher levels of both stateness and cosmopolitanism than other developing countries. They aggressively sought to build links to the world economy; they ventured out to acquire and master new technologies, knowledge and institutions, to build local capacities, to understand, use and manipulate the world economy—in other words, to manage and transform their dependence.

Much more might be written about the lessons of the Korean experience for Africa. Korea consciously engaged the world economy rather than fleeing from it. The Korean case underlies the false dichotomy that is often drawn between import-substituting industrialization and export-oriented industrialization. The Korean government deliberately set about "getting prices wrong" in order to foster rapid industrialization;[30] its role was not confined to creating an "enabling environment" but extended to what Wade has termed "big leadership"—taking the initiative to push industry in a particular direction.[31] The structure of incentives it created, however, certainly did not discriminate against exporting activities and, for the most part, fostered them while forcing firms to adjust to international market signals. Government support to industry was conditional on performance criteria, especially the expansion of exports. Limitations were placed on the role of foreign direct investment; the activities of transnational corporations were harnessed for national advantage. Clearly Korea does not conform to the laissez faire model beloved by neoclassical economists in general and by the IMF and the World Bank in particular.

Yet perhaps the most significant lessons of Korea for Africa lie in the political realm: the necessity for relative political stability; the necessity to curtail rent-seeking and corruption; the importance of a well-educated corps of economic technocrats who play a central role in policy-making and enjoy a substantial degree of autonomy from societal groups. In other words, the Korean case underlines the central importance of stateness and cosmopolitanism, both of which most African countries currently lack. Identifying these factors is one thing; engineering them is another matter.[32] As Green puts it, "The chances of Sub-Saharan Africa breaking out into Asian NIC-type economic dynamism by the year 2000 are nil. Even one such case would be surprising." But, as Gordon observes, "In both Asian and Latin American countries, fundamental reform took place only when domestic leaders put in place programs that went far beyond anything suggested by the IMF and the World Bank. This has not yet happened anywhere in Africa." Having said this, however, to rule out moving slowly and carefully in this direction, as the current Fund/Bank back to the future strategy does, would do Africa a great disservice and keep it distinctly "hemmed in" over the long haul.

The Need to Mitigate External Constraints

How can the industrial countries assist Africa to become less hemmed in? Ultimately, the reversal of economic decline will depend largely on African countries' own efforts. But if they do not receive significant assistance from the international community (which has yet to fulfill its part of the implicit structural adjustment compact), their efforts may well come to naught no matter what strategy is used. Such external aid is yet another factor that is necessary but not sufficient to ensure that countries will become less "hemmed in." External assistance in itself, however massive, will not bring about the necessary transformation unless accompanied by sustained domestic adjustment, and, in case of systematic nonreform, external actors should cease all support until a real commitment to reform is evident. On the other hand, countries that are proceeding along the difficult path of domestic adjustment will stumble, as occurred in Zambia in 1986–87, unless the international community acts effectively to smooth their way, a fact stressed by several authors in this volume.

Industrial countries and the international financial institutions need to display more flexibility in designing and implementing structural adjustment programs. Martin's article (chapter 4) illustrates the unnecessary problems that arise from an overly rigid approach to negotiations on adjustment programs. An important dimension of this is the attitude toward the role of state. While we would be the last to suggest that the performance of most African states in the quarter century after independence was anything less than disastrous, the lesson to be learned from Korea and other East Asian NICs is that the state is central rather than irrelevant to economic success. The focus should not be on removing the state completely from the economic arena, but on building effective state apparatuses that are technically proficient, run on meritocratic lines, and seek to engage with rather than flee from the world economy. As we shall see, it is encouraging that the Bank's recent reports appear to endorse this approach, even if timidly so.

The most immediate external constraint that Africa faces, however, is the debt crisis. Some have argued that the crisis is not of great import since creditors and borrowers alike recognize that African countries simply will not service and repay the debt, thereby reducing the problem to a paper abstraction. This view, however, ignores the considerable damage that the debt overhang does to economies through its impact on the psychology of investors. The possibility that a large proportion of future export earnings will have to be devoted to debt repayment inevitably has a deterrent effect on potential investors; it will also have a similar effect on African reformers, especially in an era of political liberalization.

The measures agreed by the major industrialized countries at the 1988 Toronto economic summit for the official debts (export credits) of low-income African countries have offered some temporary relief at best and merely postpone the day of reckoning. They are more significant for establishing a precedent of writing off export credits (donors in the past had only been willing to forgive development loans) than for the actual relief provided. UNCTAD estimates that the savings on interest will amount to no more than two percent of debt service payments.[33] The failure of the London economic summit in 1991 to go beyond the Toronto measures by adopting Prime Minister Major's Trinidad terms was particularly disappointing.

Having established the principle of writing off export credits, industrialized countries should now follow the recommendations of the Wass Report[34]—written by an advisory group of bankers, officials, and academics under UN sponsorship—and convert them into loans on terms similar to those available from the International Development Association (IDA), that is, annual rates of interest of 0.5% over forty years with a ten-year grace period.

The experience of Ghana, the only African country that sustained a rigorous adjustment program throughout 1980s, and of Korea and Taiwan demonstrates that a massive inflow of resources is necessary if structural adjustment is to be successful. This is even more the case if attention is to be given—as it should be—to protecting poorer groups of the population from the adverse effects of adjustment and to laying the human foundations for sustained economic growth. Ghana, however, has shown the negative effects of being a large-scale recipient of international lending on currently available terms—a worrying trend toward greater indebtedness. Its significant borrowing from the IMF—more than $1.2 billion in commitments in the period 1983–88—means, even with some money being on SAF and ESAF terms, that there is a bunching of repayments in the early and mid 1990s. The potential for a number of "successfully adjusting" countries to experience difficulties in servicing their debts to the IFIs in the next few years suggests the need for another facility that makes finance available on IDA terms.

A second general area in which industrialized countries could take supportive action is trade. Two dimensions of Africa's needs in the next decade immediately come to mind: (1) security of access for commodities and manufactured products alike, and (2) remunerative prices for African commodity exports.

Most African commodities enter their principal markets duty-free. The exceptions are certain agricultural products which compete with Northern-hemisphere domestic agriculture, e.g. beef, sugar, tomatoes, and cut flowers. In their most important market, the European Community, some African commodities enjoy a tariff advantage over those of other exporters by virtue of the provisions of the Lomé Convention. If the Uruguay Round of international trade negotiations is eventually successful, the preferential margin in the EC market on a number of tropical products will be reduced. To some extent this would be compensated by improved access for African agricultural exports to markets in other industrialized countries and by increased consumption if some of the absurdities of the current agricultural policies of industrialized countries are abandoned. The net impact is difficult to forecast; indeed, in an era of floating exchange rates, the advantages offered by tariff preferences may be of little consequence. But it is clear that Africa's commodity export prospects increasingly will depend on competitive marketing. Here industrialized countries could help by providing additional finance to assist African countries in setting up trade-promoting organizations and participating in trade fairs.

In attempting to increase exports of processed and manufacturing goods, Africa faces a number of formidable disadvantages, including inferior and expensive external transport links, unreliable infrastructure, lack of knowledge of markets, and a poorly trained and relatively expensive work force. If export-oriented manufacturing is to be attracted to Africa, it will need the incentives not only of a secure domestic working environment but also security of access to overseas markets. In Africa's relations with

Europe this was supposed to have been provided through the trade provisions of the Lomé Convention; in reality this has proved not to be the case, as African suppliers of textiles to the European market were threatened with the use of the Convention's safeguard clause in an effort to force them to agree to voluntary export restraints.[35] The impact of the European Community's short-sighted policy was to cast doubt in the minds of all potential investors about the prospects for secure access.

If industrialized countries are sincere in their support for diversification of African economies and in their demands for a secure environment for foreign investment, they should provide a guarantee of market access for the nontraditional exports of African countries. The ideal would be a commitment that no African exports would be subject to voluntary export restraints or other non-tariff or tariff barriers for an extended period, say fifteen years. This would be offered provided such exports complied with reasonable "rules of origin" (which specify how much value must be added locally for the export to be counted as a product of the country, thereby avoiding the problem of goods merely being trans-shipped through Africa from third countries to exploit the privileged access to industrialized markets). The world is gradually waking up to the uniqueness of Africa's economic problems. Just as special measures are necessary for these states in the financial sphere, similar special treatment is essential on trade issues.

The second major trade problem that Africa faces is the unstable and generally declining prices in the world markets for its principal commodity exports. Industrialized countries should cooperate with Southern countries in attempting to revive international commodity agreements. The depression of non-fuel commodity prices in the last decade deprived not only producing countries of income but also industrialized countries of markets for their exports. Successful agreements will almost certainly require industrialized countries to enforce production quotas (through application of import quotas) given the present overproduction and conflict of interest between Southern suppliers. For the NICs such as Brazil and Malaysia to be encouraged to reduce their investment in commodity production, liberalization of access for their manufactured goods to the markets of industrialized countries will be required as will more action on debt relief for the heavily indebted countries. Only if these issues are tackled globally will the current fallacy of composition problems inherent in the back to the future strategy be avoided.

There is also a good case for the introduction of a global system to stabilize the commodity export earnings of African countries, an improved and extended version of the STABEX scheme that is part of the Lomé Convention.[36] A scheme of this type can help countries cope with the problems of severe fluctuations in their export earnings. The problem with such arrangements, however, is that typically they merely offer compensation for earnings that have fallen below a trend average. In a period of falling commodity prices, they stabilize earnings around a declining trajectory (and thus need to be supplemented by international commodity agreements that attempt to maintain price levels).

The measures listed here are feasible steps that industrialized countries could take to create an external "enabling environment" for African adjustment. Many more measures might be listed, ranging from improved technical cooperation to support for African efforts to build regional economic cooperation schemes. Since adjustment on the part of African states is necessary, it is reasonable for industrialized countries to make access to benefits conditional on African governments agreeing to reform programs—but ones that are flexible enough to take into account changes in the external environment and avoid the proliferation of conditions that accompanied Fund and Bank programs in the late 1980s. Given mounting demands elsewhere in the world and the increasing preoccupation of industrialized countries with their own problems, it is not at all clear how many of these "feasible" steps will be taken. If they are not, it will be that much more difficult for African countries to become less "hemmed in."

Conclusion: Vision and Politics in the Transformation of Political Economies

The now "triumphant" industrial democracies have a brilliant vision of global transformation via the magic of the market and the ballot box, including a special back to the future version for Africa, but it is a flawed vision. It is flawed in three majors ways: (1) it underestimates the role of the state in economic transformation; (2) it misperceives the link between economic transformation and type of political regime by assuming that economic reform requires simultaneous political liberalization or democratization; and (3) it seriously underestimates the role and importance of larger contextual factors, that is, the institutions, knowledge, attitudes, and infrastructure that underpin states, markets, and regimes. These flaws and misperceptions mean that the vision is not likely to be realized in very many places in Africa or in the Third and former Second Worlds more generally, and, thus, that differentiation rather than convergence between regions and countries will mark the coming decade with confrontational rather than harmonious consequences. Each of these flaws and their consequences will be examined briefly in this concluding section.

Role of the State

While it correctly captures the fundamental importance of linkages to the world economy, the Western liberal vision has underestimated the role of the state in economic transformation in three major ways: by failing to perceive (1) the existence of the orthodox paradox, that is, that even neoclassical economic reform requires a relatively capable and important state structure; (2) that any state, authoritarian or democratic, but especially the latter, needs to buffer the sociopolitical consequences of transformation, and (3) that the liberal vision of economic transformation itself, especially its stress on minimalist states, the power of markcts, and correct policy packages, might not be the only possible path to transformation, or even the most common one.

Throughout the 1980s, Western actors responded to each of these three problem areas in partial ways. For the first problem area, they stressed the non-regime-type aspects of "governance," e.g. administrative probity and efficiency; effective legal, judicial, and regulatory mechanisms, especially for property rights and contracts; and informational and policy openness or "transparency," including such things as a relatively free press. The "laundry list" of relevant factors is now quite long. Each one of these elements probably is important but, as the list continues to grow, it is difficult to know which one to target or how to do it. For the second problem area, external actors have increasingly focused on the salience of the social costs of adjustment and policies to deal with them, particularly the creation of a social "safety net" for the most adversely affected groups. For the third problem area, they have recently made a quite interesting but still hesitant about-face, in large part by finally beginning to come to terms with the reality of Korea and other heavily statist cases of transformation: they now admit the possible importance of "market-friendly" forms of state intervention. Each of these responses constitutes an important form of learning, but it remains unclear how centrally and consistently this learning will be reflected in the programs and policies of the major Western governments and the IMF and World Bank and whether the resources exist to support new approaches.

Since the third change is particularly important, it needs to be explored a little more fully. In its reports on Africa in the late 1980s, the World Bank began to admit tacitly more of a role for the state in economic transformation. With the 1991 *World Development Report*, however, the shift became more explicit. Referring to "the remarkable achievements of the East Asian economies, or with the earlier achievements of Japan," the report asks, "Why, in these economies, were interventions in the markets such as infant-industry protection and credit subsidies associated with success, not failure?" The Bank's answer, in short, is that these "market-friendly" state interventions were "carried out competently, pragmatically, and flexibly," were terminated if they failed or outlasted their usefulness, did not distort relative prices "unduly," and were export-oriented, "moderate" rather than all encompassing, undertaken reluctantly and openly, and constantly disciplined by international and domestic markets. In sum, according to the Bank, these "market-friendly" forms of state intervention "refute the case for thoroughgoing dirigisme as convincingly as they refute the case for laissez-faire."[37] Until quite recently Western reaction to Third and Second World statism has been what Tony Killick has aptly called "a reaction too far,"[38] especially when Western behavior belies its own rhetoric, as Callaghy showed in his discussion of embedded liberalism. Effective outward-oriented transformation can quite clearly be achieved without following all the liberal economic mantras of the IMF and the World Bank. While the capabilities of African countries are weak at the moment, they need to work in this direction, however slowly and carefully.

In fact, this new view of the World Bank still significantly underestimates the type and degree of state intervention in cases such as Korea, but it does represent a major shift toward a more balanced tension between state and market, one that has long been evident in the "embedded liberal" practice, if not the rhetoric, of Northern industrial democracies. It is not a view fully shared so far by the IMF or some Western governments, however.[39] It is also not a view shared by many longtime critics of the World Bank, those seeking a "new political economy of development" which continues to stress the state over the market. This is indicated by the book title of a recent representative attack on Western "neo-liberalism": *States or Markets? Neo-Liberalism and the Development Policy Debate*.[40] A more balanced viewpoint would be *States and Markets*.

While all sides still need to seek a proper balanced tension between state and market, admitting the need for it is an important first step. It does, however, open up a major Pandora's box that Western actors have wanted to keep closed. Once you concede a serious, nonliberal role for the state, you then must decide on specific types and instances of state intervention. This is an enormously difficult thing to accomplish and clearly constitutes the current policy frontier. The elegant parsimony of the neoclassical vision has been replaced by messy ambiguity and relativity. Such an admission does not, however, imply that the state capabilities necessary to engage successfully in such intervention will exist when and where they are needed.

Economic and Political Liberalization

The cases presented in this volume, we believe, do not support the current Western faith in a tight and simultaneous link between economic and political liberalization. Our pessimism on this matter is in contrast to more optimistic views held by some of our contributors. We have seen that insulation, delegation, and buffering have been central to success at economic transformation. There appears to be a clear historical correlation between authoritarian rule and the ability to engage in major economic restructuring, but not a necessary theoretical one. The search then becomes one for what might be called "effective and sustainable democratic functional equivalents." Institutions and processes of delegation and insulation can exist under democratic conditions, as indicated in Callaghy's chapter, but they are difficult to achieve, and, above all, to sustain over time. If they are to be found, they will need to be supported by relatively high levels of resources. Even then the outcome may be very difficult to sustain, and it will depend on unpredictable political struggles, especially electoral ones, and on larger contextual factors.

Contextual Factors

As the last major flaw, the Western liberal vision has seriously underestimated the importance of larger contextual factors beyond policy change that facilitate transformation, that is, the institutions, knowledge, attitudes, and infrastructure which underpin states, markets, and regimes.[41] This powerful vision is an amazingly parsimonious one; it asserts that the magic of the market and the ballot box can be achieved by merely changing economic policy and allowing more political participation. It is also an amazingly apolitical vision as it fails to see many of the difficulties of implementation and process over time. As a result, it has significantly underestimated the time frame and costs of transformation. Clearly Western actors suffer from the "faults of analytic and policy hurry."

Because of these flaws and misperceptions in the Western liberal vision, plus the failure of the implicit bargain, the concomitant officialization and politicization of resource flows, and continued difficulties with the openness of trade, it is not likely that the vision will be realized in very many places, especially in Africa. The result will be increasing differentiation between countries and regions of Africa and elsewhere rather than accelerating convergence. This vision emerged out of the core of the international political economy—the Northern industrial democracies—and it is deeply rooted in their sociopolitical realities, dynamics, and weltanschauungs. As such, it is also deeply rooted in the international hierarchy of power, but in its contact with the Third World generally, and Africa in particular, the vision confronts local and regional realities, logics, struggles, politics, and histories and is frequently deflected by them.

The trajectory of individual African countries will be affected by a series of interlinked internal and external factors. On the internal side, relatively high degrees of stateness and cosmopolitanism are central to position a country better in the international political economy, especially the ability to monitor changes in the world economy and to bargain in a sophisticated way with all types of actors—private business groups, states, international financial institutions, and private voluntary organizations. This is particularly true for trade and credit, as the international political economy has always been more statist in these areas than most analysts are willing to admit.

Whether increased stateness and cosmopolitanism will emerge in many places in Africa, however, is very questionable, but Africa needs to work in this direction so that it can eventually go beyond the back to the future strategy. Certainly local and regional political and social dynamics will affect attempts to achieve a productive balanced tension between state and market, state and society, and state and the international arena. At bottom it is still a self-help world, and nobody should wait for external miracles that will restructure the international political economy to make it more fair or equitable. Despite all the rhetoric to the contrary, very few Western actors believe they owe Africa a living. A pervasive view among Western actors is that if the IMF and the World Bank can pull off miracles in the Africa, fine; if not, so be it: there are other places to go.

Although it is largely a self-help world, external factors are very important in determining country trajectories. These factors revolve largely around the degree of openness of the world trading order, the extent to which the implicit bargain is fulfilled, and the stability of the overall politico-strategic environment. The first two are very much in doubt, while the third depends greatly on the functioning of the new "unipolarity without hegemony" as it responds to emerging challenges.

Over the course of the 1980s, the IMF, the World Bank, and the major Western countries learned important lessons about the difficulties of implementing the liberal vision in Africa. While many more remain to be learned, these lessons now need to be applied systematically so that the gap between the vision and reality may be narrowed. This is particularly true for lessons about the implicit bargain, the need to buffer adjustment costs, the enormous challenges of simultaneous economic and political liberalization, the importance of a balanced tension between state and market, and centrality of stateness, cosmopolitanism, and larger contextual factors. If these lessons are not learned and applied, then the brilliant Western liberal vision will remained seriously flawed, in large part by the powerful realities of politics, and Africa will remain badly "hemmed in."

NOTES

1. Frederick Chiluba, "Inauguration Speech of Frederick Chiluba, November 2, 1991," typed manuscript, pp. 1–4.

2. As indicated in the introduction to this volume, by "hemmed in" we mean a situation in which the viable policy alternatives, and the capacities and resources needed to implement them, available to African governments are severely constrained as a consequence *inter alia* of volatile politics, weak states, weak markets, debt problems, and an unfavorable international environment.

3. World Bank, *Sub-Saharan Africa: From Crisis to Sustainable Growth* (Washington, D.C.: World Bank, 1989); also see Harvey Glickman, ed., *The Crisis and Challenge of African Development* (Westport, CT: Greenwood Press, 1988).

4. On governance, see Deborah Brautigam, "Governance and Economy: A Review," Working Paper, Policy and Review Department, World Bank, Washington, D.C., December 1991.

5. On the "nightmare scenario," see Economic Commission for Africa, "ECA and Africa's Development: 1983–2008," Addis Ababa, April 1983, and "Beyond Recovery: ECA–Revised Perspective of Africa's Development, 1988–2008," Addis Ababa, March 1988.

6. See Howard Stein, ed., *Asian Industrialization: Lessons for Africa* (London: Macmillan, forthcoming), especially the chapter by Deborah Brautigam, "The State as Agent: Industrialization in Taiwan 1895–1976 and Lessons for Sub-Saharan Africa."

7. Atul Kohli and Vivienne Shue, "State Power and Social Forces: On Political Contention and Accommodation in the Third World" in Joel S. Migdal, Atul Kohli, and Vivienne Shue, eds., *State Power and Social Forces: Domination and Transformation in the Third World* (New York: Cambridge University Press, forthcoming).

8. Based on discussion with Janet Roitman in September 1992 about ongoing research in northern Cameroon.

9. On democracy, uncertainty, and credibility, see Adam Przeworski, *Democracy and the Market: Political and Economic Reforms in Eastern Europe and Latin America* (New York: Cambridge University Press, 1991), and Alberto Alesina, "Political Models of Macroeconomic Policy and Fiscal Reforms," paper for a World Bank conference on "The Political Economy of Structural Adjustment in New Democracies," Washington, D.C., May 1992.

10. Quoted in "The Cupboard is Bare," *Africa News*, June 22-July 5, 1992, p. 16.

11. Ibid. and Margaret A. Novicki, "Frederick Chiluba, Champion of Zambia's Democracy," *Africa Report* 38, 1 (Jaunuary–February 1993): 37.

12. Foreign Broadcast Information Service, May 4, 1987, p. U9.

13. The data in this section are from two companion reports: World Bank, *Global Economic Prospects and the Developing Countries* (Washington, D.C.: World Bank, May 1991) and World Bank, *World Development Report 1991: The Challenge of Development* (New York: Oxford University Press, 1991);

the focus of the latter for 1991 is the record of attempted economic reform in the 1980s.

14. World Bank, *Global Economic Prospects*, p. 17.

15. World Bank, *World Development Report 1991*, pp. 28–29.

16. World Bank, *Global Economic Prospects*, pp. 6, 58 (emphases added).

17. Ibid., pp. 58, 4.

18. Quoted in Cadman Atta Mills, *Structural Adjustment in Sub-Saharan Africa: Report on a Series of Five Senior Policy Seminars Held in Africa 1987–88* (Washington, D.C.: World Bank EDI Policy Seminar Report No. 18, 1989), p. 23.

19. Cited in Chalmers Johnson, "Political Institutions and Economic Performance" in Frederic C. Deyo, ed., *The Political Economy of the New Asian Industrialism* (Ithaca: Cornell University Press, 1987), p. 136. On the expanding comparative literature on the East Asian and Latin American NICs, see Stephan Haggard, *Pathways from the Periphery* (Ithaca: Cornell University Press, 1990); Peter B. Evans, "Class, State and Dependence in East Asia: Lessons for Latin Americanists" in Deyo, ed. *The Political Economy of the New Asian Industrialism*, pp. 203–26; Gary Gereffi and Donald L. Wyman, eds., *Manufacturing Miracles: Paths of Industrialization in Latin America and East Asia* (Princeton: Princeton University Press, 1990); Robert Wade, *Governing the Market: Economic Theory and the Role of Government in East Asian Industrialization* (Princeton: Princeton University Press, 1990); and Ziya Onis, "The Logic of the Developmental State," *Comparative Politics* 24, 1 (October 1991): 109–126. On Korea, in addition to the above citations, see Stephan Haggard and Chung-in Moon, "The South Korean State in the International Economy: Liberal, Dependent, or Mercantile?" in Ruggie, ed., *The Antinomies of Interdependence*, pp. 131–189; Alice H. Amsden, *Asia's Next Giant: South Korea and Late Industrialization* (New York: Oxford University Press, 1989); Larry E. Westphal, "Industrial Policy in an Export-Propelled Economy: Lessons from South Korea's Experience," *Journal of Economic Perspectives* 4, 3 (1990): 41–59; Il SaKong, *Korea and the World Economy*, (Washington, D.C.: Institute for International Economics, forthcoming; Jung-En Woo, *Race to the Swift: State and Finance in Korean Industrialization* (New York: Cambridge University Press, 1991); Ji-Hong Kim, "Korea: Adjustment in Developing Industries, Government Assistance in Troubled Economies" in Hugh T. Patrick, ed., *Pacific Basin Industries in Distress: Structural Adjustment and Trade Policy in Nine Industrialized Economies* (New York: Columbia University Press, 1991), pp. 357–417.

20. See Robert Wade, "East Asia's Economic Success: Conflicting Perspectives, Partial Insights, Shaky Evidence," *World Politics* 44, 2 (January 1992): 270–320.

21. Edward S. Mason, "Preface" in Leroy P. Jones and Il SaKong, eds., *Government, Business and Entrepreneurship in Economic Development: The Korean Case* (Cambridge: Harvard University Press, 1980) p.vi.

22. Stephen Haggard, *Pathways from the Periphery*, p.55.

23. Alice Amsden, *Asia's Next Giant.*

24. Jones and SaKong, eds., *Government, Business and Entrepreneurship*, p. 1.

25. Irma Adelman and Cynthia Taft Morris, "Society, Politics and Economic Development: A Quantitative Approach" quoted in ibid.

26. Although there was substantial public sector involvement in Korean growth in the 1960s and 1970s, the government was formally committed to a private enterprise economy.

27. Jones and Sakong, eds., *Government, Business and Entrepreneurship,* p. 67.

28. A Ministry of Reconstruction was founded in 1955, and an Economic Development Council was formed under its auspices in 1958.

29. See Peter B. Evans, "The State as Problem and Solution: Predation, Embedded Autonomy, and Structural Change" in Stephan Haggard and Robert Kaufman, eds., *The Politics of Economic Adjustment* (Princeton: Princeton University Press, 1992), pp. 139–181.

30. The theme of Amsden, *Asia's Next Giant,* but also a major part of the argument of Jones and SaKong, *Government, Business and Entrepreneurship.*

31. Wade, *Governing the Market.*

32. See Brautigam, "The State as Agent: Industrialization in Taiwan 1985–1976 and Lessons for Africa" and "Regional Industrialization in Eastern Nigeria," report prepared for Nigeria Country Operations, West Africa Region, World Bank, Washington, D.C., 1992

33. *UNCTAD Bulletin* (May–June 1990): p. 11.

34. *Financing Africa's Recovery* (New York: United Nations, 1988). For further discussion of the debt issue, see G. K. Helleiner, "International Policy Issues Posed by Sub-Saharan African Debt," *The World Economy* 12, 3 (September 1989): 315–324.

35. See John Ravenhill, *Collective Clientelism: The Lomé Convention and North-South Relations* (New York: Columbia University Press, 1985).

36. For details of the STABEX scheme and its shortcomings, see John Ravenhill, "What is to be Done for Third World Commodity Producers? An Evaluation of the STABEX Scheme," *International Organization,* 38, 3 (Summer 1984), pp. 537–574.

37. World Bank, *World Development Report 1991,* p. 5, also see pp. 39–40.

38. Tony Killick, *A Reaction Too Far* (Boulder: Westview Press, 1990).

39. The Japanese have begun to push the IMF and the World Bank to allow more market-friendly state interventionism in their prescriptions for reforming countries.

40. Christopher Colclough and James Manor, eds., *States or Markets? Neo-Liberalism and the Development Policy Debate* (New York: Oxford University Press, 1991).

41. For a theoretical argument about contextual factors, which draws on Max Weber, see Thomas M. Callaghy, "The State and the Development of Capitalism in Africa: Theoretical, Historical, and Comparative Reflections" in Donald Rothchild and Naomi Chazan, eds., *The Precarious Balance: State and Society in Africa* (Boulder: Westview Press, 1988), pp. 67–99.

Index

Abbey, Joseph, 489
Afro-optimism, 1
Afro-pessimism, 2, 522
Agriculture, 10, 30, 43–44, 63, 248–71; and economic decline, 4, 334–37; and economic reform, 264–71, 332–53, 528–29; and infrastructure reform, 342–45; cropping patterns, 264–66; Gezira Scheme, 257; Niger Agricultural Project, 257; patterns of investment, 266–67; price reform, 339–42; producer prices, 30, 408–13, 425; share contracts, 283–85, 307–9; Tanganyika Groundnut Scheme, 257
Ahidjo, Ahmadu, 359, 361–62, 365, 368, 371, 376, 380
Aid fatigue, 109, 126; *see also* Donor fatigue
Alfonsin, Raul, 473
Amin, Idi, 187, 448
Angola, 75, 185, 187
Argentina, 472–73
Asamoah, B. B., 200
Authoritarianism, 182–83, 185, 199–200, 203, 465–66; and economic reform, 465–66, 485
Aylwin, Patricio, 481, 485

Babangida, Ibrahim, 15, 46, 202, 485, 489–91, 495–96
Bamiléké, 366–69
Banda, Hastings, 187
Banny, Jean Konan, 280
Bates, Robert, 287, 337–38, 340, 399
Bayart, Jean-François, 359, 364–65
Belaúnde, Fernando, 473
Beer, C. E. F., 287
Benin, 185, 201, 380

Berg Report, 18, 24, 108–109, 417, 426; *see also* World Bank
Berry, Sara, 3, 10–11, 16, 285–87, 529–30, 532–33
Bienen, Henry, 114, 340
Bilateral donors, 72, 99, 104–5, 116, 151–52, 166, 379
Biya, Paul, 14, 46, 357, 368–69, 371, 375–77, 380–82, 384–87, 479, 535
Black, Yondo, 380
Boahen, Adu, 200
Bolivia, 472, 475
Boone, Catherine, 499
Botchwey, Kwesi, 162, 469
Botswana, 72–73, 187, 200–201, 224–27, 230–31, 233–35, 542
Brady Plan, 99
Bratton, Michael, 203
Brazil, 32, 76, 467, 473, 554
Burkina Faso, 188, 207, 261, 300
Burundi, 224

Callaghy, Thomas, 4, 15, 45–46, 91, 96, 204, 358, 398, 442, 463, 520, 527, 531, 535, 539–40, 557–58
Cameroon, 13–14, 33, 46, 185, 187–88, 195, 199, 526, 535–36; agricultural reform, 32, 258; *Centre National de la Documentation et de la Recherche* (CENER), 376; corruption, 376–77; economic reform, 357–60, 373–89; manufacturing, 224–26, 231–32; National Coordination of Opposition Parties and Associations (NCOPA), 381–82; privatization, 378; *Rassemblement Démocratique du Peuple Camerounais* (RPDC), 367; structural adjustment, 362–64; *Union Centrale des Coopératives Agricoles de l'Ouest* (UCCAO), 369–71; *Villes Mortes*, 381–82
Canada, 156, 167
Cape Verde, 72, 201
Capitalism, 464; *see also* Economic reform
Chazan, Naomi, 3, 8, 43, 123, 180, 287, 534
Chad, 187
Chege, Michael, 1, 17, 439
Chenery, Hollis, 216
Chile, 38, 472–73, 481, 484–85, 489, 505, 509, 542
Chiluba, Frederick, 1, 17, 133, 135–39, 503, 520–22, 528, 536–37, 539–41
China, 230
Chissano, Joaquim, 54
Civil society, 8, 181, 195–97, 203, 388, 524, 527, 531–33, 541
Clientelism, 8, 46, 183, 186, 368
Collier, Paul, 505, 507
Collor, Fernando, 473
Colonialism, 10
Coleman, James, xvii
Collective action, 116, 318–22, 532
Conable, Barber, 478
Conditionality, 6, 55, 65, 91, 103–19, 123–26, 344, 468, 477, 481, 486, 506, 523, 526
Congo, 381
Consultative Groups, 64, 74, 166, 171; *see also* World Bank
Costa Rica, 484
Côte d'Ivoire, 36, 39, 46, 185, 187–88, 195, 199, 380, 386, 389-99, 532; agricultural reform, 11, 32, 257, 269, 279–326; *Caistab*, 290–91, 316; cocoa crisis, 282, 290–324; *Front Populaire Ivoirien* (FPI), 323; *Groupements de Vocation Coopérative* (GVC), 292, 314–16, 321–22; manufacturing, 224–26, 231–32, 235–36, 238, 241; *Parti Démocratique de Côte d'Ivoire* (PDCI), 281, 313, 319–20, 323; *Société d'Assistance Technique pour la Modernisation Agricole de la Côte d'Ivoire*

(SATMACI), 295, 314–15; structural adjustment, 82; *Syndicat des Agriculteurs de Côte d'Ivoire* (SYNAGCI), 323, 533
Council of African Advisors, 22–23
Crony capitalism, 35
Crony statism, 91, 96–97, 104, 115

Debt, 18–19, 21, 38, 46, 91–126, 250, 358, 491, 504, 526, 544, 552; Africa compared to Latin America, 94, 98, 101, 103
Deindustrialization, 23, 221; *see also* Industrial development
Delgado, Christopher, 333
Denmark, 167
Development dictatorships, 124
Diouf, Abdou, 15, 46, 359, 485, 496–97, 500–502, 504
Donor fatigue, 42, 524
Drought, 65, 74, 146–47

Eastern Europe, 42, 102, 104, 126, 135, 380, 465, 468, 478, 487, 508, 524, 539, 541
Economic Commission for Africa (ECA), 4, 20, 23–27, 30, 66, 69, 81, 509; *African Alternative*, 25, 66, 68; and the World Bank, 26
Economic Commission for Latin America (ECLA), 67
Economic Community of Central African States, 206
Economic Community of West African States, 206
Economic decline, 2–5, 12, 18–25, 42, 47, 72, 186–92, 249–52, 371
Economic reform, 2–17, 20–49, 54–83, 98–126, 130–73, 332–54, 357- 90, 428–58, 463–511, 520–60
EDF, *see* European Development Fund
Enhanced Structural Adjustment Facility (ESAF), 40, 58, 60–61, 101, 103
Ellis, Frank, 426
Embedded liberalism, 507–8; *see also* Political liberalization
Eritrea, 190
ESAF, *see* Enhanced Structural Adjustment Facility
Ethiopia, 24, 185, 187, 335
European Development Fund (EDF), 378; *see also* Multilateral donors
European Economic Community, 42, 82, 303, 375; *see also* Lomé Convention
Evans, Peter, 474
Exit option, 11, 287, 387; *see also* Informal economy

Finland, 222
Foreign exchange auction, 147–49, 492–93
France, 111, 167, 383,
Friedland, William, xvii
Fochive, Jean, 376

Gabon, 188, 380
Gambia, 20, 36, 61, 67, 200–201, 499
Gates, Scott, 114
Germany, 156, 167
Gersovitz, Mark, 114, 340
Ghana, 6, 15, 36, 39, 46–47, 56, 67, 76, 114, 117, 121, 185, 187–88, 196, 198, 200, 207, 251, 386, 389, 399, 430, 446, 464, 473, 475, 522, 528, 531, 536–37, 540, 542; agricultural reform, 4, 13, 30, 37, 252, 257, 269, 284, 288, 290, 299, 301–302, 307, 334, 336, 345–46, 349–50; budget deficits and economic reform, 147; debt, 132, 153–54, 166; economic reform, 43–45,130–73 ; exchange rate, 28; external financing, 170–73; manufacturing, 236; Operation Feed Yourself, 251; privatization, 35; Programme of Action to Mitigate the Social Costs of Adjustment,

(PAMSCAD), 71–73, 162; stateness, 486; structural adjustment, 7, 26, 61, 63, 65, 73–74, 81–82, 469–70, 480, 482–83, 485–89, 495, 503–4; terms of trade, 152; *see also* Provisional National Defence Council (PNDC)
Goodman, John, 505
Gordon, David, 3, 5–6, 14, 90, 526–28, 535–37, 550
Governance, 477–79, 523; *see also* Political liberalization
Gramsci, Antonio, 365
Green, Reginald, 3–5, 30, 34, 523–24, 526, 528, 530, 541, 550
Grindle, Merilee, 435
Group of Seven, 41
Guillaumont, Patrick, 250
Guinea, 30, 36, 46, 187, 300, 341
Gulhati, Ravi, 46
Guyer, Jane, 267
Gyimah-Boadi, E., 35

Hayatou, Sadou, 381
Helleiner, G. K., 105, 250
Hemmed in, 1–2, 16–17, 126, 172, 193, 242, 271, 384, 388, 504, 509, 521–22, 525–30, 533, 540–41, 551, 555, 560
Herbst, Jeffrey, 4, 12, 13, 332, 526, 529–33,
Hirschman, Albert, 11, 508
Houphouët-Boigny, Félix, 46, 187, 279, 291, 323, 325, 386, 399, 533
Humphreys, Charles, 340
Hungary, 42
Huntington, Samuel, 45
Hurd, Douglas, 479

IDA, *see* International Development Association
IFIs, *see* International Financial Institutions
ILIs, *see* International Lending Institutions
IMF, *see* International Monetary Fund
Implicit bargain, 39, 475–77, 527, 560
India, 61, 135, 465
Indonesia, 32, 222, 230, 325–26, 533
Industrial development, 3, 8–9, 16, 93, 215–43, 529–530; benign intervention, 218, 220–21, 236, 239, 529–30; harsh withdrawal, 8–9, 218, 220, 236, 529; import-substitution industrialization, 227–30; industrialization at all costs, 218, 220; manufacturing value added 222–24, 226; radical pro-industry approach, 215–222; *see also* Economic reform
Informal economy, 30, 146, 183, 189, 193–94, 280, 311, 434, 525, 529, 535
International Development Association (IDA), 39–40, 42, 66, 101, 166, 172, 552
International Bank for Reconstruction and Development, *see* World Bank
International financial institutions (IFIs/also ILIs), 1, 8, 26, 47, 82, 91–93, 95, 98–103; and debt, 112, 142, 527–53; as both lenders and creditors, 526; conditionality, 103–18; Eastern Europe, 102; external finance, 5; governance, 523; implicit bargain, 6; Kenya, 413–17; learning, 48–49; Senegal, 497–500, 502; Tanzania, 14, 417–18, 437; *see also* International Monetary Fund, World Bank
International Lending Institutions (ILIs), *see* International financial institutions
International Monetary Fund (IMF), 2, 5, 20–21, 39, 93, 95, 99–100, 104, 110, 112–13, 126, 205, 344, 386, 450, 475–76, 478, 506, 520, 542; agriculture, 351–53;

Cameroon, 357–58, 373, 378–80, 383; conditionality, 55, 91, 103–26, 193, 469, 506; conventional wisdom/fallacies, 16, 100, 557; ESAF, 40–41, 58, 60–61, 75–76, 101, 103, 165, 168, 172, 553; exchange rate, 28–30; Ghana, 3, 60, 130, 485–86, 488, 552; Japan, 468; Kenya, 413–14, 416, 445; Korea, 550; learning, 144, 471, 522, 557, 560; Nigeria, 490–91, 493–96; producer prices, 30–33, 291, 340; rights accumulation program, 101, 131, 167; SAF, 58, 60–61, 75–76, 101, 110–41, 165, 168, 172, 553; Senegal, 497–98; subsidies, 34, 36; Tanzania, 417–19, 421–22, 428–30, 436; Zambia, 60, 101, 130, 540–41; *see also* Economic reform; International financial institutions

Jabbara, Cathy, 408–409
Jackson Robert, xvii
Jaeger, William, 340
Jamaica, 473, 475, 484
Japan, 241, 468, 557
Jaycox, E. V. K., 54, 64
Joseph, Richard A., 368, 443

Kahler, Miles, 13, 115
Kane, Chiek Hamidou, 502
Kaunda, Kenneth, 7, 46, 92, 125, 133, 135, 137–38, 164, 187, 473, 503, 541
Keeling, William, 493
Kenya, 15, 39, 46, 67, 82, 107, 114, 185, 187, 195, 389, 399, 419, 421, 434–35, 504, 530–31, 535, 537; agricultural reform, 4, 13, 257, 268–69, 334, 342–47, 399–400, 402–407, 426; budget deficit, 414–16; economic reform, 435–46; exchange rate, 405- 408; Forum to Restore Democracy (FORD), 445; Kalenjin, 405, 413, 442, 444; Kenya African Democratic Union (KADU), 440; Kenya Africa National Union (KANU), 440, 445; Kenya Farmers Association (KFA), 441; Kenya Planters Cooperative Union, 441–42; Kikuyu, 405, 439–45; Luo, 444–45; manufacturing, 224–26, 231–32, 235, 238, 241; *mbari*, 249; producer prices, 408–13
Kenyatta, Jomo, 346–47, 359, 399, 439, 445, 537
Killick, Tony, 114, 416, 557
Korea, 38, 63, 230, 467, 472, 489, 509, 530, 542, 552; economic development of compared to Africa, 545–51

Lagos Plan of Action, 24, 67, 523
Latin America, 32, 95, 98, 223–24, 466, 468, 511, 541, 544, 550
Legum, Colin, 200
Lebanon, 61
Lesotho, 284
Lewis, Sir W. Arthur, 231
Liberia, 74, 115, 187, 205, 494
Libya, 135, 230
Limann, Hilla, 200, 480, 488
Lofchie, Michael, 4, 14, 16, 526–27, 530, 536–37, 538–39
Lomé Convention, 42, 553–55,
London Club, 99, 171, 491

MacNamara, Robert, 64
Madagascar, 107, 341
Malagasy, 56, 67
Malawi, 37, 46, 67, 107, 187, 190, 264
Malaysia, 32, 76, 325–26, 533, 554
Mali, 300, 341
Manufacturing, *see* Industrial development
Martin, Matthew, 3, 6–7, 46, 526, 528, 540–41

Mauritania, 36, 61, 224, 501
Mauritius, 39, 82, 200
Mellor, John, 333
Menem, Carlos, 473
Mexico, 467, 472–73, 542
Mobutu, Sese Seko, 46, 113, 473, 479, 537
Moi, Daniel arap, 346, 359, 399, 403–4, 412, 415, 435, 438, 440–44, 479, 531, 535, 537
Mozambique, 62, 64–65, 67, 73, 75, 82, 187, 190, 335, 400
Mugabe, Robert, 13, 347
Multilateral donors, 166, 344, 351, 378
Multinational corporations, 139
Mwinyi, Ali Hassan 46, 399, 418, 436, 553–54

Netherlands, 167
Newbery, David, 284
Newly industrialized country (NIC), 22, 82, 116, 216, 223, 241, 465–68, 545, 550, 554
Nkrumah, Kwame, 399
Ngayap, Pierre Flambeau, 365
Niger, 39, 187, 269, 341
Nigeria, 15, 20, 39, 47, 61, 65, 97, 102, 106–107, 135, 185, 195, 201, 258, 300, 368, 387, 443, 464, 473–75, 531, 540 ; Agbekoya riots, 287; agriculture, 257, 262–63, 267–69, 285–88, 346; agricultural reform, 257, 262–63, 267–69, 285–88, 346; auction system, 492–93; bank reform, 492–93; clientelism, 368; debt, 491, 493; exchange rate, 97; Hausa, 269, 286–87; manufacturing, 28, 224–27, 235–36, 238, 241; National Republican Convention, 202, 491; smuggling, 372; Social Democratic Party, 202, 490; structural adjustment, 61, 480, 483, 485, 489–96, 503–4, 506; Third Republic, 446; Transitional Council, 495; Yoruba, 267, 285
Norway, 444
Nyerere, Julius, 417, 428, 442, 446, 453, 455, 537, 539

OAU, *see* Organization of African Unity
OECD, *see* Organization for Economic Cooperation and Development
Official development assistance (ODA), 41–42
Ongolo, Nomo, 377
Organization for African Unity (OAU), 4, 21, 23, 25, 525
Organization for Economic Cooperation and Development (OECD), 42, 135–36, 157–58, 162–64, 545
Orthodox paradox, 13, 115, 556
Ozal, Turgut, 473, 485

PAMSCAD, *see* Ghana, Programme of Action to Mitigate the Social Costs of Adjustment
Parastatals, 194, 200, 361–62, 377, 379, 525, 529
Paris Club, 58, 74, 99, 153, 171, 358, 491, 494, 497
Patrimonial state: effect on economic reform, 536–37
Paz, Victor, 473
Pinochet, Augusto, 472
PNDC, *see* Provisional National Defence Council
Poland, 42
Political liberalization, 4, 8, 25, 38, 183, 199–208, 380–84; relationship to economic reform, 4, 15, 34, 38, 43, 45, 172, 204, 382–83, 398, 455–58, 463–511, 535, 558–59, 525–29; *see also* Economic reform, Governance
Pottier, Johan, 267
Preferential Trade Area (PTA), 206

Prebendalism, 443
Price, Robert, xvii
Privatization, 35, 525, 529; *see also* Parastatals
Provisional National Defence Council (PNDC), 38, 43, 133, 135–42, 147, 149, 154, 156–60, 163, 168–69, 200, 349–50, 483, 486; *see also* Ghana
PTA, *see* Preferential Trade Area

Ranger, Terence, 259
Ravenhill, John, 3–4, 18, 205, 446, 520, 523
Rawlings, Jerry, 7, 13, 15, 43, 46, 54, 133, 138, 142, 157, 389, 470, 479, 482, 485, 488–89
Reardon, Thomas, 261
Rhee, Syngman, 546–47, 549
Riddell, Roger, 3, 8–10, 215, 529–30
Rodrik, Dani, 105
Rosberg, Carl, xv-xviii
Rothchild, Donald, 3, 8, 180, 534
Rwanda, 61, 67, 224, 264

SADCC, *see* Southern African Development Coordination Conference
Sahn, David, 120–21
SAF, *see* Structural Adjustment Facility
SAL, *see* Structural Adjustment Loan
São Tomé and Príncipe, 201
SAP, *see* Structural Adjustment Program
Sarney, José, 473
Schattschneider, E. E., 333
Scott, James, 280
Seaga, Edward, 473, 484
Sector Adjustment Loan, (SECAL), 111
Senegal, 15, 36, 46, 67, 185, 187, 195, 200, 386, 389, 464, 535–36, 540; agricultural reform, 31, 257; debt, 497; economic reform 485, 496–504; Islamic Brotherhood, 185, 499; *marabouts*, 200, 499; *Parti Démocratique Sénégalais* (PDS), 496, 501–2; *Parti Socialiste* (PS), 200, 496–97, 500–502
Senghor, Léopold, 496
Shagari, Shehu, 202
Sharpley, J., 231
Shonekan, Chief Ernest, 495
Sierra Leone, 74, 187
Singapore, 230, 402
Sklar, Richard, 207, 389, 511
Smith, Adam, 83
Socialism, 133, 207, 430
Somalia, 61, 67, 205
South African Customs Union, 233
South Africa, 190, 230, 233
Southern African Development Coordination Conference (SADCC), 206
Soviet Union, 104, 126, 468, 488, 508
SPA, *see* World Bank, Special Program of Assistance
Stabilization Program (STAB), 54, 71–72, 74; *see also* Economic reform; Sturctural adjustment
State: autonomy, 474, 506, 536, 548; colonial state, 184; developmental state, 123, 549; post-colonial state, 8, 184; engineering of, 505, 508; role in economic reform, 556–58; state-society relations, 180–208; *see also* Crony statism; Stateness; Statism
Stateness, 182, 188, 470, 543, 550, 560; *see also* State; Statism
Statism, 8, 182, 188, 557; *see also* State; Stateness
Stiglitz, Joseph, 284
Streeten, Paul, 333
Structural adjustment, 1–3, 13, 16, 43, 49, 105, 118–26, 130, 143–44, 199, 431, 455–58; and agriculture, 8, 352–53; and budget deficits,

33–35; and conditionality, 144–45; and debt, 37–43, 151–54; and exchange rates, 28–30, 151; and external financing, 174–76; and foreign exchange, 151–54; and manufacturing, 8, 236–38; and subsidies, 146; and terms of trade, 152; Asia and Latin America compared to Africa, 126; design of, 8, 22–33, 57, 78, 242–43, 373–74, 508, 551; negotiations, 154–62; versus stabilization, 143, 464; *see also* Economic reform
Structural Adjustment Facility (SAF); see International Monetary Fund
Structural Adjustment Loan (SAL), see World Bank
Structural Adjustment Program (SAP), 8–9, 54, 63–64, 66, 72–75, 80, 82, 183, 217, 236–37; *see also* Structural adjustment
Sudan, 60, 67, 187, 190, 284, 386
Sweden, 167
Syria, 61

Taiwan, 402, 467, 472, 489, 542, 552
Tanzania, 14–16, 46, 64, 67, 73–74, 76, 78, 106–107, 187, 251, 399–402, 413, 505, 526, 536–39, agricultural reform, 30, 251, 336, 399; budget deficits, 430–31; Chama Cha Mapinduzi, 453–54; corruption, 424; economic decline, 418–28, exchange rate, 407, 429–30; parastatal reform, 424–28, 432–34; privatization, 65; structural adjustment, 61, 75, 82, 428–36, 446–58; trade liberalization, 431–32
Thailand, 38, 402, 542
Togo, 56, 67, 300, 381
Toure, Mamadou, 498, 502
Turkey, 222, 472–73, 485, 509

Uganda, 24, 36, 147, 185, 187–88, 198, 341, 386, 402, 448–49
United Nations Conference on Trade and Development (UNCTAD), 552
United Nations Educational, Scientific, and Cultural Organization (UNESCO), 36
United Nations International Childrens' Emergency Fund (UNICEF), 36, 68, 70, 80, 162; *Adjustment with a Human Face*, 36, 70
United Kingdom, 111, 156, 167, 444
United States, 111, 156, 167, 444
United States Agency for International Development (USAID), 104, 113–15, 352, 379, 402, 450, 547

van de Walle, Nicolas, 4, 13–14, 33, 124, 203, 357, 502, 526, 535–36
Vaughan, Megan, 264

Wade, Abdoulaye, 496, 501–502
Wade, Robert, 318, 550
Watts, Michael, 286–87,
Whitehead, Laurence, 464
Widner, Jennifer, 3, 10–13, 16, 279, 529, 532–33
World Bank (also International Bank for Reconstruction and Development), 2, 4–5, 16, 20–21, 24, 98, 100–101, 113, 120–21, 126, 163–64, 205, 334, 339, 450, 475–76, 478, 506, 520, 532, 541, 543–44; *Africa's Adjustment and Growth in the 1980s*, 19–20, 66; *Adjustment Lending: An Evaluation of Ten Years of Experience*, 19; *Accelerated Development in Sub-Saharan Africa*, 21, 56–57, 63, 66, 72, 337; agriculture, 306, 336–39, 351–53; Cameroon, 357, 373, 377–80; conditionality, 105,

108–9, 469, 506; Consultative Group, 57, 64, 166, 171; conventional wisdom/fallacies, 16, 100, 557; Côte d'Ivoire, 303, 319; Eastern Europe, 47; enabling environment, 477; exchange rate; 28–30; *Financing Adjustment with Growth in Sub-Sahara Africa*, 21; Ghana, 82, 143, 162; investment, 33, 42, 349, 352, 485–86, 488; Japan, 468; Kenya, 413–14, 416, 437–38; Korea, 549–55; learning, 22, 471, 522, 557, 560; Nigeria, 490–93; privatization, 35, 61, 377–78; producer prices, 11, 30–33, 291, 339–40; price reform, 12, 21, 24, 27; relations with IMF, 40, 58, 417; SALs, 110, 114, 340; SECALs, 21, 111; Special Program of Assistance (SPA), 101; *Sub-Saharan Africa: From Crisis to Sustainable Growth*, 22, 24–25, 37, 41, 76, 81, 216, 477, 522; Tanzania, 400, 411–12, 421–22, 427; Zambia, 3, 167; Zimbabwe, 64, 352; *see also* Berg Report, International Monetary Fund

Zaire, 36, 46–47, 67, 74, 82, 113, 115, 187, 266, 387, 473, 535, 537, 539

Zambia, 6, 33–34, 46–47, 67, 92, 185, 187–88, 201, 251, 257, 380, 473, 475, 503, 520–21, 526, 528, 535, 537, 539–41, 551; agricultural reform, 252, 255, 258, 262–63, 267; debt, 132, 152–54; economic reform, 130–73; external financing, 170–73; manufacturing, 224–27, 232, 235–37; Movement for Multi-party Democracy, 125, 137; structural adjustment, 7, 37, 45, 65, 114, 506

Zimbabwe, 62, 64–65, 67, 187, 531; agricultural reform, 4, 13, 334, 345, 347–50; manufacturing, 224–33, 235, 237; National Farmers Association of Zimbabwe (NFAZ), 348–49, 531, 533; structural adjustment, 64, 72–73, 82, 237